Extreme Prejudice
The Presidio "Satanic Abuse" Scam

- by -

Michael A. Aquino
Lt. Colonel, U.S. Army (Ret.)

ISBN-13:
978-1500159245

ISBN-10:
1500159247

Table of Contents

Preface

Throughout the 1960s and 1970s it was fun to be first a Satanist and later a Setian in America.

As recounted in my *Church of Satan* history, Satanists were generally regarded as the most colorful, exciting, and amusing extreme of what was popularly called the "Occult Revival" movement.[1] Both Anton LaVey's original Central Grotto in San Francisco and the various local Grottos that sprang up around the country became something akin to fashion statements in their locales. They were exciting to join or visit; their rituals and ceremonies could be counted upon to be spooky, spectacular, scary, and slapstick. A local Satanist, or better yet Priest or Priestess of the Church, was a guaranteed draw for any kind of lecture, seminar, media talk show, or Halloween party.

Even conventional churches, which one would think would be horrified at such a sinister competitor in their midst, often found themselves enjoying the novelty in spite of themselves. After all, it gave them something tangible to righteously denounce. It got them into show biz too, because local television and radio stations quickly figured out that the best debate opponent for a professional Satanist was a professional Christian.

And Hollywood happily fanned the flames. From *Rosemary's Baby* in 1966 to *The Exorcist* in 1974, showdowns between the Devil and God were big box-office.

When the Temple of Set was founded in 1975, indeed, those of us who had resigned from the Church of Satan to create this new institution felt that it was time to calm down a little. The Church had remained such a darling of the media that Satanists found their time taken up largely by public relations events. There just wasn't time for serious Black Magic, which, after all, was what becoming a Satanist was supposed to be all about.

Furthermore the Temple of Set was finally facing head-on what its predecessor had been tap-dancing around for the previous decade: that there was a serious, sophisticated, and potentially very illuminating foundation for this "religion of otherness". In this the Temple also benefitted from divesting itself completely of Judæo-Christian mythology, ideology, and symbolism. We harked back instead to pre-J/C ancient Egypt, and an interpretation of its metaphysics that promised to open a door to the divinity of each initiated individual.[2]

And so it was for the Temple's first decade as well - with one difference: that we determined from the outSet that our attention would always be devoted to our own membership's benefit. We were not there to entertain, fascinate, or stimulate the public any more. So modest and private was the Temple of Set, indeed, that the outside world scarcely knew we were there at all. That was just fine with Setians as we settled down to explore the great mysteries of philosophy, magic, and metaphysics.

And we expected it would continue pleasantly on that way forever. None of us, myself included, ever anticipated the nightmare that awaited not just Satanists/Setians, but indeed the entire "occult subculture" - and many who weren't actually part of it at all - in the 1980s.

It began in 1977 when a man named Lawrence Pazder published a book entitled *Michelle Remembers*. In this book he alleged that his wife Michelle had as an infant been kidnapped and sexually abused by Satanists, then had "repressed" all memories of the experience until he elicited them from her as an adult through "therapy sessions".

I remember that when we first heard of it, we all laughed it off as ludicrous, and certainly too transparently so for anyone to take seriously. It was soon to be found on "remaindered" sale tables, from one of which I picked up my own copy.

But away from our amused and contemptuous dismissal, it happened that many other eyes were reading the book and taking it very seriously indeed. Or, more malevolently, seeing in it a new technique for acquiring power, fame, and money by imitating its theme.

Michelle Remembers was ultimately exposed as a fraud [see Appendix #1], but by then its damage had been done, and that damage proved to be horrific and incalculable, destroying lives, families, and societies throughout many countries.

The ominous consequences of *Michelle Remembers* first came to widespread public attention in 1983, when a mentally-ill woman named Judy Johnson, on the sole "evidence" of her son's irritated anus, made an accusation of "Satanic child-molestation" against the McMartin Preschool in Los Angeles. Although the child's doctor and father

---

[1] *The Church of Satan* is available through Amazon.com in both printed and Kindle ebook editions.

[2] *The Temple of Set* is available through Amazon.com in both printed and Kindle ebook editions.

saw nothing unusual about the irritation, and although Johnson was later diagnosed as an acute paranoid schizophreniac, the damage was done and the McMartin witch-hunt was ignited. It was to end in court seven years later with no finding of any abuse by anyone at the day-care center.

The nationwide drama and sensationalism associated with *Michelle Remembers* and the McMartin case ignited an epidemic of "day-care Satanic sex abuse" witch-hunts across the United States. While many persons were prosecuted and convicted of sex-abuse as a consequence, not one instance of "Satanism" in connection with either child abuse or day-care center activity was ever demonstrated.

By the 1990s law-enforcement and governmental agencies generally, which had originally been caught by complete surprise concerning this bizarre fad, had finally had time to research it definitively. "Satanic ritual child abuse":

- does **not** exist in the United States, as reported by the FBI's National Center for the Analysis of Violent Crime in 1992, after an 11-year study. "There are many children in the United States who, starting early in their lives, are severely psychologically, physically, and sexually traumatized by angry, sadistic parents or other adults. Such abuse, however, is not perpetrated only or primarily by satanists. The statistical odds are that such abusers are members of mainstream religions ... For the last eight years American law enforcement has been aggressively investigating the allegations of victims of ritual abuse. There is little or no evidence for the portion of their allegations that deals with large-scale baby-breeding, human sacrifice, and organized satanic conspiracies." (*Investigator's Guide to Allegations of "Ritual" Child Abuse*, January 1992)

- does **not** exist in the United States, as concluded by an exhaustive national study for the National Center on Child Abuse and Neglect: "In a survey of more than 11,000 psychiatric and police workers throughout the country, conducted for the National Center on Child Abuse and Neglect, researchers found more than 12,000 accusations of group cult sexual abuse based on Satanic ritual, but **not one** that investigators had been able to substantiate. 'After scouring the country, we found **no** evidence for large-scale cults that sexually abuse children,' said Dr. Gail Goodman, a psychologist at the University of California at Davis, who directed the survey. The survey included 6,910 psychiatrists, psychologists, and clinical social workers; and 4,655 district attorneys, police departments, and social service agencies. They reported 12,264 accusations of ritual abuse that they had investigated. The survey found that there was **not a single** case among them where there was clear corroborating evidence for the most common accusation, that there was "a well-organized, intergenerational Satanic cult who sexually molested and tortured children in their homes or schools for years and committed a series of murders," said Goodman. (Daniel Goleman, *New York Times*, reprinted *San Francisco Chronicle* 11/1/94)

But in the 1980s the "SRA" myth, and monetary/publicity scams based on it, continued to rage unabated nationwide. The Department of Defense community was not immune from the epidemic. By November 1987 there had been 15 child-sex-abuse accusation scares at Army day-care centers and elementary schools alone. In late 1986 it was the turn of the Presidio of San Francisco.

Chapter 1: Gary Hambright

Caveat

The accusations against Presidio day-care teacher Gary Hambright marked the beginning of the Presidio "day-care sexual abuse" episode of 1986-87. Until in mid-1987 Chaplain Larry Adams-Thompson [hereafter abbreviated as "A-T" in my writing] and his wife Michele decided to accuse my wife Lilith and myself as well, Hambright was the sole target of parents, therapists, and investigators.

From July 1986 to July 1987, Lilith and I were living 3,000 miles away in Washington, D.C., where I was a student in the Industrial College of the Armed Forces, National Defense University. We had no idea that this episode was going on at the Presidio, nor would have felt any personal concern had we heard of it. At that point we simply weren't paying much attention to the McMartin Preschool and copycat witch-hunts, considering them just another tragic example of fundamentalist extremism gone berserk.

Therefore I did not collect information concerning the Gary Hambright situation at the Presidio, nor did I do so significantly subsequent to the Adams-Thompsons' attack on us. None of the other Presidio parents were accusing us of anything, and frankly we had no idea who Hambright was or whether he might actually have harmed any children. So we left him alone to handle his own predicament while we focused on our own.

Hence this chapter is less comprehensive than subsequent ones, assembled from what facts I did come across in the media and from one August 1989 office meeting with the public defenders who had previously handled Hambright's case. But I never had any contact with any of the accusing parents, and of course I never had access to any of the investigative documents concerning Hambright or any of the children besides Kinsey Almond/A-T.

This chapter, then, represents the most accurate, factual, and comprehensive picture I have been able to assemble of the Hambright events.

Prior to the Tobin Accusations

There were no allegations of any sort against Gary Hambright, a Baptist minister working as a teacher at the Presidio Child Development Center, prior to November 1986. This is crucially significant because in the later onslaught of parental accusations against him, he was accused of sexual abuse acts on as many as sixty day-care children from May 1985 to November 1986. Does it seem conceivable that **not a single parent would have noticed a single thing wrong with even one child before November 1986**? Even **one** such doctor or hospital visit, or police notification, would have rung an alarm bell instantly. **No such notification ever happened**, and this is the first and most glaring indicator that Hambright was in fact a completely innocent man who was unfortunate enough to be made the convenient scapegoat of a witch-hunt.

So what **did** inspire and trigger that witch-hunt at the Presidio?

On September 28, 1986 the *San Francisco Examiner*[3] began a series of eight extensive, lurid, and illustrated front-page stories sensationalizing the nationwide "day care ritual abuse" epidemic. The texts of these articles appear here as Appendices #2-9. They not only describe the witch-hunt procedures employed throughout the country, but are indicative of the state of bewilderment and uncertainty of law-enforcement and prosecutorial authorities at that point in time. Caught by surprise concerning such a bizarre epidemic, they haplessly surrendered control of local accusations to "satanic abuse" therapists, conviction-committed prosecutors, and lynch-mob-minded parents. Also discussed in the articles and diagrams were the vast lawsuits and claims filed by parents, such as $110 million in 1985 for allegations concerning the day-care center of the U.S. Military Academy at West Point, New York.

The stage was now set for San Francisco and its Presidio.

---

[3] In 1986 the *San Francisco Examiner* was the city's second major daily newspaper. Years later it failed, and in 2007 its masthead remains only on a small free daily paper.

The Tobin Accusations

On November 14, 1986, according to her later account in a 1988 magazine[4] , Joyce Tobin's (wife of Captain Michael Tobin assigned to the Presidio) 3-year-old son David came home from a day-care visit complaining that teacher Gary Hambright had bitten his penis and inserted a pencil painfully into his rectum. Joyce gave a slightly different account to KTVU television, saying that the child had made no complaints when picked up or arriving home, but that later that evening he pulled at his penis when watching television, and in answer to his brother's inquiry, said that "Mr. Gary" did it.[5]

Although a trained nurse, Joyce did not take David for a medical examination until a full week later, after a Presidio chaplain to whom her husband spoke had contacted the Army Criminal Investigation Division.[6] Then she took David not to the Presidio's Letterman Army Hospital, but to San Francisco General Hospital, where Dr. Kevin Coulter issued a report saying that David's anus showed "tears" and was enlarged.

In April 1988 on a KTVU television news documentary, Coulter admitted that he had later retracted his initial report about "tears", saying that David's anus showed only "normal grooves". Nevertheless he said that the child's anus had seemed "unusually large".

On the same documentary pediatrician Ann Parker, M.D. was asked about this statement. She responded that there are many perfectly normal causes for an enlarged anus in a child of that age, such as large bowel movements. Joyce Tobin stated in an affidavit that the child had been experiencing large bowel movements at the time.[7] Indeed she stated that he had had a large bowel movement that same evening. Other than commenting upon the size of the stools, Joyce made no mention of any defecation pain, or of any blood in the stools, etc. that might have evidenced actual anal penetration earlier that same day of a small, delicate 3-year-old child.

Neither in the adult Tobins' account for the extensive Linda Goldston magazine article footnoted here, nor in the KTVU documentary, nor in any other published source I have discovered, was any mention made of injury or damage to David's penis such as a bite with teeth might be expected to cause, particularly to a 3-year-old child. This will become significant as discussed below, since ultimately all charges against Hambright would be reduced to this single one.

Day-Care/"Satanic Ritual" Abuse Checklists

Letters were mailed to 242 Presidio parents, and checklists of "symptoms" of child sex-abuse were circulated [see Appendices #10 and #11].

Such checklists, created by "therapists" aggressively dedicated to "findings" of sex-abuse, had become nationally notorious for their inclusion of virtually every normal interest or action of a child as a "symptom". As a consequence of *Michelle Remembers*, the industry had also begun to dress up such checklists with imagined "Satanic ritual" symptoms.

One of the most well-known and widely-circulated such lists in 1986 was that of Catherine Gould [Appendix #11]. Investigators later confirmed to me that this was indeed one of the lists circulated among Presidio parents.

In this list it will be seen that many ordinary and even mutually-contradictory forms of behavior are symptoms of "Satanic ritual abuse and sexual abuse", for example a child who is either rebellious or compliant, who gets angry or play-acts or is lazy in school, or who touches his or her genitals. [Interlaced with these, hence lending

---

[4] Linda Goldston, "Army of the Night", *San Jose Mercury News West*, 7/24/88.

[5] "Nightmare at the Presidio", KTVU Channel 2 television documentary special, 4/10/88. In this film pediatrician Ann Parker commented that it is not at all unusual for children over 18 months to show an interest in, and play with their genitals.

[6] While I have not seen the name of the specific chaplain identified in print, the signatures of Larry and Michele A-T appear immediately below the Tobins' on an alarm-letter to Presidio parents circulated in approximately April 1987. No other chaplain's name appears. So I assume that it was indeed Larry A-T who initially called the CID to begin the Presidio scare.

[7] KTVU, *op.cit.*

credibility to them, are a few obviously valid warning signs, such as physical injury, the presence of semen, etc.] The checklist also warns parents that any official investigation will be incompetent, and also that even the most excellent reputation of a school or day-care facility means nothing. In short, a climate comparable to the witch-hunts of medieval Europe is created, in which anything and everything is "proof" of witchcraft and no defense is possible or admissible.[8]

Thus the mere fact of accusation meant that abuse had definitely occurred and Hambright was definitely guilty. His denials and those of all the other teachers meant nothing.[9] The absence of any physical damage to any child meant nothing. The absence of child complaints or allegations at any time in the 1-1/2 years prior to the Tobin accusation meant nothing. Indeed any inconvenient evidence of innocence was automatically ignored.

Motives for Accusation

Such was the "day-care abuse" agenda which Presidio parents, administrators, and local law enforcement investigators were now pursuing, as in so many previous instances of the national hysteria. Twenty years later it seems surprising that they could all have been so gullible and compliant. But it must be noted that the average American adult in those days knew nothing whatever about child sexual predators, "abnormal" child behavior, or psychological therapy procedures. As for the "S-word" - "satanism" - for the vast public who had not actually encountered the Church of Satan, it was a nightmare reference to secret cult activity so ghastly that the mind could scarcely picture it.[10] This played right into the hands of the "SRA therapists", who could thus attribute whatever they wished to such faceless, anonymous, heinous "satanists".

A more opportunistic explanation is, as again in previous "day-care abuse" episodes, parents soon realized that multimillion-dollar claims could be filed, while therapists and prosecutors saw an opportunity for headlines, fame, and professional advancement. Conveniently there was no risk for the parent and therapist accusers, because they always insisted that **they themselves** were not accusing anyone - they were merely "conveying the **children's** accusations". For adult accusers, therefore, it was an ideal scenario in which they were sheltered from any consequences of false accusations. They proclaimed that "little children never lie about sexual abuse", which in 1986 still worked with enough juries to have sent numerous "satanic ritual abuse"-accused adults to prison on no other evidence whatever.

That innocent victims might go to prison [and probably be severely brutalized or killed there], and that their own little children would need to be indoctrinated to believe and recite the most horrific and disgusting "sexual abuse" to themselves, were inconvenient, and therefore irrelevant considerations.

---

[8] Obviously Gould and other "SRA therapists" neither knew nor cared that their descriptions of "satanic abuse" had no basis whatever in authentic religious Satanism as it had been openly defined and practiced in the United States since the formation of the Church of Satan in 1966.

[9] In the KTVU documentary the day-care teacher with whom Hambright co-hosted his class at the center, Susan Mihata, stated that there was no private area in the center where Hambright would have been able to take a child unobserved. She further stated that she would never have allowed Hambright to leave her alone with the 30 children of the class, because that ratio of supervision would have been against the law. Mihata said that she not only never saw Hambright abusing anyone, but that she was never once interviewed or questioned by investigators. Hambright's class was also a "temporary drop off/pick up" one, with parents arriving and departing unannounced all the time. This was verified on KTVU by Federal Public Defender Geoffrey Hansen, who stated that he had reviewed all of the Center's assignment/attendance records.

[10] As noted in the Introduction, we who had openly and authentically been involved with the Satanic religion since the 1960s never anticipated that such widespread ignorance and fear of it still existed in the 1980s. To see popular fantasies of such depraved and vicious acts, sexual and otherwise, attributed to it was almost incomprehensible. The record would eventually be set straight through our public efforts and those of responsible academic and law-enforcement authorities, but not in 1986 when the "SRA" witch-hunts were at their height.

First Arrest and Charges/Dismissal

In December 1986 Hambright was arrested and charged with "lewd conduct, sodomy, and oral copulation of a 3-year-old boy" [David Tobin]. In March 1987, however, when a federal judge disallowed hearsay testimony from parents and therapists, prosecutors asked that the case be dismissed. Apparently there was no other evidence of any crime.[11]

Debbie Hickey and "Play Therapy"

The dismissal of the charges against Hambright was merely a momentary setback. By this time scores of children were in extensive programs of "play therapy" being conducted by Major Deborah "Debbie" Hickey, a psychiatrist assigned to the Presidio's Letterman Army Medical Center. According to the KTVU television documentary, Hickey proceeded to diagnose sex-abuse in several of the children, including her own. Parents were instructed not to question their own children at all - to leave questioning exclusively to Hickey.[12]

Hickey repeatedly refused to speak with the KTVU reporters, either on- or off-camera.[13] When asked by KTVU why Hickey, as a personally-interested parent, was allowed to diagnose and treat all of the children, Presidio Commander Joseph Rafferty answered only that the Letterman Hospital commander apparently did not think it improper.[14]

The accounts, as later reported by the press, were of the fantastic and incoherent variety exemplified by the Gould checklist. Children said that they had guns pointed at them, that they had played baseball with human excrement, and that "Mr. Gary" [Hambright] had a shark in a bowl on his kitchen table which he took a child home with him to feed, and that they had "played penis guitar".[15] All of this fantastic nonsense was held to somehow validate mass sexual molestation at the center.

No Physical/Medical Evidence

Apart from Hickey's "play therapy", there are no published accounts I could ever find that prior to the November 1986 Tobin accusation any child attending the Presidio center was ever taken to a doctor or emergency room for examination/care because of an apparent adult rape/sodomy, or that upon the publicizing of the scandal itself any medical examinations of any of the children had revealed any physical evidence of sexual molestation. Other than Coulter's waffling and uncertain statements concerning the Tobin child, there was therefore **no medical evidence that anything happened to any of the children**.[16]

Chlamydia?

Following medical examinations given to the children when the scare commenced, it was announced to the press that some of the children had chlamydia, a venereal disease which can be transmitted by sexual contact.[17] As

[11] *San Francisco Chronicle* 1/4/88.

[12] Colleen Parker, parent, KTVU, *op.cit.*

[13] Bob MacKenzie, KTVU, *op.cit.*

[14] KTVU, *op.cit.*

[15] Goldston; KTVU, *op.cit.*

[16] On the KTVU documentary, prosecuting U.S. Attorney Joseph Russinello stated, "In all but one of those ten cases [in the second Hambright indictment] we had no physical evidence." The "one" case was presumably that of David Tobin, with Russinello referring to Dr. Coulter's opinion concerning the size of his rectum.

[17] "An internal Army memo of 19 November 1987 concluded that there were five confirmed cases of chlamydia." Bob MacKensie, KTVU, *op.cit.*

this was the first apparent physical proof that the children had indeed been sexually abused, the press repeatedly mentioned it:

> According to [Presidio Commander Colonel] Rafferty's letter, three of the children have tested positive for chlamydia, a curable, relatively common disease that is most often sexually transmitted.[18]

> [Hambright's attorney] Bondoc said Hambright was served with a search warrant "two or three weeks ago" so that authorities could test him for chlamydia, a sexually transmitted disease. Four of the alleged victims in the case have contracted the disease.[19]

> Federal investigators have since [the first dismissal of charges] concluded that at least 58 children who attended the center were molested, and that at least a half-dozen had chlamydia, a curable venereal disease.[20]

> At least a half-dozen children had chlamydia, a venereal disease.[21]

> There were five confirmed cases of chlamydia, a sexually transmitted disease, including two of the four daughters of one family.[22]

> Referring to the victims, the parents said, "… many have documented medical evidence of sexual abuse, including rape, sodomy, and venereal disease." [23]

> Two of the Runyans' four daughters were among the victims; both had confirmed cases of chlamydia.[24]

> There were five confirmed cases of chlamydia, a sexually transmitted disease.[25]

Upon being alerted to the chlamydia allegations, Hambright's attorney hadn't waited for the search warrant test:

> Bondoc, who said his client is innocent, said he sent Hambright to his personal physician on the same day for a separate chlamydia test. "That came back negative, and I was able to confirm that the government's test was also negative. So he doesn't have chlamydia.[26] [27]

It was later brought out, however, that the tests used to detect chlamydia were so inaccurate that none of them could be used in court:

---

[18] Edward Lempinen, "More Kids Involved in Molest Probe", *San Francisco Chronicle* 8/12/87.

[19] Goldston, "10 More Claim Molestation at S.F. Presidio Child Center", *San Jose Mercury News* 8/13/87.

[20] Lempinen, "The Defense Strategy in Presidio Molestation Case", *San Francisco Chronicle* 1/4/88.

[21] Lempinen, "Angry Parents Want Trial in Presidio Case", *San Francisco Chronicle* 4/20/88.

[22] Goldston, "Army of the Night", *op.cit.*

[23] *Ibid.*

[24] *Ibid.*

[25] Goldston, "AIDS Tests Urged in Presidio Case", *San Jose Mercury News* 4/27/89.

[26] Goldston, "10 More Claim Molestation …", *op.cit.*

[27] I might note in passing here that after the A-T accusations were made, Lilith's and my own medical records verified that we had never had either chlamydia or any other venereal disease either.

The cases of chlamydia could not be used as evidence because the right kind of cultures had not been taken at Letterman Army Medical Center. When one couple called the U.S. Attorney's Office to ask if they should take their children for another culture, the answer was no.[28]

Dr. Bonnie Dattel, "an internationally recognized expert on chlamydia"[29], said that only a preliminary screening had been done by Letterman Hospital, not the conclusive, follow-up culture testing. As the children in question had then been treated for the disease, culture testing was now pointless.[30]

According to *San Francisco Chronicle* reporter Edward Lempinen, chlamydia can also be transmitted from a mother to her unborn fetus.[31] A Blue Cross pamphlet elaborates:

> **Chlamydia or NSU** (non-specific urethritis). Cause: Bacteria. Symptoms: Discharge from genitals or rectum. Pain when urinating. There may be no symptoms, especially in women. When they appear: 7-21 days. How acquired: Direct contact with infected mucus membrane (genitals, mouth, eye, rectum).[32]

In the absence of any sign of sexual violation of the children involved, it is reasonable to suppose that **if** any child had the disease, it could have been contracted in any number of ordinary, accidental ways. I am aware of no evidence to indicate that the mothers of the children in question were examined and found to be free of the disease themselves, or had no medical history of being treated for it since the birth of their children.[33] Presumably for officials to insist that this more unremarkable explanation be explored would have outraged the parents, who were already vehemently criticizing the Army, to even greater vocal indignation.

It is logical to conclude, therefore, that the **absence** of chlamydia in Gary Hambright established that:

- He **could not have given it** to any child who tested positive for it.

- He **did not contract it** through oral/genital contact from any infected child.

So, although the media kept stating that several children had "confirmed cases of chlamydia" as though this "proved" the allegations of rape and sodomy against Hambright, in actuality - assuming those children **did** have the disease, it was an **exoneration** of Hambright. This simple point was never, ever made.

AIDS?

A scare in the local media occurred when one child was initially reported as testing positively for AIDS. This test result was later shown to be false.[34] Nevertheless, as with the chlamydia, this development continued to be brought up as "additional evidence" that sex-abuse had taken place.

A second AIDS scare occurred in 1989:

> The Army has recommended that more than 60 children who said they were sexually abused at the Presidio of San Francisco be tested for the AIDS virus ...

---

[28] Goldston, "Army of the Night", *op.cit.*

[29] KTVU, *op.cit.*

[30] *Ibid.*

[31] Lempinen, "Ex-Presidio Worker Under FBI Probe in Molestations", *San Francisco Chronicle* 8/11/87.

[32] Blue Cross of California Pamphlet, "How to Prevent AIDS and Other Sexually Transmitted Diseases" 1994.

[33] Note the comment in the Blue Cross pamphlet that "there may be no symptoms, especially in women".

[34] Goldston, "Army of the Night", *op.cit.*

Bob Mahoney, speaking for the Presidio, said Wednesday the step is being taken because "there is a rumor going around that an individual who was suspected of participating in the child abuse case has AIDS" ...[35]

That "individual" was Hambright, who at that time was known to be dying of AIDS. I have seen no information that, if any of the Presidio children were tested for HIV/AIDS, any of the tests were positive. If none of the children who had been alleged to have been orally, anally, or vaginally raped/sodomized by Hambright had contracted HIV/AIDS at that time, of course, this is additional proof that the HIV/AIDS-positive Hambright did none of these things to any of them.

Second Arrest and Charges/Dismissal

Apparently solely on the basis of Hickey's "play therapy diagnoses", Gary Hambright was rearrested in September 1987 and charged with "two counts of oral copulation and ten counts of lewd & lascivious conduct between 5/1/85 and 11/21/86".

By February 17, 1988 a federal judge dismissed all but one of the charges against Hambright as being unsubstantiated. Only a single charge concerning David Tobin remained: oral copulation. Apparently even Dr. Coulter's fallback diagnosis of David's rectum had been abandoned by now. "Oral copulation" at least could be argued to leave no physical mark or damage - although David's parents had originally insisted that he had complained of his penis being **bitten** (which would presumably **have** resulted in such marks and medical exam-detectible damage).

On January 7, 1988 one of Hambright's attorneys filed the following Declaration with the court:

I, Nanci L. Clarence, declare:

1. I am an Assistant Federal Public Defender representing defendant Gary Hambright in this case.

2. Attached hereto as Exhibit A is a true and correct copy of a letter dated December 15, 1986 sent from the Director of Personnel and Community Activities, Lt. Col. Walter Meyer.

3. Attached hereto as Exhibit B is a true and correct copy of a letter dated 1 May 1987 from Joseph V. Rafferty and three pages of attachments.

4. Attached hereto as Exhibit C is a true and correct copy of a two-page memorandum from Walter W. Meyer and two pages of attachments.

5. In preparation of these motions, I have reviewed copies of FBI 302 reports provided to the defendant by this government. The quotations and paraphrases of statements made by parents and children involved in this investigation were taken directly and accurately from these 302 reports and/or other discovery provided by the government. These documents have not been attached to this declaration in the interest of protecting the privacy of the children and their families.

6. I have reviewed the videotape of an interview of David Tobin, age 3, conducted by the Army Criminal Investigative Unit ("CID") on November 21, 1986 at the Presidio of San Francisco.

7. During the interview, one of the interviewers introduced the topic of preschool by asking David whether there was anybody at preschool who should be spanked. The interviewer then asked David whether "Mr. Gary" was bad and whether he should be spanked. This question was asked repeatedly during the interview.

During the interview, David made several other statements about the defendant. In response to the interviewer's questions about "what Mr. Gary did", David answered that "Mr. Gary" bit him on his penis. Moments later, David stated that "Mr. Gary" had bit him on the arm and that Eric, another boy at daycare, bit his penis. Despite David's inconsistency on this subject, the interviewer continued to focus on the question of what "Mr. Gary" had done. In contrast, the interviewer failed to ask follow-up questions about the alleged biting incident with Eric. At another point in the interview, David denied that "Mr. Gary" had touched his penis or done anything wrong.

During the interview, the interviewer encouraged David to make use of anatomically correct dolls, apparently in an attempt to assist David's description of the alleged misconduct. However, the techniques

---

[35] Goldston, "AIDS Tests Urged in Presidio Case", *op.cit.*

employed by the interviewer in using the dolls appeared to encourage certain responses to the questions. For example, at one point, the interviewer told David to "show him what Mr. Gary did." Immediately thereafter, the interviewer told David he could take the pants off the doll. This, and other leading or suggestive lines of questioning, were used throughout the interview.

    8. I also observed that David's mother and father were each present at the interview during different intervals, and that David sat on his parent's lap during most of the interview.

    I declare under the penalty of perjury that the foregoing is true and correct of my own knowledge.

Dated: January 8, 1988
/s/ Nanci L. Clarence
NANCI L. CLARENCE
Assistant Federal Public Defender[36]

"What I saw on the videotape," said Clarence on KTVU, "was a very terrified 3-year-old sitting on his mother's lap being interrogated by a rather large, well-meaning, but somewhat gruff officer." [37]

Subsequently, on February 17, 1988, "the final count of oral copulation against the former Southern Baptist minister was dismissed by U.S. District Judge William Schwarzer after the parents of the alleged victim said their child could not withstand the rigors of the trial." [38]

A different reason was given by the Tobins to Linda Goldston: David "was removed from the case a short time later on the advice of the boy's therapist".[39]

It is easy to see why that therapist would not wish to defend the coached and extracted "allegations of David" discovered by Clarence above, and it is difficult to see how that discovery could constitute any "rigor" to David. Indeed such "rigors" would apply instead to the adults present on that videotape: the "interviewer", Michael Tobin, and Joyce Tobin.

This final exposé of the manufactured witch-hunt against Hambright may have demolished his formal prosecution, but it didn't prevent the disappointed parents from giving "righteously indignant" interviews to the media:

> Ten Army parents whose children were among the 60 apparently abused at the Presidio day-care center rebuked federal prosecutors yesterday for failing to take the case to trial ... They accused prosecutors of being "highly irresponsible" and charged that the Army's response to the apparent epidemic of abuse has been "pitiful".[40]

Clearly acknowledgment of Gary Hambright's innocence, and admission that the whole sensational episode had ultimately been exposed as nothing more than another baseless "play therapy ritual abuse" scam, was emotionally intolerable to these parents - who, it must be noted, would in that case have no grounds at all for the $74 million in claims they had filed against the Army on the grounds that the "abuse" had actually happened.

The Death of Hambright

What happened to Gary Hambright? Readers of the *San Francisco Chronicle*, whose reporter Edward Lempinen had continually written uncritical and inflammatory articles about the Presidio witch-hunt throughout its duration, learned from another reporter two years later:

---

[36] Declaration of Nanci L. Clarence in Support of Defendant's Motion for Hearing re Competency, United States of America, Plaintiff, vs. Gary Hambright, Defendant. Cr. No. 86-1139-WWS, U.S. District Court, Northern District of California, January 7, 1988.

[37] KTVU, *op.cit.*

[38] Lempinen, "Charges Dropped in Presidio Case", *San Francisco Chronicle* 2/18/88.

[39] Goldston, "Army of the Night", *op.cit.*

[40] Lempinen, "Presidio Parents Want a Trial", *San Francisco Chronicle* 4/20/88.

The Baptist minister accused of sexually abusing dozens of children at the Presidio of San Francisco's child care center in 1986 has died of AIDS in Yakima, Washington, closing a chapter in the unsolved molestation case.

Gary Hambright, 36, died November 8, his sister Carolyn Tatro of Yakima said yesterday. Hambright, a Yakima native, was twice indicted for sexually molesting children at the Presidio Child Development Center. Both indictments were dismissed, and Hambright insisted on his innocence until his death.

"This seems to be the sad, final chapter in the story," said Nanci Clarence, one of two federal public defenders who represented Hambright in the child molestation case. "Gary died with a clear conscience. It's just too bad he had to spend the final two years of his life battling these baseless charges."

Hambright's sister said he returned to live with his family in Washington after he became ill. "We loved him very much, and we wanted to be together," she said.[41]

Implications of Information Presented in this Chapter

No children were sexually molested by Gary Hambright at the Presidio of San Francisco Child Development Center during the September 1985-November 1986 period of Hambright's employment as a teacher there.

Parents were predisposed to suspect molestation and "satanic ritual abuse" because of a wave of such accusations about day-care centers across the United States, and a September 1986 series of front-page articles in a major San Francisco newspaper highlighting them.

An alternate parental motive for making day-care "abuse" allegations was knowledge, through that newspaper and other sources, of the sizable claims and lawsuit awards, extending into multimillions of dollars per family to be awarded as a result of such allegations.

In 1986-87 law-enforcement investigators were still uncertain as to how to deal objectively, methodically, and fairly with such politically and emotionally explosive allegations. It had become standard practice to place alleged child victims in the care of therapists using "play therapy" not just to treat emotionally-distressed children but to state that a physical crime had been committed against them. Such statements by therapists were made independent and in disregard of any physical evidence to the contrary. At least one such therapist was responsible for all "findings of abuse" at the Presidio.

Parents and therapists were free to make criminal accusations without fear of legal consequences to themselves, because they always took the position that they were only "repeating what the child had told them". "Play therapy" techniques included coaching, enticing, and threatening children until a desired response was elicited; any previous responses to the contrary were simply ignored.

---

[41] Bill Wallace, "AIDS Kills Minister Accused of Molesting", *San Francisco Chronicle* 1/6/90.

Chapter 2: The Larry Adams-Thompson Accusation

Among the children who had been under the care of Gary Hambright at the Presidio day-care center was Kinsey Almond/A-T, who, once she attained age 3 on September 1, 1986, was an occasional drop-off/pick-up. Hambright's classes included children only age 3 and older.[42]

On January 14, 1987 Kinsey's stepfather Chaplain (Captain) Larry A-T and her mother Michele A-T were interviewed as part of the Tobin allegations follow-up by FBI Special Agent Patricia Peyton [all sic]:

FD-302

FEDERAL BUREAU OF INVESTIGATION

Date of transcription 1/26/87

CAPTAIN LARRY ADAMS-THOMPSON and MRS MICHELE ADAMS-THOMPSON were interviewed at the Child Psychology Clinic at Letterman Hospital. They were aware that the interview was in regard to possible cases of child molestation by a teacher at the Presidio Child Development Center.

Mrs. ADAMS-THOMPSON advised that her daughter, KINSEY, had been attending the school since spring, 1986. When she turned three in September, she was transferred to "Mr. GARY's" (GARY HAMBRIGHT) class. Kinsey attended Mr. GARY's class four times in September, 1986, and twice in October, 1986. She had always enjoyed school, and liked Mr. GARY very much at first. The second and third time she attended his class, she wet her pants, which was very unusual behavior for KINSEY. She became reluctant to go to school and would get fussy, which Mrs. ADAMS-THOMPSON said was very unusual. KINSEY would tell her mother that she did not want to go to school because she did not like it.

On January 6, 1987, Mrs. ADAMS-THOMPSON took KINSEY to school for the first time in several months and KINSEY said "I don't want to see Mr. GARY." When Mrs. ADAMS-THOMPSON asked if Mr. GARY had been mean to her or tried to touch her, KINSEY replied negatively. When told she would be having a new teacher, KINSEY agreed to go. She liked the new teacher very much and now enjoys going to school.

When questioned about behavioral changes, MRS. ADAMS-THOMPSON replied that during the fall of 1986, KINSEY started waking up crying during the night. This was unusual and stopped shortly before Christmas. She also seemed to be more defiant and argumentative with family members. She described KINSEY as outgoing and said she is very comfortable with men and women and that her behavior has not altered.

Mrs. ADAMS-THOMPSON provided the following information regarding KINSEY:

Full name:	KINSEY MARIE ALMOND
Age:	Three years
Date of birth:	September 1, 1983
Address:	1431 "D" Battery Caulfield, Presidio, California
Telephone number:	752-4795
Parents:	Captain LARRY ADAMS-THOMPSON, Step-father MICHELE ADAMS-THOMPSON, mother
Siblings:	One sister, seven years, two step-brothers, nine and thirteen years.

Investigation on 1/14/87 at San Francisco, California

File # SF 70A-111158-56

by SA PATRICIA J. PEYTON/lw

Date dictated 1/14/87

---

[42] See Appendix #10.

The existence and contents of this FBI FD-302 were concealed from me by the FBI, the San Francisco Police Department, and the Army Criminal Investigation Division (CID). I first learned of it when, on September 20, 1989, Federal Public Defender Nanci Clarence sent me a photocopy. Once I read it, the efforts to suppress it were instantly understandable. It established that:

- The A-Ts had not noticed any abnormal behavior by Kinsey prior to "the fall of 1986".

- Her "fall of 1986" unusual behavior was not identifiable to sexual molestation or other bodily injury.

- She had made no statements to her parents about anyone at the Presidio day-care center hurting or touching her improperly.

- She was not assigned to Gary Hambright as a teacher until she attained age 3 on 9/1/86.

- She specifically denied that Hambright had ever "been mean to her or tried to touch her".

- During the entire period of her stays at the day-care center, she had never been taken to a doctor or hospital for examination or treatment of any physical injury or condition related or consequent to those stays.

- After becoming aware of the Tobin allegations in November 1986, the A-Ts had no hesitation about continuing to leave Kinsey at the day-care center [despite their later accusation which would imply a conspiracy of concealment by Hambright's fellow teachers and supervisors].

In short, it was strong evidence in exoneration of Gary Hambright where Kinsey Almond was concerned, and it was **conclusive** evidence in exoneration of Lilith and myself - since **we were documented to be in Washington, D.C. on every date during September-October 1986 when Kinsey was in Hambright's class at the day-care center**.[43]

On March 12, 1987 Kinsey received a thorough physical examination at Letterman Hospital's Pediatrics Clinic. Dr. John Sheridan, who conducted the examination, was aware of the ongoing day-care abuse allegations, because he headed his report "3-1/2 yr old female. Alleged victim of sexual abuse in Post Day Care Center". Therefore he had every reason to look specifically for any signs that such abuse had happened to Kinsey. He wrote his findings [sic] [emphasis mine]:

> HEENT - WNL. Chest - Clear. Abd - Benign. Skin - Clear.
> Genitalia: Ext - WNL, **Vagina - Hymenal ring intact, no disch. Rect - No evidence of laceration, normal tone.**
> Imp: **No physical evidence of abuse.**
> HIV antibody test. VDRL. GC throat, rectum, Vag Pool.[44]

Despite their knowledge of Kinsey's history as contained in the FBI FD-302 report, as well as her physically-unharmed condition as verified by this medical examination, the A-Ts had decided to schedule Kinsey for "play-therapy" sessions with psychiatrist Debbie Hickey beginning February 1987.

"Play therapy" was the most common and notorious feature of the nationwide "ritual abuse" scares, leading to usually-multiple allegations of rape, sodomy, and similar crimes where no other evidence existed to substantiate them. One private investigator observes:

---

[43] During September-October 1986 I was on active duty as a student at the Industrial College of the Armed Forces, National Defense University, where daily attendance was of course required and records kept for all student officers.

[44] Standard Form 600, Chronological Record of Medical Care, Adams-Thompson Kinsey #02-56276-34-92, Letterman Army Medical Center, 3/12/87.

The nature of the customary sexual abuse treatment given to children when there is an accusation of sexual abuse is insight oriented, dynamic, and feeling expressive psychotherapy (Wakefield & Underwager, 1988).

A child is forced to continue talking about feelings, acting out in play, and responding to questions about having been abused.

Researchers, after reviewing records of several hundred cases, have found at most a half dozen where the therapy provided to a child was anything other than insight oriented, feeling expressive therapy. With younger children, it is exclusively play therapy.

In the videotapes of therapy that researchers reviewed, they have seen children being given a toy gun and taught to shoot a Bobo doll identified as Bad Daddy, children encouraged to throw darts at pictures of the person accused, make clay figures of the person accused and then pound them with mallets and hammers, and throw dolls identified as the person accused in boxes labeled jail.

Children are reinforced for yelling screaming, saying angry and hostile things about the person accused. Children are taught to be fearful, to believe they have been victimized, and to believe people they love are wicked and evil.

Play therapy of this nature cannot be anything other than destructive and harmful to the child (Campbell, 1992a; 1992b; Russ, 1987; Trad, 1992; Casey, & Berman, 1985).

When a child who has not been abused is treated by adults who have concluded the child has been abused, it is tragically the case that the adults teach the child to be a victim. If a child continuously denies the abuse the adult believes in, the adult does not accept that no abuse occurred. Instead, the adult concludes the child is dissociating, repressing the memory, and may give a diagnosis of Multiple Personality Disorder. The child is then coerced and forced to develop this most serious iatrogenic malady. The end result may well be the destruction of the child for any normal adult life.[45]

Dr. Terence Campbell, a distinguished, board-certified psychologist, comments:

1. Any evidence supporting the effectiveness of play therapy for children is is characterized by its conspicuous absence.

2. For example, play therapy does not appear to enhance academic or intellectual achievement.

3. Treatment effects for play therapy are conspicuously absent when dealing with specific behavioral disorders.

4. Moreover, play therapy does not improve the interpersonal adjustment of children who participate in it.

5. As long ago as in 1975, a review of treatment approaches for children emphasized that the era of blind faith in the activities of play therapy had ended. In other words, play therapy amounts to what - at best - is an experimental treatment not known to be effective.

6. The parents of children participating play therapy assume their children respond positively to this treatment. These parental impressions, however, are not supported by objective data. In other words, the outcomes parents attribute to their children's therapy are influenced more by their excessively optimistic expectations than anything else.

7. Related data also demonstrate that play therapy does not effectively aid children known to have been abused. The study supporting this conclusion reported: "No consistent support was found for the hypothesis that time-limited play therapy would improve the adjustment of maltreated preschoolers who already were attending a therapeutic preschool."

8. In cases of suspected sexual abuse, however, play therapy can distort and confuse the recall of children.

---

[45] Allen Cowling - Cowling Investigations, Inc. http://www.allencowling.com

9. In these cases of distorted memory, the therapist becomes the source of what the child remembers rather than the event in question.[46]

After four "play therapy" sessions with Kinsey, Hickey informed her parents that she had "disclosed being molested".[47] Based on this, and despite their knowledge to the contrary as evidenced in the 1/14/87 FBI FD-302 and the 3/12/87 medical examination, Larry and Michele A-T in April 1987 accused Gary Hambright of sexually abusing Kinsey. The letter to Hambright from the Presidio Headquarters stated:

> You sexually abused a three-year-old child, Kinsey Adams-Thompson, on at least one occasion while she was in your care at the Presidio Child Development Center. Such act or acts took place sometime in September or October 1986 at the Child Development Center, Presidio of San Francisco.[48] [49]

Exactly what took place during the months of Hickey's "play therapy" sessions with Kinsey and the other Presidio day-care children she pronounced as "sexually abused" remained a secret for years. FOIA/PA requests were refused on the basis of the confidentiality of medical records. It is even doubtful that the FBI and the SFPD ever saw the "play therapy" records of Kinsey - for if they had seen how bizarre and incoherent they were, and compared those actual records with what Lawrence and Michele claimed they proved, their accusations would presumably have been discredited right then.

During the San Francisco Police investigation of Lilith and myself, as well as the later CID investigation, the Hickey records remained concealed. When all investigations were closed, they still remained concealed. At any time, of course, Larry and Michele A-T could have given permission for them to be released to me, but clearly that was not in their interest, as the contents would later reveal.

I finally obtained the original Hickey "play-therapy" notes in April 1991 through Discovery in my lawsuit against the Army over the fraudulent CID Report of Investigation.[50] Even then, and of course in violation of federal Discovery law, many pages had been removed and remained concealed. As it was the CID's position that the notes provided contained all information pertinent to the A-Ts' accusations and the CID Report, I reviewed and analyzed those notes on that premise. The complete notes [received] are at Appendix #12, and my analysis of them is at Appendix #13. It should be borne in mind that, in all of my 1987-3/1991 efforts to defend ourselves and prosecute Larry A-T, this crucial information was completely concealed from me.

---

[46] Terence W. Campbell, Ph.D. (University of Maryland 1970). Licensure and Certifications: Fully Licensed Psychologist (State of Michigan #01174), Licensed Marriage and Family Counselor (State of Michigan #05478). Approved and Listed: National Register of Health Service Providers in Psychology. Diplomate Status: Board Certified in Forensic Psychology by the American Board of Professional Psychology. http://www.campsych.com

[47] Larry Adams-Thompson, statement to San Francisco Police Department 8/14/87. This would have been after the 2/3/87 Hickey session, whose notes appear in Appendix #12.

[48] Letter, John R. Gunnarson, Director, Child Development Services Branch, Presidio to Gary Hambright 4/17/87.

[49] Note the specific location and date-window. Kinsey had been under Hambright's supervision only during this time period [because of her age], and then only as an unscheduled drop-off/pick-up "babysitting" child. This would have made any transportation for molestation away from and back to the center quite impossible. The date-window would become crucial later, when the CID - frustrated by our verified location in Washington, D.C. during that window - sought to solve their problem by arbitrarily revising the dates of the accusation several months back to June 1987. This illegal action by the CID will be discussed in detail later.

[50] Certificate of Service, Patrick Lisowski, 4/17/91.

In August 1987, still completely unaware of the "sex abuse" scandal at the Presidio, Lilith and I returned to our home in San Francisco after a year in Washington, D.C., where I had been a student in the prestigious Industrial College of the Armed Forces, National Defense University.[51]

On 8/12/87 Lilith and I drove to the Presidio Post-Exchange to buy a microwave oven. As far as we were concerned, it was a completely uneventful shopping trip.

Unknown to us, however, at least one of the adult A-Ts had also been present at the PX and had recognized us there. At 4:45 that afternoon Larry A-T telephoned the FBI office and initiated his accusations against us, as recorded in the FBI FD-302 of that conversation:

FD-302

FEDERAL BUREAU OF INVESTIGATION

Date of transcription 8/13/87

LARRY ADAMS-THOMPSON, address 1431 D Battery Caulfield, Presidio Army Base, San Francisco, California, telephonically contacted SA GALYEAN at approximately 4:45 pm and thereafter furnished the following information:

LARRY is the father of KINSEY ADAMS-THOMPSON and was present with her at approximately 4:00 pm on August 12, 1987, at the Post Exchange, Presidio Army Base. At that time KINSEY was observed by LARRY to become visibly frightened upon observing a male and female whom KINSEY identified as "MIKEY" and "SHAMBY". LARRY also observed the male and female and noted that the male made eye contact with KINSEY but averted his gaze from LARRY. LARRY was immediately aware that KINSEY was referring to the MIKEY and SHAMBY whom KINSEY had previously reported to them as having been at the residence where she was sexually molested by GARY HAMBRIGHT. LARRY and KINSEY then went to their automobile in the parking lot of the Post Exchange and waited for MIKEY and SHAMBY to exit the Post Exchange. LARRY stated that he was familiar with the male as being Lieutenant Colonel MIKE AQUINO, who was previously associated with a physical training program at the Presidio. LARRY had also observed the female SHAMBY to be at several functions with Lieutenant Colonel AQUINO and had been known as AQUINO's wife. Upon observing AQUINO and the female exit the Post Exchange LARRY observed the couple enter a red Isuzu Mark I automobile and then obtained the license tag number, which he wrote down as California License Number 2ENS452. LARRY and KINSEY thereafter returned to their residence where KINSEY was observed to be extremely frightened that MIKEY and SHAMBY would come to her residence and harm her. LARRY further stated that KINSEY was very talkative about the bad things MIKEY and SHAMBY had done to her along with HAMBRIGHT at the residence away from the Day-care Center.

LARRY was advised that SA FOREMAN would interview KINSEY and family in person as soon as possible.

Investigation on 8/12/87 at SAN FRANCISCO, TELEPHONE
File # SF 70A-111158
by SA HUGH W. GALYEAN/mwt
Date dictated 8/13/87

Significantly neither this FC-302 nor the ones of Michele and Kinsey that followed it were made or cited as exhibits in the CID's final 1990 Report of Investigation (ROI). Indeed they were again all concealed from me until the Discovery phase of my 1991 lawsuit *Aquino v Stone* forced their disclosure by the CID. So why had it been felt so necessary to hide them?

To begin with, there was no evidence which or how many of the A-Ts had been at the PX [although obviously at least one of the two adults was], or that any of the "recognition/behavior" events ever happened at all. Had Lilith or

---

[51] Only one U.S. Army Reserve officer each year is selected for this Senior Service College (regarded as a training-ground for future generals and admirals). I was that single USAR officer for the Class of 1987. Although our class graduated in June, my departure was delayed because I was still finishing up a Master of Public Administration degree at George Washington University, a simultaneous program offered to ICAF students.

I noticed any such close-up commotion as described, I'm sure at least one of us would have paid attention to it and probably spoken to the adult(s) on the spot. Neither at this time nor at any future time did the FBI/SFPD/CID attempt to interview anyone at the PX for witness or corroboration (such as the checkout cashier processing the microwave purchase).

Looking in detail at Larry's statements to Galyean:

- They falsified and contradicted what Kinsey had actually said in the Hickey notes during all of the six months of sessions to date. It was **Michele**, not Kinsey, who first mentioned the name "Mikey" [during the 6/30/87 session] and described "Mikey" and "Shambee" as husband and wife. On 1/27/87 "Shambee" was introduced by Kinsey as "her friend at school" who was spanked by Mr. Rogers on TV. Kinsey added that Shambee "also had **its** neck broken", indicating that "Shambee" was either an imaginary "friend" or perhaps a doll.[52]

- Kinsey had never described "Shambee" and/or "Mikey" as "having been at the residence where she was sexually molested by Gary Hambright".

- Throughout the entire PX encounter, Larry mentions **only** Kinsey and himself being present - no other family members. This would change the next day, by which time, of course, he had had plenty of opportunity to discuss the scenario with Michele and Kinsey.

At 9AM the following morning (8/13/87) SA Clyde Foreman interviewed first Michele, then Kinsey at the A-T home. Curiously he felt no need to re-interview Larry, having no questions concerning his brief telephone statement to Galyean.

FD-302

FEDERAL BUREAU OF INVESTIGATION

Date of transcription <u>8/13/87</u>

[All sic] MICHELLE ADAMS-THOMPSON, 1431 D Battery Caulfield, Presidio of San Francisco, California, was interviewed by Bureau agent who properly identified himself and explained the nature of the interview. MICHELLE ADAMS-THOMPSON provided the following information:

On Wednesday, August 12, 1987, at approximately 4:00 pm she was shopping at the Post Exchange at the Presidio of San Francisco with her husband LARRY, and her daughter KINSEY. As they walked through the store KINSEY ran to her and LARRY and told them that she had seen a man named "MIKEY" that she knew from Mr. GARY'S house.

MICHELLE recalled on prior ocassions KINSEY had described MIKEY as a man who wore an army suit "like daddies" and that he had eyebrows that went up. KINSEY also called MIKEY "the blood man".

MICHELLE picked KINSEY up and asked her to look across the aisle of merchandise and point out the individual that she was referring to. KINSEY identified a male white adult that LARRY ADAMS-THOMPSON knew as Colonel MICHAEL AQUINO.

MICHELLE discussed With KINSEY that it was important that she be positive about correctly identifying this individual. She preceded to walk past Colonel AQUINO allowing KINSEY to view him from a distance of several feet. After walking past him KINSEY told her that it was infact "MIKEY" and that she wanted to leave the store because she was afraid of him.

LARRY ADAMS-THOMPSON escorted KINSEY to the parking lot and MICHELLE followed Colonel AQUINO to the checkout stand where she observed that he provided an active duty military identification card to the clerk in order to purchase a microwave oven. MICHELLE observed him sign his name MICHAEL A. AQUINO and watched him exit the store to the parking lot.

MICHELLE, LARRY, and KINSEY drove through the parking lot where they observed Colonel AQUINO standing next to a red vehicle with California License plate 2EW5453. (This vehicle was a 1987,

---

[52] Appendices #12 & 13.

Isuzu) KINSEY observed a women standing next to the vehicle and said "Thats SHAMBY". KINSEY explained that SHAMBY was with MR. GARY and MIKEY and that she was bad with the kids.

MICHELLE discussed with KINSEY whether she could talk about MIKEY and MR. GARY with the Federal Bureau of Investigation. KINSEY said that she could talk with the Federal Bureau of Investigation and that she would tell them how MIKEY had put blood on her and had licked it off and that he had put his penis on her.

MICHELLE said that KINSEY has frequently described "Mr. GARY'S house" as a house with several stairs leading to the front door and that it is gray in color.

Investigation on 8/13/87 at PRESIDIO OF SAN FRANCISCO
File # 70A-111158-209
by SA CLYDE E. FOREMAN/mwt
Date dictated 8/13/87

Looking in detail at Michele's statements to Foreman:

- Now Michele is present at the PX too. [Additional A-Ts would be added in the future as an attempt to prop up the rapidly-collapsing the PX story.]

- Larry said that he was "with Kinsey" in the PX. Now Michele has Kinsey "running to them". Running requires a distance. Would the parents have let their 3-year-old child wander away from them in the store?

- Now Kinsey "identifies" only "Mikey". "Shamby" is not present at all in the store.

- As with Larry, Michele's statement that Kinsey said she knew "Mikey" "from Mr. Gary's house" is contradicted by the Hickey notes.

- The description of "Mikey" as "wearing an Army suit" was again Michele's, not Kinsey's.

- My "famous" pointed eyebrows were of course visible to either adult in the PX, and were known to Larry per his statement of instantly recognizing me from my assignment at the Presidio. [Evidently he had paid more attention to me than I had to him at the time.]

- Kinsey never refers to anyone as "the blood man" in the Hickey notes.

- After recognizing me, Michele picks Kinsey up and asks her to "point 'Mikey' out across the aisle of merchandise". Michele of course would have had Kinsey facing me, and the probability of more than one man in such close proximity as an aisle is low. [Nor, of course, did I notice any woman/child pointing fingers at me, which further speaks to Michele's account as pure invention.]

- Michele, apparently still carrying Kinsey, walks past me even closer, having a conversation about "Mikey". I still do not notice any such two persons.

- Michele is now looking so closely over my shoulder at the checkout stand that she can not only see my Army ID card but watch me sign "Michael A. Aquino". Are we to believe that I would not notice, and object to, someone next to me examining my financial transaction that intimately? Not to mention that my signature is a series of loops and lines which do not individually-letter "Michael A. Aquino".

- The [still only] three A-Ts are now in their car. They drive near enough to the car I am using for Kinsey to "recognize" Lilith as "Shamby". As noted above, throughout the Hickey notes Kinsey never accused "Shambee" of anything; it was only Michele who did.

- Kinsey never said in the Hickey notes that "Mikey had put blood on her and had licked it off and that he had put his penis on her." Again this is original to Michele in this FBI statement.

- As at least one adult A-T was in their car, as we drove straight to our house a few blocks away to unload the microwave, it would have been easy for him/her/them to follow us and observe that our house was a gray building with steps to its door. Once again the Hickey notes refute Kinsey's actually saying this herself; indeed every mention she made of a house throughout the sessions contradicts all actual features of our house.

Kinsey, whom her parents had now had 17 hours to privately coach and rehearse since one or both of them had seen us at the PX, was also interviewed by Foreman:

FD-302

FEDERAL BUREAU OF INVESTIGATION

Date of transcription 8/13/87

[All sic] KINSEY ADAMS-THOMPSON, was interviewed by Bureau agent with parental permission at her residence. KINSEY is known to the interviewing agent and provided the following information:

She was shown a group of five photographs containing a photograph of GARY WILLARD HAMBRIGHT. She examined the photographs and pointed out HAMBRIGHT's photo stating "Thats Mr. GARY". KINSEY said that Mr. GARY had placed his penis into her bottom, vagina, and her mouth. Mr. GARY did this on more than one ocassion and that the first time it occurred was at her school. She recalled traveling with Mr. GARY in a green car to his house where he took photographs of her. Also present at the house were MIKEY and SHAMBY. KINSEY said that the house had a bathtub with lions feet and that she was taken to the residence on more than one ocassion. Once she recalled having Cheerios with brown sugar on them for lunch. KINSEY said that MIKEY wears army clothes like my daddies. MIKEY put his penis into her mouth, bottom, and vagina just like Mr. GARY.

MIKEY, and Mr. GARY would dress up in girls clothes and Mrs. SHAMBY wore boys clothes at Mr. GARY's house. MIKEY and SHAMBY touched her private parts and Mr. GARY touched her private parts.

Interviewing agent drew a stick figure of KINSEY which she was asked to circle on the figure those areas where Mr. GARY had touched her. She first drew a black circle over the groin and chest area and a second circle over the mouth of the stick figure. A second stick figure was drawn representing Mr. GARY. KINSEY was asked if she had ever seen Mr. GARY'S penis at which point she drew a line from one stick figure to the other indicating that Mr. GARY had a penis and that he had touched her with it.

Investigation on 8/13/87 at PRESIDIO OF SAN FRANCISCO
File # 70A-111158
by SA CLYDE E. FOREMAN/mwt
Date dictated 8/13/87

Looking in detail at Kinsey's statements to Foreman:

- First, of course, what's conspicuous for its absence? **Any mention whatever of the purported PX encounter/"identification".** And this was supposedly the central point of this recontact of the FBI. But Kinsey said not a word about seeing either of us, "identifying" either of us, or connecting us with "Mikey and Shamby". Nor did Foreman, supposedly there specifically to ask her about that, ask her about that.

- Kinsey states that on at least two occasions Gary Hambright inserted his penis into her vagina and rectum, and that on at least one occasion "Mikey" did too. This is refuted by the medical examination of Kinsey, which described both her vagina and her rectum as normal and free from any signs of rape.

- Kinsey now states that she was taken to Hambright's house on more than one occasion. During the 4/7/87 "play therapy" session, however, Hickey asked Almond **twice** if she ever went anywhere with Hambright. Both times Almond said **no**. Only after Hickey still persisted asking the same question did Almond finally change her answer to yes. And, again, **Kinsey was always a random drop-off/pick-up child at the day-care center**. There would have been no time to take her anywhere else, particularly for such elaborate events as she states here, if her parents might arrive at the center at any moment to pick her up. And, obviously, they always found her there unraped, unbruised, and untraumatized.[53]

- Hambright was an epileptic who did not have a driver's license nor own a car.

- No photographs of Kinsey taken by Hambright were ever produced.

- Our bathtub is a flush-to-the-floor model with no feet, obviously [by its wear] installed many years before 1986. Nowhere else in the building is there a "footed" bathtub either.

- The "army clothes" statement was first introduced into the Hickey sessions by Michele, not Kinsey, on 6/30/87. Michele makes the same statement again in her 8/13/87 interview above, so she is obviously very dedicated to pushing it.

- No female clothing of male size was found at our home when it was searched the following day, nor for that matter male clothing of female size. Presumably no such items were ever found at Hambright's residence either, otherwise we would have heard about it.

- Kinsey never said in the Hickey notes that "Shambee" touched her anywhere, including private parts.

- The stick figure: Once again, in the only untainted [by Hickey's "play therapy" indoctrinating] FBI interview of 1/14/87, Kinsey denied that Hambright had ever even tried to touch her.

- Kinsey's "drawing a line from one stick figure to the other" being interpreted by Foreman as Hambright's "touching her with his penis" speaks more for Foreman's mental predisposition than artwork *per se*.

In summary the three A-T FBI interviews of 8/12&13/87 were a clumsy, transparent, factually- and mutually-contradictory failure for the parents and Foreman, and that is why they were instantly buried and remained so throughout all of the investigations.

But the efforts to manufacture some kind of "evidence" were not yet over for the day. Foreman and Michele were determined that Kinsey should "identify" our house as the one to which she had "been taken" [despite the aforementioned impossibility, and Kinsey's denial, of any such trip]. A CID agent, Bradley J. Potter, was taken along to write the official report.

The media would be told that this excursion resulted in Kinsey's "identification" of our house, which for years would be held up as one of the most significant "proofs" of our guilt. Once again both the existence and the actual contents of the Potter report were concealed from us until after all the investigations, leading me during that interval to suppose only that A-T had simply followed us home from the PX on 8/12/87 and made enough notes about its location and appearance to be used in Michele's 8/13/87 interview and now this excursion.

When finally obtained in 1991 in *Aquino v Stone* Discovery, the Potter report told quite a different story. Here it is: [Note: Throughout this book the address of our 1987 San Francisco home is shown as "123 Acme Avenue" out of consideration for the current residents at that address.]

---

[53] FBI FD-302 1/14/87, this chapter.

AGENT'S INVESTIGATION REPORT
ROI Number 0499-87-CID026
CID Regulation 195-1
Page 1 of 1 pages

[All sic] <u>BACKGROUND:</u> This Agent's Investigation Report is prepared in conjunction with the interview of Kinsey ADAMS-THOMPSON, conducted by SA Clyde FOREMAN, FBI, San Francisco, CA, which was conducted on 13 Aug 87.

<u>NARRATIVE:</u>

1. <u>Interview of Victim:</u>

1.1 <u>Kinsey Marie ADAMS-THOMPSON (D/SD OF CPT Larry P. ADAMS-THOMPSON; 562-76-3492; formerly residing at 1431-D Battery Caulfied, Presidio of San Francisco CA 94129):</u>

On 13 Aug 87, Kinsey was interviewed by SA FOREMAN, at her residence. SA FOREMAN had been advised by Kinsey's parents of an incident which occurred at the Presidio Main Post Exchange on 12 Aug 87. This incident involved Kinsey identifying 'Mickie & Shambi', (LTC & Mrs AQUINO), while inside the PX. SA FOREMAN conducted the interview between 0900-0945, 13 Aug 87. After the interview was conducted, SA FOREMAN advised SA POTTER that Kinsey stated she would be able to locate the house where 'Mr GARY' had taken her. Kinsey, her mother, SA FOREMAN, and SA POTTER then departed Presidio, via the Lombard Gate, past the CDC. While on Lombard Street, east bound, Kinsey was observed holding her right hand in a manner which had her thumb, index finger, and little finger extended, leaving the middle and ring fingers curled underneath. Kinsey, while holding her hand in this manner, stated to SA POTTER, 'Mr GARY showed me how to do this', or words to that effect. Kinsey did not direct SA POTTER, who was driving, where to turn, or which route to take. SA POTTER drove the the vicinity of the 100 block of Acme Avenue, San Fracisco, CA and parked the vehicle about 11/2 blocks south of the 100 block on Acme Avenue. Mrs ADAMS-THOMPSON, Kinsey, SA FOREMAN and SA POTTER then exited the vechicle and began walking in the neighborhood. While walking down Acme Avenue (north), on the east side of the street, Kinsey appeared to show a behavioral change. Approximately 10-15 feet before coming to the front of 123 Acme Avenue, Kinsey began to appear frightened and wanted to be held by her mother. Kinsey was picked up by her mother, but continued to stare at the front of 123 Acme Avenue. It was observed that four mail boxes were located adjacent to the entrance to the residence. Kinsey was taken further north on Acme Avenue, then back on the west side of the street, where Kinsey then picked out an automobile as belonging to, 'Mickie and Shanbie'. The car was subsequently identified as a red colored sedan that had been rented by/to LTC AQUINO. This information was verified by SA FOREMAN.///LAST ENTRY///

Typed Agent's Name and Sequence Number:
BRADLEY J. POTTER, 2331
Organization:
Oakland Branch Office, Sixth Region,
USACIDC, Oakland Army Base, CA 94626-5000
/s/Robert R. Buik [sp?], 2073   13 Aug 87

Passing over the oddity of why the CID Agent making this report didn't sign it himself, what do its details actually reveal?

- Foreman's statement to Potter that "Kinsey stated that she would be able to locate the house where 'Mr Gary' had taken her" was not included in the record of his interview with her that morning.

- Potter drove straight from the Presidio to Acme Avenue. Kinsey was not shown any other block or neighborhood either previously or subsequently.

- The hand sign (thumb, index, & little fingers extended) that Kinsey was observed making during the drive was presumably mentioned because Potter [or Michele A-T] assumed it to be the Satanic "Sign of the Horns". It was **not**. It was rather the American Sign Language sign (invented for the deaf, but used habitually by many people) for "I love you". It is frequently used by teachers, politicians, *et al.*; and there is even a U.S. postage stamp dedicated to it. [The Satanic Sign of the Horns has the thumb over the two lowered middle fingers. This is **not** what Kinsey was doing. Nor, it may be added, does the Temple of Set use the Sign of the Horns, as it is regarded as an obsolete Church of Satan-era gesture only.]

- Potter acknowledges that when leaving the Presidio, he received no guidance from Kinsey at all concerning what direction to take. So it was on Foreman's instructions that he went directly to Acme Avenue.

- When led on foot to 123 Acme Avenue, Kinsey "appeared frightened and wanted to be held by her mother". So Michele picked her up and held her right in front of the building, so that Kinsey could "continue to stare at it". Michele picked up Kinsey and held her in front of no other building - just that one, which she knew was our address.

- Despite this prompting from Michele, Kinsey said nothing whatever about the building. She did not point at it, scream, turn away from it, or "identify" it in any way.

- When taken back up the same block, Kinsey didn't react at all when passing 123. Evidently she and Michele were now uninterested in it, because the performance" had been done.

- Moreover it would have been impossible for Kinsey not to walk back right in front of 123, because there is no sidewalk on the other side of that block - just a wall with cars parked next to it - and that block sees constant vehicle traffic in the daytime.

- The "car identification" was meaningless, because at least one of the adult A-Ts, and possibly Kinsey, had seen the rented red Isuzu at the PX on 8/12 and written down its license number.

In summary, **Kinsey made no house "identification" whatever**, despite the guiding and prompting of her to do so at 123 Acme Avenue. Because of her parents' ignorance of actual Temple of Set symbolism, they also coached her to show the FBI/CID a "Satanic" hand gesture which we in fact do not use.

So again it is obvious why this report was concealed, even to the extent of officially denying its existence.

At this point Foreman referred Larry A-T to the San Francisco Police Department. He telephoned Sergeant-Inspector Glenn Pamfiloff and made an appointment for Larry to see him the following morning.

At 9AM on 8/14/87 Larry A-T walked alone into Pamfiloff's office and told him what throughout all the subsequent investigations I referred to as his "package story". It was the story routinely quoted in the media for years [and still is on various crank and conspiracy Internet websites today]. Unlike the hushed-up FBI reports and inaccessible Hickey notes, Pamfiloff's SFPD Incident Report was automatically a public record.

Because of both its significance and its publicity, the rest of this chapter is devoted to it. I have annotated it to show the extent of Larry A-T's deliberate lies in telling this "package story" to the SFPD:

SFPD Incident Report
(Annotated by Michael A. Aquino)
(Original Text in This Typeface)
(Annotations Indented and in This Typeface)
For readability, the symbols (P2, V, S1, etc.) are replaced in the narrative with names.

Incident No. 870910025 - Initial
Type of Incident: Child Molest
Unit Rptg: 5T10
Date(s) & time(s) of occurrence: Mon. 09/01/86–0730 to Fri. 10/31/86–1600
Date & time reported to police: Fri. 08/14/87–0900
Date & time reported to bureau or ctr: Fri. 08/14/87–0900
Name & star reported to: Pamfiloff 228
Location of occurrence: 123 Acme Ave.
Location sent to: 2475 Greenwich St.
Type of premise: Apt.
Reporting officer/star: Insp. G. Pamfiloff 228
Victim (V): Almond, Kinsey M., WF, DOB 09/01/83, Phone 752-4795.
Reportee (R/P1): Adams-Thompson, Larry P. WM, DOB 01/16/49, Phone 752-4795.
Suspect (S1): Aquino, Michael A., OtherM, 10/16/46, Alias Mikey, Address 123 Acme Ave.
(P2): Adams-Thompson, Michele E., WF 08/17/57, 1431 Battery Caulfield, Presidio 752-4795
(R2): Foreman, Clyde, WM, FBI Special Agent, 450 Golden Gate Ave, 553-7400.
(S2): Aquino, Lilith (aka Sinclair), WF 04/21/42, 123 Acme Ave. (aka Shamby)
(S3): Hambright, Gary W., WM, 07/07/53, 208 Dolores St., 861-1434.

Narrative:

On Thu. 08/13/87, 1530 hrs, Glenn Pamfiloff was told by Clyde Foreman that he had interviewed Larry Adams-Thompson, Michele Adams-Thompson and Kinsey Almond and had gotten information that Kinsey Almond had been molested in the city and county of San Francisco.

1. This "information of molestation" consisted of the three statements made to the FBI on 8/12&13/87 by Larry and Michele A-T and Kinsey, plus presumably Hickey's "diagnosis". It was refuted by the 3/12/87 medical examination report of Kinsey verifying that she was a virgin with "no physical evidence of abuse". This refutation, plus the contradictory statements of the A-Ts in the 1/14/87 FBI interview, was not provided to Pamfiloff by either Foreman or Larry A-T.

Glenn Pamfiloff phoned Larry Adams-Thompson and an appt. was made with he and Kinsey Almond, Fri. 08/14/87–0900 at Juvenile Division.
Larry Adams-Thompson stated that between the above dates and times, Kinsey Almond was dropped off at San Francisco Presidio Day Care Center approximately four or five times.

1. As Pamfiloff confirmed personally to me on 4/16/91, this meeting and conversation was exclusively between Larry A-T and himself, and that during the entire investigation he had never once talked with Kinsey at all.

2. The "above dates and times" are September 1-October 31, 1986. Note that Larry A-T was **specific and exclusive** about this window, just as he and Michele had been **specific and exclusive** to FBI SA Peyton on 1/14/87. The Aquinos were later verified to be in Washington, D.C. on all dates during this window on which Kinsey had been at the Presidio day-care center.

3. In a 2/18/87 interview with FBI Agent Foreman, Hickey also stated that "during the month of September 1986 Kinsey was moved into an hourly day care class under the direct care and control of

Gary Hambright", and that it was specifically during **this** window that the wetting incidents (supposedly symptomatic of the later-alleged "abuse") occurred.

4.   When the CID later attempted to move the A-Ts' allegations back several months to June 1986 when the Aquinos **were** still living in San Francisco, in order to "fit them to the allegations somehow", the fact that the supposed "evidence" of the wetting incidents took place in **September** was simply ignored, despite the fact that one or both of these incidents supposedly "proved" that such a crime happened at all.

Larry Adams-Thompson states that on two occasions when he picked up Kinsey Almond at the end of the day, he was informed by Gary Hambright that Kinsey Almond had wet her pants and Larry Adams-Thompson was provided with the soiled panties, and on one occasion with soiled outer pants. This was unusual as Kinsey Almond had not wet herself in approximately a year. At this time, Kinsey Almond started having nightmares, and would wet herself when frightened.

1.   There is no mention in their 1/14/87 FBI interview that either adult A-T complained to the daycare staff about this wetting, or took Kinsey for any medical examination because of it [or nightmares]. There is no mention that any of the alleged nightmares had any sexual molestation themes to them, or mention that the A-Ts took Kinsey for any psychiatric examination because of them.

2.   Again with reference to the later attempts to backdate the A-T allegations: In her 4/23/87 Sworn Affidavit, Hickey stated, and related both A-Ts as stating to her, that Kinsey's attitude and behavior were **completely normal** prior to the September-October 1986 window.

Larry Adams-Thompson states that in Jan. of 1987 he became aware a child molest investigation involving Gary Hambright at the Presidio Day Care Center.

1.   The news of the Presidio allegations begun by the Tobins was announced by letter to all Presidio parents by Lt. Colonel Meyer, Presidio HQ, on December 15, 1986 (Appendix #10).

2.   In the *San Jose Mercury News West* (11/24/88) it was stated that "On Thursday (11/20/86) Mike Tobin spoke with a chaplain at the Presidio, who contacted the Army's CID". That chaplain was probably Larry A-T, because the Tobins' and the A-Ts' names appeared together on a later April 1987 alarmist letter to other parents in furtherance of the Presidio scare.

Kinsey Almond was questioned on 01/14/87 by an FBI Agent but made no definitive statements.

1.   Larry A-T lies to Pamfiloff. From Kinsey's 1/14/87 FBI interview: "When Mrs. Adams-Thompson asked if Mr. Gary had been mean to her or tried to touch her, **Kinsey replied negatively**." That's a very definite **denial** of any abuse.

Kinsey Almond was subsequently entered into child therapy in Feb. 1987 and after four visits, the therapist informed Larry Adams-Thompson that Kinsey Almond had disclosed being molested.

1.   Larry A-T lies to Pamfiloff. Per Hickey's 2/18/87 statement to Foreman, the A-Ts entered Kinsey into therapy with her on **January** 13, 1987 (the day before the initial FBI interview containing Kinsey's **denial** of any abuse).

2.   Assuming from the Hickey transcripts that were obtained in 1991 under lawsuit Discovery that the Kinsey sessions were weekly, the fourth session would have been 2/3/87. The notes for that session [from Appendix #12]:

I asked her if Mr. Gary was a bad man - she said "no, that Mr. Gary loves me and scares me". I asked her how Mr. Gary loves her. She replied that he "hugs me & never spanks me". I asked if Mr. Gary did anything else to love her. She replied, "No." I asked if Mr. Gary kissed her. She replied, "No, but other kids kissed Mr. Gary and blow Mr. Gary in a yucky way." I asked her how, and she said, "Mr. Gary touched" in a "naked place". Asked her to show me where. She pointed to her genital region. Then said, "Mr. Gary goes pee-pee on a boy's shoe," and spontaneously said Mr. Gary had a "penis" which she said was "soft" and his did too. Said kids touched Mr. Gary's penis. When I asked how, she replied, "Like my thumb," and placed her thumb in her mouth and began to suck on it. I asked her if his penis was hard or soft. She said it was "hard" and then Mr. Gary went pee-pee" and kids would "get sick and throw up". I asked her if Mr. Gary ever did this to her, and she said, "Yes, it tasted yucky - the pee-pee and it went on my shoes." I asked if she had done this to anyone else, and she said the "little girls did this to the little boys", but could not/ would not tell me any names. I asked if Mr. Gary ever took his clothes off, and she said, "Yes." I asked if he took his shirt off, and she said, "Yes, and even showed us his boobs." I asked if she had ever taken her clothes off, and she said, "Yes." I asked her if Mr. Gary had ever touched her, and she said, "Yes, in my naked part," and said he had "spanked" her, pointing to doll's buttocks. I asked her if he had ever touched her anywhere else, and she said, "Yes," and pointed to her vaginal area and said, "On my penis. He put hot water on my penis. Don't tell my dad." Session began to end there. I asked her two or three more times if anyone else had ever done this, and she said, "No." I asked her 2-3 times if she ever played this game with anyone else, and she kept replying, "Mr. Gary." Session ended with patient telling me we shouldn't talk to anyone else about this. Patient wanted to continue to wash doll's hair, and placed doll beside the sink to let its hair dry. Patient wanted to be picked up and carried back to waiting room, which I did. Told her I would see her next week.

Obviously this session was completely inconsistent and incoherent; it is absurd that it could be used to "diagnose sexual abuse". Kinsey says that "Mr. Gary" doesn't spank her and then that he does. She states that only "other kids" performed fellatio on him, then states that she did. She said that he had "boobs". She said that she has a penis and that he put hot water on it. There is of course no mention in the A-Ts' 1/14/87 FBI interview that Kinsey ever was picked up at the day-care center in September-October 1986 making any mention or showing any signs of such shocking activity as fellatio or genital scalding, nor that prior to the Tobins' November 1986 allegations that any other child mentioned or showed any signs of such activity to parents.

3.   As Pamfiloff does not mention these inconsistencies, or the actual contents of the Hickey notes at all, in his report, it is apparent that Larry A-T concealed it from him, as it would clearly refute his account.

During the next few visits Kinsey Almond told Larry Adams-Thompson that she had been molested by Gary Hambright and a "Mikey" and a "Shamby", whose identities were unknown.

1.   There is no mention in the Hickey notes of Larry A-T ever being present at any of the sessions.

2.   In six months of sessions, from January through June 1987, Kinsey **never mentions a "Mikey" at all**. Rather it is her **mother Michele** who first introduces this name, and the allegation of "Mikey" as a molester, to Hickey and Kinsey in the 6/30/87 session. Michele also introduced the "Army officer" association during this session.

3.   "Shambee" (Hickey's spelling) appeared first on 1/27/87, introduced by Kinsey as "her friend at school" who was spanked by Mr. Rogers on TV. Kinsey added that Shambee "also had **its** neck broken", indicating that "Shambee" is either an imaginary "friend" or perhaps a doll. "Shambee" was reintroduced as "Mikey's wife" by **Michele** on 6/30/87. Kinsey never alleged any abuse, or participation in abuse by "Shambee", at any time.

4.   Therefore Larry A-T lied to Pamfiloff in every element of this statement. Just as obviously, he and Michele already had their "Army officer 'Mikey'" and his wife selected for their "Satanic ritual abuse" scam, as Michele's introduction of "Satanic cults" to Hickey during the 6/2/87 session further evidences.

On Wed. 08/12/87 Larry Adams-Thompson, Michele Adams-Thompson and Kinsey Almond were at the Presidio PX when Kinsey Almond ran to Larry Adams-Thompson and in a frightened way, clutched his leg. Larry Adams-Thompson at this time looked up and saw Michael Aquino whom he knew to be Michael Aquino; Michael Aquino was wearing a white shirt, and Larry Adams-Thompson asked Kinsey Almond if she knew the man in the white shirt. Kinsey Almond looked up but didn't respond. Larry Adams-Thompson called over Michele Adams-Thompson and again Kinsey Almond was asked if she knew Michael Aquino. At this time Kinsey Almond said "Yes, that's Mikey." Larry A-T then took Kinsey Almond outside to their car. Kinsey Almond then added "He's a bad man and I'm afraid." Michele Adams-Thompson then exited and Larry Adams-Thompson drove around to the other side of the PX. At this time Larry Adams-Thompson saw Lilith Aquino, who he knew to be the wife of Michael Aquino. Larry Adams-Thompson asked Kinsey Almond if she knew Lilith Aquino, at which time she responded, "Yes, that's Shamby." Larry Adams-Thompson, Michele Adams-Thompson, and Kinsey Almond went home and called Clyde Foreman.

1.   There is only the word of the two adult A-Ts that this incident ever happened at all. All that is known for certain is that **Larry and/or Michele** were present and saw us at the PX on that day. Larry's original 8/12/87 statement to the FBI did not mention Michele as being present. She added herself in her statement on 8/13/87. Kinsey's original 8/13/87 statement to the FBI made no mention of any such incident at all.

2.   1-1/2 years later the A-Ts, apparently in a belated effort to support their story concerning the PX, suddenly added Larry's two sons to the scene. Also just as suddenly these two boys echoed their father's story to the CID. A younger A-T daughter was added to the scene as well. From the original two A-Ts (Larry and Kinsey, if we suppose that he did not invent her presence as well), we are now up to six. Throughout the FBI and SFPD investigations, Kinsey never once stated or agreed to in any official record either her presence at the PX or any of the statements or actions attributed to her there. Only 1-1/2 years later, in an obviously coached [and clumsily performed] interview with the CID did she make any reference to the PX, purportedly saying that she had recognized me but not Mrs. Aquino there.

Following is a detailed examination of the adult A-Ts' PX allegations:

3.   On 8/14/87 Larry told Pamfiloff that "on 12 August 1987 he, Michele, and Kinsey were at the Presidio PX". No mention is made of any other members of the Adams or Thompson family together with them at the PX. In Larry's 8/12/87 FBI interview he made no mention of Michele's presence at all.

4.   On 8/13/87 Michele stated to Foreman that only she, Kinsey, and her husband were shopping at the PX. No mention is made of any other members of the Adams or Thompson family together with them at the PX.

5.   No mention was made of any other family members present throughout the subsequent 1-1/2 years while the Aquinos were being investigated and the PX account described in detail in the public media. Only when the CID interviewed Larry 1–1/2 years later on 4/10/89 did he again revise his story to say that two sons of his by a previous marriage and another girl ("our youngest daughter") were also there.

6.   In the 8/14/87 SFPD incident report Larry told Pamfiloff that, at the PX, Kinsey "ran to him and in a frightened way clutched his leg".

7. In the 8/13/87 FBI report Michele told Foreman that, at the PX, "Kinsey ran to her and Larry". In her 4/10/89 CID statement, however, she contradicts this, saying that Larry called Michele over to him after Kinsey was already with him.

8. On 4/10/89 Larry told the 6RCID that Kinsey was with her two stepbrothers in the PX, away from him and his wife, and that it was the two boys who brought Kinsey to him "saying Kinsey was acting weird". He did not say that Kinsey "ran to him". He also said that Michele was "in another area of the store" and that he had to go to her in that area when Kinsey was brought to him [alone].

Hence Larry lied when making one of his two mutually-contradictory statements. Michele also lied when making one of her two mutually-contradictory statements. [If in fact Kinsey did not "react" at all in the PX, or was not even there, as is also possible, then of course Larry lied when making both statements.] Furthermore, where would Kinsey "run from"? Did the A-Ts allow a 3-year-old infant to wander around the PX away from them? How could Kinsey run "to [Michele] and Larry" when they were in different parts of the store?

9. The two boys (who in August 87 were approximately 9 and 13 years old), interviewed 1-1/2 years later by the 6RCID, state that Kinsey was with them and that she reacted as alleged in the account Larry gave to the 6RCID [but not to the FBI or SFPD].

    a. Why are the memories of two children at such ages suddenly so precise concerning what to them would have been only a momentary behavior by their infant stepsister 1-1/2 years previously?

    b. Why were these boys not mentioned by or interviewed by Foreman or Pamfiloff at the time? They are not listed on page #1 of the SFPD incident report. They are not mentioned in Galyean's 8/12/87 or Foreman's 8/13/87 reports. [The FBI knew of their existence, however, as they were identified as relatives in Peyton's 1/14/87 report.] They would have been crucial witnesses to the "PX encounter". And why were they not mentioned by any of the news media in their intense and detailed coverage of the allegations over the next 1-1/2 years?

The boys' story is obviously a later invention, coached into them by the adult A-Ts. Presumably the boys' motivation in reciting this story is to try to shield their father from exposure of his lies in this affair.

10. On 8/14/87 Larry told Pamfiloff that he called Kinsey's attention to me - not once, but twice - and asked her if she knew me before eliciting a "Yes, that's Mikey" response.

11. On 8/12/87, however, Larry told Galyean not that he had called Kinsey's attention to me, but that she had, only once, identified both me and Lilith, in the PX "as 'Mikey' and 'Shamby'".

12. On 8/13/87 Michele told Foreman that Kinsey "told them that she had seen a man named 'Mikey' that she knew from Mr. Gary's house". Now the sudden addition of "Mr. Gary's house".

13. On 4/10/89 Larry told the CID that Kinsey twice made no answer in response to his twice-stated question: "Do you know that man?". Then he told the CID that Michele took Kinsey away from him and over to my vicinity for about five minutes. Then he said that Michele came back and that they proceeded to leave the PX. As they were doing so, he said "I heard Kinsey state 'That's Mikey, he's a bad man, get me out of this place' or words to that effect."

Larry gave one version of Kinsey's alleged statement in the PX to the SFPD and another version to the CID. In both instances he admits to prompting Kinsey repeatedly for an "identification". Both of his stories contradict the account given by Michele to Foreman only one day before his statement to the SFPD, as well as Larry's given to Galyean two days before.

14. On 8/14/87 Larry told Pamfiloff only that Kinsey "saw" me.

15. On 8/12/87 Larry told Galyean that I "made eye contact with Kinsey". [I did not, and would not have recognized her if I had.]

16. In her 8/13/87 statement to Foreman, Michele says nothing whatever about Kinsey making eye contact with me.

Larry thus gave two contradictory accounts one day apart [and immediately after the PX incident]. Furthermore, Larry told the CID 1-1/2 years later that it was the two boys who were with Kinsey when she noticed me. Larry lied in the initial contradiction, and then again if he now states that Kinsey was with the two boys at the time.

17. To Pamfiloff on 8/14/87 and to the CID on 4/10/89, Larry said that he and Kinsey saw only me in the PX, and that Lilith did not appear until later in the parking lot.

18. To Foreman on 8/13/87 Michele said nothing about Lilith being in the PX, and that her first appearance was "standing next to the car in the parking lot". Michele further said that she "followed Colonel Aquino to the checkout stand" closely enough to observe my active-duty Army ID card and to see me sign my full name on the MasterCard slip. As Lilith was standing with me in the checkout line, it would have been quite impossible for Michele not to see her if she were peering over my shoulder at the time.

19. To the CID on 4/10/89 Michele A-T said that Lilith was in the PX, that she observed us purchase the microwave together in the checkout line, and that she watched us exit together through the PX mall area. [In this interview she tried to cover up for her earlier failure to mention Lilith in the PX by implying that she didn't recognize her as my wife. In Larry's 8/12/87 telephone call to Galyean, however, he said that he recognized Lilith because she had been introduced at several Presidio functions. Presumably Michele attended those same husband/wife "command performance" social functions with her husband, so she had no excuse for not recognizing the woman with me in the PX as that same Mrs. Aquino. [Lilith possesses very striking and distinctive looks.]

Lilith was with me at all times in the PX; therefore Larry's 1987/1989 and Michele's 1987 statements that she didn't appear until later in the parking lot are obvious lies - and among the more conspicuous lies in the A-Ts' original allegations. In her 1989 statement to the CID, Michele completely contradicted her original 1987 statement to Foreman on this matter.

20. To Pamfiloff Larry said that he [alone] took Kinsey "outside to their car". He made no mention of taking the younger girl or the two boys out to the car. Why would he take Kinsey outside to the car at all if she had already "identified" someone whom Larry himself stated in the SFPD report that he recognized? As it was obvious that Lilith and I were leaving the PX, and if the goal was to calm Kinsey, why suddenly rush all of the A-Ts out into their car? Why would they not be accompanied by Kinsey's mother, who would presumably have been greatly concerned about her daughter? Neither Larry nor Michele explains this.

Obviously the A-Ts, who had already seen and recognized both Lilith and myself in the PX, wanted to see what our car looked like so that it could be added to the allegations they had already planned to make against us. Once in their own car, they followed us to our home, so that Michele could allude to Kinsey's describing its front the next day to the FBI, and try to pre-coach Kinsey into "recognizing" that as well before an FBI audience to which she "volunteered" the next day. They succeeded in coaching Kinsey to "recognize" the car (which they didn't know was only a rental car) and failed with the house.

21.   To Foreman on 8/13/87 Larry said that he "went to the car to wait for us, and saw them, and took the license number".

22.   To Pamfiloff on 8/14/87 Larry said that he drove around to the other side of the PX, where Kinsey supposedly identified Lilith as "Shamby". In this SFPD version there is no mention of our car or taking its license number.

Larry changes his story at will, as in one case he needed to drive to the other lot to find us, while in the other he merely waits for us.

23.   To Foreman on 8/13/87 Michele said that "Michele, Larry, and Kinsey drove through the parking lot where they observed Colonel Aquino standing next to a red vehicle with California license plate 2ENS453. This vehicle was a 1987 Isuzu. Kinsey observed a woman standing next to the vehicle and said, 'That's Shamby.'" [In this account Michele identified herself, her husband, and Kinsey by name but made no mention whatever of the two boys and additional girl who were suddenly introduced into this story 1-1/2 years later.]

24.   In her 4/10/89 CID statement, Michele said that Lilith was standing next to our car "alone". Michele changes her story at will concerning how many Aquinos were standing next to the Isuzu.

25.   To the SFPD on 8/14/87 Larry said that he drove around to the other side of the PX. To Foreman on 8/13/87 Michele said that he drove through the parking lot to our car.

In one version Larry drives around to the other side of the PX, while in the other he merely waits for us, sees us, and takes down the license number of our car.

26.   If Kinsey had already seen Lilith and myself in the PX, as Larry admitted to the CID on 4/10/89, why would Kinsey not have "identified" Lilith until later at our car?

27.   One could not reach the bridge-approach parking lot by driving "through the main lot" in 1987; it was necessary to drive out into the street and about 2 blocks to the east to circle around the complex, or about 2 blocks to the west to circle around it from the other side. [Barriers to a shorter route were removed following the Army's closure of the Presidio in the 1990s.]

28.   The PX has two parking lots, one on the north side of the mall and one on the south side of the mall. From the A-Ts' 4/10/89 CID statements, their car was parked in the north lot. Our car was parked in the south lot. If the A-Ts drove around to the south lot from the north lot after seeing us go through the mall, and if Michele (per her 4/10/89 statement) didn't even get into the A-T car until after we had walked through the mall doors to the south lot, they wouldn't have had time to get there [for the alleged Kinsey "identification" of Lilith] before we drove away. It was approximately a 2-blocks up/ 2-blocks back drive between the two lots, no matter which direction they might have gone.

Larry is lying about being able to "drive around to the other side of the PX" for Kinsey to see Lilith and for him to take down the license number of our car. It took so long to drive to the "bridge-approach" lot from the main lot that we would have driven away before Larry could get to that area, much less single out our car from among the others there, much less identify us inside a car. As it was August and the car was air-conditioned, and we habitually drive with the A/C on and all windows up, is Kinsey supposed to have "identified" Lilith at a distance, from inside a moving car, looking at a car suddenly pointed out to her, and at a person through rolled-up window glass? [Note: This car was a rental car which Larry would never have seen before.] Probably the A-Ts simply followed us on foot from the checkout counter through the mall doors to our rental car, then went to their own car [in either lot] and drove after us when we emerged from the south lot.

If Kinsey is supposed to have "identified" Lilith at a moment's notice, at a distance, from inside a moving car, looking at a car suddenly pointed out to her, and at a person through rolled-up window glass, then why did she not "identify" Lilith in the PX, when she would have been able to look at her as long and as closely as she allegedly did at me? Lilith was right next to me the entire time we were in the PX. It would have been impossible for Kinsey [or the adult A-Ts] to see just me and not Lilith.

On Thu. 08/13/87 morning Clyde Foreman interviewed Kinsey Almond, who stated that Gary Hambright, "Mr. Gary" whom she identified from a photo spread, had placed his penis into her bottom, vagina and mouth. Kinsey Almond states that she drove with Mr. Gary to his house where Gary Hambright took photographs of her. Michael Aquino "Mikey" and Lilith Aquino "Shamby" were present and Michael Aquino also put his penis into her mouth, bottom and vagina, just like Mr. Gary. Kinsey Almond stated that Michael Aquino and Gary Hambright dressed up in girls clothing and Lilith Aquino dressed up in boys clothing.

1. At **no** time during her interview with Foreman did Kinsey use the names of, or describe or identify in any way, either Michael or Lilith Aquino. Larry's association of the "Mikey" and "Shamby" devices of his scam-story to the Aquinos is **completely unsubstantiated** by the Foreman-Kinsey interview record.

2. While Kinsey was apparently shown a photograph of Hambright during her Foreman interview, she was not shown any photos of the Aquinos - which, through their Army ID card or California driver's license records, would have been easy to obtain.

3. Hambright was later established to be an epileptic who could not drive, had no license, and had no car.

4. On 3/12/87 Kinsey Almond was medically examined, including both her vagina and rectum, at Letterman Army Hospital. The findings of this medical examination stated specifically that there was **"no physical evidence of abuse"**.

5. Kinsey's imitation of Larry and Michele's scam-story to Foreman is completely unsubstantiated by the notes of any of the Hickey sessions.

6. No such "photographs" of Kinsey at the Aquino home ever existed, and thus were not found either during the search of our home or anywhere else.

7. No female clothing of a size which Michael could conceivably wear, or male clothing which Lilith could conceivably wear, existed, and thus was not found during the search of our home.

Kinsey Almond states the house had a bathtub with lions feet.

1. Nowhere in the Aquino building at 123 Acme Avenue did [or does] there exist a bathtub with any feet, as the search verified. All the tubs have bases flush with the floors of the bathrooms.

Clyde Foreman and Kinsey Almond accompanied by Michele Adams-Thompson responded to the 100 block of Acme and Kinsey Almond was told to see if she could recognize any of the homes that she had been to before. While walking past 123 Acme, Kinsey Almond identified that as the residence of Mr. Gary where she had met "Mikey" and "Shamby".

1. The 8/13/87 record of this trip by CID Special Agent Bradley Potter reveals that virtually every element of Larry's statement to Pamfiloff concerning it was a lie. As discussed in detail in the above analysis of the Potter report, Kinsey made no "identification" of 123 Acme at all, said nothing about "Mr. Gary", and said nothing about "Mikey" or "Shamby".

During the ensuing publicity, in which much was made of the alleged "identification" of our building, Larry remained silent about the fact that **no** such "identification" ever happened.

Clyde Foreman confirmed that Michael Aquino is listed on the mail box, and the local mail carrier advised Clyde Foreman that Michael Aquino is still receiving mail at 123 Acme. Pacific Bell shows Michael Aquino having the entire upper floor, Apt 1, Apt 2 + rear unit. Glenn Pamfiloff confirmed with PG&E that Michael Aquino is listed as receiving service at 123 Acme top and base. Michael Aquino's DMV records also list his residence as 123 Acme.

On Fri. 08/14/87, Clyde Foreman re-interviewed Kinsey Almond who stated she was filmed with a movie camera with steady lights while she bathed in a plastic lion bathtub. Kinsey Almond states the living room had black walls and a cross painted on the ceiling.

1. While I was eventually able to obtain all the other FBI interview reports cited here, no copy of a report of any 8/14/87 interview by Foreman of Kinsey, or of any other Foreman/Kinsey interview besides the 8/13/87 one, has ever appeared, or was produced in the Army investigation, etc. There is only Larry's word to Pamfiloff that Kinsey said any of these things either to Foreman or anyone else. Judging by the extent of Larry's lies to Pamfiloff throughout their 8/14/87 interview, this final "hearsay" deserves no credibility whatever. Nevertheless:

2. On 8/13/87 Kinsey said to Foreman that "the house had a bathtub with lions feet". She said nothing about a "plastic lion bathtub", bathing, a movie camera, steady lights, or a living room with black walls and a cross painted on the ceiling.

3. As noted above, no bathtubs at 123 Acme had/have any feet. All were/are flush to the floor.

4. Obviously no movie camera, no movie-camera lights, and no "plastic lion bathtub" existed, and thus was not found during the search of our home. Nor any film of Kinsey [or any other child] in our home.

5. Our living room was beige with a beige ceiling and had/has no cross painted on the ceiling. Nor did/ does any other room have a cross on the ceiling. [Very obviously Lilith and I are not Christians - why would we decorate anything in our home with a cross?]

6. The only black room in our home was the bedroom, which was so small that there is no room for any chairs, etc. in it besides the [queen-size] bed. It could not possibly be mistaken for a "living room".

7. The Hickey notes do not mention anything like this either. [In the 6/2/87 session Hickey reports Kinsey as describing "a pot hanging down from the ceiling with legs, arms, and a penis which went pee on her shoes". Perhaps Larry and Michele thought that a little elaborate for their scam story, hence decided to try a cross instead?]

* * * * * * * * * *

On the basis of this Incident Report, Pamfiloff sought and obtained the search warrant for our home reproduced here as Appendix #14. Interestingly, when I spoke with him in 1991, Pamfiloff said that it was originally the Army CID and the FBI who wanted a search warrant, but that the U.S. Attorney "wouldn't touch it". Only then did they turn to the SFPD and ask Pamfiloff to obtain one from the district attorney, which he did. "They were in a great hurry," he remarked.[54]

---

[54] Conversation, M.A. Aquino & Glenn Pamfiloff, Ellis Brooks Car Dealership, San Francisco, 8/16/91.

Implications of Information Presented in this Chapter

Larry and Michele knew that Kinsey had never shown any physical, verbal, or emotional signs of abuse to them while in Hambright's day-care supervision. They knew she had not been under his supervision at all until September-October 1986, and then only in an unscheduled, unannounced drop-off/pick-up setting in which there was obviously neither time nor opportunity to transport any child or children elsewhere for elaborate activities such as Larry would later allege to the SFPD.

Larry and Michele knew that Kinsey had been examined by Letterman Hospital and verified to be a virgin with no physical signs of any abuse.

Larry and Michele knew that Hickey's 2/3/87 "diagnosis of abuse" was both contradicted by the above facts and incoherent, inconsistent, and nonsensical on its face.

Larry and Michele knew my name and appearance from my assignment to the Presidio up to June 1986. They knew I was a "Satanist" but knew nothing about the actual and diametric distinctions between Satanism and the Temple of Set [to which we belonged since 1975]. Michele lay the groundwork for fabricating an accusation against me by introducing "Mikey, a Satanist Army officer" to Hickey on 6/30/87.

Larry and/or Michele happened to see Lilith and myself in the Presidio PX on 8/12/87. He/she/they secretly followed us to our home by car, so that Michele could describe its outside appearance [attributing it to Kinsey] to the FBI the next day. From the Hickey notes the A-Ts knew that Kinsey had denied ever being taken to a house until badgered into agreeing, that she had then denied it was Hambright's house, and had denied that Hambright was there, and had never mentioned "Mikey" or "Shamby" as being there.

The numerous, different, and mutating versions of the "PX encounter" expose it as a fabricated story by the adult A-Ts.

The CID driver was told by Foreman and Michele where to go for the "house identification". No other neighborhood was shown to Kinsey either beforehand or subsequently. She was walked in no other direction. When she neared 123 Acme, her mother picked her up, stopped, and held her facing only that house. Despite Kinsey's still saying nothing whatever, this was held to be an "identification". During the drive, Kinsey showed Foreman and Potter a hand-gesture which Larry and Michele would mistakenly think "Satanic" and also mistakenly assume that "Satanists like us" would use. Hence their coaching of Kinsey to "spontaneously" show it to the investigators.

Finally, Larry gave an extensive, detailed, and deliberately falsified statement to the San Francisco Police Department, fully expecting that we would be victimized on its basis. This was to result in years of serious damage to us, both official and in the media, about which the A-Ts never expressed any concern or remorse whatever.

When the CID, in an effort to somehow make the A-T allegations "stick", went so far as to change first the date and then the location of the "abuse" back several months to a time when the A-Ts knew Kinsey had never been in Hambright's care, and again [as a drop-off child] could not have been taken miles away into San Francisco for a stay at a house, they remained silent and cooperative with the CID's attempted manufacture of "evidence".

On 3/15/88 the A-Ts filed fraudulent claims for $3 million based on their knowingly and deliberately false allegations. On the claims form they stated that Kinsey "was sexually abused, sodomized, and subjected to mental and emotional abuse. She has suffered severe emotional and psychological stress and physical pain and will require long-term therapy".[55]

In addition to constituting false statements to law-enforcement officers, Larry A-T's statements to officials investing a possible crime on an Army post, concerning another Army officer, to the Army CID concerning all aspects of his allegations, and to the U.S. Army Claims Service constitute numerous violations of Article 133, Uniform Code of Military Justice, pertaining to the making of false official statements.

Larry's participation in the filing of the false claims is further in violation of Article 133.

In the 27 years since Larry and Michele committed these actions, they have never acknowledged, apologized for, or ever been held accountable for them.

Summarily: The only abuse that Kinsey Almond suffered at the Presidio of San Francisco was by her own stepfather and mother.

---

[55] Claim for Damage, Injury, or Death, Larry and Michele Adams-Thompson for Kinsey, 3/15/88.

The Results of the Adams-Thompsons' Claim

Until July 2008 I never knew the outcome of the A-Ts' $3 million claim. That year, however, a Probate Court Opinion was published on the Internet (Appendix #76). The story that it told was that the Army had **denied** their claim, whereupon they filed suit against it in California court. The Army agreed to a settlement of $334,720, of which half went directly to Larry and Michele, and the other half into a trust for Kinsey, controlled by Larry and Michele until Kinsey's 18th birthday. One month after that date, unless Kinsey signed the trust as a new co-trustee, her half of the claim would go to Larry and Michele.

At age 13 Kinsey left Larry and Michele and went to live with her biological father. The A-Ts' lawyer sent her father's lawyer a letter denying a copy of the trust. 28 days after Kinsey's 18th birthday, the A-Ts sued her to force her acceptance of its continuation [presumably under their control]. If the trust continued, Kinsey would not get personal control of it until she reached age 50. If she did not accept this demand, all of the trust money would be immediately paid to the A-Ts.

Kinsey filed a counterclaim against the A-Ts' attorney for aiding and abetting their breach of their fiduciary duties. She prevailed in court, the trust was dissolved, and Kinsey received approximately $260,000 damages.

From these events the following conclusions may be induced:

(1)   The Army did not award the A-Ts their hoped-for $3 million. It awarded them **nothing**. Had the Army really believed that Kinsey had been abducted, raped, and sodomized [by anyone] while in Army care, I think it is reasonable to presume that the $3 million would have been paid without question.

(2)   The A-Ts, possibly counting on the scam's publicity and the Army's discomfort over the entire affair to work to their advantage, tried a suit in California court for their money. All that they got was a negotiated settlement of just $334,720.

(3)   The A-Ts, as trustees, controlled Kinsey's half of the $334,720. When she turned 18, they attempted to continue controlling it, by forcing her to accept a minority co-trusteeship which would prevent her from receiving any remaining funds from her half until she was 50 years old. If she did not agree, the A-Ts would take all of it for themselves immediately.

I suggest that the true, financial motivation of Larry and Michele A-T in devising their 1987 allegation scheme has been *prima facie* substantiated here - even to the final, and perhaps unsurprising, obscenity of their attempting to deny Kinsey herself any part of the take from the scam in which they had used her so cruelly and cold-bloodedly as their pawn.

Chapter 3: The Cult Crusade of Sandi Gallant

In order to understand the attitude of the San Francisco Police Department when the CID and FBI requested its involvement in the A-T allegations investigation, it is first necessary to discuss the influence of SFPD Policewoman Sandra "Sandi" Gallant (*née* Daly).

An officer assigned to the SFPD's Intelligence Division in the 1980s, Gallant at some point either decided on her own or was assigned to specialize in "occult crime", In the early, pre-*Michelle Remembers* years of the decade, this was pretty much of a blank page in law enforcement circles. Crimes were crimes, and if an occasional perpetrator - like San Francisco's infamous "Zodiac" serial-killer of the 1960s - toyed with astrological or "witchy" symbols, such were regarded as mere attention-getting accents.

With no actual occult crime to investigate in San Francisco, Daly compensated by investigating occultism generally, of which San Francisco has always had a colorful abundance. Wicca and similar "white-light" New Ageism weren't of much interest to her. The most deliciously "sinister" organization was the mysterious successor to the city's campy Church of Satan - the Temple of Set.

Although since its 1975 founding the Temple had declined publicity as a matter of policy - it wished to avoid the "media circus" atmosphere that had constantly dogged the Church of Satan - its principles and activities had never been a secret from anyone with a reasonable or official need to know.[56] Officer Daly would have been quite welcome to meet with Temple officials, receive copies of our philosophical and ceremonial papers, and/or attend activities had she made any such requests in her official capacity.[57] Evidently, however, she felt that "intelligence" was not **really** "intelligence" unless it were clandestine. So at no time did she ever contact the Temple of Set or myself for information concerning us.

Nevertheless by 1981 Daly felt she knew enough about the ominous Temple of Set and its insidious leader to write a report to the SFPD about them. Here it is:

SAN FRANCISCO POLICE DEPARTMENT INTRA-DEPARTMENTAL MEMORANDUM

Intelligence Division   Day & Date: Tue., 07/07/81

TO: SUBJECT:
Captain Daniel J. Murphy   Temple of Set
Commanding Officer
Intelligence Division

Sir:

Approximately two weeks ago, information was received that a Satanic Cult named the Temple of Set would be holding a black mass in the San Francisco Fisherman's Wharf area.[58] The following background information has been obtained on this cult:

---

[56] For instance, detailed descriptions of the Temple's beliefs, organization, and religious ceremonies were provided to the Internal Revenue Service in 1975 as part of the [approved] application for official recognition as a church.

[57] Over the decades since its founding, the Temple of Set and its individual officials have periodically been contacted for advice on occult symbolism, other organizations, etc. by law enforcement agencies nationwide, for example Detective Frank Metoyer of the Los Angeles Police Department's Gang Division. This has also included participation in panels, lecture presentations, etc. such as an "Occult Crime" seminar for southern states law enforcement agencies in 1989 hosted by the Killeen, Texas Police Department. Presumably because of Gallant's activities and influence, the SFPD was one agency that did **not** contact the Temple for such advice or consultation.

[58] False. The Temple of Set has never conducted a Black Mass (more accurately the *Missa Solemnis*, a satire of the Catholic Mass, at any of its activities. Such a ritual would be performed only for an individual member's benefit, as a "disintoxication" from prior religious indoctrination and intimidation. See Appendix #14.

HISTORY

The Temple of Set is a satanic group under the leadership of one Michael A. Aquino.[59] It is a splinter group of the Church of Satan. They separated from LaVey's organization in 1975. There are several hundred members and it operates on a National level. Under Aquino's leadership are a council of nine lieutenants.[60]

The Temple of Set is seemingly obsessed with the military.[61] They have a fascination with the Nazi movement, with many of them wearing, on occasion, World War II German uniforms and insignia.[62] A more sinister aspect of their military fascination is the fact that Aquino holds a commission as a Major in the United States Army Reserve, with his specialty being Military Intelligence.[63] He purports to his members that he reports directly to the Joint Chiefs of Staff, although this is probably a gross exageration (sic).[64] It is a fact, however, that he holds a Major's commission and deals in the area of Military Intelligence. One of the organization's lieutenants, a female named Willie Browning, allegedly is a Captain in the United States Army Reserve and in an Intelligence Unit in Los Angeles. Another lieutenant, Dennis Mann, is also a Reserve officer involved in Intelligence activities.[65]

LEADERSHIP

The following background information has been obtained on Michael Aquino. Subject is a WMA, DOB 10/16/46, currently residing at 123 Acme Avenue, San Francisco. (The Reverse Directory shows a listing for a Betty Ford at this location.) Aquino is 6', 145 lbs., brown hair, green eyes, California Driver's License ######, showing a mailing address in 1976 of Box 243, Santa Barbara. Subject is listed as the registered owner of a 1979 Mercury wagon, Calif. Personalized license "XEPER". Current Department of Motor

---

[59] As above, the Temple of Set is not a "Satanic" organization or religion, since it considers all Judæo-Christian mythology, including "Satan", as inaccurate and irrelevant.

[60] False. The Council of Nine is the Temple of Set's corporate board of directors, to which the High Priest is responsible as corporate president, not the other way around.

[61] False. The Temple has no interest in or involvement with the military. There have been no such articles in its publications nor books on its reading list. Daly's sole basis for this claim seems to be that three members out of the Temple's hundreds happen to also be members of the U.S. Army Reserve.

[62] False. The Temple has never held any activity in which German military or Nazi uniforms or insignia were worn or displayed. The reason is again, quite simply, that the Setian philosophy of individualism is completely incompatible with fascist principles of state-consciousness.

[63] Why should my holding a commission as a senior Army officer be "sinister"? Quite the contrary, it indicates that my character and professionalism have been evaluated by many other officers over the years and found to merit such promotion and trust. Additionally, at the time of this report, my officer branch was Armor, not Military Intelligence.

[64] False. In 1981 I was assigned as USAR Advisor to the Commander of the Presidio of San Francisco. I had never been previously assigned to the JCS nor represented myself as such. Officer assignments are a matter of official record, which Daly could easily have checked.

[65] Neither Browning nor Mann were "lieutenants of mine" within the Temple of Set, just individual initiates with their own interests and activities.

Vehicles' records listed this vehicle as junk in June of 1979, however they issued duplicate plates on the same vehicle in August of 1979.[66]

Aquino holds a Ph.D. in Political Science and is a Professor at Golden Gate University, teaching Western European Political Affairs.[67]

Aquino is known to frequent prostitutes in San Francisco in order to become involved in various forms of Sado-Masacistic (sic) sexual activities.[68] Although Aquino is believed to be bi-sexual,[69] he resides with his girlfriend (possibly Ford), her children, and his mother.[70]

GROUP POTENTIAL

Sources state that this cult is becoming potentially more and more violent[71] as it recruits the less intellectual and more undesirable level of people such as former members of the Hells Angels and similar cycle gangs.[72] Another rumor surfacing is that they are involved in animal sacrifices.[73]
Investigation into this group is continuing.

Respectfully submitted,
Sandra C. Daly, Policewoman, Star 1918

Approved by:
Daniel J. Murphy, Captain, Star 647

SFPD-68 (9-70)

What is perhaps most striking about this report is that such a vague, inaccurate, unsubstantiated, and malicious diatribe should be accepted by a San Francisco Police Captain and Intelligence Division Commander as a valid

---

[66] While I am not sure what possible relevance this DMV information has to the Temple of Set, it is also inaccurate. I have never owned a Mercury station wagon, and the 1979 Mercury Capri that I did own in 1981 did not have "XEPER" license plates, nor had it ever been involved in any accident, much less "junked".

[67] While as a Professor of Political Science at Golden Gate University I taught many different courses, "Western European Political Affairs" was not among them.

[68] False. I have never in my life patronized any prostitute, nor do I have any interest in sado-masochism. Daly, unsurprisingly, names no names nor sources for this extraordinary assertion.

[69] False. I am a lifelong heterosexual - which Daly should know is a strict requirement for Army officers.

[70] Betty Ford was my mother, who lived in one flat while Lilith and I lived in another.

[71] The Temple of Set has no history of nor doctrines advocating violence at all, as Daly, with easy access to arrest/conviction files, could easily verify but obviously did not wish to.

[72] The Temple of Set as a matter of policy has never "recruited" anyone, nor sought the interest of any other group or organization. To the best of my knowledge in 37 years it has included no current nor former Hells Angels or other "outlaw bikers" as members. If such an individual were to request admission, however, his interest would be judged on its sincerity as fairly as anyone else's.

[73] False. Since its founding the Temple of Set has maintained an absolute prohibition of not only animal sacrifice, but any harm to or exploitation of animals at all. This is specified strictly in the Temple's membership literature, which again Daly didn't bother to consult.

"intelligence" document. Indeed one must also wonder why Daly was considered to be an competent Intelligence Division officer at all, if this represents the quality of work she produced.

Also obviously, the moment the "S-word" - Satanism - is introduced, the report enters into a special Twilight Zone of prejudice, in which anything connected with the organization or individuals is inherently "sinister", no matter how benign or irrelevant it might be in any other context.[74] Thus "Army officer", "Military Intelligence", and even teaching at a university become alarmisms, whereas if I had happened to be a Christian or a Jew such credentials would have been complimentary and commendable.

The obvious message of this officially-accepted report was that Michael Aquino and the Temple of Set were a serious and increasing danger to the city of San Francisco.

Two weeks later Daly decided to warn the U.S. Army about its Satanic peril. She telephoned Lt. Colonel T.C. Jones of the Army's Criminal Investigation Command in Falls Church, Virginia to advise him about Major Aquino and Captains Mann & Browning. Jones, not considering this a criminal matter, passed it along to Department of the Army Counterintelligence. Possibly Satanists are Soviet spies?[75]

At the Pentagon Colonel Donald Press, Director of Counterintelligence, checked with the FBI and found no record of the Temple of Set. Again not surprising, as the Temple had never been involved in or investigated for any illegal activity. Again the dreaded S-word had reared its menacing head: If a "Satanic cult" were on file anywhere, it would certainly be with the FBI. It never occurred to Press to check with the IRS for its extensive files on the Temple as a perfectly legitimate religious institution.[76]

Not knowing what else to do, but still concerned that the S-word must mean **something** worrisome afoot, Colonel Press referred the matter to U.S. Army Forces Command at Fort McPherson, Georgia.[77] From there it was passed along to the immediate commanders of the three demonic officers in question, in my case the Intelligence & Security Chief of the Sixth U.S. Army at the Presidio, Lt. Colonel John Richards.[78] Richards then responded with what Daly could have found out for herself in the first place had she bothered to ask:

AFKC-OP-IS 3d Ind
SUBJECT: Possible Adverse Suitability Information

HQ, SIXTH US ARMY, Presidio of San Francisco, CA 94129 9 DEC 1981

TO: Commander, US Army Forces Command, ATTN: AFIN-C5P, Fort McPherson, GA 30330

1. Returned without action.
2. Information mentioned in paragraph 2, basic letter, concerning Michael A. Aquino, was favorably adjudicated and Top Secret clearance granted 9 June 1981 by the US Army Central Personnel Security Clearance Facility.
3. Recommend the investigative file pertaining to Michael A. Aquino be reviewed at the US Army Central Personnel Security Clearance Facility, Fort George G. Meade, Maryland 20755.

FOR THE COMMANDER:

JOHN W. RICHARDS
LTC, GS
Chief, Intelligence and Security

---

[74] Ironically San Francisco's most famous Satanist, Anton LaVey, was not considered by the SFPD to be dangerous, presumably because he was dismissed as merely a "carnival clown" using Satanic imagery for self-advertisement.

[75] Letter, Lt. Col. T.C. Jones, Chief, Investigative Policy & Studies Division, USA CIC to HQDA (DAMI-CIS), 11/16/81.

[76] 1st Ind, Col. Donald M. Press, Director of CounterIntelligence, Headquarters, Department of the Army, 11/18/81.

[77] *Ibid*.

[78] 2nd Ind, Lt. Col. George E. Durham, Asst. Adjutant General, USA FORSCOM, 11/23/81.

Back at FORSCOM Colonel Durham decided that enough time had been wasted on Daly's monster hunt, closing the action and remarking to the Pentagon's Counterintelligence office, "The same 'not unfavorable' and inconclusive information is generally reported telephonically from other recipients of our 2d indorsement re allegations in basic letter." [79]

At the Presidio Colonel Richards hadn't bothered to mention this curious correspondence to me. I didn't learn about it until mid-1982, when Dennis Mann, having heard about it from his headquarters, asked for copies and forwarded a set to me. While no harm had been done except the wasting of various Army officials' time, I decided I'd better get in touch with this mysterious Officer Daly and clear up what might be an innocent misunderstanding on her part. At the time I had not seen and did not know about her 7/7/81 report, nor other equally inaccurate reports by her, such as a horrific misrepresentation of the Black Mass on 7/8/81 (Appendix #15).[80]

I therefore went down to the San Francisco Hall of Justice (SFPD headquarters) and paid a call on Daly.[81] She and her supervisor Sergeant Jerry Belfield acknowledged that they indeed had a file on the Temple of Set and myself, but adamantly refused to show it to me or even discuss its contents. The most they would do was allow me to add a copy of the Temple's official public informational paper to the file. On 11/29/82 I wrote to Belfield:

> This past summer you and Officer Sandi Daly were kind enough to discuss the matter of your file concerning the Temple of Set with me. While you told me that the San Francisco Police Department's policy is that I am not permitted to know what is in the file or who may have made what allegations concerning the Temple, you also said that you would include in the file any descriptive material the Temple cares to submit concerning itself.
>
> Hence I enclose, for inclusion in that file, a copy of the Temple's basic informational pamphlet and a copy of the more extensive membership letter which is sent in answer to inquiries from readers of the pamphlet.
>
> Thank you again for seeing me at such short notice, and for your courtesy during the discussion. Should the San Francisco Police Department ever have further questions concerning the Temple or any alleged affiliate, you are welcome to contact me, as its chief executive, directly.

I daresay my letter would not have been quite so gracious had I seen Daly's secret, defamatory reports "Temple of Set" and its companion "The Black Mass" (Appendix #15). Both of these remained concealed from me until 1989. In 1982 I still gave Gallant the benefit of the doubt as being a policewoman making an honest effort to learn about topics of which she was innocently ignorant.

That was my sole personal contact with Gallant until the 1987 search-warrant raid of Lilith's and my home, at which she appeared. Neither she nor Belfield had ever responded to my invitation to contact me concerning either the Temple of Set/myself or occult topics generally.

In those interim years, however, Gallant continued to write and distribute a series of SFPD-official papers with such names as "Satanic Cults/Sabbat Celebrations", "Ritual Crime Scene Clues", "Related Crimes", "Homicide Investigations", "Sabbats/Festivals: Paganism, Witchcraft & Satanism", "Colours Significant to Satanism/ Witchcraft", "Sabbats or Celebrations", "Definitions: Satanism and Witchcraft", etc. When in January 1986 *San Francisco Examiner* reporter Ivan Sharpe, who was writing a story about Satanism, sent me a set of these papers, I took the time to send him itemized, detailed critiques. Reprinting all of them here would be tedious for me and a painful reading experience for you, but I have included one at Appendix #16 as an example.

---

[79] 4th Ind, Lt. Col. Durham, *op.cit.*, 12/18/81.

[80] This is significant because in her report of the previous day, transcribed here, Daly accused the Temple of Set of planning just such a Black Mass in San Francisco.

[81] In 1986 Gallant told *San Francisco Examiner* reporter Ivan Sharpe that I had so "terrorized" the receptionist that she had left the building immediately after I arrived. Since I was merely an Army officer in dress green uniform politely asking the way to Gallant's office, I can only suppose my eyes were glowing red and smoke coming from my ears at the time. Even so, I wonder that the receptionist in San Francisco Police headquarters, of all places, should feel "terrorized" by anyone.

An additional Gallant paper - "Ritualistic Crime Profile & Questionnaire" - was distributed in 1987 by an organization calling itself the "California Consortium of Child Abuse Councils", indicating that Gallant had been distributing her materials outside of governmental law enforcement officialdom.

Following the 8/14/87 SFPD raid on our home [as recounted in Chapter #4], my attorney obtained a copy of a videotaped lecture by Gallant to other police officers on the subject of "Satanic Cults". It contained her usual, disjointed recitation of falsehoods and irrelevancies, both concerning the Temple of Set/myself and occultism generally, while stressing the newly-vogue theme of "ritual child abuse". "Children have been taken to cemeteries and placed in open graves, and to crematories and forced to have sexual activity there," Gallant told her horrified audience. And yet: "We have not been able to prove one [Satanic ritual homicide] to date."

Chapter 4: The San Francisco Police Investigation

The evening of Friday, August 14, 1987 began calmly enough at 123 Acme Avenue. I was in my study, working at the computer, while Lilith and her daughter were watching television in the sitting room. Then at 9PM there was a knock at the front door. Thinking it to be her son or brother, who were both living in the downstairs flat, Lilith opened the door - and found herself staring at a man in a suit holding a large crowbar. He identified himself as San Francisco Police, said that he had a warrant[82] to search the premises, then walked in, followed by several other men in plainclothes.

Lilith's first impression, when she got over her immediate shock, was that we were simply being robbed. Then she saw two uniformed policemen bringing up the rear of the group, which appeared to number about ten individuals. She asked one of the policemen for identification, at which he pointed to his shoulder-patch and remarked, "This is all the ID you need, lady." [Throughout the entire raid, not one of the officers would produce any identification in response to Lilith's or my requests.]

Hearing the commotion, I walked out of my study and encountered the man with the crowbar, who waved a paper at me so fast that I could not read anything on it. He said that it was a search warrant, and then told me to go into the sitting room with Lilith and her daughter, to empty my pockets on the table, and then to sit down on the couch with them and be quiet. The rest of the raiding-party had already dispersed throughout the flat and were beginning to open drawers, closets, and cupboards, rummaging through and removing many of the contents. A photographer walked around the flat, photographing the entire interior as well as articles, art objects, etc. which were called to his attention. Accompanying the raiding-party was a policewoman whom I recognized as Officer Sandi Gallant, the SFPD's "occult expert".

As would be all too evident later, once my attorneys and I had discovered the full extent of her well-poisoning activities, Gallant had apparently succeeded in convincing the SFPD that the Temple of Set, under my evil sway, was a bloodthirsty "satanic cult" just waiting to pounce upon a helpless San Francisco. Clearly when Larry A-T walked into his office to accuse us of a horrific crime, Sergeant/Inspector Glenn Pamfiloff of the SFPD Juvenile Division was therefore well-primed to anticipate another Manson Family-spectacular bust. How else to explain all of the muscle that he brought along with him to our home that evening?

It is difficult for someone who has not been through such an experience to understand just how stressful it can be. We still had not the remotest idea why this could be occurring, or what judge could possibly have authorized such an invasion. Lilith and her daughter were severely frightened, and I was trying to decide what if anything to do. Presumably the raid had been timed for late Friday evening to surprise us when we were the most tired and psychologically vulnerable - and when our chances of contacting our attorney would be minimal.

The man with the crowbar - who I would later learn was Sergeant/Inspector Pamfiloff - was across the sitting room rifling one of Lilith's personal file cabinets. I asked him if I might read the search warrant. He refused. I asked him what this raid was all about, and he made no answer. Finally I asked him if I could walk across the room to telephone my attorney, to which he nodded assent. Fortunately I found the attorney, Mark Coleman, at home and told him what was happening. He said that he would be right over, and by 10 PM he walked through the door.

It is remarkable how the presence of an attorney changes things in such situations. Coleman asked to see the warrant and was given it immediately. Noting that it was unsigned, he read it and then passed it to me. All that I could make out in a brief reading was that it was for evidence of child sexual abuse. Being unaware of any such allegations concerning ourselves, Lilith and I could make no sense of this whatever and could suppose only that it was all a grotesque mistake. Meanwhile, said Coleman, there was nothing to do but wait until the search had run its course. Following Coleman's arrival I was permitted to walk through the flat to see what was happening, though not to approach any of the raiders nor touch any item at all.

In the middle of this nightmare there were elements of surreal humor. First of all, of course, was the reaction of the SFPD and FBI raiders to the exotic decor and artwork of our home. I think they [and especially Gallant] spent as much time being tourists as conducting a search.

The library and files in my study consisted of thousands of occult papers and books, mixed in with military and academic texts and files. In a very short time the FBI agents were totally at sea. One would pick up a book of

---

[82] The SFPD Search Warrant is at Appendix #14.

Egyptian hieroglyphics or sigils of the Elizabethan magician John Dee, flip helplessly through a few pages, then drop it only to pick up something else equally obscure. They had the photographer take pictures of my ceremonial robes from the Church of Satan and Temple of Set - and also of my Ph.D. robes from the University of California, which they evidently considered equally sinister. They photographed some Don Post Hollywood masks from my collection - to include one of the original Darth Vader helmets from *Star Wars*. Then they made a real find:

Going through my files of photographs they came across an album of snapshots showing men, women, and children being tortured and killed in any number of horrific scenes, some involving the most shocking Satanic orgies. The album was confiscated with great fanfare. I stood across the room, shaking my head. In London there is a very famous tourist attraction called the London Dungeon, a wax museum which consists solely of exhibits of the occult and macabre. I had visited it a couple of years previously, and it was my snapshots of some of its exhibits that the FBI had found!

Then Pamfiloff triumphantly brandished a photograph of a laughing naked baby on a bearskin rug. "That's just Michael," said Sandi Gallant to the crestfallen Inspector. "Look at the eyebrows."

Next he dug into a small tin box from one of the closets and dramatically unfurled a Nazi battle flag, which the photographer scurried to shoot. "If you will look through the rest of that box," I said mildly, "you'll see that it contains my father's combat souvenirs from World War II, including maps, his medals, and his unit and rank insignia." Foiled again.

Walking through the halls to our living room, I was confronted by a similar scene of disarray. Paintings had been removed from the walls, art objects had been picked up and played with, and closets had been opened and their contents strewn about. Encountering Sandi Gallant, I asked her what had caused this invasion. She looked at me blandly and said that she had no idea; she had merely been invited along as an observer.

After the first hour or so it obviously became clear to the raiders that, as exotic as our home might be, it did not contain evidence of anything the least criminal. The attitude of the raiders - with the marked exception of Pamfiloff himself, who remained cold and accusatory - became less aggressive and more polite. The two uniformed officers wandered around for awhile, then left. The FBI left. Only Pamfiloff, obviously frustrated, continued to search. "This guy thinks he's a magician, so he may have some good hiding places," he remarked to another officer at one point.[83] He came to a mysterious covered object. He removed the cover and confronted our Heathkit robot 4E (named after Forry Ackerman, Hollywood's science-fiction entrepreneur). The photographer was summoned and 4E was duly mug-shotted.

By 1AM Pamfiloff had removed a number of our personal belongings and Temple of Set papers to several paper bags and cardboard boxes. I asked to inventory these; he refused to permit it. "As none of this material has anything to do with the search warrant," I said to Coleman, "why is he confiscating it?" Coleman shrugged. "He can't return empty-handed to the judge who issued the warrant." Then, as Pamfiloff departed, I asked how soon I would be able to reclaim the property. "Check with us in a couple of weeks," he said off-handedly, then was gone. Coleman stayed with us for a few more minutes, then left as well.

So at 1AM Lilith and I found ourselves standing in the middle of our home - furniture, papers, clothes strewn about us - and still totally bewildered at what could conceivably have caused such an event. After Coleman took his leave, Lilith - who had managed to keep her composure during the ordeal - finally broke down in hysterics. It was several more hours before sheer exhaustion overcame her fear and anger and she was able to catch a few hours' sleep.

It took us most of the the following day to get our home back into some semblance of order, and then on Sunday morning we went downtown to the offices of Pillsbury, Madison & Sutro, the law firm which I had previously used only for routine business affairs.

Presiding at the meeting was Maurice D.L. Fuller, Jr., a senior partner of the firm who looked just like senior partners are supposed to look: regal, white-haired, and omniscient. With him was Bernard Zimmerman, chief criminal attorney for PM&S, whose pin-striped gravity was offset by his perennial frustration with the environment in which he operated. Mark Coleman, who as a business attorney would not play in this particular game, was present primarily as a witness to the events of Friday night.

"I'm sure you came down here wanting to sue everyone involved," said Fuller, "but in affairs of this sort the real world has little in common with television dramas. The city government will back up anything the police do, and the public - to the extent they care at all about such things - generally assume that the police only do things like

---

[83] Aquino, M.A., Memorandum for Record 8/15/87.

this with justification. Any sort of litigation against the police would be extremely expensive - we're talking about several hundreds of thousands of dollars - and would by no means guarantee you a victory no matter how right you are or how wrong they are."

"The first thing we have to do," said Zimmerman, "is to get our hands on a copy of the SFPD incident report that Pamfiloff is required to file concerning this affair. Until we can review that, we won't know why this happened at all. So I advise you to just cool your heels until we can track it down."

So that is what we did for the next two weeks - until August 28, when Zimmerman called to say that he had finally obtained the search warrant and incident report and was having a courier bring copies over to us [see Chapter #2 & Appendix #14]. We read through them in utter astonishment, which quickly turned to anger at this unknown Army officer for making such a foul attack on us.

I immediately wrote to Pamfiloff [with a similar letter to Foreman]:

It is only today that my attorney was able to acquire and provide me with copies of the incident report form and your own affidavit on which the search of my San Francisco home was based. Until today my wife and I had no idea what could conceivably have caused this traumatic incident.

If you were under the impression that you were closing in on a child-molester or sex-abuser, then I can at least partially understand the abruptness of your actions. From your affidavit it is clear that you have seen more than enough cases of child abuse in recent years to make you quite adamant about putting such people out of business. My wife and I view such perversions with as much revulsion as you do, and endorse community efforts to eliminate them.

What I have more trouble understanding, however, is why the mere responses of a 3-1/2 year-old child - who was 2-1/2 when these incidents are supposed to have occurred - were considered adequate to overwhelm my lifelong reputation as a responsible, moral, and respectable individual.

For the last several years the media have repeatedly shown how so many children "sexually abused by Satanists" were merely coached by disturbed or publicity-seeking adults to say such things. Why did this possibility not cause you to look more carefully into the physical possibility of my presence in San Francisco this last year?

Moreover, if the media are correct, this child is the same one whose testimony concerning this Hambright person was disallowed by a judge on the grounds that she is too young for it to be competent.[84] Am I to assume that her stepfather has the prerogative to overrule the judge in this and merely point a finger at anyone he chooses to set this sort of thing in motion?[85]

At this point in time Lilith and I still had no idea who this "Larry A-T" was. Lilith recalled having seen a television news clip a short time earlier in which some Army captain had been denouncing a judge for having disallowed the testimony of his infant child in the Presidio scandal. We supposed that this was the same individual. [As it turned out, we were wrong. The captain on the news broadcast had been Michael Tobin (see Chapter #1).]

The Presidio had received a new commander since my departure the previous year, Colonel Joseph V. Rafferty. He and I didn't know one another, but I did know his deputy, Colonel D. Peter Gleichenhaus, very well. I telephoned him at home and asked to meet with him. The next morning Lilith and I were in his office, showing him the papers we had just received and describing what we had just been through.

Gleichenhaus said that he had known nothing about it, nor had Colonel Rafferty. The mysterious Larry A-T, he said, was a Christian chaplain (with the rank of captain), who had been assigned to the Presidio garrison shortly before my departure for Washington. At that time his name had been Thompson; shortly thereafter he had married Michele Adams and taken the combined name. Gleichenhaus added that A-T had just been reassigned to the 25th Division in Hawaii, but, as far as he knew, was still living in Presidio quarters prior to moving.

The actions I subsequently took concerning A-T are recounted in the later chapter concerning court-martial charges against him, but the focus of this one is what developed with the San Francisco Police Department.

---

[84] I was mistaken, confused by the media fragments of which I was aware at the time. David Tobin's competency to testify concerning Hambright had indeed been disallowed by a judge [see Chapter #1]. The Adams-Thompsons' allegations never proceeded to indictment or such post-indictment judicial decisions.

[85] Aquino, M.A., Letters to Glenn Pamfiloff and Clyde Foreman, 8/28/87.

In trying to make sense of the raid on our home, I could only conclude that Gallant had succeeded in spooking the SFPD with tales of Satanic horrors, and that officers such as Pamfiloff had thus merely been waiting for an excuse to break into our home and our files. Larry A-T's horrific accusation offered him the excuse he needed. I wrote to SFPD Chief of Police Jordan, protesting Pamfiloff's and Gallant's actions and requesting his help in correcting the situation (Appendix #17). This was followed by a similar letter from my attorney (Appendix #18).

As was the case with my previous letter to Pamfiloff, the SFPD responded to neither of these letters. The following month I wrote Jordan again (Appendix #19), once more receiving no answer.

It was now disappointingly clear that the SFPD had no interest in a cooperative and positive resolution of the awkward situation caused by their raid and property confiscation. The next step, advised our attorney, was to ask a judge to order the return of our property. Simultaneously, to make a formal statement of our position, we should file a claim for damages against the city. So we did. Each of our claims read:

> *Description of Accident/Occurrence & Describe the Injury and Damage Claimed:* Illegal search and seizure of property from the Aquinos and continued illegal retention of property, all in violation of the Aquinos' constitutional and other legal rights, and causing them substantial emotional distress and humiliation and substantial expense in recovering their property.
>
> *Name and/or I.D. Number of Public Employee(s) Involved:* Glenn Pamfiloff, Star #228, Sandra L. Gallant, Star #1918, Frank M. Jordan, Chief of Police.
>
> *Name(s) of Witness(es):* Mark J. Coleman, Pillsbury, Madison & Sutro.
>
> *Itemization of Claim:* Special and general damages (and punitive damages as applicable) resulting from the above incident.
>
> *Total Amount of Claim:* $1,000,000.00[86]

Our attorney was both matter-of-fact and accurate about what would happen next. "Don't expect a $2 million check. The City Attorney will routinely deny these claims and advise you that you have six months to sue the city to enforce them. Don't sue, however, because if you do, in order to retaliate the city will instantly file criminal charges against you based on the A-T allegations - even if it knows they're false and that the court will throw the case out. The SFPD will now keep their investigation open until your six-month window for suing the city has expired, even if it has realized long before that that the allegations are baseless. Only then will it announce closure. But now we'll go ahead with a court action for return of your property."

What Pamfiloff had actually confiscated from our home was not authorized by his search warrant (Appendix #14). Per his own inventory he took:

From living room: 36 video tapes, 2 loose slides, 1 notebook, misc. loose papers with names and addresses. 3 binders letters.
From master Bedroom: 6 cassette tapes, 1 roster names, 2 notebooks with names, and addresses.
From master bedroom closet: 1 packet negatives.
From rear den: 1 Radio Shack TRS80 Mod 100 computer in black case, 1 receipt from Radio Shack, 2 photo albums, 1 black binder with letters & names, 1 note pad.
From kitchen: 1 paper plate and 2 plastic gloves (from garbage).
From front study: 4 plastic negative packets, 29 photos.[87]

But what this actually consisted of was this:

1. 36 video cassette tapes: *Star Trek*, *Star Wars*, *20,000 Leagues Under the Sea*, *Cannery Row*, Carl Sagan's *Cosmos* (7 tapes - all episodes), William Shirer's *Rise & Fall of the Third Reich* (documentary), U.S. Army's *Why We Fight* (World War II training film), *Packaging American Wars* (PBS documentary on American propaganda), *The Twisted Cross* (NBC documentary), *Rosemary's Baby*, *Sphinx*, 700 Front Street (San Francisco ABC interview show), Los Angeles PBS Channel 9 interview & Manson family

---

[86] San Francisco City Form 0301-02, M. Aquino 11/9/87 & L. Aquino 11/20/87

[87] Return and Inventory on Search Warrant, Municipal Court of San Francisco, Glenn Pamfiloff, 8/14/87.

documentary, *The Green Berets*, *Rambo*, 3 tapes of meetings of the Temple of Set at the Holiday Inn, Santa Cruz, *The Seven Faces of Dr. Lao*, Lilith Aquino interview on Channel 3, Santa Barbara (2 tapes), BBC documentary on Marilyn Monroe, Zeena LaVey interview on Phil Donahue Show, *Jefferson Starship*, *History of the SS* (PBS documentary), *Fade to Black*, *The Final Conflict*, *The Omen*, *Damien-Omen II*, 1 blank tape.

2. 2 color slides - family photos, non-pornographic.
3. 3 notebook - household and city college class memos by Lilith Aquino.
4. 3 binders of Temple of Set administrative correspondence.
5. Complete set of Temple of Set executive bulletins -1986-1987.
6. Several folders of administrative papers and old membership rosters of the Temple of Set.
7. 6 audio cassette tapes: classical music, electronic music, and an answering machine tape of messages left by Linda Blood, an individual who had been regularly leaving obscene and harassing messages on our San Francisco machine.
8. Packet of photo negatives - family photos, non-pornographic.
9. 2 photograph albums - Lilith Aquino's personal albums ca. 1970-1975. No pornographic photos.
10. Radio Shack TRS-80 Model 100 computer (Temple of Set property).
11. [From kitchen trash]: paper plate & 2 plastic gloves (containing hair dye used by Lilith Aquino 8/14/87).
12. Assorted photos and negatives - all family, Temple of Set, or Church of Satan - all non-pornographic.[88]

The Temple of Set documents and correspondence were all immediately apparent as unrelated to the warrant, as were our personal notebooks and papers. The same held true for the photographs and negatives Even allowing for the SFPD to wish to review the video and audio tapes, and to examine the computer (a little first-generation Radio Shack desktop) to ensure that they contained what their labels indicated, a few days should have sufficed for all of this material to be acknowledged as irrelevant and returned to us. Instead the SFPD retained it and ignored our requests for its return, leaving the newspapers to keep sensationalizing the "36 videotapes and other items" that had been seized; "obviously the police had found something!".

On 10/28/87, after two months of this treatment, we filed suit in San Francisco Municipal Court (the same court which had issued the search warrant) to force identification and return of all of the property. This Motion to Restore Property appears at Appendix #20.

On 11/24/87 the motion was heard in court. What happened then was summarized by the 11/26/87 *San Francisco Examiner*:

Legal Move Halts Hearing for Satanist

In a rare twist, a Municipal Court hearing involving Lt. Col. Michael Aquino, president and "high priest" of a Satanic church, came to an abrupt halt Tuesday when the judge was presented a writ from a Superior Court Judge. The writ, from Superior Court Judge Timothy Reardon, was over the issue of whether a district attorney could be present at the Municipal Court proceeding, since no charges are pending against Aquino.

Municipal Court Judge Philip Moscone had ruled that Assistant District Attorney George Butterworth could not officially represent the state in the hearing. He did, however, allow Butterworth to remain in an advisory capacity and assist police Sgt. Michael Seybold of the department's legal office, who is also an attorney.

Butterworth objected, then apparently sent an aide to the higher Superior Court to seek a writ stopping the hearing. Served with the writ in court, Judge Moscone smiled and said, "I've seen this done in the movies, but never seen it done for real."

Bernard Zimmerman, Aquino's attorney, was in court Tuesday to ask Judge Moscone for the return of 36 videotapes, a computer, and address- and notebooks that were taken August 14 by Police from Aquino's Russian Hill apartment during the investigation into child molestations at the Presidio Child Care Center.

---

[88] Inventory provided to Pillsbury, Madison & Sutro, M. Aquino, upon receiving copy of Pamfiloff inventory.

The home was searched based on information from a 3-1/2-year-old girl who told authorities that Aquino and Gary Hambright had molested her in a private home off the Army base.[89] No charges have been filed against Aquino.

However, before the issue of Aquino's property can be decided, a Superior Court hearing will have to determine whether Butterworth can officially participate.

Before Tuesday's hearing was halted, Zimmerman contended police had exceeded their authority by taking more than the search warrant allowed.

We promptly communicated with the D.A.'s office, saying that we would not oppose the D.A.'s participation in the hearing if it would get the hearing going again promptly. The D.A.'s office refused to withdraw their request for the stay writ. So we next went to the Superior Court asking that, since we were not opposing the D.A.'s participation, the Superior Court itself cancel the writ and authorize the hearing to recommence. It refused.

Why the obstruction and stalling by the D.A.'s office? Apparently because the SFPD attorney wasn't handling things well, and because it was feared that the SFPD would shortly be ordered to return all of the seized property. [In his written request for the writ to the Superior Court, Butterworth stated: "I am informed and believe that there is currently pending no criminal prosecution, either locally or federally, to which the property seized in the search warrant at issue pertains."]

An order to immediately return all of the property would presumably have made the SFPD that much more vulnerable to a finding of illegal search and seizure, which neither the D.A. nor the SFPD wished to see happen.

Before the D.A. had succeeded in aborting the Municipal Court hearing, Pamfiloff (who had brought into the court a container with all the confiscated items) was called to the stand. When my attorney Bernard Zimmerman asked him what I was being investigated for, Pamfiloff responded, "Child stealing and various subsections, child abuse, child neglect, child molests, rapes." [90] It appeared that he was merely reciting a catchall laundry-list of possible child crimes, which was certainly beyond the scope of the Larry A-T allegations [and which I didn't appreciate seeing on the evening television news].

A month later contacted Walter Radtke, a current member of the Temple of Set living in San Francisco, and asked to meet with him for lunch. Radtke agreed, and in a 12/7/87 telephone call with me recounted their conversation.

"I got this phone call from Pamfiloff. He was a little bit nervous and kind of evasive, and just said he wanted to meet me somewhere. I met him in a restaurant down on the corner here. He seemed to be anxious. His main line of questioning was whether or not I had been exposed ... He wanted to know, as a Setian I°, whether or not I'd come in any contact with literature that implied or expressed the use of children in any ritualistic manner whatsoever, and I told him absolutely not. And I also told him that all the Setian literature was available to him through the Intelligence Department, Sandi Gallant; that you had released this information; that he could check up on the background and go through the reading list on his own and verify that fact.

"Then he asked me if I had much contact with any of the other members, and I said only one, with Priest Mitchell Wade on three occasions; and nothing of that nature was ever brought up in any way.

[The Bay Area O.T.O., an Aleister Crowley occult society, was then mentioned by Radtke, who gave an account of a boring ceremony that he had attended at a local art gallery. Pamfiloff then told him ...]: "of an O.T.O. person prosecuted for child molesting, and said they found letters from the O.T.O. head telling the guy to stop such activities or he would be thrown out ... essentially rationalizing that the O.T.O. was a clean organization, that they were cool, but you guys weren't.

"And then he started bringing up facts about you and your cohorts, and essentially trying to convince me that you were some kind of pervert. He said, 'Well, you know this Aquino man. This guy is like, he's known to have had homosexual liaisons and to be a pervert, and how would you like it, to have your kid ...'

---

[89] As documented in Chapter #2, Kinsey A-T said nothing of the sort. The allegations were made by her stepfather Larry A-T.

[90] Channel #2 Evening News, 10/29/87.

And he seemed .... he was essentially trying to convince me that you weren't somebody, you know, worth protecting or anything. And I told him that I had absolutely no indication of that, and in fact your material was a wholesome departure from Anton LaVey's Church of Satan. Then he dismissed Anton LaVey, saying, 'Oh, he's just a media hound, Hollywood type; he's pretty harmless.' I said, 'Yeah, Sharon Tate, right?'

"And I think he finally discovered he wasn't getting anywhere with me. He didn't try to turn me into an informer or anything, but he did request that if I received or heard of, or got any implication that there was the use of children in any ritualistic practice whether written or implied, he'd appreciate it if I sent that along.

"I said you were planning a lawsuit against him, and he just countered that rather rapidly, a little too rapidly, and said if a lawsuit were to hinder an investigation, it certainly wouldn't hinder this one. He was playing the part of merely the officer assigned to the case, but he seemed to have something of a vendetta. He said several times, in as many words, that they were out to get you, that they were going to nail you.

"I got the feeling that essentially they're trying to drum up, trying to approach potential defectors to get some sensationalized testimony out of them. It wouldn't take many. It'd take probably one. As a matter of fact I've seen cases like this where they essentially try a character assassination operation, and they'll get perjured testimony from one witness. Oftentimes it's enough with a sympathetic court and jury, etc.

"Well, Officer Pamfiloff said, and I quote: 'We've been after this guy for six years.' He kept saying, 'This guy's a kook, he's a nut, but he's really smart.' And I told him, 'If he's so damn smart, why would he act so foolishly in such a way that could easily incriminate himself?' Pamfiloff just sort of clammed up. I'd be interested to know who is in the [SFPD] Intelligence Department. Somebody is feeding that stuff from the outside ... They can be very stubborn, and if they find themselves being ground, they will generate evidence." [91]

By way of response I decided to send Pamfiloff another letter (Appendix #21). As with my previous letters to him [and anyone else at the SFPD], it went unanswered.

On 1/15/88 Pamfiloff released some of the items. When Lilith and I flew to San Francisco from my current Army duty station in St. Louis to take delivery, we asked to meet with him in his office. It was my hope that in a face-to-face dialogue we might be able to get past the stone wall that letters seemed unable to bridge.

First we reviewed the confiscated property he was still keeping:

3 video tapes containing footage of business meetings and reception at the Temple of Set Conclave, Holiday Inn of Santa Cruz, California, 10/5-7/1984. [None shows any children or contains anything the least pornographic.][92]
Several issues of *Hieroglyphs*, the Priesthood newsletter of the Temple of Set. [None of these issues contains any material the least bit relevant to child abuse or molestation, or to anything else criminal.]
Several photographs of my wife, myself, and other adult members of the Temple of Set/Church of Satan. [None contains anything the least pornographic.]
Several [non-pornographic] photographs of my wife and her son Christopher in costume, 1973.
An issue of the Temple of Set newsletter *Runes* containing an article on nostalgia [non-pornographic].
All audio-cassette tapes [non-pornographic except for Linda Blood's answering-machine statements].
Lilith Aquino's household notebooks.
Assorted Temple of Set rosters and administrative papers. [None of these papers contains any material the least bit relevant to child abuse or molestation, or to anything else criminal.][93]

---

[91] Telephone conversation transcript, Walter Radtke and M. Aquino, 12/7/87.

[92] A videocamera was set up in one of the hotel rooms the Temple used for breaks & relaxation. It was well-stocked with food. Pamfiloff retained about six hours' video of various Setians devouring veggies, chips, and dip.

[93] M. Aquino inventory for Pillsbury, Madison & Sutro, 1/20/88.

While Pamfiloff did not dispute our assertion that none of the retained property was evidence of anything criminal, he still refused to release it. This of course was still unsatisfactory, as it allowed the SFPD, and hence the press, to say that some of the materials it had confiscated were still considered relevant to the allegations and investigation.

Unfortunately the conversation then took an unproductive turn, with Pamfiloff insinuating to Lilith that entries in her notebooks were "suspicious", which incensed her [beyond her already/understandable dislike of this man who had broken into her home]. At this point Shawn Hanson, who had been growing visibly angrier at Pamfiloff's tone and questions, abruptly interjected, "This interview is over!" And so we left.

On 1/28/88 Bernard Zimmerman sent a letter to the District Attorney proposing release of the remaining property and a joint statement by the D.A. and ourselves cooperatively ending the investigation. Shortly thereafter Pamfiloff telephoned him rejecting the proposal and adding that he had now begun to question other Presidio day-care children to see if he could get "identifications" from any of them. While on one hand this signaled that the A-T allegations were now considered defunct, this new fishing expedition was a disturbing development. By now, of course, Lilith's and my faces had been all over nationwide media in connection with the A-T allegations, and anyone with an interest in that coverage could "identify" us [or coach a child to do so]. Such coached "identifications" were a notorious staple of the "ritual abuse" witch-hunts around the United States. I therefore sent Pamfiloff the letter at Appendix #22. Again it went unanswered.

And so the situation remained until 8/2/88, when the *San Francisco Chronicle* mentioned that the case had been dropped by the District Attorney's office: the customary "insufficient evidence" disclaimer rather than outright exoneration. Our attorneys had been right about one thing: Our deadline to legally enforce our claim against the city had expired a little over a month previously.

Despite the official closure of the case, the rest of our confiscated property was still not returned. Not until 1/30/90, in response to a 1/24/90 demand letter from our Army attorney Captain Thomas Tinti, did Judge Philip Moscone finally sign an order returning all of the remaining property to us, which the SFPD did without comment [or apology].[94] As for the press which had sensationalized the property seizure for years, it took not the slightest notice.

The Office of Citizen Complaints Investigation

While as explained above our attorneys had warned us against suing the City of San Francisco/SFPD until the deadline for doing so had passed, I was still intensely frustrated that Gallant and Pamfiloff, apparently on nothing more than their prejudices and whims, could just force themselves into our personal lives, wreak as much havoc as they desired, then simply waltz away without concern or accountability.

Examining the organizational and supervisory structure of the SFPD, I discovered the existence of the Office of Citizen Complaints within the San Francisco Police Commission.

The OCC, supposedly a "watchdog" agency concerning police misconduct, had until now had something of a marginal history, simply because it had no actual power to enforce its findings or punish any misbehaving police officers. The SFPD essentially ignored it as mere public relations window-dressing. Nevertheless it had recently received a new Director, who had announced his intention for improvement [see Appendix #23]. I decided to give it a try. On 4/8/88, while Pamfiloff's investigation was still open [as were our two Claims against the City of San Francisco], I filed complaints concerning both Gallant and himself (Appendices #24 & #25).

I did not expect that the OCC would or could devote much time or attention to these complaints. As noted in the *Recorder* article at Appendix #23, it was already suffering from understaffing, a sizable backlog of complaints, and a shrinking budget. Then, too, it presumably was more concerned with instances of physical harm: gunshots, baton injuries, rough arrests, unjustified arrests, that sort of thing. As angry as Lilith and I were about what Gallant and Pamfiloff had done to us, it was also true that we had never been physically manhandled, handcuffed, arrested, or even touched in any way. The death threats and home-vandalism that had resulted from Pamfiloff's raid and statements were more the consequence of press sensationalism than the SFPD *per se*.

Well, I decided to lay the facts as they were out for the OCC and see what, if anything, it might say or do about them. The case was assigned to Ms. Irene F. Rapoza, an OCC Senior Administrative Analyst as well as an SFPD

---

[94] Minute Order, San Francisco Municipal Court, Judge Phillip Moscone, 1/30/90, signed 2/20/90: "It is hereby ordered that the property seized in the investigation of Lt. Col. Aquino be returned to him or his representative."

Officer herself. Her investigation took over 1-1/2 years - complicated, she once commented to me, by Gallant's and Pamfiloff's reluctance to meet with her or provide her with all of the documents and files she requested from them. On 11/22/89 OCC Director Langer sent me the official letter of his findings, reproduced here as Appendix #26.

Prima facie I was satisfied with it. The two most important complaints concerning Gallant and Pamfiloff were "sustained", and the retention of our property and Pamfiloff's overall conduct of his investigation were judged an improper SFPD "procedure failure".

Significantly, in addition to this Appendix #26 letter, there was a much longer and more detailed official report that went from the OCC to Chief of Police Jordan. My attorneys and I were allowed to see it only within the OCC office premises, and then only if we all signed a strict non-disclosure agreement. OCC Director Langer told me that this odd provision had been insisted upon by the SFPD when the OCC first came into existence - that the OCC is not at all liked by the SFPD and that it fought its establishment and tried its utmost to limit its effectiveness. Langer added that the Police Officers Association quickly and aggressively sues any violation of the non-disclosure agreement in order to attack the OCC's effectiveness and intimidate OCC complainants.[95]

So detailed and extensive was this particular "behind-closed-doors" report, indeed, that my Army attorney Captain Thomas Tinti (who had read it) immediately wrote Langer for permission to provide it to the Army CID.[96] Langer refused, however, saying that §832.7 of the California Penal Code prohibited this absent a court order or grand jury subpœna.[97]

What transpired during the next six months was related to me by Irene Rapoza.[98] The OCC report went from the OCC to the SFPD Chief of Police, who accepted it without qualification. The report then went to the SFPD Management Control Office, which is in charges of recommending disciplinary or corrective actions within the Department. Such actions fall into one of three categories, from least to most serious: Counseling, Admonishment, or Discipline

Concerning Gallant the MCO directed her Lieutenant that she be formally counseled ("Counseling" level) concerning her collection and use of information, both on the job and in her secondary occupations (i.e. her commercial marketing of her "occult expertise" and "satanic ritual abuse" publications). The MCO further directed her Lieutenant to review and purge her files of any improper "intelligence" information.

Concerning Pamfiloff, he received written reprimands ("Discipline" level) concerning his statements regarding his investigation as well as his failure to fully cooperate with the OCC investigation. The MCO further directed the Captain of the SFPD Juvenile Division to review the entire investigation of Lilith and myself to determine policy or supervisory problems, then to institute changes as required.

The MCO further found it improper that none of my letters to the SFPD had been answered, and directed that this situation be corrected.

Further as a result of this investigation, continued Rapoza, the San Francisco Police Commission (parent organization of the OCC and the SFPD) had instructed the SFPD "to write a new general order directing that intelligence be gathered and maintained only on strictly criminal activities and organizations".

On the issue of our still-unreturned property, the OCC recommended that the SFPD consult with the City Attorney for a policy about return of property when no charges were filed. The existing SFPD policy in this regard, in the OCC's opinion, was inadequate.

And that was as much of the "tip of the iceberg" as I am legally permitted to report here from information provided directly to me at the time.

Six months later, however, the *San Francisco Examiner* (which presumably hadn't signed any nondisclosure agreements), brought much of the rest of the iceberg surging to the surface (Appendix #27).

---

[95] Conversation, Michael Langer and M. Aquino, OCC office, San Francisco, 12/4/89.

[96] Letter, Captain Thomas Tinti to Michael Langer 12/6/89.

[97] Letter, Michael Langer to Captain Thomas Tinti 12/12/89.

[98] Telephone conversation, Irene Rapoza and M. Aquino, 5/15/90.

1991: Encounter at Ellis Brooks Chevrolet

On 4/16/91, after all of the other events recounted in this book had run their course, Lilith and I were again in San Francisco, visiting an old friend of ours, the General Manager of Ellis Brooks Chevrolet. Across the showroom floor two men in suits were admiring some of the new cars. Then one of them noticed us and came over with a warm smile on his face. He shook my hand, then Lilith's. "Remember me? Glenn - Glenn Pamfiloff!"

To say that we were dumbfounded is a comic understatement. This was the officer who had been so adamant that we were child-molesters/kidnappers/worse who had escaped justice? We might now have been old college buddies at a reunion. He waved his companion over, introduced him as his current partner in the SFPD's Robbery Section, and once again it was smiles and handshakes all around. Lilith and I were still too astonished to plumb our emotions for any residual indignation, so somewhat surreally found ourselves matching the two officers' cheerfulness.

Although Pamfiloff gave the impression that he had essentially lost interest in our case the moment the SFPD closed it in 1988, he now commented that he himself had never really wanted to open it to begin with. It was originally the CID/FBI who had wanted a search warrant for our home, he said, and only when the U.S. Attorney "wouldn't touch it" did they come to him and ask him to obtain one through the SFPD.

He confirmed that he had never once met or spoken to Kinsey A-T herself - only her stepfather Larry. He added that over the course of his investigation he had talked with "many, many other children", and that not one of them had "identified" or made any accusations against either of us.

It was a shame how the Army had hounded us, he continued, and he was glad to hear that our ordeal was finally over. More smiles and handshakes, followed by "Good luck!" wishes from both officers, and they left the dealership ... while Lilith and I stared at one another, still stupefied.

2000: Encounter on the Internet

On 4/19/2000 I received, once again "out of the blue", the following email:

Dear Michael,
    I've noticed my name come up, over the years, within your organization and friends. Recently I've done a search on your name and seen the bombardment that you've been experiencing.
    Well, maybe it's time for the real "lead investigator" to set all the Presidio Day Care Center stuff straight.
    Send me your direct phone number, and I'll give you a call.
Sincerely,
Glenn

P.S. I tried to approach this when we met on Van Ness, at the car dealership, about 7-8 years ago, but I guess it didn't connect.

We exchanged telephone numbers, and a few hours later had a friendly telephone conversation. I learned that he was now retired from the SFPD and living with his wife in a pleasant East Bay town. The following morning I received another email from him:

Dear Michael,
    I enjoyed yesterday's conversation and look forward to getting together on Tuesday.
    Hopefully I'll be able to correct some of the injustices that have been heaped upon you in the "Presidio Day Care Center" investigation.
Sincerely,
Glenn

Later that same day, having reviewed some of my recent Internet posts defending Lilith and myself against the still-occasional "Presidio" mud-throwing efforts against us, Pamfiloff emailed again:

Dear Michael,

I've read your recent messages, regarding the particulars of the investigation against you.

You must remember that I worked with most of those investigating you. You seem to want to break down every little iota to its nexus, but I want to try to keep it at its most basic. "No evidence against you" doesn't need to be answered with specifics.

If no other children, of the 100+ interviewed identified you, nor any of the children identified your home, as a respected child abuse investigator I would have to assume, that you were not involved with these children.

This is the entire point of my contacting you.

I'm sure that if you were the evil man that so much of the media makes you out to be, especially with your notoriety, at least one of "Dr.Lt.Col.'s" children would have attributed some nefarious act to you.

Well, I found no evidence, other than the first, very doubtful identification of you at the PX, and the very stretched identifications within your home, and a few, very stretched relationships, that in anyway could find you guilty of any child abuse.

My hope is to put this information into the public sector, to clear you of any relationship with Mr. Hambright, of which my investigation found none, and to clear you of any involvement with the children of the Presidio Day Care Center.

I do not purport to have full knowledge of your life's activities, nor to acquit you of the myriad of attacks that you have sustained.

I do not in any way wish to affiliate myself with your church, but I do wish to make sure that justice is done in the Presidio Day Care Center matter, and that an innocent man can have some peace from the media onslaught that he has undeservedly received for these many years.

I will attempt to get the truth out, and with our meeting of this coming week, I hope that we can achieve a mutually acceptable means of achieving just that.

Respectfully yours,
Glenn

While it was true that a statement of "no evidence" from the case's lead investigator had an authoritative simplicity to it, I thought he might not understand that the subject of that investigation certainly did not have that luxury, but indeed had to "break down each and every iota". I responded the same evening:

Dear Glenn,

> You seem to want to break down every little iota, to its nexus, but I want to try to keep it at its
> most basic. "No evidence against you" doesn't need to be answered with specifics.

My apologies for the admittedly exhaustive analyses. Particularly during the CID investigation, I was made to feel that it was my responsibility to account for "every iota" of anything that investigators could conceivably twist into something "suspicious". So I got quickly into the habit of dissecting everything in microscopic detail, turning the brightest possible light on it.

> Well, I found no evidence, other than the first, very doubtful identification of you at the PX

"Very doubtful" boils down to nothing more than the say-so of the **two adult** A-Ts, who were established to have lied about numerous elements of that event.

> and the very stretched identifications within your home,

"Very stretched" boils down to Larry A-T's lucky guess that one of the rooms in the home of a "Satanist high priest" just might be painted black. But he got the room wrong, and there was no pentagram on its ceiling. And he lied to you about attributing even **that** image to a Hickey-session:

In all of the Hickey session notes there is not a single mention of a "black room" anywhere - not by Hickey, not by Kinsey. As for an object on the ceiling, there is not a single mention of a pentagram. The Hickey session note that Larry A-T personally revised into what he told you was this on 6/2/87:

> "Asked her if there was a big pot that hung down from the ceiling there with legs sticking out. Said it had legs, arms, and a penis. Said the 'dead people' were 'blue' in color. Said the penis went pee on her shoes."

That's it. I think you will agree that there was no pot full of blue dead people hanging from the ceiling of our bedroom and peeing on your shoes as you walked in that evening!

> and a few, very stretched relationships.

I'm not sure what you're referring to here. Neither Lilith nor I ever had any contact with the A-Ts [and to this day we don't know what any of them look like, since we've never even seen photos of them]. We never had any contact with Hambright, or anyone else at the daycare center. We never had any contact with any of the "copycat" cranks, etc.

> My hope is to put this information into the public sector, to clear you of any relationship with Mr.
> Hambright, of which my investigation found none, and to clear you of any involvement with the
> children of the Presidio Day Care Center.

I understand and very much appreciate this, as does Lilith.

> I do not purport to have full knowledge of your life's activities, nor to acquit you of the myriad of
> attacks that you have sustained.

I quite understand that. I take full responsibility for my own life, warts and all. As for the various SRA-lunatic-fringe ravings that resulted from all the Presidio publicity, that's to be expected from our "colorful" American social spectrum. I ignore most of the over-the-top drools, and just answer honest public inquiries as frankly and courteously as possible.

FYI The most recent of the drooling category is some conspiracy-theorist in England who's decided that I am an agent of a race of lizard-men planning to take over the planet. **That's** a new one!

> I do not, in any way, wish to affiliate myself with your church, but I do wish to make sure that
> justice is done in the Presidio Day Care Center matter, and that an innocent man can have some
> peace from the media onslaught that he has undeservedly received for these many years.

Thank you. A pleasant weekend to you and Mrs. Pamfiloff, and I look forward to seeing you Tuesday.
Sincerely,
Michael

As it turned out he fell ill - I sensed from his voice on the telephone that he was not in the best of health - and we were not able to meet. A month later I sent him another letter, feeling that there was a final, crucial point I needed to make. I have not heard from him since, and would like to think that this does not mean that his health worsened critically.

May 27, 2000

Dear Glenn,

Enclosed are photocopies of your original Incident Report and of the search warrant papers. In addition to the original Incident Report, here also is my annotated transcript of the same Report. I didn't know all this information in August 1987, and obviously you had no way of knowing it either when Larry Adams-Thompson showed up in your office and gave you his little story. It took me years to piece the truth together, to search out all the documentation, and often much FOIA tooth-pulling to get papers which I was obviously never supposed to see.

But here it is, and once again I think the sum total of it is pretty clear: Adams-Thompson and his wife weren't by any stretch of imagination "innocent victims just concerned about their little girl". They knew that nothing had happened to her. They knew we had never done anything to her. They also knew that they had an opportunity to defraud the government of $3 million, and all they had to do was hide behind "that's what Kinsey told us" and "that's what the therapist told us" - then sit back and watch public hysteria over the well-known "Satanism" of the Aquinos railroad us into prison, probably there to be ourselves raped or beaten to death as reportedly often happens to persons convicted of child sex crime.

I know that in our phone calls you've said that you thought the Adams-Thompsons were nice people. If I could see in their actions just an honest mistake, I would say so. But what is down in cold documentation here are not one, nor a few, but a virtually endless stream of lies, changing stories, and maneuverings by both of them to get their $3 million over the dead bodies of myself and my wife. To say nothing of their cold-blooded decision to bring up their little girl believing that she had been kidnapped and gang-raped when none of that had ever happened at all.

Lilith and I spent years of fear and stress defending ourselves against what those two vicious people tried to do to us. It severely damaged our health, terrified our families, destroyed my pending promotion to full colonel, and as you've seen on the Internet has been seized upon by any number of unstable crackpots to stalk us in lunatic conspiracy theories. So yes, we're deeply bitter about it. The fact that the Army didn't have the guts to court-martial Adams-Thompson, but instead cooperated in their scheme and paid them their money, makes it all the worse.

Our respect for human integrity and decency has certainly been revived by your contact and offer to provide us with your letter. Lilith and I want you to know again how very much we appreciate it.

Sincerely,
Michael

And so after all of the stressful, disheartening, and embittering events of the San Francisco Police investigation of Larry and Michele A-T's vicious little scheme, enhanced by Sandi Gallant's years of equally-squalid well-poisoning at the Department, it ultimately transpired that Glenn Pamfiloff and Michael & Lilith Aquino finally found and made a quiet, mutually respectful, and I think I may indeed say friendly peace with one another.

During one conversation Pamfiloff mentioned that over his many years in the SFPD Juvenile Division he and his partner had "investigated, prosecuted, and helped to incarcerate hundreds of pedophiles and child molesters". He would have been less than human if such a depressing and revolting series of cases didn't take a grinding toll on his own nerves, enjoyment of life, and respect for the human race generally.

Perhaps if Larry A-T had come to him ten years earlier with his concocted story, Pamfiloff might have been less inclined to rush to judgment, more careful to examine the accuser before agreeing to examine the accused. But the Glenn Pamfiloff of 1987 had probably come to carry within him a simple, dark hatred of all monsters who injure children, and this - together with Sandi Gallant's "expert" assurance that Michael and Lilith Aquino were indeed two such monsters, instantly imbued him with a single-minded determination to slay those monsters. If I am correct in this, my logical, reasonable letters to him weren't unconvincing in their content; they were just distractions in their entirety, to be brushed aside in favor of the original, dedicated pursuit.

But as Glenn Pamfiloff's final encounters prove, there was ultimately a greater humanity in him, a sense of decency and integrity, that any past horrors of his police career could not completely overwhelm. He was, in the final reckoning, a Good Cop.

Chapter 5: Court-Martial Charges Against Larry Adams-Thompson

The Elephant in the Dark Room

Larry A-T was an official Christian chaplain of the Army Corps of Chaplains, with the government-mandated mission of representing and promoting Christianity to all soldiers with whom he came into contact.

I, on the other hand, was "quite the other thing": from 1970 to 1975 a Priest of Satan, and thereafter High Priest of the ancient Egyptian god Set. The Army didn't have any Satanic or Setian chaplains, of course, nor do I think it would have been comfortable if I had requested equal time in the post chapel for a Satanic Mass or Setian invocation of the ancient gods.

Throughout my Army career I had addressed this situation by simply keeping my religion to myself, except when asked about it by friends, senior officers, or security clearance officials. Then I would discuss it frankly and honestly, with appropriate tolerance and courtesy towards conventional religions.

Until 1987 this had sufficed reasonably well, though the higher in rank I became, the more of a curiosity and gossip-object I found myself. By all accounts I had an exemplary and blemish-free service record, but the United States Army couldn't quite assimilate the idea of an officer conjuring up dæmons and Egyptian gods, and doing a bit of Black Magic on the side. Even my "normal" behavior while on duty was unsettling; like H.P. Lovecraft's sinister Joseph Curwen in The Case of Charles Dexter Ward, I was "suspected of vague horrors and dæmonic alliances which seemed all the more menacing because they could not be named, understood, or even proved to exist."[99]

Despite this, once Army commanders and colleagues managed to get over their original qualms, as they invariably did, they found themselves enjoying this "oddity" in the otherwise-undisturbed social climate of the service. Amusingly this always included the local chaplains, who obviously enjoyed the opportunity for some very "different" theological and metaphysical conversations. Indeed in 1977 my current headquarters went so far as to award me a monstrously-decorated certificate which proclaimed:

The 306th Psychological Operations Battalion
presents
The Esoteric Order of Dagon
to
Major Michael Aquino
In recognition of his knowledge of Mysteries unnatural, unnamable to the uninitiate and unspeakable to the profane, the above-named officer is hereby designated an
Honorary Unit Chaplain
with license to celebrate masses, extract and hear confessions, and keep away from this battalion all ghoulies and ghosties and long-leggity beasties and Things that go Bump-in-the-Night.

While assigned to the Presidio of San Francisco Headquarters 1981-86, I had known the two chief Protestant and Catholic chaplains, both colonels, as good friends, I hadn't had any personal contact with A-T, an assistant Protestant chaplain who had arrived on the post shortly before I left in June 1986 for my next assignment in Washington, D.C. As I would later learn, however, A-T and his wife were very interested in Lilith and myself - whom they saw at occasional Headquarters social functions.

After Larry A-T made his allegations against us, our respective religious affiliations and offices became "an elephant in a darkened room" - an unacknowledged, unspoken, but very real factor in the ways we were respectively treated by the various officers, headquarters involved. Essentially those who did not know anything about me other than my religion - which to them was simply the "S-word" making such horrific "SRA" headlines across the country - attempted to reject contact/dialogue with me as much as they legally could, while A-T on the other hand was a sanctioned icon of the Corps of Chaplains to be sheltered and protected.

---

[99] Lovecraft, Howard Phillips, *At the Mountains of Madness and Other Novels*, Sauk City: Arkham House, 1964, page 115.

Bluntly, it was unthinkable that an official Army Christian chaplain could be court-martialed and punished for a crime against Satanists. Jesus Christ is Good, after all, and the Devil is Evil. **Everyone** knows that.

Except that the U.S. Constitution, and the Uniform Code of Military Justice based upon its principles, actually **didn't** know that. Instead they held that American justice, including military justice, should be indifferent to religion and focus instead upon the statements and actions within a given incident. It was with the Constitution and UCMJ in mind that I sought such justice. I soon realized that, as Batman observed in *The Dark Knight Returns*, "the world only makes sense when you **force** it to".[100]

First Discovery

As recounted in Chapter #4, for the two weeks following the surprise raid on our home Lilith and I had absolutely no idea why it had taken place or who was responsible for apparently making criminal allegations against us. On 8/28/87 our attorneys finally obtained a copy of Glenn Pamfiloff's filed SFPD Incident Report [see Chapter #2], and so I learned that the instigator was one Captain Larry Adams-Thompson, whom I then located in a Presidio directory as Captain (Chaplain) Larry P. Thompson. I immediately wrote to him at his Presidio address [on my St. Louis, Missouri letterhead]:

August 28, 1987

Dear Captain Thompson:

After a year's assignment in Washington, D.C., my wife and I were able to pay a short visit to our San Francisco residence early this month. At 9 PM on Friday the 14th, a team of San Francisco police officers and FBI agents arrived at our front door with a warrant to search the premises, and for the next four hours my wife and I could do nothing but stand by in shock and bewilderment while our entire home and personal effects were ransacked. After the police finally left, and after I had endeavored to comfort my wife, who was severely frightened by this unexplained invasion, it took me the rest of the night and the following day to restore our strewn-about clothes, papers, and personal effects to some semblance of normalcy.

That night we were told nothing more than that the officers were searching for "evidence of child molesting". Not until today was my attorney able to acquire a copy of the enclosed form from the S.F.P.D. I now find out that **you** are the individual who is responsible for this incident.

I have no way of knowing what sort of leading questions you may have put to your stepdaughter at the P.X., if indeed you did not fabricate that incident entirely. But if you had taken just a moment to check with the Presidio Headquarters, or the officer records section of COMPACT, you would have learned that I had been assigned as a resident student at the National Defense University from August 1986 through July of 1987. There is no possible way my wife or myself, who have been living in an apartment in Washington, D.C. for the last year with our S.F. home closed up, could have been involved in the Presidio day-care scandal, even if we were that kind of people - which we are most emphatically not.

Even during my assignment to the Presidio from 1981 to July 1986, my wife and I never had anything to do with the child-care center, nor with this Gary Hambright person, nor with your stepdaughter, nor - as far as I can recall - with you. Why you now decided to abuse us so maliciously I cannot possibly imagine.

By your vicious, irresponsible, and thoroughly disgusting accusations you have brought about the violation of my home, severe trauma to my wife and family, and an insult to my own integrity that is especially foul and loathsome, based as it is upon the sexual abuse of little children. Only if you send me immediately a letter of complete and unqualified apology and retraction for this disgraceful conduct of yours will I consider not taking legal action against you, either via civil suit or per applicable provisions of the UCMJ.

Sincerely,
/s/ Michael A. Aquino
Lt. Colonel, Military Intelligence

cc- Commander, Presidio of San Francisco
Inspector Glenn Pamfiloff, S.F.P.D.
Special Agent Clyde Foreman, F.B.I.

---

[100] Miller, Frank, *The Dark Knight Returns*. New York: DC Comics, 1996, page #192.

No answering letter was received, but on September 10th, by which time Lilith and I were back in St. Louis, an unsigned pornographic card stating "BLOW IT OUT YOUR ASS YOU POMPOUS JERK!" arrived in our St. Louis mailbox [otherwise unknown to any participant in the Presidio scam]. I wrote to Captain A-T (who I had learned was now assigned to the 25th Infantry Division in Hawaii):

September 10, 1987

Dear Captain Adams-Thompson:

To date I have received no letter from you in answer to mine of August 28th. On the other hand, I have today received an extremely vulgar card (copy enclosed) which, while unsigned, was postmarked in San Francisco on the day you would have received my letter at your Presidio of San Francisco address.

That you were still taking delivery of mail at that address when my letter arrived is established by the lack of a forwarding address filed with the PSF post office at that time. [My envelope was marked "address correction requested", and a USPS card would automatically have been sent to me had you had a change-of-address on file by the time my letter passed through the PSF post office for local delivery.]

I might also add that by 9/2 virtually no one in San Francisco - and certainly no one likely to send a card like this - had been advised of my new St. Louis address except yourself. Since you have already shown evidence of your true character by the disgusting and utterly false accusations you furtively made against my wife and myself, I conclude that this card represents all the consideration you gave to my letter - and all the concern you have for the harm you have done to two innocent people. If so, it is not surprising that you didn't sign it, as that would have committed you to a statement that you could **not** use your infant child to "hide behind".

If you care to deny having sent this card, I would welcome a letter from you to that effect - and repudiating its message.

Sincerely,
/s/ Michael A. Aquino
Lt. Colonel, Military Intelligence

This letter was unanswered as well.

On 12/1/87, therefore, I wrote to Major General James Crysel, Commanding General of the 25th Division, recounting the situation in as much detail as I knew at the time, ending:

... I therefore conclude that Adams-Thompson deliberately intended to smear my good name, that of my wife, and that of our church with this abominable accusation, counting on media sensationalism and public ignorance not only to compound the damage to us, but also to shield him from the consequences of falsely and maliciously accusing a fellow Army officer of a serious felony.

To date it appears that he has been quite successful in this. No official actions have been taken against him whatever. The Presidio Judge Advocate's office excuses such inaction as being a necessary consequence of the "ongoing investigation" into the Presidio scandal as a whole. This is absolutely unjustified, since the facts surrounding Adams-Thompson's behavior in this incident [cited in this letter] are all clearly established, and since Adams-Thompson's false accusations against me are not connected with any molestation activities which may have been perpetrated at the day-care facility by Hambright or anyone else. To delay justice in Adams-Thompson's case is not only to allow him to savor what he has done; it is to indefinitely perpetuate and aggravate the continuing public ordeal of my wife and myself.

While Adams-Thompson has been free to enjoy his new duty station in Hawaii, my family and I have gone through three months of protracted agony because of his vile accusation. We have been questioned by scores of military associates, family friends, and business associates. We and our church have been caricatured sensationally and inaccurately by many commercial media. Our personal privacy and the religious privacy of our church have been and continue to be regularly violated as though we are mere freaks for public entertainment; we are forced to respond to continued inquiries only to try to preclude at least the more bizarre distortions in the inevitable coverage [which reporters are quite skilled in phrasing to circumvent libel]. We have learned to our distress that even the most polite declining of interviews usually results in hostile distortions by the reporters in question.

My wife and I have received several death and arson threats on our telephone answering machine. Our San Francisco home has been vandalized, forcing me to spend over $3,000 in repairs and protective reinforcement. Our tenants in the building have also been harassed and traumatized by vandalism. The building has become a "tourist attraction" in the city, with groups of people ogling it daily.

After a lifetime of cordial relations with the San Francisco Police Department, I now find myself in an adversarial legal battle against them because of their bureaucratic refusal to reverse the search/confiscation action they took solely on the strength of Adams-Thompson's accusation. This legal action has already cost over $6,000 in attorney's fees, and will certainly cost several tens if not hundreds of thousands of additional dollars if we are forced to pursue the matter into state and/or federal court to restore the good name and property of ourselves and our church.

Add to this the countless man-hours the Department of the Army has now had to devote to responding to reporters concerning this affair, and the damage to the Army that has nonetheless resulted from some reporters' crude castigations of the Army for my religious "oddity" as though it were something despicable. Even my Top Secret security clearance, though not compromised in the least by my religion nor even relevant to this situation, has been headlined as though it were a scandal in itself.

And add to this the very notion that a Lieutenant Colonel in the Army "may be linked to child-molesting at the Presidio" [as the stories "carefully" state], which necessarily reflects that much more adversely upon the Army officer corps as a whole.

I think that Chaplain Adams-Thompson fully deserves to be dishonorably discharged from the Corps of Chaplains and from the U.S. Army for his disgraceful and unethical actions and the severe damage resulting from them, which ill-dignify the moral and Constitutional standards which the Corps of Chaplains is expected to defend and exemplify. I am advised that I can prefer charges against him under Articles #133 and/or #134 of the UCMJ, whose elements of proof may be reasonably determined to include such behavior as Adams-Thompson's. I am fully aware, however, of the sensationalistic domestic and foreign media coverage that would certainly descend upon the court-martial of a Christian chaplain in defense of an officer who is a Satanic Priest - particularly in view of the grotesque stories which have already appeared in newspapers, magazines, and television about Adams-Thompson's accusation and my religion.

I think that any administrative actions which the Army can take to preclude such a spectacle would clearly be in the Army's best interests. For these reasons I am willing to accept a letter of reprimand by yourself to Adams-Thompson, placed permanently in his official file and identifying explicitly and without equivocation his unethical behavior and religious discrimination in this case. If I am advised in writing by 1 January 1988 that this has been done, I will initiate no UCMJ action against him.

If either you or higher commanders should decide not to issue such a letter of reprimand to Adams-Thompson by this date, then for my honor, the honor of my wife and family, and the honor of the religion we follow in accordance with the provisions of the United States Constitution, I will commence with such legal action against Adams-Thompson as is available to me under the UCMJ. It should be understood that such a legal action, if I am forced to undertake it, would be most actively pursued with all the resources at my disposal - and I expect that its administrative handling and eventual disposition would be as meticulously observed and commented upon by the national media as they have done since Adams-Thompson activated their interest. I cannot see such a situation being to the benefit of the U.S. Army or its Corps of Chaplains, and sincerely hope that administrative action to rectify the injustice perpetrated by Adams-Thompson will make it entirely unnecessary.

Respectfully,
/s/ Michael A. Aquino
Lt. Colonel, Military Intelligence

First Court-Martial Charges

While under the Uniform Code of Military Justice any commissioned officer may prefer court-martial charges, it is traditional professional courtesy to allow commanding officers of problem individuals the first opportunity to address that problem. Hence this initial communication to General Crysel. When after a month I had received no response whatever, however, I formally swore to charges against A-T on 1/4/88 and sent them to the 25th Division for disposition. The Charge Sheet (DD Form 458) read:

CHARGE 1: VIOLATION OF THE UCMJ, ARTICLE 133

SPECIFICATION 1: In that Chaplain (Captain) Lawrence P. Adams-Thompson, U.S. Army, Third Brigade, 25th Infantry Division, Schofield Barracks, Hawaii, on active duty, did, while assigned to the Headquarters of the Presidio of San Francisco, California, on or about 12 August 1987, knowingly and with malicious intent make false statements and representations defaming the characters of Lieutenant Colonel Michael A. Aquino and Mrs. Lilith Aquino.

SPECIFICATION 2: In that Chaplain (Captain) Lawrence P. Adams-Thompson, U.S. Army, Third Brigade, 25th Infantry Division, Schofield Barracks, Hawaii, on active duty, did, while assigned to the Headquarters of the Presidio of San Francisco, California, on or about 2 September 1987, answer a letter from Lieutenant Colonel Aquino demanding an apology for and retraction of Adams-Thompson's actions in Specification 1 with an obscene and disrespectful card mailed to Lieutenant Colonel Aquino.

The Charge Sheet was accompanied by sworn statements by Lilith and myself, once more detailing all that we knew at the time; Pamfiloff's SFPD Incident Report; the two letters I'd sent to A-T; and the obscene card received. Our sworn statements appear here as Appendices #28 & #29. They are particularly significant not just because of what they say, but because of the extensive amount of additional evidence that they were made in as-yet ignorance of. In other words, a proper investigation of the charges would have exposed many more supporting facts and documents - from the FBI & CID reports to the Hickey notes - as discussed in Chapter #2. As will be shown here, that investigation into these charges would never be made.

Article #133 of the Uniform Code of Military Justice is *prima facie* simple and direct:

Article 133. Conduct unbecoming an officer and a gentleman

Any commissioned officer, cadet, or midshipman who is convicted of conduct unbecoming an officer and a gentleman shall be punished as a court-martial may direct.[101]

Behind this short statement, however, are quite detailed elements of such offenses and explanations concerning them. These are reprinted here in Appendix #30.

In this instance, Specification #1 was clearly the essential one, with Specification #2 [concerning the card] being included simply because, if it were determined by investigation to be from Larry A-T, it was a #133 violation as well.[102]

For readers who may not be familiar with the UCMJ, the formal preferral of charges is an extremely serious action. The preferer must sign the charges and specifications under oath before another commissioned officer, state that he has personal knowledge of the matters set forth therein, and swear that they are true in fact to the best of his knowledge and belief. To put this another way, the deliberately false preferring of charges would itself be an actionable and punishable violation of Article 133.[103]

At first the process appeared to be proceeding normally. The 25th Division acknowledged receiving the charges.[104] Lt. Colonel William Hagan, the Staff Judge Advocate, advised General Crysel accordingly:

---

[101] *Uniform Code of Military Justice*, §933, Art. 133, page A2-33.

[102] And arguably UCMJ Article 134 as well, which among other things prohibits "the depositing or causing to be deposited obscene matters in the mail" . *Manual for Courts-Martial*, 1984, Part IV: Punitive Articles, page #IV-134.

[103] *Rule for Courts-Martial* 306 (c) (5), page II-28.

[104] Memorandum, HQ 25th Infantry Division to LTC M. Aquino, Subject: Allegations of False Accusations, 1/12/88.

Headquarters 25th Infantry Division

APYG-JA (27)   21 January 1989

MEMORANDUM THRU: Chief of Staff; Assistant Division Commander (Operations)
FOR: Commanding General

SUBJECT: Court-Martial Charges - Captain (Chaplain) Adams-Thompson

1. Purpose. To inform the Command Group about court-martial charges preferred by LTC Michael Aquino, ARPERCEN, St. Louis, Missouri, against CPT (Chaplain) Adams-Thompson, Headquarters and Headquarters Company, 3d Brigade, for allegedly initiating a false complaint (TAB A).

2. Discussion.

a. LTC Aquino alleges that during September 1987[105], CPT Adams-Thompson, through his daughter, initiated false child abuse charges against LTC Aquino. The allegedly false complaint resulted in a search of LTC Aquino's home in San Francisco and the seizure of several items of personal property (TAB B).

b. LTC Aquino claims that CPT Adams-Thompson was motivated by religious differences with LTC Aquino, who is the High Priest of the Temple of Set, a Satanic group.

c. Rule for Courts-Martial (R.C.M.) 303 requires that the accused's immediate commander conduct a preliminary inquiry to determine if the offenses occurred. I will forward the charges and allied papers to the Cdr, 3d Bde informing him about this requirement (TAB C). CID will assist the commander's inquiry.

3. Recommendation. That you approve forwarding the charges and allied papers to the Cdr, 3d Bde for compliance with R.C.M. 303.

/s/ William Hagan
Lt. Colonel, Judge Advocate
Staff Judge Advocate

I sat back to await the investigation of the RCM #303 officer, which I presumed in due course would include interviews with Lilith and myself. What happened instead was this:

Headquarters 3rd Brigade
25th Infantry Division

APVG-ZZO-CO   15 May 1988

MEMORANDUM THRU: Staff Judge Advocate; Chief of Staff;
Assistant Division Commander (Operations)
FOR: Commanding General
Approved: /s/ J.C.

SUBJECT: Court-Martial Charges - Chaplain (Captain) Adams -Thompson

1. Purpose. To inform you of the proposed disposition of charges preferred by Lieutenant Colonel Michael A. Aquino against CPT Adams-Thompson.

2. Discussion.

a. LTC Aquino preferred court-martial charges against Chaplain Adams-Thompson on 4 January 1988 alleging that during September 1987, Chaplain Adams-Thompson, through his daughter, initiated false child abuse charges against LTC Aquino (Tab C).

b. LTC Aquino claims that Chaplain Adams-Thompson was motivated by religious differences with LTC Aquino, who is the High Priest of the Temple of Set, a Satanic group.

c. LTC Hagan sent the charges to me advising of the requirement to conduct a preliminary inquiry under Rule for Courts-Martial (R.C.M.) 303 (Tab B).

---

[105] Correctly from the Charge Sheet August 1987.

d. I asked the local CID office to assist in the investigation. The report of investigation and allied papers are attached at Tab A.

e. Under R.C.M. 404a, I propose to dismiss the charges for lack of substantiating evidence.

3. Recommendation. That you take no action and allow me to dismiss the charges.

/s/ Michael J. Sierra
Colonel, Infantry
Commanding

This was followed on 5/27/88 by a Memorandum from the 25th Division's Staff Judge Advocate to Colonel Sierra, recommending that he formally dismiss the charges, which Sierra did by his initials.[106] Which in turn was followed by this letter to me:

Headquarters 25th Infantry Division

APVG-JA   2 June 1988

MEMORANDUM FOR: Lieutenant Colonel Michael A. Aquino

SUBJECT: Allegations of False Accusations

1. The inquiry into the charges you preferred against Chaplain (Captain) Adams-Thompson has been completed. The investigation failed to uncover any evidence to support the charges.

2. On 27 May 1988, the commander dismissed the charges.

/s/ William Hagan
Lt. Colonel, Judge Advocate
Staff Judge Advocate

This made no sense to me. The next step was obviously to ascertain why this decision had been made. On 6/23/88 I sent an answering letter:

Dear Colonel Hagan:

I have just returned from leave and have received your letter of June 2nd stating that Chaplain Adams-Thompson's commander has dismissed the court-martial charges I preferred against Adams-Thompson, on the grounds that the preliminary examination "failed to uncover any evidence to support the charges".

I have consulted with the ARPERCEN Command Judge Advocate's office and am advised that, as the individual preferring the charges, I may make a Freedom of Information Act request to receive a copy of the preliminary investigation report and all supporting documentation upon which Adams-Thompson's commander based his decision. By this letter I make this FOIA request.

I further request to know if Adams-Thompson's immediate commander has taken or is contemplating any non-judicial punishment of Adams-Thompson in lieu of a court-martial action. Please include the commander's name and unit.

I further request the name and mailing address of the next higher commander in Adams-Thompson's chain of command with court-martial jurisdiction.

A prompt response to these requests will be greatly appreciated, as it has now been nine months since Adams-Thompson's defamatory actions against my wife and myself, and six months since I preferred the charges.

Sincerely,
/s/ Michael A. Aquino
Lt. Colonel, Military Intelligence

---

[106] Memorandum, Captain Theodore Dixon to Colonel Michael Sierra, Subject: "Court-Martial Charges - Chaplain (Captain) Adams-Thompson - ACTION MEMORANDUM", 5/27/88.

On 7/5/88 Colonel Hagan responded that Colonel Sierra had since been reassigned, but that the new 3rd Brigade commander was not considering any action against A-T. Hagan further said that Major General Crysel was also being reassigned as of 7/7/88. Finally:

> The local CID coordinated the investigation into your allegations. I forwarded your request for the investigation report to them. I have been informed that the local CID has forwarded your request to the Commander, San Francisco Field Office, 6th Region USACIDC, Presidio of San Francisco.[107]

In other words, Colonel Sierra hadn't appointed an RCM #303 investigating officer at all, but had nominally assumed that role himself. Then, instead of conducting his own investigation as required under 303, he had simply referred that task to the local CID, which in turn had referred it to the CID San Francisco Field Office - exactly the same office, of course, which had endorsed and pushed A-T's allegations to begin with.

Shortly thereafter the San Francisco Field Office CID commander wrote to say that his office was not authorized to release the investigative report, but that my FOIA request had been forwarded to the national Criminal Investigation Command (CIC) headquarters, which did have that authority.[108] It seemed that the 3rd Brigade's RCM #303 report was becoming more and more bureaucratically elusive, if not indeed evasive. Since General Crysel was now gone as well as Sierra, I decided to refocus the issue with the new 25th Division Commander, Major General Charles P. Otstott. On 8/23/88 I wrote him:

Dear General Otstott:

On January 4, 1988 I preferred court-martial charges against a member of your command, Captain (Chaplain) Lawrence Adams-Thompson, for a violation of Article #133 of the Uniform Code of Military Justice directed against my wife and myself, copy enclosed. I was informed by your Staff Judge Advocate that a preliminary inquiry would be conducted accordingly.

During the next four months neither my wife nor myself was ever contacted by any investigating official or agency for an interview concerning our sworn statements or any other pertinent information. Then on May 18 the then-3rd Brigade Commander Colonel Sierra dismissed the charges "for lack of substantiating evidence".

In response to my Freedom of Information Act request of June 23 for a copy of the documentation upon which Colonel Sierra based his decision, I have received no copy of any investigation of Specification #1 from the 25th Division. I merely received a letter from SJA Lt. Colonel Hagan diverting this request to the CID. The CID field offices in Hawaii and San Francisco responded in turn by diverting it to the CIDC headquarters in Virginia.

Two months have now elapsed since the filing of that FOIA request with your SJA. It is fairly obvious that no timely provision to me of any investigation papers of Specification #1 will be forthcoming. Add to this the lack of any interview with my wife or myself during the 4-month "inquiry", and it is reasonable to conclude that no thorough inquiry under Rule for Courts-Martial #303 was ever conducted at all -that the charges were merely stalled for four months, until shortly before the PCS of both the brigade and the division commanders, and then were dismissed on nothing more than a pretext.

With regard to Specification #2 - obviously the lesser of the two specifications - the only FOIA evidence that any inquiry ever took place was a handwritten note (not even a sworn statement) from the Adams-Thompsons denying it. After the dismissal of the charges, I requested by FOIA a copy of Adams-Thompson's travel voucher to Hawaii. While there are still unanswered questions in my mind about Specification #2, I think that sufficient doubt concerning it has now been established to warrant its being dropped, and I do so request.

On the other hand, the initial strong evidence concerning Specification #1 has been added to considerably by the information I have accumulated since preferring the charges in January of this year -

---

[107] Letter, William Hagan to Michael Aquino 7/5/88.

[108] Letter, Captain Stuart S. Taylor to Michael Aquino 7/18/88.

and which I had expected to discuss with an investigating officer or agency. This additional evidence appears in my sworn statement of this date, enclosed with this letter.[109]

In my opinion the dismissal of the charges against Adams-Thompson is a miscarriage of justice and a violation of the purpose of the Uniform Code of Military Justice and the Constitution of the United States. I accordingly request that you reinstitute the charges, with Specification #1 only.

A grievous harm was done to my wife and myself by Lawrence AdamsThompson on no evident provocation but a religion held by us that he personally dislikes. To date he has not only escaped accountability for this malicious act, but continues to function as an Army chaplain, entrusted with the moral and spiritual instruction of American soldiers and their families. This is an individual whose actions in the Presidio of San Francisco scandal have caused serious harm to innocent people. His more extensive role as a possible instigator and aggravator of that scandal should be a subject of focus by the investigating officer, as that scandal has caused tremendous damage to the installation generally, the public image of the U.S. Army, and the many individuals who have suffered because of it.

Please understand that I am firmly resolved to obtain justice in this case no matter to what level of the chain of command, or of the United States Government generally, I am forced to pursue it. I am willing to abide by the decision of a General Court-Martial where Adams-Thompson's acts are concerned, but I do not think it is appropriate for such a verdict to be preempted by an administrative fiat.

Respectfully,
/s/ Michael A. Aquino
Lt. Colonel, Military Intelligence

cc- Commanding General, U.S. Army Western Command
Commanding General, U.S. Army ARPERCEN
Chief of Chaplains, Department of the Army
Commanding Officer, Presidio of San Francisco
San Francisco Police Commission

On 9/30/88 Otstott responded:

MEMORANDUM THRU: Major General [sic] Paul L. Babiak
US Army Reserve Personnel Center
FOR: Lieutenant Colonel Michael A. Aquino
Headquarters and Headquarters Company, US Army Reserve Personnel Center

SUBJECT: Dismissal of Court-Martial Charges Against Chaplain (Captain) Adams-Thompson

1. This responds to your letter dated 23 August 1988.
2. I have considered your letter and the attached materials.
3. The investigation is finished. I do not intend to reopen the investigation nor do I intend to reinstate any charges against Chaplain (Captain) Adams-Thompson. I am satisfied that your allegations do not have substantive merit.
4. I return the written materials and the video tape.

/s/ Charles P. Otstott
Major General, USA
Commanding

It appeared that whatever doors General Crysel had wished to keep closed were going to remain so under his successor. I therefore took the case to the next higher headquarters above the 25th Division, the U.S. Army Western Command:

---

[109] Appendix #31.

October 14, 1988

Lieutenant General Charles W. Bagnal
Commanding General, U.S. Army Western Command
Fort Shafter, HI 96858

Dear General Bagnal:

In January 1988 I preferred court-martial charges against Chaplain (Captain) Lawrence Adams-Thompson, currently assigned to the 25th Infantry Division, for a malicious and defamatory allegation he made concerning my wife and myself. I was informed by the division staff judge advocate that these charges would be investigated in accordance with Rule for Courts-Martial #303.

Four and one-half months later I was informed that the charges would be dropped for "lack of substantiating evidence". I had in fact provided a detailed packet of substantiating evidence to the 25th Division, and at no time during the "investigation" were my wife or myself - the victims of Adams-Thompson's action - ever contacted by any investigating official.

I then requested a copy of the "investigation" conducted by the brigade commander. The 25th Division SJA then told me that this was not an investigation actually conducted by the brigade commander, but rather a CID report used by him. I duly requested a copy of this CID report. I have since been informed by the U.S. Army Crime Records Center that the report is apparently that of the Presidio of San Francisco child-care center scandal, and is not yet releasable. In short, the information I received from the 25th Division that the brigade commander's specific investigation into the charges I preferred was supported by a CID investigation into those specific charges is incorrect.

The conclusion I drew from the above is that a proper, impartial, and complete investigation of the charges in accordance with Rule for Courts-Martial #303 was not in fact conducted, and that the charges were accordingly improperly dismissed by the outgoing division commander, Major General Crysel.

On August 23, therefore, I requested the new division commander, Major General Charles P. Otstott, to reinstate the charges and initiate a proper preliminary investigation. In support of such an investigation I provided an updated and expanded packet of evidence, a copy of which was also sent to you as the next senior commander.

Today I received the enclosed letter from Major General Otstott. Although many of the items of evidence contained in the packet sent to him were never considered in the "preliminary investigation" and are clearly relevant to the charges, and although there was a conspicuous mishandling of the investigation in the lack of any interviews with my wife or myself, and although no documentation of the investigation (the supposed CID report) appears to exist at all, still General Otstott refuses to even reopen the preliminary investigation -which of course would not pre-commit him to any particular disposition upon its proper completion.

I do not believe that this is a proper application of the Uniform Code of Military Justice. Extreme personal harm has been done to my wife and myself by Chaplain Adams-Thompson - a wrong which Article #133 of the UCMJ exists to redress, if so determined by a properly constituted and conducted court-martial. The seeking of justice under the UCMJ is a right guaranteed to all soldiers, not a favor to be dispensed or withheld peremptorily. I ask your help in seeing that these charges are reinstituted and that a proper and thorough inquiry is conducted prior to their consideration for disposition. As two commanding generals of the 25th Division have committed themselves to the handling of the case as it stands to date, I further request that, to ensure impartiality, the inquiry and subsequent decisions concerning disposition be removed to your level of command.

If you have not retained the packet of documentation previously sent to you, please advise me and I will forward the packet sent to [and returned by] General Otstott.

Respectfully,
/s/ Michael A. Aquino
Lt. Colonel, Military Intelligence

cc- Commanding General, 25th Infantry Division
Chief of Chaplains, United States Army
Commanding General, U.S. Army Reserve Personnel Center
Commander, Presidio of San Francisco

By 10/20/88 this letter was sitting on General Bagnal's desk - evidently something of a hot potato, because a week later he privately memoed his Staff Judge Advocate "What should we do now? Letter from me?" [110] Another week later the letter went out:

Headquarters, United States Army Western Command

APCG   8 November 1988

MEMORANDUM FOR: Lieutenant Colonel Michael A. Aquino

SUBJECT: Court-Martial Charges Against Chaplain (Captain) Lawrence Adams-Thompson

    1. I have received and considered your letter of 14 October 1988 requesting that the charges preferred by you against Chaplain Adams-Thompson be reinstituted and reinvestigated by this command.
    2. Rule 303, Rules for Courts-Martial, requires a preliminary inquiry into the charges you preferred. Such an inquiry was conducted to the satisfaction of Major General Crysel, who then dismissed the charges. His successor in command, Major General Otstott, declined to reopen the investigation or reinstate the charges, which he found to be without substantive merit.
    3. You are entitled to your opinion that the R.C.M. 303 inquiry into your charges was not conducted properly or thoroughly However, I do not share your opinion. Your request that the inquiry be reopened and the charges be reinstated is denied.

                    /s/ Charles W. Bagnal
                    Lieutenant General, USA
                    Commanding

As with the 25th Division, General Bagnal offered not a word of explanation as to his "without substantive merit" denial. While I could have appealed this denial again to the next [four-star] higher headquarters, it seemed obvious that this Christian chaplain was simply going to be protected, period. Whether the decision came from his two-star commander or from some higher authority was evidently not going to be shared with me.

    Meanwhile, every few months I continued to receive a form letter from the CIDC's U.S. Army's Crime Records Center advising me that the investigative report of the San Francisco and/or Hawaiian CID in support of Colonel Sierra's RCM #303 investigation was "currently ongoing with an undetermined completion date".[111] Since it had now been well over a year since that investigation was closed by Sierra, I decided to write back:

                                              September 15, 1989

Mr. Wilbur L. Hardy, Director
U.S. Army Crime Records Center, USACIC

Dear Mr. Hardy:
    I have received your letter to me of September 7, 1989 once again denying my FOIA/PA request for all CID documents relating to the court-martial charges I preferred against Chaplain Lawrence Adams-Thompson, 25th Infantry Division, in January 1988.
    You state that these documents "are part of an ongoing investigation with an undetermined completion date". I enclose, however, a copy of a letter from the 25th Infantry Division stating that the charges against Adams-Thompson were dismissed. If the investigation was "complete" enough for the 25th Division commander to dismiss the charges, then it is "complete" enough for your denial to be in violation of 5 U.S.C.
    This 9/7/89 letter from you appears to be merely the latest in a series of maneuvers by the CID to prevent me, as both the officer who preferred the charges and the individual victimized by Adams-

---

[110] Memorandum, Lt. General Charles Bagnal to Colonel Jacunski, 10/27/88, FOIA.

[111] Letters, Robert Brisentine and Wilbur Hardy, Directors Crime Records Center, to Michael Aquino 9/7/88, 1/9/89, 3/29/89, 5/10/89, 5/24/89, 9/7/89.

Thompson's criminal actions, from examining the "investigative report" which the 6th Region CIDC sent to the 25th Division concerning those charges. These evasions by the CID began in response to my original request for that "report" on 6/23/88. and have continued to this date.

It is my belief that examination of this material will expose the thorough inadequacy and bias of that "investigation", and indeed the deliberate effort of the 6th Region CID to conceal critical evidence in substantiation of those charges from the Commanding General of the 25th Division and the Commanding General, WESTCOM. Such an act by the 6th Region CID constitutes an act of misprision of serious offense and obstruction of justice in violation of Article 134 UCMJ. Concealment of this same information by the Director of the Crime Records Center would place you in the position of being an accessory to this same violation of the UCMJ.

An examination of this material is further important to the exposure of a prejudicial investigation subsequently instigated by the same 6th Region CID against me, in which documents and information proving both my innocence and AdamsThompson's guilt and establishing the unlawful bias of the 6th Region CID - to include the "investigative report" sent to the 25th Division - were deliberately concealed from me and my legal counsel.

I have formally requested Major General Cromartie[112] to investigate the conduct of the 6th Region CID Headquarters in this affair, to reopen the criminal investigation of Chaplain Adams-Thompson, and to dismiss the fraudulent investigation of myself accordingly. The documents I first requested on 6/23/88 - well over a year ago - are important additional evidence in support of all three of my requests.

I therefore request that you comply immediately both with 5 U.S.C. and the UCMJ, and furnish me with these documents without further delay.

Sincerely,
/s/ Michael A. Aquino
Lt. Colonel, Military Intelligence

Copies to:
Lieutenant General Charles W. Bagnal, Commanding General, WESTCOM
Major General Eugene R. Cromartie, Commanding General, USACIC
Major General Charles P. Otstott, Commanding General, 25th Infantry Division
Colonel Carl L. Lockett, Commander, 6th Region CID

That letter evidently singed tailfeathers at the CIC. On 10/20/89 I received a reply - not from the Crime Records Center but from the CIC's Staff Judge Advocate:

As to your request for the CID investigative report concerning the charges you preferred against Chaplain Adams-Thompson in January 1988, no such report exists. Those charges were determined to be unfounded; therefore no Report of Investigation resulted.[113]

Indeed? I responded directly to General Cromartie:

October 27, 1989

Major General Eugene L. Cromartie
Commanding General, USACIC

Dear General Cromartie:

I have just received the attached letter #A from your Staff Judge Advocate Lt.Col. Green. I will address other aspects of Lt.Col. Green's letter in a separate response to you, but this one is concerned specifically with the following remarkable paragraph from that letter:

---

[112] Commanding General, USA Criminal Investigation Command (USACIC).

[113] Letter, Lt. Colonel Brent Green to Michael Aquino, 10/20/89.

As to your request for the CID investigative report concerning the charges you preferred against Chaplain Adams-Thompson in January 1988, no such report exists. Those charges were determined to be unfounded; therefore no Report of Investigation resulted.

Please permit me to call your attention to the following:
Attachment #B (Letter, SJA 25th Division to me, 4/15/88) states:

> The commander asked that the local CID office assist in conducting the inquiry. The local CID office requested assistance from the Presidio of San Francisco CID office. I have been told that both of those offices are preparing their final reports concerning your allegations. Once these reports are received, they will be given to Captain Adams-Thompson's commander for review and disposition.

Attachment #C (Letter, Colonel Sierra to Commanding General, 25th Division, 5/13/88) states in paragraph #2.d.:

> I asked the local CID office to assist in the investigation. The report of investigation and allied papers are attached at Tab A.

Attachment #D (Letter, SJA 25th Division to me, 6/2/88) is the letter advising me that the charges had been dismissed.

Attachment #E (Letter, myself to the SJA, 25th Division, 6/23/88) requests a copy of "the investigation report and all supporting documentation upon which Adams-Thompson's commander based his decision".

Attachment #F (Letter, CID Hawaii District Office to me, 7/1/88) indicates that my request has been forwarded from the Hawaii District office of the CID to the San Francisco Field Office as the "controlling office".

Attachment #G (Letter, SJA 25th Division to me, 7/5/88) states in paragraph #4:

> The local CH) coordinated the investigation into your allegations. I forwarded your request for the investigation report to them. I have been informed that the local CID has forwarded your request to the Commander, San Francisco Field Office CID.

Attachment #H (Letter, myself to CID Hawaii District Office, 7/8/88) responds to Attachment #F and makes it quite explicit what report I had requested, i.e. the CID reports referred to by Lt. Colonel Hagan in Attachment #B and by Colonel Sierra in Attachment #C.

Attachment #1 (Letter, myself to CID Hawaii District Office, CID San Francisco Office, et a!., 7/20/88) makes my request further explicit in paragraphs #4 and #5:

- The complete documentation of the final report prepared by your office in Hawaii in support of Colonel Sierra's inquiry. In his letter to me of 15 April 1988, Lt. Colonel Hagan stated that both your office and the San Francisco Field Office were preparing final reports concerning the charges I preferred. I wish to see the report from your office as well as the one prepared by the San Francisco Office.

- The complete documentation of the final report prepared by the San Francisco Field Office in specific support of Colonel Sierra's inquiry.

Attachment #J (Letter, Commander CID San Francisco Field Office to me, 7/18/88) acknowledges the existence of the information I requested in Attachment #E, but states that authority to release it is held by your headquarters.

Attachment #K (Letter, Commander CID Hawaii District Office, 7/27/88) acknowledges my request and states that it was forwarded to the San Francisco Field Office as "the office controlling this investigation".

To this point in time we have five officers (Lt.Colonel Hagan, Colonel Sierra, Chief Warrant Officer Walker, Captain Taylor, and Captain Hastedt) who have all acknowledged the existence of the report in question. Colonel Sierra has in fact based his recommendation to the 25th Division Commanding General upon it. Now we proceed forward in time to the CID Crime Records Center.

Attachment #L (Letter, Director CID CRC to me, 9/7/88) acknowledges my original request (Attachment #E) and states:

> Your request will be retained in this center until our field element forwards a copy of the investigative record for releasability review. Upon receipt of this record, it will be reviewed for investigative thoroughness and legal sufficiency prior to release.

Attachment #M (Letter, Director CID CRC to me, 1/9/89) again acknowledges my original request (Attachment #E) and states that a response to me will be delayed.

Attachment #N (Letter, Director CID CRC to me, 3/29/89) again acknowledges my original request (Attachment #E) and states that a response to me will be delayed.

Attachment #0 (Letter, Director CID CRC to me, 5/10/89) again acknowledges my original request (Attachment #E) and states that a response to me will be delayed.

Attachment #P (Letter, Director CID CRC to me, 5/24/89) again acknowledges my original request (Attachment #E) and states that a response to me will be delayed.

Attachment #Q (Letter, myself to Commander, 25th Infantry Division, 8/3/89) restates my request for the CID report identified in Attachment #E.

Attachment #R (Letter, SJA 25th Infantry Division to me, 8/16/89) acknowledges Attachment #Q and the existence of pertinent "CID documents", and refers that part of the request to the CID.

Attachment #S (Letter, Director CID CRC to me, 9/7/89) acknowledges Attachment #Q and states:

> Your request and several documents that originated with this command were referred to this headquarters by the SJA Schofield Barracks and were received on or about August 15, 1989.
>
> A review of the referred documents and coordination with our Sixth Region Headquarters has determined that the documents are a part of an ongoing investigation with an undetermined completion date.

Attachment #T (Letter, myself to Director CID CRC, 9/15/89) acknowledges Attachment #S; points out that the "ongoing investigation" excuse used in Attachments #M, N, 0, P, & Q is invalid as substantiated by Attachment #D; and requests compliance with my request (Attachment #E) as required by 5 U.S. Code.

Further in my letters to you personally of 8/3/89, 8/30/89, 9/27/89, and 10/18/89, I restated my request (Attachment #E), identified the CIC's noncompliance with it in violation of 5 § 552 U.S. Code and AR 340-17, and requested immediate compliance with the law by your direction to the CRC as its commander.

As demonstrated by the above documentation, one of two mutually-contradictory situations now exists:

(a) If this current 10/20/89 letter from your Staff Judge Advocate Lt.Col. Green is correct, two senior officers of the 25th Division, two commanders & one Chief Warrant Officer of CID field offices, and two Directors of the CID Crime Records Center have made false official statements supporting the existence of the documents referred to in Attachments #B and #C. Such false official statements are in violation of Article #133 UCMJ, and you as the Commanding General of the CIC are required to title those officers accordingly.

(b) If on the other hand all those officers and CRC Directors were telling the truth, then Lt.Col. Green has just made a false official statement and you are required to title him accordingly. This is not a minor matter, but a subject of critical importance to the Army, as he well knows. Actions to cover up the crimes of Adams-Thompson as described in the January 1988 court-martial charges I preferred against him constitute not only an act of misprision of serious offense and obstruction of justice in violation of Article 134 UCMJ, but also serve to facilitate the deliberate defrauding of the U.S. Government of several million dollars by Adams-Thompson via his fraudulent claims, and possibly the further defrauding of the U.S. Government of up to $66 million in unjustified claims by other parents participating in the phony Presidio "child molestation" scam.

I request a resolution from you as to whether #(a) or #(b) is correct, and what action as CIC Commanding General you will take as required against the officials who have violated the UCMJ accordingly. If you determine #(b) to be correct, then I once more request that you direct the CRC to comply with 5 § 552 U.S. Code and AR 340-17 and, without further evasion, excuse, or delay, provide to me the documents identified in Attachments #B & #C and requested by me in Attachment #E.

Respectfully
/s/ Michael A. Aquino
Lt. Colonel, Military Intelligence

Attachments as identified

Copies to:
Honorable Michael P.W. Stone, Secretary of the Army
General Carl E. Vuono, Chief of Staff, United States Army
General Robert W. RisCassi, Vice Chief of Staff, United States Army
Lieutenant General Henry Doctor, Inspector General of the Army
Lieutenant General Charles W. Bagnal, Commanding General, WESTCOM
Major General William F. Ward, Chief, Army Reserve
Major General William K. Suter, Judge Advocate General of the Army
Major General Norris L. Einertson, Chief of Chaplains, Department of the Army
Mr. Joseph G. Hanley, Chief of Public Affairs, Department of the Army
Major General Charles P. Otstott, Commanding General, 25th Infantry Division
Colonel Bobby R. Sanders, Commander, ARPERCEN
Colonel Joseph V. Rafferty, Commander, Presidio of San Francisco
Colonel Carl L. Lockett, Commander, 6th Region CID

General Cromartie did not answer me, but on 11/27/89 the Director of the USA Crime Records Center suddenly managed to find the nonexistent report after all, and sent it to me. It appears here as Appendix #32.

Second Court-Martial Charges

Upon receiving the mysterious, elusive, and purportedly nonexistent CID report used to justify the dismissal of the original court-martial charges against A-T, I repreferred the charges and sent them once again to the 25th Division. I reiterated the First Specification from the original charges, for which by now I had accumulated [and was enclosing] additional and more conclusive evidence. I dropped the original Second Specification [concerning the obscene card] because it was far less significant than the First Specification. And I added a new Second Specification, because by this time I had learned of A-T's filing of a $3 million claim based on his allegations:

CHARGE 1: VIOLATION OF THE UCMJ, ARTICLE 133

SPECIFICATION 1: In that Chaplain (Captain) Lawrence P. Adams-Thompson, U.S. Army, Third Brigade, 25th Infantry Division, Schofield Barracks, Hawaii, on active duty, did, while assigned to the Headquarters of the Presidio of San Francisco, California, on or about 12 August 1987, and in related instances thereafter, knowingly and with malicious intent make false statements and representations defaming the characters of Lieutenant Colonel Michael A. Aquino and Mrs. Lilith Aquino.

SPECIFICATION 2: In that Chaplain (Captain) Lawrence P. Adams-Thompson, U.S. Army, Third Brigade, 25th Infantry Division, Schofield Barracks, Hawaii, on active duty, did, on or about 15 March 1988, file one or more false claims, based upon the false statements and representations identified in

Specification 1, such claim or claims totaling at least $750,000 and possibly as much as $3,000,000, and such claim or claims thus constituting a deliberate attempt by him to defraud the United States Government.[114]

Along with this Charge Sheet went a letter from myself to Major General Otstott, explaining the repreferral (Appendix #33). Included with this was an extremely comprehensive analysis - "Chaplain Lawrence A-T's Violations of Article 133, UCMJ" - which by this time I had been able to assemble from my continued research [including extensive FOIA/PA requests]. Provided not only to Otstott in this instance, but to many other concerned officials and headquarters from this time on, this document has never been questioned or refuted in any detail whatever. Here it appears as Appendix #33.

Nevertheless Otstott dismissed the charges (Appendix #34). I appealed his decision to Lt. General Bagnal (Appendix #36). His successor as WESTCOM Commander, Lt. General Kicklighter, declined to overrule Otstott (Appendix #37).[115] I wrote back to correct Kicklighter and request his reconsideration (Appendix #38). No answer.

I have reproduced this series of correspondence as Appendices because of their length. Altogether the letters establish that Otstott and Kicklighter were still determined that under no circumstances would this chaplain be investigated, much less court-martialed for either Specification. None of the facts I cited was invalidated, nor was I admonished for, in effect, implying that the dismissal of the original charges, and suppression of these repreferred ones, was **itself** a UCMJ violation of Article #134, Misprision of Serious Offense and Obstruction of Justice.

Two two-star Generals and two three-star Generals had now all stood up against the door of Chaplain Larry A-T's accountability for his actions before a court-martial, to keep it firmly wedged shut.

And that was that. A Lt. Colonel may lead a General [or several of them] to water, but he most assuredly cannot make him drink.

Implications of Information Presented in this Chapter

By January 1988 Larry A-T was aware of enough personal information about Lilith's and my Washington, D.C. location in September-October 1987 to know that we could not possibly have had any contact with his stepdaughter Kinsey, even if he had credited Hickey's assertion that the child had been molested by Hambright during that window. Nevertheless A-T took no action whatever to withdraw or apologize for his allegations against us to SFPD Inspector Pamfiloff.

This same proof of our non-involvement was available to A-T's new unit, the 25th Infantry Division. It initiated no corrective action concerning him upon my request.

When in January 1988 I preferred court-martial charges against A-T, the 25th Division refused to conduct the required RCM #202 into the elements of proof I provided. Further, additional elements of proof, such as FBI documents and the Hickey notes, which I did not at the time know about but which a RCM #202 investigation would have exposed, conclusively supported the first specification of the charges.

The 25th Division commander dismissed the charges, and the senior U.S. Army Western Command commander upheld his dismissal. Both refused to address the elements of proof in the charges' supporting documentation.

Why these commanders so adamantly and abruptly protected A-T from UCMJ accountability is open to anyone's speculation. I think it was simply the established prestige and influence of the Corps of Chaplains within the Army, together with ignorance, fear, and prejudice concerning the "S-word" - Satanism. It was politically unthinkable to prosecute a Christian chaplain for a crime against a Satanist, even if it had happened.

It took me almost two years - to November 1989 - to obtain the RCM #202 investigation report, which was repeatedly concealed from me, even to the point of denying its existence, until exposure of the concealment became too conspicuous. The report turned out to contain no inquiry into the elements of proof of the charges whatever.

---

114 Charge Sheet, DD Form 458, 11/29/89. Accuser: Lt.Col. Michael A. Aquino, Witness: Col. Bobby R. Sanders, Commander, ARPERCEN, St. Louis, MO.

115 At this time I was unaware that Kicklighter, in his immediate past assignment as Director of the Army Staff, had been the Department of the Army's action officer to "deal with the matter of Lt. Col. Aquino" following the October 1988 Geraldo River "Satanism" special on NBC network television [see Chapter #6]. Thus there was a clear conflict of interest in Kicklighter's decision concerning A-T, about which he neglected to inform me.

I re-preferred charges, adding A-T's $3 mission defrauding of the government, in November 1989. Considerable additional elements of proof were added. Yet these charges were also immediately dismissed by the 25th Division and Western Command, again without investigation into any of those elements.

Senior dismissing officer this time was Lt. General Claude Kicklighter, who, as Director of the Army Staff at the Pentagon in November 1988, had on the orders of Secretary of the Army John Marsh convened a secret, and possibly illegal, meeting of senior Department of the Army officials to "deal with me" [see Chapter #6]. Kicklighter did not reveal this conflict of interest to me when suppressing the A-T court-martial charges.

As in November 1988 the Judge Advocate General of the Army had secretly ordered that the Army initiate a new criminal investigation of me based on A-T's allegations, it was obvious that an investigation into, and court-martial of A-T for falsifying those same allegations was not going to be permitted.

Despite the eventual, conspicuous, and ignominious failure of TJAG and the CID to fabricate a case against Lilith and myself, any investigation into A-T's actual violations of the UCMJ remained permanently prohibited.

Chapter 6: Geraldo, Jesse, and Behind-Closed-Doors

Geraldo Rivera's "Satanism!" NBC Special

In 1988 both the United States Army and I could have done without Geraldo Rivera.

The Presidio of San Francisco "child abuse" episode, Larry A-T's attack on Lilith and myself, and the consequent events and actions summarized in the preceding five chapters hadn't, of course, taken place in a social vacuum. Across the United States, as well as overseas in such countries as the United Kingdom, "satanic ritual abuse" hysteria was continuing to rage, with new accusations against day-care providers, babysitters, and family relatives a regular occurrence in the news.

Unsurprisingly the tabloid media milked this cash cow enthusiastically. The spirit of Moloch prevailed. The more lurid the latest scandal, the more people could be counted upon to tune their televisions to it.

Preeminent among the "satanism" fear-merchants was a new daytime television talk-show host, Geraldo Rivera. Presenting himself as merely a concerned investigative journalist, he was rather a sensationalist predecessor to the bottom-feeding, tabloid-trash television shows to come, such as that of Jerry Springer. By mid-1988 Rivera's daytime shows were regularly presenting "victims of satanists", "reformed ex-satanists", "teen satanists", "anguished parents of satanists", "witnesses of satanic crimes", and anything else invoking the dreaded S-word he and his publicists could entice in front of a camera. Ratings soared as audiences shuddered in delicious horror that "such things were happening **even in our own, normal American neighborhoods!**".

Later that year Rivera announced his personal *pièce de résistance*: a two-hour, prime-time NBC television special on "Satanism". I discussed this with the Temple of Set in the October 1988 issue of its *Scroll of Set* newsletter:

> On October 25th Geraldo Rivera, he of Al Capone's basement vault and the treasures of the *Titanic*, will be anchoring a two-hour NBC special report on Satanism in the United States. I have been invited to participate in the special as part of a discussion panel. The other members of the panel have not been finalized, but possible names include Father James LeBar of New York City and Roy Masters.
>
> "Reverend" LeBar styles himself "Consultant of Cults for the Archdiocese of New York". Under this title he operates a hate-group entitled the Interfaith Coalition of Concern about Cults. I am surprised - perhaps I shouldn't be - to see the following institutions affiliated with it: Greek Orthodox Archdiocese of North & South America, Jewish Community Relations Council of New York, the Roman Catholic Archdiocese of New York, and the Council of Churches of the City of New York.
>
> LeBar actively disseminates a selection of distorted, disinformational sheets concerning Satanism and the Temple of Set similar to those disseminated by Sandi Gallant & Co. He never informed us that he was doing this, and of course never asked us for one of our informational statements. This past May, when I first learned of his furtive little hate-campaign, I promptly sent him a letter taking him to task for his bigotry. Of course there was no reply; such types operate only in the dark and when others' backs are turned.
>
> Roy Masters' name is new to me. I understand that he is a Christian fundamentalist, operating in Los Angeles and Oregon, who specializes in "deliverances" [presumably from demonic possession?]. Any Setian who knows anything about this individual is asked to send me as much information as possible as quickly as possible.
>
> The broadcast will also feature a live hook-up with the Oklahoma State Penitentiary, where someone named Sean Sellers is serving a jail sentence, presumably for a "Satanic" crime. Again, any Setian who may have heard of this individual or knows anything about him is requested to provide me with details as soon as possible.
>
> Scheduled also to be present at the penitentiary with Sellers is professional ex-Satanist Mike Warnke. I already know most of what I need to know about Warnke. But again, if any Setian has any current information concerning him or his activities, now is the time to pass it along. [This article was written before the Lexington, Kentucky news media exposed Warnke's entire "Satanic" story as being a fabrication.]

Anton LaVey has not responded to Rivera's invitation to appear on the special. On August 8th, however, a weird event took place in San Francisco that the producers of the special witnessed and filmed:

At the bottom of San Francisco's "tenderloin" area - so-called because of the abundance of sex-shops, prostitutes, derelicts, and flophouses, is the Strand Theater. The Strand, located on Market Street, is a rather decrepit old movie house that shows 3rd- or 4th-run movies, an occasional oddball film festival (such as Kenneth Anger's *Magic Lantern Cycle*), or a rental-event.

The Strand was rented on 8/8/88 for what was billed as "An Evening of Apocalyptic Delight: A Tribute to the Zodiac Killer", consisting of the film *The Other Side of Madness* about the Manson Family, a Jonathan Reiss movie entitled *A Bitter Message of Hopeless Grief*, and a gig by a local rock band called "NON", which I gather is of the punk/metal variety.

One of the featured participants, apparently, was Zeena LaVey, the daughter of Anton & Diane LaVey, who read some extracts from the *Satanic Bible*. Apparently there were some black-clad teenagers in the audience waving the Sign of the Horns and howling "Hail, Satan!" while this was going on, because the Geraldo team caught it on film.

This caused a minor furor in the Bay Area over the next several days, as a number of people in the audience who had merely come to see the show were not thrilled about being depicted on national television as "Satanic/Nazi" punk-rockers! Attorneys were accordingly engaged, and a *Geraldo* organization spokesman assured the indignant citizens that no faces would be shown for whom signed releases had not been obtained.

There is a certain comic element in this, but what is of concern to me is the impression that the Strand affair creates of the Church of Satan as a rather sleazy operation. During its substantive operation from 1966 to 1975 it went about its business in a responsible and sophisticated fashion - which isn't to say that it didn't enjoy pulling society's leg on occasion. I am providing Rivera with some background material to illustrate the original Church's - and Anton LaVey's - actual depth.

Concerning the NBC broadcast Rivera has said: "Whether or not you believe in Satan, there is no doubt that Satanism is a very real, widespread, and in many ways dangerous phenomenon in this country. Jayne Mansfield and Sammy Davis, Jr. were both Satanists. Now Davis claims not to be, but we have photographs of him in worship services. And there's lots more. It's well into the tens of thousands."

Upon seeing this comment I have provided Rivera with some relevant facts to increase the broadcast's accuracy. Mansfield was certainly a Satanist, but the case is a bit different with Sammy Davis, Jr. Following the 1972 airing of his movie *Poor Devil*, I presented him with an honorary degree as a Warlock II° in the Church. It was understood by Davis, myself, and Anton LaVey that this was a gesture of appreciation for his sensitive and tolerant portrayal of Satanism in the film - and was **not** intended to "convert" him from whatever personal religion he might hold.

The honorary membership presented to Davis was known throughout the Church of Satan, and of course he was welcomed by many Grottos and members of the Priesthood during his tours and travels. If he had his picture taken together with some of them, I daresay it was more in the spirit of friendliness than in the performance of formal Black Magic operations.

This is not to say that Davis' interest in the Church of Satan wasn't sincere. It was. But it is fair to say that it was more a philosophical interest than an actively ritualistic or ceremonial one.

Rivera has also gone south to Los Angeles to look in on the notorious McMartin Preschool "Satanic child abuse" trial, which - incredibly! - is still grinding on after all these years. In fact it is not anticipated to conclude until April of 1989.

After the initial wave of mass accusations in that witch-hunt subsided, only two people are still under indictment: Raymond Buckey, 30, and his mother, Peggy McMartin Buckey, 61.

The *Los Angeles Daily News* reported on August 11th that attorneys for both the prosecution and defense were apprehensive about Rivera's being filmed among the courtroom spectators. I don't know why, and I don't really think the attorneys do either - except that the "Satanism" accusations thrown around during the original McMartin scandal were so idiotic and absurd that recalling them to the public's attention in a "Satanism" news special can't help making the continuing trial look all that much more deplorable.

I have provided Rivera with extensive documentation concerning the continuing national epidemic of "Satanic child abuse" witch-hunts created by the "industry" of therapists and fundamentalist hate-groups. Perhaps he will use this opportunity to really put the torch to this obscene movement. It would take courage to do so, but Rivera has shown on his daytime show that he is not afraid of speaking controversial and even unpopular truths. If he does in this instance, a great many past, present, and potential future victims of the "child abuse industry" will be in his debt.

Why did I agree to participate in this television special as a panelist? First, as High Priest of the Temple of Set, I felt that I had an *ex officio* responsibility to publicly stand up for our religion, particularly in what was evidently going to be one of television's most widely-watched specials in recent history. If the environment were biased and hostile, I would simply have to do my best to make it less so.

Secondly, Rivera said that he intended to include the Presidio episode. The inference was clear: Either you accept my invitation to defend yourself, or you will be at the mercy of whoever else we can find to talk about you.

Shortly before the special's 10/25 taping in New York City, I wrote Rivera:

I hope that you will indeed use this broadcast to clear up misinformation concerning contemporary Satanism. The preposterous stereotypes projected by the religious lunatic fringe are already largely discredited among people who have taken the time to examine the facts. As with any other craze, it is simply a question of time until the rest of the public realizes the extent of the distortions and malicious defamations which have occurred, and shrugs off the fad in disgust. Your broadcast can be the spearhead of this expose - or it can be one of the last efforts to prop up an already moribund hate-campaign. I hope that you will have the courage and the journalistic integrity to make it the former.

In your previous letter to me, you said that you would be asking my opinions concerning Sean Sellers and Mike Warnke.

According to published accounts in the local media at the time of his crime, and per a televised interview he gave to a Texas television station several months ago, there is no indication that Sean Sellers was ever part of an organized Satanic group which encouraged or orchestrated the murders of which he was convicted.

Sellers has stated that he was "trained" into Satanism by playing "Dungeons and Dragons". This makes about as much sense as being "trained" into Satanism by seeing a horror movie. Children and adolescents habitually play any number of fantasy games while they grow up. I'm certain young Jerry Rivers [Rivera's real name] did as well. Did they warp your soul or enslave you to the Devil? Well, they may have prompted you to become an attorney, which is almost as bad. [Rivera had been a practicing attorney before career-changing into television.]

Sellers has stated that, after being sucked into Satanism via "D&D", he "became a vampire and had a craving for blood". Obviously he is not a vampire, nor can humans drink blood without getting violently sick. Why should his claims about Satanic involvement be any more credible than those about his being Count Dracula?

Sellers has stated that "every Satanist uses drugs". In fact the Church of Satan and Temple of Set have consistently and adamantly insisted that their members stay clear of illegal drugs. The occasional violator, when discovered, has been expelled unless it has been verified that he or she is under corrective medical treatment.

As a minor, Sellers was presumably brought up as a member of a conventional church which, together with his parents and school, assumed responsibility for his moral instruction and emotional development. If a religion is to be blamed for the murders that he committed, it stands to reason that it should be the one which indoctrinated him throughout his childhood, not one with which he had no formal connection whatever.

While, like "Tod", "Sam", and "Kurt" on your 10/6/88 daytime show, Sellers spins stories of a massive and clandestine "Satanic underground", the same objection arises that applies to all the other "accounts" of this nature - including that of the equally-pathetic "ex-Satanist Elaine" on your 11/19/87 daytime show. Despite all the horrendous crimes in which these people claim to have been involved, and the long associations they claim with the many other people in the cults in question, no other member of any such cult has ever been identified or prosecuted. Nor have any of the "escaped ex-Satanists" ever been prosecuted for the crime orgies in which they say they were involved (usually as leaders).

As a Satanist for the last twenty years, I am well familiar with the lore and symbolism of the religion in its many ritual and ceremonial applications. If any of these "ex-Satanists" were recounting actual Satanic activities, I would recognize the terminology, the settings, and the procedures. Not one of them has demonstrated knowledge beyond the comic-book level. [I exposed one such "ex-Satanist" on the Oprah Winfrey Show in just this way.]

If a cult or gang were engaged in such serious crimes as regular human sacrifice (=murder), I seriously doubt that any participant would be allowed to just drop out and waltz into the talk-show circuit. Despite your studio gimmicks such as screens and masked faces, any such gang would have first-hand knowledge of a disaffected member from the moment he or she ceased cooperating. Retaliation would presumably be immediate. Yet there is no evidence that any of these "ex-Satanists" ever had any difficulty bowing out of a "murder ring".

I see Sellers as no different from any wrongdoer who is anxious to project the responsibility for his deeds on to something - anything - else other than himself. "The Devil made me do it" is the first act in this cliché, soft-shoe routine. The second act is being Born Again, as per Susan Atkins and Charles Colson. [If you've already been reBorn once, as Jimmy Swaggart and Jim Bakker, then I guess you've got to go round a second time.]

My views concerning Mike Warnke are much the same as those concerning Sellers, save that Warnke isn't a convicted murderer. Since he first surfaced in 1972 as star of Morris Cerullo's traveling "Witch Wagon" revivalist road show, Warnke's claims about his "Satanic" past have come across like so much snake oil.

Two evenings ago I listened to an extensive taped interview given by Warnke in which he claimed to have been a leader in a 1,500-strong Devil-cult in the Los Angeles area. The Church of Satan had members all over Los Angeles. If any other Satanist group of this size, involved in either criminal or non-criminal activities, had existed, we would have certainly known about it. There is no indication that any of the crimes alleged to have been perpetrated by this large cult ever took place, or that anyone from it was ever identified or arrested, or that Warnke himself was arrested for having been a leader in it, or that he has ever suffered so much as a wart for having made a profession for himself writing books and making media appearances about it. His book *The Satan Seller* talks horrifically about this cult, but once again includes not one specific item of information which can be used to verify its existence.

You already have the extensive documentation on the other subjects of your show which I have provided you by mail. Certainly you have enough data to know that the "criminal conspiracy" image of Satanism projected by religious hate-groups is simply wrong - not in a few respects but in every respect.

Satanism is a legitimate religion which has evolved through the years into a respectable, creative, and positive alternative for thoughtful individuals. We do not claim it is suitable for everyone, but we think it deserves to be judged on its own merits - not to be persecuted out of existence by bigots who fear that it might look more attractive than the alternatives in which they have an emotional or financial stake.

Are you going to suppress the truth about this, or are you going to reveal it?

The show was indeed a hatchet job on Satanism, with Rivera using the S-word in an alarmist sense to characterize any and every sort of extreme criminal activity, ritual/non-ritual and real/imaginary. I had glumly expected this, but felt that whatever objections & clarifications I could make would be better than none at all. As it turned out, there was almost no time for any of the panelists or invited guests in the audience (including Lilith) to talk, as Rivera filled most of the 2 hours with film-clips. But such comments as I was able to make were well-received, and Rivera himself was courteous and respectful both on- and off-camera.

Although the producers had also invited Anton LaVey to attend, he refused to come - but did send his daughter Zeena in his stead. Under the circumstances she rose to the challenge and handled herself well.

Numerous reviews, as well as video of that special, can be Googled on the Internet. While immediately attracting a huge national viewing audience, it quickly came under severe criticism for its many exaggerations and falsehoods, resulting in an eventual public apology for it by the NBC president.

In a subsequent letter of mine in answer to a correspondent who asked my impressions of the broadcast at the time, I said:

It is an accepted principle in Western society that legitimate churches have the right to define the religion they represent. Opponents of the religion or cranks do not have that right.

The first thing that I said to Rivera is thus the essence of the matter. The criminals, psychos, and assorted cranks that were shown on the filmclips were not and are not Satanists, but rather the failures and wreckage of the other moral and religious systems in which they were raised and educated.

Rivera's use of the term "Satanism" as a theme for this special merely harks back to Nazi Germany, when it was fashionable to label all crime as "Jewish". For awhile the Nazis went through the motions of distinguishing "good Jews" and "bad Jews" - the implication being that some people could have some redeeming qualities despite the general contamination of their religion. The most that I can say for Rivera is that he singled out the Temple of Set and Church of Satan as "good Jews".

Judging from feedback the Temple of Set has received - a surge in membership inquiries and not a single piece of hate mail - the viewer public seem to have come to the same conclusion and rejected the show's propaganda. I think that this reflects well upon the good sense of the citizenry.

Senator Jesse Helms (1)

Well, not all of the citizenry, unfortunately. Jesse Helms, the notoriously reactionary Senator from North Carolina, saw the broadcast and was instantly enraged that a United States Army Lt. Colonel should actually dare to espouse a Satanic religion.

This was not Helms' first attack on Satanism. In September 1985 he had quietly introduced an amendment into the 1986 Congressional budget bill. This Amendment #705 read:

No funds appropriated under this act shall be used to grant, maintain, or allow tax exemption to any cult, organization, or other group that has as a purpose or that has any interest in the promoting of satanism or witchcraft: provided that for purposes of this section, "satanism" is defined as the worship of Satan or the powers of evil and "witchcraft" is defined as the use of powers derived from evil spirits, the use of sorcery, or the use of supernatural powers with malicious intent.

The effect of this legislation, if passed, would have been to strip federal, and hence state, tax-exempt status as a religion from religious institutions such as the Temple of Set and various neopagan/witchcraft groups. It was this status which formalized, where the U.S. government was concerned, a particular religion's right to be recognized as such in terms of First and Fourteenth Amendment Constitutional protections. Helms wasn't interested in whether donations were tax-deductible; he wanted Satanism and witchcraft outlawed.

Despite a major Helms-sponsored letter-writing campaign in support of #705, it was stripped out of the budget bill in committee, other legislators feeling that it was too blatantly unConstitutional.

Now Senator Helms was determined to save America's armed forces from the Devil. He instructed his Legislative Assistant to contact the Secretary of the Army forthwith:

Jesse Helms
North Carolina

United States Senate
Washington, D.C. 20510

October 26, 1988

The Honorable John O. Marsh, Jr.
Secretary of the Army

Dear Secretary Marsh:

I am writing first as a citizen of the great nation of ours and secondly as an employee of our federal government, concerning a cancer in the military, specifically a cancer within the Army.

Last evening I viewed a program hosted by Geraldo Rivera on Satanism and Witchcraft. I was appalled to learn that a Colonel Aquino of the United States Army was a founder of the Temple of Set, a satanic cult. I believe he is stationed in St. Louis.

To my view, this is disheartening. Here is a military man who has taken an oath to defend God and country who practices a religion that is completely contrary to the oath he swore to uphold. If you or any member of your staff saw this telecast I am confident your reaction was identical to mine.

This individual should not be allowed to remain in the Army, his military service record notwithstanding. I am respectful of any individual's right to his first amendment prerogatives to worship. However, I cannot believe the Constitution is intended to protect those individuals who have a belief system that espouses the killing and sacrifice of infants and the ritual torturing of children.

I would appreciate your looking into the existence of satanic worship in the Army and it's [sic] adherents. Perhaps it may be necessary to hold Congressional hearings to consider appropriate legislation in this matter.

Kindest regards,

Sincerely,
/s/ Wayne Ronald Boyles, III
Legislative Assistant to Senator Jesse Helms

Behind Closed Doors (1)

On 11/2/88 the Department of the Army instituted Tasking Control Document #8811318Z concerning Helms' letter. Action Officer was initially SALL (Secretary of the Army Legislative Liaison), who briefed Secretary Marsh 11/4/88:

Expresses concern about his learning that an Army officer, featured on a recent talk show on Satanism and Witchcraft, was the founder of the Temple of Set, a satanic cult. Asks that this matter be looked into.

On 11/8/88 Secretary Marsh personally tasked the "matter" to the Judge Advocate General of the Army, with a handwritten comment to additional addressees the Army Chief of Staff, Vice Chief of Staff, General Counsel, Director of the Army Staff, and Criminal Investigation Command: "What do we do about this? /s/ M"

Interestingly this staffing directive went to the Army's legal and criminal staff, not - as would be appropriate in the case of a religion inquiry, to the Chief of Chaplains (who was not even info-copied). As far as Secretary Marsh was concerned, the Temple of Set was not entitled to the dignity of an actual religion; instead it was assumed to be of legal/criminal concern. Nor, of course, did either Helms or anyone at the Department of the Army think to ask **me** about any of this, nor even alert me to the correspondence. I was, of course, only a telephone call away in my Army ARPERCEN office in St. Louis.[116]

Upon receiving his copy of Marsh's memo, the Director of the Army Staff assumed the action responsibility and memoed his assistant:

Department of the Army

8 November 1988

To: Colonel Williams
    1. For action.
      a. Task out.
      b. I need an IPR[117] on this.
      c. The IPR should be the same group that met earlier.
    2. This is a difficult area.

/s/ K
Claude M. Kicklighter
Lt. General, GS
Director of the Army Staff

This is the same General Kicklighter who would subsequently be reassigned as Commanding General of the U.S. Army's Western Command and who in that capacity, in April 1990, would prevent the second court-martial charges against A-T from proceeding to investigation and trial [see Chapter #5].

---

[116] I obtained copies of these documents only years later, through FOIA/PA filings and lawsuit Discovery.

[117] In-Progress Report.

The tasking went to the Judge Advocate General, who on 11/10/88 reported back to Kicklighter that the IPR "will include TJAG, DCSPER, OCAR, OCLL, PA, DACH, and M&RA.[118] Target dates for presentation are 21 or 22 November." [119]

On 11/23/88 the JAG responded to the DAS with an "Information Paper" for the impending IPR, reproduced here as Appendix #42. In addition to its numerous factual errors, two aspects stand out about this paper:

(1) The Army officer who was the subject of it was neither informed about it, invited to contribute to/ proof it, nor attend the meeting. This amounted to **a serious violation of Army personnel procedure**, according to which all actions concerning evaluation or proposed actions concerning any soldier are required to be only through properly-authorized and constituted boards.

(2) My religious affiliation, and my presence in the Army while holding it, was addressed as a "problem to be solved", expressly including ways to eliminate me at least from active duty, if not indeed from the Army altogether. Clearly **not** on the table was the Constitutionally-mandated option of simply leaving me alone, leaving my religion alone, and both publicly **and within the Department of the Army** refusing to compromise this mandate.

The IPR meeting finally took place on 11/29/88. However **not** mentioned in either the pre-meeting Information Paper nor in any supplement to it, nor in any record of the meeting itself as provided to me under FOIA/PA was the fact that the Judge Advocate General had **already** on 11/23/88 initiated a new criminal investigation of me on the basis of A-T's allegations. [These actions within TJAG are discussed in detail in Chapter #7.] Thus several days before the supposedly-top-level meeting which was to decide "what to do about me", General Overholt had already made its agenda irrelevant by fiat. In view of the seniority and parity of the other meeting participants, he would presumably have taken this preemptory action **only** by direction and with express approval of higher authority, in this case Secretary of the Army Marsh per his personal tasking of Overholt on 11/8/88 [see above].

I learned about the 11/29/88 IPR meeting only in June 1989, seven months later, through FOIA/PA references to it, and promptly sent TJAG a FOIA/PA demand for it. Also assuming General Kicklighter to still be DAS, I then wrote to him as convening official:

August 31, 1989

Dear General Kicklighter:

On November 29, 1988 an In-Progress Report on the subject of the Satanic religion was held in the Pershing Conference Room by your decision. Under the Freedom of Information Act and Privacy Act, both in my capacity as an individual soldier and in my capacity as chief executive officer of the Temple of Set, an incorporated Satanic church, I request copies of all papers presented at, all minutes taken at, and all decisions, directives, and items of correspondence resulting from that meeting.

As the nation's senior military officer representing the Satanic religion in official capacity, I am surprised that I was neither invited to participate in this meeting not offered the opportunity to provide an informational paper to it. The result was a meeting to discuss a particular legitimate American religion without any representation by or input from that religion.

The office of the Chief of Chaplains is not qualified to fulfill either function, as the Corps of Chaplains embraces only Christian and Jewish officials whose metaphysical assumptions and theological backgrounds are quite different from those of Satanists. The only handbook on the subject published for chaplains, DA Pam #165-13 (April 1978), had to be contracted out to the Institute for the Study of American Religions at a time when ISAR itself knew little about the subject. We have since been in touch with ISAR, and have contributed accurate material about our religion to its *Encyclopædia of American Religion*, I might add.

---

[118] = The Judge Advocate General, the Deputy Chief of Staff for Personnel, Office of the Chief or the Army Reserve, Office of the Chief of Legislative Liaison, Public Affairs, Chief of Chaplains, and Morale & Recreation Activities (!?).

[119] Memorandum, author's name blacked out on FOIA copy, Office of the Chief of Staff, 11/10/88. A major portion of this memo was also blacked out on the FOIA copy.

Since I "dared" to defend my integrity and that of my religion on a Geraldo Rivera broadcast which was designed to slander it, I have unfortunately become the recipient of official discrimination and persecution within the Army. Some of this may be due to individual prejudice and disregard for the law. Some of it, however, may be due to Rivera-type misinformation being circulated about me, about the Temple of Set, and/or about the Satanic religion generally. It is my responsibility as the senior Satanist in the Armed Forces not only to ensure that my own Constitutional rights and those of our church are respected, but also to ensure that the rights, safety, and careers of the many commissioned and enlisted members of all of the Armed Forces who are Satanists are not jeopardized in violation of the law.

I would very much appreciate your understanding of the constructive intent of my request, and your providing the maximum possible information to me accordingly.

Respectfully,
/s/ Michael A. Aquino
Lt. Colonel, Military Intelligence

I never received a response to this letter from General Kicklighter (a violation of the legal requirements of the Freedom of Information Act and Privacy Act). On 10/30/89 I reiterated my FOIA/PA demand to his successor as DAS, Lt. General Ellis D. Parker, and only this time was informed by TJAG that my original FOIA/PA demand to DAS would be honored.[120]

Here I may note for the reader that I had quickly realized that multiple FOIA/PA demands to each office, official, or agency identified with a relevant piece of information would sometimes yield significantly more results, as recipient A would be unaware of what recipient B had decided to conceal from me. Such are the perils of large bureaucracies trying to conceal rats in the woodpile, as it were.

By this time readers will also have noticed my habit of sending copies of every factual or FOIA/PA demand letter of mine to a great many Department of the Army senior officers. This was not for either advertisement or drama, but deliberately to deny all such recipients "deniability" of any illegal actions being committed against Lilith and myself. As mentioned in Chapter #5, the UCMJ prohibits not only false official statements under Article #133, but any action in either obstruction of justice or concealment of a crime ("misprision of serious offense") under Article #134. While it was highly unlikely that all of these distinguished addressees would actually face court-martial under #133/#134, I daresay the more they officially knew, the less comfortable they felt about complicity in their continued silence.

What I eventually received now were copies of the pre-meeting "Information Paper" (Appendix #42) and some of the pre-meeting memoranda here quoted. Some of the memoranda contents were heavily blacked-out. No list was provided to me of papers **not** sent (also required by the FOIA/PA). Most conspicuously, no after-action report of the meeting's **results** was provided. For an IPR involving so many senior officers at Department of the Army level, such a report was mandatory. What was I not allowed to see? Obviously the decisions made concerning "what to do about me", which, if they were thus kept secret, were improper and illegal. That such decisions were in fact taken and implemented will also become quite evident in the chapters to come.

Also denied to me was a specific list of just which officers had been present at the IPR meeting. On 10/10/89, in a response to an earlier FOIA/PA demand of mine, TJAG wrote:

A number of **draft** documents are being withheld from you in their entirety, although the final version of most of these documents is being or has been released to you. Ten other documents are also being withheld from you in their entirety. The documents consist of predecisional internal advice, recommendations, and subjective evaluations, release of which could potentially cause governmental harm by revealing the deliberative process. The basis for withholding the documents is FOIA exemption 5 (5 U.S.C. 552(b)(5); AR 340-17, paragraph 3-200 No. 5).

You will note that names and addresses have been deleted from several of the documents being released to you. This information has been deleted to protect the personal privacy of individuals other than yourself. The basis for withholding the information is FOIA exemption 6 (5 U.S.C. 552(b)(6); AR 340-17, paragraph 3-200 No. 6) ...

---

[120] Letter, Colonel William J. Lehman, TJAG, to Michael Aquino 11/14/89.

There are several pieces of paper in two attorneys' files which are handwritten notes to themselves. These are being considered the personal records of those attorneys, and are not being released to you because only agency records, not personal records, are subject to the FOIA.[121]

That was not at all satisfactory to me. I wrote back to the Secretary of the Army:

October 17, 1989

Dear Sir:

On October 16, 1989 I received the enclosed packet of papers from the DA Judge Advocate General's Administrative Law Division. I also enclose a copy of the original letter of mine to which this packet is a response. I hereby appeal Colonel Lehman's letter as follows:

Paragraph #2: I hereby appeal **all** of the decisions to withhold the documents identified as being withheld from me. A review of the papers provided in the packet establishes a **clear pattern** of intentional, illegal, and prejudicial discrimination against my religion and my personal freedom to practice it as provided by the First and Fourteenth Amendments to the Constitution. The withholding of additional papers in which officials of the government provide "predecisional internal advice, recommendations, and subjective evaluations" which, because of their prejudicial nature, **violate the Constitution**, cannot conceivably be supported on the mere excuse that the revelation of such papers would "cause governmental harm". Agencies and officials of the United States Government have no "right" to conceal their violation of the laws they are sworn to uphold. To the contrary, the government and the people of the United States are harmed by the **concealing** of such prejudice at high governmental levels, which permits it to continue in future instances.

Paragraph #3: I appeal the denial of all names and addresses to me. Because of this campaign of innuendo against my religion, my church, my wife, and myself, a deliberately fraudulent and prejudicial criminal investigation was initiated against me by the U.S. Army CID. To expose this fraudulent investigation it is necessary for me to identify all persons who may have contributed to it by administratively prejudicing the outcome, by making false and malicious allegations, or by otherwise compromising the objectivity of the Army's investigative procedures in this case. Such attempts to corrupt the investigation, to the extent that they constitute deliberate concealment of the truth, constitute acts of misprision of serious offense and obstruction of justice in violation of Article #134 UCMJ. Protection of the personal privacy of individuals who may have committed crimes cannot be used as justification for concealing those crimes.

Paragraph #6: I appeal the denial of the attorneys' notes again on the grounds that, to the extent they may identify the attorneys as acting or giving advice in violation of the Constitution, they constitute important evidence of the nature of the deliberate campaign of defamation undertaken against me. If these are U.S. government attorneys, then their making of notes to themselves in support of a government assignment, on government time, in government offices, and on government salary clearly establishes that those notes and all other papers of theirs involved with the assignment, are government property. I may cite the example of President Nixon's "personal" tapes as an example; these have been clearly held to be government property despite his claim that they should have been privileged as "personal memoranda for his memoirs".

Paragraph #7. I request a list of all documents contained in the JAG files which were generated by the CID and/or the Personnel Security Branch, and which have been referred to these agencies for FOIA/PA action. This is important so that I may follow up to see if these agencies do in fact comply with the law concerning the release of this material to me, and also so that I may identify precisely what documents these agencies felt it appropriate to provide to the JAG for its files. Provision of such documents to the JAG for separate files, if a clear justification for such provision cannot be demonstrated, may constitute a violation of applicable provisions of the Privacy Act and other laws preventing the creation and maintenance of unofficial, defamatory dossiers within the government.

In my 6/5/89 letter to which Colonel Lehman's letter is in answer, I requested an official statement describing precisely what is meant by the phrase "to deal with him". I am not aware of any license which the Army has to take action against any soldier simply because he may be exercising his Constitutionally-

---

[121] Letter, Colonel William J. Lehman, TJAG, to Michael Aquino 10/10/89.

guaranteed right to freedom of religion. I restate my request for an explanation why such language as "to deal with him and other Army members who practice Satanic worship" was considered appropriate. I presume that the Army does not "deal with Jews", for example.

Respectfully,
/s/ Michael A. Aquino
Lt. Colonel, Military Intelligence

Enclosures:
- Letter, Lt.Col. Aquino to the Judge Advocate General, June 5, 1989
- Cover letter and packet received in answer, October 10, 1989

Copies to:
Honorable Michael P.W. Stone, Secretary of the Army
General Carl E. Vuono, Chief of Staff, United States Army
General Robert W. RisCassi, Vice Chief of Staff, United States Army
Lieutenant General Henry Doctor, Inspector General of the Army
Lieutenant General Charles W. Bagnal, Commanding General, WESTCOM
Major General William F. Ward, Chief, Army Reserve
Mr. Joseph G. Hanley, Chief of Public Affairs, Department of the Army
Major General Charles P. Otstott, Commanding General, 25th Infantry Division
Colonel Bobby R. Sanders, Commander, ARPERCEN
Colonel Joseph V. Rafferty, Commander, Presidio of San Francisco
Colonel Carl L. Lockett, Commander, 6th Region CID

A response came shortly thereafter:

Department of the Army
Office of the General Counsel

December 8, 1989

Dear Colonel Aquino:

This responds to your letters of October 17, and November 21, 1989, which we received on November 29, 1959. You have appealed the partial denial of your request under the Freedom of Information Act (FOIA) and the Privacy Act (PA). You requested copies of all documents maintained by the Office of The Judge Advocate General (OTJAG) pertaining to you or the Temple of Set. That office partially denied your request on October 10, 1989.

You received all requested information except for draft versions of final documents that were released to you, personal notes of attorneys in OTJAG, and predecisional material. OTJAG also redacted the names and addresses of numerous third parties to protect their personal privacy. Upon review, we have determined that the remainder of the documents were properly withheld under Exemptions 5 and 6 of the FOIA. Therefore, we deny your appeal.

Draft and predecisional documents have been withheld under Exemption 5 of the FOIA, 5 U.S.C. section 552(b)(5), which protects from disclosure inter- or intra-agency memoranda that would not be available by law to a party other than an agency in litigation with the agency. Specifically, this information is withheld under the "deliberative process privilege," the general purpose of which is to prevent injury to the quality of agency decisions.

Exemption 6 of the FOIA authorizes the withholding of information when its disclosure would result in a "clearly unwarranted invasion of personal privacy." 5 U.S.C. section 552(b)(6). To determine whether release of the requested information constitutes such an invasion of privacy, we must balance any qualifying public interest in disclosure against the privacy interests in withholding the document at stake. In this case, there appears to be no public interest in the release of the names or addresses, particularly of constituents who have exercised their Constitutional right to petition Congress. On the other hand, release of this information could lead to harassment of the named individuals and would invade their protectable privacy interests. Therefore, names and addresses have been redacted. See *Department of Justice v. Reporters Committee for Freedom of the Press*, 109 S. Ct. 1468(1959).[122]

As noted above, the documents you requested included the personal notes of OTJAG attorneys. Because these notes were created and used solely by the preparer, were not circulated, and were not filed with Army records, these notes are not agency records. As personal notes, they are not subject to release or access under the FOIA or the PA, respectively.

In accordance with Army policy, records originating within Criminal Investigation Command and the Office of the Deputy Chief of Staff for Intelligence are considered records of those offices, not OTJAG, and were referred to those offices for a release determination. OTJAG notified you of these referrals. The fact of referral is not a proper subject for appeal.

Finally, you asked for an explanation of certain terminology contained in the 23 November 1988 Information Paper provided in response to your request. As no records exist that are responsive to this portion of your request, this issue is not subject to appeal under the FOIA. See Army Regulation 340-17, paragraph 5-300a.

This letter constitutes final action on behalf of the General Counsel, who has been designated by the Secretary of the Army to consider appeals under the FOIA. You may, if you so desire, seek judicial review of this determination in accordance with the FOIA provisions.

> Sincerely,
> /s/ Darrell L. Peck
> Deputy General Counsel (Military/Civil Affairs)

So that was as far as the FOIA/PA would take me in this inquiry.

Senator Jesse Helms (2)

We now return to December 1988. TJAG had secretly initiated its criminal investigation of me on 11/25/88, and the secret 11/29/88 IP meeting had been held. On 12/8/88 the official response to Senator Helms went back, containing no hint of either incident:

Department of the Army
Office of the Secretary of the Army
Washington, D.C. 20310-1600

Office, Chief of Legislative Liaison

8 December 1988

Dear Senator Helms:

This responds to Mr. Wayne Boyles' letter of October 26, 1988, to Secretary Marsh regarding the October 25, 1988, NBC television program on satanism. Specifically, he inquired about the portion of the program pertaining to the United States Army and Army Reserve Lieutenant Colonel Michael Aquino.

The Army understands your assistant's concerns. Let me assure you, the Army by no means encourages "devil worship." I am sure Mr. Boyles' understands that the principle that requires toleration of the religious beliefs of Lieutenant Colonel Aquino is the same one that protects the religious freedom that all Americans enjoy.

Enclosed is an Army news release that addresses the NBC program *Devil Worship - Exploring Satan's Underground* and the misstatements and innuendo pertaining to the United States Army. We believe it will greatly assist you in replying to your constituents should they also express concern.

I trust that you will find this information helpful.

> Sincerely,
> /s/ John J. McNulty, III
> Lieutenant Colonel, U. S. Army
> Chief, Special Actions Branch
> Congressional Inquiry Division

---

[122] This case had nothing whatever to do with the concealment of the identity of Army officials at a possibly illegal official meeting.

This wasn't at all what Senator Helms wanted to hear. He wrote back to Secretary Marsh, this time personally:

Jesse Helms
North Carolina

United States Senate
Washington, D.C. 20510

January 9, 1989

Dear Jack:

Except for two or three trips back to Washington, I've been working out of our Raleigh office since the Senate adjourned in late October. Yesterday in going through a stack of material sent to me in Raleigh, I ran across a December 27 clipping from *The Washington Times*[123] about a Lt. Col. Michael Aquino who identifies himself as a "Satanist" and who claims that this is his "religion".

Either the man needs psychiatric help, or the Army doesn't need <u>him</u>. The fact that he has twice appeared on national television seems to me to demonstrate that he doesn't have all four wheels on the ground.

This is not a matter of freedom of religion. Satanism is not a religion.

I tried yesterday to reach you at your home through the White House switchboard, but learned that you are in Germany. When you get back, would you give me a ring? Maybe there's something I missed in translation, but I do not understand how the Army decided to "stand by" Colonel Aquino - if indeed the newspaper account is accurate.

The most charitable thing that can be said of the colonel is that he is a nut. If that is the case, I might have some sympathy for him but I still do not believe that he should be "handling budgets" for the Army Reserve Personnel Center - or anywhere else. Perhaps I am dismayed at his arrogance as much as anything else.

In any event, please let me have the Army's side of it - and I sure would appreciate a call from you.

Sincerely,

/s/ Jesse

Behind Closed Doors (2)

This letter set off an even more energetic flurry of memos:

Department of the Army
Office of the Secretary
Memorandum

17 January 1989

For General Overholt[124]

Mr. Marsh asks that you see him concerning the attached letter from Senator Helms on Lieutenant Colonel Aquino.

Please call this office for a time on the Secretary's schedule.

/s/ Richard F. Timmons
Colonel, General Staff
Executive

* * * * *

---

[123] Appendix #39.

[124] The Judge Advocate General of the Army.

Department of the Army
Office of the Chief of Legislative Liaison
Memorandum

18 January 1989

General Overholt
Sir:

I understand that you've been designated to speak to Senator Helms on Aquino. Correspondence attached.

Senator Helms' office will call me tomorrow (he's in Baker hearings now).

/s/ Colonel Cruden
OCLL

* * * * *

Routing and Transmittal Slip

30 January 1989

1. Lt. Colonel Kaplan [sp?]
2. Colonel Semper [sp?]
3. Brigadier General Hansen
4. Colonel Murphy [sp?]
5. Major General Suter[125]
6. Major General Overholt

Sir, attached is a proposed info paper[126] for Sen. Helms re LTC Aquino for your meeting - I think this covers all of the areas you indicated.

/s/ Lt. Colonel Burton

* * * * *

John B[127] -

I saw Senator Helms. Will let you know what happened.

/s/ HRO
Hugh R. Overholt
Major General, USA
The Judge Advocate General

In addition to the FOIA/PA denial of General Overholt's briefing paper for Senator Helms, any report of that meeting that Overholt prepared for Secretary Marsh - as he almost certainly would have - was also absent and unmentioned in my FOIA/PA responses. When the Secretary of the Army sends a Major General/the Judge Advocate General of the Army across Washington to personally brief a U.S. Senator on a matter, rest assured that said General will write up the result for the Secretary on return to the Pentagon. Whatever was in that report, it was evidently essential that Lt. Colonel Aquino - the subject of that meeting - **not** see it.

When later that year I obtained copies of the Helms correspondence and the consequent memoranda from various Pentagon offices through FOIA/PA, I thought it would be interesting to write to Jesse Helms directly to see if he would have the courage to say to my face what he had been saying behind my back:

---

[125] The Assistant JAG of the Army.

[126] This paper was denied to me in response to my FOIA/PA demand.

[127] Presumably Lt. Colonel John Burton, TJAG action officer who had prepared the "Information Paper" (Appendix #42).

August 3, 1989

Dear Sir:

Under the provisions of the Freedom of Information Act and the Privacy Act, I request copies of all letters, memoranda, and other paperwork either originating from or received by your office relating to myself, the church to which I belong (the Temple of Set), and the Satanic religion generally. This request excludes letters from constituents, but includes all answers to them by you or your staff. It specifically includes all letters between yourself and any other official, agency, or department of the United States Government

I am willing to reimburse the government for reproduction costs involved. As this information may be used for a Department of Defense investigation, however, I request that these costs be waived.

Respectfully,
/s/ Michael A. Aquino
Lt. Colonel, Military Intelligence

Helms didn't have that courage:

Jesse Helms
North Carolina

United States Senate
Washington, D.C. 20510

September 19, 1989

Dear Lt. Colonel Aquino:

In response to your letter requesting copies of material originating from my office which relates to you or the church to which you belong, I suggest you contact the Senate's Legal Counsel.

Sincerely,
/s/ Jesse Helms

Which of course was a stone wall.

Other Congressional Inquiries

While Jesse Helms was the first and most vehement critic from Capitol Hill, the Department of the Army also received inquiries - for the most part just routinely passed along from constituents' letters - from several other Senators and Representatives. A final list prepared by the Army's Public Affairs Office, Office of the General Counsel, and Office of the Judge Advocate General included: Senator William L. Armstrong, Congressman Herbert H. Bateman, Congressman Charles E. Bennett, Senator Lloyd Bentsen, Senator Jeff Bingaman, Senator Christopher S. Bond, Senator Bill Bradley, Senator John H. Breaux, Senator Dale Bumpers, Senator Robert C. Byrd, Senator Lawton Chiles, Senator Thad Cochran, Senator Alan Cranston, Congressman William L. Dickinson, Senator Bob Dole, Congressman David Dreier, Congressman Bill Frenzel, Senator Charles E. Grassley, Congressman Lee Hamilton, Senator Howell Heflin, Senator J. Bennett Johnston, Congressman Jerry Lewis, Senator Richard G. Lugar, Senator John Melcher, Congressman G.V. Montgomery, Senator Don Nickles, Senator Sam Nunn, Senator John D. Rockefeller IV, Congressman Lamar Smith, Congressman Neal Smith, and Senator Strom Thurmond.

To each of these Lt. Colonel McNulty sent a personalized copy of his original 12/8/88 letter to Senator Helms.

The Vice Chief of Staff and the Chief of Staff of the Army

Following the Geraldo special the second-highest-ranking officer in the Army, Vice Chief of Staff General Arthur E. Brown decided to share his own thoughts with NBC in December 1988. Because of the length of this letter, it appears here as Appendix #40.

I did not learn of the existence of this letter for another six months, by which time General Brown had been replaced by General Robert RisCassi. I accordingly wrote RisCassi the letter at Appendix #41. No response.

By this time I was becoming quite tired of seeing mis/disinformation concerning the Temple of Set, myself, and the Setian/Satanic religion generally circulated by high-level Army officials. Accordingly I wrote to General Carl Vuono, Chief of Staff of the Army and its seniormost officer:

June 2, 198

Dear Sir:

The enclosed letter from Major General Ward discusses documents concerning me which have been withheld from me under my FOIA request because they are notes in preparation for an In-Process Review for you.

Many documents containing significantly erroneous information concerning myself and my religion have been circulating throughout the Department of the Army in the last few years. In several cases the information was so erroneous that decisions based upon it could cause serious and unwarranted harm to myself, my religion, and other members of the U.S. armed forces who are affiliated with this religion. As an example I enclose a copy of the letter written to the President of NBC by the former Vice Chief of Staff on your letterhead, together with my letter of this date to General RisCassi correcting the misinformation therein.

While I do not ask you to provide me with copies of informal notes concerning myself, I do request that, before making any decision based upon them, you advise me of any statements or purported facts contained therein, so that I may either confirm or correct them as appropriate.

Respectfully,
/s/ Michael A. Aquino
Lt. Colonel, Military Intelligence

No answer was forthcoming, nor did the Army ever respond to my requests to the Vice Chief and Chief of Staff to check proposed official statements concerning the Setian/Satanic religion with me before issuing them.

Implications of Information Presented in this Chapter

The San Francisco Police Department's investigation of A-T's allegations concerning Lilith and myself quickly established our innocence; we were verified to be 3,000 miles away in Washington, D.C. on all dates when Kinsey had been left with Hambright at the Presidio day-care center. When that investigation was closed in August 1988, the Army considered it over with. Simultaneously the Army had suppressed any investigation or accountability of A-T for instigating it.

While the entire episode might have ended there, it was dragged back into national, and the Army's, attention by the sensationalistic Geraldo Rivera "Satanism" NBC television special in October 1988. This elicited a storm of public complaint to the Congress about an Army Lt. Colonel being a Satanist, as well as two especially vehement demands for my termination by Senator Jesse Helms, a reactionary but influential personal friend of Secretary of the Army John Marsh.

Marsh tasked the Judge Advocate General of the Army, Major General Overholt, to "do something about me". As my service record was, in TJAG's own words, "superlative", the only possible way to force me out of the Army was to resurrect the A-T allegations, which TJAG so did on 11/23/88 by initiating a new CID/TJAG investigation.

From the SFPD investigation (closed almost four months before on 8/1/88), the CID/TJAG had full knowledge of our innocence, but assumed that the pressure and publicity of a revived criminal investigation would intimidate me, and frighten my wife, into resigning my commission [as would be explicitly recommended to me by CID/TJAG investigators]. Failing that, the investigation could be [and was] used to illegally remove me from the full-time AGR program, returning me at least to the part-time Reserve. From the outset of the sham investigation, no actual court-martial charges were ever contemplated.

Summarily the Secretary of the Army had decided that, whatever my service record and however good an officer I might be, my religion simply made me more of a liability than an asset. Since that religion was Constitutionally protected, some other way had to be found to get rid of me, and the A-T allegations were the only "other way" possible.

During the entire November 1988 timeframe, when these decisions were being made in the Pentagon, I knew nothing whatever of them. No questions were asked of me, no suggestions invited. Since an illegal course of action was being undertaken in order to "deal with me", I was obviously to be treated as an "external target", not respected as a fellow professional soldier with a shared interest in the good of the Army.

Chapter 7: The CID/TJAG "Reinvestigation"

On 12/13/88 I was suddenly informed that my Army personnel records had been flagged.[128] Learning that this was on the initiative of the San Francisco Field Office of the CID, I immediately telephoned that office and was connected to its head, Special Agent Robert Birck. He said that a "preliminary investigation" had been open on me since August 1987, that this had been closed out with a "final report" on 11/22/88, and on the basis of that report he personally decided to open a full-scale criminal investigation of me.

As I would gradually verify over the next year, **none** of this was true: No documents from or referring to any such "preliminary investigation" or its "11/22/88 final report" were ever identified by or obtained from under FOIA/PA demands or later federal lawsuit Discovery from the SFPD, FBI, TJAG, or the CID. My Top Secret security clearance had **not** been suspended [as **any** CID criminal investigation would require], nor had my personnel file been flagged. These actions **only** happened on 11/23/88.

And was the decision to initiate an actual investigation on 11/23/88 really Birck's? If a matter has garnered such attention that the Secretary of the Army and a number of the Army chiefs at the 2-. 3-, and 4-star level are conferring about it, its further course of resolution is assuredly **not** going to be personally decided by a mere CID special agent out in a local field office. Clearly Birck just said and did as he was told by TJAG through his CID chain of command, period.

The timing was of course significant: a short time following the Geraldo show and its aggravating public-relations aftermath. But Birck's statement about purely-local justification rang very false indeed. If, as Birck was now claiming, the SFCID had taken A-T's allegations seriously at the time he made them, it would have been obligated to open a formal investigation and flag my records **right then in August 1987**, regardless of what the SFPD might be doing. An officer genuinely under suspicion of the horrific crimes Chaplain A-T alleged would **never** be allowed to continue his career flag-free, with highest-level security clearance, and without the formal restrictions of a CID investigation, for another 1-1/3 years.

Also the SFPD investigation had been formally closed on 8/1/88. If the SFCID for some obscure reason felt that it didn't need to formalize its own investigation as long as the SFPD was conducting one, then why - again in the case of such a serious allegation - wait for almost four months before taking action?

"Birck's" 11/23/88 decision traveled to TJAG headquarters in Washington so fast that on the very same date Lt. Colonel Stephen J. Smith of TJAG's Criminal Law Division sent a letter to the Assistant Judge Advocate for Military Law stating that "LTC Michael A. Aquino, the avowed Satanist[129] , would be titled for kidnapping, sodomy, conduct unbecoming an officer, urging the court-martial of another without basis, and conspiracy. The titling determination was based on a review of evidence previously gathered by the CID, the FBI, and the City of San Francisco." [130]

All of this was simply another lie:

As noted above, the CID had previously gathered **no** evidence, conducted **no** investigation, written **no** report.

As for the FBI, it had washed its hands of the A-T allegations on 9/30/87, when its public spokesman, U.S. Attorney Joseph Russoniello announced at a press conference in San Francisco that "after a lengthy investigation, his office in conjunction with the FBI had concluded that Mr. Hambright had acted alone and there were no co-perpetrators. He further stated that there would be no other arrests in connection with the Presidio day-care center. Colonel Joseph Rafferty, Presidio Commander, was at present and echoed Russoniello's statements." [131]

---

[128] "Flagging" means suspension of all possible favorable personnel actions, such as awards, promotions, schooling, etc. while the flag is in effect.

[129] If, as the CID/TJAG would exhaustively claim, my religion was not a factor in this decision or investigation, why was it appropriate to make special mention of it here?

[130] "Titling" is a formal statement by the CID that it thinks a given crime has taken place. It is issued tentatively at the onset of an investigation and may or may not be finally stated at its conclusion. "Titling" is not comparable to a civilian indictment, however: no arrest is made and no charges preferred.

[131] Letter, Bernard Zimmerman (Pillsbury, Madison & Sutro) to SFPD Chief Frank Jordan 8/2/87.

As for the San Francisco Police Department, it had formally ended its investigation on 8/1/88 with Deputy District Attorney Michael Williams announcing that there was "insufficient evidence to prosecute" Lilith or myself concerning the story which he [inaccurately] attributed to Kinsey A-T instead of her stepfather.[132] Also noteworthy here are SFPD chief investigator Glenn Pamfiloff's comments to me on 4/19/2000, quoted in full in Chapter #4:

> You must remember that I worked with most of those investigating you. You seem to want to break down every little iota to its nexus, but I want to try to keep it at its most basic. "No evidence against you" doesn't need to be answered with specifics.
> If no other children, of the 100+ interviewed identified you, nor any of the children identified your home, as a respected child abuse investigator I would have to assume, that you were not involved with these children.
> This is the entire point of my contacting you.
> I'm sure that if you were the evil man that so much of the media makes you out to be, especially with your notoriety, at least one of "Dr.Lt.Col.'s" children would have attributed some nefarious act to you.
> Well, I found no evidence, other than the first, very doubtful identification of you at the PX, and the very stretched identifications within your home, and a few, very stretched relationships, that in anyway could find you guilty of any child abuse.
> My hope is to put this information into the public sector, to clear you of any relationship with Mr. Hambright, of which my investigation found none, and to clear you of any involvement with the children of the Presidio Day Care Center.

Hence there was **no** "previously gathered evidence for sodomy, kidnapping, or conspiracy". As for "urging the court-martial of another without basis", one wonders how the SFCID could determine this when it declined to investigate any of the elements of those charges at all, recommended dismissing those charges in disregard of those elements, and did its utmost to cover up its actions in those regards for 1-1/2 years [see Chapter #5].

Nor could the CID possibly cite any "conduct unbecoming an officer" concerning me, as all I had done was, through proper channels and always in accordance with Army Regulations, to insist that my wife and I had committed no crime whatever, and to formally request that the officer who had maliciously lied about this be held officially accountable for those lies.

Notwithstanding the above inconvenient details, Major General William K. Suter, the Assistant Judge Advocate General at Department of the Army, rushed to inform his boss General Overholt:

---

[132] "Army Officer's Case is Dropped", *San Francisco Chronicle* 8/2/88.

Routing and Transmittal Slip

25 November 1988

To: TJAG

    1. CIDC has titled LTC Aquino. CID JA summary is attached.

    2. I briefed VCSA[133], DAS[134], and MG Ward[135]. LTC Steve Smith prepared memo and EXSUM[136] - I signed. Steve is contacting PAO[137], OGC[138], Presidio[139], Leonard Wood (GCM auth)[140], and ARPERCEN[141]. Steve will brief you Monday. (We also notified Claims Service.)[142]

/s/ William K. Suter
Major General, USA
The Assistant Judge Advocate General

A remarkably busy and exciting day for General Suter just because of a "sudden decision" by a lowly field agent at the lowest level of field office in the entire CID.

But such lofty intrigues were unknown to me at the time [and would remain so in this detail for years]; the significant thing was that this CID investigation **had** been opened.

I promptly asked my PM&S attorney Shawn Hanson to follow up. On 12/14/88 Captain Mark W. Harvey, Judge Advocate of the 6th Region CID, sent him a letter containing a number of questions for me to answer:

If LTC Aquino is willing to waive his rights and discuss the offenses under investigation, with the assistance of counsel, let me first begin by commenting that if LTC Aquino has **not** committed these offenses, USACIDC hopes to establish his innocence, and assist in clearing his name. USACIDC's responsibility is to discover the evidence so that it can be determined whether a crime has been committed, and if possible identify the person(s) that committed the crime. LTC Aquino's statement will be made an exhibit in any USACIDC report that may be created in this case. LTC Aquino's cooperation with this investigation will also be documented within USACIDC files.

Further, if LTC Aquino provides certain leads or evidence that shows the allegations to be without merit, I will insure that USACIDC personnel follow those leads, to the maximum possible extent, in order to properly document his innocence.

I had decidedly mixed feelings about Harvey's honeyed promises. While I wanted very much to trust his professionalism, integrity, and word, I had not forgotten that it was this same 6th Region/San Francisco Field Office CID which had deliberately acted to quash the court-martial charges I had preferred against A-T with a token "report of investigation" ignoring all its elements of proof. On 1/1/89, therefore, I wrote to Harvey:

---

[133] Vice Chief of Staff of the Army, General RisCassi [see Chapter #6].

[134] Director of the Army Staff, Lt. General Kicklighter [see Chapters #5 & #6].

[135] Major General Ward, Chief of the Army Reserve.

[136] Executive summary of the memo.

[137] Public Affairs Office

[138] Office of the General Counsel.

[139] Commanding General 6th U.S. Army and Commander, Presidio of San Francisco.

[140] Commanding General, Fort Leonard Wood, the general court-martial authority covering the St. Louis, Missouri area.

[141] U.S. Army Reserve Personnel Center, St. Louis - my unit of assignment.

[142] U.S. Army Claims Service, the agency handling monetary claims from the A-Ts and other Presidio parents.

Dear Captain Harvey:

Mr. Shawn Hanson of Pillsbury, Madison & Sutro has provided me with a copy of your December 14th letter to him.

While you can expect my full cooperation with any objective investigation designed to establish the truth about the Presidio child-care scandal, I will not lend any legitimacy whatever to a biased investigation designed to conceal the truth, to frame innocent people for crimes which never occurred, and to facilitate the defrauding of the United States Government for $66 million. The way in which this investigation proceeds from this point forward will indicate to me, and to many other observers, which one of the two kinds of investigations is actually taking place.

If this investigation of me were honestly and ethically opened, I can only suppose that it is because the CID has only an incomplete and confusing picture of the entire sequence of pertinent events to date, and that - as you stated in your letter to Mr. Hanson - you are accordingly interested in ensuring that you have a complete and clear picture. The documents I am enclosing will enable you to do that. There should then be no reason not to terminate the investigation of me without delay, to remove the flag on my personnel file, and to restore my security clearance. Mrs. Aquino and I have now been investigated, vandalized, harassed, and threatened for well over a year because of Adams-Thompson's attack on us, and we have had quite enough of it.

I have several misgivings concerning this latest in the series of investigations:

(1) As the enclosed historical documents show, it very quickly came to light that Chaplain Adams-Thompson's allegations against my wife and myself were utterly without foundation. It takes no "great leap of faith" to see this; the facts are clear and conspicuous for any intelligent individual to appreciate, and have been carefully and exhaustively presented many times. Nevertheless the CID is now opening this new investigation based once more upon those allegations, as if the facts proving them false simply do not exist at all.

(2) Based on stories which have recently appeared in the *San Francisco Chronicle* and *San Jose Mercury News West*, CID investigators and spokespersons have been making statements to Presidio parents and to the media that a crime was indeed committed and I have already been "titled" for it, with the necessary implication being that this investigation is merely a going-through-the-motions exercise with its outcome predetermined before it began. Particularly in view of the hysterical, "lynch mob" climate of the Presidio scandal, such statements are highly prejudicial, encourage the manufacture of allegations by anyone hoping to benefit in the $66 million claims action against the U.S. Army, further endanger the personal safety of my wife and myself, and impugn my professional and personal reputation as an officer.

(3) Although Adams-Thompson's allegations were shown to be without any basis whatever, and I am thus entitled to the same presumption of non-involvement in the scandal as any other soldier, I am nonetheless being uniquely singled out for continued treatment as a "suspect" in the Presidio scandal generally, evidently for no other reason than my religion (which neither advocates nor tolerates any crimes against children). The reference in your letter to "children" (plural) and the questions you sent which range far beyond the date of Adams-Thompson's original allegations clearly indicate such a fishing expedition. I see the classic signs of a witch-hunt, in which, if one alleged crime is disproven, other allegations are quickly manufactured in order to somehow justify the original attack and "get" the individual.

(4) As the enclosed "paper trail" shows, from the very first day I first learned of Adams-Thompson's attack on my wife and myself, I moved methodically through the appropriate procedures established by the Army to correct injustices - from a letter to Adams-Thompson personally, to requests for non-judicial corrective action by his commanders, to UCMJ charges as appropriate. What I have seen in response is a year-long pattern of the deliberate sheltering of Adams-Thompson from accountability for his vicious actions, apparently because he is a Christian minister in the Corps of Chaplains and I am a Satanist, and that for public relations purposes the Army will not consider court-martialing a Christian minister on behalf of a Satanist, no matter what harm the minister did to him and his wife.

(5) Further, according to your letter, the very fact that I "dared" to ask that Adams-Thompson be called to account for his attack under the UCMJ, as it is the right of every wronged soldier to request, is now itself being used to threaten and intimidate me further - by allegations that I prepared a false charge sheet and lied in the sworn statements in support of it. The facts and reasoning in those sworn statements are *prima facie*

the truth, and they support the charge sheet accordingly. No objective analysis can lead to any other conclusion.

As I look at these five general aspects of this investigation, I do not see a fair, objective, and non-prejudicial picture at all. This is not the way American justice is supposed to be administered, and it is not the way the United States Army is supposed to conduct investigations either. In my 19-year career as a commissioned officer, I have frequently been an investigating officer, presided in Article 32B inquiries, and served in summary, special, and general courts-martial capacities. I know the difference between a search for the truth and its concealment, and I know the difference between an objective investigation and a prejudicial one. I have never tolerated the latter in the case of any other soldier in the Army, nor will I tolerate it now where I am concerned.

As for the questions you submitted to Mr. Hanson: I have not the slightest qualms about any of them. However, as I stated at the beginning of this letter, I will not serve to lend any atmosphere of legitimacy to any attempt to invent nonexistent crimes or to fabricate evidence by persons with a vested interest in profiting from the Presidio scandal. My attorneys know my feelings, and are presently reviewing the questions to decide which if any of them are reasonable for the CID to ask of me in this situation.

Sincerely,

/s/ Michael A. Aquino

Lt. Colonel, Military Intelligence

As Major Harvey had invited me to suggest leads for the CID to pursue to evidence Lilith's and my innocence and Larry A-T's guilt, I sent him a letter detailing twelve such leads on 1/5/89 (Appendix #44). As I had seen no sign that the CID was the least interested in implicating A-T, and indeed was actively preventing such implication, I had little expectation that any of these leads would be investigated. I was correct; the letter was ignored. But I had wanted it down for the record that Harvey had received a response to his invitation.

On 1/27/89 I sent Harvey my answers to his questions (Appendix #45). Indeed I didn't just answer them in a letter; I swore to my answers in an official statement. If these answers are beginning to strike you, the reader, as rather repetitious by now, I had precisely the same reaction when [re]typing them. The factual situation, as compiled in Appendix #34, was about as straightforward and self-evident as anything could be. But perhaps the SFFOCID simply wanted some of the points freshly stated for their own bureaucratic records.

Since I was now officially under CID investigation, I requested and was assigned an Army attorney from the Trial Defense Service of TJAG. The effectiveness of such representation within the military justice system has always been debatable. By investigating and/or charging a soldier, the chain of command has already established its interest and predisposition in the matter. Even more so than in civilian jurisprudence, military prosecutors and the commanders who assign them their missions are interested only in "mission accomplishment", which translates to a successful prosecution and conviction. Finding the soldier innocent is simply not part of that scenario.[143]

While the TDS is given *pro forma* recognition and cooperation, it is treated more as an intrusion and an annoyance than an equal investigative or legal authority. JAG officers assigned to TDS receive mixed signals accordingly: They are expected to go through the motions of defending their clients, but not to the extent of embarrassing, impeding, or much less defeating the CID/TJAG prosecution machinery - certainly not if they expect successful long-term careers in TJAG, that is.

I was assigned Captain Thomas M. Hayes III, a Senior Defense Counsel. He immediately started sending extensive, detailed letters to Harvey, calling his attention to all of the so-far-ignored exculpatory evidence and urging that A-T's motives and actions be seriously investigated as well - by an independent investigator:

I have seen no evidence that the chaplain's background and possible motives for falsely accusing LTC Aquino have been examined. This lack of thoroughness is disturbing and should cause concern to those commanders who have been asked to ack on the charges against the chaplain.

---

[143] In 1986, while assigned to Presidio Headquarters, I had been appointed president of a court-martial concerning a local recruiting sergeant. My questioning in court brought out that it was his commander, not him, who had violated Army regulations in recruiting procedures. In deliberations I argued strongly that the sergeant should be found completely innocent, and so he was - to the obvious frustration of the CID and the prosecuting JAG - but to the tearful, stunned delight of the sergeant and his family. On that day military justice deserved its name.

I suggest several actions to remedy this problem. First, and independent investigator should be appointed to examine the charges against the chaplain. This will allow for a greater level of neutrality and lack of predisposition in gathering information and forming an opinion on the veracity of LTC Aquino's complaint. It is easy to understand the difficulty that those who are investigating the serious charges surrounding the Child Development Center would have with remaining objective in examining the motives of the chaplain. Second, LTC Aquino should be invited to the Presidio in order to explain his reasoning for swearing out the charges in a face-to-face setting.[144]

When Harvey ignored his first memorandum, Hayes sent a follow-up on 2/2/89. In this one, in addition to restating his earlier points, Hayes added:

I have learned that the CID is pursuing private telephone records through the Department of Defense Inspector General subpœna process. I request on behalf of my client that you withdraw your request for these records through this process. Use of the provisions of the Inspector General Act of 1978 for this purpose is inappropriate.

When I had refused the CID blanket access to my financial and telephone records, to preclude "fishing expedition" efforts to manufacture evidence[145] , and when the 6RCID was unable to obtain subpœna authority through TJAG channels, it took the illegal step of invoking the Defense Department Inspector General's federal subpœna authority to obtain them. This authority is legally to be used only for authentic Inspector General investigations, not CID/TJAG ones.

Harvey ignored Hayes' second memorandum as well and continued his illegal use of IG subpœnas. [While through these he received our telephone records, there was of course nothing the least incriminating in them.]

Hayes did not appreciate Harvey's disdain for his TDS office and communiqués. On 2/17/89, therefore, he went over Harvey's head to Major General Eugene Cromartie, Commanding General of the Criminal Investigation Command (CIC) at the Department of the Army (Appendix #46). I followed this with a letter of my own to Cromartie on 3/6/89 (Appendix #47). On 3/21/89 Hayes sent a memorandum to the new 6RCID investigator, Special Agent (Warrant Officer) Dan Cates, again restating his concerns, emphasizing the significance of the Hickey notes in impeaching A-T and requesting that A-T be flagged accordingly (Appendix #48).

Finally on 4/7/89, in response to Hayes' memoranda and my own letter to Cromartie, Harvey finally sent Hayes an answer (Appendix #49). In it Harvey made no mention of the illegal IG subpœnæ, nor of an independent investigation of A-T, nor of Hayes' request that A-T be flagged. I myself responded to Harvey's memorandum on 4/24/89 (Appendix #49), correcting numerous false statements by Harvey therein and questioning the CID's announced policy that no other flags would be considered during this investigation. In effect this meant that A-T was automatically "protected" while I was automatically in a "target". Harvey ignored this letter as well.

By now it was reasonably clear to both Hayes and myself that we were dealing with a CID which had a predetermined bias and agenda. Unfortunately neither Hayes nor I had any power to force correction of this - for example by reassigning the entire investigation to another CID Region or to an agency outside of the CIC altogether (such as the FBI). Equally obvious was that the CIC Commander, Cromartie, was completely in agreement with Harvey's actions [and inactions]. The deck was stacked from the bottom to the top.

Subsequent contact and correspondence between us was accordingly carried on less with the expectation of honest and fair investigation than merely to go on record with as much factual and exposé information as possible, to make any fraudulent CIC agenda as difficult as possible to frame.

In a 5/18/89 memorandum-for-record, for instance, Harvey brought up recent "copycat" allegations by a child named Angelique Jefferson, whose mother had contacted Pamfiloff saying that Angelique had "recognized me on TV". He also made an issue over a black panther statue which he had seen in our St. Louis home [when invited there for a two-day face-to-face interview a short time previously]. Finally he took issue with the Church of Satan's Black Mass, about which he had read in *The Devil's Own*, an earlier edition of my history *The Church of Satan* (an updated copy of which I had given him in St. Louis) (Appendix #51). Once again I replied in detail concerning all

---

[144] Memorandum, Captain Thomas Hayes to Major Mark Harvey 1/13/89.

[145] See my 1/1/89 letter to Major Harvey above, and Appendix #45, Q&A 4.

these topics to Harvey in two separate 5/31/89 letters (Appendices #52 & #53). Seeing that Harvey, a Catholic, was particularly upset by the concept and contents of the Black Mass, I pointed out to him that it was no more offensive to him than his own church's Rite of Exorcism was to us, and enclosed a copy of same so that he could see for himself (Appendix #54).

Upon receiving his faxed copies of my two 5/31/89 letters to Harvey, Hayes decided that he smelled a very pungent rat in the woodpile where Harvey's imminent final CID report was concerned. But if we could have a chance to review and critique that report before the CID command structure formally committed itself to it, the framing-agenda might still be frustrated. That same date, therefore, Hayes sent an official request to the 6RCID commander asking that he and I be permitted such a review, which Hayes said could be within the confines of a CID office if necessary (Appendix #55). Without reason, elaboration, or justification, Acting 6RCID Commander Lt. Colonel Christopher Cole immediately responded to Hayes: "I regret to inform you that this request is denied." [146]

Assessing the entire situation and scenario at this point in time, I decided to write to the 6RCID commander, Colonel Webster Ray, myself. Now quite aware of the framing agenda, I speculated that only an "all cards on the table" solution between myself and these anonymous, faceless witch-hunters at Department of the Army level might bring a mutually-acceptable conclusion to this travesty. While earlier letters of mine had intentionally been shared with the widest possible audience of high-level concerned officials, therefore, this one was copied only to Secretary of the Army Marsh, Army Chief of Staff General Vuono, Chief of the Army Reserve General Ward, and CIC Commander General Cromartie. Addressing the letter to the 6RCID commander was a mere formality.

In this letter I bluntly summarized the bias and agenda of Harvey's sham "investigation". I recognized its actual purpose of trying to force me out of the Army. I mentioned my illegal non-selection for AGR retention on full-time active duty, and said that I would not expose or contest it if the CID did not formally frame me for the A-T allegations. Additionally I would abandon any further efforts to expose A-T or see him brought to justice. Summarily Lilith and I were exhausted and disgusted by the entire, sordid campaign against us, and would settle for its just being ended with no official dishonor to us (Appendix #56).

I might as well have saved my breath [or in this instance my fingertips]. On 6/30/89 Colonel Ray informed Captain Hayes that he would be "titling" me for the A-T allegations. Harvey also provided Hayes with a copy of the report's cover sheet detailing the "titling". Absurdly, a week later Ray sent me a letter saying that he had "reviewed your letter of 20 June", period, and that "I will make my final titling decision based on my careful review of the final report." [147] As he had told Hayes of his titling action a week previously, and as he considered the contents of my 6/20/89 letter not worth bothering about, it was once more evident that the 6RCID, including its commanding officer, was merely a rubber-stamp in a much-higher-level-predetermined outcome.

Hayes sent me a copy of the report cover sheet, and on 7/4/89 I replied to Harvey concerning it. As I had not yet received Ray's 7/6/89 letter, at this moment I still considered it possible that my 6/20/89 letter was being seriously considered behind-the-scenes, hence wrote my letter with that in mind (Appendix #57). Harvey's reply was as evasive as Ray's: "It would be inappropriate for me to comment on the contents of your letter." [148]

On 7/31/89, having heard nothing further from any CID representative, I telephoned Colonel Ray, who confirmed that he had signed the titling action. I discussed my reactions to this in an 8/3/89 letter to General Cromartie (Appendix #58). On 8/24/89 Harvey replied to this on behalf of Ray (who had departed command of the 6RCID on 8/11/89): "Colonel Ray asked me to respond on his behalf that it would be inappropriate for him to comment on the contents of your letters." A 10/20/89 letter from Cromartie's Staff Judge Advocate said that Cromartie had approved Ray's titling action and that, if I wished, I could submit an "amendment request" concerning it through channels once I had read it.[149] In short, my contention that the generation of the report *per se* constituted major and multiple violations of the UCMJ was completely ignored.

I might note at this juncture that I had now gone on formal record as accusing the 6RCID investigators, SJA, and Commander - as well as the Major General commanding the entire U.S. Army Criminal Investigation

---

[146] Memorandum, Lt. Colonel Christopher Cole to Captain Thomas Hayes 6/2/89.

[147] Letter, Colonel Webster Ray to Michael Aquino 7/6/89.

[148] Letter, Major Mark Harvey to M. Aquino 7/6/89.

[149] Letter, Lt. Colonel Brent Green to M. Aquino 10/20/89.

Command if he endorsed them - of numerous major and serious violations of Articles #133 & #134 of the UCMJ. I did this before an information-copy audience of several other Department of the Army senior officials. Had I been the **slightest** bit incorrect in my statements and assessments, I as a Lt. Colonel would have been in serious [and in this case authentic] violation of the UCMJ myself.

But throughout **all** of my correspondence, sworn, and verbal statements, **not once** did any such senior officer **ever** accuse me of a factual violation in this regard. Considering the strength and candor of my letters, I think it is justifiable to conclude that I was never reproved because all recipients **knew full well that I spoke truth**. Because this truth happened to be politically unacceptable, the only possible response was to remain mute in the face of it.

It took me until 11/30/89 to get a copy of the 6RCID Report of Investigation (ROI). The CID was clearly in no hurry for me to see it, and when I did pry a [heavily censored] copy loose, I saw why. To Cromartie on that same date I wrote:

> After an initial reading of the CID report of investigation concerning me, I am absolutely astounded that the CID would dare to represent such an absurd document as this as the basis for a criminal titling action. It is incumbent upon you, as Commanding General, to rescind the fraudulent titling of Mrs. Aquino and myself **immediately**, to order this "report of investigation" recalled and destroyed, and to initiate disciplinary action against the CID personnel involved for such an outrageous and illegal abuse of their investigatory and titling license.
>
> I enclose an analysis[150] covering just the cover letter[151] of this report. While I intend to draft a similar analysis of the rest of the report, you have no excuse whatever for delaying its invalidation and the removal of the titling actions one moment further.
>
> I am advised by the Director of the Crime Records Center that news media are already requesting copies of this report. If it is provided to the media, I will of course provide all of the documentation containing the truth to those same media. Quite obviously the result would be a scandal which would utterly disgrace the entire CID and the United States Army. Accordingly your immediate action to rescind the titling and invalidate the report is all the more important.

As by now routine, this letter and its enclosure was copied to every major commander and official in the U.S. Army concerned in any way with the A-T affair. As also by now routine, Cromartie did not respond to it.

On 12/22/89 I sent Cromartie [with copies to all of the same Army officials] a follow-up letter addressing the detailed section of the ROI following its cover letter, the "Narrative/Summary of Significant Information". This letter and its accompanying analysis of that Narrative appear as Appendix #61. Again there was no response from Cromartie personally. A week later, however, I did receive this letter:

Department of the Army
United States Army Criminal Investigation Command

December 28, 1989

Dear Colonel Aquino:

This is in reply to your request of November 30, 1989, for amendment of U.S. Army Criminal Investigation Command (USACIDC) Report of Investigation (ROI) numbered 88-C1D026-69259. Your request was received at this headquarters on December 11, 1989.

Your amendment request will be processed under the provisions of paragraph 4-4b, Army Regulation 195-2, which provides, in part:

> "Request to amend USACIDC reports will be granted only if the individual submits new, relevant and material facts that are determined to warrant their inclusion in or revision of the report. The burden of proof is on the individual to substantiate the request. Requests to delete a person's name from the title block will be granted only if it is determined that there is no probable cause to believe that the individual committed the offense for which he/she is listed as a subject. It is

---

[150] Appendix #60.

[151] Appendix #59.

emphasized that the decision to list a person's name in the title block of a USACIDC report of investigation is an investigative determination that is independent of whether subsequent judicial, nonjudicial, or administrative action is taken against the individual."

Your request is under consideration and you will be advised when a determination has been made.

If you have any questions regarding this matter, please write to the Director, U.S. Army Crime Records Center, Attention: Freedom of Information/Privacy Act Division (PA89-1548), 2301 Chesapeake Avenue, Baltimore, Maryland 21222-4099.

> Sincerely,
> /s/ Wilbur L. Hardy, Director
> Crime Records Center

This was the same Wilbur Hardy who [see Chapter #5] had worked so exhaustively to deny me a copy of the "nonexistent" CID report of investigation into my charges against A-T. Apparently Hardy was now tasked to divert my current correspondence from its focus upon the CID's *modus operandi* into a routine amendment request. It didn't sell. I wrote back [with copies to the "usual everybody" throughout the Department of the Army]:

January 6, 1990

Dear Mr. Hardy:

I am in receipt of your letter of December 28, 1989.

My 11/30/89 letter to General Cromartie does **not** request mere "amendment" of the 6th Region CID's report of investigation #88-C1D026-69259. Rather it specifies the **complete and total invalidation** of that report, and the removal of the fraudulent titling actions contained within it, as being flagrant violations of the Constitution, the Uniform Code of Military Justice, Army Regulations, and CIDC regulations.

As General Cromartie is well aware from my 11/30/89 and 12/22/89 letters and enclosures addressing just the cover-letter and narrative portions of that report, its contents substantiate **none of the titling actions whatever**. It is nothing more than a clumsy, ignorant, and coarse attempt by Major Mark Harvey, with the complicity of ex-commander Colonel Ray, to smear myself, Mrs. Aquino, and our religion with an incoherent ramble of lies, falsified "evidence", statements deliberately misquoted/misinterpreted/edited out-of-context, and interviews which have no conceivable relevance to the investigation but were clearly solicited and included simply for purposes of character assassination. Harvey, whose Catholic selfrighteousness is obviously incensed by the theology and philosophy of a legitimate religion embarrassing to his own, presumes to use his office in the CID to mount an amateur Inquisition.

Obviously Harvey assumes that in so doing he will be protected from personal accountability by the CID "organization", which now faces the awkward task of trying to explain the 6th Region's massive violations of UCMJ Articles 133 and 134 pertaining to false official statements, misprision of serious offense [of Chaplain Adams-Thompson], attempted manufacture of evidence, and obstruction of justice. I have been indexing all such violations in my continuing review of the report, and a detailed list of them when I am finished will be a major paperwork exercise in itself.

This report is an utter disgrace to the CIDC, and to the U.S. Army which depends upon the CIDC to set and maintain exemplary standards of ethics, impartiality, and respect for the law in its investigations. For you to try to represent the report as a properly-prepared document for which normal AR 195-2 "amendment" procedures are appropriate is, under the circumstances, ludicrous.

It is incumbent upon General Cromartie to rescind and invalidate the report in its entirety immediately. As for Harvey and anyone else found to be responsible for creating it, it is an outrage that such incompetent and unprincipled individuals should be entrusted with positions which they can abuse to violate the law so arrogantly, and to attack honorable soldiers and their families so viciously and wantonly.

Honest errors due to "best guesses" in investigations where all the facts are not available, or where the individual under investigation is uncooperative or obstructive, are quite understandable. Such an excuse cannot be claimed for this ROI, however. The CID investigators received full and complete cooperation at all times, as both the Trial Defense Service and I assumed that the CID was an ethical and professional institution. The documented facts exonerating Mrs. Aquino and myself, and proving beyond a doubt the criminal actions of Adams-Thompson, are both abundant and indisputable. The ROI, with an editorial bias comparable only to the most grotesque anti-Semitic propaganda of Nazi Germany, simply ignores the multitude of facts which establish the truth, invents falsehoods, twists whatever facts it cannot disregard, and clumsily attempts to fabricate "incriminating evidence" where none exists.

This is such an obscene caricature of how a CIDC investigation should not be conducted that I am surprised I should have to go through the motions of exposing this report at all. I would have thought that such a vulgar piece of trash would have been rejected the moment it arrived on General Cromartie's desk.

Sincerely,
/s/ Michael A. Aquino
Lt. Colonel, Military Intelligence

As 1989 came to a close, and with my personal communications to the CID appearing wholly and simply to be ignored, I decided that it was time to retain a civilian attorney specializing in military cases. One name stood out beyond all the rest: Gary Myers.[152] He agreed that at this stage of things, Army officialdom would pay attention only to an attorney, and that the Army's own Trial Defense Service officers, while well-intentioned, simply did not have the license, skill, or adrenaline to pursue justice aggressively.

Myers' first step was to indeed file a formal Appeal of the CID ROI and its "titling" actions. This Appeal appears at Appendix #62. It was submitted on 1/31/90; six months then elapsed in silence. When the 7/30/90 official reply finally arrived, it removed all titlings from Lilith's name and removed all titlings from my name with the exception of:

LTC Aquino should remain titled as a subject for the offenses of conspiracy, kidnapping, sodomy, indecent acts or liberties with a child, indecent acts, and false swearing.[153]

None of the factual contents of Gary Myers' appeal was addressed or even mentioned. The one-sentence reason for retaining the titlings quoted above was: "The evidence of alibi offered by LTC Aquino was not persuasive." [154]
In an immediate response to the Judge Advocate General I wrote:

This document reaffirms the titling of Lt. Colonel Aquino for "conspiracy, kidnapping, sodomy, indecent acts or liberties with a child, indecent acts, and false swearing". The decision to retain these titlings was made by Colonel Francis A. Gilligan, Chief, Criminal Law Division, Office of the Judge Advocate General, Department of the Army. **Colonel Gilligan was in possession of abundant evidence proving all of these allegations to be false.** This document is therefore a false official statement by Colonel Gilligan in violation of Article 133, UCMJ.

Gilligan falsely implies that I have practiced "nudity and indecent acts within the confines of a private religious ceremony". I have done **neither**, and there is **no** evidence to indicate that I have. This statement by Gilligan is therefore evidence of a false official statement by him in violation of Article 133, UCMJ.

Gilligan falsely states that "the evidence of alibi offered by Lt. Colonel Aquino is not persuasive". Gilligan knows that the CID **fraudulently altered** the date of accusation from September-October 1986 to June 10, 1986 when it was established that I was not in San Francisco on a "workable" date in September-October 1986. The statement provided by Graham Marshall that there were **no** children anywhere in our residence at 123 Acme Avenue on June 10, 1986 was **conclusive**. The CID would later try to evade this by shifting the alleged location to a downstairs apartment - which was immediately disproven by Commander William Butch, USNR, resident of that apartment. This statement by Gilligan is therefore evidence of a false

[152] http://www.mcmilitarylaw.com/

[153] Letter, Colonel Francis A. Gilligan, Chief, Criminal Law Division, Office of the Judge Advocate General, Department of the Army to Deputy Commander, USA Criminal Investigation Command, SUBJECT: Review of Amendment Request by LTC Michael A. Aquino, 30 July 1990.

[154] *Ibid.*

official statement by him in violation of Article 133, UCMJ. It is further evidence of an act by him to obstruct justice in violation of Article 134, UCMJ.[155]

Subsequently I discovered more about how Gilligan's decision had been made, and commented in a letter to my own Commanding General at ARPERCEN:

October 18, 1990

Brigadier General Thomas J. Kilmartin
Commanding General
U.S. Army Reserve Personnel Center
Dear General Kilmartin:

Enclosed is a copy of a letter just received from the CID responding to my request to have the fraudulent investigative report and titling of Mrs. Aquino and myself expunged.

According to my attorney, what actually took place at DA was that **the CID's own legal counsel recommended expungement**. However the significance of the CID's admitting to such a blatant act of corruption, falsification, and character assassination as the report constitutes was such that the decision was bucked to TJAG, where it languished for months while some face-saving solution for the Army was sought. There was, of course, **no** such solution. The evidence of our innocence was overwhelming and conclusive, as it always had been from the beginning.

Therefore this letter from the CID, as dictated by TJAG, represents a clumsy effort at trying to protect and conceal some remnant of the criminal actions committed against us - giving us part of the relief we requested on the hope that we would then just go away and endure the rest.

The "maltreatment of a subordinate/Article #30" titling was placed in the original report to find some way of dealing with the court-martial charges that I twice preferred against Adams-Thompson for his crimes against us (false official statements) and the U.S. government (false claims). Both times the Army suppressed the charges I preferred against him with no proper inquiry into or. refutation of the evidence as presented. If the "maltreatment of a subordinate" titling is now removed, then the CID in essence **admits that those charges I preferred were justified**. In that case I am of course innocent and he is guilty of criminal actions as charged.

The "conduct unbecoming an officer" titling was placed in the original report purely and simply as an effort to attack my religion, which is and always has been a legitimate religion involving no criminal or undignified conduct on my part whatever. The CID knew this from the beginning, yet deliberately set out to misrepresent it - and in doing so blatantly violated the First Amendment and AR 600-20 - in an attempt to assassinate my character [and draw attention away from the fact that the report **could not in the least substantiate** the Adams-Thompson accusation against Mrs. Aquino and myself]. The removal of this titling admits the criminal actions by the CID which that character-assassination effort constitutes, which of course means that the officers who wrote it and approved it should now be charged for their crimes (false official statements and acts of religious discrimination). That would involve (at minimum) charges against the Major who wrote the report, the Colonel who approved it at the Sixth Region CID, and Major General Cromartie for approving it at the CID headquarters.

The removal of all titlings from the name of Mrs. Aquino, while retaining them against my name, is perhaps the most conspicuous evidence of the official corruption which has marked this affair from the start. [Even the phrase "insufficient evidence" is indicative. There is not "insufficient evidence"; there is **no evidence whatever**.] Adams-Thompson's fake "child-abuse" allegations were directed against **both** of us, who were alleged to have "committed every crime" together. If the CID now admits that there is no reason whatever to title Mrs. Aquino, then there is equally no reason to title me - save, once again, to try to cover up the fact that the **entire** report, and the entire attempt to falsify any kind of case against me, is a deliberate lie from start to finish.

I am utterly disgusted at such corruption and dishonesty. As I indicated to you previously, I have therefore instructed my attorney to commence immediately an action against the Army in United States District Court to have the remaining titlings expunged.

---

[155] Memorandum, M. Aquino to the Judge Advocate General of the Army 7/30/90.

I continue to respect those many ethical and honorable soldiers with whom it has been my privilege to serve throughout my Army career, and whose contribution to our nation's security has brought honor and dignity to the Army. Accordingly it is all the more inconceivable to me that this same Army should tolerate such dishonesty and corruption as the CID, and any higher officials dictating its conduct in this affair, have shown.

Respectfully,
/s/ Michael A. Aquino
Lt. Colonel, Military Intelligence

Administrative channels within the Army to invalidate the Report of Investigation now having been exhausted, the only remaining recourse was to sue the Army concerning it in federal court. That is the subject of the next chapter.

Chapter 8: The Lawsuit

The situation as of November 1, 1990: The CID investigation of Lilith and myself had been concluded. Administratively its "titlings" of Lilith for everything, and myself for everything but the A-T allegation, had been removed. No court-martial charges or any other punitive action (such as non-judicial punishment or even a letter of reprimand) had been taken against me. My Top Secret/Special Compartmented Intelligence security clearance had been immediately restored. My full-time (Active Guard & Reserve = AGR) tour of duty had come to an end on 8/31/90, hence I had been returned to the part-time Army Reserve. Herein I had been assigned to an Individual Mobilization Augmentee (IMA) position as a Space Intelligence Officer at Headquarters, U.S. Space Command. As with other part-time Reservists, this required two weeks' active duty with that headquarters each year. All of my Officer Efficiency Reports to date continued to give me the highest possible ratings in all categories.

Thus I could have just "walked away" from the CID investigation and report.

I was, however, incensed that such injustices had been perpetrated, and officially sanctioned at the highest levels of the Army, against Lilith and myself. My attorney Gary Myers advised that my only option was to sue the Army in federal court.

Myers further advised that a full-blown lawsuit embracing, essentially, all of the personalities and actions in the foregoing chapters of this ebook, would be expensive, costing several hundreds of thousands of dollars. Numerous witnesses, subpœnæ, statements, motions, court-time, appeals, transportation, housing, legal assistance staff, etc. As I had already spent well over one hundred thousand dollars to date defending ourselves, I certainly did not have the resources for such an expensive and indefinite lawsuit.

There was one option, Myers said: a Motion for Summary Judgment. Essentially this is a federal court hearing in which each side presents a written brief and an oral argument before a judge. There are no witnesses or testimony, and of course no jury. The judge simply considers the written and oral arguments and makes his own decision about them. This would merely cost tens of thousands of dollars. I decided to pursue this option.

What could I expect to accomplish? Initially, since federal court Discovery would apply, I would obtain a complete, uncensored copy of the CID Report of Investigation (ROI). [The copy the CID had finally provided to me as described in the previous chapter had been extensively blacked-out, such that it had been possible for me to refute it only by inferring or guessing much of its contents.]

How much more than this might happen was dependent upon the judge's decision, what orders if any he might issue, and of course the Army's willingness to comply with them, much less to initiate corrective action of its own based upon the decision. I hoped that at least the ROI would be officially discredited and ordered discarded in its entirety [to include of course the remaining titling]. While a titling itself is not recorded outside the CID's own records - it was not, for instance, included in my official U.S. Army Personnel Records file (OMPF) - its existence **anywhere** outraged me.

As for the Army's investigating, prosecuting, and punishing all those who **had** violated the Uniform Code of Military Justice throughout this entire affair, I knew there was very little chance of that happening. I had by now identified, documented, and reported numerous such violations (comparable to civilian felonies) by a great many officers up to the highest general officer ranks. Conspicuous among these were the Commanding General of the entire Army Criminal Investigation Command and the Judge Advocate General of the Army. Not to mention a trail leading all the way to the Secretary of the Army himself. Would the United States send all of these people to jail just to deliver justice to one lieutenant colonel and his wife? Not very likely.

Well, as Don Quixote might have said to the windmills, *"En garde!"*

On 11/15/90 Myers filed the *Complaint for Declaratory Judgment and Damages* with the U.S. District Court in Virginia [proximate to Washington, D.C.]. This Complaint appears at Appendix #63.

Along with it were submitted a number of "Interrogatories", being questions for the CID whose answers were now court-mandated. These Interrogatories, the CID's responses to them, and my critique of those answers to Myers, appear at Appendix #64. Nothing new was learned from the CID's answers; they were clearly just Major Harvey's continued evasion and lying. As with the ROI itself, it was if nothing else obvious that he had been officially assured that he could [continue to] do so with impunity.

The evident ease and casualness with which Harvey and other CID/TJAG officers lied, moreover, was a phenomenon that was very slow and difficult for me to comprehend and accept. U.S. commissioned officers are expected to adhere to an extremely rigorous, indeed inflexible code of official integrity. Lying in official statements or documents is formally a court-martial offense, but - in the entire military culture - it just **isn't done**. "An officer's word is his bond", and the armed forces have long been accustomed to taking that strictly and seriously.

Prior to the A-T affair I had throughout my career never interacted very much with either the Judge Advocate General's Corps or the Criminal Investigation Command. For most soldiers "JAGs" were just there to provide soldiers with free/routine legal advice and services, and the CID was an odd conglomerate of warrant officers and civilians called in to investigate the occasional government property theft or personnel misconduct. Since JAG attorneys were also commissioned as officers, I assumed that they would be indoctrinated into, and just as conscientiously adhere to the standards of integrity and truthfulness expected of all other officers.

As I think has been amply evidenced here, this did not turn out to be the case at all. The CID and its TJAG superiors all lied routinely, easily, and repeatedly; and such behavior was sanctioned all the way to the top of their chains of command.

It seemed then, and still seems today to me almost incredible that the Army could function with such indifferent corruption in its legal and investigative branches, but there it was nonetheless. Following the A-T affair I would never again trust any JAG office/officer [of which/whom I consider the CID merely a "facilitating" device]. I would caution anyone considering a military career to take my experience here into account as well.

Taking over from Major Harvey at this stage of things was JAG Major Patrick Lisowski from the Department of the Army's TJAG Litigation Division.

After receiving the TJAG/CID's response to his Interrogatories, Gary Myers went on to draft and file his brief with the District Court (Appendix #65). In lieu of reprinting Lisowski's brief completely, I have in Appendix #66 quoted its substantive parts and identified the numerous falsehoods contained therein.

Shortly thereafter Myers filed a reply brief (Appendix #67). In this reply brief he contests Lisowski's strenuous efforts in his brief to blanket-exempt all TJAG/CID ROIs from judicial review under the U.S. Privacy Act. The significance of such an exemption, if successful, would be that *de novo* judicial consideration of the ROI's evidence would not occur, that the "preponderance of the evidence" standard for any conclusions from that evidence would also not be applied, and that the ROI author would be exempt from punitive damages and attorney costs.

The much weaker Administrative Procedure Act, which the CID argued should apply instead of the Privacy Act, would also require much stronger and explicit evidence of governmental misconduct than the Privacy Act.

In short, the strategy of Lisowski was to argue that the judge had no authority to look into the ROI itself, nor to evaluate the validity of its contents: it was the inviolate prerogative of TJAG/CID to write whatever it wished into its reports.

Following the filing of briefs, oral arguments were scheduled for 5/31/91. A transcript of these arguments appears as Appendix #68.

District Court Judge Claude M. Hilton issued his ruling on 7/1/91 (Appendix #69). Ignoring all of Myers' factual points concerning the case, while uncritically reciting Lisowski's lies as "truth", Hilton obligingly swept aside the Privacy Act and found that under the Administrative Procedure Act TJAG/CID was free to have whatever opinions it wished. Not a single one of Myers' legal points was even mentioned, much less refuted.

So glaring was the bias in this district court ruling that Gary Myers strongly urged an appeal to the federal Fourth Circuit Court of Appeals. Despite the considerable court and legal expense involved, I agreed. If it had been unthinkable that the district court would condone the numerous crimes committed by TJAG/CID and embodied in this ROI, it was impossible that three senior judges of an appeals court would also sanction such a miscarriage of justice.

Myers' appeal brief (Appendix #70) devoted most of its body to an extensive, exhaustive, detailed, and forceful argument as to why the Privacy Act should indeed be allowed as the judicial standard for this case. His object was quite simple: If the Privacy Act prevailed, then the district court judge, under its *de novo* requirements, would be **forced** to personally examine all of the "evidence" in the ROI in terms of its accuracy, factuality, and objectivity. In the remainder of his brief Myers once again listed a number of the ROI's lies and omissions.

Historically the Fourth Circuit Court of Appeals had set strong and repeated legal precedent for the applicability of the Privacy Act in cases such as this. Accordingly Myers felt quite certain that it would uphold its previous rulings and require that Act here.

Once again Lisowski's main goal was at all costs to **prevent** the Privacy Act from being applied. Where he referred to the case itself, he once again freely and repeatedly lied to the appeals court, as again documented in Appendix #71.

The unanimous decision of the three-judge panel of the appeals court, when it was issued on 2/26/92 was, if anything, even more startling and incredible than that of the district court. Once again all of Myers' arguments were simply ignored as if he had never written or spoken them, whereas Lisowski's were all accepted and parroted without any question whatever. The court's ruling, annotated to detail the extent of this, appears as Appendix #72.

Most unexpected in this ruling was the court's 180° turn **rejecting** all of its previous rulings and precedents concerning the Privacy Act. The implications of this went far beyond my particular case, virtually freeing all federal investigative agencies from judicial accountability for the conduct of their investigations and content of their reports.

All a stunned Gary Myers could think of to do was to file an immediate request for his appeal to be reheard *en banc* by the entire court (beyond the three-judge panel). This request appears as Appendix #73. Upon receiving my copy I wrote to Gary:

March 14, 1992

Dear Gary:

Received today the brief for rehearing *en banc*. As with your earlier briefs, it looks [to my rational, if not legalistic eyes] faultless. But I have been astounded and dismayed by first the district and then the 3-judge appeals decisions, so don't know what to expect any more. It seems to me that, from the day when Adams-Thompson made his first accusation, this entire affair has been driven by an Alice in Wonderland "logic" in which all constants are variables at the pleasure of the Army: If a law, rule, or fact gets in the way, just ignore it or arbitrarily change it.

After all of the "changes" I have seen the Army calmly manufacture to try to get the titling to "fit", the latest is Lisowski's invocation of - and the appeal judges' blessing of - various items in our apartment which (a) no child mentioned, (b) were not on the search warrant, (c) were never confiscated as "evidence" during the search, and (d) are irrelevant since [in the interrogatory answers] the Army dodged Graham Marshall's alibi by proceeding to move the "location" out of our flat entirely [thereafter dodging Cdr. Butch's alibi of his flat by simply ignoring it altogether]. The court therefore sanctions the CID's right to keep changing not only dates and locations but the presence/absence of physical evidence at whim. This sets a charming precedent for the future of criminal investigation, don't you think?

I am beginning to get the feeling that the moment someone hears the "S-word" - **Satanism** - logic and sanity fly out the window to be replaced with some sort of weird "Inquisition mind-set" which dictates: "Fry this guy, no matter whether he is right or wrong. It is inconceivable that a **Satanist** could be innocent of anything -particularly an especially heinous accusation!"

In another context, as I read the *en banc* brief, I see the seriousness of the general legal point you are making. If the 3-judge decision stands, the ripples go far beyond my case to a blanket *carte blanche* for the CID, FBI, etc. to say and do whatever they wish with virtual immunity. That is a frightening prospect, particularly given the irresponsibility and falsification the Army has displayed in just this situation.

Lilith and I continue to be very grateful to you and John Wickham for your valiant efforts not simply in support of our cause, but in support of the more general principles of truth and justice in the courts which are at issue here.

/s/ Michael

The following month, without explanation or comment, the court denied Myers' request for an *en banc* rehearing. Even Lisowski - who, Myers said, had originally remarked to him that he didn't expect the Army to win this case - called Myers to express professional sympathy.

Only one option remained: a further appeal to the United States Supreme Court. Merely the filing fees for this would have been over forty thousand dollars, and there was no guarantee that the court would accept the case even then. Still, Gary Myers and his associate John Wickham (son of a former 4-star general and Army Chief of Staff) informed me that they would donate their own fees and expenses if I wished to go ahead. I wrote back to Gary:

April 25, 1992

Dear Gary:

I was going to wait until I had received your package of papers before sending this letter, in case there was something therein which called for a comment from me. The package has not yet arrived, however, so I'll post this letter now.

First Lilith and I would like to thank both you and John Wickham again for your legal efforts on our behalf. We think that you both did a valiant job, and of course deserved to prevail in the district and appeals courts. That you did not speaks simply to the failure of the court system to administer justice as it is supposed to do.

That brings me to your gracious offer to carry the fight to the Supreme Court for costs only, with you and Mr. Wickham donating your time.

Given the nature of the current Supreme Court, we think this would simply be a waste of our funds and your & Mr. Wickham's valuable time [and dignity].

The cold fact is that we received not so much as a crumb of consideration from the district court, and equal indifference from the appeals court.

There was not a single word in support of our position, not a single dissent from any judge, not even the slightest indication that any of the judges had even **bothered to read** any of the meticulous and conclusive briefs you filed. You might as well have been writing and talking to a brick wall.

Lisowski's crocodile-tears of "surprise and sympathy" to you are the height of hypocrisy under the circumstances.

Until and unless the courts are going to pay attention to the law and the truth, you and Mr. Wickham should not tolerate being made to look like fools in this demeaning and insulting fashion.

We have already identified the reasons for this situation:

(1) No court is going to declare a "Satanist" innocent of anything, even if he **is**.
(2) "Child-molestation" remains automatic justification for witch-hunts, even when the fakery used to instigate such scams has been exposed.
(3) The Army Corps of Chaplains cannot be criticized.
(4) The Army Medical Corps cannot be criticized.
(5) The Army CID cannot be criticized.
(6) The Army Judge Advocate General's Corps cannot be criticized.
(7) "Army parents" - i.e. those who participated in the Presidio scam - cannot be criticized.
(8) A flock of generals and colonels who violated the law to participate in our framing and the Adams-Thompson cover-up cannot be criticized.
(9) Ex-Secretary of the Army Marsh cannot be criticized.
(10) Senator Jesse Helms cannot be criticized.

Ergo the Army has informed the courts that this case is **not** to be won by plaintiff, period.

These truths being self-evident [to borrow a phrase from Jefferson], what can be done at this point?

First I intend to pursue Harvey's personal violation of the ROI confidentiality and Lisowski's [and his bosses'] lies in court through the Army and possibly Defense Department chain of command. Obviously I don't expect anything to come of this. But I want to go through the motions, if only to satisfy my curiosity as to what wiggling and squirming by more generals and colonels will occur. To date, as you've seen, TJAG and the IG are having fun throwing the hot potato back and forth between the two of them, presumably in an effort to prevent it from landing once again on the Chief of Staff's or Secretary of the Army's desk.

Once this Keystone Kops farce has been played out, then it's time to get serious again. At your convenience I would like to hear your thoughts on a lawsuit against the Army for Harvey's Privacy Act violation, pure and simple. The idea is not to waste further time on the titling action itself, as that is obviously a political sacred cow. But narrowly and specifically on Harvey's violation of the ROI confidentiality. That, it seems to me, should be impossible for the Army to defend or excuse. And here we are talking not about a gaggle of politicians and generals, but about just one major. I doubt that the Army would armtwist the courts quite so earnestly in his case.

If we win a judgment against Harvey, we will then be in a financial position to invest further big funds in the "main case". It seems to me that the way to go relates to the Army's numerous and documented lies to the courts, as I have extensively listed. It **cannot** be acceptable for attorneys to deliberately lie to courts. Whether the solution lies through petitions to the same courts, or protests with bar associations, or whatever, I will be interested in pursuing it.

When and if we prevail, then the way is presumably clear to retrying the main case with the Army **prevented** from lying. Even if the courts still resist applying the Privacy Act, we should prevail under the Administrative Procedure Act. At that point there will simply be nothing for the Army to say to prevent it.

Carthago delenda est.

/s/ Michael

I had commenced correspondence within the Army to formally protest Major Lisowski's lies to the district and appeals courts in December 1991 - to both the Judge Advocate General and the Inspector General of the Army. I was nonetheless reasonably certain that, as with Harvey, Lisowski knew beforehand that his courtroom lies in this case were both sanctioned and protected.

Summarily the Inspector General disclaimed any authority to investigate misconduct by the Judge Advocate General, and the Judge Advocate General responded that he saw nothing illegal or unethical in the actions of any JAG officer involved in the case.

Finally, feeling as though I might as well make the attempt, I sent two letters (Appendices #74 & #75)) to the seniormost officer of the Army, Chief of Staff General Gordon Sullivan. If he wished, he had the power to overrule the Judge Advocate General. Evidently he did not so wish; both my letters went unanswered.

And that was the end.

I had exhausted all avenues, all resources; I could do nothing more.

Epilogue

Meanwhile ...

Among the strangest aspects of this entire, bizarre affair was that, apart from the CID and TJAG, the United States Army and I were getting along just fine - as we always had previously - from the time of A-T's allegations to 1994, when I requested transfer to the Retired Reserve. My Officer Efficiency Reports for this period contained nothing but the highest praise - including of my integrity and moral character. And, for that matter, thereafter to the present, as in 2006 I was again transferred to the Army of the United States, wherein I remain a lifelong Lieutenant Colonel (Retired) with full pay and benefits.

From the time of A-T's original attack against Lilith and myself, not a single officer in my chain of command ever indicated the slightest doubt as to our innocence and integrity. Off-duty we were always invited to all command social functions, and always greeted warmly by other officer families as well.

Throughout the CID/TJAG ordeal, I routinely kept my own commander, Brigadier General Paul Babiak of the Army Reserve Personnel Center, personally updated on all communications and developments. He knew he was always welcome to ask me any questions he wished, all of which were courteous and supportive.

When my Active Guard & Reserve assignment at ARPERCEN ended on 8/31/90, I was presented with a Certificate of Appreciation by General Babiak's successor, Brigadier General Thomas J. Kilmartin, and Lilith and I were given a rousing farewell party.

Subsequently I was assigned in the part-time Army Reserve as an Individual Mobilization Augmentee (IMA) to Headquarters, United States Space Command, Peterson Air Force Base, Colorado. As a Military Intelligence officer I was first sent to the Joint Space Intelligence Operations Course administered by the Air Force for the Army Space Institute, then assigned to the office of the Deputy Chief of Staff for Intelligence, SPACECOM and NORAD. I served in this office until 1994, when I decided to request transfer to the Retired Reserve.

At that time, by order of the [new!] Secretary of the Army, I was awarded the Meritorious Service Medal covering the entire previous ten years. This of course included the duration of the A-T attack, the investigations, and the lawsuit. I saw in this medal a symbolic and subliminal, if not explicit apology for what had been done to me under the previous Secretary.

In addition to the trust and confidence shown in me by my own commanders and fellow officers, the U.S. Army Intelligence & Security Command - which has authority and absolute discretion over all personnel security clearances - had made it clear from the beginning that it would take no part in the disgraceful agenda of TJAG/CID. Security clearances are not in the least bound by any formal legal procedures or constraints: If AISC feels that you are a risk for any reason whatever, your clearance evaporates instantly and there is **no** appeal, including through the courts. [Without at least a Secret clearance, a commissioned officer cannot function at all, hence would have to leave the Service.]

In short, had AISC felt there was any substance to the A-T attack, my clearance would have been revoked the moment he made it, and even if I were never charged with any crime or court-martialed, it could still have denied that clearance permanently.

In my case this was especially significant because from 1976 to 1986 my clearance had been at the highest general classification - Top Secret (TS) - and thereafter at the even more rarified Top Secret/Special Compartmented Intelligence (TS/SCI). It scarcely needs saying that personnel even suspected of having committed any crimes whatever, much less serious ones, do not get such clearances.

When the CID opened its investigation on 11/23/88, my security clearance was automatically and routinely suspended. The moment the investigation was concluded with no charges, AISC instantly restored me to TS/SCI as before. The bogus "titling" was obviously treated with the contempt and disregard it deserved.

In 1991 my clearance came up for its regularly-scheduled re-evaluation by the Defense Investigative Service (DIS), which handles all such investigations throughout the Department of Defense. TS/SCI requires the most extensive and exhaustive such examination, called a Special Background Investigation (SBI). Towards the end of the process there is at least one personal interview, and when mine took place, I told the two DIS Agents that they were welcome to ask me anything about the entire A-T affair. It was not in the least necessary, they responded. My TS/SCI clearance was renewed, and remained effective until my retirement request was approved in 1994.

Through a Glass, 2014

For many years it was extremely difficult for me to look back on the A-T episode without intense anger and frustration. Like many other victims of "satanic ritual abuse" scams during the 1980s' hysteria and witch-hunts, Lilith and I could have been imprisoned and possibly seriously injured or killed in prison for a "crime" that had never happened, just so that a chaplain and his wife could waltz comfortably into their future with a $3 million fattening of their bank account. It wouldn't have been any better had they known us or had any actual reason to hate us; but it was quite clear that they were utterly indifferent to us except as a convenient means to their monetary claims scheme.

The FBI and the SFPD quickly realized the scam for what it was, and washed their hands of it as soon as gracefully possible. Obviously holding any of the Presidio's "media martyred parents" to account instead was, in the climate of the national mania, not possible either.

There the matter might have ended had it not been for Geraldo Rivera's continued tabloid-television sensationalizing and agitation about "satanic crime", which dragged me back into the controversial national [indeed international] spotlight.

At that point, as a result of pressure from Jesse Helms and other Senators and Congressmen, Secretary of the Army Marsh and/or his senior military generals decided that Lt. Colonel Michael Aquino had simply become more of an inconvenience than an asset to the Army, and would have to be removed at least from the visibility of full-time active duty. That I might not personally deserve this was regrettable but politically irrelevant.

The CID was accordingly instructed to open an investigation on 11/23/88 based on the A-T allegations. Since these were already known to be false, no actual court-martial was ever contemplated; the idea was simply to intimidate me into resigning my commission [as CID Agent Cates bluntly and explicitly suggested over lunch at our first meeting]. Failing that, I would at least be discontinued from the full-time AGR and returned to the less-visible part-time Reserve.

What had **not** been anticipated was the intensity, tenacity, and precision of my resistance to this agenda. A great many generals and colonels were placed in the unexpected and decidedly uncomfortable position of being party to[156], or in knowing tolerance of[157] crimes under the Uniform Code of Military Justice for their roles in the affair. They were all saved from accountability for the same reason: that the agenda remained blessed from the very top. Neither actions nor inactions in furtherance of it would be officially acknowledged or penalized.

The infamous ROI was the most transparent kind of travesty. Had any of the command recipients believed even one of its "titlings", I would of course have been court-martialed instantly. There was plenty of time to finalize the ROI before the statute of limitations ran on the A-T accusation, and of course no statute had run on any of the other CID tag-ons like "false swearing". The CID Region Commander was told **in advance** that he would "approve" it [as Captain Hayes was informed], and the general court-martial authority was also told **in advance** that he would "decide" that there be no court-martial consequently [as Gary Myers was informed].

My own chain of command and the Army Intelligence & Security Command refused any participation in this entire farce.

The civil lawsuit process brought an uncertain new dimension to the affair. Clearly the Army had not anticipated such exposure and accountability, and its only recourse was to get the courts to disallow the *de novo* spotlight and "preponderance of the evidence" standards of the U.S. Privacy Act. Fortunately for TJAG/CID, both the district and appeals courts sheltered them by rejecting that Act. Evidently the courts realized that the shock- and ripple-effects of exposing the truth in this case could go much farther throughout the Army command structure and Congress than would be politically desirable.

In retrospect I also think that my own professional conduct throughout the entire episode won me some grudging respect from the nameless and faceless orchestrators of the agenda. I could still not be allowed to win absolutely and completely, but it was also clear that I was just as good an officer now as I had been throughout all of my military career. Once symbolically removed from the AGR, I would thus be allowed to continue my Reserve career in positions of the highest trust and prestige [as indeed happened].

---

[156] False official statement (violation of Article 133, UCMJ). Manufacture of evidence, obstruction of justice (violation of Article 134, UCMJ).

[157] Misprision of serious offense (violation of Article 134, UCMJ).

Am I still incensed that Lilith and I weren't fully and openly vindicated, that A-T wasn't court-martialed and imprisoned for what he did to us, and that Majors Harvey and Lisowski didn't join him in Fort Leavenworth for what they did? Certainly. All of them went on to comfortable promotions - A-T retiring from the Corps of Chaplains as a full Colonel. [Absent a complete exoneration, and possibly not even then because of the shadow of A-T's scam, my own prospects for further promotion were destroyed, all of the "promote ahead of contemporaries" recommendations in my Officer Efficiency Reports and my Senior Service College "anointing" notwithstanding. Nor would it have helped that all Colonel promotions require Senate confirmation, which Jesse Helms would have sabotaged. Had it not been for the A-T scam, of course, Geraldo Rivera could not have used it to force my appearance on his "special", hence I would not have come to Helms' attention.]

The CID's illegal manipulation of the AGR continuation board terminated my full-time career one tour before I could qualify for Active Army retirement benefits: a higher retirement pension and immediate medical coverage instead of my present Reserve benefits.

Three years of criminal investigation, despite everyone involved knowing the "crime" was fictitious, was stressful and exhausting. Indeed, since Lilith and I realized that the investigation was agenda-, not fact-driven, we had no way of knowing what fate was intended for us. We considered it entirely possible that we would be murdered "accidentally" to prevent the extent of the felonies committed against us from being exposed.

Defending yourself in a series of governmental criminal investigations requires much more than personal initiative and articulation. Legal representation during the entire ordeal exceeded $200,000 [in 1980s funds], forcing us to liquidate many of our retirement savings and assets.

The international media circus caused by the A-T scam also inspired years of "copycat" allegations and defamation, all as baseless as A-T's original, from the lunatic fringe. We routinely receive death-threats to this day; before the A-T scam, despite our unusual and exotic religion, there had been none.

But this is not a perfect world, nor is there usually perfect justice. Neither the United States Army nor Lilith & I had asked for or anticipated this entire nightmare. All things considered, it came out as well as could be expected given the harsh politics of the "real world" at that time.

In the last analysis the FBI, the SFPD, and the U.S. Army did well by Lilith and myself in the face of a completely unexpected and out-of-control national "satanic ritual abuse" witch-hunt mania. The FBI eventually issued an authoritative research paper discrediting the "SRA" urban myth,[158] the SFPD disbanded the "intelligence" office which had misguided its own investigations, and the Army stood by me as an officer throughout the rest of my career and subsequent Reserve retirement.

I have written this book in 2014, twenty-seven years after our ordeal began, neither to complain nor to boast, but rather just to set down what actually happened, for the benefit of anyone who may have heard about and/or been interested in any of this. So here are the facts; here are the documents. And that's it.

---

[158] Supervisory Special Agent Kenneth V. Lanning, *Investigator's Guide to Allegations of "Ritual" Child Abuse*. Quantico, VA: Behavioral Sciences Unit, National Center for the Analysis of Violent Crime, FBI Academy, January 1992.

Appendix 1: *Michelle Remembers*

"The Debunking of a Myth: Why the Original 'Ritual Abuse' Victim May Have Suffered Only from her Childhood Fantasies"

- by Denna Allen & Janet Midwinter
Victoria, British Columbia
The Mail on Sunday
London, England
September 30, 1990
Page 41

Michelle Pazder is a plump, middle-aged woman with one daughter. She has an ordinary nine-to-five job working as a receptionist in her husband's surgery in the Canadian provincial town of Victoria, British Columbia. Yet, incredible as it seems, Michelle Pazder is a key figure in the current Satanic abuse controversy to whom the extraordinary happenings in England can be directly linked.

Thirteen years ago she lay on a psychiatrist's couch and poured out tales of such unimaginable horror that the Vatican launched an investigation and Hollywood offered her a film contract. Michelle described how, as a five-year-old, she had been offered to Satan. From deep inside her mind came memories long buried: How she had witnessed debauchery, murder and the sacrifice of babies, the mutilation of snakes and kittens. How she was made to drink blood at the altar of Satan. Her torment was to last nearly two years. And she named the person guilty of giving her to the Devil - her own mother.

The psychiatrist who recorded all this in many months of therapeutic sessions was Dr. Larry Pazder. Both were married to other people. He is now her husband. The Pazders' book, *Michelle Remembers*, was an immediate international best-seller. But, more importantly, many child care experts believe it was the "seed work" which began the current wave of hysteria about Satanists. Robert Hicks of the U.S. Justice Department said: "Before *Michelle Remembers* there were no Satanic prosecutions involving children. Now the myth is everywhere."

The book was pounced upon by fundamentalist Christian groups, interest spread like wildfire across the States, and the crusade crossed last year to England. An important conference at Reading University, attended by social workers from all over the country, heard "experts" describing Michelle's experiences.

It was Dr. Pazder who coined the phrase "ritual abuse", which has been used by the Rochdale Social Services Department to justify their drastic action in taking 16 children into care.

But did Michelle, now aged 40, tell the truth? Did these things actually physically happen to her? Is *Michelle Remembers*, published in this country by Michael Joseph and now being treated with such respect by a powerful child welfare lobby, fact - or fiction? For the past two weeks *Mail on Sunday* reporters have been investigating.

Dr. Pazder, who has since been consulted in more than 1,000 "ritual abuse" cases, was reluctant to speak to us at length. He would not allow us access to Michelle, his wife and star witness. He said: "For Michelle to go on talking about these things is too painful. She is totally free of Satan today. She is a wonderful person, full of freedom and love."

But every other witness we have interviewed described these happenings as "the hysterical ravings of an uncontrolled imagination".

Some, including a Roman Catholic bishop, give Michelle the benefit of the doubt - that she did genuinely **believe** these things happened to her. But they are firmly convinced that, in real life, they did not - and have to be explained as the workings of her subconscious.

In the book Michelle says she was introduced to the Satanic ring by her mother in the basement of her home in 1955. She was just five.

Dr. Pazder conceals the family's true identity and home address. But we discovered she was the daughter of Jack and Virginia Proby, who lived with Michelle's two sisters at 2078 Newton Street, Victoria - a white-painted house, set among neat hedges and suburban lawns.

The first witness is Michelle's father, Jack Proby. Mr Proby, now 74, admits he was not the perfect father, and it was a difficult marriage. But he is outraged at what Michelle and her psychiatrist have done to the memory of his wife, who died in 1963:

It was the worst pack of lies a little girl could ever make up. The book took me four months to read, and I cried all the time. I kept saying to myself: "Dear God, how could anyone do this to their dead mother?"
There never was a woman on this earth who worked harder for her daughters. There was no hanky panky or devil-worshipping.

I asked my lawyer if I could sue them. He said I would win, but it would cost me $5,000. So instead I took out a Notice of Intent against their publisher, which meant if they ever went beyond a literary contract I would sue. That meant they couldn't get their movie deal.

Mr. Proby itemized, as examples, three specific points where he says Michelle lied:

Book: Michelle said she had no religious upbringing.
Father: "She went to church every Sunday with her mother and sisters. The three of them were confirmed together."

Book: Michelle said she was twice poisoned during Satanic rites.
Father: "She was treated for poisoning, but it had nothing to do with devil-worship. Once she drank turps and paint mixture while I was cleaning my brushes. Another time she ate shoe polish."

Book: Michelle describes a horrible car accident which was re-lived by the devil-worshippers in which Satan himself appears.
Father: "What I do recall was us once coming across a fatal crash in our car. We saw two cars smashed together, and a woman lying in the road bleeding to death. Her intestines were hanging out, and it was a horrible sight. Michelle started to scream, and we could not stop her for ages."

Mr. Proby's testimony is backed by several independent witnesses. Dr. Andrew Gillespie, who was the family doctor, said, "I believe it was something she pictured in a lot of conversations with Dr. Pazder and an over-active imagination. I remember her mother as a kindly woman. She died of cancer when Michelle was 14. There were several poisoning episodes in which the children got into mischief, but they were not serious."

A neighbor, Alice Okerstrom, agrees. "I dismissed the book as crazy. The mother was a nice, gracious lady. A little girl could not have been tortured without someone hearing."

Diana Lockyer, whose husband was head of the cancer unit at the local hospital, was a close friend of the Probys. She too was "outraged" at the book. Her daughter Gillian was Michelle's best friend. Gillian said: "Virginia was like a second mother to me. I certainly never had a bad feeling about her."

The next important witness is Michelle's first husband, Doug Smith, a chartered surveyor. Although he would not speak to us directly, a close friend said he was extremely bitter. Not once during their marriage or the birth of their daughter did Michelle ever mention her experience, which included such hideous psychological torture as being imprisoned in a cage with live snakes and being forced to eat a soup of worms.

Michelle went to Dr. Pazder for therapy sessions and eventually left her husband. Dr Pazder was also married, with four children.

The Royal Canadian Mounted Police says there has never been one prosecution in Victoria for Satanic practices. And a Canadian author who is an expert on the occult, Jean Kozocari, said. "There was never any Satanism in Victoria in the 1950s. The most interesting group there were wife swappers."

Finally the conclusions of the Roman Catholic Church: When the book first appeared, Bishop Remi de Roo spent many hours interviewing Michelle and listening to tapes of her therapeutic sessions. He then arranged for her to fly to the Vatican to meet Cardinal Sergio Pignedoli, then head of the Secretariat for Non-Christians.

When the book was published in 1977, the Bishop wrote in a preface: "I do not question that for Michelle the experience was real. In time we will know how much of it can be validated. It will require prolonged and careful study. In such mysterious matters hasty conclusions could prove unwise."

In the meantime "ritual abuse" become a buzz-phrase among social workers, who believe that Michelle and her doctor bravely lifted the lid on practices which had going on for years without outsiders realizing it.

So what does the Roman Catholic Church now believe? Bishop de Roo's office told us, "He wants to distance himself from these people. More than ten years ago he asked the couple to provide him with details, but they never supplied all the information he required."

Dr. Pazder himself admits he is working in areas that are difficult to define. "It's an area where if you jump in too quickly, you get hysteria. People start seeing Satanists around every corner."

He says *Michelle Remembers* gave victims a voice to be heard and not be labeled crazy.

We then asked Dr Pazder, "Does it matter if it was true, or is the fact that Michelle believed it happened to her the most important thing?"

He replied: "Yes, that's right. It is a real experience. If you talk to Michelle today, she will say, 'That's what I remember.' We still leave the question open. For her it was very real. Every case I hear I have skepticism. You have to complete a long course of therapy before you can come to conclusions. We are all eager to prove or disprove what happened, but in the end it doesn't matter."

One wonders what the parents of Rochdale would have to say about that!

Appendix 2: *Examiner* "Satanic Ritual Abuse" Series #1

A Presumption of Guilt: "Warped" Child, Twisted Justice
- by A.S. Ross
- Paul Avery contributed to this report
San Francisco Examiner
Sunday, September 28, 1986, page #A-1

Allegations of ritualistic child abuse have been cropping up in police reports, therapists' files, and child welfare caseloads nationwide. They have taken a destructive toll of accused and accuser. This is the first of two Examiner *reports on the pursuit of these allegations. Today: How cases are being mishandled.*

My God, what has happened to our community? People are asking, Have we got sexual abuse that has turned into a horrible cancer - murders, Satanic cults? Or do we have brainwashed children Accusing innocent persons of nonexistent crimes?

- Glenn Cole, Foreman of the 1984-85 Kern County Grand Jury

The same question asked by Glenn Cole has been raised in dozens of other U.S. communities as hundreds of children have leveled bizarre accusations of sexual abuse, Satanic rituals, and grotesque murders against preschool teachers, baby sitters, neighbors, family, and friends.

From Bay Area suburbs and southern California beach communities to small towns in the Midwest and working-class neighborhoods in the South, authorities have spent millions of dollars and hundreds of thousands of hours trying to find the answer. Mostly they have not succeeded. Tomorrow the California Attorney General will release results of an unprecedented, nine-month investigation of a Kern County mass-molestation case. It is expected to be highly critical of the authorities' handling of the case.

Kern County became a textbook example of how so-called ritualistic child-abuse cases, inflated by overzealous investigators with little hard evidence, have seemingly careened out of control. At the height of the county's 18-month probe into what has been called the "Gonzales-Thomas molestation ring", nearly 80 adults were implicated and more than two dozen children said to have been killed in Satanic ceremonies. Sheriff's deputies dragged lakes, dug up back yards, and searched homes looking for bodies. They found none, nor any other evidence of murder, but they did charge six people with child molestation.

Successive grand juries have already harshly criticized the Sheriff's Department and the county's Child Protective Services. The 1984-85 grand jury accused them, among other things, of leaking children's testimony to local service clubs and church groups before charges had been brought. The 1985-86 grand jury, went further, echoing criticisms made of several similar cases across the country: "A presumption of guilt appeared to pervade the transcripts available within the Welfare Department case files, and guilt by association was sufficient to bring charges against individuals."

Superior Court Judge Robert Baca angrily blames authorities for making the children involved "virtual prisoners" who were "brainwashed" to shore up shaky molestation cases against the adults. "The molestation, if there was, is not what caused this warped child," Baca said of 9-year-old Michael Nokes, a key witness in the case. "The blame is on the system. For the sake of the prosecution's case, this child was taken into the system and completely warped."

The Widening Circle

Like similar cases with ritualistic overtones in Los Angeles, Sacramento, and Memphis, the Kern County case started out small enough. In June 1984 Gerardo Gonzales, a 29-year-old mechanic, was arrested after 5-year-old Brooke Hastings told authorities that Gonzales and a man she knew as "Thomas" had molested her and a friend three times. Under separate interrogation, Gonzales' 6-year-old daughter Melissa said her father had abused her and her 3-year-old brother Tyson. She identified the other man as Will Thomas, a local preacher and Gonzales' karate instructor. Gonzales has been in county jail awaiting trial ever since. Thomas is free on $50,000 bail.

The case had problems from the outset. According to Kern County Sheriff's files, Brooke twice failed to identify Thomas from a photograph, and Tyson at one point told investigators that Brooke was "lying". More significantly, at a preliminary hearing for Gonzales and his wife Cheryl, who had also been charged, Melissa denied repeatedly - over two days of questioning - that she had been molested. Asked why she originally said she had been, Melissa replied: "First I said they didn't. Then he (a Sheriff's deputy) said they didn't believe me, so I had to say they did happen."

Nonetheless the investigation proceeded. More adults were named; more children were taken from parents and placed in county shelters and foster homes. Fresh stories emerged of drugs, boards, chains, and handcuffs. Photographs were said to have been taken, but none was ever found.

Among the ever-widening circle of adults being accused were Michael Nokes' parents: Brad, 28, an oil-rig operator and Mary, 32. They were charged after a 7-year-old girl identified Mary Nokes as the wife of "the man with the pony tail" who had allegedly molested the girl and other children. In the course of hundreds of interrogations, Michael Nokes was to tell investigators that he was molested on scores of occasions by dozens of adults - including his parents, aunts, uncles, grandparents, family friends, ministers, a Child Protective Service worker, and an assistant district attorney. But his early and repeated denials that he had been molested, records show, were ignored. On one occasion, according to a Sheriff's report, Michael said that he had lied about the molestations because CPS worker Cory Taylor told him to. Michael added that he had not told the truth because "he didn't think Cory would believe him".

In a tape-recorded interview with a detective hired by the Nokes family, Michael said Taylor told him she knew he had been molested, and she told him to "tell it or we're going to sit in this room all day until you do".

"I just don't recall it," Taylor said in an interview. "I'm sure I wouldn't have said those things." Taylor, who interviewed Michael twice, said she felt the two of them "just didn't hit it off". At a recent court hearing, Michael's therapist, Dr. Jay Fisher, said such interviewing techniques would have a "profound negative effect" and may have been why Michael later named Taylor as an abuser as well.

By March 1985 Michael's stories, and those of Melissa Gonzales and several other children, had progressed from the incredible to the grotesque to the hallucinatory. In a March 21 report, Michael told investigators that children were taken to Will Thomas' church to "pray to the Devil". The assembled adults, according to Michael's testimony, smeared the children with excrement, forced them to drink blood, and sacrificed animals, including birds, cats, dogs, turtles, snakes, wolves, and a "baby bear".

Two weeks later the stories turned to killing humans. In one episode, Michael said, he, Melissa, and the adults hurled knives into one of Michael's cousins. "Once all the knives were thrown by the adults and the chanting was over," according to Michael's testimony as described in an investigator's report, "that baby Jonathan's head looked like the ring that was around Jesus' head."

Altogether 77 Bakersfield adults were swept up by the bewildering allegations. They were supposed to have stabbed to death as many as 29 infants, burned them in fire-pits, and even eaten some of them. Investigators seemed to dismiss charges by parents, defense attorneys, and grand jury members that such stories were childish fantasies, perhaps embellished in therapy sessions.

The Sheriff's Department's exhaustive search for evidence of ritual murder continued, only to come up dry. "Baby Jonathan", now 3-1/2, along with other children identified by Michael and others as being murdered, is alive and at home with his parents - who had at one time been accused of being part of the Satanic ring. Three months after the Satanic stories surfaced, in the wake of a collapsing investigation, the grand jury asked the state Attorney General to enter the case.

The Reckoning

"I still believe the children were telling the truth," said Sheriff Larry Kleier. "They don't tell these ritualistic things out of nowhere." Sheriff's Lt. Brad Darling, who headed the county's Satanic task force, believes a malignant group of Satanists who allegedly left dead dogs on detectives' front porches and used "divide and conquer tactics" helped stymie the investigation.

Last October District Attorney Edward Jagels declared the investigation "essentially complete". During the probe 21 children were removed from their parents. Five of them, including Michael Nokes, his younger sister Angela, and Melissa Gonzales, have seen little or nothing of their parents since then.

Fifteen adults, including the six defendants, voluntarily took and passed lie-detector tests. Gerardo and Cheryl Gonzales and Will Thomas still face more than 40 counts each of child molestation. Their trial is scheduled to begin October 27.

Leroy George Stowe, Jr., a hospital technician, was sentenced to 30 years in prison after a jury, persuaded by testimony of Michael Nokes and Stowe's youngest son, convicted him in March 1985 of abusing one of his three children. But soon after Stowe entered Folsom Prison, Judge Baca released him on bail pending appeal when questions arose about Michael's credibility.

Brad and Mary Nokes face 133 counts of child abuse, charges that were reinstated in July by a state appeals court. A lower court dismissed the charges in May 1985 after the county welfare department would not let defense doctors physically examine Michael. In a Catch-22 ruling, the appeals court said such an examination might have been too traumatic for Michael if he had already been abused. "I really don't know what they put him through," said Mary Nokes, who has not seen Michael for more than 18 months. "I can only guess."

One person who is familiar with Michael's ordeal is Marge Judd, his current foster mother. "I don't know any more than any of you as to what traumatized Michael Nokes," she said, "but I'm the woman that holds him at 2 in the morning when he is screaming in his bed, when he is saying, 'Make them leave me alone, Mom. Get them away.' I don't know who he is talking about any more than you do. I just know that this little boy, something is scaring him very much."

Appendix 3: *Examiner* "Satanic Ritual Abuse" Series #2

Satanism or Mass Hysteria?
Experts Split on Reasons for Rise in Abuse Cases
- by A.S. Ross
- Ivan Sharpe contributed to this report
San Francisco Examiner - Sunday, September 28, 1986, page #A-8.

Child-abuse cases tinged with ritualistic or Satanic overtones have sprung up all over the country in the last three years. In California and eight other states, an *Examiner* survey has found that 13 cases have reached court and at least 17 more have been investigated.

Police, therapists, and children's advocates believe that Satanic rings are molesting and killing children as part of some grotesque ritual. Defense attorneys and religious scholars accuse the authorities of creating a climate reminiscent of the 17th-century Salem witch trials.

Caught in the middle are traumatized children; jailed, emotionally-shattered, and economically-ruined parents; and a legal system unable to cope with a phenomenon nobody understands. But while many of the investigations, usually based on uncorroborated testimony of children, have collapsed for lack of physical evidence, so others have arisen.

The first such case to surface was the McMartin Preschool case in Los Angeles. The national coverage given to its lurid allegations of "naked movie-star games" and references to robes and candles may have triggered a rash of "copy cat" allegations, some observers believe.

Key law-enforcement offers offer a grimmer explanation. "For some reason, in the 1980s," said San Francisco Police Officer Sandra Gallant, "children are being sexually abused and possibly even murdered during what appears to be Satanic-type rituals." Gallant, regarded as an expert on occult crimes by other law-enforcement agencies, has called for a task force to combat what she regards as a nationwide conspiracy.

Others dispute her views. "I'm afraid what we're seeing is mass hysteria," said Evangeline Brown, a Contra Costa County deputy public defender who represented a Concord man accused of molesting his 7-year-old daughter during Satanic rites. "I'm convinced there are many people being wrongly accused in this climate of fear."

A review of court documents and police reports, and interviews with parents, children, and law-enforcement officials indicate that most of these cases have rested solely on the unsubstantiated word of children. Often investigators have tainted cases by asking children leading questions and prematurely disclosing rumors to already-fearful parents. "It's been an atrocity the way these cases have been handled," said Don Casey, a Dade County, Florida assistant district attorney. Last October Casey gained one of the few convictions in a ritualistic child-abuse case, involving a baby-sitting service operator in Miami.

The greatest difficulty for investigators is that, with rare exceptions, there has been no physical evidence to support the children's stories of rituals, drugs, costumes, and human and animal sacrifices. Photographs the children say were taken have never been found. Supposed murder victim, have turned up alive. "It's difficult with 4-year-olds," said an investigator connected to the Fort Bragg case. "Our problem is to try to sort out what's real and what's imagined."

The human toll of these investigations, wherever they have led, has been high.

• The daughters of a Sacramento restaurant manager, whom the children accused of being involved in human sacrifices and of making "snuff" films, suffer from what doctors describe as "severe emotional trauma". They are confined to psychiatric treatment centers in San Francisco - at a cost to taxpayers of more than $300,000.

Last October a judge dismissed charges against the father, Gary Dill, and four other defendants. The judge said the girls were victims of their "severely mentally ill" grandmother, who had planted the stories in their heads. Dill now has a $5/hour auto parts job in San Francisco. He has seen his children once in three years.

Sacramento attorney Wade Thompson, who represents Dill, said the daughters may never recover fully. "You hate to say any human beings are beyond repair," he said. "But the chances of these kids returning to normalcy are slim to none."

• Millions of dollars in civil suits are still pending against Scott County, Minnesota authorities in a case labeled a "tragedy" by state Attorney General Hubert H. Humphrey III. Grim stories of murder, kidnapping, and mutilation involving more than 60 adults and more than 100 children surfaced 2-1/2 years ago in the tiny Minnesota River Valley town of Jordan. The FBI and state investigators ultimately determined the stories were fabricated. At one point 24 adults were charged with a variety of child-abuse felonies. Only one was convicted after confessing.

The state Attorney General's report said that the case suffered from a "fundamental lack of evidence" and "prolonged interrogation" of the children that resulted in "confusion between fact and fantasy". The case is returning to haunt Jordan. The prosecutor, R. Kathleen Morris, who at one point faced impeachment proceedings, is running for election as Scott County District Attorney in November. Her opponent has been using the handling of the Jordan case as an issue. Morris still believes the stories and says, "If it hadn't been for the press, these kids wouldn't have been returned to their parents."

• Failure to prosecute purported Satanic child molesters in Los Angeles and Fort Bragg has left parents frightened and bitter. A number have moved. "I know something terrible happened to my daughter," said Audrey Sullins, a 35-year-old Fort Bragg mother who believes her 4-year-old daughter was used in gruesome rituals involving crosses and coffins. A four-month Mendocino County Sheriff's investigation last year turned up no physical evidence and resulted in no arrests.

• Six of the original seven defendants in the McMartin Preschool molestation case in Los Angeles have lost their homes and been declared legally indigent. In the wake of the longest - and at $4 million the most expensive - pretrial proceeding in California, five of the accused were freed last January after the district attorney decided the case against them was "incredibly weak". The two remaining defendants face trial next month on more than 100 counts of molestation.

In the face of such problems, some prosecutors are attempting to play down Satanic allegations, convinced that such stories harm what they regard as otherwise-provable child-abuse cases.

In the 1985 Concord case, in which jurors deadlocked 6-6, Deputy District Attorney Hal Jewett said jurors who voted for acquittal later told him they did not believe the girl's allegations of devil-worship and murder. "I wanted the jury to focus on child sexual abuse. I wanted to de-emphasize the Satanic aspect as much as possible," Jewett said. "But it was something you either had to swallow whole or reject whole. I had absolutely nothing to corroborate the girl's stories of Satanic worship. I have no doubt that, if she hadn't talked about that, they would have believed she was a victim of molestation."

"We're doing children a disservice if we bring these cases to court only to see them dismissed," said Rita Swann of CHILD, Inc., a children's advocacy group based in Sioux City, Iowa. "To bandy about charges that can't be substantiated ... will make the public cynical about the issue, and make them less likely to believe a child's story of sexual abuse in the future."

Cases from the Bay Area and the West

PORT ANGELES, Wash. — Surfaced February 1986. A preschool owner and son faced three counts of "indecent liberties" involving five children. Children's allegations included use of feces, sticks and hooded robes and that adults "cut the babies." The son was evaluated twice for competency to stand trial and was declared competent in the second evaluation. "We're just going to have to deal with the weird stuff at the trial," a Clallum County prosecutor said.

FORT BRAGG — Surfaced January 1985. Sheriff's Department conducted six-month investigation of Jubilee Day Care Center after more than a dozen children, some as young as 4, said they had been ritually abused, filmed or photographed and had witnessed child murders. License was revoked over unrelated molestation charges. Authorities brought no criminal charges, citing lack of physical evidence. "All we really have is the testimony of very young kids, who probably couldn't qualify as competent witnesses," former Assistant District Attorney Hugh Cavanagh said.

CONCORD — Surfaced August 1983. Vehicle mechanic was accused by stepdaughter of being part of satanic cult that forced her to kill an infant and eat feces as well as engage in ritualistic sex abuse in early 1980s. Jury split 6-6 in May 1985. No new trial is scheduled.

ATHERTON — Surfaced May 1985. A 17-year-old Woodside High School honor student accused her stepfather and 10 other adults of sexually abusing her. She said she had witnessed blood-drinking, animal mutilations and human sacrifice. Dead cats were found in girl's locker and back porch, according to investigators, who said the girl had marks indicating physical abuse. The case was investigated by Atherton Police Department, the San Mateo County sheriff and the district attorney's office. No charges were brought. The case is "active but not closed," said Elaine Tipton, an assistant district attorney.

FREMONT — Surfaced spring 1985. A 5-year-old boy said he was picked up at school by an adult and taken to a house, possibly a church, where he was sexually abused by at least two men and was photographed. He said he had observed mutilation of animals and human beings. Case was investigated by Fremont Police Department and Alameda County district attorney's office. "It's a suspended case, but not forgotten," said Fremont police Detective Vince Mastracci.

CORNELIUS, Ore. — Surfaced January 1985. The investigation involved nine children, some as young as 3, and three adults at a day-care center. "Little by little, children have talked of robes, candles and murder," an investigator said. Local police and the Washington County district attorney's office investigated. No arrests made.

ATASCADERO — Surfaced August 1985. Police dug for bodies of 15 children and infants they were told were ritually slain and buried in a thicket near the home of a couple previously sentenced to more than 500 years in prison for child molestation in Kern County (not related to alleged "Gonzales-Thomas ring"). Police found only animal bones. No charges were filed.

SACRAMENTO — Surfaced June 1984. Charges against Gary Arthur Dill, 34, and four other defendants were thrown out last October by a municipal judge after Dill's two daughters testified they had made up stories of grotesque abuse and "snuff" films on their grandmother's orders. The two girls were in the McAuley Neuropsychiatric Institute at St. Mary's Hospital in S.F., being treated for "post-traumatic stress syndrome" for months after the supposed reason for the treatment had been judged to be false. "Sadly," Judge Ronald Robie commented, "health professionals and law enforcement officials were unable to recognize or do anything about the senseless harm being done to these children."

RENO — Surfaced March 1984. The owner of a baby-sitting service and two workers faced 69 charges of sexual molestation and mental harm involving as many as 26 children. Several children had talked of chanting, singing and a "naked movie-star game." Trial date postponed until report of three psychiatrists appointed by the court to evaluate interviews with children was complete.

BAKERSFIELD — Surfaced June 1984. The so-called "Gonzales-Thomas ring" was alleged to have engaged in mass molestation, satanic rituals and child murders. Leroy George Stowe Jr. is appealing a 30-year molestation sentence. Five other defendants face hundreds of molestation charges. No evidence of murders or satanic rituals found. Report on yearlong investigation by state attorney general into handling of this and other Kern County mass-molestation cases is expected Monday.

Information compiled from FBI and local police reports, court transcripts and other documents, and interviews with law enforcement officials and defense attorneys

CARSON CITY — Martha Helen Felix, 37, and nephew Felix "Paco" Ontiveros, baby-sitting service operators, face trial on 29 counts of felony child abuse involving 14 children. Children made reference in a September 1985 preliminary hearing and elsewhere to animal-killings, blood-drinking and other rituals. Photos belonging to defendants of "mummified children" were found and produced at preliminary hearing. No evidence of mutilated animals was found.

LOS ANGELES COUNTY — Surfaced October 1984. Sheriff's task force and state Department of Social Services investigated allegations "strikingly similar" to the McMartin Pre-School case at preschools in several communities, including Torrance, Pico Rivera, Whittier, Placentia, Covina and Lomita. Testimony in Torrance case included references to animal and human sacrifices and to hooded figures in dark robes dancing and chanting in a circle. Several preschools temporarily shut down. The task force spent more than $1 million, identified 56 suspects, searched homes and businesses and interviewed 100 adults and several hundred children. No criminal charges have been filed. The task force was disbanded last October. "We are not cutting off parents or closing the books," said Lt. Richard Willey.

MANHATTAN BEACH/The McMartin Pre-School case — Surfaced August 1983. Ray Buckey, 27, and his mother, Peggy McMartin Buckey, 60, face trial Oct. 21 on 100 counts of child abuse. A substantial number of the 349 children who told therapists at the Children's Institute they had been molested also described satanic rituals involving hooded adults in local churches and graveyards, animal sacrifices and blood-drinking. More than 100 other charges were dropped against five other defendants, including the school's owner, 77-year-old Virginia McMartin, after an 18-month preliminary hearing. District attorney said the evidence was "incredibly weak."

● **The Manhattan Ranch Pre-School case** — Surfaced summer 1984. After a 16-week trial, a teacher's assistant, Michael Ruby, 17, was released after the jury deadlocked on 11 counts of child molestation. Although pretrial testimony relating to underground passages and a haunted house was played down by the prosecution, jurors said children's contradictory testimony was the main reason for the impasse. No new trial is scheduled.

Across the country, 'a climate of fear'

NILES TOWNSHIP, Mich. — Surfaced August 1984. Allan Barkman, a teacher at the Small World Preschool, 90 miles east of Chicago, was convicted in April 1985 of molesting a 4-year-old boy and sentenced to 50 to 75 years. In court testimony and in interrogations, children alleged they were driven to barns near the Indiana border to be photographed and that Barkman snapped off the head of a chicken. His wife, who children said had dressed up in a witch's costume, was not charged. The conviction is being appealed.

DES MOINES, Iowa — Surfaced June 1985. Five adult members of a "Wicca" coven were convicted or pleaded guilty to several hundred counts of sexual abuse involving teen-age boys going back to 1979. Evidence seized by police included a set of "initiation rites for Satan." No evidence of ritualistic abuse or violence was found. Prosecutors, who said police were tipped off to the ring's activities by another member of the coven, believe occult activities were not connected to the sex ring.

SPENSER TOWNSHIP, Ohio — Surfaced March 1985. Lucas County sheriff's deputies excavated suburban woods and fields around Spenser Township, looking for 50 to 60 bodies after allegations that children had been sacrificed in satanic rituals during the previous 16 years. Many of them were newborns whose births were never recorded, Sheriff James Telb said. Police say they found "various ritualistic emblems" but no bodies.

PARKER, Ariz. — Surfaced October 1983. Four children told police in Omaha, Neb., and Parker that other children were being kidnapped from shopping malls by a satanic cult, drugged, abused and sacrificed. Police found no evidence. No charges have been filed.

Information compiled from FBI and local police reports, court transcripts and other documents, and interviews with law enforcement officials and defense attorneys.

WEST POINT, N.Y. — Surfaced July 1984. A yearlong FBI investigation concluded that there were "indications" of abuse at the West Point Child Development Center, but "insufficient evidence to prosecute" after investigators interviewed 950 people including hundreds of children aged 2-6. Army physician Walter Grote refused a promotion to major in 1985, accusing West Point officials of covering up the "presence of ritualized/satanic child abuse at West Point." Eight families of allegedly abused children have filed a $110 million lawsuit against West Point and the Army.

MALDEN, Mass. — Surfaced September 1984. The Fells Acre Day Care case. Gerald Amirault, 32, was convicted of 15 counts of child abuse, including rape and indecent assault, and sentenced to 30 to 40 years in state prison. Nine children, some as young as 3, testified that Amirault, known as "Tookie," sexually molested them in a "magic room" wearing a clown suit and white paint on his face. One child testified about birds and squirrels being killed, but this was not corroborated. Amirault's wife, Cheryl, 28, and his mother, Violet, 62, the owner of the school, face trial on similar charges.

JORDAN, Minn. — Surfaced September 1983. Twenty-four adults were accused of sexually abusing dozens of children. They were also alleged to have committed murders and mutilations. After a guilty plea by one suspect on straightforward molestation charges, and acquittal of another couple, all other charges were abruptly dropped. A state attorney general's report found extensive fabrication of the stories of torture and murder.

MAPLEWOOD, N.J. — Surfaced December 1985. Kelly Michaels, 24, a day-care center teacher in an affluent New Jersey suburb, awaits trial on 236 charges involving 31 children, aged 3-6, in what an Essex County prosecutor termed "repulsively bizarre acts" involving urine, feces, bloody tampons and peanut butter and jelly. Between October 1984 and April 1985, Michaels is alleged to have assaulted children with silverware, to have dressed in a black robe, played the piano in the nude and to have told the children she had "attributes like God." Released on her own recognizance, Michaels was recently evaluated by two psychiatrists and pronounced fit to stand trial, which may start in November.

LUZERNE COUNTY, Pa. — Surfaced March 1985. Male and female counselors at a church summer camp outside Wilkes-Barre allegedly molested a 6-year-old girl and her 8-year-old brother, forced them to have sex with animals, including oral sex with a goat, and to eat the raw heart of a dismembered deer. Still under investigation.

RICHMOND, Va. — Surfaced in fall 1984. Two children alleged they were abused in their home and forced to witness the murder of another child, whose mutilated body police had discovered about a year earlier. Police said they have found candles and other ritualistic paraphernalia, but said the children "would freeze up . . . we couldn't tell whether they were telling the truth or fantasizing." No allegations of rituals were raised in spring 1985 trial, in which one adult was convicted of a misdemeanor: contributing to the delinquency of a minor.

MIAMI — Surfaced September 1984. The Country Walk Day Care case. Francisco Fuster was convicted last October on 14 counts of child abuse, and sentenced to a minimum of 165 years in prison. His wife, Ilena, confessed and testified for the prosecution. She received a 10-year sentence. Testimony from the children, who were 1 to 3 years old at the time of the abuse, included references to anal rape with a crucifix, masks, animal killings, chanting and feces eating.

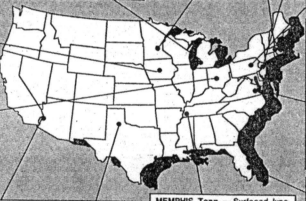

KING COUNTY, Texas — Eight children, aged 4 to 15, allege they were sexually molested by as many as 10 adults who, they say, injected them with drugs, forced them to eat body parts and to watch the murder of an adult and a child. Also said cauldrons, ropes, knives and skeletons were used in rituals. State agencies investigating. No charges filed.

MEMPHIS, Tenn. — Surfaced June 1984. Four adults, including the Rev. Paul Shell, face trial on 18 counts of child abuse involving up to 26 children, who said Shell and three other teachers at the Georgian Hills Early Childhood Center wore masks and robes, burned the children with candles, locked them in cages and baptized them in the name of the devil. Awaiting judge's ruling on a trial.

Appendix 4: *Examiner* "Satanic Ritual Abuse" Series #3

Going to Trial despite a Questionable Probe
- by A.S. Ross
San Francisco Examiner - Sunday, September 28, 1986, page #A-8.

Investigators knew they had problems with the Georgian Hills Baptist Church case long before it went to court. A confidential memo to the FBI written by two Memphis investigators, dated February 5, 1985, and obtained by the Examiner, said the allegations were "so irrational and so unbelievable" that "nothing has surfaced that connects anybody to the criminal act".

The case began with the June 1984 arrest on molestation charges of Francis Ballard, 54, a former Georgian Hills teacher. Particularly shocking to the parishioners of what one described as a "conservative, Bible-preaching church" were publicized accounts of the children, who said that they were drugged, filmed, burned with candles, and locked in cages. They reportedly saw animals slain, and said their parents' lives were threatened if they told the "secret".

But, the memo said, because of the difficulties of interviewing children so young, "they required a lot more leading than would be desirable with older victims". Also, the memo said, some parents probably "coerced or improperly extracted" information from their children. The memo also said: "When re-questioned, those children who had denied (being molested) ... admitted to also being abused."

Yet three months after the memo was written, the pastor of the church, the Rev. Paul Shell, 65; part-time teacher Betty Stimpson; and her son Jeff, 24, were indicted by a grand jury on 14 counts of aggravated rape involving 26 children ages 2-5.

As in most cases of this sort, the children's testimony is the crux of the prosecution's evidence. The defense is likely to challenge how that testimony was obtained. Dr. Ben Bursten, Chairman of the Psychiatry Department of the University of Tennessee, was asked by prosecution to listen to tapes of one child being interviewed by authorities. In a court affidavit he was highly critical of their methods. "In my opinion," he said, "the interviewers put words in the child's mouth. They virtually accused the child of holding back secrets when the information they wished was not forthcoming."

In a telephone interview, Bursten said one investigator told a child, "I can look in your eyes and tell what you know," and then, "Unless you tell it, it is always in there."

"That is a terrible thing to say to a young child who is led to believe adults can magically ferret inside their minds," he said.

A prosecution psychiatrist defended the technique, saying children are unlikely to make spontaneous disclosures of abuse to parents or investigators.

Asked how strong a case he thought there was, an assistant prosecutor said, "I frankly do not know ... It's just going to be the kids. Their credibility is going to be the major issue in this case."

A trial date is pending.

Appendix 5: *Examiner* "Satanic Ritual Abuse" Series #4

A Presumption of Guilt: Child-Abuse Cults: How Real?
Experts are divided over credibility of children's testimony.
- by A.S. Ross
- Ivan Sharpe contributed to this report
San Francisco Examiner - Monday, September 29, 1986, page #A-1.

Allegations of ritualistic child abuse have been cropping up in police reports, therapists' files, and child-welfare caseloads nationwide. They have taken a destructive toll of accused and accusers alike. This is the second of two Examiner *reports on the pursuit of these allegations. Today: The search for Satanic cults.*

The eerie phenomenon of young children branding teachers, parents, and family friends as murderous devil-worshippers over the past three years has defied clear explanation. Court cases and investigations throughout California and the nation have crumbled either for lack of evidence or because of bizarre, unbelievable testimony.

But to a core of police investigators and child advocates, ritualistic and Satanic child abuse is the latest twist in the long history of crimes against children. They compare their lack of success in proving it exists to the societal skepticism that surrounded allegations of incest in the not-so-distant past. "I predict in five years the courts will believe children when they say they are involved in Satanic rituals," said Sandra Baker of the Sacramento Child Sexual Abuse Treatment Program.

San Francisco Police intelligence Officer Sandra Gallant agrees. "It can't be just coincidence that kids are telling the same stories across the country," said Gallant, whom other law-enforcement agencies regard as an expert on "Satanic" crimes. "The rituals are detailed and very consistent. A young child could not make them up."

Disbelievers, however, say that is precisely what the children are doing. "The phenomenology of the Salem witch trials is being created all over again," said theologian Aidan Kelly of Holy Family College in San Mateo. "That is, innocent adults are being accused by hysterical children."

Like the religious cult debates of the 1970s, groups of competing experts have traveled around the country, proclaiming their views in courts, community meetings, and television studios. "Talk of Satanic child-abuse has become the pop-art of the child-abuse field," said Aline Kidd, a psychology professor at Mills College.

Child-abuse cases with ritualistic or Satanic overtones have figured in 13 court cases in California and eight other states. At least 17 more have been investigated. But in their pursuit of answers, investigators and child advocates have been relying on, and conveying to other agencies, information and sources that are often questionable - and sometimes wrong. Critics say that such misinformation adds to the fear and confusion. For example:

• The prosecutor in a forthcoming ritualistic child-abuse case said she had relied on a book written by Canadian psychiatrist Larry Pazder for background information on the subject. The book, *Michelle Remembers*, is a synthesis of taped psychotherapy sessions in which a patient of Pazder's recalls fantastically grotesque childhood memories of being in a Satanic cult that, among other things, cut up bodies and stitched them back together in bizarre anatomical configurations.

No corroborating evidence has ever been offered to support the stories. "It was Michelle's fantasy, and Pazder encouraged it," said Gordon Melton, Director of the Institute for the Study of American Religions at the University of California, Santa Barbara.

Nonetheless Pazder said in an interview that he has acted as a consultant to the Los Angeles Police Department and to parents throughout the country.

• Child advocate Ken Wooden said on a Phil Donahue television show on Satanism that there was evidence people were "committing what appears to be human sacrifices and incredible child abuse. I mean incredible tales of kids being molested while in the incubator, little babies." Asked during an interview what the evidence was to support such startling statements, Wooden said: "All I know is I'm getting similar stories from little kids all over the country, telling me similar things." Asked what other evidence there might be, Wooden replied, "Their drawings, their knowledge, their sophistication."

(Wooden is the founder of the National Coalition for Children's Justice. He co-produced an ABC News *20/20* segment entitled "The Devil Worshippers", which was largely devoted to ritualistic child abuse, in May 1985. He also mailed a detailed questionnaire on what to look for in ritualistic abuse cases to 3,500 prosecuting attorneys across the country last year.)

One Pennsylvania prosecutor, who called Wooden "my mentor", said he had sent his own investigators to be "debriefed" by Wooden after a child-abuse case with ritualistic overtones surfaced near Wilkes-Barre, Pennsylvania last year.

There have also been instances of police investigators' passing on to other concerned groups erroneous information on current cases.

Kern County Sheriff's Lt. Brad Darling told a child-abuse symposium in San Jose last April that tests at the home of a family suspected of being involved in mass molestations and child murders revealed evidence of "blood spatters, blood smears, and blood wiped away ... wherever the children said they occurred". Darling, who headed Kern County's Satanic child-abuse task force for five months last year, told Los Angeles County Sheriff's investigators the same thing in May 1985, according to a police memo obtained by the *Examiner*. At the time the L.A. authorities were investigating a rash of ritualistic child-abuse allegations that had surfaced in the wake of the celebrated McMartin Preschool case.

However a May 25, 1985 Kern County laboratory report obtained by the Examiner stated that its tests of the areas were "negative". In an interview Darling expressed surprise about the lab report.

At the San Jose symposium, according to a transcript of his remarks obtained by the *Examiner*, Darling had also said that, during the Kern County investigation, it "seem(ed) almost like SOP (Standard Operating Procedure). You got up, and you picked the dead dog up off your porch, or the dead chicken, or whatever it was ... they anointed your house with over the evening." In an interview he said he had heard that dead chickens had been found at a detective's house "two or three times", and that a dead dog had been found once outside of a therapist's house.

In Kern County stories of Satanic rituals had circulated in individual and group therapy sessions attended by allegedly-molested children. Explaining the stories, Carolyn Heim, the children's therapist, once told a reporter that she believed some of the allegedly-sacrificed children were what she called "altar babies". "An altar baby is a baby that is conceived for the purpose of sacrifice," Heim said. "That is a home birth; there is never a recorded birth certificate."

That such bizarre and unsupported notions have gained credence among investigators, critics say, does not reflect a new wave of religious superstition but rather what defense attorney Walter Urban has called "the burgeoning child-abuse industry". "The whole thinking is that there is a huge number of pedophiles in the United States who were virtually unheard-of and totally unknown until the 'experts' discovered them," said Urban, who defended preschool teacher Betty Raidor in the McMartin case. "They won't accept a denial from the children that nothing happened because they're the 'experts'," he said. "They say, 'I know something happened. You're just afraid to tell me.' And all of a sudden the kid's starting to roll."

Referring to techniques he saw used by therapists in videotaped interviews with children in the McMartin case, Urban said: "The children are encouraged to play; they're encouraged to freely associate. And all of a sudden you have kids talking the way kids do. They talk about monsters and bodies and blood and kill, kill, kill."

Others have pointed to what Kenneth Lanning of the FBI's Behavioral Research Unit has described as a "cross-contamination of ideas" in which children and parents involved in mass-molestation cases compare stories with others.

But many child experts say it's extremely unlikely, if not impossible to influence large numbers of children into telling similarly-detailed stories. "Besides," said Dr. Roland Summit, a psychologist attached to UCLA-Harbor Medical Center, "there is no professional in the world that I know of who would come up with a screwball story ... (or) implant something in the child ... that could lead to criminal charges."

Despite the collapse of so many ritual abuse cases, Summit and others still believe the events took place. Sacramento County District Attorney Rich Lewkowitz said the dismissal of charges in Sacramento's "snuff film" abuse case last year "reinforces a belief in my mind ... that there is an entrenched prejudice to disbelieve children, especially when it has to do with something gruesome and horrific."

They point to the conviction of a Miami baby-sitting service operator last December as evidence that ritualistic abuse is real. The County Walk Babysitting Service, up to a year ago, was apparently the scene of nightmarish abuse, involving masks, feces & urine, and a "cut off your head" game, according to court testimony that resulted in a life term for Cuban ex-convict Francisco Fuster. Fuster's wife testified that he raped her with a cross and strung her up on a punching bag in front of the children. Prosecutors told the *Examiner* that even more bizarre and grotesque allegations were kept out of the trial for fear of jeopardizing the case.

But how typical these cases are, and whether they are the work of isolated individuals or of organized groups, is disputed. "It's probably small groups of adults doing it as part of a sexual perversion," said San Francisco FBI Agent Joe Davidson, who was assigned last year to help keep track of ritual child-abuse cases. "It's a brainwashing type of technique used to scare and control the kids and members of the group."

Some academic observers agree. William Holmes of Northeastern University's Center for Applied Social Research has closely studied a case in Maiden, Massachusetts, where a day-care worker was recently convicted of molesting children while dressed in a clown suit. He said the use of "mystical elements" like costumes and masks in child abuse "is not done just for the sexual pleasure, but for the domination of a helpless victim ... to assert the authority of whoever is in charge."

"I don't think we need to worry about a Satanic conspiracy," said Professor Jeffrey Burton Russell of UC Santa Barbara, author of a four-volume work on the history of the Devil. "I do think we need to worry, like we've always had to, about individual psychopathic people roaming around."

Appendix 6: *Examiner* "Satanic Ritual Abuse" Series #5

How the Specter of Satanism led to L.A. Uproar in Child Care
- by Ivan Sharpe
San Francisco Examiner - Monday, September 29, 1986, page #A-6.

LOS ANGELES - Parents dug for bones, played detective in sleazy bars, trailed suspects, crept through graveyards at night, and threatened vigilante action. Determined to expose what they believe is the Devil's work, they put up "wanted" posters of suspected Satanic child abusers and offered rewards for pornographic photos of their children.

Preschool owners, teachers, and their attorneys met secretly to share stories of ruined lives. They organized protests and bought full-page newspaper ads suggesting that children with fertile imaginations could be led into saying anything.

From a single allegation of molestation in a respected preschool just south of Los Angeles, the specter of Satanism was to darken the entire Los Angeles basin. The Sheriff's Department formed a special task force, and it spent a year investigating the near-epidemic number of allegations.

Both accused and accusers say they have been assaulted, vandalized, and terrorized. And with a blizzard of lawsuits filed, almost everyone involved in Los Angeles' uproar over Satanism seems to be suing everybody else.

A Simple Beginning

It was August 1983 when a mother told Manhattan Beach police that her 2-year-old son allegedly had been molested by "Mr. Ray" at the Virginia McMartin Preschool. Questioned by an investigator, the boy indicated that other children also had been molested. Further questioning of others produced seemingly unending accounts of children being photographed in the nude.

Police were perplexed. Hundreds of children had gone to the 28-year-old McMartin nursery school. Lacking the personnel to interview all of them, police mailed letters to McMartin parents asking them to question their children about possible abuse at the school.

The stories of weird rituals did not begin to emerge until weeks after therapist Kee MacFarlane and her assistants at the Children's Institute began talking to the children in September 1983 at the request of the District Attorney's office.

MacFarlane remembers when the stories of ritualism first began. It was a 7-year-old talking about witches. "I didn't think much of it," she said. "I didn't believe it. I remember saying to a co-worker that I had a kid who seemed a little delusional."

Initially Virginia McMartin's grandson, Ray Buckley, was arrested. But he was soon released because of lack of evidence, only to be re-arrested six months later along with his mother, sister, grandmother, and three former teachers in what then-District Attorney Robert Philibosian, who was running for re-election, hailed as the biggest child-molestation case in U.S. history.

The counts grew to more than 200 against McMartin, the 77-year-old founder of the school; her daughter and co-owner Peggy McMartin Buckley, 27; Peggy Ann Buckley, 28; and teachers Betty Raidor, 65; Mary Ann Jackson, 57; & Babette Spitler, 36.

The preliminary hearing was an 18-month legal and emotional marathon, the longest in California history. It cost $4 million and produced 540 volumes of testimony. Along with allegations of rape and sodomy, episodes in which children were supposedly stripped and photographed during "naked movie star games", some young witnesses testified about hooded adults in churches and graveyards, grotesque animal sacrifices, and blood-drinking. The children said they were tortured and terrorized into silence by the slaughtering of rabbits, turtles, and birds, coupled with threats against their parents.

Parents were jubilant in January when Municipal Judge Aviva Bobb ordered all seven defendants to stand trial on 135 counts of child sexual molestation and conspiracy.

One week later District Attorney Ira Reiner announced that, although he believed the children had been molested at the school, he was dropping charges against five of the defendants because the evidence against them was "incredibly weak". Only Ray Buckley and his mother, Peggy McMartin Buckley, still stand accused. They are scheduled to be tried October 21 on 100 counts.

The Conspiracy Theory

None of this made any sense to McMartin parents, who launched an unsuccessful effort to persuade state Attorney General John Van de Kamp to reinstate the dropped charges.

Therapist MacFarlane said in an interview that 349 McMartin children had described some kind of sexual abuse. A substantial number, she said, had also described sadistic rituals.

Only 14 eventually testified in court. Some parents did not want to expose their children to the stress of the courtroom, but others later said prosecutors had told them their children's stories were too unbelievable. Prosecutors were less than pleased, for example, by one child's account of City Attorney James Hahn and movie star Chuck Norris molesting and whipping children tied to a pole.

MacFarlane scoffs at suggestions that she and other therapists brain-washed children into repeating startling stories of Satanic rituals. "I was very cautious about bringing this up with other children," she said. "There are some children who focus on this as the primary thing, and others who don't describe anything like that at all. I don't know whether that means some were involved and others weren't."

But what skeptics scathingly refer to as the contagion of fantasy, parent groups darkly describe as a huge Satanic conspiracy involving morticians and business people throughout southern California.

The Sheriff's task force and state Department of Social Services investigated the flood of allegations in the wake of the McMartin case at preschools in several southern California communities, including Torrance, Whittier, Placentia, Covina, and Lomita. The task force identified 56 suspects, searched several homes and businesses, and interviewed 100 adults and several hundred children. Several schools were shut down temporarily. But in October 1985, one year and $1 million later, the task force disbanded without making a single arrest.

Since then some parents have taken matters into their own hands. Last November Robert Currie, 52, the most vocal McMartin parent, vowed at a Hollywood press conference, with seven young alleged victims hidden behind a curtain, that "we are going to show that ritualistic abuse is happening all across the country". He set up a complaint hot-line to exchange information.

Currie and other parents then offered a $10,000 reward for pornographic pictures of children in the McMartin case. He was arrested for gun possession as he was waiting for an informant outside a low-rent Los Angeles nightclub last year.

Other parents rented a backhoe and excavated a vacant lot next to the preschool, hoping to substantiate their children's tales of tunnels and animal sacrifices. They unearthed some turtle shells and a few animal bones, which the police said proved nothing.

Two months later Pico Rivera mother Vickie Meyers led another small band of parents on a dig at the former site of the burned-out Old Molokan Church in Norwalk, where children in another alleged abuse case had supposedly witnessed Satanic sacrifices. They were luckier, uncovering hundreds of sawed bones in trash bags. But analysis showed they were animal bones - remains, a church member said, of meals. Meyers, her husband, and their three children moved last year after a judge dismissed molestation charges against two Pico Rivera couples. The judge said one 8-year-old boy was lying and another boy had admitted he lied.

The ordeal has been traumatic for the children, their parents, and former suspects. Once, with a reporter present, Meyers' 7-year-old son Jeffrey tried to choke himself while en route to testify in the case. "I wanted to kill myself so I wouldn't have to go to court," he later explained. In the courthouse cafeteria, when his mother and therapist tried to persuade him to talk to an attorney, he suddenly clasped his hands over his ears, began sobbing, and screamed, "I don't want to remember."

Fear, quarrels with spouses over children's behavior, and feelings of revenge have sent many parents to family therapists.

Although she is now free, former McMartin defendant Betty Raidor will never forget the red wristband she had to wear in jail to separate her from other inmates. It bore the words "Lewd acts with a child". She and her husband have sold their large home and depleted their $45,000 life savings to pay legal expenses. Nonetheless, Raidor said, she harbors no ill will. "I don't feel bitterness toward anyone," she said. "I have nothing but affection and sadness in my heart for the children."

Appendix 7: *Examiner* "Satanic Ritual Abuse" Series #6

Police Believe in Violent Cults
- by A.S. Ross
San Francisco Examiner - Monday, September 29, 1986, page #A-7.

"1 think every investigator in the field has made mistakes," says San Francisco Police intelligence Officer Sandra Gallant. "We're in a re-grouping process." Since 1980 Gallant has investigated "occult" and "Satanic" crimes and has consulted with other police departments. She also trains federal and local investigators about these topics. She is recommended frequently by other law-enforcement agencies as the primary expert on ritualistic and Satanic child abuse.

Gallant says, "There are just not clear-cut answers" to the phenomenon. "How much of it is real? How much of it is fantasy?" Despite the questions, she firmly believes that murderous, child-molesting Satanic cults exist

Testifying in Contra Costa County in May 1985, Gallant, who had been called as an expert witness in a case involving a 9-year-old girl who had accused her stepfather of abusing her and killing others in Satanic settings, said that the eating and drinking of human wastes, ferocious abuse of children, and even human sacrifice are both present and past characteristics of Satanic worship.

And in a detailed memo widely circulated among law-enforcement agencies last year, Gallant provides a description of a 200-year-old "Satanic Black Mass" whose celebrants would "cut the child's throat on the belly of (a naked) woman, and its blood will be caught in a chalice. The sacrifice of animals, young children, and infants was apparently commonplace," the memo added. "The stories that we are hearing today, in 1985, ring true of the practices held then."

But little evidence has surfaced to support Gallant's assertions, both then and now. Many modern historians dismiss the historical description as a myth, and believe that "black masses" - if they took place - were little more than theatrical, if obscene parodies. "Yes, there have been sexual psychopaths all through history," said historian Jeffrey Burton Russell of U.C. Santa Barbara. "But the notion of groups or any kind of organization doing it (ritualistic child abuse) over any period of time -there is simply no evidence of that."

Gallant acknowledges the difficulties police face investigating allegations of ritual abuse. "The problem is we are not finding any bodies," she says. "We are not finding any bodies, period."

Gallant says she is drawing up new guidelines for investigators. "I really feel they need to document the information as soon as they get it," she said. "In the past, they would not make assumptions that were not proven."

Appendix 8: *Examiner* "Satanic Ritual Abuse" Series #7

Van de Kamp Rips Probe of Molestation Cases
- by Joe Bigham, Associated Press
San Francisco Examiner - Monday, September 29, 1986, page #A-7.

BAKERSFiELD - State Attorney General John Van de Kamp said Monday that Kern County law enforcement and social agencies had mishandled an investigation of child-molestation cases that led to unfounded allegations of Satanic child sacrifices. At a press conference in Bakersfield, Van de Kamp called the highly-publicized investigation "one of the most complicated and bizarre in the nation".

The investigation began in June 1985 when Sheriff Larry Kleier said his office was checking allegations by a group of molested children that as many as 80 people were involved in a Satanic cult that practiced the sacrifice of infants. While some molestation convictions were eventually returned, no evidence of any cults or child killings was ever found.

Van de Kamp issued these criticisms:

• The Sheriff's Department did not always perform effectively in its role as chief investigator. The Attorney General said deputies had relinquished control and turned over the direction of their investigation to people untrained in the requirements of criminal law.

• Proper procedures for interviewing child witnesses were not followed, reports were inadequate, and little effort was made to find corroborating evidence.

• The District Attorney's legal assistance to the Sheriff's Department was "less than thorough".

Appendix 9: *Examiner* "Satanic Ritual Abuse" Series #8

State Blasts Kern's Handling of Bizarre Child-Abuse Case
- by Paul Avery
San Francisco Examiner -September 30, 1986, page #A-1.

BAKERSFIELD - Kern County authorities have been severely criticized by state Attorney General John Van de Kamp for their handling of a bizarre child molestation case. He said the findings of a year-long, $500,000 state review of the case showed that the county Sheriff's Department, District Attorney's office, and Child Protective Services unit shared blame for an investigation that got out of hand.

The case broke into the news last year. At the time the Kern County Sheriff Larry Kleier said he was "absolutely convinced" that a cult of 77 men and women had sexually molested 60 children and murdered as many as 29 infants during devil-worship rites in Bakersfield homes and churches. But Van de Kamp said his investigators - although not trying "to prove or disprove allegations of Satanic rituals or infanticide" - had found nothing that backed up Kleier's oft-repeated statement. "No physical evidence was found to substantiate such claims, while indeed much was found to disprove them," Van de Kamp said Monday at a crowded news conference in Bakersfield. He released an 80-page summary of the state's review. Also present during the hour-long session at the county library were about 100 Bakersfield residents, among them 15 lawyers and 30 or so of the people accused, though not charged. Frequent angry and emotional outbursts came from the audience. One woman shouted at Van de Kamp that dozens of children in Kern County had been "kidnapped from innocent parents" by Sheriff's deputies and Child Protective Services workers. Most of the audience applauded.

Van de Kamp directed his harshest criticism at the Sheriff's Department: "Deputies relinquished control and direction of their investigation to people untrained in the requirements of criminal law. Proper procedure for interviewing child witnesses was not followed. Reports were inadequate. And little effort, and I underscore this, was made to find corroborating evidence for children's statements."

The allegations of Satanic rituals and sacrifices of infants that investigators drew out in interrogations of some of the children "greatly eroded their credibility as witnesses," Van de Kamp said. "Many charges depended entirely on the veracity of the children. Once that was open to serious question, there could be little thought of taking those cases to court. Although 77 adults were named as suspects in the case, only six persons were ever arrested and charged with child-molest offenses. One man was convicted and sentenced to state prison for a 30-year term. He is presently free while his case is on appeal. The other five men and women charged are awaiting trial."

Kleier's office said he was unavailable to directly comment on the Attorney General's findings, but Sgt. Randy Raymond, Kleier's spokesman, later released a statement. "(The Attorney General's review) offers a number of suggestions that will be reviewed and put into effect where necessary and desirable," the statement read in part. "Child abuse and Satanic worship are not unique to Kern County. We have cooperated openly with the Attorney General in this investigation to hopefully learn better ways of accomplishing our goals. Be assured that the Kern County Sheriff's Department will continue to investigate and seek prosecution of child molesters and others who prey on our children."

District Attorney Edward Jagels also was unavailable to comment on the state review. His secretary said he was "out of town" but wouldn't say where. Van de Kamp criticized Jagels' office for failing to "press the Sheriff's Department for better reports and evidence until long after such deficiencies could be easily remedied".

The county's Department of Human Services, Van de Kamp said, generally "met its responsibilities in accordance with state and county policies. Yet one (Child Protective Services) worker contributed greatly to the confusion and unprofessionalism surrounding the case by assuming the role of criminal rather than civil investigator. And the case was further complicated by the unfortunate and poorly documented interaction by a number of (alleged) child victims in group therapy." Bill Curbow of the Department of Human Services said he felt the review's findings were accurate and that new guidelines and methods of dealing with "these kinds of complicated cases" would be implemented as soon as possible. Van de Kamp's office entered the case last year at the request of a Kern County grand jury after it investigated the three agencies' actions. Additionally many of the individuals accused of taking part in the alleged Satanic rituals and infant murders also asked the Attorney General to investigate. They said they were victims of a witch hunt.

Appendix 10: Presidio Headquarters Letter to Parents

Obtained by M.A.A. FOIA/PA Request

[All sic.]

DEPARTMENT OF THE ARMY
Headquarters, Presidio of San Francisco
Presidio of San Francisco, California 94129

December 15, 1986

Reply to the Attention of: Director of Personnel and Community Affairs

Dear Sponsor:

The Commander, Presidio of San Francisco has been apprised of a single incident of alleged child sexual abuse reported to have occurred at the Presidio Child Development Center. Immediately upon receipt of the report, proper law enforcement authorities were notified and concurrently the child was provided a thorough physical examination by physicians trained to handle cases of this nature. Thereupon, the child and the parents began a professional program of treatment to deal with the situation. Also on the day notification was received, the civilian employee believed responsible was removed from his position and subsequently assigned new duties away from the Center.

We have no reason to believe that other children have been victimized, but feel compelled to advise you of the facts as we know them and request your cooperation.

Our records reflect that the employee implicated in this incident may have provided care to your child during an eighteen-month period ending in November 1986. The following five time periods are involved:

1) September 1985 to May 1986: Preschool for Children 3 years of age, held in Room 2, Building 572.
2) September 1985 to May 1986: After School Hourly Care for School Aged Children, ages 5 to 12 years, held in Rooms 13 and 14, Building 563.
3) June 1986 to August 1986: Hourly Child Care Program for Children, ages 3 to 5 years, held in Room 3, Building 572.
4) September 1986 to November 1986: Preschool Hourly Care Program (Morning), Children ages 3 to 5 years, held in Room 13, Building 563, and
5) September 1986 to November 1986: Afternoon Kindergarten Program and afternoon Hourly Care Program, Children ages 3 to 6 years, held in Room 14, Building 563.

We have been in touch with health care professionals and experts in this area. Procedures have been developed which we believe will fully inform you of the facts and provide full services to your children. Also, this process permits professionals the opportunity to elicit from any youngsters who might have been exposed to this suspect relevant information concerning any possible inappropriate contact without further traumatizing the youngster involved.

The Presidio of San Francisco has established a Child Care Help Line, 561-5502, for parents to call with any questions they might have. The line is manned during regular duty hours by Ms. Cheek and the Family Advocacy Case Management Team. An answering service is provided so that parents can request a call back should they call after duty hours.

Our health care professionals have put together the enclosed check list of the most often exhibited symptoms of child abuse. In the event your child or children exhibit any of these symptoms, we request you not question them or conduct any kind of interrogation. You should contact Ms. Cheek or a member of the Team at telephone number 561-5502. We have arranged to have trained professionals, with your approval, interview your child. Improper questioning might well impede a child's ability to recall events, color his or her recollection and, in effect, make it difficult if not impossible to get a true reading of what really did happen.

As a follow-up, we are committed to providing treatment, care and counseling for any of the patrons of the Child Development Center who may seek our assistance. We will, of course, continue working with law enforcement authorities to support any criminal prosecution that might be warranted.

Please call the Child Care Help Line at 561-5502 if you have any questions.

Sincerely,
/s/ Walter W. Meyer
Lieutenant Colonel, U.S. Army
Director, Personnel and Community Activities

Enclosure

Facts for Families

According to the American Academy of Child Psychiatry the behavior of sexually abused children can include:

- Unusual interest in or avoidance of all things of a sexual nature.
- Sleep problems; nightmares.
- Depression or withdrawal from friends or family.
- Seductiveness.
- Statements that their bodies are dirty or damaged, or fear that there is something wrong with them in the genital area.
- Refusal to go to school, or delinquency.
- Secretiveness.
- Aspects of sexual molestation in drawings, games, fantasies.
- Unusual aggressiveness.
- Other radical behavioral changes.

Other authorities say the following behavior may also be considered:

- Difficulty in walking or sitting.
- Torn, stained, or bloody underclothing.
- Complaints of pain or itching in the genital area.
- Bruises or bleeding in external genitalia, vagina, or anal area.
- Displaying sophisticated or unusual sexual knowledge or behavior.
- Statements by the child that he or she has been sexually assaulted by a caretaker.

Appendix 11: Catherine Gould "Satanic Ritual Abuse" Checklist

<u>Catherine Gould, Ph.D. - Clinical Psychology</u>
12011 San Vicente Blvd., Suite 402 Brentwood, CA 90049
16161 Ventura Blvd., Suite 224 Encino, CA 91436 Telephone (213) 455-2260

May 23, 1986

<u>Symptoms Characterizing Satanic Ritual Abuse</u>
<u>Not Usually Seen In Sexual Abuse Cases</u>

Preschool Age Children

1. Preoccupation with urine and feces. Use of words for urine and feces that are not used at home (especially "baby" words like "poopoo").
2. Discussion of feces or urine on the face or in the mouth. Constant discussion of urine and feces at the dinner table.
3. Urine or feces strewn or smeared in the bathroom.
4. Inability to toilet train a child because the child is afraid (as opposed to not ready to be toilet trained or in a power struggle with the parent). The child may reveal fears of having to eat the feces if (s)he uses the toilet.
5. Preoccupation with passing gas. Using mouth to make gas sounds repeatedly, attempting to pass gas purposefully, wild laughter when the child or someone else passes gas. Use of words for passing gas which are not used at home.
6. Aggressive play that has a marked sadistic quality. The child hurts others intentionally, and seems to derive pleasure from doing so. Child destroys toys.
7. Mutilation themes predominate. Child acts out severing, sawing off, twisting or pulling off body parts. Aggressive words include cut, saw, slice, chop. Taking out eyes or removing other parts of the face and head are common themes.
8. Harming animals, or discussion of animals being hurt or killed.
9. Preoccupation with death. Child "practices" being dead, asks if (s)he will die at age 6 (the Satanic number), asks whether we eat dead people. Questions are distinguishable from normal curiosity about death by their bizarre quality.
10. Fear that there is something foreign inside the child's body - e.g., ants, ice, a bomb.
11. Fear of going to jail, being tied up or caged. References to the police coming after the child.
12. Fear of ghosts and monsters. Child's play frequently involves ghosts and monsters.
13. Fear of "bad people" taking the child away, breaking into the house, killing the child or the parents, burning the house down.
14. Child is clingy and may resist being left with babysitters, especially overnight.
15. Child's level of emotional or behavioral disturbance or developmental delay seems inconsistent with the parents' level of functioning.
16. Preoccupation with the devil, magic, potions, supernatural powers, crucifixions. Questions about these topics in families who do not believe in or discuss them are significant.
17. Odd songs or chants by the child that are sexual or otherwise bizarre, or that have a "you better not tell" theme.
18. Numbers or letters always written backwards (as opposed to a child who sometimes or often reverses numbers or letters). This is the "devil's alphabet".
19. References to drugs, "pills", candy, mushrooms, "bad medicine", or injections that seem peculiar for a preschool age child. References to drug-like or diaretic effects.
20. Constant fatigue, illness, flare-up of allergies. Vomiting.
21. References to people at school who are not school personnel. (This is because other adults join teachers for the abusive activities).
22. References to "my other Daddy", "my other Mommy", or "my other family" (meaning "at school").

23. References to television characters as real people. (This is because perpetrators take on names like "Barney Flintstone" so child's disclosures will be dismissed as television-inspired fantasies).
24. References to people in scary costumes, especially monsters, ghosts, devils, Dracula.
25. References to sexual activity with other children at school.
26. Discussion of being taken to people's houses or other locations (junkyard, church, hospital, another school) that are not normal school outings for which parents have given permission.
27. References to pictures or films being taken at the school at times other than when school pictures would normally be taken. Peculiar descriptions or references to nudity, sexual acts, unusual costuming, or animal involvement when discussing photography at school.
28. Marks on the child's back, unusual bruising, especially in patterns.
29. Nightmares or dreams of any of the above.

<u>Symptoms Characterizing Satanic Ritual Abuse</u>
<u>And Sexual Abuse</u>
Preschool Age Children

1. Low self-esteem, feeling of being "bad". Child feels deserving of punishment.
2. Child is fearful, clingy, regresses to "baby" behavior. Separation anxiety.
3. Child is angry, aggressive, acts out.
4. Child acts wild, uncontrolled, hyperactive.
5. Child is accident prone or deliberately hurts self.
6. Child is negativistic, resistant to authority. Child mistrusts adults.
7. Child is overcompliant with authority, overly pleasing with adults.
8. Child shows rapid mood changes.
9. Child is withdrawn, does not play, or plays in lethargic, unfocused way.
10. Child exhibits short attention span.
11. Child does not learn.
12. Child's speech is regressed and babyish. Child has delayed speech or speech disorder. Child's speech production decreases significantly.
13. Somatic complaints - stomachaches, nausea, vomiting.
14. Nightmares, sleep disorders.
15. Child is fearful of being touched. Child fears having genital area washed.
16. Child touches genitals or masturbates excessively. Child touches or tries to insert finger in rectum.
17. Child pulls down pants, pulls up dress, takes clothes off inappropriately.
18. Child touches others sexually or asks for sex.
19. Child is sexually provocative or seductive.
20. Child complains of vaginal or anal pain, burning when washed, pain when urinating or defecating.
21. Semen or blood stains on child's underwear.
22. Detailed and age-inappropriate understanding of sexual behavior.
23. "Hints" about sexual activity.
24. Complaints that an adult or older child is "bothering" the child.
25. Reference to blood or "white stuff" in genital area.
26. Statement that someone removed the child's clothes.
27. Statement that older child or adult exposed themselves to the child.
28. Statement that an older child or adult touched or penetrated child's bottom, vagina, rectum, mouth, etc.
29. Statement that child touched an older child's or adult's bottom, vagina, penis, rectum, etc.
30. Statement that the child witnessed sex acts.
31. On exam, relaxed sphincter, anal or rectal laceration or scarring, child relaxes rather than tenses rectum when touched.
32. On exam, enlargement of vaginal opening, vaginal laceration or scarring in girls. Sore penis in boys. Blood or trauma around genital area.
33. On exam, venereal disease.

Characteristics of Schools in which Satanic Ritual Abuse Occurs

1. It is our experience that so-called "open" schools are as prone to Satanic ritual abuse as are closed schools. That is, being able to walk directly into the classroom does not guarantee safety. We believe that a "watch" person alerts perpetrators that a parent is arriving, and the child is quickly produced.

2. We have found that several of the offending schools have two-way mirrors in the classrooms. These are almost never "single perpetrator" cases. Rather, from what the children tell us, the whole school seems to be involved. Therefore, the ability to look into the classroom and see what is going on provides no deterrent.

3. Personnel at offending schools usually do not seem obviously "strange". After a child discloses abuse at the school, the parent rarely thinks in retrospect that she should have suspected it based on the teachers' behavior. Some personnel at offending schools may even be. exceptionally "solicitous" of the child's academic progress. When the child does not progress (because (s)he is being abused) the school may recommend (s)he be retained an extra year.

4. The expense, prestige, religious or educational affiliation of a preschool seem to provide no assurance that the school is safe. Children from expensive, prestigious preschools have made extensive arid detailed allegations of abuse. Similarly, children from college and university affiliated preschools have alleged abuse. Religiously affiliated preschools have also numbered among the offenders.

5. Satanic ritual abusers tend to infiltrate preschools in clusters, by geographic area. As in the case of the South Bay, in which 7 offending preschools were identified, there is rarely a single school involved in a given area. Currently, we are aware of clusters of offending schools in the Newbury Park, Whittier, and Riverside areas (see maps).

6. It is unrealistic to believe that confronting the school with the child's allegations of abuse will produce anything other than denials that such activity is going on. The school may submit to "investigation" by the police, which usually involves little more that "talking to" the preschool director. Sometimes the school will threaten to sue the parents if they file a complaint.

Police Investigation of Complaints of Abuse in Preschools

1. Police will often discount the allegations of the child if, when they interview the child (s)he does not disclose to them directly. Police often do not understand that the child's life and the family have been threatened if (s)he tells. The police also tend not to understand that a standard part of Satanic ritual abuse involves perpetrators dressing in police costumes. Many small children will not talk to even a plainclothes police officer because, in the words of one child, "she is a teacher."

2. Police usually will not interview other children at the preschool because they want to avoid a "panic" or the school losing all its students after parents' suspicions are aroused. The net result is that parents at most schools in which a child has complained of abuse are never notified of the allegations, and have no opportunity to seek medical or psychological help for their children.

3. Police will normally keep a case open for a few months, warning the family not to contact other parents or publicize the case in any way because these actions could "jeopardize the investigation." In all cases I have been involved in, no serious efforts at investigation were ever made. Cases are usually dropped after a few months.

Appendix 12: Hickey "Play Therapy Notes" - Kinsey Almond

"Play Therapy" Record: Kinsey Almond
27 January - 10 August 1987
Major/Lt.Colonel Deborah L. Hickey
Letterman Army Medical Center
Presidio of San Francisco, California

- transcribed by -
Lt. Colonel Michael A. Aquino
23 September 1991
[corrected only for punctuation and completion of abbreviated names]

[Pages #1-5 missing.]

27 January 1987

Attempted to find out who she played goo-goo games with. Said she played with "Shambee", her friend at school. Said "Shambee" went up the stairs, through the door, went to bed, and did poo-poo for which Shambee was spanked by a man. Attempts to name man wound up to Mr. Rogers on TV, who "just belongs on TV" and is "not a teacher". Patient said Shambee also had its neck broken - couldn't elaborate on this. Attempts to ask if something scary had happened to her. She replied that on Halloween she and her sister ...

[Pages #7-10 missing.]

3 February 1987

I asked her if Mr. Gary was a bad man - she said "no, that Mr. Gary loves me and scares me". I asked her how Mr. Gary loves her. She replied that he "hugs me & never spanks me". I asked if Mr. Gary did anything else to love her. She replied, "No." I asked if Mr. Gary kissed her. She replied, "No, but other kids kissed Mr. Gary and blow Mr. Gary in a yucky way." I asked her how, and she said, "Mr. Gary touched" in a "naked place". Asked her to show me where. She pointed to her genital region. Then said, "Mr. Gary goes pee-pee on a boy's shoe," and spontaneously said Mr. Gary had a "penis" which she said was "soft" and his did too. Said kids touched Mr. Gary's penis. When I asked how, she replied, "Like my thumb," and placed her thumb in her mouth and began to suck on it. I asked her if his penis was hard or soft. She said it was "hard" and then Mr. Gary went pee-pee" and kids would "get sick and throw up". I asked her if Mr. Gary ever did this to her, and she said, "Yes, it tasted yucky - the pee-pee and it went on my shoes." I asked if she had done this to anyone else, and she said the "little girls did this to the little boys", but could not/would not tell me any names. I asked if Mr. Gary ever took his clothes off, and she said, "Yes." I asked if he took his shirt off, and she said, "Yes, and even showed us his boobs." I asked if she had ever taken her clothes off, and she said, "Yes." I asked her if Mr. Gary had ever touched her, and she said, "Yes, in my naked part," and said he had "spanked" her, pointing to doll's buttocks. I asked her if he had ever touched her anywhere else, and she said, "Yes," and pointed to her vaginal area and said, "On my penis. He put hot water on my penis. Don't tell my dad." Session began to end there. I asked her two or three more times if anyone else had ever done this, and she said, "No." I asked her 2-3 times if she ever played this game with anyone else, and she kept replying, "Mr. Gary." Session ended with patient telling me we shouldn't talk to anyone else about this. Patient wanted to continue to wash doll's hair, and placed doll beside the sink to let its hair dry. Patient wanted to be picked up and carried back to waiting room, which I did. Told her I would see her next week.

[Page #14 missing.]

24 February 1987

… A couple of questions. She said yes. I asked her if Mr. Gary's pee-pee was white or yellow. She replied it was white. I then asked her to name some colors of chalk in can. Had difficulty doing this. I then picked up white and yellow pieces and asked her what color Mr. Gary's pee-pee was. She said it was both, and said Mr. Gary's penis was hard when he went pee-pee on the kids. I asked her if the "goo-goo game" was the game she played with Mr. Gary. She said, "Yes." I asked her if she ever played the goo-goo game with anyone else - she said no. I asked her if she could tell me what the game was - she said it was "farts and pee-pee" and didn't want to talk about it. She then said she "didn't fart anymore". I asked if she could just tell me a little about the goo-goo game. She said Mr. Gary would make sounds "like a baby" goo-goo-wah-wah, and then kids would pee on him. I asked her if Mr. Gary ever touched her. She said, "Yes." I asked her to show me where. She touched her genital/vaginal area. I asked her if he ever touched her "buns". She said, "Yes." I asked her how. She said he would push/press on/in her buns. I asked with what. She said, "With a needle." I asked where he got the needle. She said he picked it up off his shoe. She then said she didn't want to talk about it anymore. I said okay but told her I would have to tell her parents. She didn't want me to. I asked how come. She said because they "get sad". I said her parents loved her very much, to which she said yes, and that we had to tell them because they care very much about her. She reluctantly agreed to this. I told her we might have to tell the police/FBI too. She didn't want to do this. I asked her if she remembered talking to a lady in the playroom. She asked if this was "Trish". I said yes, and that Trish was an FBI/policeman. She seemed surprised, but agreed I could tell the FBI, and agreed to talk with them "about this". I told her she was very brave, and that her parents wouldn't be angry with her. She asked if time was up. I said no. She …

[Pages #17-28 missing.]

24 March 1987

I asked her what they did. They "were naughty". How? "They said, 'Shut up.'" I told her that I didn't think people went to jail because they said "shut up". Session ended there.

* * *

Impression: Some themes of jail, some of sibling rivalry, some of [?], some mischievousness. Full affect.

* * *

P: (1) Last session planned for next week. (2) After that RTC PRN basis.

30 March 87

Spoke to mother today. States she and Kinsey were in store yesterday. Kinsey began to mumble under her breath. Mother overheard her saying "bad man", "no touch me/us", "no kissing", "I don't like me", "I'm not good." Patient at another time was asked to go play in her yard. Patient became upset, saying was afraid of "bad man". Mother asked who, response "Mr. Gary". Was afraid Mr. Gary would be in her yard, wanted to know if her parents told him to stay away, not to come around her anymore. Began to talk of "firesticks" in the yard, brought sticks in for father to light on the stove, told her parents Mr. Gary would "put fire sticks in his mouth". Kinsey last week more tearful, crying at times to point of passing out. Kinsey did this when an infant.

* * *

Impression: More traumatic material.

* * *

P. (1) Continue with sessions past tomorrow.

7 April 1987

Patient began by giving me a piece of bubblegum and one for herself. In playroom. Asked her if she ever went to Mr. Gary's house - "No, my mommy asked me that too." Asked her if she ever went anywhere with Mr. Gary. Initially said no, then said she went with him 2-3 times with "Sassy" to "Sassy's" house. Said Sassy was Todo girlfriend. Said Shambee and Sassy were the same person. Said their house was upstairs and there were no stairs around. Said car was blue, house was blue, and bathtub was blue, but was drawing with a blue marker at the time. Said Sassy and Todo were white, blonde hair, but said Mr. Gary had black hair, then switched it to poo-poo colored hair (wigs?). Said Sassy and Todo were older than Mr. Gary. Said "lion bathtub" was a bathtub with a picture of a small lion on the wall. Said they went there for a "party". Said they had a camera which she said was a movie camera, and she was in the movies. Showed her a videocamera in the clinic, and said it was the same camera ("wonderful camera"). Said they all had their clothes off and would poo-poo on each other. Said that is where they played the goo-goo game. Said that the big people would touch the kids in their private parts, that was where she put Mr. Gary's penis in her mouth and Mr. Gary put his penis in her bottom. Asked her if that was where the firesticks were. Said yes, that Mr. Gary would take the firesticks and put them in dolls and toys and break them. Said they were not sparklers, but could not describe. Asked her if there was a gun there. "Yes, Mr. Gary told Sassy he would kill her." Why? "She did something bad." What. "Poo-pooed on him." Said Todo was cut - Cut himself for doing something bad - poo-pooed on Mr. Gary. Why would Mr. Gary threatened/ tell he was going to kill someone? "I don't know; he just did." Said there were books. What kind? Golf books and golf balls. Said there was a computer there. Said there was no table or chairs and no bed. Said they didn't live there, but other times said that was where Sassy and Todo lived. Said they had "two" toys, then said they had all kinds of toys, to include "dinosaurs that bite" and "hurt". Said that was where she cleaned up the floor as well. Repeated 2-3 times that Evan was there with her, and that another boy was James. Said Mr. Gary put a boy's head under water and "hurt a boy" …

[Page #33 missing.]

21 April 1987

Patient to playroom - Did not want to talk about recent trip to visit father. Wanted to play "school bus" in which two buses - yellow and red - were "going to San Francisco". Everyone had to get in them. Patient refused to answer who was driving red school bus. Patient played this. During this time I asked her if the place Mr. Gary had taken her had a garage, a tree house, and a swing set. Said, "Yes." Asked her what color the swing set was. "Blue." Asked her if there was a fence there. "Yes." Asked her where you could see this from. "Far away." Asked her if this is where the lady drove them. "Yes." Asked her what color the car was. "Red and white." There followed on a comment Kinsey made about Mr. Gary calling her "doo-doo face". I told her I met Evan. Initially seemed pleased and said Evan was with her at the party. She then said she knew this and that Evan had seen "Dr. Sheridan" too. Later said she didn't know Evan. I feigned surprise, to which she laughed and said, "Yeah, I know Evan." After bus sequences patient moved to sink to "wash dishes". Patient did this for awhile, then switched to washing the doll's hair and the doll being "Timothy" and she being "Michelle". Much conversation about doll "staying still" and "sitting down" so Michelle could wash hair. Patient: Was water getting in Timothy's face? During this sequence I asked Kinsey if Dena was at party. Said yes, also said Kara and Katie were there too. Some confusion on my part about Katie vs. Katherine vs. Kara. Kara is Katie (who is Kathryn) sister. Session ended with patient finishing Timothy's hair. Patient reluctant to stop play, but did so with assurances we could play again next week.

Impression: Seems gradually more open and comfortable about discussing traumas - seems comforted in knowledge that she is not only child undergoing similar experiences.

Add: Also spoke with Kinsey about speaking to Mr. Foreman. Kinsey: "David's dad?" Said I didn't know, but said was policeman that gave her the crayons. Change in facial expression to somber - didn't reply yes or no. Seemed to want to think about that.

[Page #36 missing.]

28 April 1987

Patient to playroom. Spent first several minutes talking on playphone with Mr. Foreman. Mr. Foreman to Kinsey, to Kristin, to Michelle, to Judy. Mr. Foreman to house, "go somewhere". States she was scared. First said wasn't house, then was. Then said she was afraid to talk about it, was afraid of MP, was afraid she would get into trouble with Mr. Foreman if she "told". Said Shannon told her she would have to go to bed and never get up, said her "first dad" told her he would get her into trouble. Told her Mr. Foreman would never get her into trouble, that he would make sure she was safe, and that he wanted to help kids so that nothing bad would happen to them. Said place they went to was where Mr. Gary took them. Asked if she ever played in playground there. "No." - somber voice, head straight, no facial contact. Asked what Sassy looked like. Said she had black hair like mine (brown) and yellow eyes like mine (green). Asked if she wore glasses. "Yes." Asked if she had short hair or long hair. Said, "Short." Asked what hair Todo had. "Green." To play hide and seek, then began to play hide and seek in room and lights out and some talk of being scared. Said this was how she played hide and seek with Todo. Then had to go to bathroom. Saw Sally on way back to room. Asked if Sally was at Mr. Gary's. No response. Began to play with boy doll, dog, and woman doll. Woman doll in confrontation with tiger. Tiger trying to bite woman, woman victorious in knocking tiger down and "not being scared", dog then did likewise. Boy in vehicle where tiger was a "little scared", but the light was on so it was okay. Patient then asked me if Clyde was Mr. Foreman. Said yes. Patient then saw wolf puppet, which she called a "mask". Mask then proceeded to bite my fingers, nose, and ears. Then patient became the "doctor" who made my ears better by a series of shots. Session ended there.

* * *

Spoke to mother briefly after the session. States husband tired, will be going on brief vacation. Discussed couples sessions after return from vacation as needed. Mother stated that after visit with Mr. Foreman Kinsey told her mother that she "couldn't tell Foreman everything she remember" as opposed to "couldn't remember everything".

* * *

Impression: Themes of being scared, occurrences of visit.

12 May 1987

Mother and patient here today. Patient to playroom. Began to play with doll house - mother, father, two brothers. Brother in bathtub, tried to get shirt off so wouldn't get wet so mother wouldn't be mad at him. Asked Kinsey if I could ask a question about the house Mr. Gary took her to. Said, "Yes." Asked what color hair man with Mr. Gary had. "Brown." Did he have glasses? "Yes." Did he have hair on his face? "Yes." Where? "All over." Did you ever see him at the school? "Yes." What about the lady, what color hair did she have? "Blonde." Did you ever see her at the school? "Yes." Does she work there? "Yes." Do you know her name? "Cathy." Do you know the man's name? "Yes," but wouldn't say. Is that the lady I saw on the day I was there and you were really crying? "Yes." Whose house was it you went to? "Cathy's." Then: "I have to go to bathroom." Went to bathroom. After bathroom said she didn't want to talk about Mr. Gary. Then played scene in house where kid has nightmares about his teacher and had to go to his parents' bed because he is scared. Asked what the dream was about. "My teacher." Asked what about that teacher. Moved to sink to wash doll's hair. Asked me to get ET ready for bed and put blanket under him. Then said she was washing ET's husband's hair, and he would take a nap with ET. Did this, got paper towels from bathroom. Then they slept feet against each other. Patient called me on phone, asked if I could come over to her house. She said her mother said this was okay. Then asked me if I knew Clyde. Said yes. Asked me if he had a boy. Said yes. Asked me if his name was Alex. Said no, I had a little girl. Then played telephone again. This time Kinsey came to my house. Went to "beautiful doll house" and began to play, then took down hand puppets of doctor and woman and infant. Conversation: Mother told doctor infant couldn't go to her house; mother wouldn't let her. Then moved to play with guns, shooting them briefly. Then to F - P and [?] with dogs with fluffy ears, people, policeman can't go there. Asked Kinsey if Sally went to house with her. She asked with her and Evan? I said yes. She said she sure did. I asked if Evan's brother went with them. She said Brandon Fox did. I then asked if Collin did. She said, "yes." I asked if David went with her too. Said, "No." I asked her again about the name of the lady with Mr. Gary at the house. "Cathy." Is that the lady who was there the day you were crying? Unknown. How do you know it was her house? No response. Who told you it was her house? "She did." Cathy did? "Yes." Did Mr. Gary say it was her house? "No." How many adults were with Mr. Gary? "Two." A man and a woman? "Yes." These people are Sassy and Todo? "Yes." Did they have their [clothes off?]? "Yes." How many times did you go to this house? "Two times." Did Cathy have a piano? "No." Patient then continued to play with [Fisher-Price?] house, saying it was a dog school. I told Kinsey I was sorry I didn't know who the lady was on the day I saw her, because if I had I wouldn't have left her there. Kinsey responded, "You sure shouldn't," and kept playing. Patient reluctant to stop play.

* * *

Mother said Kinsey had nightmares "about her teacher" on two nights prior to returning to San Francisco. Mother told her to talk back to her dreams, which Kinsey apparently did. Kinsey's grandfather showed Kinsey mementos of the fire department and then asked Kinsey to go there. Kinsey initially excited, but on day of trip said she didn't want to go. Kinsey went and had a good time listening to what firemen did, playing on truck, etc. Upon getting into car, Kinsey said aloud, "Mr. Gary lied to me." Mother didn't explore that with other people present.

* * *

Impressions: More material for catharsis.

* * *

Inform Mr. Foreman of above info.

19 May 1987

Patient here with Aunt Colette. Mother at airport with father. Father going to Hawaii. Patient wanted to play with checkers. Played short game of checkers by placing checkers on various squares. Then wanted to play with wood blocks. Began to build with them. Asked her if she had anything to drink at Mr. Gary's house. Said, "No." I said Evan told me he had. She then said she had a "red drink". Anything else? "A green drink." Asked if there were scary things there. Said, "No." Then said there were ghosts and scary faces in Disneyland. Then began to talk about "dead people." When I got closer, she said, "I told Mr. Gary not to talk about dead people," and said she had to go to the bathroom. Once back in playroom, I showed her the gargoyle. Said she hadn't seen this. Showed her the [Ol?] evil figure - said it was a "hawk" and it was "bad". Asked her if she had seen this before. She said, "Yes, but no wings." Patient then faltered and asked, "Is this Mr. Gary?" I said I didn't know. What did she think? No response. I then asked if there was a black baby at the house after Kinsey asked about where the baby was. She said, "Yes." Asked if this were real baby or a fake. Said it was "real". Asked if it was a boy or a girl. Said it was a "girl". Asked what its name was. Said "Kay-kay," then said that wasn't her name and she couldn't remember. Asked what happened to the baby. At that point she said the baby was really at home with its parents; it really wasn't there. Asked if there were animals there. Said, "Yes." Asked if they were real or fake animals. Said they were "real" but refused to answer what kind of animals they were. Then I asked if she knew what a cross was. Said, "Yes." Asked if there were crosses at this house. "Yes, bad ones." Why were they bad? "Went pee-pee on people." Asked if there was a bible there. Said, "Yes, a bad one." Had "poo-poo on it". Said it was funny looking. Didn't want to talk about this anymore, and appeared scared/frightened. Then moved to play with "man-doll" who was "naked" although doll was female doll in red dress. Asked if this were a man doll. Said, "Yes." Asked her if she ever saw a man wear a dress. Said, "Yes," but wouldn't answer where she saw this. Then pulled legs apart. Said there were "private parts" and that it "hurt to pull legs apart". Then said doll went pee-pee. Then put dolls on bean bag pillows. Then played telephone and said she didn't want to see Dr. Hickey anymore, well, maybe later. Then saw box of animals and gingerly picked up alligator, calling it a dinosaur. Seemed fearful alligator would bite her and verbally commented on this. Told her it was pretend, the teeth were made of rubber, and it was okay, it wouldn't hurt her. Then picked up dinosaur and said it was an alligator. Then had alligator bite dinosaur. Then picked up giraffe. Said it was a zebra. Tried to ride it. Then played going to the airport to go to Hawaii. Just prior to this played zebra was "bad" and had to go to "jail". Then went to other side of room picked up three rings and said you used this to "pull down boys underwear" but wouldn't elaborate. After …

[page #46 missing.]

26 May 1987

Patient here with father today. Playroom - wash dishes. I'm baby, she's mom, then big sister. Then play with "black baby" and ET. Asked her if she saw man I was talking with just before session. "Yes." What color? "Black." Black baby at house? "Yes." Said baby had a baby in its stomach. Said people went pee-pee and poo-poo on it, and that it had a pee-pee bath, not a "lion bath". Said it couldn't walk but could crawl, wore diapers, and had no teeth. Only black person there. Went to bathroom - went pee-pee. Back to playroom. Began to wash baby's hair, then decided to play with other toys and said she "didn't want to talk about what happened at the house". Took out dinosaurs = "bad because they fight", alligator, camel, and giraffe (calls this a zebra). Then had to go back to bathroom to poo-poo. Came back, picked up telephone, told me to "take my clothes off". Said no, we couldn't do that. Said to pretend to do this, that we would play [Captain Cereal?] …

[Pages #48-50 missing.]

2 June 1987

Asked patient if I could ask her a question. "Yes." Was the lion bathtub really a plastic swimming pool? "Yes." - smiled. Asked her what room this was in. Said she would "tell me later", that she didn't want to talk about it. Asked her if there was a big pot that hung down from the ceiling there with legs sticking out. Said it had legs, arms, and a penis. Said the "dead people" were "blue" in color. Said the penis went pee on her shoes. I told her that I thought the legs and arms were really mannekins or dummies like you see in a store, and asked her if she saw the beach mannekin in the PX. Patient seemed to listen to this, then asked about the "dead people Dr. Steve brought from the hospital" and that Dr. Steve had brought them there. That Dr. Steve was there with Mr. Gary at the house. Then said she went to two houses with Mr. Gary. Said Dr. Steve spanked Mr. Gary for being bad on his buns for going poo/saying poo. Patient said Dr. Steve was Dr. Steve of Carolyn, Sharon, Steve, etc., and said her mother knew him. Patient then wanted to draw with markers. Session time up. Moved into my office.

* * *

Asked mother about Dr. Steve, who mother states is a neighbor. States Kinsey never went to hospital with him, has never known anybody who has died, whose association/experience with hospital with peds and my office, and could offer no explanation for Kinsey's association of hospital/dead people and Dr. Steve. Mother stated she would think about this some more. Seemed totally surprised by Kinsey's statement. Mother asked if I thought the people involved with this were practicing a Satanic cult as part of a procedure to insure successful pornographic/sexual exploitation of children or the exploitation was [20?] the Satanic cult practice. Said I didn't know.

Also spoke with mother about Kinsey's concerns about asking questions when things didn't seem quite right. Mother seemed surprised and reassured Kinsey that she could do this.

* * *

Impression: Working through her experience.

9 June 1987

Patient and mother here today. Mother states Kinsey wants to talk with Clyde.

* * *

To playroom. Brought in playdoh; began playing with this. Asked Kinsey why she wanted to talk with Clyde. Said she wanted to tell him about Mr. Gary. That "Mr. Gary was mean" and "put his penis in here" - pointing to her mouth. Patient then continued to play with water, making a mess and then cleaning this up. Patient then wanted to play with paints and painted on paper. Then said she was the mommy and I was the baby and that I should go upstairs to my room and play while she made lunch. Said she was making fruit salad. Patient had brought in pictures. Said she lost Disney pictures down the elevator. Spoke of trip to fire station again and had patient tell me what she was doing in each of the pictures. Patient seemed more comfortable this week in doing so. I then asked patient if I could ask her a question. Seemed reluctant but said okay. Asked her how she knew Dr. Steve was at the house Mr. Gary was at. Did she see his clothes or his face? Said he was dressed like a doctor but that she saw his face too. Returned to making fruit salad by putting water and playdoh together. Then said, "I hate you," "You're dumb." I asked what was that about. Said I had told her she was dumb. Told her I didn't say that, that I thought she was smart, that sometimes I may have asked questions she couldn't answer, but that was okay because they were hard questions. Patient listened to this but said nothing.

Patient continued with her playdoh and water combo. At end of session looked at playdoh and water combo and called it "sick". Patient helped clean up mess.

* * *

Upon returning to office, spoke with mother. Patient was very afraid of ghosts in Disney's haunted house, seemed uncomfortable. On Halloween went with father. At one house, man jumped out. Patient became extremely upset and had to be taken …

[Page #55 missing.]

23 June 1987

> *[Note by M. Aquino: The following Hickey entry refers to a "Dr. S." It is not clear whether this is the same "Dr. Steve" previously identified by Almond, or a "Dr. Sheridan" who was apparently treating children at the Letterman Medical Center, or to some other "Dr. S."]*

Patient said she saw Dr. S. yesterday, that he touched her in her private parts and took some blood pointing to left arm. Asked her if she knew why. Discussed how Dr. S. wanted to make sure she was healthy and didn't have any germs that would make her sick. Patient seemed to understand this, then said that Mr. Gary had touched her in the same place as Dr. S. Asked where. Said in her private parts. Asked with what. Said with a needle. Patient then began to paint with brush and watercolors. Patient later moved to floor to play with a bus and a family going onto the bus. Asked patient if anyone else had ever touched her where Mr. Gary did. No response. Asked if anyone else was with Mr. Gary. Patient said she didn't want to talk about it. Patient then wanted to play getting dressed up in blanket cape and hat, but decided against this when another hat could not be found. Patient then decided to wash the doll in the sink and did so. Later moved back to play with playdoh and make "crystal balls", which we did until the session ended.

* * *

Impressions: Continued working through.

30 June 1987

Mother relates patient talking more about events. Has scheduled separate appointment time for this. Patient relates "Mikey" being "Shambee's" husband. Told mother Mikey wore an "Army suit" - Patient's term for Army greens. States had a stripe on pants.

* * *

To playroom. Wanted to play with markers and playdoh. Drew various ranks for patient. Patient picked out WO2 as being Mikey's rank and then told me to add a third dot on both WO ranks drawn. Asked what letters were on name plate. Patient said, "AK." Patient then wanted to play with the playdoh. Said Mikey put his penis in her mouth and peed on her. Said Mikey put poo-poo in her mouth. Meanwhile was taking playdoh and making balls with them. Then began to wet playdoh, saying it was like poo-poos. Had to go to bathroom. Said she had real playdoh in toilet. Back in playroom had various dolls named Dinky/Tinky, Tomo, Naughty, Nadi, and Pinky [?] at house. Said Pinky was a girl, all others were boys. Asked if Kari Anna was name of baby. Said, "Yes." Asked if Jaime was at house. Said, "Yes," but would not elaborate on the material. Had everyone go to bed after being yelled at by lady. Then had plane by the house and people catching a flight. Play ended there.

* * *

Impressions: Patient able to discuss more details of events/share them with her mother.

2 July 1987

Met with mother. Patient talking more frequently now about events. Mother keeping track.

* * *

Impressions: Patient disclosing to mother.

* * *

P: (1) Contact FBI with info to contact mother.

7 July 1987

Patient here today with mother and grandmother (maternal). Patient and sister to go with grandparents for approximately one month.

Patient had picture taken with me in playroom so that she could "talk with me" with grandmother as needed on trip.

* * *

Patient brought all materials into playroom. Began session making tortillas out of playdoh. Once into making tortillas, asked patient if she knew her mother came to talk with me. Said, "Yes." Asked her if it was true that Nancy was Shambee. Said there were two mothers there - Nancy and Shambee, they were the "good mothers". Said there were two sisters there, also that Nancy and Shambee had girls too. Said the "new" kids were Kinsey and Cristen, but not she and her sister. Asked if there were pets there. "Yes, black ones." Said one's name was Sadi. Sadi was a black dog, and said there were other dogs as well, all black. Asked if there were other pets. "Yes," but wouldn't elaborate. Asked if Nancy and Shambee worked at the school - Said ...

[Pages #60-62 missing.]

10 August 1987

Patient here with her mother today. Mother states patient did fairly well on vacation. Upon return home began to experience nightmares again. Last night awoke at 2 with nightmares.

* * *

Patient gave me a piece of gum she brought with her to large playroom. Patient initially wanted to go back to small playroom, but settled in to old themes quickly. Patient began by playing with playdoh. Patient was mother and I was daughter. She was making tortillas and I was to make "crystal balls" but was sent "upstairs" to do this. While doing this, asked patient if she remembered the baby at the house Mr. Gary brought her to. Said, "Yes," they were "Mr. Gary's babies". Asked what happened to the baby. Used her left hand, indicating a vertical movement over xiphoid process encompassing chest and abdominal cavity, saying that Mr. Gary "cut the baby open" with a knife. Then what? Said Mr. Gary had her cut his stomach with a knife, indicating a horizontal movement back and forth over her midsection. Then what? The other police "took him to jail with his baby". Where did the baby come from? "He stole them from the circus." What color? "Brown and black." How many? "Four." Were they boys or girls? "A boy and girls." Patient becoming anxious, moved to putting balls, brown, in cups of water at the sink. Began to talk of Mr. Gary going poo-poo in his pants at school and then again at the house. I commented that the balls of playdoh in the water looked like poo-poos. Patient said it wasn't, but was a "tomato" in a "cup of coffee". Patient then began to take playdoh and smear it on the blackboard, making crosses. Asked if she had done this before/seen this done before? "Yes." "At Mr. Gary's house." After this patient returned to playdoh. Patient then said that I had "broken the lamp" and we needed to "talk about it". Patient began to lecture me in a quiet, controlled tone of voice and finally said, "Honey, I'm sorry, but this requires a spanking," and called Larry to "come up here" to give me a spanking ...

Appendix 13: M. Aquino Analysis of Appendix #12

Analysis of Hickey "Play Therapy" Record: Kinsey Almond
- by -
Lt. Colonel Michael A. Aquino
26 September 1991

1.   Completeness of the Record.

The Hickey record pages are numbered at the bottom. The following numbered pages are missing from the record provided by the CID with the ROI, hence are wrongfully denied to plaintiff in *Aquino v Stone* under discovery: 1-5, 7-10, 14, 17-28, 33, 36, 46, 48-50, 55, 60-62, all after 64.

As the CID provided only 32 pages to plaintiff, **at least 32 additional pages have been concealed and suppressed**.

Since so much importance is placed by the CID on Almond's credibility as an "accuser", and in Hickey's professional ethics and competence, the **entire** record is material and essential.

Nevertheless it is obviously the CID's official position that the denied pages contain nothing of any significance to this case whatever, so the following analysis takes the CID at its word in this respect.

2.   Context of the Record.

These interviews did not take place in a single, tight sequence, but rather over a loose, seven-month period. During this period:

- The Presidio "day-care child-abuse" theme, in whose November 1986 instigation the adult Adams-Thompsons were involved, continued to be promoted as established truth.

- Activist parents maintained close contacts with one another, exchanging all information useful in promoting the episode.

- The high media profile of the episode, and the involvement of many investigative agencies and personnel, and Washington D.C. interest established a commitment to produce one or more guilty parties. An ultimate finding that the entire episode was in fact baseless became politically unthinkable.

- The activist parents proceeded to file [as of 11/27/89] 74 claims against the government for $74,500,000. Clearly they all had a strong financial motive to promote the episode and see it officially sanctioned as "truth".

3.   Deborah Hickey.

- Hickey diagnosed "sex abuse" in scores of children, including her own, in connection with the scam.

- Hickey introduced references to the "devil" into her sessions with the children (Fox session 5/18/87).

- Hickey initiated statues of "gargoyles" in her sessions with the children.

- Hickey had **no** known training in the diagnosis or treatment of "ritual child sex abuse".

- Hickey has **no** education in **or** experience concerning the authentic Satanic religion.

- Hickey regularly introduced **leading questions** into her sessions. Tales of "sex-abuse" did not originate spontaneously from the children, but only in response to specific and pointed questions from Hickey.

- When Hickey received an "unhelpful" answer from Almond, such as a denial that Hambright did anything to her, she would refuse to accept it or change the subject, and would persist in the question until Almond said something that Hickey could characterize as a "helpful" answer, i.e. supportive of a "sex-abuse" diagnosis.

- On 23 April 1987, in a sworn affidavit, Hickey said that on 2/3/87 Almond "stated that she needed to get a gun to kill the bad man". This is **not** in the actual Hickey notes of that session.

- On 23 April 1987, in a sworn affidavit, Hickey said that on 2/3/87 Almond "identified this bad man as Mr. Gary". This is **not** in the actual Hickey notes of that session. In fact, the notes state that Hickey initiated a question to Almond "if Mr. Gary was a bad man", and Almond answered, "**No.**"

- On 23 April 1987, in a sworn affidavit, Hickey said that on 2/3/87 Almond "**spontaneously** said Mr. Gary had a penis which was **soft**". This is **not** in the actual Hickey notes of that session. In fact, the notes state that **Hickey initiated** a question to Almond "if his penis was hard or soft", and Almond answered, "**Hard.**"

- On 23 April 1987, in a sworn affidavit, Hickey said that on 2/3/87 Almond "**described** Mr. Gary as having taken his clothes off **on several occasions**". This is **not** in the actual Hickey notes of that session. In fact, the notes state that Hickey initiated a question to Almond "if Mr. Gary ever took his clothes off", and Almond answered, "Yes." (no mention of more than one occasion).

- On 23 April 1987, in a sworn affidavit, Hickey said that on 2/24/87 Almond "named the gluteal region as being 'buns'". This is **not** in the actual Hickey notes of that session. In fact, the notes state that **Hickey initiated** a question to Almond "if Mr. Gary ever touched her **buns**", and Almond answered, "Yes."

- On 23 April 1987, in a sworn affidavit, Hickey said that in "other sessions similar to the 2/3 and 2/24 ones" Almond "would use a small doll and a large doll, and place the head of the small doll against the genital area of the large doll, or describe an action in which the large doll was 'peeing' on the small doll". **No** such actions are described in the actual Hickey notes of the sessions.

- On 23 April 1987, in a sworn affidavit, Hickey said that "Kinsey has also expressed very specific fears of disclosing this information to others because of a fear that Mr. Gary would 'kill her' with 'a gun' and through Mr. Gary's use of 'firesticks' which he would light and put in his mouth. Kinsey … made it clear to me she was afraid of the 'firesticks'." **No** such actions are described in the actual Hickey notes of the sessions. The subject of "firesticks" was introduced to Hickey on 3/30/87 by Almond's mother Michele Adams-Thompson, **not** by Almond herself. Hickey initiated a question to Almond if the firesticks were "in her bottom", to which Almond answered, "Yes." **Hickey** initiated the subject of a gun to Almond, to which Almond responded, "Yes." There was **no** discussion by Almond of any gun-threat to her, nor any fear of Hambright because of it.

- On 23 April 1987, in a sworn affidavit, Hickey said that "During this time, Kinsey has experienced feelings of poor self-esteem, fears and phobias which include fear of going into her own yard to play because of her concern that 'Mr. Gary would be there', regressive behaviors, including becoming easily frustrated, crying over minor events, e.g. tieing her shoes, impaired interpersonal relationships, isolative behaviors, and a loss of the bright, spontaneous effect which is normally part of her character" **No** such actions are described in the actual Hickey notes of the sessions. Almond is described as playing happily with the toys provided by Hickey throughout all of the sessions, and **never** crying or being frustrated. She **never** told Hickey that she was afraid that Hambright might be in her yard. Again this was alleged to Hickey **by her mother**, Michele Adams-Thompson.

4.   "Shambee".

"Shambee" (Hickey's spelling) appears first on 1/27/87, introduced by Almond as "her friend at school" who was spanked by Mr. Rogers on TV. Almond added that Shambee "also had **its** neck broken", indicating that "Shambee" is either an imaginary "friend" or perhaps a doll.

There is no record of the FBI/SFPD/CID interviewing either teachers or other children at the Presidio day-care center to see if anyone used or was known by the name "Shambee".

According to documents introduced by the CID as evidence, there is no mention of "Shambee" by any other child.

On 4/7/87 Almond said Shambee and Sassy were the same person, and that Sassy was Todo's girlfriend. After this neither Almond nor Hickey used the name "Shambee" anymore, discussing only "Sassy".

"Shambee" is reintroduced as "Mikey's wife" **by Michele Adams-Thompson** on 6/30/87.

On 7/7/87 Almond told Hickey that "Nancy and Shambee were good mothers."

On 7/7/87 Hickey asked Almond if Shambee worked at the school. Almond's answer - and anything else she may have said as a follow-up on the next three pages of Hickey's record - **has been concealed by the CID** by withholding those pages.

5.   "Sassy."

There is no record of the FBI/SFPD/CID interviewing either teachers or other children at the Presidio day-care center to see if anyone used or was known by the name "Sassy".

According to documents introduced by the CID as evidence, there is **no** mention of Sassy by any other child. [Almond said that several other children had been at Sassy's house.]

Almond said Sassy had **blonde** hair (4/7/87), then that Sassy had "**black** hair like Hickey" (who has **brown** hair) (4/28/87), then that Sassy had **blonde** hair again (5/12/87)

Almond said Sassy "had **yellow** eyes like Hickey" (who has **green** eyes) (4/28/87).

Almond switched Sassy's name to "Cathy" (5/12/87), then back again to "Sassy" in the same session.

There is no record of the FBI/SFPD/CID interviewing either teachers or other children at the Presidio day-care center to see if anyone used or was known by the name "Cathy".

According to documents introduced by the CID as evidence, there is **no** mention of Cathy by any other child.

6.   Almond's Attitude and Credibility.

Throughout all of the sessions Almond shows no signs of being an injured or severely-traumatized child. Left to herself, she plays happily with the toys provided by Hickey. **All** "molestation" themes and questions are **initiated by Hickey**, and Almond repeatedly indicates that she doesn't want to talk about such things and returns to her playing. From the notes it is quite clear that her reluctance is not because of fear, but rather lack of interest in Hickey's subject.

- On 4/7/87 Hickey asked Almond **twice** if she ever went anywhere with Hambright. Both times Almond said **no**. When Hickey still persisted, Almond then said **yes**.

- On 4/7/87 said that Sassy & Todo's house "was **upstairs** and there were **no stairs around**".

- Said the car [in which she went to the house] was **blue** (4/7/87), **red & white** (4/21/87).

- Said Sassy and Todo were white and had **blonde** hair (4/7/87), then that Sassy had "**black** hair like Hickey" (who has **brown** hair) and Todo had **green** hair (4/28/87).

- Said Hambright had **black** hair (4/7/87), then **poo-poo-colored** hair (4/7/87)

- Said Hambright put his penis in her bottom (4/7/87), contradicted by medical examination 3/12/87.

- Answered "yes" when Hickey asked her if there were "firesticks in her bottom" (4/7/87).

- Said Sassy and Todo lived [at the house] and then said that they **didn't** (4/7/87).

- Said Sassy and Todo had "**two**" toys, then said they had "**all kinds of**" toys (4/7/87).

- Said Sassy and Todo had "dinosaurs that bite and hurt" (4/7/87).

- Almond said Sassy "had **yellow** eyes like Hickey" (who has **green** eyes) (4/28/87).

- On 4/7/87 said that she went to **Sassy** & Todo's house. On 5/12/87 said that the lady's name was **Cathy** and that it was her house (no mention of Todo).

- Almond said that she was accompanied to the "house" by Sally, Evan, Brandon Fox, Jaime. **None** of these persons agreed with her statements about the house - and Jaime identified it as a house which was confirmed by Jaime's mother to belong to "Katie".

- On 5/12/87 Almond said that it was **Cathy's** house and that **Cathy** was the name of the woman with Hambright at the house. Then during the same session, when Hickey asked Almond if "**Sassy** and Todo" were there, Almond said, "Yes," and that there were **only two** adults there with Hambright.

- On 5/19/87 Almond said she had had **nothing** to drink at "Mr. Gary's house", then immediately said she had had "**a red drink**" and "**a green drink**".

- On 5/19/87 Almond said there was a baby at "**the house**", then said it was "really **at home with its parents**". On 8/10/87 she said that the police took Hambright "**to jail with the baby**" and that it originally came "**from the circus**".

- On 5/19/87 Almond said the baby's name was "**Kay-kay**", then said "that **wasn't** her name and she couldn't remember".

- On 5/19/87 Almond **twice** identified a **female** doll in a **red dress** to Hickey as a "**naked man-doll**".

- On 5/19/87 Almond identified a toy **alligator** to Hickey as a **dinosaur**. Then immediately afterward identified a toy **dinosaur** to Hickey as an **alligator**. Then identified a toy **giraffe** as a **zebra**, both on this date and again on 5/26/87.

- On 5/19/87 Almond said that the baby at the house was **white**. On 5/26/87 she **twice** said it was **black**.

- On 6/2/87 Almond said that there was a pot hanging down from the ceiling with "legs, arms, and a penis which went pee on her shoes"

- On 5/19/87 and 5/26/87 Almond said that there was **one** baby at the house. On 8/10/87 she said that there were **four**.

7.   Michele Adams-Thompson.

On several occasions accompanied Almond to therapy sessions and alleged "sex-abuse-substantiating" conduct by Almond to Hickey which Hickey did not witness or substantiate herself.

- On 3/30/87 Michele said to Hickey that Almond "became upset, saying she was afraid of the 'bad man' (Hambright)." This **identical** wording would be used by the adult Adams-Thompsons - again **not** by Almond **herself** - in their 8/87 allegations against Mrs. Aquino and myself.

- On 3/30/87 Michele told Hickey that Almond was "last week more tearful, crying at times to point of passing out". Unsubstantiated by any of Almond's behavior in any of the Hickey sessions.

- On 6/2/87 Michele introduced the subject of "Satanic cults" to Hickey. On 6/30/87 Michele introduced "Mikey the Army officer/Shambee's husband" to Hickey.

8.   "The House" [to which Almond was alleged to have been taken]

On 4/7/87 Hickey asked Almond **twice** if she ever went anywhere with Hambright. Both times Almond said **no**. When Hickey still persisted, Almond then said **yes** - to Sassy and Todo's house.

On 4/7/87 Almond said that Sassy & Todo's house "was **upstairs** and there were **no stairs around**".

On 4/7/87 Hickey asked Almond if the house "had a garage, a tree house, and a swing set, and a fence", and Almond said, "Yes." [Our home in San Francisco has **none** of these.]

In Hickey's notes concerning other Presidio children, accounts concerning "trips to a house", its description, and people connected with it vary markedly. For example, in the 5/31/87 Hickey entry concerning Jaime Parker: "[Jaime's mother said] Jaime visited Trinity, and Trinity lives in the general area of Katie and may be confusing stories. Then said Katie had approached her and **said she used to take kids to her house** to go to the bathroom when they would go to Sanchez Park."

There is no record of any FBI/SFPD/CID investigation of "Katie" or search warrant ever served on her house to investigate its design, decor, bathtub, etc.

9.   "The man with Hambright at the house" [to which Almond was alleged to have been taken]

Almond said he was "Todo" (4/7/87) who had first **blond** hair (4/27/87) and then **green** hair (4/28/87).

Almond said the man had **brown** hair (5/12/87). [My hair is so dark brown that people generally describe it as **black**.

Almond said the man had "hair all over his face" (5/12/87). [I had no facial hair at all in 1986-87, having a regulation Army haircut with no mustache.]

Almond said she had seen the man at the school (5/12/87).

Almond said that the house was "**Sassy & Todo's**" (4/7/87), then **Cathy's** (5/12/87).

Almond said that the man was "Dr. Steve" (6/2/87).

10. "Dr. Steve".

"Dr. Steve" was the only real person specifically and repeatedly (6/2/87) (6/9/87) identified by Almond as being with Hambright at "the house". She said that he was "dressed like a doctor" and that she recognized him because she "**saw his face**".

Almond said that he "brought dead people from the hospital" to the house (6/2/87)

Almond said that he "spanked Mr. Gary" (6/2/87).

On 6/2/87, in answer to Hickey's question, Almond's mother Michele Adams-Thompson admitted that she knew who "Dr. Steve" was and that he was a neighbor of the Adams-Thompsons at the Presidio of San Francisco.

Neither Hickey [as indicated in her notes] nor Michele Adams-Thompson reported this identification to the FBI/SFPD/CID. There is no record that "Dr. Steve" was ever questioned, served with a search warrant, investigated, or titled on the strength of this **authentic, unsolicited identification** by Almond. There is no explanation of Michele Adams-Thompson's personal relationship to "Dr. Steve".

11. "Mikey".

"Mikey" was never mentioned initially by Almond, and there is no mention of this name whatever until 6/30/87 - after Michele has introduced the idea of a "Satanic cult" to Hickey on 6/2/87.

On 6/30/87 it is Michele, not Almond, who introduces "Mikey" to Hickey, alleging that "Mikey is Shambee's husband". Michele then alleges to Hickey that Almond told her that "Mikey wore an 'Army suit' with a stripe on the pants". **None** of these allegations by Michele were checked by Hickey in her 6/30/87 direct-questioning of Almond, and Almond made **no mention of any of them** during the session.

Hickey showed Almond a selection of Army officer rank insignia, from which Almond picked out a **Chief Warrant Officer 2** insignia, then asked that it be modified to a **Chief Warrant Officer 3** insignia. [Neither insignia looks remotely like a Lieutenant Colonel's insignia.]

Hickey asked what letters were on the nameplate. Almond answered "**AK**", which of course is not on my nameplate.

Almond said (6/30/87) that Mikey "put his penis in her mouth and peed on her, and put poo-poo in her mouth". During all of the preceding sessions she had made the same statements concerning (a) Hambright, (b) "little boys", (c) all of the children at "the house", (d) Sassy, (e) Todo, (f) the cross, (g) the bible, (h) the female doll, (i) the penis in the pot hanging from the ceiling with arms and legs in it, and (j) Dr. Steve.

The only other mention of the name "Mike" (not "Mikey") by a Hickey-therapized child was by Jaime Parker. On 7/17/87 Jaime said that "Mr. Mike" spanked kids and her. The CID underlined this entry and put a star beside it in the margin. On 7/8/87, however, Jaime identified this **same** individual as "Frank" and said that "he watched the news and didn't want her mom to make cookies". The CID did not underline this entry nor put a star beside it in the margin.

12. "Todo".

The CID was to make an issue out of the fact that the SFPD found one page from Mrs. Aquino's telephone notebook containing a list of names and telephone numbers, one of which was for a "Mike Todo".

As Mrs. Aquino explained to the CID in her May 1989 interview, that page of the notebook contained a list of persons and their phone numbers who called in answer to an ad in the *San Francisco Chronicle* for rental of a flat we own at 121 Acme Avenue. [The flat was rented to someone else.]

We never met this "Todo", and apparently Mrs. Aquino spoke to him only that once on the phone. In the interview she suggested that the CID trace him through the phone number he gave - and for that matter verify the nature of the list by calling the other persons on it.

The CID responded that Todo's phone number was disconnected, but apparently they made no effort whatever to trace him through phone company records, or for that matter to verify the flat-rental-ad nature of the list with any of the other names on it.

Appendix 14: SFPD Search Warrant for Aquino Home

MUNICIPAL COURT OF THE CITY AND COUNTY OF SAN FRANCISCO
STATE OF CALIFORNIA
AFFIDAVIT FOR SEARCH WARRANT

The undersigned, Glenn Pamfiloff, being first duly sworn, deposes and says upon reasonable and probable cause that:

1. The following described property, to wit: See "List of Property to be Seized" attached hereto and incorporated herein by reference as though fully set forth.

2. Is located at 123 Acme Avenue, San Francisco, CA (top unit residence of Michael A. Aquino and basement) and the persons of Michael A. Aquino and Lilith Aquino who reside in said residence.

3. And comes within the provisions of California Penal Code Section 1524 as noted below:

a. Subdivision 2: Property or things used as a means of committing a felony.

b. Subdivision 3: Property or things in the possession of a person with the intent to use it as a means of committing a public offense or in possession of another to whom he may have delivered it.

c. Property or things which are evidence which tends to show a felony has been committed or that a particular person has committed it.

4. Property or things that are evidence that tend to show sexual exploitation of children.

The following facts establish the reasonable and probable cause upon which your affiant's statements are based: See attached Affidavit of Glen Pamfiloff, which is attached hereto and incorporated herein as though fully set forth.

WHEREFORE, affiant prays that a search warrant issue commanding the immediate search of the persons and premises above designated for the property or things above described, and that such property be brought before a magistrate or retained as provided in Section 1536 of the California Penal Code.

/s/ Glenn Pamfiloff
Affiant

Subscribed and sworn to before me this 14th day of August 1987.
/s/ George ?
Judge of the Municipal Court
In and for the City and County of San Francisco, State of California

LIST OF PROPERTY TO BE SEIZED

1. Camera equipment and video equipment intended for taking, producing, and reproducing of photographic images, including but not limited to cameras, instant or otherwise, video reproduction equipment, lenses, enlargers, photographic papers, film, chemicals, Polaroid cameras, attachments for remote taking of photographs.

2. Phone books, phone registers, correspondence, or papers with names, addresses, or phone numbers which would tend to identify any juvenile.

3. Photographs, movies, video tape, negatives, slides, and/or undeveloped film depicting nudity and/or sexual activities involving juveniles with juveniles and juveniles with adults.

4. Correspondence, diaries, and any other writing, tape recordings, or letters relating to any juvenile and/or adults which tend to show the identity of juveniles and adults and sexual conduct between juveniles and adults.

5. Magazines, books, movies, photographs, and/or drawings, artifacts or statues depicting nudity and/or sexual activities of juveniles for adults, as well as collections of newspapers, magazines, and other publication clippings of juveniles.

6. Indicia of occupancy consisting of articles of personal property tending to establish the identity of the person or persons in control of the premises as described above, including but not limited to rent receipts, canceled mail, keys, utility bills, and phone bills.

7. Women's clothing, including but not limited to lingerie, underclothing, stockings, nylon or otherwise, garter belts, etc.

8. Sexual aids, including but not limited to dildoes, vibrators, lotions, etc.

9. Bathtub with lion's feet.

10. Photographs of described feature, fixtures and personal belongings described by minor victim including the following:

    a. Bathtub with lion's feet.

    b. A cross on the ceiling of the residence and walls painted black.

    c. Hard or hardwood floor described by minor victim.

11. Fingerprints (latent prints) of minor victim and/or victims located within the residence.

AFFIDAVIT OF GLENN PAMFILOFF

1. Your affiant is an Inspector of the San Francisco Police Department having been a police officer for 17 years, almost eight of which he had been assigned as an inspector in the Juvenile Detail of the San Francisco Inspectors Bureau. Affiant has specialized in child molesting cases including child pornography. Affiant further states that he has taken classes in child pornography as well as lectured to numerous educators and child welfare workers in the field of child pornography. Further affiant has been the training officer in child pornography for the San Francisco Police Department for the last three years. He has investigated hundreds of cases of child pornography and sexual abuse as well as read material on the above subject. He has talked to child molesters, pedophiles and people who deal in filming, selling and buying pictures of and paraphernalia used in child pornography.

Affiant has read research reports, and articles on the subject of child pornography and child exploitation. I have viewed pictures, movies, video tapes and commercially distributed child pornography depicting juvenile girls and boys posing in a sexually provocative manner and engaging in sexual acts with each other and adults.

Affiant has corresponded with adults, while working covert investigations, who have explained to affiant in detail how they managed to seduce their juvenile victims into sexual activity and picture-taking sessions.

Affiant has also investigated other child pornography cases in conjunction with the U.S. Postal Inspectors Office, U.S. Customs and numerous other police agencies in the field of child pornography.

Based on affiants experience, training and expertise, it is affiant's opinion that adults who participate in child molestation and photograph or film incidents of child molestation rarely, if ever, dispose of their sexually explicit material, especially when it is used in the seduction of their victims and the materials are treated as prized possessions. These materials have been found in prior investigations to be concealed in safety deposit boxes, private commercial storage spaces, beneath homes, buried, in automobiles, hidden inside of legitimate books, etc.

2. Child molesters often correspond and/or meet with each other, share information and identify their victims as a means of gaining status, trust, acceptance and psychological support.

3. Child molesters rarely destroy correspondence from other molesters or victims unless requested to do so. They will conceal this material in the same manner as their explicit material.

4. Child molesters in most cases, will photograph their victims engaged in sexual activities with the molesters, other adults and other children. These pictures, films, video or other media will always be kept and are treated as prized possessions.

5. Child molesters will also use the material, material received from other molesters and commercially obtained material to illustrate to the victim what activity they wish them to engage in.

6. Child molesters to risk of discovery, often maintain their own photo developing equipment. This includes use of modern state-of-the-art instant developing equipment, such as polaroid, video recorders, etc. They will patronize large volume developing labs that deal strictly in hardcore adult pornography material to avoid detection.

7. Child molesters will often maintain lists of names, addresses, phone numbers of individuals with whom they have been in contact that share the same interests in child sex as they do. These names, addresses and phone numbers are sometimes written in phone books, address books, or on scraps of paper. At times they are computerized onto home computers for easier retrieval.

8. Child molesters will maintain names, addresses, phone numbers of victims, victim's friends, or victims of other pedophiles, athletic rosters and school rosters in the same manner as described above.

9. Child molesters may use sexual aids that are usually sold in adult bookstores and arcades, such as dildoes, vibrators, and lotions to stimulate their victim and/or selves.

10. Child molesters often maintain diaries of their experience and communications with others. They may take the form of formal diary books, note paper, or any other type of writing material.

11. Child molesters collect material on all subject matter dealing with child psychology, family sociology, child physical development and text dealing in the artistic depictions of youthful figures.

12. All the material for seizure will identify children who are being sexually exploited through child molestation, child pornography and child prostitution. The materials will also identify other adults who are engaging in the sexual exploitation of children by these means. In addition, these materials will demonstrate the sexual proclivity, inclination, preference and activities of the person under investigation, providing evidence which will tend to show that the person under investigation has committed felony child molestation (288 P.C.); misdemeanor child molestation (647A P.C.); and/or the producing, distributing, selling, trading, or the exchange of child pornography (311 and its attendant sub-section of the penal code), and contributing to the delinquency of a minor (272 P.C.).

Your affiant states that in his capacity as an Inspector for the San Francisco Police Department assigned to the Juvenile Division investigating child molestation cases, he was notified on August 13, 1987, by Clyde Foreman of the Federal Bureau of Investigation of a molestation of a minor child in the City of San Francisco. The minor child was said to be a 3-1/2 year old minor who was molested at the home of Michael A. Aquino at 123 Acme Avenue, San Francisco, CA on or about September 1, 1986 through October 31, 1986.

The information given by victim, witnesses and investigators during affiant's investigation is included in San Francisco Police Report No. 870910025 dated August 14, 1987 and authored by your affiant, Inspector Glenn Pamfiloff. Said report and its full contents is fully incorporated by reference herein as "Exhibit A" as though fully set forth.

Affiant has verified that suspect Michael A. Aquino currently lives at 123 Acme Avenue, San Francisco CA by the following information provided by Clyde Forman of the San Francisco Office of the Federal Bureau of Investigations:

1. Investigator Forman visited the residence and confirmed that Michael A. Aquino is listed on the mail box at 123 Acme Avenue, San Francisco, CA.

2. Investigator Forman stated that he interviewed the U.S. Mail Carrier and Michael A. Aquino is receiving mail at said address.

3. Investigator Forman stated the Pacific Bell informed him that their records show Michael A. Aquino having and occupying the entire upper floor including apartment no. 1, no. 2, and a rear unit.

4. Affiant then confirmed with Pacific Gas and Electric Company that Michael A. Aquino is listed in their records as receiving service at 123 Acme Avenue "top and base".

5. Affiant checked records of the California Department of Motor Vehicles and Michael A. Aquino's listed address is 123 Acme Avenue, San Francisco, CA.

Affiant further states that Investigator Clyde Foreman of the F.B.I. visited the residence and building at 123 Acme Avenue, San Francisco, CA on August 13, 1987. Investigator Foreman found the residence to be located within a gray stucco or plaster three level fourplex. The address appears in gold letters on the right side of the door frame. There are brick steps leading to a brick porch. The residence is the [numerical] building on the [compass] side of Acme Avenue from the intersection at [Adjacent] Street. The residence has white leveler blinds in all of the windows facing Acme Avenue.

The undersigned further states and declares that he has disclosed and provided the office of the District Attorney and the Court reviewing this affidavit, as part of his application for a search warrant, all known material facts, whether favorable or unfavorable to either side, including all information which may be exculpatory.

WHEREFORE affiant prays that a search warrant issue commanding the immediate search of the persons and premises above designated for the property and things above described, and that such property be brought before a magistrate or retained as provided in Section 1536 of the California Penal Code.

/s/ Glenn Pamfiloff

AFFIANT

Subscribed and sworn to before me this 14th day of August 1987.

/s/ George ?

Judge of the Municipal Court

In and for the City and County of San Francisco, State of California

Appendix 15: SFPD "Black Mass" Report by Sandi Daly [Gallant] & Michael Aquino Critique

SAN FRANCISCO POLICE DEPARTMENT INTRA-DEPARTAL MEMORANDUM

Intelligence Division Wed., 07/08/81

TO: SUBJECT:
Captain Daniel Murphy   Satanic Rituals
Commanding Officer   The Black Mass
Intelligence Division

INTRODUCTION

The witches Mass is a parody of the Christian Mass which is adapted to the worship of their own Gods. The black host, bearing the Devil's symbol, is elevated and followers cry out in adoration of him. The witches have preserved the custom of bread and wine for communion, however, they leave out the confession of sins. Followers form a cross or semi-circle around the altar and prostrate themselves on the ground prior to being given communion. After this, the Devil coupled with them and a sexual orgy would begin. Black candies, red and/or black altar cloths and red or black gowns are used, as well as the chapel being hung in red and black. On occasion, a slaughtered child is offered in sacrifice to the demons.

HISTORY

Centuries ago, black masses were used frequently to attract love or money, and even to kill. In one instance, a mass was said over a naked woman and papers were placed under the altar cloth bearing the names of those it was hoped to either attract to love or kill.

One Satanic priest baptized a child in holy oil, strangled him, and offered his corpse as a sacrifice to the Devil.

On many occasions young virgin females are placed naked on the altar and the priest will copulate with her while saying the mass.

MODERN MASSES

It is not uncommon, today, for animals to be used and sacrificed in Black Masses. Usually these will be black cocks, doves or chickens. Their eyes, hearts and tongues are ripped out. In some cases, the parts are placed on the altar and consecrated (depending on the animal used). In other cases, the parts are dried in the sun, ground to powder and preserved for another ritual such as the Mass for the Dead. In this mass, the priest, calls on God to free him from the fear of hell and to make the demons obedient to him. A yellow candle, which has been lit, is extinguished. The throat of a young male lamb is slit and the skin of the lamb is rubbed with the powdered organs of the cock.

Priests still follow the Catholic rites closely, but substitute "Satan" for "God" and "evil" for "good." Christian prayers are reversed and parts of the Mass read backwards. The Satanist Prayer is used.

"Our Father which WERT in heaven
Thy will be done, in heaven as
it is on earth
Lead us INTO temptation
Deliver us NOT from evil ..."

The purpose here is to degrade the Christian service and transform it as a ritual of the magical force to the glory of Satan.

Black Masses are usually kept very secretive because of the types of rituals recited during them. Satanists believe that when anyone invokes the Devil with intentional ceremonies that "the Devil comes, and is seen."

Respectfully submitted,
Sandra C. Daly, Policewoman, Star 1918

Approved by:
Jerry D. Belfield, Sergeant, Star 1540
SFPD-68 (9-70)

Comments Concerning Gallant's Report:
"Satanic Rituals: The Black Mass" (7/8/81)
- by -
Michael A. Aquino
Sent to the San Francisco Police Department 8/15/89

This report, which was obviously prepared to spotlight and dramatize Gallant's statement in her "Temple of Set" report of the previous day (7/7/81) that the Temple would be performing a Black Mass on Fisherman's Wharf that month, is an absurd jumble of the most ignorant, horrific, and false myths concerning the *Missa Solemnis* or Black Mass of Satanism. It bears no resemblance whatever to the *Missa Solemnis* (Black Mass) of the Church of Satan (as retained in the archives of the Temple of Set).

The Black Mass of Christian legend was merely a propaganda device used by medieval Christian institutions in order to terrorize their members against anything non-Christian. [Much the same tactics are being used by present-day Christian fanatics and extremists to attack other religions generally and the Satanic religion in particular.] There is no evidence that anything like Gallant's Black Mass was ever conducted in actuality. It appears only in fictional accounts, most prominently J.K. Huysmans' novel *Là-Bas* (*Down There*). [Enclosed is an extract from the April 1989 *Scroll of Set* newsletter, containing an analysis of *Là-Bas* by one of our Belgian members, introduced by me.]

Gallant has no excuse whatever for representing disgusting Christian propaganda as indicative of the Black Mass as practiced by the Church of Satan and retained in the archives of the Temple of Set. The text of this ceremony is commercially published in Anton LaVey's *The Satanic Rituals* (Avon Books #W359, 1972) and thus would have been readily available to Gallant had she made any effort at all to obtain it. [A photocopy of this section of the *Satanic Rituals* is enclosed.] What she chose to do instead was to provide the San Francisco Police Department with deliberate and extremely defamatory misinformation concerning a legitimate religion. In doing so she strove to create a climate in the SFPD in which other officers (such as Glenn Pamfiloff) who trusted her "intelligence", would look for any opportunity to break into our home and seize Temple papers in anticipation of finding verification of all the horrors Gallant had been predicting. This is exactly what happened in August 1987 when Chaplain Adams-Thompson's allegations during the Presidio witchhunt provided Pamfiloff an excuse to do so [and Gallant an opportunity to accompany him].

Concerning the Black Mass of the Church of Satan, as retained in the archives of the Temple of Set:

The authentic *Missa Solemnis* is a completely legal religious ceremony. Its purpose is to criticize the god of another religion which has abused the Satanic religion and its god. Thus it occupies exactly the same place in Satanic religious ritual that the Rite of Exorcism does in Catholic religious ritual. [For purposes of comparison, a copy of the Catholic Church's Rite of Exorcism is enclosed.]

It should be noted that the Black Mass is a private ceremony for Satanists only. The Church of Satan and Temple of Set have never compelled anyone, member or not, to attend or witness the *Missa Solemnis*. This ceremony would be conducted only for individuals who request it, and then in private ceremonial facilities.

[By contrast, I must add, many unwilling persons have been forced to undergo Catholic exorcisms during the last two thousand years - usually with accompanying torture and eventual execution once the "devils" had been "cast out". Even today, when Christian churches are prohibited from torturing or killing those who resist their indoctrination (= are "possessed"), they usually manage to impose varying degrees of penance or even physical punishment on those whom they exorcise.]

The *Missa Solemnis* contains statements and judgments which would be offensive to a Catholic. Similarly the Rite of Exorcism contains statements and judgments which are extremely offensive to Satanists. If Gallant is going to attack the practice of one religion criticizing another, then let her send Captain Murphy intelligence memoranda concerning Catholic priests in San Francisco who conduct ritual exorcisms as well. [Gallant, however, has no business passing judgment on the beliefs or ceremonies of **any** church as long as no laws are broken.]

In his *Satanic Rituals*, in the section concerning the Black Mass, Anton LaVey writes:

> While the Black Mass maintains the degree of blasphemy necessary to make it effective psychodrama, it does not dwell on inversion purely for the sake of blasphemy, but elevates the concepts of Satanism to a noble and rational degree. This ritual is a psychodrama in the truest sense. Its prime purpose is to reduce or negate the stigma acquired through past indoctrination. It is also a vehicle for retaliation against unjust acts perpetrated in the name of Christianity.

Further concerning these two points:

(1) Reduce past indoctrination: The Setian/Satanic religion has always placed great importance on freeing the individual from crippling, self-destructive superstition and indoctrination. By satirizing and lampooning a vehicle of psychological control and intimidation used by an individual's former religion to keep him docile and fearful, we demonstrate the impotence of that vehicle and free the individual from its domination.

A Black Mass is tailored to its participants by the officiating Priest. A Black Mass employing Christian symbolism would not be meaningful for persons with crippling inhibitions or superstitions stemming from Buddhist or Islamic indoctrination. The Christian-symbolism Black Mass, however, was naturally most appropriate within a Church of Satan membership which had generally come from a Christianity-dominated background.

(2) Retaliation against unjust acts perpetrated in the name of Christianity: Christianity has been hurling the most vehement and unjustified abuse at Satan and Satanism in its rituals, literature, statements, and actions for the past two thousand years. [Gallant's propagandistic "description" of the Black Mass is a case in point.] The genuine Black Mass is a reaction and a response to this campaign of vilification.

Although Christian intolerance and persecution of "heretics" date from antiquity, attacks on nonChristians grew steadily. More times than can be counted the populations of conquered "heathen" cultures were given the choice to convert or be put to the sword. Wars such as the Crusades were regularly funded and fought simply to spread Christianity's sphere of control, taxation, and exploitation.

The Middle Ages and the Renaissance witnessed the uninterrupted slaughter of accused witches and Satanists throughout Europe. Not content with just murdering "infidels" and "heretics", Christians invented history's most ghastly torture devices for prolonging their death agonies: iron masks that were heated red-hot then spiked to victims' faces, iron maidens, racks, boots, screws, and back-breaking wheels that are still preserved in scores of European museums. If unfortunates survived such tortures, death by burning at the stake was their reward. Accused Satanists tortured and killed in the European witch-craze have been estimated by historians as approximately 13 million.

To this may be added the Thirty Years' War, the extermination of whole pre-Columbian civilizations, and the Christian pogroms against Jews. Christianity's history is awash in the blood of those who either tried to escape it or who simply wished to live their lives free from it. We have good reason to reject it as a terrible plague of intolerance, misery, and cruelty - in its historical record a stark mockery of the messages of peace, brotherhood, and love it insists that it represents.

If the more bigoted, vicious, and fanatic elements of contemporary Christianity did not go out of their way to try to harm us, there would doubtless be no motive for the *Missa Solemnis* to ever be performed. It would become simply a historical curiosity. But if the Temple of Set's religious beliefs are flagrantly distorted and misrepresented by Sandi Gallant, and if its private, non-criminal papers are confiscated by Glenn Pamfiloff on the excuse of a search warrant which has nothing to do with them, and if Christian clergymen such as Chaplain Adams-Thompson can make the most vicious attacks upon us and be sheltered by society when they do so, then obviously the anger and resentment which inspired Satanists to create the *Missa Solemnis* are indeed justified.

Appendix 16: Sandi Gallant "Satanism and Witchcraft" Definitions

[Gallant entries and definitions in these Italics.
Aquino 1986 comments in this regular typeface.]

DEFINITIONS - SATANISM AND WITCHCRAFT
Information Furnished by Officer Sandi Gallant
San Francisco Police Department
Intelligence Division
(415) 553-1133

ACOLYTES — *Initiates*
A Christian term referring to an assistant at a liturgical mass. Not used in Satanism.

ALPHA — *Main ritual room*
Not used by Satanists to identify a ritual room [or anything else except a letter of the Greek alphabet and a type of brain-wave].

ALTAR — *Ritual table*
Ritual table used in any religion.

ATHAME — *Ritual knife*
Ritual knife used by nature-worshipping neopagan groups (Wiccans) - not by Satanists.

BELL — *Rung to begin and end rituals*
Used to begin and end some Satanic rituals. Also used in virtually every other religion for the same reason.

BLACK MAGIC — *Use of power for evil purposes*
As employed by Satanists, this term has nothing to do with the "use of power for evil purposes". From the *Crystal Tablet of Set*:

> **Lesser Black Magic** is the influencing of beings, processes, or objects in the objective universe by application of obscure physical or behavioral laws.

> **Greater Black Magic** is the causing of change to occur in the subjective universe in accordance with the Will. This change in the subjective universe will cause a similar and proportionate change in the objective universe.

[These are both extremely complex concepts, and involve several chapters in my book The Temple of Set.]

BLK WIDOW SPIDER — *Mark of death*
No significance beyond being a poisonous spider. Not used in Satanic rituals.

BLOOD — *The part of man which survives death. In drinking it you acquire his divine quality*
A physiological component of man which dies at the same time he does. In drinking it I understand you acquire diarrhea.

CELEBRANT — *Presiding priest (Sacrifist)*
The presiding priest in any religion.

CELEBRANTS — *Junior mothers and fathers*
More than one celebrant. [What in the world are "junior mothers and fathers"?]

CHAPTERS — *Branches of church organization*
May be branches of other church organizations, but not Satanic ones. Branches of the Church of Satan were called Grottos, and those of the Temple of Set are Pylons.

CIRCLE — *9' diamater on floor. Magic done inside for protection and concentration*
Satanists do not use a "circle on the floor for protection and concentration". Protection from what? The same dæmonic forces they consider allies? Tosh.

COVEN — *Branch of organization. Ideal number in witchcraft is 13. May range from 4-20 members*
Term used in Wicca (neo-pagan "white witchcraft") only. Not used in Satanism.

COVENANTOR	*Ministers of lowest rank*	
	Not used in Satanism. Presumably a Wiccan term.	
DEGREE	*Ranking within organization*	
	Initiatory recognition of wisdom and expertise.	
DEMONCRACY (sic)	*Worship of an evil nature*	
	Presumably *demonocracy*. Possibly a form of democracy for demons?	
DISCIPLE	*Lay member*	
	Not used in Satanism. Christian term referring to Matthew, Mark, Luke, John, *et al*.	
EARS	*Signify wisdom and spiritual development*	
	Funny-looking things on your head you hear through.	
ESBAT	*Coven meetings*	
	Both "esbat" and "coven" are Wiccan terms, not used in Satanism.	
EVANGELIST	*Represents Satan at rituals*	
	Propagandist for Christianity, not used in Satanism.	
EYES	*The "evil eye" is feared*	
	Organs through which you see. Neither "good" nor "evil" in themselves.	
FINGER	*Holds spiritual powers. Index finger is known as "poison, witch or cursing finger". Must not use it to touch a wound or it will never heal.*	
	Good for picking nose and signaling in traffic disputes.	
FIRE	*Symbolizes Satan*	
	May symbolize Satan. Also symbolizes Jehovah, who appeared as a pillar of fire to Moses and also as a burning bush.	
GOAT	*Believe Satan appears in form of a goat*	
	Part of the Sigil of Baphomet, representing Satan as *Ba-neb-Tettu* (the "Ram Lord of Mendes") from ancient Egyptian religion.	
HAIR	*Holds character. In witchhunt times it was believed sorcerers* (sic) *magical potency was in his hair*	
	Keeps head warm. In [non-Gallant] witchhunt times, it frequently contained lice.	
HEAD	*Central powerhouse of the body. Believed to be the seat of the soul and to contain potent magical powers*	
	Keeps eyes, hair, and ears from falling apart.	
HEART	*Symbol of eternity and the seat of emotion and intellect. Hearts may be eaten in order to acquire characteristics of victim. By controlling the heart of another, you control his entire being*	
	Pump for blood. Not eaten by Satanists.	
HIGH PRIEST	*Top leaders - male gender*	
	Chief religious official and organizational executive in the Church of Satan and Temple of Set. Used in Wicca as a ceremonial role only, and in Verdi operas, etc. as the villain.	
HIGH PRIESTESS	*Top leaders - female gender.*	
	Title held by Diane LaVey (Mrs. Anton Szandor LaVey) exclusively in the Church of Satan. The title would only be used in the Temple of Set were a female to become chief religious official [in which case there would be no High Priest]. Wiccan covens are usually headed by women, who generally call themselves by this title.	
ICONS	*Sacred ornate frames decorated with red cloth*	
	Eastern Orthodox Christian devices - not used in Satanism.	
INITIATE	*New member*	
	Any member of the Temple of Set [not just a new one].	
INVERTED CROSS	*Mockery of christian cross*	
	The only use for an inverted cross in Satanism would be as a shock/satire element in a Black Mass (*Missa Solemnis*).	
INVERTED PENTAGRAM	*Five pointed star with single point downward*	
	Symbol of the Temple of Set.	

IPSISSMUS — *Highest order held in Satanism. Rarely attainable during a lifetime.*
Correct spelling: *Ipsissimus*. Highest degree in the Temple of Set [held by M.A. Aquino]. Previously used in various non-Satanic occult organizations in Western civilization, such as the British Orders of the Golden Dawn and Silver Star.

I.P. MESSENGER — *Minister of lowest rank*
A term particular to the Process Church of the Final Judgment. Its full meaning is "Inner Processean Messenger", and refers to one of the higher intermediate ranks in that organization [not a "minister of lowest rank"].

MAGICK — *Science art causing change to occur in conformity to thy will*
This peculiar spelling specifically indicates the ceremonial system of Aleister Crowley. It is not used by Satanists except to refer to that system. [Gallant's [misquoted] definition is taken from Crowley's *Magick in Theory and Practice*.]

MASS — *Ceremony*
Term referring to a ceremony in many religions, principally Catholicism.

MASTER — *Top leader*
The term "Master of the Temple" identifies one of the senior degrees of initiation in the Temple of Set and the Church of Satan [as well as in many predecessor systems of Western Rosicrucianism and Freemasonry].

MENTOR — *Senior brothers sisters*
Greek term for "teacher". Not used as a formal designation in Satanism.

MINOR LUMINARY — *Lieutenants to leaders*
Astronomical term for a less-brilliant star. Has nothing to do with Satanism, except that some Satanists are amateur astronomers.

MISSAL — *Book with rituals and teachings*
Catholic book with rituals and teachings. Not used in Satanism.

NECROMANCY — *Conjuring spirits of the dead to magically reveal the future or influence course of events*
Religious rituals involving the invocation of deceased persons, as in the Easter services of Christianity. [Satanists do not consider "spirits of the dead to magically reveal the future or influence the course of events".]

NESTS — *Branches of groups*
Bunches of twigs in which birds live.

NUDITY — *Believed essential to raising forces through which magic works*
Human beings with no clothes on. [Not considered "essential to raising forces through which magic works".]

O.P. MESSENGER — *Student Ministers*
Another Process Church term: "Outer Processean Messenger" [junior in rank to the IP Messenger - see above].

PENTACLE — *Disc shaped talisman*
Not a "disc-shaped talisman". It is a term used to refer to a variety of pentagram- or pentagon-based magical designs drawn by medieval occultists for ceremonial operations.

PENTAGRAM — *Five pointed star w/single point upward*
Satanists use this symbol with a single point downward [not upward]. Wiccans use a point-upward pentagram.

PROPHETS — *Senior brothers and sisters*
Process Church term for high-level members. Not used in Satanism.

PROVISIONAL
MASTER — *Lieutenants leaders*
Term not used in Satanism.

RESPONDERS — *At rituals he states natures of Lucifer and Christ*
Term not used in Satanism.

RIGHT PATH	*Path taken in white magic*
	Correct term: "Right-Hand Path". Generally describes "white light" occistuism.
RITUAL	*Tool to focus individual power of group members on a common concern or object*
	Standardized recitations or pageants used in any religion.
SABBAT	*Significant holidays and celebrations of which there are eight during the year*
	Judæo-Christian term for a religious holy day, now used by neo-pagan Wiccan groups. Not used by Satanists.
SACRIFIST	*Presiding priest - represents Christ*
	Why in the world would a presiding Satanic Priest represent Christ?
SANCTUM	*Main ritual room*
	Old Latin term, commonly used to refer to a private office or study. Does not refer to a Satanic ritual room.
SATANISTS	*Practitioners of satanic worship*
	This figures.
SERPANT (sic)	*Serpant w/horns is symbolic of the demons*
	[Correct spelling: *serpent*]. Personally I have never seen a "serpent with horns", but if I did, I can't imagine why I would consider it "symbolic of the demons".
SERVERS	*Ritual assistants*
	Christian religious ritual assistants. [Not used in Satanism.]
SHRINE	*Ritual table*
	Term not used to refer to a "ritual table" in Satanism. Used in the Jewish faith for this purpose.
SKULL	*Human or animal used in rites*
	Keeps head, hair, eyes, and ears from falling apart. Used in some Satanic ceremonies, Catholic religious shrines, and anatomy lessons.
SORCERERS	*Those who have made a pact with the devil*
	Popular term generally referring to senior practitioners of the Left-Hand Path [see above]. Sorcerers do not have to make "pacts with the Devil".
SUPERIORS	*Junior mothers and fathers*
	A Catholic term referring to the head of a religious order of priests or nuns. Not a title used in Satanism. [I ask again: What in the world are "junior mothers and fathers"?]
TALISMAN	*An object believed to hold magical powers*
WARLOCK	*Male Practitioner of satanism or witchcraft*
	Male practitioner of Satanism [not Temple of Set]. Term not used in neopagan witchcraft (Wicca).
WATER	*Symbolizes Christ*
	Water does not symbolize Christ to Satanists. Rather it signifies any number of water-aligned deities and dæmons, such as the Kraken, Poseidon, Typhon, Dagon, Leviathan, Nessie, and Cthulhu.
WHITE MAGIC	*Uses magical powers to do good*
	As employed by Satanists, this term has nothing to do with "using magical power to do good". Harmless pageantry.
WITCH	*Female practitioner of satanism or witchcraft*
	Female practitioner of Satanism [not the Temple of Set]. In Wicca a practitioner of either sex.
WITNESS	*Student ministers*
	Term not used in Satanism.

Appendix 17: Letter, M. Aquino to SFPD Chief Jordan 9/7/87

Lt.Col. Michael A. Aquino
Post Office Box #4507
St. Louis, Missouri 63108

September 7, 1987

Chief of Police Frank M. Jordan
San Francisco Police Department
Hall of Justice
850 Bryant Street
San Francisco, California 94103

Dear Chief Jordan:

I believe that my wife, myself, and the church to which we belong (and of which I am the chief executive officer) have been treated by SFPD officers in a manner contrary to the standards of justice which the Department maintains. I am writing to ask your help in correcting the matter, in the continuing absence of an answer by Sergeant/Inspector Glen Pamfiloff to my letter of August 28 (copy enclosed).

The problem is a two-fold one: (1) a recent search of my residence and seizure of my property - and property of my church - by Sergeant/Inspector Glen Pamfiloff of the Juvenile Division, and (2) The "intelligence" activities of an officer named Sandi Gallant. The sequence of events is recounted in the enclosed issue of the *Scroll of Set*, newsletter of my church. A current informational paper concerning this church is also enclosed for your information, as is a copy of my personal resumé.

Where Sergeant/Inspector Pamfiloff is concerned, it is my feeling that:

(1) Pamfiloff failed to adequately research the allegation before obtaining the search warrant. Had he called the Presidio Headquarters to ascertain my whereabouts during the, period the incidents are said to have occurred, he would have learned that I was assigned as a full-time student in the National Defense University, Washington, D.C. [as an Army Lt. Colonel on active duty]. It would have been equally easy for him to verify my wife's residence there with me, both through NDU and through the Washington apartment building where we leased our apartment.

(2) Pamfiloff acted solely upon the hearsay statements of the stepfather of a 3-1/2 year-old child, who was supposedly providing detailed information about a sex-abuse incident that happened when she was 2-1/2. This same child's testimony concerning one Gary Hambright was ruled incompetent by a judge, and the child's stepfather promptly gave statements to the San Francisco media expressing his indignation at the judge's decision.[159]

(3) The child, apparently in the company of an FBI agent and her stepfather, was taken to my house on [a San Francisco] Hill and erroneously identified it as the home of Hambright.[160]

---

[159] At the time I wrote this letter, I was still confusing media stories about the Tobins with A-T's accusations.

[160] Actually Kinsey A-T had not "identified" our home at all, as the actual CID report of that trip would verify, but that report was concealed from me until Discovery in *Aquino v Stone* in 1991. Here I was responding to Pamfiloff's assertion in his Incident Report.

(4) Since neither my wife nor I have ever met this child, and since she has never been to any of our homes [including the one in San Francisco], I assume that her "identification" of myself and my wife, and her "recognition" of the [San Francisco] Hill building, were the result of coaching and prompting by her stepfather. In Pamfiloff's Incident Report it is stated that the stepfather prompted the child several times before getting any "identification" from her in the PX.

The child is said to have recalled and identified - from age 2-1/2, a year earlier - the difference between men's and women's clothing, "lion's feet" on a bathtub, and a movie camera [as distinct, presumably, from a still camera]. The bathtub was inconsistently described as a "bathtub with lion's feet" and a "plastic lion bathtub".

Such implausible detail and recall from an infant, together with the inconsistency of her description of the bathtub, should have alerted Pamfiloff to the probability of coaching by her disgruntled stepfather, rather than bona-fide information. He also knew, presumably, that a judge had recently ruled this same child incompetent to testify in court.

(5) On the basis of this incompetent information and erroneous building identification, Pamfiloff applied for and obtained a search warrant.

(6) Upon executing the warrant, Pamfiloff was able to ascertain immediately that the child's supposed "interior descriptions" did not fit my flat. This, together with the insubstantiality of the accusations made by the stepfather, should have justified his terminating the search immediately. Nevertheless it continued.

(7) At the conclusion of the search, Pamfiloff had found nothing whatever relevant to child-molesting, which is not surprising since neither my wife nor I are or ever have been child-molesters. Nevertheless he confiscated a number of personal articles and official papers of our church - none of which have anything to do with child-molesting. As of this date these articles still have not been returned.

(8) A police photographer was present during the search, and took pictures both at random and of whatever articles she was directed to by Pamfiloff or other personnel present. There is now therefore a complete set of photographs of the interior of my home, and any number of personal effects and papers in it, in the SFPD archives. As my wife and I have never committed any crimes, and as the premises have never been involved in the commission of any crimes, I do not think the SFPD possession of these photographs to be warranted.

With regard to the actions of Sergeant/Inspector Pamfiloff, therefore, I respectfully request the following:

(1) That my personal property, and the property of my church, be completely returned to me without further delay, and that you instruct the SFPD not to retain in its files any copies of any of this material, whether photographs or papers.

(2) That you order that all of the photographs taken of my home and property during the search be destroyed, along with their negatives.

(3) That you order the immediate cessation of any efforts by Pamfiloff to continue with this misdirected and unjustified investigation, and that you advise the San Francisco office of the FBI and the San Francisco office of the CID of your decision.

Where Officer Sandi Gallant is concerned, it is my feeling that:

(1) She is maintaining "intelligence" files on a legitimately credentialled church with no record of any criminal involvement or doctrines.

(2) She is presumably maintaining a similar file concerning myself, who also have no record of any criminal involvement.

(3) She has openly and without qualification associated the term "Satanic" with child-molesting, in disregard that there are at least two legitimate, formally-incorporated Satanic churches - the Temple of Set and the Church of Satan - which have nothing whatever to do with child-molesting.

(4) She continues to represent herself to the media and to law-enforcement agencies as an "expert" on Satanism, and on occultism in general, despite her conspicuous unfamiliarity with these fields.

With regard to the actions of Officer Sandi Gallant, therefore, I respectfully request the following:

(1) That you order the immediate destruction of any files she or her office may be maintaining on the Temple of Set or myself, the maintenance of such files being a violation of the First and Fourteenth Amendments to the Constitution providing for non-discrimination against religions and equal protection of the law. Further that you forbid her to amass any new "intelligence" on the Temple or myself in the absence of any properly documented and warranted Police action.

(2) That you order her to cease associating the terms "Satanic" or "Satanism" with crimes in general, and child-molesting in particular. These are terms particular to a bona-fide and officially-recognized religion in the United States which is not in any sense a criminal activity. Its religious terminology should not be associated with the crimes of individuals any more than the term "Christian" is associated with the crimes of individuals using its symbolisms irresponsibly [for example, Jim Jones].

(3) That you order her to cease representing herself as an expert on either occultism in general or Satanism in particular -fields which require years of serious study. [If you wish, the Temple of Set can recommend a curriculum of study for her which will give her a solid grounding in this subject matter.] Whether she represents herself as an expert in child-molesting as a criminal matter is SFPD business, of course.

You should also know that I have formally requested the U.S. Army to take disciplinary action against the captain/chaplain who falsely accused myself and my wife. It is also my intention to file a civil suit against him for his actions.[161]

I should also add that, to date, I have contacted neither the media nor any community or governmental office above the SFPD concerning this entire affair. My family has lived in San Francisco for the last hundred years, and I have always regarded the SFPD as a thoroughly reputable, responsible, and distinguished institution. I have no desire whatever to see it embarrassed before the public eye, or for that matter before outside government review systems, because of the actions of two individual officers. I am therefore hoping that you can correct this situation through your own administrative systems, so that no further concern need be paid to it.

In conclusion I would like to reaffirm my personal support, and the support of the Temple of Set, for the Department's efforts on behalf of justice. If we can ever be of any assistance to you or your officers in this regard, please feel welcome to contact us.[162]

> Respectfully,
> /s/ Michael A. Aquino

---

[161] As recounted in this book, I twice filed court-martial charges against Larry A-T, both of which were suppressed in violation of the Uniform Code of Military Justice. I was unable to file civil suit against him or his wife, because they had been careful to make their accusations only to law-enforcement officials, which provides personal legal immunity.

[162] The SFPD did not answer this letter.

Appendix 18: Letter, Bernard Zimmerman to SFPD Chief Jordan 9/18/87

LAW OFFICES OF
PILLSBURY, MADISON & SUTRO
225 BUSH STREET
POST OFFICE BOX 7880
SAN FRANCISCO, CALIFORNIA 94120

September 18, 1987

Frank N. Jordan
Chief of Police
850 Bryant Street
Room 525
San Francisco, CA 94103

Dear Chief Jordan:

This firm represents Lt. Col. and Mrs. Michael A. Aquino.

On August 14, 1987 Inspector Pamfiloff and other officers of your department executed a search warrant on the Aquino residence. For your convenience I enclose a copy of the "warrant", not signed by a judge, that was presented to them during the search. As you can see from the inventory, a substantial number of personal items were seized by your officers as well as items belonging to the Temple of Set, a church organization of which Lt. Col. Aquino is High Priest.

On September 7, 1987 Lt. Col. Aquino sent you a letter of complaint about the search, containing a number of requests, including that his property and the property of his church be returned. To date he has received no response to his letter.

Shortly after the search I contacted Inspector Pamfiloff, orally and in writing, to request a copy of the complete search warrant, its supporting affidavit, the police report of the seizure, and the return of the seized property. Enclosed please find a copy of my letter of August 20, 1987. Inspector Pamfiloff's response was that he would get back to me when he completed processing the seized property.

Thereafter Inspector Pamfiloff filed his affidavit and report. I obtained a copy from the clerk. After learning of the charges Inspector Pamfiloff was investigating, and discussing them with my clients, I called Pamfiloff. I was told he was on disability leave and that the case had been reassigned to Sgt. Eisenman.

I called Eisenman and advised him that my clients could not possibly have committed the acts in question. I told him that they had lived continuously from June of 1986 through August of 1987 in Washington, D.C., where Lt. Col. Aquino had been ordered to attend the National Defense University, and that during the period in question Lt. Col. Aquino was attending classes daily except for certain periods which we could document and which were generally related to his receiving medical treatment.

I offered to meet with Sgt. Eisenman to provide him with as much detail as I could so he could confirm my clients' story. Sgt. Eisenman's response was that the Police Department could do its own investigating.

I called back a few days later only to be told that the investigation was continuing. I offered to identify military personnel in Washington, D.C. who could confirm my clients' whereabouts, but Sgt. Eisenman replied that my help was not needed. I have subsequently called Sgt. Eisenman on several occasions and he has not returned those calls.

As of this date, my clients stand falsely accused of a very serious charge, and your department seems to be making no effort to contact the appropriate military personnel in Washington, D.C. to develop the information which will clear them. Nor has your department returned any of the seized property.

On behalf of the Aquinos I hereby request that you forthwith conduct an internal investigation into this matter with two ends in mind:

One is to clear the Aquinos and return their property to them. We stand ready to cooperate with your department in this regard.

Another is to determine whether your officers acted properly in obtaining and executing the warrant, in failing to return the seized property timely, and in failing to timely conduct the necessary investigation to clear my clients. Again we stand ready to cooperate with your investigating officers and to disclose full particulars of the manner in which we believe your officers acted irresponsibly, some of which are set forth in Lt. Col. Aquino's letter to you.

I frankly do not understand why your officers would prefer to believe the unsubstantiated statement of a three-year-old girl over the statement of a Lt. Colonel in the United States Army and the other military personnel who stand ready to support him. I hope it is not because your officers are prejudiced against the Aquinos because of their religious affiliation. I am sure you are as interested as the Aquinos are in getting this matter resolved, and trust you will give this letter your prompt attention.[163]

Yours very truly,
/s/ Bernard Zimmerman

---

[163] The SFPD did not answer this letter.

Appendix 19: Letter, M. Aquino to SFPD Chief Jordan 10/18/87

Lt.Col. Michael A. Aquino
Post Office Box #4507
St. Louis, Missouri 63108

October 18, 1987

Chief of Police Frank M. Jordan
San Francisco Police Department
Hall of Justice
850 Bryant Street
San Francisco, California 94103

Dear Chief Jordan:

To date I have received no answer to my letter to you of September 7, 1987 concerning your review of the actions of Sergeant/Inspector Glenn Pamfiloff and Officer Sandi Gallant. My attorney, Mr. Bernard Zimmerman of Pillsbury, Madison & Sutro, has been left with the impression that the SFPD is uninterested in any effort to settle the situation cooperatively and constructively through administrative procedures, and that the only course open to me is thus formal litigation.

This is very disappointing to me because, as I indicated in my 9/7 letter, I have never in my life regarded the SFPD as an adversary. I will of course do what I am forced to do to preserve my rights and reputation as a citizen, but I deplore having to do so because of a situation which my common sense tells me is completely unnecessary.

If you are in fact conducting your own administrative review of the actions of Pamfiloff and Gallant, I would very much appreciate word from your office to that effect. If I am informed that you have indeed begun such an internal investigation, I would want to wait until you had a reasonable time to complete it before acting on my attorney's advice.

Further concerning the activities of Sandi Gallant:

Officer Gallant is currently distributing to law-enforcement agencies and private child-abuse action organizations the enclosed papers, which freely and repeatedly attribute various illegal practices to "Satanism". The very fact that these papers are being distributed in the name of the San Francisco Police Department has the effect of conveying the Department's endorsement of them, and of implying that "Satanism" is in fact a criminal activity rather than the code of beliefs of a legitimate and law-abiding religion.

With my 9/7 letter to you I enclosed a statement of the Temple of Set's actual ethics and thoroughly-legitimate standards, so there should be no question as to what we believe and practice. We stand ready at any time, as we always have, to discuss our philosophy with any representative of yours.

Sandi Gallant's papers, in addition to seriously misleading law-enforcement and private agencies concerning legitimate Satanism, also contain a great many errors of fact which I have addressed in my attached critique. I have assembled this critique not only to demonstrate Gallant's incompetence as an advertised "expert" on Satanism, but also because the SFPD's continued endorsement and dissemination of these papers may very well mislead other law-enforcement civic agencies concerning the topics addressed, with the ultimate effect of possibly confusing crime investigations and ultimately embarrassing you both in official channels and in the media as the authority under whose license Gallant is advertising herself.

As I mentioned in my 9/7 letter, the Temple of Set has more information on occultism in general, and on Satanism in particular, than any other institution in existence. We have regularly been consulted by academics, the press, and other law-enforcement agencies accordingly, and have invariably done our best to assist them. You may wish to contact Detective Metoyer of the Los Angeles Police Department (213) 485-2962 and Detective Smith of the L.A.P.D. Gang Division (213) 485-2501 for two verifications of this.

It accordingly strikes us as more than a little absurd that the Police Department in our own city should not only not avail itself of our assistance in research which it considers important, but instead approaches us like the Ghostbusters assaulting a haunted house. I would like to think that Sandi Gallant's enthusiasm for her personal media image does not overrule your own concern and responsibility for the entire Department's professional precision and reputation.

If you had been provided with accurate information concerning the Temple of Set and the Satanic religion, I am certain you would understand my indignation at the Pamfiloff/Gallant raid on my San Francisco home this past August. In fact, if you had been provided with accurate information, I doubt that such an event would have occurred in the first place. It is for this reason that I am more concerned with the quality of the "intelligence" being fed your officers by Gallant than I am with the specific actions of Pamfiloff, who - as a consequence of believing such "intelligence" - may have honestly assumed that he was setting out that evening to confront all manner of nameless horrors and brain-curdling blasphemies at my San Francisco home.

Gallant has never voluntarily provided copies of her "intelligence" papers either to me or to the press, claiming repeatedly that they are "official police business". It is quite obvious now that they are nothing of the sort - that they contain no information sensitive to any police procedure or investigation. It is more conspicuously the case that she did not want them seen by persons such as myself who know enough about the subject material to expose them for their thoroughly inadequate and unprofessional substance.

Accompanying Gallant's "intelligence papers" is the enclosed "Ritualistic Crime Profile and Questionnaire". Based as it is on her "intelligence papers", I see no need to critique it for you, as I trust the point concerning its thorough inadequacy is made. I also note on the Questionnaire that Captain Daniel Murphy has requested that it "not be duplicated or distributed without prior written consent of the Intelligence Department of the SFPD". While the Temple of Set will honor this request, **child abuse action groups are not doing so**, with the result that yet one more set of misleading papers from Gallant attributed to your Department is in uncontrolled circulation.

I would appreciate some indication from you as to the disposition the matters mentioned in my 9/7 letter. As stated in that letter and reemphasized in this one, I very much wish to resolve these matters cooperatively and constructively, rather than adversarily.[164]

Sincerely,
/s/ Michael A. Aquino

---

[164] The SFPD did not answer this letter.

Appendix 20: Motion to Restore Property, San Francisco Municipal Court

PILLSBURY, MADISON & SUTRO
BERNARD ZIMMERMAN
SHAWN HANSON
225 Bush Street
Post Office Box 7880
San Francisco, CA 94120
Telephone: (415) 983-1179

Attorneys for Lieutenant Colonel and Mrs. Michael Aquino

Dated: October 28, 1987.

Municipal Court of the City and County of San Francisco. State of California

In re: 36 video tapes, etc. seized from LIEUTENANT COLONEL and MRS. MICHAEL AQUINO

MEMORANDUM OF POINTS AND AUTHORITIES
IN SUPPORT OF MOTION TO RESTORE PROPERTY

On August 14, 1987 the San Francisco Police Department executed a search warrant on the home of Lieutenant Colonel and Mrs. Michael Aquino. The Aquinos were given an unsigned copy of the warrant, a true and correct copy of which is attached to the declaration of Bernard Zimmerman as Exhibit A. The police seized a substantial amount of property. A copy of the inventory as given to the Aquinos is attached to the Zimmerman declaration as Exhibit B. It does not list all the seized property (Zimmerman Decl.).

Almost three months have now passed. The Aquinos have not been charged with any crime. The Police Department has refused to return their property despite repeated oral and written requests.[165] True and correct copies of the written requests are attached to the Zimmerman declaration as Exhibits C, D, E. The Police Department has provided no explanation for its continued retention of the property. Instead it has taken the position that its policy is to require the owner to retain an attorney and go to court to obtain an order for the return of property. The Police Department will not seek such an order. Accordingly the Aquinos have now moved this Court for an order restoring all the seized property to them.

---

[165] Since this motion was first prepared, the Police Department first offered to return the property, then changed their mind and then offered to return some of it. The Aquinos have no idea what the Police Department's actual position is except that no property has yet been restored to them (Zimmerman Decl.).

ARGUMENT

Penal Code section 1540 provides as follows:

> If it appears that the property taken is not the same as that described in the warrant, or that there is no probable cause for believing the existence of the grounds on which the warrant was issued, the magistrate must cause it to be restored to the person from whom it was taken. Leg. H. 1872 (Pen. Code § 1540)

In addition this Court, as the repository of the seized property, has the power to release improperly seized or retained property under both Penal Code section 1536 and "the inherent power of the court to control and prevent the abuse of its process" (*Buker v. Superior Court* (1972) 25 Cal. App. 3d 1085).

In this case, there is no reason why the property should not be returned and many reasons why it should.

First, a review of the incomplete inventory discloses that the property seized is not the same as the property described in the warrant. For example, nothing in the warrant describes a computer or any of the 36 videotapes which, as the evidence to be produced in the courtroom will show, are mostly commercially released videotapes of movies such as *Star Trek*. Even as to those items of seized property, such as "miscellaneous loose papers with names and addresses", which have some superficial relation to property described in the warrant, the evidence at the hearing will clearly establish that the papers seized do not contain names or addresses which would tend to "identify any juvenile".[166]

The seized property does include membership lists and similar records of a religious organization, the Temple of Set, of which Lt. Col. Aquino is High Priest. As such the property should be restored since its seizure and continued retention violates the freedoms of religion, privacy, and association guaranteed by the United States and California Constitutions. For example, in *NAACP v. Alabama* (1958) 357 U.S. 449, the Supreme Court struck as unconstitutional an order requiring the NAACP to produce its membership lists.

> Inviolability of privacy in group association may in many circumstances be indispensable to preservation of freedom of association, particularly where a group espouses dissidents beliefs. (id.)

Nor is. there any probable cause for believing the existence of the grounds on which the warrant was issued. The Police Department knew or should have known that the information upon which the affidavit in support of the warrant was based was inaccurate.

Assuming, however, for purposes of this motion that the warrant was properly issued, there is certainly no longer any probable cause to connect the Aquinos with any of the alleged crimes in connection with which the property was seized. The investigation into those crimes has been conducted by the Federal Bureau of Investigation and the United States District Attorney's Office. As the Police Department well knows, the Honorable Joseph Russoniello, United States Attorney, recently announced that after an extensive investigation of those alleged crimes, a federal grand jury returned an indictment against one Gary Hambright and that no further arrests would be made because there was no evidence of any co-perpetrator (Zimmerman Decl.).

Moreover, the Aquinos were living in Washington, D.C. during the period when the alleged crimes were committed, where Lieutenant Colonel Aquino was regularly attending the National Defense University while on assignment by the United States Army (Zimmerman Decl.).

Instead, it appears that the only reason the Police Department has not returned the Aquinos' property is because of a policy or practice it has of requiring the owner of the property to retain counsel and affirmatively move this Court for a return of property. Such a policy or practice constitutes a deprivation of the rights to be free from

---

[166] Similar constitutional considerations require a prompt determination of whether the property was properly seized. (See *Roday v. Superior Court* (1961) 55 Cal. 789, 799).

unconstitutional searches and seizures, and to not be deprived of property without due process of law guaranteed by the Fourth and Fourteenth Amendments of the United States Constitution and by Article 1 of the California Constitution.

[Section 1540] does not put the burden on the citizen of suing to get the property back. It makes it the duty of the magistrate to see to its restoration by a mandatory "must". There is no discretion about it. Upon ascertaining that the property taken is not that described in the warrant - and it is not difficult to do that - he must not **order** its return, but must "cause it to be restored". Further, the statute says nothing about ownership; it deals only with possession. (*Stern v. Superior Court* (1946) 76 Cal. App. 2d 772, 784) [emphasis in original.]

These rights belong not only to the Aquinos but to all other citizens who are subject to the policy and practice of the San Francisco Police Department. This practice is an abuse of this Court's process, and this Court should order an end to it.[167]

For the foregoing reasons and for any additional reasons which may be adduced at the hearing, Lieutenant Colonel and Mrs. Michael Aquino respectfully request this Court to order that all property seized from them be restored forthwith, that an order issue directing the San Francisco Police Department to henceforth move the Court for an order permitting it to return property when it concludes that it has no reasonable basis for continuing to retain it and for an award of attorneys' fees incurred in obtaining said order.

---

[167] Under Section 10255 of the Code of Civil Procedure, the Aquinos are entitled to their attorneys' fees for vindicating this important public right.

JEFF BROWN
Public Defender

PETER G. KEANE
Chief Attorney
Grace Lidia Suarez
Deputy Public Defender
555 Seventh Street
San Francisco, California 94103
(415) 553-1671
Attorneys for *Amicus Curiæ*

Date: Nov. 24, 1987
Time: 9:00 a.m.
Dept.: 18

IN THE MUNICIPAL COURT OF THE STATE OF CALIFORNIA
IN AND FOR THE CITY AND COUNTY OF SAN FRANCISCO

In re: 36 video tapes, etc. seized from LIEUTENANT COLONEL and MRS. MICHAEL AQUINO

APPLICATION FOR LEAVE TO APPEAR AS *AMICUS CURIÆ*

TO THE HONORABLE PHILIP MOSCONE, JUDGE OF THE MUNICIPAL COURT:

The San Francisco Public Defender hereby applies for leave to appear as *amicus curiæ* in support of petitioners.

The Public Defender of the City and County of San Francisco represents the vast majority of indigents arrested by the police in this county and from whom property is seized.

As is shown in the attached declarations, the repeated refusal of the San Francisco Police Department to return property seized from arrestees or suspects constitutes an ongoing deprivation of the constitutional rights of these clients of the Public Defender, and a substantial expenditure of City funds budgeted for the use of the Public Defender's Office. The Public Defender has a deep and abiding interest in a fair resolution of this problem.

WHEREFORE, the San Francisco Public Defender respectfully requests leave to appear as *amicus curiæ* and to file a brief in support of petitioners.

Respectfully submitted,
JEFF BROWN
Public Defender

By:
Grace Lidia Suarez
Deputy Public Defender
Attorneys for *Amicus Curiæ*

BRIEF *AMICUS CURIÆ*

INTRODUCTION

Amicus believes that the actions of the San Francisco Police Department in the present case do not present an isolated instance of police misconduct, but rather a policy of the police, which encourages its officers to refuse to return property, whether seized with or without warrant, even when the property is neither contraband nor evidence in any pending case.

Support for the Public Defender's belief is found in his own, his deputies' and employees' experiences. The declarations of some of them are attached to this brief.

This policy or practice results in harm to hundreds of indigent suspects and arrestees, who are deprived of property sometimes necessary for survival. It also results in the waste of thousands of taxpayers' dollars in salaries paid to the deputy public defenders and office employees who must aid these people in obtaining their property, as well as the waste of judicial resources consumed in pointless hearings on motions for return of property.

Amicus hopes that this Court, through a strongly-worded Order commanding the return of Lt. Colonel Aquino's property, will send a clear message to the San Francisco Police Department that the courts will not abide the illegal retention of the property of citizens.

BY RETAINING PROPERTY WHICH IS NEITHER CONTRABAND NOR EVIDENCE IN A PENDING CASE, THE SAN FRANCISCO POLICE DEPARTMENT AND ITS OFFICERS VIOLATE THE CONSTITUTIONAL RIGHTS OF THE AFFECTED CITIZENS

The Fifth Amendment to the United States Constitution provides that no person shall "be deprived of ... property, without due process of law; nor shall private property be taken for public use without just compensation".

The Fourth Amendment protects citizens "against unreasonable ... seizures". The California Constitution, Articles 13 and 19, provides similar protections.

The California Supreme Court has stated in no uncertain terms its opinion that a government agency violates the law when it refuses to return property one of its agents has seized. In *Minsky v City of Los Angeles* (1974) 11 Cal. 3d 113 it stated:

Governmental officers who seize an arrestee's property bear the duty to provide a receipt, to safeguard, and to pay and deliver such property as the prisoner directs except "when otherwise ordered by a court of competent jurisdiction" (Government Code section 26640) (*Minsky*, supra at 119; emphasis added)[168]

The Court added,

... we find that the government in effect occupies the position of a bailee when it seizes from an arrestee property that is not shown to be contraband (*cit. om.*). The arrestee retains his right to eventual specific recovery, whether he seeks to regain tangible property ... or ... money ... (*Minsky*, supra at 121)

The Court reaffirmed its holding in *Minsky* in 1978 (*Holt v Kelly* (1978) 20 Cal. 3d 560, reiterating that "respondent [the Trinity County sheriff] [was] under a duty to return the claimed property to petitioner". (*Holt* supra at 564)

Government Code section 26640 details the duties of government agents who seize property from arrestees:

The sheriff[169] shall take charge of, safely keep, and keep a correct account of, all money and valuables found on each prisoner when delivered at the county jail. Except when otherwise ordered by a court of competent jurisdiction, the sheriff shall pay such money or sums therefrom or deliver such valuables as the

---

[168] It should be noted that although Government Code section 26640 refers to "the sheriff", the *Minsky* court found "no valid distinction between the duty of a county sheriff and the duty of city police officers with respect to an arrestee's property" (at 119, fn. 5).

[169] and the police (see footnote 1 supra).

prisoner directs and shall pay and deliver all the remainder ... to the prisoner upon his release from the jail (emphasis added).

In *Handschuh v Superior Court* (1985) 166 Cal. App.3d 41, 212 CR 296, the Court of Appeal held that person whose property had been taken under color of a search warrant and subsequently lost or destroyed could maintain an action under Title 42, United States Code section 1983[170] , which holds that

> Every person who, under color of any statute of any State ... subjects, or causes to be subjected, any citizen of the United States to the deprivation of any rights, privileges, or immunities secured by the Constitution and laws, shall be liable to the party injured in an action at law ... or other proper proceeding for redress. (*Handschuh* supra at 43)

This action could be brought even though the aggrieved party has a civil remedy for conversion of the property, since it constituted a violation of "the substantive guarantees of the Constitution" (quoting *Al-Mustaf a Irshad v Spann* (ED Va. 1982) 543 F. Supp. 922, 926).[171]

There is no authority for the police or any other governmental agency to retain possession of property which is not contraband, stolen property, or evidence (see *People v Superior Court* (McGraw (1979) 100 Cal.App.3d 154, 160; Penal Code Section 1411 (stolen property); *Buker v Superior Court* (1972) 25 Cal. App.3d 1085 (money)). The entire statutory scheme (Penal Code Sections 1407-1422) envisions the return of all property to its owner or possessor with the exception of dangerous or deadly weapons, narcotic or poison drugs, explosives, or items prohibited by law (Section 1419).

CONCLUSION

The actions of the San Francisco Police Department in the present case seem totally unwarranted. Furthermore they appear to be part of the larger pattern of illegal behavior observed by *amicus*. This Court should grant petitioners' motion for return of property and warn the Police Department that, by retaining property without justification, it is violating the constitution, state law, and judicial decisions.

---

[170] In the State court.

[171] It is ironic to note that the defendants in *Handschuh* were also San Francisco police officers. This practice seems to have been going on for some time.

Appendix 21: Letter, Michael Aquino to SFPD Inspector Glenn Pamfiloff 12/10/87

Lt.Col. Michael A. Aquino
Post Office Box #4507
St. Louis, Missouri 63108

December 10, 1987

Sergeant/Inspector Glenn Pamfiloff
Juvenile Division, San Francisco Police Department
2475 Greenwich Street
San Francisco, California 94123

Dear Inspector Pamfiloff:

I have recently seen television footage of you testifying on the stand at the hearing concerning the return my property and that of the Temple of Set. When Mr. Zimmerman asked you if there were other matters under investigation concerning me, you answered: "Child stealing and various subsections, child abuse, child neglect, child molests, rapes." You have also been quoted to me as expressing a desire to "nail" me for child molestation, and expressing your conviction that I and a close circle of intimates are perverts and homosexuals and chronic abusers of children.

I continue to be as perplexed by all of this as I was when you made your surprise visit to my home last August. Either you are a reputable officer who has been grossly misinformed, or you are an unprincipled one embarked on a personal crusade in which the truth is an unimportant annoyance to you. As when I wrote you my earlier letter concerning Adams-Thompson's false allegations, I would prefer to believe that you set store by your professional integrity and would not use your office to abuse persons for reasons that have nothing to do with lawbreaking.

The purpose of this letter is to set certain facts before you, and to invite you to write me personally concerning these or other issues of concern to you. If I can support my responses with documentation, I will be pleased to do that as well. As I have continually stressed to Chief Jordan and yourself, it is very exasperating for me to be forced to take legal action against the Police Department for a situation as absurd as this. While I will of course do what is necessary to clear my name and that of my church, I would much prefer that the situation be resolved in cooperation with the Police rather than at their expense.

1. Concerning my personal morality:

As you know, I am a professional Army officer. I have eighteen years' worth of annual officer efficiency reports written by superiors in daily contact with me, with whom I have socialized on off-duty time as well as on-duty. All have been aware of my religion. Copies of the last several years' OERs are enclosed. You will notice that each OER requires a rating for the subject's moral qualities, and that I have consistently received not only the highest rating, but in several cases additional comments in commendation of same.

You are also aware that, periodically throughout my military career, I have been routinely investigated by the Defense Investigative Service for security clearances up through Top Secret/Special Compartmented Information/Special Intelligence Access. Such Special Background Investigations (SBIs) are exceedingly thorough and go back through the previous 15 years of the subject's life. If I were a degenerate, a criminal, a pervert, or a homosexual, I am quite sure that it would have come out in at least one of these several investigations - which focus as much upon the subject's private, personal life as upon his professional one. The results of all of these investigations have been entirely clean of anything reprehensible, as I'm sure you have verified through the DIS.

Enclosed is a copy of my current personal resumé. I am providing it so that you can see the sorts of interests I have held throughout my life, and the professional paths I have followed. Many of these activities have resulted in distinctive awards and special recognitions to me, which necessarily reflect my character as an individual in addition to the specific work in question. I have received many high offices and honors in the Boy Scouts of America - an environment in which the slightest deviant behavior would not be ignored or excused.

In these three examples please note that I have focused upon evaluations of me made not by myself, but by other people in regular contact with me over extended periods of time, who are not members of the Temple of Set.

Also enclosed are photocopies of a chapter I wrote in my National Defense University thesis this past year in Washington on the subject of ethics. While you're at it, why don't you drop by the Political Science Department of Golden Gate University and take a look at the lesson plans I wrote for my courses in political philosophy, which emphasize the development of Western civilization's moral and ethical traditions? [The course outlines to ask for are those which I prepared for Humanities #143-C: Dynamics of Western Culture.]

2. Concerning the interests and activities of the Temple of Set:

Again I would like to begin my comments by referring to documentation.

Among the materials you confiscated from my home was my complete file of the past year's issues of *Hieroglyphs*, my newsletter as High Priest of the Temple of Set to the entire Priesthood of Set - the officials of the entire institution. As you read through them, I am sure that you saw that they had nothing even remotely do do with pedophilia or any other degenerate activity. Where they talked about integrity, in fact, they emphasized the high standards of integrity upon which the Temple of Set has always insisted. These issues of *Hieroglyphs* would dispel, I. think, any notion that pedophiliac activities are being carried on within the "secret inner circle" of the Temple. That "inner circle" - the Priesthood of Set - is concerned with maintaining the Temple's high ethical standards, not with abusing them.

In those same issues of *Hieroglyphs* you also saw a report on the past three years' financial transactions of the Temple, itemized by category. You saw that there are not the kinds or sizes of sums or transactions that would presumably appear if the Temple were trafficking in child pornography or anything else illegal. [Where my personal finances are concerned, you know that I am well off as a consequence of commercial real estate holdings, hence have no motive at all to supplement my income by means of pornography.]

In case you don't have a reasonably current copy of the *Crystal Tablet of Set*, our principal membership "guidebook", I am sending you one under separate cover. The point in doing this is simply to illustrate the immense time and effort the Temple of Set -and I myself - have devoted to developing its religious philosophy, and for you to see for yourself that this philosophy couldn't possibly be less concerned with sexual perversions concerning children. The sheer mass and complexity of this philosophy are the product not of some hastily-contrived "cover story", but of years and years of exhaustive research, dialogue, and writing by many dedicated people.

You have now seen both the "inner" and "outer" communications of the Temple of Set to its membership. You have seen our repeated and strong statements in support of legality in general, and in opposition to sexual or any other kind of abuse of children, animals, etc. - statements of policy that go back to our founding in 1975. What else can you possibly expect a church do to make its policies clear in this regard?

3. Concerning the allegations of Sandi Gallant concerning "Satanic child abuse":

I assume that Gallant is responsible for the image in your mind of Satanists as fiendishly clever maniacs who not only rape, sodomize, and murder children but also breed them so that they can rape, sodomize, and murder them that much faster. In Gallant's mind the absence of any evidence of such a nationwide assembly-line of rape, sodomy, and murder certainly doesn't mean it isn't happening; it just means that we Satanists are even more fiendishly clever than people suspect!

I am reminded of a test for witchcraft used in. the middle ages. The accused was bound hand and foot and thrown into a river. If she floated, she was guilty (the "waters of God had rejected her") - and was taken out to be burned at the stake. If she sank and stayed down, she was innocent - but of course she also drowned. Is this the kind of "test" we are now being subjected to - one in which it is unacceptable for us to be innocent, even though we are?

Gallant has a cozy situation going for her. She has been able to make allegations to fellow officers behind closed doors for years, but has never once made these allegations, and submitted her evidence for them, before any individual such as myself who has the knowledge and background to correct her. When I once asked her to do so, some years ago in the privacy of her own office, she refused with her classic response: "Official police business." That kept her ignorance from being exposed, of course, but the long-term result is that other officers like you are now paying the price for it.

I'm sure that you have seen my detailed critique to Chief Jordan of the set of Gallant's "intelligence" papers which the California Consortium of Child Abuse currently provides to inquirers. Since then my attorneys have also obtained extensive additional information concerning her allegations and statements, all admissible for court purposes. In the face of this evidence, how can you continue to let this woman manipulate you? By relying and acting on her wild fantasies, you and the Department are now in a publicly embarrassing situation that can only get worse as the media continue to bring the facts out.

I have made no secret to Chief Jordan of my opinion of Gallant as a "Satanic expert". I think that she is thoroughly incompetent and dangerously unprofessional as a police officer, since her fantasies and misinformation lead directly to the harassment and persecution of innocent people by other officers who have trusted her "intelligence".

4. Concerning Gallant's sources of information prejudicial to me or the Temple:

There are two of these whose names have been regularly brought up to me: Lewis Dale Seago and Linda Osborne Blood. Both are ex-members of the Temple of Set who were expelled for violation of our ethical standards. Both carry a grudge because of this.

Dale Seago was a high-level initiate of the Temple who was expelled for making slanderous statements concerning me and for several other acts of unethical behavior in his capacity as a senior Temple officer. He was manipulated into such behavior by his wife Amber, whom he loved very deeply, and who unfortunately happened to be having an affair behind his back [about which I had the thankless task of telling him]. When Amber was exposed, she left the Temple and made it her goal to get her husband thrown out as well. Shortly after she succeeded in this, she abandoned him. Shamed and humiliated before all of the friends and associates with whom he had worked for over a decade, he is now scarcely an objective source of information. Additional distasteful details are unnecessary here, but would certainly come out if it were necessary to impeach his testimony in court.

Linda Blood joined the Temple of Set enthusiastically in 1979 and participated actively in it. Unfortunately she also developed a sexual crush on me, which I refused to reciprocate. Her sexual fixation became so conspicuous and obnoxious that she was ultimately expelled from the Temple [by Seago, in fact, with whom she had had an affair]. She then went on a continuous campaign of leaving venomous and sexually obscene messages on the telephone answering machines of my old, terminally-ill mother, my wife, and myself. After a year of waiting for these to abate, I complained to the Lexington, Massachusetts Police Department and they took action which halted her for a time. Then she moved to another city and the calls began again, persisting to this day. Since these calls regularly contained many screaming and shrieking accusations that I was a homosexual, a sado-masochist, and almost every imaginable kind of sex-pervert, I can only suppose that Blood is the source of your above-quoted allegations. Needless to say, it would be quite easy to establish her prejudice, bias, and sexual-obsessive motives. [We have all of her answering-machine messages on tape, a copy of which accompanied my letter to the Lexington Police.] As for her experiences in the Temple of Set, we have scores of letters from her saying how much she enjoyed it, its activities, and the friends she made therein. I daresay that her frustrated sexual passions hardly justify her subsequent bitter and caustic attacks on the Temple or myself.

5. Other disaffected ex-members of the Temple of Set:

You can keep searching for these, of course, and I'm sure you will find at least some. But you would be wise to ascertain why such individuals were expelled from the Temple before you rely upon their accounts. As you have seen from our literature, we do not allow people with disruptive, destructive, or degenerate interests or behavior to enter the Temple - or to remain in it if their true colors are only discovered later on. If you wish to identify any such sources of information to me, I will be happy to tell you exactly why they were expelled from the Temple - or why they left in annoyance when the Temple did not support their particular interests. If you don't know this, it would just be embarrassing for the Department when it eventually does come out.

* * *

If, after considering this letter, you see fit to work towards a dignified and cooperative close to this affair that will reflect well upon the SFPD and enable the Temple of Set to continue its legitimate and decent existence as a church in the San Francisco community without further unjustified confrontations, I will do my part to help.

Sincerely,
/s/ Michael A. Aquino

Appendix 22: Letter, Michael Aquino to SFPD Inspector Glenn Pamfiloff 3/7/88

Lt.Col. Michael A. Aquino
Post Office Box #4507
St. Louis, Missouri 63108

March 7, 1988

Sergeant/Inspector Glenn Pamfiloff
Juvenile Division, San Francisco Police Department
2475 Greenwich Street
San Francisco, CA 94123

Dear Inspector Pamfiloff:

My attorney Mr. Shawn Hanson has advised me that you have now begun questioning children from the Presidio day-care center in an effort to elicit "identifications" of me in your investigation of the Presidio scandal.

From the information which I have voluntarily provided to you over the past several months, including the sworn statements of my wife and myself and supporting documentation in the court-martial charges which I have preferred against Chaplain Adams-Thompson, it should be abundantly clear to you that we never had **anything** to do with the Adams-Thompson child, much less the Presidio day-care center. We both have an established **lifetime** history of never having abused **any** children at **any** time for **any** reason. And as you know from my resumé, I have not had just an average life but one consistently marked by the highest moral and professional evaluations and recognitions.

From your confiscation of my wife's and my personal property during your surprise search of our home, you further know that neither of us had **any** pedophiliac materials whatever. And from both your confiscation of executive papers and your review of the general membership materials of the Temple of Set, you know that there is **nothing whatever** in its doctrines or practices that either tolerates or advocates the abuse of children, ritually or otherwise. [Indeed, from the papers I provided you, you are aware that hundreds of priests and ministers from **conventional** churches have been involved in pedophilia. Since the Temple of Set is conspicuous for having **no** involvement whatever with any crime, including this one, since its founding 13 years ago, why should it be singled out for persecution in this instance?]

Accordingly I fail to see any reason why you should be deliberately trying to produce "identifications" of my wife or myself from other Presidio day-care children. There is no reason to single us out for special mention to the children any more than any other military family who has been assigned to the Presidio in the past - **less**, in fact, since as you know the Army had reassigned us to Washington, D.C. long before the Presidio scandal ever occurred.

Since Adams-Thompson's false accusation first dragged us into this entire affair, I have done considerable research concerning the rash of "abuse" scandals around the country these past few years. I have of course noted the recurring incidents of "identifications" from infants elicited by questioners using techniques which were deliberately engineered to produce predetermined answers - and which were later exposed as such. From Mr. Hanson's account of your statements to him during your recent telephone conversation, I am concerned that exactly this kind of technique is being employed here. If so, and if any further injustices should be inflicted on my wife and myself because of deliberately manufactured "evidence", I will pursue every legal recourse to expose and prosecute anyone responsible. I think that the court-martial charges I have already preferred against Adams-Thompson should substantiate my resolve in this regard.

Mr. Hanson tells me that you again raised the issue of a polygraph test, saying that "it is the only way to clear us". I thought we discussed that during our meeting in January, but let me review it to ensure that there is no misunderstanding. First, as U.S. citizens, we have the right to be presumed innocent unless proven guilty of a crime, hence in the absence of any factual evidence should not have to submit to a humiliating exercise in order to "prove" our innocence.

Secondly, all of my attorneys at PM&S have strongly advised against a polygraph test on the grounds that the results can be erroneous for any number of reasons. [My wife was told the same thing by professional polygraph administrators during her San Francisco City College criminology degree program.]

Finally and most fundamentally, I do not believe that there are the slightest grounds for you or anyone else to presume that my wife or myself is a liar. For years I have held -and despite this disgraceful episode **continue** to hold - the highest level of national security clearance granted by the United States: "Top Secret/Special Intelligence Access". This kind of clearance is **not** granted to liars. You have in your possession sworn statements, under penalty of perjury, from both of us concerning the Presidio affair. If you wish sworn statements from us concerning any matter not covered by those statements, you are welcome to so advise me at any time. [May I suggest a polygraph examination be administered to Adams-Thompson concerning the points brought out in my sworn statement concerning him?]

I would also like to reemphasize, as I believe I mentioned during our January meeting, that within the Army the swearing to false statements in support of something as serious as court-martial charges is **itself** a criminal offense punishable under the Uniform Code of Military Justice. Whether or not you ever charged me with anything in San Francisco, if it were ever established that any element of my sworn statement were false, the Army would prosecute me for that reason. Accordingly I think you will agree that it would have been exceedingly stupid of me to say anything in that statement of whose truth I had the slightest doubt.

Mr. Hanson also said that you would like to have a chronology of any travel of mine to and from San Francisco since being assigned to Washington. My initial response to that is that I do not see why my mere presence in my native city, where I have maintained my home of record since I was born there in 1946, should **in itself** associate me with any crime which may take place in the city limits. Suppose I had still been assigned to the Presidio Commander's staff during 1986-87. Would that **in itself** make me more of a suspect? In which case why don't you suspect **every** person living on or near the Presidio during the scandal?

Nevertheless I have no qualms whatever about substantiating my whereabouts as it may be necessary. As you know, active-duty soldiers must account for their movements officially. They are either at their place of assignment or on official leave. I have on file all leave-and-earnings statements (LESs) and official travel documents, together with records of expenses, airline tickets, charge-card statements, and other documents needed for my tax and military records. I have accounted completely for all of the time when I was assigned to the National Defense University, as Mr. Zimmerman has verified to you. If you will identify to Mr. Zimmerman any specific day or days you have reason to feel are critical to your investigation, he will be able to provide you with information concerning my location at that specific time and with such supporting documentation as is available. Mr. Zimmerman has advised me not to provide blanket statements in the absence of such specific requests, on the grounds that to do so would make me vulnerable to manufactured "evidence" in the form of alleged incidents invented for any day during which I may have been in the city.

I had thought that in the course of our January meeting you would have resolved any reasonable doubts you might have had concerning the Temple of Set, my wife, and myself. As I mentioned to you at the time, I would have been happy to have met with you in August, and to have had you over to the house to inspect our bathtub, without having to involve attorneys. Because of the way we were in fact treated, however, we were forced to conclude that we were being deliberately and maliciously persecuted for no better reason than to prop up Sandi Gallant's ridiculous "Satanism" scare-stories.

Accordingly we have had to defend our personal safety - and the good name of our **legitimate** church - by careful attention to the guidance of Pillsbury, Madison & Sutro. If this makes your job more difficult, consider that it makes my preferred way of discussion more difficult as well. Despite that, I think that my wife and I have bent over backward to be cooperative, and to try to positively resolve an extremely ugly, shocking, and traumatic situation which has savaged our lives for the past half-year. It would be a welcome gesture to see the San Francisco Police Department appreciate this, and to leave two innocent people alone.

Sincerely,
/s/ Michael A. Aquino

Appendix 23: San Francisco Office of Citizen Complaints Article

New OCC Leadership Praised For Improving Investigations
by Peter Aronson, *Recorder* Staff Writer
The Recorder, Newspaper for U.S. District Court, Northern California Superior Court, City and County of San Francisco, and the Municipal Court of San Francisco
April 13, 1988

Despite severe understaffing, a continuous budget crunch, and a huge case backlog, the new leadership of the San Francisco Office of Citizen Complaints appears to be making a serious effort to transform the office into a *bona fide* police watchdog agency.

That's the view of John Crew, head of the American Civil Liberties Union police practices unit.

On Tuesday the OCC released to *The Recorder* preliminary statistics for 1987 that, according to Crew, show the OCC seems to be investigating complaints more thoroughly than under the leadership of former OCC Director Frank Schober, Jr., who resigned last May amid complaints that too few citizen complaints were being sustained.

Last year 98 of the allegations made in 1,501 complaints against police officers in San Francisco were found to have merit, according to the OCC's new Director, Michael A. Langer.

In 1986 only 37 allegations made in 1,535 complaints were sustained by the OCC, Crew said.

"By conservative estimates it appears that in 1987 they sustained at least twice as many allegations as before," Crew said. "It's hard to draw a conclusion because Langer has been there only a short time, but it is encouraging."

Langer said be is too new on the job to say whether the statistics indicate the office is becoming more effective as a watchdog. He said the OCC is completing a detailed statistical analysis of the OCC's 1987 case load and hopes to release it to the city's Police Commission this week.

He and Crew cautioned that the preliminary statistics released Tuesday should not be misinterpreted. The 98 allegations sustained came from a total of 2,575 allegations lodged by citizens in 1,501 complaints in 1987. Langer would not say what types of complaints were upheld or how many different officers were named in the allegations.

In general, Langer said, complaints against officers range from verbal abuse and improper arrest to unnecessary force.

Police Chief Frank Jordan refused comment on the OCC statistics.

Another close observer of the OCC, Peter G. Keane, Chief Attorney in the San Francisco Public Defender's Office, said it's difficult to draw a conclusion from the tentative figures, but he said another barometer indicates Langer is having a positive impact.

"The Police Officers Association is pissed off with him," Keane said. "That is the watershed index." He said POA leaders were angry with Langer's acute attention to citizen complaints, as compared to the lackluster investigations under the Schober administration.

But POA president Bob Berry said that, contrary to Keane's impression, the Association believes Langer is a very credible administrator who is doing a fine job under difficult budgetary constraints. The only problems so far have been a few procedural changes - the type that have occurred under prior OCC administrations.

"I think that comment by Peter Keane is way out of line. We have some procedural problems, but they are constant," he said. "I don't have any problems with Langer."

Langer, a former Chief of Detectives for the Skokie, Ill., Police Department, was named to the $56,000-a-year job in November after a nationwide search.

"My impression is that he's trying to do a good job," said Drucilla S. Ramey, Executive Director of the Bar Association of San Francisco. Citing one difference between Langer and Schober, Ramey said Langer wants willing BASF members to conduct discipline appeal hearings *pro bono*, while Schober did not.

Langer said this cost-saving measure - the savings would be $64,000 - could be adopted during the city's effort to reduce the projected $172-million deficit. He said the Police Commission, which oversees the OCC, must approve this and other recommended changes.

The OCC's $857,000 annual budget supports a 14-member staff. With one employee on sick leave and another transferred for disciplinary reasons, the office has only six investigators and four clerks.

He said each OCC investigator must handle more than 200 cases. He said in 1978 each, investigator with the OCC's predecessor, the Police Department's Internal Affairs Division, handled 23 cases.

"I think we owe the citizens of San Francisco a good job, and I don't think we can do that job unless we get more people," Langer said. "A major, major problem is lack of people."

Langer said the office initially asked that its budget for 1988-89 be increased to $1.3 million, which would enable it to increase its staff to 22 employees. But that request was nixed, as were subsequent lower requests, Langer said.

Now the director said he is faced with the problem of having to cut a budget that is already too low. The most recent request calls for a 2- to 3-percent budget cut.

If that is approved, Langer said that by shifting resources, the office would hope to hire two more investigators.

This would require that the office make extreme cuts in other areas, including eliminating all overtime pay, cutting word processing and all travel and reducing training.

An additional personnel problem is that some members of the present OCC staff are not working hard enough, Langer said. He said he is monitoring the staff closely and that he will seek their dismissal if their work habits don't improve.

The total effect of the staff problems, Langer said, is that the office will not be able to wipe out a chronic backlog of complaints that now stands at 500 to 600 cases.

Crew said that the city charter requires the city to fund the OCC so that it can promptly and properly investigate citizen allegations of police misconduct.

"If the city doesn't give it the necessary resources, we'll have to look at whether the city is fulfilling its legal responsibility," Crew said.

Although Langer said he cannot promise prompt investigation of the complaints, he said he is confident that every allegation is being thoroughly investigated by his staff.

"I want people to know there is honesty and integrity in this office," he said. "If you get a complaint and it's signed by Langer, I know the disposition is correct."

Appendix 24: OCC Complaint - Officer Sandra Gallant, Star 1918

April 8, 1988

Narrative of Incident

1. Since at least July 21, 1981 Officer Gallant has been maintaining confidential "intelligence" files on the Temple of Set, a legitimate church with no record of any criminal actions, statements, or doctrines. The Temple of Set was incorporated in California in 1975 as a church, and qualified in that same year for federal and state tax-exempt recognition as such. [Tab A]. The singling-out of a church involved in no illegal activity for police surveillance is a violation of the First and Fourteenth Amendments to the U.S. Constitution pertaining to freedom of religion and equal protection of the law.

2. As part of this "intelligence" effort, Gallant has similarly maintained confidential files on myself, as the Temple's chief executive. I have no criminal record whatever, nor is there any probable cause to assume that I am involved in anything criminal. The "investigation" of a U.S. citizen for no other reason than his religion and religious office is a violation of the First and Fourteenth Amendments to the U.S. Constitution pertaining to freedom of religion and equal protection of the law. [A copy of my personal resumé is attached at Tab B.]

3. On July 21, 1981 Gallant (maiden name Daly) initiated contact with the U.S. Army to insinuate that the existence of the Temple of Set as a "Satanic cult" should be considered grounds for possible adverse action against myself and two other Army officers as members of the Temple. The Temple's legitimate status is well-known to the Army; therefore Gallant's effort failed. [Tab C]

4. Gallant's effort to initiate administrative action against the other officers and myself became known to me through one of the other officer's discovery of the Tab B correspondence in his official file. I promptly went to Gallant's office at the Hall of Justice and saw Gallant and her associate Sergeant Jerry Belfield. Gallant and Belfield admitted that they were keeping files on the Temple of Set and myself, but refused to tell me what allegations they might contain, even when I made it explicitly clear that I sought such information only in order to provide documentation and other evidence of our legality and social responsibility pertaining to any allegation. I did not insist upon knowing the name of any informant. The most that Gallant would do was to permit me to add a copy of the Temple of Set's official information paper [Tab D] to the file.

5. Since that time Gallant has never once contacted the Temple of Set or myself for information, or to obtain our/my version of information in her files. She has admitted to being in contact with at least two ex-members of the Temple of Set who were expelled from the Temple for ethical misconduct, and who have since embarked on a campaign of vindictive misinformation about the Temple and myself. This is unprofessional of Gallant in that, under the guise of "intelligence", she accumulated adverse statements about the Temple and neither made nor tolerated any effort to critique such statements and present an objective picture. Thus she deliberately created a distorted and defamatory image of the Temple of Set and myself, which she then proceeded to represent as objective truth to the San Francisco Police Department and other governmental and non-governmental persons and organizations.

6. For several years it was impossible for me to find out what Gallant might be saying about the Temple, its religion, and myself - because she only spoke and provided files to law-enforcement agencies. Gradually she began giving media interviews in which she denounced our religion - Satanism - as horrifically criminal. [Tab E] In fact no registered member of the Temple of Set has ever been prosecuted for or convicted of any such crimes as Gallant has regularly alleged.

7. At an unknown date between 1981 and 1987, Gallant delivered a lecture on "Satanism" to a law-enforcement group - presumably the San Francisco Police Department. This lecture was virtually a continuous stream of

distortions and several outright lies concerning the Satanic religion, the Temple of Set, and myself. This lecture was taped, and in November 1987 my attorneys (Pillsbury, Madison & Sutro of San Francisco) obtained a copy of it. Included statements by Gallant, and my corrections to them, are contained at Tab F. [A copy of the video tape can be provided should you require it.]

8. In 1985 Gallant produced and began to distribute to private organizations as well as governmental ones, a series of "intelligence papers" on Satanism. These papers contain severe and defamatory distortions and falsifications concerning the Satanic religion. Since Gallant never checked any of this information with us, and never provided me with a copy of these papers, I was not able to respond or object to them until 1987, when we received a set from the California Consortium of Child Abuse Councils (a private, non-government organization). A copy of the Gallant papers is included at Tab G, and my commentary to them is included at Tab H.

9. I have recently been informed that, on October 23, 1986, Gallant spoke at a restricted-access Symposium on Child Abuse in Riverside, California. Reportedly she flashed a photograph of me on a screen, identified me, and said, "We haven't got anything on him yet, but we're going to get him." [This account was provided to me by a private investigator working for a Los Angeles legal firm, who has asked to remain unidentified for fear of persecution. This source would probably be willing to confirm this account to an authorized investigator from your office.]

10. Being ignorant of the actual extent or impact of Gallant's defamatory campaign, we did not take any action concerning it - until August 1987, when she and Sergeant/Inspector Glenn Pamfiloff used the excuse of an obviously-groundless child-abuse allegation to execute a search-warrant on my San Francisco home. Although the search warrant was only for "evidence of child abuse", no such evidence was found or taken. Many official files and papers of the Temple of Set were confiscated, however - documents containing no illegal material whatever, but simply consisting of membership and administrative records of the church. [A more detailed account of this incident is provided in my complaint filed against Sergeant/Inspector Pamfiloff on this same date.]

11. Following the August 1987 incident I wrote two letters of protest to Chief of Police Frank Jordan, neither of which was even answered at all. Copies of these letters are attached at Tabs I and J.

12. After it became clear that the S.F.P.D. would not on its own initiative correct the actions of Officers Gallant and Pamfiloff, my attorneys filed a motion in San Francisco Municipal Court to force the return of the Temple of Set's and my confiscated property. [Tab K] The District Attorney's office has succeeded in aborting both scheduled hearings before Judge Moscone to date - presumably to prevent Moscone from seeing how conspicuously the confiscated property has nothing to do with the search warrant, and also to prevent Gallant and Pamfiloff from being questioned on the stand and the actual nature and quality of Gallant's "intelligence" records from being exposed in court and to the public.

13. In current interviews, such as that given to the *Kansas City Times* for its March 26, 1988 edition and the *Santa Barbara News-Press* on March 14, 1988 [Tab L], Gallant has stated "that there is no proof that the Temple of Set is involved in crime". This would seem to make the continued retention of our, seized property, and indeed the continued maintenance of an intelligence file on us, all the more unjustified.

14. Since it is apparent that we are being prevented from exposing the facts of this situation in Municipal Court, we would normally pursue the alternative of legal action in the State or Federal Courts. Before considering such a step, however, I am requesting that your office, without seeking to find fault or fix blame for past actions, act to correct the situation to what under law it should properly be. Hopefully this will resolve the problem constructively and with the minimum of trouble to all concerned. I request:

a. That any files Gallant or her office may be maintaining on the Temple of Set or myself be destroyed, the maintenance of such files being a violation of the First and Fourteenth Amendments to the U.S.

Constitution. Further that she be prohibited from amassing any new "intelligence" on the Temple or myself in the absence of any specific judicial order to do so.

b. As Gallant continues to associate the terms "Satanic" and "Satanism" with crimes in general, and with child-molesting in particular [Tab L], that she be ordered to cease the use of these religious terms when describing alleged crimes of a secular nature. These terms identify a *bona fide* and officially-recognized religious persuasion in the United States which in no sense advocates any criminal behavior. Its religious terminology should not be associated with the crimes of non-affiliated individuals misusing its symbols any more than the term "Christian" should be used to describe crimes committed by persons using its official symbols inappropriately.

c. That Gallant be ordered to cease representing herself as an expert on either occultism in general or on Satanism in particular. As the attached documentation clearly establishes, she is an expert on neither, and her inaccurate accounts have caused great damage to the safety, security, and reputations of decent and law-abiding followers of the Satanic religion throughout the nation.

If these actions [and those requested in my related complaint of this date concerning Sergeant/Inspector Pamfiloff are taken, I will be satisfied that a good-faith effort by the City of San Francisco to correct this situation has been made, and my wife and I would consider it appropriate withdraw our claims against the City of San Francisco.

I verify that the above statement is true and correct to the best of my knowledge and belief.

/s/ Michael A. Aquino
[Notarized]

Appendix 25: OCC Complaint - Inspector Glenn Pamfiloff, Star 228

April 8, 1988

Narrative of Incident

1. On August 14, 1987 Sergeant/Inspector Glenn Pamfiloff obtained and executed a search warrant [Tab A] on my home in the city of San Francisco. This action was improper in that he did not adequately research and evaluate the allegation before seeking the search warrant. Nor did he take any actions short of the drastic search warrant - such as contacting me for an office interview, or coming by my home and asking to look at the premises - to explore the allegation. In short he approached me not as a responsible citizen with an impeccable and distinguished civic record, but as someone whose home it was appropriate to forcibly invade, family to frighten, and personal and religious property to confiscate.

2. A detailed account of the obviously false and malicious nature of the allegation is contained at Tab B. In the form of sworn statements by my wife and myself, this information has also been provided to the U.S. Army in support of court-martial charges which I have preferred against Chaplain Adams-Thompson.

3. Upon executing the search warrant, Pamfiloff was able to ascertain that the child's supposed "interior descriptions" did not match the actual interior of my home. This, together with the spurious nature of the chaplain's allegations, should have justified his terminating the search. Nevertheless it continued.

4. At the conclusion of the search, neither Pamfiloff nor Officer Sandi Gallant nor the team of other officers accompanying them had found any evidence of child molesting. Nevertheless Pamfiloff confiscated a number of articles and papers belonging to our church (the Temple of Set) and to my wife and myself. A list of what he confiscated is shown at Tab C.

5. My attorneys were not able to obtain a copy of the Police Incident Report [Tab D] until August 28, so neither my wife nor I had any idea what the reason for Pamfiloff's raid had been. Upon seeing the Incident Report, I wrote Pamfiloff the letter at Tab E. He did not reply to it.

6. When it became clear that Pamfiloff did not intend to respond to my letter, I wrote the letters to S.F.P.D. Chief Jordan contained at Tabs F and G. Jordan did not reply to either of them.

7. In October 1987 the search of my home was featured in the San Francisco and national news media. The S.F.P.D. regularly referred to my wife and myself as "suspects", stated that we were "under investigation", and stated that "videotapes" had been among the items confiscated from our home. The obvious implication was that the videotapes contained something pedophiliac or otherwise criminal, whereas in actuality they contained nothing of the sort [see Tab C]. The effect of the wording of the S.F.P.D. statements was to cause great harm to my wife's and my reputations, to provoke vandalism against our home, and to provoke anonymous threats of murder against us on our telephone answering machine.

8. After it became clear that the S.F.P.D. would not on its own initiative correct the abuse of the search warrant and confiscations, my attorneys filed a motion in San Francisco Municipal Court to force the return of the Temple of Set's and my confiscated property. [Tab H] The District Attorney's office obtained stay orders to abort both the first hearing and its follow-up before Judge Moscone - apparently to prevent Moscone from seeing how obviously the confiscated property has nothing to do with the search warrant, and to prevent Pamfiloff's conduct of the "investigation" from being exposed.

9. During the first Municipal Court hearing - before the stay order was served - Pamfiloff was briefly questioned on the stand and stated that he was investigating me for "child stealing and various subsections, child abuse,

child neglect, child molests, rapes". After seeing this on a television news broadcast [a copy of which can be provided to your investigator if needed], I wrote Pamfiloff the letter at Tab I. He did not reply to it.

10. On December 2, 1987 Pamfiloff telephoned a San Francisco member of the Temple of Set, Walter Radtke, and asked to meet with him. During the meeting, as recounted in Radtke's letter to me later that same day: "Officer Pamfiloff repeatedly stressed throughout our conversation his desire to nail you for child molestation, stressing his conviction that you were perverts, homosexuals, and chronic abusers of children".

11. After the first Municipal Court hearing was halted by the D.A.'s office via a stay order obtained from the Superior Court (which we did not contest but which the D.A. refused to withdraw anyway), the S.F.P.D. agreed to release most of the confiscated property to me. In January 1988 my wife and I flew to San Francisco to take delivery on it. At the same time we also requested a meeting with Pamfiloff to review the rest of the property still being withheld by him.

12. On January 15, 1988 my wife, my attorney Shawn Hanson, and I met with Pamfiloff at his office. [Pamfiloff taped the conversation but we did not.] The withheld property was reviewed and its irrelevance to any criminal activity clearly established. A list of the withheld property is at Tab J.

13. On January 28, with no further action by Pamfiloff to restore the property, my attorney Bernard Zimmerman wrote the District Attorney's office the letter at Tab K.

14. Shortly thereafter Pamfiloff telephoned my attorney Shawn Hanson to reject the proposed solution & joint statement, and to say that he was now conducting interviews with Presidio day-care children to see if any of them would "identify" me. On hearing this, I wrote Pamfiloff the 3/7 letter at Tab L. He did not answer it.

15. On March 17, following the Superior Court's rejection of the D.A.'s stay order, the Municipal Court hearing was scheduled to resume. [Tab M] This time the D.A. prevented it from even beginning by another stay order, now obtained from the Appellate Court. Again we indicated that we would not contest it, and again the D.A. refused to withdraw it and allow Moscone to hear the case.

16. Since it is apparent that we are being prevented from exposing the facts of this situation in Municipal Court, we would normally pursue the alternative of legal action in the State or Federal Courts. Before considering such a step, however, I am requesting that your office, without seeking to find fault or fix blame for past actions, act to correct the situation to what under law it should properly be. Hopefully this will resolve the problem constructively and with the minimum of trouble to all concerned. I request:

    a. That all of my wife's and my personal property, and that of our church, be restored to us without further delay, and that the S.F.P.D. not retain any copies of this material.

    b. That any and all photographs taken of my home, my wife, and/or myself during the search of our home be destroyed along with their negatives as being an unjustified and unconstitutional invasion of our privacy.

    c. That Pamfiloff be ordered to cease this abusive, harassing, and completely unjustified "investigation" of my wife, myself, and our church; and that he as an individual not be assigned to any future investigation which might involve our church or ourselves, as his prejudice against us has been conspicuously and conclusively established.

If these actions [and those requested in my related complaint of this date concerning Officer Gallant] are taken, I will be satisfied that a good-faith effort by the City of San Francisco to correct this situation has been made, and my wife and I would consider it appropriate withdraw our claims against the City of San Francisco.
I verify that the above statement is true and correct to the best of my knowledge and belief.

/s/ Michael A. Aquino

[Notarized]

Appendix 26: Office of Citizen Complaints Findings Letter

The Police Commission
OFFICE OF CITIZEN COMPLAINTS
City and County of San Francisco
555 Seventh Street #252
San Francisco, California 94103
(415) 553-1407

November 22, 1989

Dr. Michael A. Aquino
P.O. Box 4507
St. Louis, MO 63108

Dear Dr. Aquino:

Re: OCC Case # 0468-88.

The Office of Citizen Complaints has conducted an investigation into your complaint referenced above.

As a result of our investigation of your allegations that the search warrant for your home was not properly executed; that letters written to SFPD members were not answered, and complaints not forwarded to OCC; that the named member made improper statements regarding your guilt and character; and that a proper investigation has not been conducted, we have preliminarily found that the actions you complained of are improper under the rules and regulations of the San Francisco Police Department. Accordingly our preliminary[172] disposition of these allegations is "Sustained".

As a result of our investigation of your allegations that a named member is keeping improper intelligence files on you and your religion; that this same member is accumulating negative information and not trying to present an objective picture in these files; that this same member improperly contacted your employer with confidential information; that this same member has presented a defamatory image of your religion, both on and off duty, we have preliminarily found that the actions you complained of are improper under the rules and regulations of the San Francisco Police Department. Accordingly, our preliminary disposition of these allegations is "Sustained".

As a result of our investigation of your allegation that a search warrant for your home was not properly obtained, we have preliminarily found that our investigation failed to disclose evidence to substantiate your complaint. Accordingly our preliminary disposition of this complaint is "Unfounded".

As a result of our investigation of your allegations that retention of your property was improper; that you were refused the opportunity to speak with the named member about the contents of the intelligence file and refused the opportunity to place rebuttal information therein; that the named member made a statement to a public meeting implying you were guilty of criminal activity before any conviction for same; and that the SFPD did not handle media contacts properly so as to present a neutral picture regarding yourself to the media, we have preliminarily found that our investigation has failed to disclose sufficient evidence to enable us to determine the validity of the allegations made in your complaint. Accordingly our preliminary disposition of these allegations is "Not Sustained".

---

[172] According OCC investigating officer Irene Rapoza, neither Gallant nor Pamfiloff protested the findings of this report by the required deadline to do so. Therefore all of the "preliminary" findings in this letter became "final". Conversation, M. Aquino and Irene Rapoza, 12/18/89.

As a result of your allegations that retention of your property was improper, and that a proper investigation was not conducted, we have preliminarily found that the current procedure followed by SFPD is not proper. Accordingly, our preliminary disposition is "Procedure Failure".

If you are not satisfied with these dispositions, you have the right to request an investigatory hearing on your complaint. If you wish to request a hearing, please submit your request in writing no later than ten days from the date you receive this letter. Send your request to Larry Shockey, Hearing Coordinator, at the above address.

I have discretionary authority to empanel an investigatory hearing if I determine that such a hearing will facilitate the fact finding process. Accordingly your letter should establish one of the following grounds for a hearing: (a) there is additional evidence, such as witness statements or other information, that contradicts, or supplements, or is not disclosed by the investigative report; (b) there is reason to question the conclusion of the investigative report; (c) an appearance in person by the parties would further the fact finding process; (d) there are other factors that you believe make an investigatory hearing necessary.

Please tell us your reasons for submitting the request for a hearing, and be as specific as possible. We will notify you by mail whether your request has been granted or denied.

In order to assist you in determining the grounds for a hearing, you may make an appointment and visit our office to discuss our preliminary disposition and to review the evidence upon which that disposition was based. If you wish to take advantage of this opportunity, please call Irene F. Rapoza at 553-1407 to make that appointment.

Thank you for bringing this matter to our attention. If we can be of further assistance, please feel free to contact us.

Very truly yours,
/s/ Michael A. Langer
Director

MAL:IFR:hs

Appendix 27: "Massive S.F. Police Shakeup" - *S.F. Examiner*

"Massive S.F. Police Shake-Up"
New Chief Casey to Reassign 16 of 22 Captains, Abolish Department Intelligence Unit
by Larry Maatz of the *Examiner* Staff
Malcolm Glover of *The Examiner* Staff contributed to this report.
December 19, 1990

In one of the most far-reaching shake-ups in the history of the San Francisco Police Department, newly-appointed Police Chief Willis Casey is disbanding the Department's controversial Intelligence Division and is reassigning 16 of the force's 22 captains. Within the week Casey also will announce the reassignment of more than half the department's 78 lieutenants. "Simply put, it's time for a change," Casey said late Tuesday. "I can't make it any more clear than that."

Casey plans to announce the changes Wednesday evening to the Police Commission, along with his appointment of two new patrol commanders, Captains Richard Shippy and James Arnold.

The reassignment of the Department's captains comes as no surprise, Casey having made it clear as he assumed command in November that a shake-up was due. "There's nothing punitive about it," he said Tuesday. "I just want a new mix. I want to confront people with new challenges, new situations. A lot of these people have been where they are for far too long. They really don't know what they can do. I want to give them the chance to surprise themselves about how good they really are."

But the dismembering of the Department's Intelligence unit, long the target of protest, minority and lifestyle groups, comes as a bombshell. Again Casey said, it was time for a change. "This didn't come on me yesterday," he said. "I've been thinking on this for a long time, but I couldn't act on it. But now I can. This is 1990, going on 1991. Whatever may or may not have been appropriate in the '50s just isn't appropriate now. This is a police department, not the CIA."

Of the Intelligence Division's 22 officers, 14 assigned to gang-taskforce work are being moved to the Vice Division. "Their work largely revolved around Chinatown gambling anyway," Casey said, "so better that they work there."

Of the remaining officers, two will be assigned to investigate hate crimes under a newly formed Special Investigation Division, and the other eight will be reassigned within 30 days, Casey said.

"I want the officers in this Department to be developing intelligence relative to fighting crime and then acting on it," Casey said, "so I'm putting those officers with that expertise in jobs where they can act on it, and I'm going to expect them to do just that. I don't think it's a proper police function to gather [intelligence] information on various groups just because it's there and then file it away.

"If we can't act on it in the service of this city, then it's a waste of our time," Casey said, "and with our manpower shortage, we can't afford that kind of waste."

Casey said the captains' reassignments came after nearly three weeks of interviews, and that all the captains had been assured they would have a minimum of two years on their new assignments to put their ideas to work.

"I've made it clear to them that they're going to be given more freedom of action than they've ever had," Casey said. "I also made it clear that I'm going to hold them accountable for their actions."

Appendix 28: Michael Aquino Sworn Statement - First A-T Charges

I, Lieutenant Colonel Michael A. Aquino, want to make the following statement under oath:

1. From approximately October 1986 to the present time, the Presidio of San Francisco child-care center has been the subject of many allegations concerning sexual abuse of the children left there. A Baptist minister who worked at the center, one Gary Hambright, has been indicted for such abuse but has not yet been tried. The investigation at the Presidio has been conducted by the FBI in conjunction with the Army CID and the San Francisco Police Department.

2. Prior to July 1986 I was assigned to the Presidio headquarters as USAR Advisor to the Presidio Commander. Some time before my reassignment to Washington in July 1986, Adams-Thompson arrived on post and was also assigned to the Presidio headquarters.

3. From July 1986 through July 1987 my wife and I were living in Washington, D.C., where I was a student in the resident course of the Industrial College of the Armed Forces, National Defense University, Fort McNair.

4. Following the end of the ICAF year (extended through July 1987 because of my participation in a George Washington University M.P.A. option), my wife and I traveled to San Francisco to visit our home-of-record there for a month before moving on to St. Louis for my next PCS assignment.

5. On 12 August 1987 Chaplain Adams-Thompson, without my knowledge or the knowledge of the Presidio Commander, falsely accused me and my wife to the FBI and the San Francisco Police Department of having sexually molested his infant stepdaughter at Gary Hambright's home during the period September-October 1986. Adams-Thompson alleges that he made the accusation based solely on comments elicited from his 3-year-old stepdaughter (who was age 2 in October 1986).

6. Approximately a week before Adams-Thompson made his accusation, a federal judge had ruled that unsupported statements elicited from another 3-year-old child would be incompetent due to the child's age, hence inadmissible in court. This ruling was highly publicized in the San Francisco media, and Adams-Thompson was certainly aware of it. According to the official SFPD Incident Report (Attachment #A), Adams-Thompson's stepdaughter was questioned by the FBI on 14 January 1987 and did not make any statements about being molested at all, much less by my wife or myself, or at our San Francisco home. Only after intensive child-therapy, which has become nationally notorious for conditioning young children to fabricate molestation stories [see paragraph #22 below], did Adams-Thompson represent that his stepdaughter was molested. To date it has not been established that the child was ever molested at all.

7. I have never had anything to do with either Kinsey M. Almond (Chaplain Adams-Thompson's stepdaughter) or any other child involved with the Presidio day-care center. I have never molested any child in my life. I have never used or been known by the nickname "Mikey".

8. The officer corps of the Presidio headquarters garrison is not large, and it would have been quite conspicuous to Adams-Thompson that I had not been present for garrison activities for over a year. It would have been equally easy for him to have ascertained that I had been reassigned to Washington in July 1986, merely by asking the officer personnel office or any senior officer in the garrison headquarters. Since only one USAR officer per year is selected nationwide to attend ICAF, my selection was well-known at the Presidio.

9. Therefore, even if Adams-Thompson's stepdaughter did make an allegation, Adams-Thompson had two reasons not to initiate formal action as a consequence: (a) the established incompetence of 2/3-year-olds in even current testimony, and (b) the ease with which he could have acted to ascertain my Washington PCS assignment

during the entire Presidio child-care scandal. Instead he disregarded the former and took no steps concerning the latter before contacting the FBI.

10. On 12 August 1987 my wife and I went shopping at the Presidio PX. We were unaware of the presence of Adams-Thompson and/or any other members of his family, nor would have recognized them in any case as we had never met them. According to the facts as set forth in Attachment #A, Adams-Thompson stated that his stepdaughter reacted to my appearance upon seeing me at the PX. Since I have a prominent widow's peak and sharply-pointed eyebrows (Attachment #B/ICAF 1987 Yearbook), it is not uncommon for children [or even adults] to react to me. Adams-Thompson did not call my attention to his presence or ask me any questions. Instead he prompted his stepdaughter several times to elicit what he alleges was the child's identification of my wife and myself as two individuals who had molested her about ten months earlier at the home of Gary Hambright.

11. Adams-Thompson's statement that my wife did not appear until later in the PX parking lot is false, since at no time was she separated from me during our shopping trip. The notion that his stepdaughter could have identified either of us is also false, since we have never met any members of the Adams-Thompson family. [Adams-Thompson himself obviously recognized me from my Presidio assignment a year earlier, since he accused me by name to the FBI. I was not in uniform during the PX shopping trip, hence was not wearing a nametag.]

12. The detailed story which Adams-Thompson says he received from his stepdaughter is impossible for a 3-year-old infant to have assembled, much less recalled from a year earlier at age 2. It includes such details as the identification of a movie camera [as distinct from a still camera] and other details which no 2-year-old would either notice, recognize, or retain. It is genital-obsessive to a disgusting degree: certainly the product of an adult perversion rather than a 2-year-old's actual perception. The story was quite clearly fabricated by an adult and tutored into the child - either by Adams-Thompson himself or by some other adult who had instructed her.

13. After Adams-Thompson made his allegations to the FBI, an FBI agent then drove the child to my San Francisco street address, presumably still in the company of Adams-Thompson. Allegedly the child then identified my building as the "home of Gary Hambright". This too is impossible, as the child had never been inside the building [nor has any other member of the Adams-Thompson family - nor Gary Hambright (whom we have never met) - nor any other child involved with the Presidio day-care center]. If she identified the building, it is either because she was taken there in advance and instructed to "identify" the building later, or because the "identification" was deliberately coached from her either by Adams-Thompson or by the FBI agent. Both Adams-Thompson and the FBI agent knew that my building was not the residence of Hambright, furthermore, because Hambright's actual address elsewhere in San Francisco is included on the SFPD incident report (Attachment #A).

14. As a consequence of these accusations by Adams-Thompson, the San Francisco Police Department obtained and exercised a search warrant on my home on 14 August 1987 - from 9 PM to 1 AM, to the utter surprise and shock of my wife and myself, who could do nothing but watch while our entire flat was ransacked and our most personal effects pawed through and photographed. The police found that the interior "descriptions" alleged to have been given by the Adams-Thompson child did not match the interior of my home, and they found no evidence whatever of any child abuse/pornography activities. They confiscated a selection of family and church papers & photographs, and other articles so that, in my attorney's opinion, they would not have to return to the judge empty-handed. Since it is SFPD policy to not return seized property until a judge orders it, I have had to initiate litigation accordingly. On 24 November 1987 San Francisco District Attorney George Butterworth stated in a Declaration to the Superior Court, under penalty of perjury: "I am informed and believe that there is currently pending no criminal prosecution, either locally or federally, to which the property seized in the search warrant at issue pertains." No charges based on either Adams-Thompson's or any other allegations have been filed against my wife or myself.

15. I did not learn of Adams-Thompson's actions until 28 August 1987, when a copy of the SFPD Incident Report was made available. As Adams-Thompson was at that time still assigned to the Presidio, I immediately advised the Deputy Commander of the Presidio, Colonel D. Peter Gleichenhaus. Simultaneously I sent Adams-Thompson a letter (Attachment #C) affirming my noninvolvement and demanding a letter of apology and retraction for his conduct. He sent no letter by way of reply. On the same day that my letter would have been delivered to his

Presidio address, however, an unsigned card (Attachment #D) with no return address was posted to my St. Louis address from San Francisco. It shows a repulsive male transvestite and the printed message "BLOW IT OUT YOUR ASS!" together with the typed message "YOU POMPOUS JERK!". That Adams-Thompson sent this card is suggested by the date of its posting, together with its addressing to my new St. Louis address, of which no one in San Francisco other than family and a few close friends was as yet aware. [Adams-Thompson knew the address, of course, because it appears as the return address on the 28 August letter I had sent to him.]

16. On 10 September I sent a second letter (Attachment #E) to Adams-Thompson at his subsequent duty assignment with the 25th Infantry Division. I enclosed a photocopy of the card and requested him to deny having sent it if he were not the source of it. No answer was ever received. For these reasons I conclude that he indeed sent the card. [The "transvestite" theme also appears in the allegations he made to the FBI/SFPD concerning my wife and myself - neither of whom are or ever have been transvestites.]

17. I thus conclude not only that an Army officer and chaplain made an irresponsible and knowingly false criminal accusation against another officer and his wife, but also that, when the facts were subsequently brought to his attention and an informal apology requested, his response was one not only of no regret whatever, but indeed of vulgar and obscene insolence.

18. Why should Adams-Thompson have behaved this way towards my wife and myself, since we had had no previous contact with him or his family whatever?

19. During my assignment to the Presidio garrison, it was well-known on post that I was, as High Priest of the Temple of Set, the chief official of the nation's largest and most prominent legitimate Satanic church. Although I did not advertise or encourage publicity within the military in any way, my unusual religion was common knowledge to the post commanders under whom I served, the Presidio Catholic (Colonel Christoph) and Protestant (Colonel Autry) chaplains, and most if not all of the other officers, enlisted personnel, and civilians on post. As one of the subordinate garrison chaplains, it is inconceivable that Adams-Thompson was not also aware of it.

20. At no time did Adams-Thompson speak to me about it, nor make any other inquiry to the Temple of Set about its standing, beliefs, or practices. Had he done so, he would have learned that since its founding in 1975 it has remained a legitimate religious institution, incorporated in California and possessing full state and federal tax-exempt recognition as a church. It has no record whatever of any misdemeanor or felony activities. Its public information documents make it quite explicit that it neither engages in nor advocates any illegal activities whatever, nor permits anyone under the age of 18 to affiliate or to attend any of its functions. [My religious affiliation has been continuously known to the Army since my commissioning in 1968, and has never been the basis for any adverse official concern or action.]

21. I find it inescapable to conclude, therefore, that Adams-Thompson's actions towards my wife and myself were the result of religious intolerance and bigotry: the fear and hatred of a passionate, professional Christian clergyman for something which he [ignorantly] thought to be a threat to his preferred religion. Hence his actions were not motivated by a sincere, logical conviction on his part that my wife and I had in fact molested his stepdaughter, but rather by his cold and deliberate perception of an opportunity to inflict great harm upon us and our church with a devastating accusation.

22. In *San Francisco Chronicle* coverage of the Presidio child-care scandal on 10 August 1987, it was made clear that the parents making the allegations were very much aware of the extremely sensational McMartin and Kern County "Satanic child-abuse" cases of the previous two years, in which young children - proved later to have been coached to make false statements by parents, therapists, and law-enforcement officials -obediently reported sexual abuse, murder, and cannibalism at the hands of "Satanic cults" at day-care centers. After exhaustive investigation and the ruining of the lives of many innocent persons who had neither abused children nor been Satanists (legitimate or otherwise), both scandals ended with the allegations of "Satanic child abuse" being shown to be completely without basis. The Kern County case in particular ended with the California Attorney General

severely criticizing the investigators and officials involved for the impulsive and unprofessional way in which they had proceeded.

23. The publicity accorded these two cases - and a flurry of subsequent "copycat" cases around the country - have nonetheless generated a media image of Satanists as habitual child-abusers or child-murderers. As law-enforcement officials have repeatedly admitted, however, not a single such connection between child-abuse and Satanism has ever been established. The published texts of contemporary legitimate Satanism, most prominently Anton LaVey's *Satanic Bible* and the Temple of Set's *Crystal Tablet of Set*, contain strong and explicit prohibitions against any and all harm to children, sexual or otherwise. [See Attachment #F.]

24. I therefore conclude that Adams-Thompson deliberately intended to smear my good name, that of my wife, and that of our church with this abominable accusation, counting on media sensationalism and public ignorance not only to compound the damage to us, but also to shield him from the consequences of falsely and maliciously accusing a fellow Army officer of a serious felony. To date it appears that he has been quite successful in this. No official actions have been taken against him whatever. The Presidio Judge Advocate's office excuses such inaction as being a necessary consequence of the "ongoing investigation" into the Presidio scandal as a whole. This is absolutely unjustified, since the facts surrounding Adams-Thompson's behavior in this incident [cited in this statement] are all clearly established, and since Adams-Thompson's false accusations against me are not connected with any molestation activities which may have been perpetrated at the day-care facility by Hambright or anyone else. To delay justice in Adams-Thompson's case is not only to allow him to savor what he has done; it is to indefinitely perpetuate and aggravate the continuing public ordeal of my wife and myself.

25. My family and I have endured four months of protracted agony because of Adams-Thompson's vile accusation. We have been questioned by scores of military associates, family friends, and business associates. We and our church have been caricatured sensationally and inaccurately by many commercial media. Our personal privacy and the religious privacy of our church have been and continue to be regularly violated as though we are mere freaks for public entertainment; we are forced to respond to continued inquiries only to try to preclude at least the more bizarre distortions in the inevitable coverage. We have learned to our distress that even the most polite declining of interviews usually results in hostile distortions by the reporters in question.

26. My wife and I have received several death and arson threats on our telephone answering machine. The most recent one was on January 1, 1988, in which an anonymous caller stated that we would both be killed this year. Our San Francisco home has been vandalized, forcing me to spend over $3,000 in repairs and protective reinforcement. Our tenants in the building have also been harassed and traumatized by vandalism.

27. After a lifetime of cordial relations with the San Francisco Police Department, I now find myself in an adversarial legal battle against them because of their bureaucratic refusal to reverse the search/confiscation action they took solely on the strength of Adams -Thompson's accusation. This legal action has already cost over $6,000 in attorney's fees, and will certainly cost several tens if not hundreds of thousands of additional dollars if we are forced to pursue the matter into state and/or federal court to restore the good name and property of ourselves and our church. [See Attachment #G: letter to my attorney, Mr. Bernard Zimmerman, dated December 27, 1987.]

28. Add to this the countless man-hours the Department of the Army has now had to devote to responding to reporters concerning this affair, and the damage to the Army that has nonetheless resulted from some reporters' crude castigations of the Army for my religious "oddity" as though it were something despicable. Even my Top Secret security clearance, though not compromised in the least by my religion nor even relevant to this situation, has been headlined as though it were a scandal in itself. And add to this the very notion that a Lieutenant Colonel in the Army "may be linked to child-molesting at the Presidio" [as the stories "carefully" state], which necessarily reflects that much more adversely upon the Army officer corps as a whole.

Affidavit

I, Lieutenant Colonel Michael A. Aquino, have read or have had read to me this statement which begins on page 1 and ends on page 5. I fully understand the contents of the entire statement made by me. The statement is true. I have initialed all corrections and have initialed the bottom of each page containing the statement. I have made this statement freely without hope of benefit or reward, without threat of punishment, and without coercion, unlawful influence, or unlawful inducement.

/s/ Michael A. Aquino

Subscribed and sworn to before me, a person authorized by law to administer oaths, this 4th day of January 1988.

Witnesses:
Major Patrick D. Barry
First Sergeant Sam J. Nicholas
HHC ARPERCEN
9700 Page Boulevard, St. Louis, MO 63132

Authority to Administer Oaths: AR 600-11

Appendix 29: Lilith Aquino Sworn Statement - First A-T Charges

I, Lilith Aquino, want to make the following statement under oath:

1. From July 1986 through July 1987 my husband, Lieutenant Colonel Michael A, Aquino, and I were living in Washington, D.C., where he was a student in the resident course of the Industrial College of the Armed Forces, National Defense University, Fort McNair.

2. Following the end of the ICAF year (extended through July 1987 because of my husband's participation in a George Washington University M.P.A. option), my husband and I traveled to San Francisco to visit our home-of-record there for a month before moving on to St. Louis for my husband's next PCS assignment.

3. On 12 August 1987 my husband and I went shopping at the Presidio PX. We were unaware of the presence of Adams-Thompson and/or any other members of his family, nor would have recognized them in any case as we had never met them. I accompanied my husband at all times during the shopping trip, as it was for the purpose of purchasing a microwave oven as a gift for my daughter. En route from the store to the parking lot, I had to open three glass doors for my husband, who was carrying the oven.

4. I have never met either Chaplain Lawrence Adams-Thompson or any member of his family, nor had any member of his family over to our San Francisco home at 123 Acme Avenue, San Francisco.

5. I have never had anything to do with either Kinsey M. Almond (Chaplain Adams-Thompson's stepdaughter) or any other child involved with the Presidio day-care center. I have never molested any child in my life. I have never used or been known by the nickname "Shamby".

Affidavit

I, Lilith Aquino, have read or have had read to me this statement which begins on page 1 and ends on page 2. I fully understand the contents of the entire statement made by me. The statement is true. I have initialed all corrections and have initialed the bottom of each page containing the statement. I have made this statement freely without hope of benefit or reward, without threat of punishment, and without coercion, unlawful influence, or unlawful inducement.

/s/ Lilith Aquino

Subscribed and sworn to before me, a person authorized by law to administer oaths, this 4th day of January 1988.

Witnesses:
Major Patrick D. Barry
First Sergeant Sam J. Nicholas
HHC ARPERCEN
9700 Page Boulevard, St. Louis, MO 63132

Authority to Administer Oaths: AR 600-11

Appendix 30: Article 133 of the *Uniform Code of Military Justice*

59. Article 133 - Conduct unbecoming an officer and gentleman

a. *Text*.

"Any commissioned officer, cadet, or midshipman who is convicted of conduct unbecoming an officer and a gentleman shall be punished as a court-martial may direct."

b. *Elements*.

(1) That the accused did or omitted to do certain acts; and

(2) That, under the circumstances, these acts or omissions constituted conduct unbecoming an officer and gentleman.

c. *Explanation*.

(1) *Gentleman*. As used in this article, "gentleman" includes both male and female commissioned officers, cadets, and midshipmen.

(2) *Nature of offense*. Conduct violative of this article is action or behavior in an official capacity which, in dishonoring or disgracing the person as an officer, seriously compromises the officer's character as a gentleman, or action or behavior in an unofficial or private capacity which, in dishonoring or disgracing the officer personally, seriously compromises the person's standing as an officer. There are certain moral attributes common to the ideal officer and the perfect gentleman, a lack of which is indicated by acts of dishonesty, unfair dealing, indecency, indecorum, lawlessness, injustice, or cruelty. Not everyone is or can be expected to meet unrealistically high moral standards, but there is a limit of tolerance based on customs of the service and military necessity below which the personal standards of an officer, cadet, or midshipman cannot fall without seriously compromising the person's standing as an officer, cadet, or midshipman or the person's character as a gentleman. This article prohibits conduct by a commissioned officer, cadet, or midshipman which, taking all the circumstances into consideration, is thus compromising. This article includes acts made punishable by any other article, provided these acts amount to conduct unbecoming an officer and a gentleman. Thus, a commissioned officer who steals property violates both this article and Article 121. Whenever the offense charged is the same as a specific offense set forth in this Manual, the elements of proof are the same as those set forth in the paragraph which treats that specific offense, with the additional requirement that the act or omission constitutes conduct unbecoming an officer and gentleman.

(3) *Examples of offenses*. Instances of violation of this article include knowingly making a false official statement; dishonorable failure to pay a debt; cheating on an exam; opening and reading a letter of another without authority; using insulting or defamatory language to another officer in that officer's presence or about that officer to other military persons; being drunk and disorderly in a public place; public association with known prostitutes; committing or attempting to commit a crime involving moral turpitude; and failing without good cause to support the officer's family.

d. *Lesser included offense*. Article 80 - attempts.

e. *Maximum punishment*. Dismissal, forfeiture of all pay and allowances, and confinement for a period not in excess of that authorized for the most analogous offense for which a punishment is prescribed in this Manual, or, if none is prescribed, for 1 year.

Appendix 31: Michael Aquino Sworn Statement - First A-T Charges, Updated/Expanded

I, Lieutenant Colonel Michael A. Aquino, want to make the following statement under oath:

Concerning the background of the 1986 Presidio child-care scandal:

1. In recent years there has been a nationwide epidemic of "child-care center sex abuse" scandals, all imitating the highly-publicized McMartin Preschool case in Los Angeles. Sometimes the mass accusations have been directed against parents, more often against professional day-care workers. Such scandals have almost always begun in the same way: sensational allegations by one or two individuals, followed by the intensive and exhaustive grilling of children by "child therapists" specializing in the invention of sex-molestation symptoms, followed by spiraling mass investigations and indictments, followed by the eventual collapse of the case after immense, extensive damage to the innocent parties involved. A thorough analysis of the epidemic is included as Attachment #A (*Commercial Appeal*, Memphis, Tennessee, January 17-22, 1988).

2. This epidemic has extended to U.S. military services as well, including 15 U.S. Army day-care centers and elementary schools by November of 1987. In late 1986 it was the turn of the Presidio of San Francisco.

3. On September 28, 1986 the *San Francisco Examiner* began a series of eight front-page stories, with many dramatic maps and photographs, describing the "day-care sex abuse" epidemic sweeping the country. A copy of this series of articles is enclosed as Attachment #B.

4. Approximately a month after this series of articles appeared, the wife of a captain assigned to the Presidio, Joyce Tobin, decided that her son might have been anally raped by a Presidio day-care worker by the name of Gary Hambright. Nevertheless she did not take the child for a medical examination until a week later. Then she took the child to a civilian community hospital, where Dr. Kevin Coulter issued a report saying that the child's anus showed "tears" and was enlarged. Based upon this the Tobins complained to the Presidio Commander, and in December 1986 a "task force" containing representatives from the professional sex-abuse office where Coulter worked was advising the Army to expect multiple victims.

5. In April 1988 on a KTVU television news documentary [Attachment #C], Coulter admitted that he had later retracted his initial report about "tears", saying that the Tobin child's anus showed only "normal grooves". Nevertheless he said that the child's anus had seemed "unusually large". On the same documentary pediatrician Ann Parker, M.D. was asked about this statement. She responded that there are many perfectly normal causes for an enlarged anus in a child of that age, such as large bowel movements. Tobin's own mother stated in an affidavit that the child had been experiencing large bowel movements at the time.

6. Letters were mailed to 242 Presidio parents, and a checklist of "symptoms" of child sex-abuse was circulated [see Attachment #C]. Such checklists, created by "therapists" professionally dedicated to the finding of sex-abuse, have become nationally notorious for their inclusion of virtually every normal interest or action of a child as a "symptom". As a consequence of *Michelle Remembers*, a book written by one of these opportunists, the industry has now dressed up such checklists with "Satanic ritual" symptoms. [See Attachment #A, pages #30-31.] A copy of one of the more widely-circulated and often-copied lists by therapist Catherine Gould is enclosed as Attachment #D.

7. In this list it will be seen that many ordinary and even mutually-contradictory forms of behavior are symptoms of "Satanic ritual abuse and sexual abuse", for example a child who is either rebellious or compliant, who gets angry or play-acts or is lazy in school, or who touches his or her genitals. The checklist also warns parents that any official investigation will be incompetent, and also that even the most excellent reputation of a school or day-care facility means nothing. In short, a climate comparable to the witch-hunts of medieval Europe is created, in which anything and everything is "proof" of witchcraft and no defense is admissible.

8. In the predictable pattern other children were interviewed by a therapist, reportedly one Debbie Hickey either assigned or contracted to the Presidio's Letterman Army Medical Center. According to the KTVU documentary, Hickey proceeded to find symptoms of sex-abuse in several of the children, including her own. The accounts, as later reported by the press, were of the fantastic and incoherent variety normal to previous episodes of the epidemic. Children said that they had guns pointed at them, that they had played baseball with human excrement, and that "Mr. Gary" [Hambright] had a shark in a bowl on his kitchen table which he took a child home with him to feed. All this was supposed to "prove" mass sexual molestation at the center.

9. Apart from this "therapy", there are no published accounts that any child attending the Presidio center was **ever** taken to an emergency room for examination/care because of an apparent adult rape/sodomy, or that upon the publicizing of the scandal itself any medical examinations of any of the children revealed any evidence of sexual molestation. Apart from Coulter's waffling and uncertain statements concerning the Tobin child, there is no medical evidence that anything happened to any of the children.

10. As a consequence of medical examinations given to the children when the scandal commenced, it was first given out to the press that five of the children had chlamydia, a venereal disease which can be transmitted by sexual contact. It was later brought out, however, that the tests used to detect chlamydia were so inaccurate that none of them could be used as evidence. Since nothing more was heard about the chlamydia allegations, it is reasonable to assume that rechecks of the same children by more reliable testing procedures either did not occur or produced negative results. According to *San Francisco Chronicle* reporter Edward Lempinen, chlamydia can also be transmitted from a mother to her unborn fetus. In the absence of any sign of adult rape on the children involved, it is reasonable to suppose that if any child had the disease, it was contracted this way. No evidence has been published to indicate that the mothers of the children in question were examined and found to be free of the disease themselves, or had no medical history of being treated for it since the birth of their children. Presumably for the Army to insist that this more probable explanation be investigated would have angered the women in question, who were already vehemently criticizing the Army, to even greater antagonism.

11. A scare in the local media occurred when one child was initially reported as testing positively for AIDS. This test result was later shown to be false. Nevertheless, as with the chlamydia, this development continued to be brought up as "additional evidence" that sex-abuse had taken place.

12. In February 1988 a federal judge dismissed all of the charges against Hambright as being unsubstantiated. Only the original charge concerning the Tobin child remained. Significantly by this point in time, the charge in the case of the Tobin child had been changed from sodomy to oral copulation. This suggests that even Coulter's amended report of an "enlarged anus" and the circumstances surrounding the initial complaint that began the whole episode were now considered too spurious to take seriously.

13. Finally the Tobins, who were now faced with being the sole accusers of Hambright, suddenly refused permission for their child to be used as evidence "on the advice of his therapist". Therefore the U.S. Attorney dropped the remaining charge against Hambright in February 1988.

14. Joyce Tobin and a few other parents appeared actively and enthusiastically in local newspaper, magazine, and television talk-show interviews during the scandal. Following the dropping of the charges against Hambright, these parents, according to the April 20, 1988 *San Francisco Chronicle*, "accused prosecutors of being 'highly irresponsible' and charged that the Army's response had been 'pitiful'". They angrily protested the opening of a new day-care center at the Presidio. And finally they filed 53 claims against the Army for a total of $55 million. These claims remain pending at this time.

15. In summary, based upon all published evidence to date in all of the San Francisco bay area media and the *Army Times*, **there is not a single piece of evidence other than coached "therapy" that any child was ever sexually abused or molested at the Presidio daycare center**. Accordingly the $55 million claims against the U.S. Army are not substantiated. The media-courting militancy of the ringleader group of parents is most probably explained by the realization that they have already gone too far in hurling the accusations that caused such a

damaging witch-hunt. To backtrack on them now would be to admit that they had caused grievous and totally unjustified harm to innocent people -and might subject them to defamation legal suits as well.

Concerning the attack on my wife and myself
by Captain (Chaplain) Lawrence Adams-Thompson:

16. For several years prior to July 1986 I was assigned to the Presidio headquarters as USAR Advisor to the Presidio Commander. Some time before my reassignment to Washington in July 1986, Captain (Chaplain) Lawrence Adams-Thompson arrived on post and was also assigned to the Presidio headquarters as an assistant post chaplain.

17. From July 1986 through July 1987 my wife and I were living in Washington, D.C., where I was a student in the resident course of the Industrial College of the Armed Forces, National Defense University, Fort McNair.

18. Following the end of the ICAF year (extended through July 1987 because of my participation in a George Washington University Master of Public Administration degree option), my wife and I traveled to San Francisco to visit our home-of-record there for a month before moving on to St. Louis for my next PCS assignment.

19. On 12 August 1987 Chaplain Adams-Thompson, without my knowledge or the knowledge of the Presidio Commander, contacted the FBI and the San Francisco Police Department and falsely accused me and my wife of having sexually molested his infant stepdaughter at Gary Hambright's home during the period September-October 1986. Adams-Thompson alleges that he made the accusation based solely on comments elicited from his 3-year-old stepdaughter (who was age 2 in September 1986).

20. According to the official SFPD Incident Report (Attachment #E), Adams-Thompson's stepdaughter was questioned by the FBI on 14 January 1987 and denied being molested by Hambright or anyone else. There is no evidence to indicate that the child was ever taken by her parents to Letterman Army Medical Center, hospital emergency room, or medical doctor at any time during the September-October 1986 time period for examination or treatment of the kind of injuries that a 2-year-old would necessarily sustain had she been both sodomized and raped by two adult males. Had there been any such evidence, it wouldn't have taken the FBI until January to interview the child, nor would any denials by her at that time have been taken seriously, nor for that matter would she have had any reason to deny such an assault. It also would have been included in the SFPD report, which it is not. It is therefore evident that until they decided to have the child therapized, the Adams-Thompsons had **no** grounds to think that she had been assaulted -and in fact every physical/medical/anatomical reason to know that she had **not** been assaulted. [By a FOIA request to LAMC I acted to verify these facts from the SFPD incident report. This information has been denied to me, but should be pursued by the investigating officer. See Attachment #F.]

21. Adams-Thompson, apparently the chaplain who had counseled the Tobins to initiate their actions to begin the scandal and witch-hunt the previous year, placed his stepdaughter in therapy in February 1988 despite his knowledge of her lack of any corresponding injury and her denial of abuse during the FBI interview. After four sessions the therapist purportedly told Adams-Thompson that his stepdaughter was one of the "victims" and produced the "Mikey & Shamby at Hambright's house" story. [SFPD report]

22. Exactly how much of this story the therapist [presumably the same Debbie Hickey whose "therapy" had created the avalanche of other fantastic abuse accounts] invented, and how much Adams-Thompson and his wife invented, will not be known until a written record of the therapy sessions is obtained. The investigating officer should obtain a copy of this record.

23. If the details of the story contained in the SFPD report are not included in the therapy record, then it is evident that that story was simply invented whole cloth by Lawrence and/or Michele Adams-Thompson.

24. If the story appears on the therapy record, the Adams-Thompsons may still have invented it if they coached the child to recite it before or between the therapy sessions. Whether the AdamsThompsons or the therapist invented

the story, however, the clear fact remains is that because it directly contradicts what the Adams-Thompsons knew to be the physical condition of the child during the time-period in question, they had every reason to know that it was a false account.

25. It was stated in the SFPD report that the Adams-Thompsons thought their daughter was molested because she "started having nightmares and would wet herself". It is obvious that 2-year-olds may occasionally wet themselves or have nightmares for many reasons having nothing to do with sexual attack. In the absence of any physical evidence whatever, it is preposterous for the Adams-Thompsons to have concluded from ordinary infant events such as these that rape and sodomy had occurred.

26. At this point I state for the record that I have never had anything to do with either Kinsey M. Almond (Chaplain Adams-Thompson's stepdaughter) or any other child involved with the Presidio day-care center. I have never molested any child in my life. I have never used or been known by the nickname "Mikey". Neither Kinsey Almond, nor Gary Hambright, nor any other Presidio day-care child or worker has ever been inside my San Francisco home.

27. The officer corps of the Presidio headquarters garrison is not large, and it would have been quite conspicuous to Adams-Thompson that I had not been present for garrison activities for over a year. It would have been equally easy for him to have ascertained that I had been reassigned to Washington in July 1986, merely by asking the officer personnel office or any senior officer in the garrison headquarters. Since only one USAR officer per year is selected nationwide to attend the Industrial College of the Armed Forces, my selection was well-known at the Presidio.

28. Therefore Lawrence Adams-Thompson had a clear reason not to initiate any accusation against anyone, and even more of a reason not to initiate one against an officer who he had known to be gone from the garrison for over a year. Nevertheless he made the accusation against us.

29. Concerning the 12 August 1987 account by Adams-Thompson in the SFPD report:

a. On that day my wife and I went shopping at the Presidio PX. We were unaware of the presence of Adams-Thompson and/or any other members of his family, nor would have recognized them in any case as we had never met them. Adams-Thompson stated that his stepdaughter reacted to my appearance upon seeing me at the PX. Since I have a prominent widow's peak and sharplypointed eyebrows (Attachment #G/*ICAF 1987 Yearbook*), it is not uncommon for children [or even adults] to react to what they consider an unusual appearance.

b. Adams-Thompson did not call my attention to his presence nor ask me any questions. Instead he prompted his stepdaughter several times to elicit what he alleges was the child's identification of my wife and myself as two individuals who had molested her about ten months earlier at the home of Gary Hambright. Why did Adams-Thompson not immediately leave his stepdaughter with his wife, who he states was also at the PX, and discuss the matter with me? It is unreasonable for him to have felt in any personal danger from a field-grade officer surrounded by crowds of shoppers. Had he not wanted to bring up the subject there, he could have requested that we meet immediately with the Presidio Chaplain (Colonel Jerry Autry) or the Commander or Deputy Commander or any other appropriate military official for a discussion. Instead Adams-Thompson left the PX without making his presence known to me or my wife at all.

c. Adams-Thompson's statement that my wife did not appear until later in the PX parking lot is completely false, since at no time was she separated from me during our shopping trip. We had gone to the PX specifically to purchase a microwave oven. Both of us picked it out from the floor samples, and then my wife held the two sets of glass doors open for me as I carried the heavy oven out to our car.

d. The account that his stepdaughter could have identified either of us is also false, since we have never met any members of the Adams-Thompson family. [Adams-Thompson himself obviously recognized me from my

Presidio assignment a year earlier, since he accused me by name to the FBI. I was not in uniform during the PX shopping trip, hence was not wearing a nametag.]

30. Instead of consulting either with Colonel Autry or the post Commander or Deputy Commander concerning such a serious allegation against a senior officer and former member of the Presidio headquarters, Adams-Thompson went immediately to the FBI and the San Francisco Police Department. Thus, in addition to having every reason to know his accusation was false to begin with, he also made it in a way which would obviously result in the maximum damage to my wife and myself, and avoided any consultative action within his chain of command which might have shortstopped that accusation. For these reasons I conclude that the elements of proof of a violation of Article #133 - of Adams-Thompson's making a knowingly false and malicious official statement - clearly exist in this case. Both he and I were officers on active duty; the incident occurred on a U.S. Army installation, and its evident intent was deliberately to defame and harm myself and my wife.

31. It is now appropriate to examine the detailed story which Adams-Thompson says he received from his stepdaughter either directly or via the therapist. At face value the story was clearly concocted by an adult, not the child. It is impossible for a 3-year-old infant to have assembled, much less recalled from a year earlier at age 2, a story with such features as the identification of a movie camera [as distinct from a still camera] and other details which no 2-year-old would either notice, recognize, or retain. The story is genital-obsessive to a disgusting degree: certainly the product of an adult perversion rather than a 2-year-old's actual perception. The story was quite obviously fabricated by an adult and tutored into the child -either by Adams-Thompson himself, the therapist, or by some other adult who had instructed her. [The details of the Adams-Thompson account will all be found in the chart of "similar tales" on pages #21-22 of Attachment #A.]

32. When Adams-Thompson made his allegations to FBI agent Clyde Foreman, the first thing Foreman should have done was to ask for medical verification that his stepdaughter had in fact been double-raped and sodomized. When such a medical report could not be produced, Foreman should have asked for the child to be taken immediately to LAMC for such a physical examination. There is no evidence that Foreman did this. The absence of medical evidence that the child had been raped or sodomized, therefore, was merely ignored by both the Adams-Thompsons and Foreman.

33. After Adams-Thompson made his allegations to Foreman, Foreman then drove the child to my San Francisco street address, in the company of Michele Adams-Thompson. Allegedly the child then identified my building as the "home of Gary Hambright". This too is impossible, as the child had never been inside the building [nor has any other member of the Adams-Thompson family - nor Gary Hambright (whom we have never met) - nor any other child involved with the Presidio daycare center]. If she identified the building, it is either because she was taken there in advance and instructed to "identify" the building later to the FBI agent, or because the "identification" was deliberately coached from her either by Adams-Thompson or by the FBI agent. It would have been easy to do this simply by calling the child's special attention to my building, just as AdamsThompson had done to me in the PX. Both Adams-Thompson and the FBI agent knew that my building was not the residence of Hambright, furthermore, because Hambright's actual address elsewhere in San Francisco is included on the SFPD incident report (Attachment #E).

34. Although the original story was that the child was taken to Gary Hambright's house, there is no evidence that the FBI agent or any other investigating official ever drove the child to Gary Hambright's block or address for a possible "identification" of the building where she was supposedly molested. Presumably this should have happened in February 1987 after the therapist produced the molestation story. If such an on-site identification had been tried and failed, then it would have shown the story to be that much more spurious. If it had been tried and yielded an "identification", there would then have been no reason to seek an "identification" of a totally different building halfway across the city. The inescapable conclusion is that **no** building identification of Hambright's residence was ever attempted as a consequence of the original story. Obviously the story had not been considered worth investigating even to that extent - until Adams-Thompson saw my wife and myself in the PX and decided to use it for a deliberate attack against us. Suddenly an identification was attempted against my home supposedly on the grounds of the same story.

35. For that matter, there is no evidence that during or following the therapy-produced story in February 1987 either the FBI or the SFPD ever acted to search Gary Hambright's house, confiscate any items of his kept there (for example, a still or movie camera if he owned such an item), or otherwise take the Adams-Thompson story seriously prior to its employment against my wife and myself.

36. Since only Michele Adams-Thompson and FBI agent Clyde Foreman were present for the "building identification", whatever leading questions or coaching methods were used on the child cannot be determined from the facts known. Presumably neither would now admit to having deliberately coached an identification. However it is obvious from the behavior of the Adams-Thompsons prior and subsequent to this moment that they had deliberately set out to defame and damage my wife and myself. A coached "building identification" would have represented only a minor obstacle.

37. As a consequence of Adams-Thompson's accusations, San Francisco Police Department Juvenile Division officer Glenn Pamfiloff then obtained and exercised a search warrant on my home on 14 August 1987 - from 9 PM to 1 AM, to the utter surprise and shock of my wife and myself, who could do nothing but watch while our entire flat was ransacked and our most personal effects pawed through and photographed. The police found that the interior "descriptions" alleged to have been given by the Adams-Thompson child did not match the interior of my home, and they found no evidence whatever of any child-abuse/pornography activities. They confiscated a selection of family and church papers & photographs, and other articles so that, in my attorney's opinion, they would not have to return to the judge who approved the search-warrant empty-handed.

38. Since it is SFPD policy to not return seized property until a judge orders it, I had to initiate litigation accordingly. In January 1988, after a motion to return the property had been filed in San Francisco Municipal Court, Pamfiloff returned almost all of it. That same month he, my attorney, my wife, and I jointly inventoried the rest of it and established that none of it was evidence either of the Adams-Thompson allegations or of anything else illegal. [I have filed a formal complaint concerning Pamfiloff's actions in this case with the Office of Citizen Complaints, San Francisco Police Commission. This complaint is under active investigation at this time.]

39. On 1 August 1988 the San Francisco District Attorney's office announced that it was closing its investigation into the Presidio scandal, and that no charges would be filed against my wife or myself.

40. After the raid on my home, I did not learn of Adams-Thompson's allegations until 28 August 1987, when a copy of the SFPD Incident Report was finally made available. As Adams-Thompson was at that time still assigned to the Presidio, I immediately contacted the Deputy Commander of the Presidio, Colonel D. Peter Gleichenhaus. My wife and I met with him in his office on that morning. Gleichenhaus indicated that he had never been contacted by Adams-Thompson about the matter, either before or after Adams-Thompson had contacted the FBI and SFPD. He said that Adams-Thompson was being transferred to the 25th Division in Hawaii, but as far as he knew was still in quarters at the Presidio.

41. The moment I left Gleichenhaus' office I posted from the Presidio branch post office a letter (Attachment #H) affirming my non-involvement and demanding a letter of apology and retraction for his conduct. He did not bother to reply.

42. I thus conclude not only that an Army officer and chaplain made a malicious and knowingly false criminal accusation against another officer and his wife, but also that, when the facts were subsequently brought to his attention and an informal apology requested, his response was one of unconcern. Judging from his wife's statement in paragraph #43 below, his only regret is that his maneuver didn't succeed in doing more damage to us than it did.

43. On 2 August 1988, after the majority of the above-cited facts had long since been established and the innocence of my wife and myself was clearly evident, and after we had endured a year of agony because of the allegations, Michele Adams-Thompson had only this to say [quoted in the *San Jose Mercury News*]: "The district attorney's decision not to file charges is certainly not surprising in lieu (sic) of how the authorities have bungled

everything else. No one agency has distinguished themselves (sic). It all seemed to be a really sad failure of all agencies to do their jobs properly."

44. Therefore the unconcern of the Adams-Thompsons for all factual evidence remains clear. That the various government agencies involved ultimately failed to support them doesn't in the least change their minds; rather they merely attack those agencies *en masse* as inept and irresponsible.

45. Michele Adams-Thompson also stated to the *SJMN* that she has kept her child in constant therapy. Since there is no medical evidence that the child was ever abused, the only reason for such treatment would be to reinforce the story introduced as a consequence of the February 1987 therapy sessions. If the child were to backtrack to the original statement of "no molestation" originally given to the FBI in January 1987, obviously, it would be very inconvenient and awkward for Captain and Mrs. Adams-Thompson.

46. The question of motive remains. Why should Lawrence Adams-Thompson have behaved this way towards my wife and myself, since we had had no previous contact with him or his family whatever?

47. During my assignment to the Presidio garrison, it was well-known on post that I was, as High Priest of the Temple of Set, the chief official of the nation's largest and most prominent legitimate Satanic church. Although I did not advertise or encourage publicity within the military in any way, my unusual religion was common knowledge to the post commanders under whom I served, the Presidio Catholic (Colonel Christoph) and Protestant (Colonel Autry) chaplains, and most if not all of the other officers, enlisted personnel, and civilians on post. As one of the subordinate garrison chaplains, it is inconceivable that Adams-Thompson was not also aware of it.

48. At no time did Adams-Thompson speak to me about it, nor make any other inquiry to the Temple of Set about its standing, beliefs, or practices. Had he done so, he would have learned that since its founding in 1975 it has remained a legitimate religious institution, incorporated in California and possessing full state and federal tax-exempt recognition as a church. It has no record whatever of any misdemeanor or felony activities. Its public information documents make it quite explicit that it neither engages in nor advocates any illegal activities whatever, nor permits anyone under the age of 18 to affiliate or to attend any of its functions. [My religious affiliation has been continuously known to the Army since my commissioning in 1968, and has never been the basis for any adverse official concern or action.]

49. I find it inescapable to conclude, therefore, that Adams-Thompson's actions towards my wife and myself were the result of religious intolerance and bigotry: the fear and hatred of a passionate, professional Christian clergyman for something which he [ignorantly] considered a threat to his preferred religion. Hence his actions were not motivated by a sincere, logical conviction on his part that my wife and I had in fact molested his stepdaughter, but rather by his cold and deliberate perception of an opportunity to inflict great harm upon us and our church with a devastating accusation.

50. In *San Francisco Chronicle* coverage of the Presidio child-care scandal on 10 August 1987, it was established that the parents making the allegations were very much aware of the extremely sensational McMartin and Kern County "Satanic child-abuse" cases of the previous two years, in which young children -proved later to have been coached to make false statements by parents, therapists, and law-enforcement officials -obediently reported sexual abuse, murder, and cannibalism at the hands of "Satanic cults" at day-care centers. After exhaustive investigation and the ruining of the lives of many innocent persons who had neither abused children nor been Satanists (legitimate or otherwise), both scandals ended with the allegations of "Satanic child abuse" being shown to be **completely** without basis. The Kern County case in particular ended with the California Attorney General severely criticizing the investigators and officials involved for the impulsive and unprofessional way in which they had proceeded. [See Attachment #B, documents A and H.]

51. The publicity accorded these two cases - and a flurry of subsequent "copycat" cases around the country - have nonetheless generated a media image of Satanists as habitual child-abusers or child-murderers. As law-enforcement officials have repeatedly admitted, however, **not a single such connection between child-abuse and**

Satanism has ever been established. The published texts of contemporary legitimate Satanism, most prominently Anton LaVey's *Satanic Bible* and the Temple of Set's *Crystal Tablet of Set*, contain strong and explicit prohibitions against any and all harm to children, sexual or otherwise. [See Attachment #1.] See also the exposure and discrediting of the "Satanic" theme in Attachment #A, pages 17-31

52. I therefore conclude that Adams-Thompson deliberately intended to smear my good name, that of my wife, and that of our church with this abominable accusation, counting on media sensationalism and public ignorance not only to compound the damage to us, but also to shield him from the consequences of falsely and maliciously accusing a fellow Army officer of a serious felony. To date it appears that he has been quite successful in this.

53. After these charges were initially preferred on 4 January 1988, they were referred to Adams-Thompson's brigade commander for a preliminary inquiry. After five months, during which time neither my wife nor myself was contacted by any investigating authority to discuss our sworn statements, any statements by Adams-Thompson, or any other pertinent evidence, I received a letter saying merely that the charges had been dismissed "for lack of substantiating evidence".

54. As is clear from this sworn statement and its 4 January 1988 predecessor, there is **abundant** substantiating evidence of the charges. It is not the function of a preliminary inquiry to pass preemptory judgment upon charges. The right of judgment is reserved to a formally constituted court-martial. It is the right of one soldier who believes he has been victimized by another in violation of Article #133 of the Uniform Code of Military Justice to seek justice according to the procedures provided for in that code.

55. My family and I have now endured one year of protracted agony because of Adams-Thompson's vile accusation. We have been questioned by scores of military associates, family friends, and business associates. We and our church have been caricatured sensationally and inaccurately by many commercial media. Our personal privacy and the religious privacy of our church have been and continue to be regularly violated as though we are mere freaks for public entertainment; we are forced to respond to continued inquiries only to try to preclude at least the more bizarre distortions in the inevitable coverage. We have learned to our distress that even the most polite declining of interviews usually results in hostile distortions by the reporters in question.

56. My wife and I have received several death and arson threats on our telephone answering machine. During one such message on January 1, 1988 an anonymous caller stated that we would both be killed this year. Our San Francisco home has been vandalized, forcing me to spend over $3,000 in repairs and protective reinforcement. Our tenants in the building have also been harassed and traumatized by vandalism.

57. After a lifetime of cordial relations with the San Francisco Police Department, I had to initiate first legal actions and then a Police Commission complaint concerning the search/confiscation action they took solely on the strength of Adams-Thompson's accusations. The legal actions have already cost over $40,000 in attorney's fees alone.

58. Add to this the countless man-hours the Department of the Army has now had to devote to responding to reporters concerning this affair, and the damage to the Army that has nonetheless resulted from some reporters' crude castigations of the Army for my religious "oddity" as though it were something despicable. Even my Top Secret security clearance, though not compromised in the least by my religion nor even relevant to this situation, has been headlined as though it were a scandal in itself. And add to this the very notion that a Lieutenant Colonel in the Army "may be linked to child-molesting at the Presidio" [as the stories "carefully" state], which necessarily reflects that much more adversely upon the Army officer corps as a whole.

59. I therefore request that the Commanding General of the 25th Infantry Division immediately reactivate the charges I have preferred against Chaplain (Captain) Lawrence Adams-Thompson and refer them for trial by general court-martial.

60. I fully appreciate the public relations awkwardness of a situation in which the United States Army court-martials a Christian chaplain in defense of a Satanist High Priest. Certainly this is an unwelcome prospect in a country in which the majority of the citizenry are Christian. However I must point out that 14th Amendment to the United States Constitution, the supreme law of the land, guarantees equal protection of the laws to all citizens regardless of their religion, and the 1st Amendment to the Constitution further guarantees freedom of all law-abiding religions and churches in this nation. I must also point out that Article #133 of the UCMJ specifically applies since both Adams-Thompson and myself were and are active-duty commissioned officers covered by the Code. Any false or malicious action or statement that he made concerning me, regardless when or to whom made, is covered by the Code. Finally I must point out that whatever distaste the Army or the Corps of Chaplains feels for this situation is not the result of any initiative by my religion, my wife, or myself. I have conducted myself as an officer and a gentleman, respecting soldiers of all faiths, since my commissioning in 1968. It is Captain Lawrence Adams-Thompson who has forced this situation into existence, by deliberately and without the slightest provocation acting to harm my wife and myself. I seek justice under the law, as is guaranteed to every American citizen, and under the Uniform Code of Military Justice, as is guaranteed to every American soldier.

Affidavit

I, Lieutenant Colonel Michael A. Aquino, have read or have had read to me this statement which begins on page 1 and ends on page 11. I fully understand the contents of the entire statement made by me. The statement is true. I have initialed all corrections and have initialed the bottom of each page containing the statement. I have made this statement freely without hope of benefit or reward, without threat of punishment, and without coercion, unlawful influence, or unlawful inducement.

/s/ Michael A. Aquino

Subscribed and sworn to before me, a person authorized by law to administer oaths, this 23 day of August 1988.

Witnesses:
Captain Acie T. Angel, Executive Officer
Carolyn Pozdel
HHC ARPERCEN
9700 Page Boulevard, St. Louis, MO 63132

Authority to Administer Oaths: AR 600-11

Appendix 32: CID Investigation Report - First A-T Charges

AGENT'S INVESTIGATION REPORT
CID Regulation 195-1
ROI Number 0038-88-CID108

Basis for Investigation

On 19 Jan 88, COL Michael J. SIERRA, Commander, 3d Brigade, 25th infantry Division (Light), requested CID assistance in investigating court-martial charges preferred by LTC Michael AQUINO against Chaplain (CPT) Larry P. ADAMS-THOMPSON.

Narrative

1. COORDINATION WITH SAN FRANCISCO FIELD OFFICE (SFFO), SIXTH REGION, USACIDC, PRESIDIO OF SAN FRANCISCO (PSF), CA:

1.1 On 24 Jan 88, COL SIERRA'S request for assistance was forwarded to the SFFO.

1.2 On 15 Mar 88, a message was received from the SFFO, PSF, CA. The message addresses questions asked by representatives of the Staff Judge Advocate, 25th inf Div (L). The following are excerpts from that message:

On 4 Mar 88, SA Kent T. WATSON, SFFO, contacted CPT Mitchell F. BOOMER, Criminal Law Branch, SJA, PSF, CA. CPT BOOMER opined that sufficient probable cause does not exist, at this time, to support titling LTC AQUINO for any criminal offense.

On 8 Mar 88, SA WATSON contacted CPT BOOMER pertaining to the charges made by LTC AQUINO against CPT ADAMS-THOMPSON. CPT BOOMER opined that specification 1 had no merit as no evidence exists that indicates CPT ADAMS-THOMPSON, on or about 12 Aug 87, knowingly and with malicious intent, made false statements and representations defaming the characters of LTC and Mrs. AQUINO. CPT ADAMS-THOMPSON reported, in good faith, what he believed to be a felony offense, committed by LTC AQUINO. CPT BOOMER opined that specification 2 has no merit as no evidence exists to indicate CPT ADAMS-THOMPSON did, on or about 2 Sep 87, answer a letter from LTC AQUINO with a disrespectful card, mailed to the St Louis, MO, address of LTC AQUINO.

The Sari Francisco Police Department (SFPD) and the SFFO are continuing the preliminary investigation pertaining to LTC AQUINO, and, at this time, no evidence or information exists which indicates a false complaint was made by CPT ADAMS-THOMPSON and/or his family members. Therefore, any action taken toward CPT ADAMS-THOMPSON, or LTC AQUINO, prior to the completion of the SFPD and SFFO preliminary investigation, would be premature and not advisable. A completion date for this investigation can not be determined at this time; however, upon identification of any significant information, which may require appropriate command action, your office will be notified.

2. INTERVIEW OF CHAPLAIN (CPT) ADAMS-THOMPSON:

2.1 On 25 Feb 88, at the request of the SFFO, ADAMS-THOMPSON was interviewed by SA FACUNDO. ADAMS-THOMPSON rendered a sworn statement detailing how he felt that he was threatened by AQUINO.

3. COORDINATION WITH SJA:

3.1 On 24 Mar 88, all information obtained in this inquiry was coordinated with CPT Theodore DIXON, Trial Counsel, 25th Inf Div (L).

Status

No further investigative action is being pursued by Hawaii District, Seventh Region.

/s/ SA Ralph P. Facundo
Hawaii District, Seventh Region, USACIDC
14 April 1988
* * * * * * * * * *

AGENT'S INVESTIGATION REPORT
CID Regulation 195-1
ROI Number 0038-88-CID108

Basis for Investigation

On 18 Feb 88, this office received a Request for Assistance (RFA) from SA Robert BURKE, Operations Officer, San Francisco Field Office, 6th Rgn, USACIDC, Presidio of San Francisco, CA. SA BURKE requested that this office interview and obtain a statement from CPT (Chaplain) Larry P. ADAMS-THOMPSON, HHC, 4th Battalion, 27th Infantry, 25th Infantry Division (Light), Schofield Barracks (SB), HI 96857, concerning whether or not ADAMS-THOMPSON felt that he was being threatened by LTC Michael AQUINO, formerly assigned to a unit at Presidio of San Francisco, CA (NFI), in an effort to have ADAMS-THOMPSON stop his stepdaughter from pursuing a sexual assault complaint made by her against AQUINO.

Narrative

1, VICTIM INTERVIEW

1.1 CPT ADAMS-THOMPSON: At 1438, 25 Feb 88, ADAMS-THOMPSON was interviewed by SA FACUNDO and completed the rendering of a typed sworn statement detailing how he felt that he had been threatened by AQUINO.

Status

No further investigative activity is required at this time.

/s/ SA Ralph P. Facundo
Hawaii District, Seventh Region, USACIDC
25 February 1988

SWORN STATEMENT
Location: Schofield Barracks, HI
Date: 25 February 1988
Name: Adams-Thompson, Larry Parker
Social Security Number: 562-76-3492
Grade: Captain
Organization: HHC 4/27th Inf, 25th Inf Div (L), Schofield Barracks, HI 96857

I, Larry Parker Adams-Thompson, want to make the following statement under oath:

Q: There is currently a criminal investigation being conducted in which your stepdaughter, Kinsey, been identified as a victim, and in which LTC Michael AQUINO is identified as a suspect. Do you feel that AQUINO is trying to threaten you, so that you will have your step-daughter retract her statements?

A: Yes.

Q: Explain how you feel that you have been threatened by AQUINO?

A: I have received two letters from AQUINO. Copies of those letters are in possession of the CID Office, Presidio of San Francisco, CA and the CID Office, Hawaii. Also I have seen a copy of a newsletter which I believe was prepared by AQUINO, in which AQUINO had written an article concerning how he was being persecuted and that I (he mentioned me by name in the article) was going to get my "just dues ... just reward ... or he'll get his ...", or something to that effect.[173]

Q: Did you feel that the comments made in the letters, and newsletter were threatening?

A: Yes, and that the charge sheet was another way of threatening me.

Q: Has AQUINO ever made a direct threat against either you, or a member of your family?

A: Other then the statements made in the letters and newsletter, AQUINO has never verbally threatened me, nor any member of my family.

Q: Where is the copy of the newsletter?

A: I have a copy of the newsletter and the CID Office in CA has a copy of the newsletter.

Q: Did you respond to either of the letters that AQUINO sent you?

A: No.

Q: Do you feel that AQUINO has the means to carry out the threats outlined in his letters to you?

A: Yes, when I read what he had written I believed at that time that he would carry out his threats.

Q: Did you receive the letters from AQUINO, in which he threatened you, through the U.S. Mail?

A: Yes.

Q: Is there anything that you want to add to this statement?

A: No.

Affidavit

I, Larry Parker Adams-Thompson, have read or have had read to me this statement which begins on page 1 and ends on page 2. I fully understand the contents of the entire statement made by me. The statement is true. I have initialed all corrections and have initialed the bottom of each page containing the statement. I have made this statement freely without hope of benefit or reward, without threat of punishment, and without coercion, unlawful influence, or unlawful inducement.

/s/ Larry P. Adams-Thompson

Subscribed and sworn to before me, a person authorized by law to administer oaths, this 25 day of February 1988.

Witnesses:

SA Ralph P. Facundo, 2562

Authority to Administer Oaths: Art 136 (b) (4), UCMJ

---

[173] In the October 1987 issue of the *Scroll of Set*, newsletter of the Temple of Set, I wrote:

"What about Army Chaplain Lawrence Adams-Thompson, blissfully enjoying his new assignment in Hawaii after setting in motion this malicious damage to the Temple of Set, Lilith, and myself?

"I have requested the Presidio Commander to initiate a formal reprimand as a permanent entry in Adams-Thompson's official file - this again as a way of addressing the matter without the time, publicity, and expense that would accompany formal court-martial charges. If Adams-Thompson can be handled this way, so much the better.

"Adams-Thompson can be reprimanded [or court-martialed] for violating Articles #133 and/or #134 of the Uniform Code of Military Justice - relating respectively to 'Conduct Unbecoming an Officer and Gentleman' and 'all conduct of a nature to bring discredit upon the armed forces'. Such a violation focuses on his irresponsibility for making a formal accusation concerning my wife and myself to the FBI when reasonable care on his part would have made it clear that such an accusation was unjustified. This is assuming that he did not deliberately fabricate his stepdaughter's detailed allegations, which in light of her 2-year-old age at the time I consider far more probable. Also relevant is his profession as a Christian clergyman; I certainly doubt that he would have made such an outrageous accusation against any Lieutenant Colonel who was **not** known to be a prominent Satanist.

"As of this writing, the Army Criminal Investigation Division (CID) has opened a preliminary investigation concerning Adams-Thompson. Further decisions or actions by either the Army or myself await the outcome of this investigation."

Appendix 33: Letter, Michael Aquino to Major General Otstott 12/1/89

December 1, 1989

Major General Charles P. Otstott
Commanding General
25th Infantry Division
Schofield Barracks, HI 96857-6000

Dear General Otstott:

Enclosed is a DD Form 458 in which, on November 29, 1989, I have preferred charges against Chaplain Lawrence Adams-Thompson, an officer under your command, for violations of the Uniform Code of Military Justice as indicated.

As you know, I originally preferred charges against this individual on January 4, 1988. Those charges were inquired into by Colonel Michael J. Sierra, Adams-Thompson's brigade commander, in accordance with Rule #303 MCM.

Colonel Sierra's conclusions concerning Specification #1 of those charges were based upon a report of investigation provided to him by the CID, stating that "there was a lack of substantiating evidence", which he included as Tab A to his recommendations to your predecessor Major General Crysel.

As has since been revealed, as verified by documents which I have sent to you subsequently and together with this letter and charge sheet, the San Francisco Field Office of the CID was in fact in possession of a **considerable body** of evidence to substantiate Specification #1. Hence the CID's report of investigation to Colonel Sierra caused him to be deliberately misled. This action by the San Francisco Field Office of the CID constitutes misprision of serious offense and obstruction of justice in violation of Article 134 UCMJ, which I have brought to the attention of the CIC Commanding General, Major General Cromartie, for investigation.

Since the dismissal of those original charges, the CID has gone to extraordinary and illegal lengths to prevent my seeing the CID report of investigation provided to Colonel Sierra, even to the extent of the Staff Judge Advocate of General Cromartie's headquarters stating to me on 10/20/89 that "no such report exists". The Crime Records Center, after illegally denying me a copy of the "nonexistent" report for well over a year, finally complied with the law and sent it to me three days ago.

What that CID investigation report reveals is that the "investigation" consisted of the Hawaii Field Office of the CID simply referring the entire matter to the San Francisco Field Office. The San Francisco Field Office conducted **no investigation at all**, but simply called a Captain Boomer at the Presidio Judge Advocate's office, who gave it as his "opinion" that "no evidence exists".

It is obvious that, in offering this "opinion", Captain Boomer neither researched **any** of the contents in the sworn statements & supporting documentation provided by Mrs. Aquino and myself, nor had knowledge of FBI & CID documents **known to the San Francisco Field Office of the CID** which fully substantiated Specification #1. As for the San Francisco Field Office, it merely passed Boomer's "opinion" along to the Hawaii Office, which rubber-stamped it as an "Agent's Investigation Report" on 4/14/88 and passed it along to Colonel Sierra.

Perhaps most incredibly, the same Hawaii Field Office Special Agent (Facundo) conducted an interview with Adams-Thompson on 2/25/88 in which the **only** subject that was discussed was whether Adams-Thompson (whom Facundo identified as "victim"!) felt "threatened" by the fact that UCMJ charges had been preferred against him. Not a **single** question material to the charges was asked by Facundo.

Although Colonel Sierra should not be faulted for the incompetence and UCMJ violations of the CID, it **was** his responsibility to examine the report of investigation provided him by the CID for thoroughness and pertinence to the charges. Obviously the ROI did not address any of the details of Specification #1 at all, and just as obviously Facundo's interview with Adams-Thompson didn't address them either. Accordingly it was Sierra's responsibility to refuse to accept the ROI and send the CID back to do the investigation correctly and thoroughly. Sierra did not do this.

It also seems reasonable to me that a #303 inquiry officer should make an attempt to interview all parties to the charges himself. There is no record of Sierra interviewing Adams-Thompson. Certainly Sierra did not interview, or even contact either Mrs. Aquino or myself as the two individuals who had provided sworn statements in support of the charges. [Nor did either the Hawaii or the San Francisco CID, nor did Captain Boomer.]

In short, a proper Rule #303 inquiry was **not** conducted into the charges. That Rule specifically requires the commander to:

"... gather all reasonably available evidence bearing on guilt or innocence and any evidence relating to aggravation, extenuation, or mitigation." [R.C.M. #303]

It is clear that a decision was made, either by the San Francisco Field Office of the CID or by higher authority, that Adams-Thompson would be "automatically innocent" in disregard of the facts. That meant that Mrs. Aquino and I had to be framed as "automatically guilty" in disregard of the same facts. As a consequence the Sixth Region Headquarters of the CID, higher headquarters of the SFFO, has issued a fraudulent report titling us for the Adams-Thompson allegations and, of course, for making "false" sworn statements in support of the 1/4/88 UCMJ charges against Adams-Thompson. If our sworn statements - which were **absolutely true** in accordance with all information known to us at the time they were sworn - were not denounced, then the acts wrongfully committed by the CID in Captain Sierra's #303 inquiry would have been exposed, which in turn would have established the bias of the CID in issuing the fraudulent report against us.

These actions by the San Francisco Field Office and Sixth Region CID headquarters were also apparently in response to high-level political pressure that would make it "out of the question" for a Christian chaplain to be prosecuted for crimes committed against an officer and his wife who happen to be adherents of the Satanic religion. **This is in direct violation of the Fourteenth Amendment to the Constitution's provision for equal protection of the laws.**

The instigation of the phony Presidio "child-molestation" scandal, the AdamsThompsons' decision to attack a Satanist family as part of it, and the zeal of the SFPD and CID in reinforcing this attack cannot be considered apart from the "Satanic child-molestation" hate-propaganda promoted by religious extremists around the country. This campaign has since been exposed as utterly baseless, as the enclosed report by the FBI's senior expert on the subject indicates.

Furthermore the officers in the SFPD responsible for prejudicing that agency against our religion and ourselves, and for using Adams-Thompson's allegations as the basis for persecution and harassment of us, have since been censured by the San Francisco Police Commission for these actions (copy of SFPC letter of findings enclosed).

I am advised by Captain Thomas Tinti of the U.S. Army Trial Defense Service, Presidio of San Francisco, that if a #303 inquiry has been improperly conducted, it is appropriate for the charges to be re-preferred and a correct #303 inquiry performed.

"A decision to take no action or dismissal of charges at this stage does not bar later disposition of the offenses under subsections (c)(2) through (5) of this rule." [R.CM. 306(c)(1)]

I do not at this time take issue with Colonel Sierra's recommendation that Specification #2 of the 1/4/88 charges be dismissed. Documentation later provided to me in response to my FOIA request to the 25th Division indicated that, despite the facts stated in support of that original Specification #2 in my 1/4/88 sworn statement, it is improbable that Adams-Thompson personally deposited the obscene card in question in a San Francisco mailbox.

In addition to repeating Specification #1 of the original charges, this present Charge Sheet adds a new Specification #2 based upon a further criminal act committed by Adams-Thompson in relation to Specification #1. This criminal act involves his attempt to defraud the United States Government by capitalizing on the sheltering he has received from the crimes he committed in Specification #1. Copies of the claims forms in question are enclosed. Although the names of the claimants have been concealed from me, Major Harvey of the 6th Region CID informed my Army attorney Captain Hayes that they were in fact filed by the Adams-Thompsons. The new #303 inquiry officer should, of course, obtain uncensored copies of these documents to verify this.

It is important to note that, in addition to the $750,000-$3,000,000 of which Adams-Thompson is attempting to defraud the government, other instigators of the Presidio of San Francisco scam are also trying to defraud the government to a total of $74,500,000. Cooperation by the 25th Division in the coverup of the truth concerning Adams-Thompson's crimes, in addition to being a UCMJ violation in itself, would facilitate not only his defrauding of the government, but also - by lending unwarranted legitimacy to the scam - facilitate the massive defrauding of the government by the other instigators.

The enclosures provided with this letter and Charge Sheet, many of which have previously been sent to you, represent only a portion of the official documentation in substantiation of these charges. The investigating officer should of course obtain uncensored copies of all of these documents, as well as other documents which may exist in the files of the 6th Region CID, San Francisco Police Department, and FBI which further evidence Adams-Thompson's criminal actions but which have been concealed to date.

Please be advised that the conduct of the #303 inquiry into these charges by the 25th Division will be closely observed, and if necessary brought to the attention of appropriate senior commanders, the Department of the Army Inspector General, and other governmental and non-governmental officials and institutions concerned with the enforcement of the First and Fourteenth Amendments to the Constitution and applicable religious-freedom provisions of AR 600-20.

> Respectfully,
> /s/ Michael A. Aquino
> Lt. Colonel, Military Intelligence

Enclosures (also sent to recipients of copies of this letter):
- DD Form 458,11/29/89.
- Adams-Thompson's violations of Article 133 UCMJ, updated 11/29/89.
- Letter of findings, San Francisco Police Commission, 11/22/89.
- CID Agent's Investigation Report 4/14/88.

Enclosures sent only with original of this letter:
- CID Agent's Investigation Report 2/25/88:.
- Sworn statement of Adams-Thompson 2/25/88.
- FBI Form FD-302,1/14/87.
- FBI Form FD-302, 8/13/87.
- San Francisco Police Department Incident Report, 8/14/87.
- CID Agent's Investigation Report, 8/13/87.
- Sworn statement, L. Adams-Thompson, 4/10/89.
- Sworn statement, M. Adams-Thompson, 4/10/89.
- FBI report on Satanism, FBI Academy, October 1989.
- CID report concerning medical examination of Kinsey Almond, 3/12/87.
- Claims forms submitted by the Adams-Thompsons, 3/15/88.
- Letter, U.S. Army Claims Service to Lt. Col. Aquino, 11/27/89.

Copies to:

Honorable Michael P.W. Stone, Secretary of the Army
General Carl E. Vuono, Chief of Staff, United States Army
General Robert W. RisCassi, Vice Chief of Staff, United States Army
Lieutenant General Johnny H. Corns, Inspector General of the Army
Lieutenant General Charles W. Bagnal, Commanding General, WESTCOM
Major General William F. Ward, Chief, Army Reserve
Major General William K. Suter, Judge Advocate General of the Army
Major General Norris L. Einertson, Chief of Chaplains, Department of the Army
Major General Eugene L. Cromartie, Commanding General, U.S. Army CIC
Major General Daniel R. Schroeder, Commanding General, Fort Leonard Wood
Colonel Bobby R. Sanders, Commander, ARPERCEN
Colonel William D. Swift, Commander, Presidio of San Francisco
Colonel Carl L. Lockett, Commander, 6th Region CID
Colonel John T. Lane, Inspector General, ARPERCEN
Lt.Colonel Nolan H. Goudeaux, Headquarters, Trial Defense Service
Major Harold Brown, Tort Claims Division, U.S. Army Claims Service
Captain Thomas Tinti, Trial Defense Service, Presidio of San Francisco
Mr. Joseph G. Hanley, Chief of Public Affairs, OCAR, Department of the Army
Mr. Bob Mahoney, Public Affairs Office, 6th Army & Presidio of San Francisco
Mr. Gary R. Myers, Attorney
San Francisco Police Commission
Pillsbury, Madison & Sutro, Attorneys

Appendix 34: Larry A-T's Violations of Article 133, UCMJ

Chaplain Lawrence Adams-Thompson's Actions in Violation of Article 133, UCMJ
by
Lt. Colonel Michael A. Aquino
- initially prepared May 3, 1989 -
- updated as of November 29, 1989 -

A. Prior to August 1987.

1. On 1/14/87, after the Presidio child-care witch-hunt had been in process for two months, Chaplain Adams-Thompson and his wife Michele were interviewed by FBI Special Agent Patricia J. Peyton (FBI #FD-302, 1/14/87). Adams-Thompson's stepdaughter (Michele's daughter) Kinsey Almond was apparently not present. From the transcript of the FBI report:

    a. "Mrs. Adams-Thompson advised that her daughter Kinsey had been attending the school [Presidio Child Development Center (CDC)] since spring 1986. When she turned 3 in September, she was transferred to 'Mr. Gary's' (Gary Hambright) class."

    b. "When Mrs. Adams-Thompson asked if Mr. Gary had been mean to her or tried to touch her, Kinsey replied negatively."

2. In this interview - only 2-1/2 months after the time-period in which Adams-Thompson would later allege so many different and dramatic sexual atrocities occurred - the Adams-Thompsons stated Almond's **denial** of any abuse. They made **no** mention of any emergency medical care of Almond, such as would have been necessary had she been abused as they would later allege. They made **no** mention of anyone other than Hambright at all, nor of any reason to think that Almond had been abducted from the day-care center at any time. They did not accuse Hambright of anything.

3. When the Sixth Region CID (6RCID) established that Mrs. Aquino and I had been in Washington, D.C. on all dates in September-October 1986 on which Almond had been at the Presidio day-care center, Adams-Thompson cooperated with the 6RCID in "revising" the dates of his 8/87 allegation against us to the May-July 86 time period. Evidently he and Michele assumed that their statement to Peyton that Almond had **never** been under Hambright's care or control until **September** 86 had either been lost or was just not noticed. [It has been found and is hereby noticed.]

4. According to a 12/15/86 letter from Lt.Colonel Walter W. Myer, Director of Personnel and Community Activities, HQ Presidio, at **no** time during his entire employment at the CDC did Gary Hambright supervise children under the age of 3. As Kinsey Almond did not turn 3 until 9/1/86, this further verifies that Hambright could **not** have had her under his care or control in May-July 86.

5. This 1/14/87 FBI interview is both the closest to the September-October 1986 time-period and the **only** one in which the Adams-Thompsons did not possess information concerning ourselves which they could manipulate to try to construct plausible lies. If any of the atrocities later invented by Adams-Thompson were true, it is obvious that **specific medical signs** of them would have appeared **at the time of the incident** and would been documented in this most immediate interview accordingly.

6. On 3/12/87 Kinsey Almond was medically examined. The findings of this medical examination stated specifically that there was "**no physical evidence of abuse**".

7. Nevertheless, not later than April 1987 Adams-Thompson made an allegation against Gary Hambright for sexually abusing Almond. "Such act or acts took place sometime in September or October 1986 at the Child Development Center, Presidio of San Francisco." [Letter, Presidio CDS Director to Hambright, 4/17/87]. Adams-Thompson was specific about the time and location, and no allegation was made of the child being transported elsewhere, of anyone else being involved, or of any other time period being involved.

8. In the 8/14/87 SFPD Incident Report Adams-Thompson states that, subsequent to the Peyton interview, he entered Almond into therapy with Debbie Hickey, an Army therapist who at the time was diagnosing multiple cases of child sex-abuse [including in her own children] despite physiological/medical evidence to the contrary. He states that Hickey informed him that Almond had been molested. None of Hickey's notes as revealed by the 6RCID to date, however, verify that Hickey ever made such an abuse-diagnosis to Adams-Thompson.

9. Despite Adams-Thompson's April 87 allegations, however, it is clear that neither the FBI (investigating) nor the U.S. Attorney's Office (prosecuting) Hambright thought that any harm had come to Almond at all. Her name was **not** included in either the initial or the superseding indictments which were brought against Hambright [and which were ultimately all dismissed by the court].

B. The August 1987 "Package Story".

10. In formal statements to the FBI and San Francisco Police in August 1987, Adams-Thompson suddenly changed his April 87 allegation entirely, now saying that Almond had been taken off the Presidio and that Mrs. Aquino and myself were involved.

11. During the course of its 1988-89 investigation, upon finding that neither Mrs. Aquino nor I were in the San Francisco area at any time during September-October 1986 when Almond had been left at the Presidio day-care center, the 6RCID arbitrarily changed the dates of the allegation back several months to a time when I was still assigned to the Presidio. Although Adams-Thompson's April and August allegations had clearly specified the September-October 1986 time period, he remained silent and made no objection while the 6RCID "further adjusted" his already-repeatedly-changed allegations.

12. In August 1987 Adams-Thompson made an allegation against Mrs. Aquino and myself of rape and sodomy concerning Kinsey Almond, knowing all the time that Almond is a **virgin** and showed **no signs of any physical damage** such as would have been immediately and conspicuously evident in the case of a 3-year-old, requiring immediate emergency medical treatment. [He of course was aware of the 3/12/87 medical examination of Almond which found that there were no signs of abuse whatever.]

13. Although Adams-Thompson alleged that the rape/sodomy happened between 1 September and 31 October 1986, there is **no** evidence that he ever noticed **anything** wrong with Almond, nor took her for an emergency medical examination of this nature at any point during that period [nor during the later-invented May-July 86 period].

14. Although two rapes and two sodomies, which Adams-Thompson alleges were committed by two adult males, would also have severely traumatized a 3-year-old, there is **no** published evidence that he **ever** noticed anything wrong with Almond nor took her for psychiatric help during September/October 1986 [nor during the later-invented May-July 86 period].

15. In August 1987 the Adams-Thompsons made a big issue about Almond's being "upset" at seeing me in the Presidio PX, and "upset" in the vicinity of 123 Acme. If this same child was supposedly abducted and molested in September/October 1986 [or during the 6RCID-invented May-July 1986 period], why wouldn't she have shown far more obvious signs of being "upset" at **that** time? Obviously the "evidence" of Almond's being "upset" in August 1987 means **nothing**.

Adams-Thompson made repeated, official, and deliberately false allegations of violent and depraved crimes against his stepdaughter which, at the time he made the allegations, he knew had never taken place. He modified these allegations several times in order to try to fit them to the known circumstances of whomever he was trying to victimize at the moment (Hambright and/or Mrs. Aquino & myself).

16. On August 13, after seeing my wife and myself at the Presidio post exchange, Adams-Thompson and Michele contacted FBI Special Agent Clyde Foreman, the agent in charge of the general Presidio investigation since it was originally incited. In Foreman's report of this contact (FBI #FD-302 8/13/87), the Adams-Thompsons offer a substantially different story of the "PX encounter" than they would give to SFPD Inspector Pamfiloff the following day, and a substantially different story than they would give to the 6RCID in 1989. Specific discrepancies are indicated below, in a discussion of the "package story" which Adams-Thompson offered to Pamfiloff.

17. On August 14 Adams-Thompson made a statement to SFPD Inspector Pamfiloff. In this statement the "package story", which Adams-Thompson invented in its entirety solely to harm Mrs. Aquino and myself and to slander our religion, appears for the first time.

18. In the SFPD Incident Report, Adams-Thompson stated to Inspector Pamfiloff that "in January of 1987 he became aware of a child molest investigation involving Gary Hambright at the Presidio day-care center". In fact that investigation commenced two months earlier, in November 1986, and Adams-Thompson was aware of it from the beginning.

19. The first official notification of the investigation to Presidio parents was a letter from Lt.Colonel Walter Meyer, 12/15/86. However, in the *San Jose Mercury News West*, it was later reported that the initial accusation of molestation at the Presidio came about after the parents (the Tobins) had asked the advice of a chaplain at the Presidio. This was in November 1986. As the Adams-Thompsons' signatures appear immediately after the Tobins' in an inflammatory letter sent to Presidio parents in early 1987 to fuel the fires of the witch-hunt, it is probable that Adams-Thompson was indeed the chaplain who set the hysteria in motion in November.

*Adams-Thompson lied to Pamfiloff about the time he became aware of the Presidio child-care scandal, presumably to conceal or excuse the fact that he had not made any complaints concerning his stepdaughter **during** the September-October 1986 time period. He said nothing to Pamfiloff about his and Michele's key activities in promotion of the hysteria. He lied to Pamfiloff about Almond's **denial** of abuse at the time of the Peyton FBI interview, saying instead that Almond had "made no definitive statements" at the time.*

20. In the SFPD Incident Report, Adams-Thompson stated to Inspector Pamfiloff that Kinsey Almond "was subsequently entered into child therapy in February 1987 and after four visits the therapist informed Adams-Thompson that Almond had disclosed being molested. During the next few visits Almond told Adams-Thompson that she had been molested by Gary Hambright and a 'Mikey' and a 'Shamby' whose identities were unknown". The notes of Debbie Hickey as made available to date do **not** substantiate that Almond told either Adams-Thompson or Hickey that she had been molested during any of these sessions, or that she told him that "Mikey" and/or "Shamby" had done anything, or that she even associated "Mikey" and "Shamby" as a couple.

21. In her 4/10/89 statement to the CID, Michele Adams-Thompson states that it was not Almond who introduced the subject of "Satanism" into the therapy sessions, but Debbie Hickey, who had provided Michele with an article which Hickey had highlighted entitled "The Devil Made Me Do It". Commencing with the 6/2/89 therapy session, Michele states that she brought up the subject again with Hickey.

22. In his 4/10/89 statement to the CID, Lawrence Adams-Thompson admits that he recognized me from the time I had still been assigned to the Presidio Headquarters, and also that he knew at that time that I was a member of the Temple of Set.

This information establishes that prior to any attempt to turn "Mikey" into a Satanist and an Army officer in the therapy sessions, both Lawrence and Michele Adams-Thompson were aware of me and my religion. It also establishes that Debbie Hickey was circulating "Satanic child molestation" propaganda to the parents of the children whom she was "therapizing".

23. In the 8/13/87 FBI report, Michele Adams-Thompson "recalled on prior occasions Kinsey had described Mikey as a man who wore an Army suit 'like Daddy's' and that he had eyebrows that went up. Kinsey also called Mikey 'the blood man'."

24. In the Hickey notes, however, Almond **never** describes "Mikey" as "wearing an Army suit like Daddy's"; it is again **Michele** who alleges this to Hickey (6/30/87) - a month after Michele's 6/2/87 introduction of "Satanic child molestation" into the Hickey sessions - when it had evidently occurred to the Adams-Thompsons that Mrs. Aquino and I, as the Presidio's famous Satanists, might be suitable victims for allegations in addition to or in lieu of Hambright. In the Hickey notes neither Michele nor Almond makes any mention of "eyebrows that went up", nor of "the blood man", nor of association of blood with "Mikey" in any way. Michele conveniently "forgot" to mention to Foreman that, in the Hickey sessions, Almond had picked out a Chief Warrant Officer 2 rank insignia as being that which "Mikey" supposedly wore, and had told Hickey that the letters "AK" appeared on his nametag.

This is just one of many instances of Michele Adams-Thompson "recalling" things in a transparent attempt to fabricate a bogus "identification". Obviously Michele had seen my distinctive eyebrows the previous day in the PX. Chaplain Adams-Thompson, present at this interview, did not intervene to correct her inventions, nor to supply the information which she conveniently "forgot". In general, the Adams-Thompsons seem to be equally accomplished at "forgetting" inconvenient facts and at "remembering" convenient "associations" after being exposed to new information.

25. Prior to the Adams-Thompsons' invention of the "package story" and tutoring of it to her, in fact, there is **no** published record of Kinsey Almond **ever** stating to anyone that she was ever sexually attacked, raped, or sodomized by anyone anywhere. There is **only** the sudden appearance of the "package story" as recited by Almond to Foreman on 8/13/87 and dramatically elaborated upon by Lawrence Adams-Thompson to Pamfiloff on 8/14/87. The **only** time that such a story from Almond herself would have been untainted, of course, would have been immediately **at the time of the incident in question. No such statement or anything remotely resembling it was ever made.** The first official interview, by the FBI Agent Peyton in January 1987, elicited **no** such statement from Almond [or her mother or stepfather]. Even in April 1989, after her mother and stepfather had had years to drill her, her attempted recitation of her stepfather's "package story" to 6RCID interviewers was a ludicrous fiasco (CID report 8/11/89, para. 4.1).

26. There is **no** published record that Hickey diagnosed Almond as having been sexually abused by anyone anywhere. There are, in the Hickey notes, only incoherent ramblings of the sort common to all children of this age, cross-fertilized with the same pseudo-"Satanic ritual" nonsense popularized for such scams as that at the Presidio by the book *Michelle Remembers* and the McMartin fiasco in Los Angeles, and as introduced into the "therapy" by Hickey and Michele themselves (CID statement, Michele Adams-Thompson, 4/10/89).

27. Although on 8/14/87 Adams-Thompson told Pamfiloff the extremely elaborate "package story" of what was supposed to have happened to Almond during her "abduction", **not a single element** of this "package story" appears in Michele's interview with Foreman only 24 hours earlier.

Adams-Thompson lied when he told Pamfiloff that Almond had told him the "package story". He told Pamfiloff nothing about the incoherent ramblings of Almond during the Hickey sessions, nor of Almond's mentioning five other individuals, nor that Almond had not associated "Mikey" and "Shamby" together during the sessions, nor that Almond had never accused anyone of molesting her during the sessions.

28. In the "package story" of Almond's "abduction" which Adams-Thompson told to Pamfiloff, he stated that Almond said that "she drove with Mr. Gary to his house".

29. In her 8/13/87 statement to Foreman, Michele alleged only that Almond had referred to "Mr. Gary's house". She made no mention of Hambright "driving" Almond there or anywhere else.

30. In an FBI Form FD-302 dated 8/13/87 (which has been concealed from me but described to my attorney Captain Hayes), Almond purportedly said that she traveled "with Mr. Gary in a **green** car to **his** home". She did not mention anyone else in the car, nor going to any other location.

31. As verified by the U.S. Public Defender's Office in San Francisco, Gary Hambright is an epileptic who **cannot** drive, having neither driver's license nor car.

Adams-Thompson had to come up with a way to "transport" Almond from the day-care center to our building. [In all "day-care sex-abuse" scams, "off-site transport" is the ploy commonly used to "explain" abuse which could not possibly happen in the observable environment of a day-care center itself.] He knew that there was no indication that anyone like Mrs. Aquino or myself had ever been to the center. Therefore he would have to portray the teacher, Hambright, driving Almond away. He either did not know that Hambright cannot drive and owns no vehicle, or he simply forgot this fact while inventing the "package story" at short notice. Nor has he explained how the red Isuzu, if it were supposedly "our" car in September-October 1986 (which it was not), would have driven itself to the CDC, changing its color to green on the way, to be available for Hambright's use if Mrs. Aquino and I were both at home at the time. Later the Adams-Thompsons tried to get around this problem, and presumably Hambright's driving incapacity, by proposing that Mrs. Aquino drove Hambright and Almond in "Shamby's" car, which had once again changed its color to red.

32. Adams-Thompson told Pamfiloff a "package story" which he claims Almond told to FBI Agent Clyde Foreman on the previous day (13 August 1987). At that time Adams-Thompson knew full well that this package story was nothing more than a selective rearrangement of garbled nonsense that Almond [and Michele] had told Debbie Hickey. Adams-Thompson did not make this clarification to either Foreman or Pamfiloff. This would have been crucial to the credibility of the child's story.

33. Not a single element of this "package story" appears in Michele's 8/13/87 statement to Foreman.

34. In an FBI Form FD-302 dated 8/13/87 (which has been concealed from me but described to my attorney Captain Hayes), Almond purportedly said that Mr. Gary drove her to his home, which had a bathtub with lion's feet, that Mikey wore Army clothes, and that she was raped and sodomized by both Mr. Gary and Mikey. She apparently made no mention of any of the other features of Adams-Thompson's "package story".

Adams-Thompson deliberately omitted mention of the actual, disconnected nature of Almond's therapy ramblings in order to convince Foreman and Pamfiloff that she was telling a coherent story of abduction, sodomy, and rape. He did this to incite Foreman and Pamfiloff to action against my wife and myself. The "package story" was obviously invented by Adams-Thompson and Michele following the encounter at the PX, recited in part by Almond to Foreman on 8/13/87, and elaborated upon by Adams-Thompson for Pamfiloff the next morning (8/14/87).

If Almond herself made the statements as cited from the FBI FD-302 8/13/87, then it is easily refutable. Hambright cannot drive and had no car. 123 Acme is not his home. 123 Acme contains no bathtub with lion's feet. It is insane to think that, if I were going to commit such crimes as these, I would do so in full Army uniform, at my own home, and using anything resembling my own name. Finally Almond has been medically examined and found to be a virgin with no signs of rape or sodomy.

35. Adams-Thompson arbitrarily added details to the "package story" which do not appear in the Hickey notes, such as a movie camera and "a living room with black walls and a cross painted on the ceiling". If Almond mentioned these features to Foreman herself prior to Adams-Thompson's relaying this account to Pamfiloff,

then Adams-Thompson obviously coached it into her following the Hickey sessions, to add a "Satanic/film-pornographic" touch to the planned "package story".

36. None of these details appears in Michele's 8/13/87 statement to Foreman, or in the purported 8/13/87 statement of Almond to Foreman.

In addition to allowing law-enforcement officials to think that his stepdaughter had told a coherent "package story", Adams-Thompson added details to that story himself to make it more horrendous than merely a rearrangement of the Hickey notes would support.

C. The August 12, 1987 Presidio Post Exchange Incident.

The next section of this summary concerns the "PX incident" of 8/12/87, in which Lawrence and Michele Adams-Thompson alleged that Kinsey Almond "identified" Mrs. Aquino and myself. The follow analysis examines the changes and inconsistencies in Lawrence and Michele's accounts in detail. It is important to note, however, that at the time of their original attack in August 1987, there is only the word of the two adult Adams-Thompsons that this incident ever happened at all. All that is known for certain is that Lawrence and/or Michele saw us at the PX on that day.

a. There is no evidence that Almond was with them.

b. There is no evidence that Almond reacted to anyone as they alleged.

c. There is no evidence that Almond "identified" anyone as they alleged.

1-1/2 years later the Adams-Thompsons, apparently in a belated effort to prop up their story concerning the PX, suddenly added Lawrence's two sons to the scene. Also just as suddenly these two boys echoed their father's story to the CID. A younger Adams-Thompson daughter was added to the scene as well, doubling the original number of Adams-Thompsons said to be at the PX on that day. It is just as easy for the Adams-Thompsons to have invented the presence of Almond, and her behavior, in the original stories they told Foreman and Pamfiloff. There is no contemporary record of Kinsey Almond herself verifying either her presence at the PX or any of the statements or actions attributed to her there. Only 1-1/2 years later, in a ludicrously coached [and ineptly recited] interview with the 6RCID did she make any reference to the PX, purportedly saying that she had recognized me but not Mrs. Aquino there.

Following is a detailed discussion of the adult Adams-Thompsons' PX allegations:

37. On 8/14/87 Adams-Thompson told Pamfiloff that "on 12 August 1987 he, Michele Adams-Thompson, and Kinsey Almond were at the Presidio PX." No mention is made of any other members of the Adams or Thompson family together with them at the PX.

38. On 8/13/87 Michele stated to Foreman that only she, Almond, and her husband were shopping at the PX. No mention is made of any other members of the Adams or Thompson family together with them at the PX.

39. No mention was made of any other family members present throughout the subsequent 1-1/2 years while the Aquinos were being investigated and the PX account described in detail in the public media. Only when the 6RCID interviewed Adams-Thompson 1-1/2 years later on 4/10/89 did he again revise his story to say that two sons of his by a previous marriage and another girl ("our youngest daughter") were also there. Suddenly there are six Adams-Thompsons at the PX instead of the original three.

Adams-Thompson lied to Pamfiloff, the FBI, and/or the 6RCID about the number of members of his family present at the PX and their involvement. Since by April 1989 the Adams-Thompsons had had 1-1/2 years to consider ways of trying to strengthen their allegations, the 1989 accounts must be considered spurious where contradicted by the 1987 ones.

40. In the 8/14/87 SFPD incident report Adams-Thompson told Pamfiloff that, at the PX, Almond "ran to him and in a frightened way clutched his leg".

41. In the 8/13/87 FBI report Michele Adams-Thompson told Foreman that, at the PX, "Kinsey ran to her and Larry". In her 4/10/89 CID statement, however, she contradicts this, saying that Adams-Thompson called Michele over to him **after** Almond was already with him.

42. On 4/10/89 Adams-Thompson told the 6RCID that Almond was with her two stepbrothers in the PX, away from him and his wife, and that it was the two boys who brought Almond to him "saying Kinsey was acting weird". He did not say that Almond "ran to him". He also said that Michele was "in another area of the store" and that he had to go to her in that area when Almond was brought to him [alone].

Adams-Thompson lied when making one of his two mutually-contradictory statements. Michele also lied when making one of her two mutually-contradictory statements. [If in fact Almond did not "react" at all in the PX [or was not even there], as is also possible, then of course Adams-Thompson lied when making ***both*** *statements.] Furthermore, where would Almond "run from"? Did the Adams-Thompsons allow a 3-year-old infant to wander around the PX away from them? How could Almond run "to [Michele] and Larry" when they were in different parts of the store?*

43. The two boys (who in August 87 were approximately 9 and 13 years old), interviewed 1-1/2 years later by the 6RCID, state that Almond was with them and that she reacted as alleged in the account Adams-Thompson gave to the 6RCID [but not to the FBI or SFPD].

    a. Why are the memories of two children at such ages suddenly so precise concerning what to them would have been only a momentary sulk by their infant stepsister 1-1/2 years previously?

    b. Why were these boys not mentioned by or interviewed by Foreman or Pamfiloff at the time? They are not listed on page #1 of the SFPD incident report. They are not mentioned in Foreman's 8/13/87 report. [Foreman knew of their existence, however, as they were identified as relatives in Peyton's 1/14/87 report.] They would have been crucial witnesses to the "PX encounter". And why were they not mentioned by any of the news media in their intense and detailed coverage of the allegations over the next 1-1/2 years?

The boys' story is obviously a later invention, coached into them by their father. Obviously the boys' motivation in reciting this story is to try to keep their father from facing criminal prosecution for his actions in this affair - which of course he would have represented to them as truthful and honorable. As young teenagers from a fundamentalist-Christian family, it is not difficult to see them cooperating with their father in any "white lie" requested to attack "the Devil". Nor need he have even represented it to them as a "lie". All he had to do was tell them what he insists happened, and make it clear that he expected them to back him up to the CID.

44. On 8/14/87 Adams-Thompson told Pamfiloff that he called Almond's attention to me - not once, but twice - and asked her if she knew me before eliciting a "Yes, that's Mikey" response.

45. On 8/13/87 Michele told Foreman that Almond "told them that she had seen a man named 'Mikey' that she knew from Mr. Gary's house". [No prompting at all in this version - and the sudden addition of "Mr. Gary's house"].

46. On 4/10/89 Adams-Thompson told the 6RCID that Almond twice made no answer in response to his twice-stated question: "Do you know that man?". Then he told the 6RCID that Michele took Almond away from him and over to my vicinity for about five minutes. Then he said that Michele came back and that they

proceeded to leave the PX. As they were doing so, he said "I heard Kinsey state 'That's Mikey, he's a bad man, get me out of this place' or words to that effect."

Adams-Thompson gave one version of Kinsey's alleged statement in the PX to the SFPD and another version to the CID. In both instances he admits to prompting Almond repeatedly for an "identification". Both of his stories contradict the account given by Michele to Foreman only 24 hours before his statement to the SFPD.

47.   On 8/14/87 Adams-Thompson told Pamfiloff only that Almond "saw" me.

48.   On 8/13/87 Adams-Thompson told Foreman that I "made eye contact with Kinsey". [I did not, and would not have recognized her if I had.]

49.   In her 8/13/87 statement to Foreman, Michele says nothing whatever about Almond making eye contact with me.

Adams-Thompson thus gave two contradictory accounts one day apart [and immediately after the PX incident]. Furthermore, Adams-Thompson told the 6RCID 1-1/2 years later that it was the two boys who were with Almond when she noticed me. Adams-Thompson lied in the initial contradiction, and then again if he now states that Almond was with the two boys at the time.

50.   To Pamfiloff on 8/14/87 and to the CID on 4/10/89, Adams-Thompson said that he and Kinsey saw only me in the PX, and that Mrs. Aquino did not appear until later in the parking lot.

51.   To Foreman on 8/13/87 Michele Adams-Thompson said nothing about Mrs. Aquino being in the PX, and that her first appearance was "standing next to the car in the parking lot". Michele further said that she "followed Colonel Aquino to the checkout stand" closely enough to observe my active-duty Army ID card and to see me sign my full name on the MasterCard slip. As Mrs. Aquino was standing with me in the checkout line, it would have been quite impossible for Michele **not** to see her if she were peering over my shoulder at the time.

52.   To the CID on 4/10/89 Michele Adams-Thompson said that Mrs. Aquino was **in** the PX, that she observed us purchase the microwave together in the checkout line, and that she watched us exit together through the PX mall area. [In this interview she tried to cover up for her earlier failure to mention Mrs. Aquino in the PX by implying that she didn't recognize her as my wife. In Lawrence Adams-Thompson's 8/12/87 telephone call to the FBI, however, he said that he recognized Mrs. Aquino because she had been introduced at several [Presidio] functions. Presumably Michele attended those same husband/wife "command performance" social functions with her husband, so she had no excuse for not recognizing the woman with me in the PX as that same Mrs. Aquino. [Mrs. Aquino possesses very striking and unforgettable looks, I may add.]

Mrs. Aquino was with me at all times in the PX; therefore Adams-Thompson's 1987/1989 and Michele's 1987 statements that she didn't appear until later in the parking lot are obvious lies - and among the most conspicuous lies in the Adams-Thompsons' original allegations. In her 1989 statement to the CID, Michele completely contradicted her original 1987 statement to Foreman on this matter.

53.   To Pamfiloff Adams-Thompson said that he [alone] took Almond "outside to their car". He made no mention of taking the younger girl or the two boys out to the car. Why would he take Almond outside to the car at all if she had already "identified" someone whom Adams-Thompson himself stated in the SFPD report that he recognized? As it was obvious that Mrs. Aquino and I were leaving the PX, and if the goal was to calm Almond, why suddenly rush all of the Adams-Thompsons out into their car? Why would they not be accompanied by Almond's mother, who would presumably have been greatly concerned about her daughter? Neither Lawrence nor Michele explains this.

Obviously the Adams-Thompsons, who had already seen and recognized both Mrs. Aquino and myself in the PX, wanted to see what our car looked like so that it could be added to the allegations they had already planned to make against us. Once in their own car, they may also have followed us to our home, so that they could try to coach Almond into "recognizing" that as well before an official audience. They succeeded with the car (which they didn't know was only a rental car) and failed with the house.

54.   To Foreman on 8/13/87 Adams-Thompson said that he "went to the car to wait for us, and saw them, and took the license number".

55.   To Pamfiloff on 8/14/87 Adams-Thompson said that he drove around to the other side of the PX, where Kinsey supposedly identified Mrs. Aquino as "Shamby". In this SFPD version there is no mention of our car or taking its license number.

Adams Thompson changes his story at will, as in one case he needed to drive to the other lot to find us, while in the other he merely waits for us.

56.   To Foreman on 8/13/87 Michele said that "Michele, Larry, and Kinsey drove through the parking lot where they observed Colonel Aquino standing next to a red vehicle with California license plate 2ENS453. This vehicle was a 1987 Isuzu. Kinsey observed a woman standing next to the vehicle and said, 'That's Shamby.'" [Note that in this account Michele identified herself, her husband, and Almond by name but **made no mention whatever** of the two boys and additional girl who were suddenly introduced into this story 1-1/2 years later.]

57.   In her 4/10/89 CID statement, Michele said that Mrs. Aquino was standing next to our car "**alone**".

Michele changes her story at will concerning how many Aquinos were standing next to the Isuzu.

58.   To the SFPD on 8/14/87 Adams-Thompson said that he drove around to the other side of the PX. To Foreman on 8/13/87 Michele said that he drove through the parking lot to our car.

In one version Adams-Thompson drives around to the other side of the PX, while in the other he merely waits for us, sees us, and takes down the license number of our car.
If Almond had already seen Mrs. Aquino and myself in the PX, as Adams-Thompson admitted to the 6RCID on 4/10/89, why would Almond not have "identified" Mrs. Aquino until later at our car?

One cannot reach the bridge-approach parking lot by driving "through the main lot"; it is necessary to drive out into the street and about 2 blocks to the east to circle around the complex, or about 2 blocks to the west to circle around it from the other side.

59.   The PX has two parking lots, one on the north side of the mall and one on the south side of the mall. From the Adams-Thompsons' 4/10/89 CID statements, their car was parked in the north lot. Our car was parked in the south lot. If the Adams-Thompsons drove around to the south lot from the north lot after seeing us go through the mall, and if Michele (per her 4/10/89 statement) didn't even get into the Adams-Thompson car until **after** we had walked through the mall doors to the south lot, they wouldn't have had time to get there [for the alleged Almond "identification" of Lilith] before we drove away. It is approximately a 2-blocks up/2-blocks back drive between the two lots, no matter which direction you go.

Adams-Thompson is lying about being able to "drive around to the other side of the PX" for Almond to see Mrs. Aquino and for him to take down the license number of our car. It takes so long to drive to the "bridge-approach" lot from the main lot that we would have driven away before Adams-Thompson could get to that area, much less single out our car from among the others there, much less identify us inside a car. As it was August and the car was air-conditioned, and we habitually drive with the A/C on and all windows up, is Almond supposed to have "identified" Mrs. Aquino at a distance, from inside a moving car, looking at a car suddenly pointed out to her, and at a person through rolled-up window glass? [Note: This car was a rental car which Adams-Thompson would never have seen before.] Probably the Adams-Thompsons simply followed us on foot from the checkout counter through the mall doors to our rental car, then went to their own car [in either lot] and drove after us when we emerged from the south lot.

If Almond is supposed to have "identified" Mrs. Aquino at a moment's notice, at a distance, from inside a moving car, looking at a car suddenly pointed out to her, and at a person through rolled-up window glass, then **why did she not "identify" Mrs. Aquino in the PX***, when she would have been able to look at her as long and as closely as she allegedly did at me? Mrs. Aquino was right next to me the entire time we were in the PX. It would have been* **impossible** *for Almond [or the adult Adams-Thompsons] to see just me and not Mrs. Aquino.*

D. The 123 Acme Avenue "Identification" Trip.

60. To Pamfiloff on 8/14/87 Adams-Thompson stated that on 8/13/87: "Michele and Kinsey, accompanied by Foreman, responded to the 100 block of Acme, and Kinsey was told to see if she could recognize any of the houses that she had been to before. While walking past 123 Acme, Kinsey identified that as the residence of Mr. Gary where she had met 'Mikey' and 'Shamby'."

61. The 8/13/87 record of this trip by CID Special Agent Bradley Potter reveals that **virtually every element of Adams-Thompson's statement to Pamfiloff concerning it was a lie.** [Quotes from this report as follows fill in the probable names that were blanked out from the copy of this report provided to me on 11/27/89.]

62. Adams-Thompson made no mention to Pamfiloff that CID Agent Potter also went along on the trip. This is significant in that Potter's account of the trip **contradicts** Adams-Thompson's "package story" account of it.

63. Potter acknowledges that "Almond did not direct SA Potter, who was driving, where to turn or which route to take. SA Potter drove the the (sic) vicinity of the 100 block of Acme Avenue, San Francisco".

64. The 8/11/89 CID report states that "Kinsey was told that she would be traveling to an area where she should examine the houses to see if she recognized any of the homes as a place where she had gone before." As this guidance to her was given **immediately after** the same persons had led her through a recitation of Adams-Thompson's "package story", it is obvious that the child was meant to connect the two situations and produce the house from that story.

65. The 8/11/89 CID report states that the adults drove Almond up and down the 100 block **twice**, each time eliciting **no response from her whatever**. Then, obviously determined that the child would do **something** that could be represented as an "identification", they parked the car and walked her down the same street. By now, of course, it was obvious to Almond that whatever they wanted her to "recognize" was **on that block and that block only** [among the thousands in San Francisco!].

66. Potter states: "While walking down Acme Avenue (north), on the east side of the street, Almond appeared to show a behavioral change. Approximately 10-15 feet before coming to the front of 123 Acme Avenue, Almond began to appear frightened and wanted to be held by her mother. Almond was picked up by her mother, but continued to stare at the front of 123 Acme Avenue." [The 8/11/89 CID report says that Almond grabbed her mother's legs, but Agent Potter's report of the same day as the trip does **not** specify this.]

67. The 8/11/89 CID report states that, as soon as Michele picked up Almond as they were **approaching** 123, she started talking to her telling her that "she was safe and no one would hurt her". Since Almond had just been led through the "package" story that morning, and since she had been told to identify a building, and since she had been shown that it would be on the 100 block of Acme, for her mother to pick her up and make comments like these to her as they came up to 123 is about as obvious a cue as can be imagined.

68. Although the 8/11/89 CID report editorially states that Almond said at this moment that 123 was the location in the "package story", this is **absolutely refuted** by the CID 8/13/87 Potter report, in which it is quite explicit that Almond **made no statements concerning 123 whatever**.

69. Potter states: "Almond was taken further north on Acme Avenue, then back on the west side of the street, where Almond then picked out an automobile as belonging to 'Mickie and Shanbie' (sic). The car was subsequently identified as a red colored sedan that had been rented by LTC Aquino."

70. The CID 8/11/89 report editorially states that Michele and Almond "were directed to cross the street and Almond was asked to examine five vehicles parked at the curb". This is another example of the deliberate editorial distortions of the 8/11/89 report, as it is totally unnecessary to cross to the west side of Acme to examine the cars there [and, as noted below, it is dangerous]. However, if such instructions were given to Almond, her attention was again narrowed to five cars from all the ones along the block, **none of which she had reacted to spontaneously**.

71. The CID 8/11/89 report editorially states that Almond picked out the red Isuzu as "Mrs. Shamby's" car and said that she had ridden in it with her. This was of course **after** Michele and Lawrence Adams-Thompson had connected that car with us at the PX, but **before** they discovered it to be only a rental car.

*From Potter's on-site/same-day account it is clear that **Almond did not "identify" 123 Acme at all**. She did not say anything about it, point at it, or refer to it **in any way whatever**. Potter made a personal assumption only - that Almond "**appeared** to show a behavioral change", whatever that is supposed to mean. Almond made **no** statement that she was "frightened" or that she wanted to be held by her mother; all that Potter's report establishes is that Michele Adams-Thompson chose to pick Almond up and hold her in front of 123 Acme, which of course dramatized that location to her audience (Potter and Foreman) - and to Almond as well, who otherwise might have walked right past it. There is no indication that Almond was looking at 123 when "she began to appear frightened", nor that she was in fact "frightened" at all. She didn't, for example, either cry or try to run away.*

*Even while being held stationary by Michele in front of 123 Acme, Almond said **nothing** about the building and made **no** gestures concerning it. That she "continued to stare at it" is not an "identification". Nor, if her mother was holding her stationary in front of it so that Almond's face was turned toward it, is it surprising that Almond would continue to look at the building. [Her only option would be to close her eyes or wrench her head around sideways.]*

*It is significant to read in Potter's report that Almond "was taken back on the west side of the street". There is no sidewalk on most of the west side of that block; rather cars are parked alongside a massive wall. There is a great deal of fast-moving traffic from nearby Bay Street and Fisherman's Wharf driving south on Acme, and it is particularly dangerous to walk on the west side of 123 Acme because the intersection approaching it from the north is a blind one over a hill. It would have been all the more dangerous to walk up the block on the west side with a small child. The party would have had to walk out in the middle of the street, at risk of being hit by southbound traffic. Most probably the party walked up the east side of the street again, **in which case 123 Acme was passed again with no reaction or comment whatever from Almond**. Even if the party walked up the west side of the street, dodging traffic, 123 is just as visible from that side of the (2-lane) street as from the sidewalk in front of it. As there is only the blank concrete wall across from it on the west side, there is nothing else to look at at that point of the block. Yet, as noted, Almond paid **no attention to it whatever**.*

*Obviously, from seeing the car [and calling Almond's attention to it] at the PX the previous day, the Adams-Thompsons concluded that it was our personally-owned car, hence coached Almond in advance to "identify" it if she saw it again as well as to "identify" whatever building she was shown by her mother in the presence of the FBI agent. What Adams-Thompson did **not** know was that the Isuzu was a **rental** car which we had had for only a few days.*

*As noted above, the 8/11/89 CID report editorially states that Almond was specifically told to examine a group of five cars, thus (a) cueing her that she was once again supposed to produce something from the "package story", (b) cueing her that it was supposed to be a car, and (c) cueing her that she should make her choice from **only those five*** *cars* exclusive of all the others on the street. As she had already been coached concerning the red Isuzu the Adams-Thompsons [and possibly Almond herself] had seen at the PX the day before, she knew what was expected of her.

*During the ensuing publicity, in which much was made of the alleged "identification" of our building, Adams-Thompson remained silent about the fact that **no such "identification" ever happened**, and also remained silent about the "identification of the Isuzu" fiasco - which, when the rental-nature of the car became known, would have revealed that "identification" to have been coached. [If Adams-Thompson knew about Hambright's inability to drive a car anywhere, he also remained silent about that.]*

72.   In Foreman's own 8/13/87 report of his interview with Michele, no mention whatever is made of this supposed "identification trip". Assuming that Foreman took Michele and Almond to 123 Acme prior to writing this report, however, another of Michele's "recollections" occurs: "Michele said that Kinsey has frequently described 'Mr. Gary's house' as a house with several stairs leading to the front door and that it is gray in color."

The Hickey notes do not substantiate Michele's "sudden recollection" that Almond had "frequently described 'Mr. Gary's house' as a house with several stairs leading to the front door and that it is gray in color". Nor do any entries in Michele's constantly-changing "journal". Throughout the 7-month period of Almond's "therapy" sessions with Hickey, there was no mention whatever of any house belonging to "Mikey" [or "Shamby"], nor of any gray house, nor of any house with stairs leading to the front door. This "sudden recollection" by Michele obviously post-dates her seeing our building, either on 8/12/87 in the company of Adams-Thompson & Almond or on 8/13/87 in the company of Foreman and Potter before Foreman wrote this report. The trip to 123 Acme took place early in the morning (9:45 AM) on 8/13/89, making it highly probable that Foreman's report was written at a later time in the day.

Could Almond have reacted to our building during the northward walk on 8/13/87 without conspicuous prompting, holding, and direction of her eyes toward it by Michele at that moment? She could if she had been taken there before on 8/12/87 and pre-coached to "identify" it. The Adams-Thompsons have acknowledged that they clandestinely observed Mrs. Aquino and myself in the PX, and that they clandestinely followed us to our rental car, and that they were in their own car at the time with Almond. As we live only ten minutes away from the Presidio, and as we went directly home with the microwave, and as we had no reason to drive quickly, it would have been quite easy for the Adams-Thompsons to follow us in their car, observe the house we entered, and coach Kinsey to "identify" it the next time she saw it. From Potter's report it is clear that it was still necessary for Michele to pick up Almond and hold her with her eyes towards the building to pretend that an "identification" took place. Obviously none did.

E. After August 1987.

73.   After the SFPD raid revealed that the interior of our home did **not** match the "package story", Adams-Thompson remained silent while Mrs. Aquino and myself went through an extended ordeal in the "witch-hunt" atmosphere surrounding the Presidio scandal. Although all the facts - from the actual interior of our home to my established assignment to ICAF during the period of his allegation - would have demonstrated our innocence to someone who had merely made "an honest mistake", Adams-Thompson remained silent and unremorseful. He remains so to this day, apparently quite satisfied with the intense harm he has caused to two innocent people, and equally unconcerned with the embarrassment and waste of resources he has caused the FBI, the San Francisco Police Department, and the United States Army.

74.   On 15 October 1987 Kinsey Almond, in the company of Michele Adams-Thompson, was interviewed by FBI Special Agents James Nice and Patricia Bradley. Sole purpose of the interview was to show Almond 35 photographs taken of our San Francisco home during the evening of the 8/14/87 forceable invasion and search of our home. Almond made no response to any of the photos verifying that she had ever been inside the building. [She asked Agent Nice if it were **his** house!] Rather she merely gave incoherent responses which I have discussed in a separate 9/27/89 paper to the Commanding General, CIC.

75. After showing Almond [and Michele] all of the photos with no questions, Nice showed them again, asking Almond if she recognized anything. This time she recited another obviously-coached phrase ("the haunted house") six times. She made no mention of "Mr. Gary", "Mikey", "Shamby", or any other name in either the Hickey notes or Chaplain Adams-Thompson's "package story" to the SFPD. She mentioned no element of that "package story" whatever. She made no reference to anyone resembling Michael or Lilith Aquino. She made no response to 24 of the 35 photos, and to the others she gave completely nonsensical answers. Almond's comments in this second run through the photos were **in every case** completely inconsistent with her responses in the first run.

76. Although Adams-Thompson was apparently not present for this interview session, he certainly heard about it later from his wife Michele, and learned that Almond had not validly "identified" anything in the photos nor said anything at all to support any detail whatever of his "package story" to the SFPD. Nevertheless he did not retract his allegations. Obviously the child's failure to substantiate his attack was not important to him as long as investigators were continuing to try to "make it stick".

77. It is reasonable to assume that, after the story of Adams-Thompson's allegations broke in the national media, he was informed of everything in that media which disproved his "package story", to include a detailed television-tour of our home.

78. On 20 December 1988 LTC William Hagan, SJA of the 25th Division, provided Adams-Thompson with copies of every letter, document, sworn statement, etc. which I had previously provided to the 25th Division in support of the UCMJ charges I preferred against Adams-Thompson for his malicious actions (a stack of documents over 1 inch thick). At the time the CID interviewed the Adams-Thompsons in 1989, therefore, they had had abundant opportunity to revise their accusations any way possible to avoid incriminating themselves and to attempt to further the CID's evident effort to make any kind of a case against us.

*More than anything else, Adams-Thompson's behavior **after** learning about the results of the 8/14/87 invasion, and **after** learning of the results of the 10/15/87 FBI interview with Almond, puts the lie to the notion that he was "merely a neutral person" without malice towards us. By his silence and disregard of the revealed falsehoods of the "package story" that he had told Pamfiloff, he acted to sustain our ordeal, obviously in hope that we would ultimately be prosecuted, convicted, and imprisoned for a crime **which he knew from the beginning had never occurred at all**.*

79. On 2/25/88 Adams-Thompson was interviewed by CID Special Agent Ralph Facundo of the CID. In this interview he said that I had "made statements in two letters and a newsletter" that he interpreted as a "threat".

80. The first letter (8/28/87) stated my discovery that Adams-Thompson had been responsible for the false accusation against us that had caused our home to be raided and ransacked and ourselves and our families terrorized during the night of 8/14/87. This letter concluded:

> By your vicious, irresponsible, and thoroughly disgusting accusations you have brought about the violation of my home, severe trauma to my wife and family, and an insult to my own integrity that is especially foul and loathsome, based as it is upon the sexual abuse of little children. Only if you send me immediately a letter of complete and unqualified apology and retraction for this disgraceful conduct of yours will I consider not taking legal action against you, either via civil suit or per applicable provisions of the UCMJ.

81. The second letter (9/10/87) provided Adams-Thompson with a copy of a vulgar card which I believed to have been sent by him in response to my 8/28/87 letter. This letter contained no elaboration upon the conclusion of the 8/28/87 letter whatever, but simply concluded:

If you care to deny having sent this card, I would welcome a letter from you to that effect - and repudiating its message.

82. No threat against Adams-Thompson was made in the *Scroll of Set* newsletter. Articles in the *Scroll* between the time of Adams-Thompson's attack and this interview merely stated that I had requested his chain of command to take appropriate administrative action concerning him, and that, if it would not, I would prefer court-martial charges against him. There was no statement incorporating "just dues … just reward … or he'll get his" as alleged by Adams-Thompson.

Neither the letters nor the Scroll of Set *newsletter contained any threats whatever. Adams-Thompson was merely informed that, if on his own initiative he did not act to correct the serious and unjustified harm he had caused to Mrs. Aquino and myself, I would seek to have these matters corrected through the legal systems of the United States and the U.S. Army. If Adams-Thompson were an innocent man, there is no reason why he should have to feel "threatened" by judicial review of his actions. Adams-Thompson therefore lied in the 2/25/88 CID interview about the contents of the letters and the wording of the* Scroll of Set.

When asked during the same interview for a copy of the Scroll of Set *newsletter in question, Adams-Thompson stated that he had a copy of it, but he did not produce it. For him to have done so would have revealed that the threatening wording he alleged it to contain did not in fact appear therein.*

83. On 4/10/89 Chaplain Lawrence Adams-Thompson was interviewed by CID Agent Cates. Among his statements were the following:

> Kinsey made various disclosures to her therapist Dr. (LTC) Hickey at Letterman Army Medical Center, Presidio of San Francisco, CA, indicating that she had been sexually assaulted by one of her teachers, Mr. Gary Hambright, and also that she had been taken to his residence. Kinsey also mentioned the names of "Shamby" and "Mikey" as people who had been present at Mr. Hambright's house. The disclosure of these names occurred shortly after she began seeing Dr. Hickey. However I only heard about this from my wife (with whom Kinsey had been talking about the incidents), and from Dr. Hickey. Prior to August 87 I did not hear about "Shamby" and/or "Mikey" directly from Kinsey.

Immediately after stating under oath that Kinsey had made these "disclosures" to Hickey, Adams-Thompson revises this assertion to only hearsay information from Hickey and Michele. Therefore his statement that such "disclosures" were in fact made is incompetent. Of course, if Lawrence and Michele Adams-Thompson invented the "package story" themselves in August 1987, then this sworn statement by Adams-Thompson is an outright lie, which he is attempting to hedge by projecting the responsibility on to Michele and/or Hickey.

F. Fraudulent Claims Against the Government.

84. On 3/15/88 Adams-Thompson, Michele Adams-Thompson, and the two of them together on behalf of Kinsey Almond, filed claims totaling at least $3 million against the U.S. Army for the supposed abuse of Kinsey Almond and the "serious emotional and mental distress" they as mother and stepfather "suffered" as a result. [The names on the claim-forms were deleted on the copies provided to me, but Captain Hayes was informed by Major Harvey that they were in the names of the two adult Adams-Thompsons and the two of them on behalf of Kinsey Almond.]

As at the time Adams-Thompson and Michele knew full well that this abuse had never happened, the filing of such claims constitutes a deliberate attempt by both of them to defraud the U.S. Government.

G. Conclusions.

The above facts establish that in not just one but a great many instances Lawrence Adams-Thompson invented, told, and then attempted to sustain lies deliberately designed to cause the greatest possible harm to another officer and his wife. He perpetrated these lies in the form of formal statements to and interviews with investigating officials of the FBI, the San Francisco Police Department, and the U.S. Army 6RCID. He regularly attempted to modify those parts of the lies which had become conspicuously weak, as highlighted by me in the supporting statements accompanying the 4 January 1988 UCMJ charges which I preferred against him. He has further attempted to defraud the U.S. Government by making false monetary claims based upon them.

All of these actions clearly evidence Adams-Thompson's repeated, deliberate, and extreme violations of Article #133 of the Uniform Code of Military Justice, and he should be charged and prosecuted accordingly by General Court-Martial.

Appendix 35: Letter, Major General Otstott to Michael Aquino 12/29/89

Headquarters 25th Infantry Division (Light)

APVG-CG   29 December 1989

MEMORANDUM FOR: LTC Michael A. Aquino

SUBJECT: Request for Inquiry

1.   You asked that I reopen the inquiry conducted into the charges that you preferred against Captain Lawrence Adams-Thompson of this command.

2.   I decline to do so. In my opinion, COL Sierra's inquiry complied substantially with the requirements of R.CM. 303. COL Sierra dismissed the charges; MG Crysel, the 25th Infantry Division (Light) Commander and General Court-Martial Convening Authority, ratified that decision; and, later, upon your application, LTG Bagnal, Commander, WESTCOM, reaffirmed those subordinate commanders' decisions.

3. The "new" charge relating to what you see as a fraudulent claim is, in my opinion, supported by much of the same evidence as was delved into during the original inquiry and, therefore, does not justify an additional investigation. What you have provided us and others during the past year and more, together with what we gathered during the original inquiry, adequately supports the original decision and my determination to let the matter rest.

4. You raise no new evidence, only opinion. That you, as complainant, may be dissatisfied with official disposition of charges that does not accord with your view of justice is not surprising. The UCMJ, as any other criminal code, exists not as a private vehicle for righting perceived wrongs. Instead, duly constituted authorities have the duty to inquire and decide in accordance with the law and their consciences. Three commanders, acting upon the advice of legal officers, have so done. Nothing you have raised sufficiently shifts the burden upon the Army to reopen the inquiry.

5. Accordingly, I dismiss the charges you preferred on 29 November 1989.

/s/ Charles P. Otstott
Major General, USA
Commanding

Appendix 36: Letter, Michael Aquino to Lt. General Bagnall 1/5/90

January 5, 1990

Lieutenant General Charles W. Bagnal
Commanding General, U.S. Army Western Command
Fort Shafter, HI 96858-5100

Dear General Bagnal:

I have just received the enclosed 12/29/89 letter from General Otstott dismissing the 11/29/89 charges which I preferred against Chaplain Lawrence Adams-Thompson.

The reasons which General Otstott gives for dismissal of the charges are not factually correct and do not justify his dismissal of the charges. General Otstott's comments follow in Italics with my annotations in regular type:

In my opinion, Colonel Sierra's inquiry complied substantially with the requirements of R.C.M. 303.

- RCM #303 requires the commander (in this case Colonel Sierra, Adams-Thompson's brigade commander) to "... gather all reasonably available evidence bearing on guilt or innocence and any evidence relating to aggravation, extenuation, or mitigation".

- Colonel Sierra did not interview or even contact either of the two victims of Adams-Thompson's crime (Mrs. Aquino and myself).

- There is no record in Colonel Sierra's correspondence to General Crysel (CG of the 25th Division at the time of his #303 inquiry) that Sierra ever personally interviewed Adams-Thompson about the details of the charges as contained in my sworn statement in support of them.

- Colonel Sierra based his recommendation for dismissal upon a CID report of investigation which contained no actual investigation into the details of the principal charge (Specification #1) whatever. Colonel Sierra's acceptance of such an inadequate report from the CID was improper.

- It is therefore quite clear that Colonel Sierra did **not** comply with the requirements of RCM #303 in his inquiry.

Colonel Sierra dismissed the charges; Major General Crysel, the 25th Infantry Division (Light) Commander and General Court-Martial Convening Authority, ratified that decision; and, later, upon your application, Lieutenant General Bagnal, Commander, WESTCOM, reaffirmed those subordinate commanders' decisions.

As demonstrated above, Colonel Sierra's dismissal of the charges was improper in that he failed to conduct a thorough and relevant inquiry as required by RCM #303:

- Colonel Sierra represented to General Crysel that he had conducted a proper inquiry, and obviously General Crysel took him at his word.

- It is just as understandable for a succeeding division commander (General Otstott) to defend the actions of his predecessor, and for the higher headquarters commander (yourself) to defend the actions of two general officers under your command.

- If the above deficiencies in Colonel Sierra's #303 inquiry were not identified by any of these three general officers, however, it is apparent that their review of Sierra's handling of the inquiry was not sufficiently precise.

- The fact that three superior officers failed to identify the deficiencies in the inquiry, therefore, does not in itself excuse those deficiencies nor justify the continued acceptance of that inquiry as adequate.

The "new" charge relating to what you see as a fraudulent claim is, in my opinion, supported by much of the same evidence as was delved into during the original inquiry and, therefore, does not justify an additional investigation.

- The "new" charge - that of Adams-Thompson's efforts to defraud the government of as much as $3 million in false claims money - is indeed supported by evidence.

- It is **not** true, however, that this evidence "was delved into during the original inquiry". The vast majority of documentary evidence provided with these new charges was either concealed from Colonel Sierra by the CID at the time of his inquiry or had not yet been collected and correlated (as in the 84-item fact sheet of Adams-Thompson's crimes accompanying the 11/29/89 charges).

- An additional investigation into Adams-Thompson's attempt to defraud the government is therefore indeed justified.

What you have provided us and others during the past year and more, together with what we gathered during the original inquiry, adequately supports the original decision and my determination to let the matter rest.

- The evidence which I have provided to the 25th Division has never been evaluated by Colonel Sierra, nor in the present instance by General Otstott. Not one item identified in the list of Adams-Thompson's violations has been addressed in any 25th Division document. [I possess a set of the correspondence from Colonel Sierra to the 25th Division Judge Advocate and Commanding General on this matter.]

- Accordingly General Otstott cannot state that "the evidence supports the original decision".

- A "determination to let the matter rest" conveys the implication that the charges will not be investigated because they are inconvenient and troublesome. I appreciate that it would be extremely politically unpopular for a Christian chaplain to be prosecuted for a crime against a soldier and his wife who happen to be members of a non-favored religion. However this is **not** a nation of political expediency, nor of preferential treatment to only certain religions. It is a nation of **law**, most principally the Constitution which all Army officers, including General Otstott, are sworn to uphold. The First and Fourteenth Amendments to that Constitution require General Otstott to order an inquiry into any crime supported by factual evidence, including this one, whether or not it was committed by a chaplain.

You raise no new evidence, only opinion.

- Provided with the 11/29/89 charges are thirteen items of documentary evidence not available to Colonel Sierra at the time of the original 1/4/88 charges.

- One of these items is a 15-page, 84-item analysis of Adams-Thompson's violations of Article 133 UCMJ. Each numbered entry in this analysis is established, documented fact, with "opinion" (i.e. analysis) appearing as separate, un-numbered annotations in Italics.

- General Otstott's statement is thus incorrect.

That you, as complainant, may be dissatisfied with official disposition of charges that does not accord with your view of justice is not surprising.

- I am not a "complainant", but a commissioned officer who has formally preferred charges with due consideration to the serious nature of such an action, and, as General Otstott also knows, after first exhausting every less-formal avenue to see Adams-Thompson brought to account for his crimes.

- It is a UCMJ convening authority's right to dispose with charges, of course, and I would accept such disposition if it were in fact based upon a properly-conducted and factually-substantiated RCM #303 inquiry. Quite obviously this is not the case with either the 1/4/88 charges or these 11/29/89 charges.

- "My view" of justice is not at issue. Justice itself is the issue. If an investigation is not properly conducted, then it is impossible for justice to be served as required by law. If such an investigation produces evidence that substantiates dismissal of the charges, that is "my view" of justice. If the investigation produces evidence that substantiates the formal consideration of that evidence by a court-martial, that too is "my view" of justice.

The UCMJ, as any other criminal code, exists not as a private vehicle for righting perceived wrongs.

- I am not attempting to use the UCMJ as such a "private vehicle".

- On the other hand, the UCMJ **does** exist to provide for the protection of soldiers and others against crimes perpetrated by persons subject to the code, as Adams-Thompson is. It offers a means by which apparent crimes can be formally and methodically evaluated, and the apparent perpetrators either exonerated or punished as the UCMJ prescribes.

- A UCMJ commander's disposition authority should not be invoked to prevent the thorough and objective investigation of apparent crimes.

Instead, duly constituted authorities have the duty to inquire and decide in accordance with the law and their consciences.

- It is precisely my point that duly constituted authorities have the duty to inquire -and **only then** to decide. They do **not** have the prerogative, as in this instance, to make decisions **without** conducting a proper, relevant, and thorough inquiry into the evidence presented.

- A person's conscience is a measure of what he believes to be the moral right and wrong of a situation. Because of the controversial and emotionally-charged religious dimensions to this case, "conscience" is all the more unreliable a basis for a disposition decision. Such a decision should be based upon the facts of the situation, not upon the convening authority's moral opinions.

- Most importantly, the United States is a society in which justice is established by **law**, **not** by the moral opinions of persons in positions of authority. It is precisely the purpose of law to provide standards of social conduct which apply to all citizens regardless of their personal moral outlook.

Three commanders, acting upon the advice of legal officers, have so done.

- The actions of General Otstott, General Crysel, and Colonel Sierra, as discussed above, are unsupported by the evidence in this case and were also influenced by deliberate attempts by the CID to suppress evidence and mislead the #303 inquiry officer.

- There is no documentation to indicate that the legal advisor of General Otstott reviewed Colonel Sierra's report to ensure its compliance with RCM #303 upon my request to him to reinstitute the 1/4/88 charges following General Crysel's dismissal of them.

- The only evidence of legal advice to Colonel Sierra is a 5/27/88 memorandum from Captain Theodore Dixon, Assistant SJA of the 25th Division, recommending dismissal of the charges following Sierra's submission of his paperwork. There is no indication whatever in this memorandum that either Dixon or any other legal officer examined that paperwork for completeness, pertinence to the charges, or compliance with RCM #303. As Sierra's paperwork was not returned to him for correction and completion as required by RCM #303, it is obvious that the SJA office of the 25th Division did not review it adequately, if at all.

Nothing you have raised sufficiently shifts the burden upon the Army to reopen the inquiry.

- None of the evidence and documentation I have provided, either with these 11/29/89 charges or with the 1/4/88 charges, has been investigated as required by RCM #303.

- There is thus no "burden to be shifted" to the Army. The burden was and remains with the Army - specifically with the 25th Division - to comply with the Uniform Code of Military Justice and conduct a proper, thorough, and relevant RCM #303 inquiry.

The realities of this situation are quite clear to me, and I presume to both you and General Otstott as well. At issue here is not just this specific case, but indeed whether United States law applies equally and fairly to all soldiers regardless of their religion, or whether some are to be protected against accountability for crimes which they may commit because of their "favored" religious office while others are to be denied equal protection of the law, and deliberately persecuted, because of their "non-favored" religious faith.

I request that you order General Otstott to comply with United States law, reinstitute the 11/29/89 charges, and direct that a proper RCM #303 inquiry be conducted forthwith.

> Respectfully,
> /s/ Michael A. Aquino
> Lt. Colonel, Military Intelligence

Copies to:
  Honorable Michael P.W. Stone, Secretary of the Army
  General Carl E. Vuono, Chief of Staff, United States Army
  General Robert W. RisCassi, Vice Chief of Staff, United States Army
  Lieutenant General Johnny H. Corns, Inspector General of the Army
  Major General William F. Ward, Chief, Army Reserve
  Major General William K. Suter, Judge Advocate General of the Army
  Major General Norris L. Einertson, Chief of Chaplains, Department of the Army
  Major General Eugene L. Cromartie, Commanding General, U.S. Army CIC
  Major General Charles P. Otstott, Commanding General, 25th Infantry Division
  Major General Daniel R. Schroeder, Commanding General, Fort Leonard Wood
  Colonel Bobby R. Sanders, Commander, ARPERCEN
  Colonel William D. Swift, Commander, Presidio of San Francisco
  Colonel Carl L. Lockett, Commander, 6th Region CID
  Colonel John T. Lane, Inspector General, ARPERCEN
  Lt.Colonel Nolan H. Goudeaux, Headquarters, Trial Defense Service
  Major Harold Brown, Tort Claims Division, U.S. Army Claims Service
  Captain Thomas Tinti, Trial Defense Service, Presidio of San Francisco
  Mr. Joseph O. Hanley, Chief of Public Affairs, OCAR, Department of the Army
  Mr. Bob Mahoney, Public Affairs Office, 6th Army & Presidio of San Francisco

Appendix 37: Letter, Lt. General Kicklighter to Michael Aquino 4/4/90

Headquarters, United States Army Western Command

APJA[174]   18 April 1990

MEMORANDUM FOR: Lieutenant Colonel Michael A. Aquino

SUBJECT: Request for Inquiry

1. This replies finally to your letter to Lieutenant General Charles W. Bagnal, U.S. Army, Retired, concerning your charges against Chaplain (Captain) Adams-Thompson.

2. I decline to reopen an investigation into those charges.

3. From the beginning of this controversy, the only substantive issue has been whether Chaplain Adams-Thompson's young daughter, Kimberly, told the truth when she related her story to the San Francisco Police. During Colonel Sierra's inquiry, the original investigator stated that he interviewed Kimberly outside the presence of her parents. That investigator was trained in investigating such offenses. He did not believe that Kimberly was coached by her parents. Further, Chaplain Adams-Thompson and his wife deny coaching Kimberly. The investigator found Kimberly credible and sought a warrant based upon her statement. A neutral magistrate found that probable cause existed and issued a warrant.

4. Nothing you have sent causes me to question the initial conclusions of that investigator. You state that Chaplain Adams-Thompson coached his daughter; he denies it. The only other evidence available on that issue is the San Francisco Police investigator's conclusions based-upon extensive training and experience in this area.

5. Colonel Sierra, Major General Crysel, Major General Otstott, Lieutenant General Bagnal, and now, I have considered this evidence and have decided to dismiss charges against Chaplain Adams-Thompson. Absent newly discovered evidence, I will not conduct further inquiry into this matter.

/s/ Claude M. Kicklighter
Lieutenant General, U S Army
Commanding

---

[174] This indicates that this letter was drafted by the Staff Judge Advocate rather than the Commanding General personally.

Appendix 38: Letter, Michael Aquino to Lt. General Kicklighter 4/23/90

April 23, 1990

Lieutenant General Claude M. Kicklighter
Commanding General
U.S. Army Western Command
Fort Shafter, HI 96858-5100

Dear General Kicklighter:

I have today received the April 18, 1990 letter from your Staff Judge Advocate's office over your signature. The many factual falsehoods in its statements made by your SJA embarrass you as the signer of that letter. Moreover, to the extent that the letter may appear to be an action to obstruct justice, it reflects adversely upon WESTCOM command responsibilities.

The reasons the SJA gives for declining to reinstitute the court-martial charges against Chaplain Lawrence Adams-Thompson and see that a proper RCM #303 inquiry is conducted, as U.S. law requires, are not factually correct and accordingly do not justify a decision to prevent the UCMJ from being properly applied. The SJA statements follow in Italics with my corrections in regular type:

From the beginning of this controversy, the only substantive issue has been whether Chaplain Adams-Thompson's young daughter, Kimberly, told the truth when she related her story to the San Francisco Police.

- This is not a mere "controversy" to be resolved as such. Formal court-martial charges have been preferred in accordance with the UCMJ. Formal procedures are required to inquire into those charges. Those procedures were not followed, as detailed in my 1/5/90 letter to your predecessor General Bagnal. It is your responsibility as a commander to ensure that your subordinate commanders follow the UCMJ properly, thoroughly, and objectively when it has been formally invoked by an officer (myself) with the right to prefer charges.

- Chaplain Adams-Thompson has no daughter named "Kimberly", and the actual child in question is not his daughter at all. He is the stepfather to Kinsey Almond, his wife's daughter by a previous marriage. It is this child which he deliberately used as a means for him to make false and malicious allegations against Mrs. Aquino and myself.

- Almond **never** related **any** story to the San Francisco Police. As is clearly stated on the official SFPD report, it is **Chaplain Lawrence Adams-Thompson** who made the allegations, inventing a fictitious incident which he alleged to have happened to his daughter. Documentary evidence previously provided to you verifies that she herself told **no** such story.

During Colonel Sierra's inquiry, the original investigator stated that he interviewed Kimberly outside the presence of her parents. That investigator was trained in investigating such offenses. He did not believe that Kimberly was coached by her parents.

- I possess and have reviewed the documentary records of Colonel Sierra's inquiry. There is **no** record of his **ever** speaking with the original investigator (Sergeant/Inspector Glenn Pamfiloff, SFPD).

- The official SFPD record does **not** substantiate that Pamfiloff ever interviewed Kinsey Almond [not "Kimberly"] outside the presence of her parents. The record establishes that she was taken to Pamfiloff by **Chaplain Adams-Thompson** on the morning of 8/14/87, and that **he alone** did the talking to Pamfiloff.

- Whether trained to investigate such allegations or not, Pamfiloff conducted this particular investigation improperly, **as has been formally and officially determined** by the Office of Citizen Complaints, San Francisco Police Commission. He has since been reassigned to another division of the SFPD where he will not have the opportunity to conduct any further such juvenile investigations.

- Since Almond made no statements to Pamfiloff herself, he would have had no reason to offer an opinion whether "coaching" took place or not. Nor, as noted above, did Colonel Sierra ever speak with him.

Further, Chaplain Adams-Thompson and his wife deny coaching Kimberly.

- Documentary evidence previously provided to you establishes, **by comparison of official FBI, SFPD, and CID records**, that the Adams-Thompsons have lied many times since they first participated in the Presidio of San Francisco "child abuse" fraud.

- The essence of the charges preferred against Adams-Thompson is that (a) he has made a false official statement and that (b) he has initiated false claims against the U.S. government in an effort to defraud it of several million dollars.

- The Adams-Thompsons are aware of the penalties they may face when their criminal actions are ultimately exposed.

- Any unsupported "denial" by them under these circumstances does not constitute grounds to prevent court-martial charges from being properly and thoroughly investigated as required by law.

The investigator found Kimberly credible and sought a warrant based upon her statement.

- As noted above, Pamfiloff interviewed **only Chaplain Adams-Thompson** and thus could **not** evaluate Kinsey Almond's [not "Kimberly"] credibility at all. Nor did Pamfiloff make any statement in his report concerning Almond's credibility.

- Pamfiloff sought a warrant based upon **Chaplain Adams-Thompson's** allegations, **and** based upon malicious religious propaganda against me from another officer in the SFPD (whom the OCC of the Police Commission has **also** officially cited for that violation of SFPD procedures and ethics).

- The OCC of the Police Commission has officially determined that the warrant in question was improperly executed.

- The San Francisco Municipal Court has ordered **all** property seized under that warrant returned to Mrs. Aquino and myself, and it has been so returned by the SFPD.

A neutral magistrate found that probable cause existed and issued a warrant.

- Your SJA has no grounds to establish the "neutrality" of the magistrate who authorized the warrant.

- There is no record that the magistrate in question critically examined Pamfiloff's affidavit at all.

- Pamfiloff's affidavit contains **nothing** in support of his request for the warrant except a recital of the fake, unsupported allegations made to him by Chaplain Adams-Thompson.

- The mere issuance of the warrant under such conditions as these is not grounds for the court-martial charges against Adams-Thompson to be improperly dismissed.

Nothing you have sent causes me to question the initial conclusions of that investigator.

- In fact, your Staff Judge Advocate's letter neither responds to nor refutes **any** of the numerous facts substantiating the charges against Adams-Thompson, nor **any** of the numerous facts substantiating improper disposition of those charges by the 25th Division.

- There is no evidence that **any** of this material was seriously evaluated by your SJA at all. The numerous errors and inaccuracies in the letter which the SJA provided for you to sign - without even the name of the Adams-Thompson stepdaughter being correct! - is evidence of this negligence.

- As noted above, Pamfiloff's "initial conclusions" were based simply upon Adams-Thompson's personal allegations and religious propaganda. Subsequently the district attorney's office declined to file any charges based upon those "initial conclusions", and the OCC/San Francisco Police Commission issued an official finding against Pamfiloff for improper conduct of that investigation. **These later established facts** supersede his "initial conclusions" as relevant to your decision.

You state that Chaplain Adams-Thompson coached his daughter; he denies it.

What I have stated - and formally charged - is that Chaplain Adams-Thompson made false official statements as specified in the Charge Sheet and substantiated by the supporting documentation provided to the 25th Division and to you. Since his stepdaughter [not his "daughter"] never once successfully recited the story which he has tried to attribute to her, it is evident that any "coaching" of her which he and his wife may have attempted has been quite unsuccessful.

As noted above, any unsupported denial which Adams-Thompson may make concerning the charges must be weighed against the proven facts and documentary evidence of his many false statements as provided with the charges. It is thus not a question of "my word against Adams-Thompson's", but rather of Adams-Thompson's word against documentation which proves him to be a liar.

The only other evidence available on that issue is the San Francisco Police investigator's conclusions based upon extensive training and experience in this area.

Together with the charges, I provided the 25th Division and WESTCOM **abundant** evidence - including a 15-page, 84-item detailed and documented summary of Adams-Thompson's violations of #133 UCMJ - pertaining to the charges. **None of this evidence has been refuted, or even mentioned, by either the 25th Division or your SJA in this latest letter.**

- The suppression or concealment of material evidence in support of a crime is itself a violation of the UCMJ's Article 134 relative to obstruction of justice (*Manual for Courts Martial* 1984, IV, #96).

- Pamfiloff's "initial conclusions" and "extensive training/experience" have been discussed adequately above.

Colonel Sierra, Major General Crysel, Major General Otstott, Lieutenant General Bagnal, and now, I have considered this evidence and have decided to dismiss charges against Chaplain Adams-Thompson.

- Colonel Sierra conducted an improper, incomplete, and inadequate RCM #303 investigation, as documented by me to General Otstott and General Bagnal.

- General Crysel dismissed the initial charges based solely upon Colonel Sierra's improper, incomplete, and inadequate RCM #303 investigation.

- General Otstott, in his 12/29/89 letter to me, gave reasons for dismissing the re-preferred charges which, as documented in my 1/5/90 letter to General Bagnal, were not factually correct and do not justify his dismissal of the charges.

- General Bagnal neither replied to nor refuted any of the points contained in my 1/5/90 letter to him.

- This 4/18/90 letter signed by you neither replies to nor refutes any of the points contained in my 1/5/90 letter to your predecessor General Bagnal.

- Under these circumstances the dismissal of the charges against Adams-Thompson is improper and unjustified, absent conduct of a proper RCM #303 investigation in which pertinent evidence as provided is neither suppressed nor ignored.

Absent newly discovered evidence, I will not conduct further inquiry into this matter.

- Such evidence has **already** been provided to the 25th Division and yourself. To date it has merely not been acknowledged, addressed, nor refuted.

I again request that you order General Otstott to comply with United States law, reinstitute the 11/29/89 charges, and direct that a proper RCM #303 inquiry be conducted forthwith.

Respectfully,
/s/ Michael A. Aquino
Lt. Colonel, Military Intelligence

Appendix 39: "Army Stands by Satanist", *The Washington Times*

Army Stands by Satanist, Despite Cry from Public
- by Peter Almond
The Washington Times
December 27, 1988, page #A1

Lt. Col. Michael Aquino has given the Army a devil of a time over the past few weeks.

He appeared on Geraldo Rivera's television talk show in late October. Looking like Dracula in "satanic" clerical garb, he declared his belief in Satanism. Since then, Army officials have been bombarded by demands for his dismissal.

"We've had hundreds of phone calls from people complaining about him, from all over the country," said Army spokesman Lt. Col. Greg Rixon. "At one count, we had 75 letters, more than we've had on any other issue."

Col. Aquino told viewers that his firm belief in Satanism is as legitimate as anyone else's beliefs. He added that the Army does not object to his beliefs.

A few months earlier, Col. Aquino and his wife Lilith had made a similar appearance on Oprah Winfrey's show.

One of Col. Aquino's most vehement critics is an Army recruiter in West Seneca, New York. Told by a potential recruit he no longer wanted an Army career because it harbored such men, Sgt. 1st Class Robert Moak wrote the *Army Times*:

"Is this not the Army of 'values?' It seems inconsistent with what I know of all the tenets of devil worship for the Army to allow this practice. I know that religious freedom is fundamental to our form of government, but give me a break. The Army can certainly abridge such freedoms if they are found to be 'prejudicial to good order and discipline.'"

The Army steadfastly rejects such criticism.

"Lt. Col. Aquino is protected by the U.S. Constitution. He serves admirably in his unit in St. Louis," said Col. Rixon. "I've known about him for two years. By all accounts he is an exemplary officer.

"I believe it would be impossible to make a case that Lt. Col. Aquino is a divisive influence. He is very careful to inform his commander of his activities relating to his religious beliefs. He practices nothing, to our knowledge, that interferes with his work."

The Army is keeping open a much-publicized inquiry against Col. Aquino involving alleged child sex abuse at the Presidio in San Francisco in 1986.

However, according to the Army and Col. Aquino, San Francisco police have closed the case without charging him.

A military intelligence analyst by trade, Col. Aquino, 42, has been in the Army for 19 years. He dispatched helicopters on special operations psychological missions in Vietnam in 1969-70, receiving the Bronze Star and Air Medal.

He left the Army in 1972[175] and became a Merrill Lynch broker. He got a political science doctorate at the University of California in San Francisco[176] , and returned to the Army in 1981.[177] He spent last year at the Industrial College of the Armed Forces at Fort McNair and is now handling budgets at the Army Reserve Personnel Center in St. Louis.

"The Army has known about my religious beliefs for nearly 20 years," he said in an interview. "But it's not what people think."

He is a member of the Temple of Set, a group of "less than 1,000." Contrary to information in the Army Chaplain's 1978 handbook, he said, "Setians have no fertility rites. They do not drink blood, molest children or perform other deviant acts popularly ascribed to them," he said.

---

[175] Correctly: transferred from the Regular Army to the Army Reserve.

[176] Correctly: the University of California, Santa Barbara.

[177] Correctly: went from part-time (Troop Program Unit) to full-time (Active Guard & Reserve) status in the USAR.

The church's beliefs, he said, require a "college-level education" to understand. Setians believe Judeo-Christian religions have established Satan - "the oldest god ever known to humanity" - as a "straw man" to justify their guilt for man's ejection from the Garden of Eden.[178]

Lt. Col. Aquino said his upturned eyebrows and black widow's peak are natural features. His wife, Lilith - a legal name-change based on the Jewish legend of Adam's first wife, who became a child-attacking demon at the creation of Eve - is "naturally pale," he said.[179]

He said the furor over his TV appearances has led him to "tone down" his physical looks, but the Army has not pressured him and he feels no conflict between his values and the Army's.

"The Constitution is for everyone," said Col. Rixon, a Roman Catholic. "If it's Michael Aquino [as a target] today, it's Buddhists tomorrow. Who knows? It's much safer to tolerate that which is bizarre and outside the mainstream of American Judeo-Christian beliefs than slice that principle so fine it all disappears."

In West Seneca, Sgt. Moak said he thought about leaving the Army because it has not objected to Col. Aquino's beliefs.

But his *Army Times* letter prompted a response from Army public affairs that he said "calmed me down a little."

"I'm not a religious guy, but it's still distasteful, at best," he said. "I have a hard time accepting Satanism as a religion. It's not just atheism; it's believing in the opposite of God. I still hold it's a problem. It's potentially a bad situation if you allow this in the field."

Meanwhile, Col. Aquino and his wife reportedly spent Christmas quietly reading books.

"I don't begrudge Christians celebrating Christmas at all," he said.

---

[178] An inaccurate quote, probably because of the reporter's confusion. I would have said that Set is one of, if not the earliest gods known to humanity, pre-dating Judæo-Christianity by several thousand years, and later corrupted by those religions into its "Satan".

[179] Lilith chose her name not because of this reporter's quoted attribution, but because she liked its sound, and because in his *Satanic Bible* Anton LaVey whimsically referred to Lilith as "Adam's first wife, who taught him the ropes".

Appendix 40: Letter, Army Vice Chief of Staff to the President of NBC 12/2/88

Department of the Army
Office of the Chief of Staff
Washington, D.C. 20310-0200

2 December 1988

Mr. Robert Wright
President and Chief Executive Officer
National Broadcasting Corporation
30 Rockefeller Plaza
New York, New York 10112

Dear Mr. Wright:

By now I'm sure you believe you've received more than enough criticism of your recent presentation, "Devil Worship - Exposing Satan's Underground." I intend to add to that criticism by providing counterpoints to a number of inaccurate and misleading statements, implications and innuendoes about the Army made during the show.

First, I will address Lieutenant Colonel Michael Aquino's Temple of Set. The show cut to a recording of the Temple of Set's answering machine which says, "The Temple is the only international religious institution fully recognized by the United States Government." The narrator then said that, "Indeed, the Army does recognize satanism as a legitimate religion."

The implication here is that the Army sanctions or endorses Lieutenant Colonel Aquino's church. In fact, the Army does not endorse the satanic cult. As proof of this so-called endorsement, the narrator said, "The Army ... supplies chaplains with this guide for ministering to the satanic soldier."

The guide shown on the screen is Department of the Army Pamphlet 165-13 (Religious Requirements and Practices of Certain Selected Groups: A Handbook for Chaplains). The pamphlet serves as an informational tool about beliefs and practices of many religious groups to help chaplains and commanders to respond to questions. It clearly is not an endorsement of satanic practice.

A second area where the broadcast implied the Army endorses satanic practices followed from the statement, "Yet, unofficially, some charge that Army bases have become sanctuaries for devil worshipers." Rest assured that Army commanders and law enforcement officers do not tolerate lawlessness on Army installations. Vandalism, as portrayed, would indeed be investigated by proper authorities if it had occurred within an area under Army jurisdiction.

The narrator also said, "Just last month, under a full moon, I took a midnight tour of the Presidio grounds." Later he said, "... operating right here on the Army base." The narrator may indeed have toured the Presidio grounds at midnight (it's an open post), but he certainly didn't film satanic graffiti, "... right here on the Army base," since the bunkers he showed are on grounds of the Golden Gate National Recreation Area, outside the jurisdiction of the U.S. Army. Colonel Joseph Rafferty, Commander of the Presidio, personally explained to the narrator that the bunkers filmed for the show were not on Army property.

I was particularly troubled by the implication that the Army tolerates child abuse committed in the name of satan. Clearly, we do not. Yet that is exactly what the broadcasting technique seemed to convey when it was said, "It was here, parents and others allege, that as many as 60 young children were ritualistically abused by soldiers (pause) of satan." Using the word "soldiers" instead of "followers", as well as pausing dramatically between "soldiers" and "of satan," unfairly implied that ritualistic child abuse was widespread and deeply rooted in the military community. As you know, allegations of ritualistic child abuse have indeed surfaced at the Presidio. Let me assure you, we are actively investigating the allegations which are within our jurisdiction and are cooperating fully with investigations by local and other federal authorities.

Since this show aired, we have received dozens of calls and more than seventy-five letters challenging us to defend the "fact" that we are harboring satanists like Michael Aquino. Our answer is simple. We don't "harbor" satanists. What we do is ensure that all soldiers are afforded the full privilege of their Constitutional rights.

Your audience was poorly served by your show, and you bear substantial responsibility for that. The show wove a web of innuendoes designed to place the Army in the worst possible light. The American public, the Army, and all soldiers deserve more than that from your network.

> Sincerely,
> /s/ Arthur E. Brown, Jr.
> General, United States Army
> Vice Chief of Staff

[While not included with General Brown's letter to Mr. Wright, the following staff paper was provided to Brown for his use in drafting that letter. - M. Aquino]

THE FOLLOWING POINT/COUNTERPOINT PAPER WAS PREPARED BY OCPA-MRD[180] FOR USE BY VCSA. OTJAG[181] SUGGESTED MANY CHANGES FROM THE ORIGINAL VERSION THAT ARE NOW INCORPORATED IN THIS DRAFT. THIS DRAFT WAS APPROVED 31 OCTOBER 1988. (LTC Greg Rixon/ 77589)

Point/Counterpoint
Geraldo Rivera's *Devil Worship - Exposing Satan's Underground*

Point 1: The show cuts to a recording of the Temple of Set's telephone answering machine which says, "The Temple is the only international religious institution fully recognized by the United States Government." Rivera then goes on to say that "Indeed the Army does recognize satanism as a legitimate religion."

Counterpoint 1: For LTC Aquino and Rivera to claim government recognition of the Temple of Set is specious. The U.S. Army does not endorse any specific religious group.

Point 2: The Army "... supplies chaplains with this guide for ministering to the satanic soldier."

Counterpoint 2: The guide shown on the screen is DA Pamphlet 165-13 (*Religious Requirements and Practices of Certain Selected Groups: A Handbook for Chaplains.*) The pamphlet addresses the beliefs and practices of many religious groups, and is provided to chaplains and commanders to assist in many ways. For instance, it is used to help chaplains advise soldiers who may be questioning their own faith, or may be considering adoption of a new religion. It is provided to assist in evaluating the sincerity, accuracy and depth of belief of those soldiers considering conscientious objector status. The pamphlet also helps commanders make operational decisions, since it can provide insight into the impact military operations may have on local citizens of a predominant religious group. The pamphlet is **not** designed to assist chaplains in ministering to the satanic soldier, or any other soldier. The section addressing the Church of Satan merely outlines what adherents to this group profess, and how they express their beliefs. The pamphlet is informational in nature, not directive.

---

[180] Office of the Chief of Public Affairs, Department of the Army.

[181] Office of the Judge Advocate General of the Army.

Point 3: Rivera states "yet, unofficially, some charge that Army bases have become sanctuaries for devil worshippers."

Counterpoint 3: Army commanders and law enforcement officers do not tolerate lawlessness on Army installations. Vandalism, as portrayed by Rivera, would indeed be investigated by proper authorities if it had occurred within an area under Army jurisdiction.

Point 4: Rivera goes on to say, "Just last month, under a full moon, I took a midnight tour of the Presidio grounds." He later says, "operating right here on the Army base."

Counterpoint 4: Rivera may indeed have toured the Presidio grounds at midnight (it's an open post,) but he certainly didn't film satanic graffiti "...right here on the Army base" since the bunkers he showed are on grounds of the Golden Gate National Recreation Area outside the jurisdiction of the U.S. Army. Colonel Joseph Rafferty, commander of the Presidio, personally explained to Rivera that the bunkers he filmed were not on Army property. Rivera disregarded this information in order to further sensationalize his charges against the Army.

Point 5: "Joseph," a former Army officer, says that satanic organizations were "active" on the Presidio with the full knowledge of Army authorities. Colonel Rafferty says he is unaware of any satanic activity.

Counterpoint 5: The implication here is that the Army must stop or punish satanic activities on an Army base regardless of the form they take. Clearly, if the hideous crimes described by Rivera throughout the show were performed on base, they would be investigated and appropriate judicial action would be taken. However, peaceful and **legal** religious belief and practice will not be judged or tested by the Army. In the absence of any evidence of criminal activity, neither the Army, nor any other government agency, can impose itself.

Point 6: "Satanism may be a constitutionally protected religion, but, similar to another recent case at the United States Military Academy at West Point, here (PSF) charges surfaced connecting ritual child abuse at the Presidio Day Care Center to the devil cult."

Counterpoint 6: Allegations of ritualistic child abuse have indeed surfaced at both West Point and Presidio, San Francisco. However, to date no charges of ritualistic abuse have been substantiated. Despite intense effort by the respective U.S. attorneys, evidence sufficient to support a prosecution was lacking. No connection between the cases at West Point and Presidio, San Francisco has ever been made by any competent agency.

Point 7: "It was here, parents and others allege, that as many as 60 young children were ritualistically abused by soldiers ... of satan."

Counterpoint 7: Here Rivera's broadcasting technique was misleading. His theatrical pause between the words "soldiers" and "of satan" implied that the child abuse alleged to have occurred at the Presidio was performed by soldiers. No soldier has ever been implicated in the cases at either West Point or the Presidio.

Point 8: Rivera asks LTC Aquino, "You are still a serving officer, a colonel, in the United States Army. Do you feel it is inconsistent with a high ranking officer pledged, sworn, to uphold the Constitution of the United States, that you are also a practicing satanist?"

Counterpoint 8: A soldier's religious **beliefs** cannot, and should not, be tested or questioned in any way. The **practice** of his or her religion is another matter. If any soldier commits a crime in the name of his or her religion, he or she can he prosecuted for it.

The same First Amendment that protects NBC's or Geraldo Rivera's right to publish and broadcast protects soldiers' rights to religious beliefs outside the mainstream of Judeo/Christian tradition. Justice Jackson, writing in another context in 1943, said, "Freedom to differ is not limited to things that do not matter much. That would be the mere shadow of freedom. The test of its substance is the right to differ as to things that touch the heart of the existing order."

Appendix 41: Letter, Michael Aquino to Army Vice Chief of Staff 6/2/89

June 2, 1989

General Robert W. RisCassi
Vice Chief of Staff, United States Army
Pentagon Building #3E666
Washington, D.C. 20310

Dear Sir:

I have just received a copy of the enclosed letter from the previous Vice Chief of Staff, General Brown, to the President of NBC. This letter contains several misleading statements concerning the contents of the Geraldo Rivera October 25, 1988 show in general, and concerning myself and my church, the Temple of Set, in particular. While I realize that this letter is now six months old, I would appreciate these corrections being filed with it so that, if used as the basis for further decisions, it does not continue to convey inaccurate information.

(1) No claim was made by Rivera [or myself] that the Army **endorses** Satanism. The Temple affirms that it is formally recognized by the United States Government, which it is as a tax-exempt church formally approved by the Internal Revenue Service. While the Army does not "endorse" any religion, DA Pamphlet 165-13 does recognize the existence of many unusual religions, Satanism among them. Under the name "Congregation of Set", the Temple of Set is specifically mentioned in this pamphlet. [The Institute for the Study of American Religions, contractor for that pamphlet, has since developed a far more sophisticated file on the Temple of Set. For further information contact Rev. J. Gordon Melton, Director, TSAR, University of California, Santa Barbara, CA 93106.]

(2) On page #2 of his letter, General Brown equates Satanism with "lawlessness" and "vandalism". This nation's two Satanic churches, the Temple of Set and the Church of Satan, neither prescribe nor tolerate either lawlessness or vandalism by their members.

(3) There is no graffiti by Satanists in the bunkers of either the GGNRA or the Presidio. For one thing, legitimate Satanists are not the type to deface public buildings with graffiti. For another thing, authentic Satanic symbolism is both unique and precise, and would be easily distinguishable from scrawlings by non-Satanists inspired by Hollywood monster-movie nonsense.

(4) The Temple of Set and the Church of Satan do not tolerate child abuse. The Satanic religion respects children and does not harm them in any way. In fact, minors have never been permitted to affiliate with the Temple or even to attend any of its functions. [This simply reflects the Temple's policy that children should not receive religious indoctrination, but should rather be free to decide upon a metaphysical orientation of their own upon reaching responsible adulthood.]

(5) For the record, I have yet to see any clear evidence that even a single child was abused in the Presidio of San Francisco scandal. Until I see such evidence, I think it is simply one more incident of deliberately-inflamed hysteria in the nationwide epidemic of phony child-abuse witch-hunts which has caused so much damage over the last few years.

I appreciate General Brown's affirmation that the Army is committed to affording all soldiers, including myself, the full privilege of their Constitutional rights. Since the Geraldo Rivera show, however, the CIDC has flagged my file, suspended my security clearance, and conducted a criminal investigation of me for an alleged crime which was clearly maliciously fabricated by an Army chaplain. I do not consider this treatment, and the sheltering of the chaplain to date against accountability for his actions, to constitute the full privilege of my rights under the First and Fourteenth Amendments to the Constitution. I await correction of this flagrantly unjust situation by the Department of the Army at this time.

Provided to General Brown in support of his letter was a "Point/Counterpoint" paper prepared by OCPA-MRD. This paper too contains significant misinformation concerning myself and my religion which I could have corrected had the paper been staffed through me. To be specific:

Point/Counterpoint #1: For me to claim U.S. Government recognition of the Temple of Set is not "specious". As noted above, the Internal Revenue Service - the agency of the United States Government which recognizes the legal standing of churches for purposes of tax-exempt certification, so recognized the Temple of Set in 1975.

Point/Counterpoint #2: If the U.S. Army does not endorse any specific religious group, then why does it commission and pay the salaries of chaplains, who are serving officially as representatives and promoters of certain religious institutions? The U.S. Army further funds the building and maintenance of Christian chapels on its installations. I appreciate the fact that American society generally approves of this violation of the church/state principle as a convenience to soldiers. Nevertheless it is in fact a very tangible endorsement of Christianity by the Army.

The paper insists that DA Pamphlet 165-13 "is not designed to assist chaplains in ministering to the Satanic soldier, or any other soldier". DA Training Circular 16-24 (9 June 1978) clearly establishes, however, that the Army **does** require commanders and chaplains to recognize and meet the needs of "less familiar religions" as well as Christianity. To quote from this publication:

> The commander is responsible for the religious life of the command, which includes meeting the religious needs of military personnel, their dependents, authorized civilians, and retired personnel and their dependents. The staff officer responsible to the commander for seeing that this is accomplished is the chaplain.
>
> Less familiar religions are included within this responsibility. The facilities provided by the commander should be made available to all religious groups for use as needed. Normal participation gives priority in scheduling to General Protestant and Catholic services. Other religious groups are accommodated in a cooperative manner so as to best meet the needs of all.
>
> The chaplain can neither be required to perform any task which conflicts with the requirements of his/her own religious denomination, nor to participate in or conduct a service in conflict with his/her beliefs. However, the recognition of religious needs of others and the effort to meet these needs in terms of facilities, personnel, and planning is a responsibility of the chaplain.

Point/Counterpoint #3: The paper casually equates "devil worship" with "lawlessness" - obviously an equation upon which General Brown relied when drafting his letter to NBC. As noted above, this is non-factual and a prejudicial statement against the Satanic religion and its adherents.

Point/Counterpoint #4: As noted above, there is no genuine Satanic graffiti in either Presidio or GGNRA bunkers.

Point/Counterpoint #5: "Joseph" is actually Captain Lewis D. Seago, USAR, a former member of the Temple of Set who was expelled from it for misconduct in 1982. At the time Seago, whose identity was concealed by Rivera, made his statement on camera, he knew full well that no "Satanic organizations had been active on the Presidio". Following Seago's expulsion, I was the only member of the Temple of Set on the Presidio, and no activities of the Temple of Set were conducted on post. [On the evening that the Rivera broadcast aired and I first heard Seago's statements, I immediately telephoned Colonel Rafferty and communicated this information to him. Rafferty told me that Captain Seago had not identified himself to him nor cleared the content of his statements with him.]

In fact the October 25, 1988 Geraldo Rivera broadcast contained far more errors than the position paper provided to General Brown identified. Enclosed is an analysis of that broadcast prepared by the Council for Democratic and Secular Humanism, together with a copy of my own commentary on that analysis. I think you will find that a far different picture of the subject emerges from that which Rivera tried to sell.

As the senior representative of the Satanic religion as well as a commissioned officer in the Army, I respectfully request that official Army statements concerning this religion be staffed through me for comment before being finalized by the Department of the Army. I am interested not only in ensuring that our religion is described accurately, but also in enabling the Army to respond to questions concerning it as accurately as it does to questions concerning more familiar religions, which I presume are staffed through representatives of those religions in the Corps of Chaplains.

Under the Freedom of Information Act and the Privacy Act, I further request that copies of any other correspondence or other papers concerning myself, the Temple of Set, and/or the Satanic religion generally being maintained by your office be provided to me. My interest in reviewing such material is, as above, to correct any misinformation contained therein.

> Respectfully,
> /s/ Michael A. Aquino
> Lt. Colonel, Military Intelligence

cc- General Carl E. Vuono, Chief of Staff, United States Army
Major General William F. Ward, Chief, U.S. Army Reserve
Major General Eugene R. Cromartie, Commanding General, USACIDC
Commander, U.S. Army Reserve Personnel Center
Colonel Joseph V. Rafferty, Commander, Presidio of San Francisco
Colonel Webster D. Ray, Commander, Sixth Region, USACIDC
Lt. Colonel Wayne Price, U.S. Army Trial Defense Service
Lt. Colonel Greg Rixon, Department of the Army Public Affairs Office
Captain Thomas Hayes, U.S. Army Trial Defense Service
Mr. Gary R. Myers, Attorney at Law
Ms. Irene Rapoza, Senior Analyst, San Francisco Police Commission
Pillsbury, Madison & Sutro
Office of the Inspector General, ARPERCEN
Command Equal Opportunity Office, ARPERCEN
Command Freedom of Information Act/Privacy Act Office, ARPERCEN

Appendix 42: TJAG Information Paper - Involvement of Army Members in Satanic Worship, 11/23/88

DAJA-AL

LTC John Burton/76000
23 November 1988

INFORMATION PAPER

SUBJECT: Involvement of Army Members in Satanic Worship

1. Purpose. To inform the Director of the Army Staff of the status of LTC Michael Aquino and the options available to deal with him and other Army members who practice satanic worship.

2. Background. On 25 October 1988 LTC Michael Aquino appeared on an NBC special concerning satanism which focused, in part, on alleged satanic worship practices at or near the Presidio. LTC Aquino is an AGR Civil Affairs officer who was formerly stationed at the Presidio but is currently assigned to ARPERCEN. During his interview with the narrator, LTC Aquino acknowledged that he is an Army officer but stated that he does not view his satanic worship as conflicting with his status as an officer. The narrator implied through misstatements and, innuendoes that satanic rituals were being performed on Army bases, that child abuse was involved, and that the Army condoned such practices. PAO[182] prepared-a point paper (Tab A) and issued an ARNEWS message (Tab B) rebutting each misstatement and clarifying the Army's position.

3. Discussion.

    a. Status of LTC Aquino (BIO at Tab C).

        (1) He has been on continuous active duty as an AGR[183] officer since 1981. He was commissioned as an Armor officer (ROTC-DMG[184]) in 1968, serving on active duty (including Vietnam) until July 1972 and in USAR units from 1973 to 1981. He branch transferred to Civil Affairs in 1981.

        (2) He converted to satanic worship in the early 70s[185] and later formed his own satanic church, the Temple of Set, which was granted tax exempt status as a valid religious organization by the IRS in June 1976.[186]

---

[182] Department of the Army Public Information Office.

[183] Active Guard and Reserve, a highly-selective full-time active duty program for Reserve/National Guard soldiers.

[184] ROTC Distinguished Military Graduate. A designation awarded to only a very few top ROTC cadets, commissioning them in the Regular Army rather than the Army Reserve, on par with West Point graduates.

[185] Correctly: 1969, when I joined the Church of Satan. However I did not "convert" from anything, never having been a member of any other religion previously.

[186] Correctly: The Temple of Set was founded in June 1975, California State tax-exemption in October 1975, federal tax-exemption in June 1976.

(3) As Tab D reflects, various individuals in the Army have been aware of his satanic worship activities and ideas since 1972[187] , when he provided a Church of Satan "position paper" to, a chaplain at the US Army Chaplain school. He later wrote to the Office of the Chief of Chaplains in 1982 to correct what he believed were misstatements in DA Pam 165-13 concerning satanic worship.[188] He has also appeared on other TV shows and in magazine articles (Tab D and Tab E).

(4) He graduated from the ICAF resident course in 1987, after being recommended by a USAR SSC[189] board in 1986. His OMPF[190] has apparently never reflected his satanic worship practices or ideas; on the contrary, his OMPF is superlative in every respect.[191] It appears that the Chief, Army Reserve, was briefed on LTC Aquino's satanic worship before the SSC board recommendation was approved (Tab E).

(5) He currently has 11 years of active duty (for retirement under 10 USC 3911) and 20 "good years" for retirement under 10 USC 1331 (i.e., pay begins at age 60). He is 42 years old and has an MRD[192] of 13 July 1996 for years of service. His DOR[193] as LTC is 13 June 1985. He has a TS[194] clearance, which was issued in 1981 and validated in 1986, with full knowledge of his satanic worship. DIS[195] has cleared him for SCI.[196]

(6) His AGR status will be routinely reviewed by a "continuation board" in January 1989. The board is required to retain him in an AGR status if he is "fully qualified" and a position is available (which it is; he is in it). Otherwise, by regulation he can only be REFRAD[197] by DAADB[198] procedures for misconduct, moral or professional dereliction or substandard performance of duty. The Secretary of the Army retains plenary authority under 10 USC 681 to REFRAD him in the best interests of the Army.

---

[187] Correctly: Since I joined the Church of Satan in 1969, all of my commanders were aware of my religion. In addition to numerous local & regional newspaper & broadcast interviews, I was profiled in the 6/19/72 issue of *Time* magazine: "The Occult: A Substitute Faith". Upon leaving my assignment on the faculty of the U.S. Army Armor School later that year, I was presented officially with [another] Army Commendation Medal and unofficially with an elegant Sikh dagger "to be used for sacrificing virgins, if you can still find any"!

[188] This letter appears as Appendix #43.

[189] Senior Service College, the highest and most exclusive level of professional education in the Department of Defense. Only one U.S. Army Reserve officer is selected for each year's Industrial College of the Armed Forces (ICAF) class, and I was that officer for the Class of 1987.

[190] Official Military Personnel File.

[191] Why would "superlative military performance in every respect" be **contrary** to Satanic religion? A clearly prejudicial statement.

[192] Mandatory Retirement Date.

[193] Date of Rank.

[194] Top Secret, the highest category of security clearance.

[195] The Defense Investigative Service, which conducts background investigations for security clearances.

[196] Special Compartmented Intelligence, extremely restricted and specialized access above Top Secret. I retained TS/SCI until my retirement in 1994.

[197] Relieved From Active Duty.

[198] Department of the Army Disciplinary Board.

(7) There have been numerous Congressional inquiries, principally the routine forwarding of letters from constituents who were reacting to the misstatements and innuendoes made on the 25 October NBC show. The only non-routine letter is at Tab F.[199]

b. Options for dealing with LTC Aquino and other Army members who profess or practice satanic worship.

(1) If his **actual conduct** constitutes a UCMJ offense (including "conduct unbecoming") or moral or professional dereliction or substandard performance of duty, then judicial, nonjudicial, or adverse administrative action (e.g., LOR[200]) can be taken, as well as follow-on actions such as REFRAD or discharge if warranted. Although the Secretary could exercise his plenary authority to REFRAD LTC Aquino, there would have to be a clearly articulated basis for doing so in the best interest of the Army.

(2) LTC Aquino's satanic worship has not apparently interfered with his duty performance, nor has he made a statement which would suggest a potential conflict. The CID initiated an inquiry into allegations that LTC Aquino was involved in child abuse at the Presidio, but held its inquiry in abeyance pending action by both federal and San Francisco authorities. The CID initiated a formal investigation (SSI), with LTC Aquino listed as a suspect, on 23 November 1988.

(3) His appearance on TV shows and in magazine interviews have apparently been during his off-duty time, not at government expense, and not in his official capacity or in uniform. As such, his actions are protected by the First Amendment, from the perspective of both free speech and free exercise of religion.

(4) Part of the Army's current concern stems from the narrator's misstatements and innuendoes rather than from LTC Aquino's statements. PAO has prepared a letter from VCSA to the President of NBC expressing his disappointment over the show's misstatements and innuendoes (Tab G).[201]

c. Satanic worship by Air Force and Navy members. The Navy has not had any recent incidents involving satanic worship. Approximately 3-4 years ago, there was an alleged satanic ritual funeral performed for a deceased sailor. The Air Force is currently reviewing a request by a satanic worship group that has requested permission to use a base chapel to conduct services.[202]

4. Recommendations.

a. Do not issue "top down" guidance to ARPERCEN or the continuation board concerning LTC Aquino.[203]

b. Avoid any perception of command influence in the criminal allegations against LTC Aquino. Allow CID to continue its inquiry; allow the local command to determine whether charges should be preferred and an Article 32 investigation conducted.[204]

c. Do not eliminate DA Pam 165-13 and DA Pam 165-13-1 which describe satanism, along with other little known "religions", for informational purposes.

d. Reply to Congressional inquiries by providing a copy of the ARNEWS release.

---

[199] The 10/26/88 letter from Senator Jesse Helms' office [see Chapter #6].

[200] Letter of Reprimand.

[201] Appendix #40.

[202] Neither of these incidents involved the Temple of Set.

[203] Such instructions were in fact illegally issued to the AGR continuation board, as discussed in Chapter #8.

[204] As the chapters dealing with the CID investigation and post-investigation conduct by the CID and TJAG show, this "Information Paper" proposal was ignored.

Appendix 43: Letter, Michael Aquino to the Chief of Chaplains 4/15/82

Department of the Army
Headquarters, Presidio of San Francisco
Presidio of San Francisco, California 94129

AFZM-DRCS   15 April 1982

Chaplain (Colonel) John J. Hoogland
Director, Personnel and Ecclesiastical Relations
Office of the Chief of Chaplains
Headquarters, Department of the Army
Washington, D.C. 20310

Dear Chaplain Hoogland:

I was recently contacted by Chaplain (Colonel) Meredith R. Standley, Command Chaplain at Fort Ord, for information concerning the Church of Satan and Temple of Set. Chaplain Standley alerted me to the existence of DA Pamphlet 165-13 *Religious Requirements and Practices of Certain Selected Groups*, a copy of which I subsequently obtained from the Sixth Army Chaplain. The sections in this publication dealing with the Church of Satan, Satanism, and witchcraft in general contain various factual errors. Chaplain Standley recommended that I forward my comments to you for possible incorporation in changes to or future editions of this publication. These comments are enclosed. All points contained therein are backed by personal experience and/or sound research practices. (I hold a Ph.D. from the University of California, which should attest to my research capabilities.)

I see no need to include a description of the Temple of Set in a revised 165-13, as our beliefs and practices do not interface or conflict with the professional practices and expectations of the armed forces. There are no services that the Corps of Chaplains can perform for the Temple of Set other than to verify to commanders that it is a legally-incorporated and state/federally tax-exempt religious institution (which you can verify through the Internal Revenue Service).

On the general subject of Satanism and Black Magic, I recommend that the Corps of Chaplains discourage military personnel from involvement with groups or organizations other than the Temple of Set. This recommendation is not born simply of a desire for sectarian monopoly. In 14 years I have seen the rise and fall of innumerable "Satanic" groups. The blunt truth of the matter is that virtually all of them - with the significant exception of the pre-1975 Church of Satan and post-1975 Temple of Set - ultimately proved to be excuses for drug abuse, sexual exploitation, or financial rackets. Warning soldiers against such hazards does not, in my opinion, abuse their freedom of religion as much as it evidences concern for their personal health and safety. Often by the time an individual learns the truth in such cases, he is involved to an awkward and even dangerous degree.

We have found, moreover, that exposure to the theories and practices of Black Magic can be highly disturbing and traumatic to immature individuals. Consequently the Temple of Set screens applications carefully and introduces new members to concepts only as they demonstrate their ability to understand and apply them with intelligence and judiciousness. We feel most strongly that any approach to the Black Arts which does not evidence extraordinary care in this area is unethical and irresponsible.

I myself am the senior member of the Priesthood in the only legally-recognized (through non-profit incorporation and full tax-exemption) "Satanic" (we prefer the non-Christian term "Setian") religious institution in the United States. As such, and as an Army officer of 14 years' Active and Reserve service, I would be pleased to assist the Corps of Chaplains with questions which may arise in this area. My Presidio Autovon number is 586-4772, and my residential number is (415) ###-####.

                                                            Sincerely,
                                                            /s/ Michael A. Aquino
                                                            Major, Civil Affairs

CF: Chaplain (COL) M.R. Standley

Appendix 44: Letter, Michael Aquino to Captain Mark Harvey 1/5/89

January 5, 1989

Dear Captain Harvey:

In your December 14, 1988 letter you said: *If Lt. Colonel Aquino provides certain leads or evidence that shows the allegations to be without merit, I will ensure that USA CIDC personnel follow those leads, to the maximum possible extent, in order to properly document his innocence.*

Following is a list of such leads. The manner in which these are followed up by the CID will be of considerable interest to me in ascertaining how objective your investigation is. Therefore I request that you keep me, through Captain Hayes of the Trial Defense Service, advised on the steps which are in fact being taken to pursue these leads.

Five months elapsed from the time I preferred court-martial charges against Adams-Thompson until they were dropped by the 25th Division. During that time apparently the only "investigation" which was done of the principal specification (#1) was to comment that "Adams-Thompson was just repeating what his stepdaughter told him" [and therefore he is innocent of any malicious act]. If your investigators are going to proceed from the naïve assumption that Army chaplains are incapable of lying, and that whatever Kinsey Almond is alleged to have said could not possibly have been the invention of her stepfather, mother, and/or Debbie Hickey, then I would have serious reservations about your ability to deal with a case such as the Presidio scandal. As I have documented to you, the nationwide epidemic of such scandals is notorious for the deliberate indoctrination of children by parents, investigators, and "therapists" out of desires for career advancement, financial profit, media glamor, and/or personal vendettas. If the CID understands this, then there shouldn't be any great mystery about the Presidio affair. If you don't understand it, then you will simply be dupes for those who created, aggravated, and are still attempting to exploit the scandal for their personal advantage and profit.

I have one further comment to make before going into the leads, and I ask that you consider it carefully:

Unlike the Adams-Thompsons and the other Presidio witch-hunters, I have no investment in the Presidio scandal. I do not stand to realize millions of dollars in claims money, nor suffer the consequences of having perpetrated a cruel hoax on the Presidio community, nor be responsible for the indoctrination of scores of infants and children into lurid sex fantasies which they can scarcely begin to comprehend, nor be responsible for ruining the lives and careers of innocent victims of allegations. My wife and I were minding our own business when Adams-Thompson suddenly attacked us out of nowhere. On the excuse of his allegations, we were then set upon savagely by an officer of the San Francisco Police Department which, as we later learned to our surprise, had allowed another officer to pursue a covert campaign of defamation against us for several years.

Defending ourselves against this unexpected, unprovoked, undeserved, and vicious attack has now cost us over $50,000 in legal fees and vandalism repairs to date. It has seriously affected our health. It has seriously shaken the trust and confidence we previously had in "investigative" agencies. While I would like to believe, as you told me, that the CID is a disinterested, objective, fact-finding body, I will need to see a lot more than sham investigations [of Adams-Thompson], stonewalled FOIA requests [for information crucial to the proof of our innocence], and prejudicial statements to the press by national CID officials to take you at your word. If it appears that you are indeed investigating objectively, then I will cooperate with you as much as possible. But if it appears that you are merely operating from a hidden agenda to persecute my wife and myself regardless of the truth, I will certainly not cooperate with that.

1. Find out if there is any record of the Adams-Thompsons taking their stepdaughter to Letterman Army Medical Center (LAMC) **in September/October 1986** for treatment for any physical symptom significant of rape and sodomy by two adult males. If there is no such record, then it is obvious that at the time in question they had

no reason whatever to think that any sexual abuse as later alleged by them in August 1987 had happened to the child.

2. Get the record of the January 1987 FBI interview with Kinsey Almond/AdamsThompson, in which there was no conclusion of sex-abuse, and compare it to the later "Mikey/Shamby" story produced after the four "therapy" sessions in February 1987. Why should the "therapy" story be considered more credible than the earlier FBI interview results, given the reputation of such "therapists" for manufacturing fake "sex-abuse symptoms"?

3. Find out if there is any record of the Adams-Thompsons taking their stepdaughter to LAMC for medical examination **in January 1987** after she denied to the FBI interviewer that she had been molested by anyone. If there is no such record, then it is obvious that even after the Presidio scandal had been set in motion and Kinsey Almond had been interviewed, the Adams-Thompsons **still** didn't think that any sexual abuse as later alleged by them had happened to the child.

4. Find out if, after the child had been subjected to "therapy" indoctrination in February 1987 by Debbie Hickey, the Adams-Thompsons **then** took the child to LAMC for a physical examination. Obtain the results of any such medical examination and have them assessed by an expert pediatrician such as Ann Parker, M.D. (who was interviewed as an expert in the KTVU television documentary on the Presidio scandal). If no such examination occurred, then it would be obvious that even after the "therapy" sessions the Adams-Thompsons **still** didn't think that any sexual abuse (i.e. the double rape and double sodomy supposedly revealed by the "therapy" sessions) had in fact happened to the child.

5. Obtain written records of all four of the Hickey "therapy" sessions in February 1987 and see how consistent they are with one another, and to what extent the "Mikey/ Shamby" story was created and progressively indoctrinated by Hickey as opposed to being later invented or embellished by Lawrence and/or Michele Adams-Thompson. Investigate the background of Hickey as to her license, professional qualifications, and reputation as an automatic abuse-finder in childcare witch-hunts. Consider the possibility that, in order to protect himself/herself, the therapist may have altered these "therapy" records at a later date. Investigate whether Hickey has attended "how to create child-abuse scandals" workshops with leading profiteers such as Catherine Gould.

6. I understand that the phrase "Mikey likes it" was a popular television advertisement phrase, and I have seen it nowadays on stickers, buttons, and carwindow ornaments. Review children's television shows, comics, etc. of the 1985-86 era to see if there was a cartoon character, super-hero, animal, etc. named "Shamby". Find out whether there are any records of these names appearing in other Hickey therapy-stories.

7. Provide copies of the FBI interview and the four "therapy" sessions to Lee Coleman, M.D. for an expert opinion. Dr. Coleman is the Director of the Center for the Study of Psychiatric Testimony, 1889 Yosemite Road, Berkeley, CA 94707 - (415) 527-7512. Dr. Coleman is a nationally-famous authority on the use of quack "therapy" to manufacture child-abuse scares, and has been called to testify in court as an expert witness in many scandals similar to that at the Presidio.

8. Compare the records of the January FBI interview and the February 1987 "therapy" sessions to the story told by Lawrence and Michele Adams-Thompson to FBI Special Agent Clyde Foreman in August 1987 [after seeing Lilith and myself at the Presidio PX]. Obtain a copy of the report that Foreman presumably wrote within the FBI concerning the story told to him.

9. What is the religious affiliation and history of Clyde Foreman? Is he a Christian or a member of the same church in which Adams-Thompson is an ordained minister?

10. Find out why, if the "Mikey/Shamby" therapist-story was indeed produced in February 1987, the child was not taken immediately to Gary Hambright's address for a possible house-identification. [The therapist-story was that the child said she was taken to "**Mr. Gary's** home", not to someone else's home.]

11. Review the February 1986 Hickey "therapy" records to see if there is any description of a building besides "Mr. Gary's home" given. [Consider that Hickey or the Adams-Thompsons may have doctored these records later in order to protect themselves.] If Almond supposedly went into meticulous detail concerning the interior of the building ("hardwood floors"), why not the color, shape, size, etc. of the exterior? Certainly this would have been of interest to an ethical therapist trying to uncover a crime. What I expect you will find is that there was **no** such description, because at that time it had not yet occurred to Adams-Thompson to use the story to attack my wife and myself.

12. In August 1986 Adams-Thompson took his allegations against us immediately to the FBI, which acted on them immediately, whereupon the SFPD acted immediately. Yet the therapy story was developed in **February** (six months earlier). Did Adams-Thompson go running to the FBI at **that** time [remembering that the therapy-story named Hambright and Hambright's home]? Did the FBI take Almond on an "identification ride" to Hambright's residence at that time? Did the SFPD obtain and execute a search warrant on Hambright's residence seeking the same list of "features detailed by Almond" that appeared six months later on the SFPD report and search warrant used against us? I suspect you will find that **none** of this happened.

13. Investigate the supposed "identification trip" to our San Francisco home. Is there any verifiable record of Almond having described the color, size, shape, or location of a building **before** the trip was made? Why wasn't she driven to the block on which Hambright's residence was located? Why wasn't she driven to various city blocks at random and given an opportunity to "identify" a building? Exactly **who** said that Almond "identified" our building? Is it in an official FBI report, or did Michele Adams-Thompson just allege this later to the SFPD? According to the SFPD report, the "identification" was made while walking the child past our building. Obviously this increases the opportunity for prompting or coaching as to that specific building, whose address both Foreman and Michele Adams-Thompson knew beforehand. Why not just stop the car at a "neutral" location on the street and ask Almond if anything there was familiar to her?

14. Once Almond had allegedly "identified" our building, why was the child not immediately interviewed in depth concerning specific interior features of the premises which could be verified upon a search by authorities? For example: "Did you go upstairs or downstairs [it is obviously a multistory apartment building]?" "What does the entrance way look like, and what color is it?" "What did the rooms look like?" If Almond had in fact been there before, all such details could have served to validate a search - **or to further invalidate it**. What happened is that there was **no** attempt to obtain further details from Almond before going ahead with the search. As far as I am concerned, the reason for this is that Sandi Gallant and Glenn Pamfiloff simply wanted an excuse to get inside our home and confiscate Temple of Set papers, and the fewer inconvenient facts which might get in their way, the better. The "interior description" was deliberately left as vague as possible, so that a mismatch would not come back to haunt them any more than necessary. [Even so, the mismatch is obvious.]

15. Find out why, when the U.S. Attorney's Office issued its multiple indictments against Gary Hambright for doing terrible things to multitudes of Presidio children, the Adams-Thompson allegation was not taken seriously enough to be included. Whether or not my wife and I or anyone else was involved, the "therapy" story clearly named "Mr. Gary" and his house. Michele Adams-Thompson has publicly criticized the Army investigators for their "mishandling" of the allegations against us, so it wouldn't seem that the Adams-Thompsons would have balked at having Kinsey Almond included on the list of offenses for which Hambright was charged. According to the original therapy-story, the double rape and double sodomy had been done at his home, and he had been one of the rapists/sodomizers. So why was a charge which the Adams-Thompsons now feel is appropriate to make against my wife and myself not equally appropriate to make against Hambright? If they tried to make it, why wasn't it accepted as one of the indictments?

16. It has been reported in the media that the Adams-Thompsons have kept the child in continuous "therapy" since they made their attack on my wife and myself. Investigate how they selected the "therapist", what the reputation of that "therapist" is as a professional abuse-finder, and what monetary benefits accrue to that "therapist" both from the clients and from outside private & governmental grants based on "child-abuse" cases opened. Obtain copies of any written reports by that "therapist" and compare them with (a) the January 1987 FBI interview, (b) the February 1987 "therapist" reports, and (c) with information concerning my wife, myself, and the appearance of our home to which the Adams-Thompsons were exposed **after** the August 1987 raid (either by police/FBI/CID contact or by the extensive public media coverage of ourselves and our home).

17. I recommend that CID agents investigate the past sexual histories of Lawrence Thompson and Michele Adams, including interviewing their previous marital and extramarital sex partners as discovered. If Kinsey Almond is being interviewed, question her as to whether she was ever sexually touched or molested by either her mother, her stepfather, or another immediate family member.

18. Find out what church Lawrence Adams-Thompson is ordained by, what his personal record in that church is, what that church's official position towards Satan and Satanism is, and what it expects its ministers or priests to do about "Devil-worship".

19. Find out why, in conducting a five-month preliminary inquiry into the court-martial charges I preferred against Adams-Thompson, neither Brigade Commander Colonel Sierra, nor any representative of his, nor the CID (which was supposedly investigating the charges for Sierra) ever once contacted either my wife or myself to discuss any of the details of our sworn statements.

20. Find out why the San Francisco Police Department has refused to return the rest of our personal and church property seized in the August 1987 raid, despite the fact that nothing contained in it is evidence of anything the least criminal, child-abuse related or otherwise, and despite the fact that the District Attorney closed the investigation of us without filing any charges. [I am entirely willing for that remaining confiscated property to be examined by CID investigators.]

21. Contact Ms. Irene F. Rapoza, Senior Administrative Analyst, Office of Citizen Complaints, San Francisco Police Commission, 555 Seventh Street #252, San Francisco, CA 94103, telephone (415) 553-1407 and request access to a copy of her forthcoming investigative report on case #0468-88. This is the complaint which I filed against SFPD officers Sandi Gallant and Glenn Pamfiloff for abuse of their offices in violation of the Temple of Set's and its members' Constitutional rights, defamatory statements and actions against me, and use of the Adams-Thompson allegations as a mere excuse to terrorize my wife and myself and confiscate and retain personal and church material having no relation to any criminal activity whatever.

22. What are the religious affiliations and histories of all CID special agents assigned to the investigation of me? Are any of them Christians, or members of the same church in which Adams-Thompson is an ordained minister? If any of this is the case, what steps have been taken to verify their ability to be objective in the investigation of a Satanist and head of the nation's preeminent Satanic church?

[Concerning the Presidio Child-Care Scandal investigation generally]:

1. Find out who the Presidio chaplain was who initially [in October/November 1986] advised Captain and Mrs. Tobin to go to the authorities with an allegation of child sex-abuse. Was it by any chance Adams-Thompson?

2. Find out what roles Lawrence and Michele Adams-Thompson each played in aggravating the rumors and hysteria in the subsequent Presidio scandal.

3. Find out why, after the Tobins' initial accusations of anal rape with "tears" had been retracted by Dr. Kevin Coulter, the allegations made against Hambright concerning the Tobin child were switched to "oral copulation" - which was apparently never mentioned at the time of the initial allegations. Is this another

instance where the "crime" is hastily reinvented when the initial accusation is found to be false? Unlike anal rape, of course, "oral copulation" cannot be proved or disproved by medical examination, and thus is all the more convenient for "therapists" as an allegation.

4. Find out how many parents actually took their children to LAMC for medical examinations for any physical problems which could have been sex-abuse-related **at the time such abuses are now alleged to have occurred - not months later when the witch-hunt was set in motion**. Investigate the results of those pre-scandal examinations, if indeed any actually occurred.

5. Under separate cover I am sending you copies of the following two books:
    • Mary Pride, *The Child Abuse Industry* (Westchester, IL: Crossway Books, 1986).
    • Paul & Shirley Eberle, *The Politics of Child Abuse* (Secaucus, Lyle Stuart, 1986)
    These books document the ongoing national "child-abuse industry" series of manufactured day-care scandals, and the exploitation of the concept of "therapy" for personal gain. If you do not read them, you are investigating in the dark.

6. Take the time to read **thoroughly** Attachment #A (*Commercial Appeal*, Memphis, Tennessee, January 17-22, 1988) to my sworn statement of 23 August 1988. Judging by what I have seen so far, your investigation of the Presidio affair seems to be proceeding in ignorance of the history and character of the ongoing fake child-care/child-abuse epidemic.

7. Under separate cover I am sending you the section of Arthur Lyons' *Satan Wants You: The Cult of Devil Worship in America* (New York: Mysterious Press, 1988) discussing the idiotic allegations that Satanists molest/abuse/ sacrifice/breed/etc. children. It exposes the religious hate-group network around the country which has seized upon such allegations as an opportunity for attacking the legitimate Satanic religion.

8. Contact FBI Supervisory Special Agent Kenneth Lanning, FBI Academy, Quantico, Virginia for information as to whether any legitimate Satanist church such as the Temple of Set or Church of Satan has ever been involved in child-abuse crime. Lanning is the FBI's principal expert on the subject of Satanism and "Satanic crime". Note that the Temple of Set has been in existence since 1975, and the Church of Satan since 1966, and that thousands of individuals have come and gone from these organizations in these 22 years. If they were engaged in sexual abuse or other criminal acts towards children, it would certainly have surfaced long before now. [Lanning is a considerably more reliable source of information on this subject than Geraldo Rivera, I might add.]

9. Examine the allegations by parents and "therapists" from the standpoint of monetary motives. The parents who are anxious to prove some kind of molestation have a $66 million stake from the federal government in doing so. They may also be able to get thousands of additional dollars from the Crime Victim's Compensation law in California. As for "therapists": The 1974 Mondale Act provided for huge federal grants to states if they passed mandatory child-abuse reporting laws, which they proceeded to do. California's law became effective in 1981. In order to receive this money, state and local child-abuse protective service agencies are under constant pressure to generate as many new cases as possible. The manufacture of child-abuse cases is now a very big and lucrative business.

10. Investigate the professional backgrounds and credentials of every "therapist" who has been involved in the Presidio scandal [if in fact there were more than just Hickey]. This profession is nationally notorious for slack or nonexistent credentialing procedures, and many individuals represent themselves as "therapists" or "family counselors" who have little or no accredited training in the field. In California, the practicing of "therapy" without a license is only a misdemeanor. For further information, contact: Marriage, Family, and Child Counseling; Behavioral Sciences Examiners Board; 1021 "O" Street, Room A198; Sacramento, CA 95814. Telephone: (916) 445-4933.

11. Find out why Debbie Hickey, who according to the KTVU documentary diagnosed sex-abuse in her own children, was permitted to proceed with mass-diagnoses of child-molestation of all the other children at the Presidio child-care center. Find out why Hickey refused to be interviewed by the KTVU documentary team about this.

12. Many non-medical-degreed "psychologists" specializing in the "child-abuse finding" field have similarly-questionable backgrounds and credentials, and are simply interested in the financial profits to be made. Checklists of "Satanic ritual abuse symptoms", such as that circulated at the Presidio in the developing stages of the scandal, are simply geared towards the generation of new business, in that they cite almost any ordinary behavior of a child as "evidence of abuse". For further information, contact: Psychology Examining Committee; Board of Medical Quality Assurance; 1430 Howe Street; Sacramento, CA 95825. Telephone: (916) 920-6383.

> Sincerely,
> /s/ Michael A. Aquino
> Lt. Colonel, Military Intelligence

cc- Major General William F. Ward, Chief of the U.S. Army Reserve
Brigadier General Paul L. Babiak, Commanding General, ARPERCEN
Colonel Joseph V. Rafferty, Commander, Presidio of San Francisco
Lieutenant Colonel Greg Rixon, PAO, Department of the Army
Ms. Irene Rapoza, San Francisco Police Commission
Mr. Bernard Zimmerman, Pillsbury, Madison & Sutro
Mr. Shawn Hanson, Pillsbury, Madison & Sutro
Captain Thomas Hayes, Trial Defense Service, Presidio of San Francisco

Appendix 45: Michael Aquino Answers to CID Questions 1/27/89

I, Lieutenant Colonel Michael A. Aquino, want to make the following statement under oath:

I. CID questions. [CID questions are in *Italics*. My sworn answers are in regular type.]

1. *Please give the dates and addresses when LTC and Mrs. Aquino lived in San Francisco in approximate terms.*

1. 123 Acme Avenue was originally purchased by my grandfather, Dr. Campbell Ford, in 1921, and it was my home from birth in 1946 until 1961, when I moved to Santa Barbara with my father. My mother, Mrs. Betty Ford, inherited the property and resided there until her death in December 1985. When I was commissioned in the Regular Army in 1968, 123 Acme became my legal home of record, although with my military and subsequent civilian assignments I resided in other locations. In September 1980, following completion of my Ph.D. degree in Santa Barbara, Lilith and I moved to 123 Acme and resided there until 20 July 1986, when we moved to Washington, D.C. for my resident attendance at the Industrial College of the Armed Forces. We returned to live at 123 Acme Avenue in early August 1987. We resided there until 1 September 1987, when we returned to St. Louis and I reported to my present assignment.

2. *Specifically, provide the dates when LTC and Mrs. Aquino were in San Francisco between January 1986 and July 1987. The period from May 1, 1986 to August 31, 1986 is particularly critical. 3. If not in San Francisco, please provide the location and a method of verifying the location of LTC and Mrs. Aquino between January 1986 and July 1987.*

2-3. To this date I have not been advised of any specific date or time when, or location where I am alleged to have committed any alleged crime being investigated by the CID. I am advised by Captain Thomas Hayes of the U.S. Army Trial Defense Service that to volunteer the answers to questions #2 and #3 is inappropriate unless the CID informs me of such a specific allegation and the specific date/time/location involved. I will then respond to the best, of my information concerning my location and activities at the specific point in time.

4. *Please have the Aquinos sign a consent for the USA CIDC to obtain their financial records for 1986.*

4. At this time Mrs. Aquino and I do not consent to the CID obtaining our personal financial records, as we would consider it an unwarranted and unnecessary invasion of our personal privacy. If the CID informs me of the specific date/time/location of any specific allegation, I will be willing to provide copies of my financial records for that specific date to the U.S. Army Trial Defense Service, Presidio of San Francisco. The CID will then be welcome to examine those records in the Trial Defense Service office, but not to copy or remove them.

5. *In 1986 did LTC Aquino have any pictures of lions in his home at 123 Acme Avenue, San Francisco?*

5. No. And if the Hickey "therapy" account was of "a bathtub with lion's feet", I do not see why that should be arbitrarily extended or generalized into "pictures of lions in my home".

6. *In 1986 did LTC Aquino have a bathtub with lion's feet in his home at 123 Acme Avenue, San Francisco?*

6. No. The bathtub is a built-in model, flush to the walls and floor, and is modem in style. It was installed at some point prior to 1980 by my mother, who lived in the flat through 1985. The bathtub is shown on camera in the KTVU Channel #2 television documentary *Nightmare at the Presidio*, broadcast 10 April 1988 in San Francisco.

7. *In order to obtain suitable character references to ensure a balanced investigative report, please provide the name, address, and telephone number of LTC Aquino's five closest military friends in 1986.*

7. [Provided.]

8. *Please provide the name, address, and telephone number of LTC Aquino's five closest civilian friends in 1986.*

8. [Provided.]

9. *Provide the names, addresses, and phone numbers of as many witnesses as possible (not more than 10) who have seen the inside of 123 Acme in 1986.*

9. The following individuals saw the flat regularly during January-July 1986: [Provided.]

10a. *On 4 January 1988 Lilith Aquino made a sworn statement to Major Berry that indicated size had lived in Washington, D.C. with her husband from July 1986 until July 1987, when the Aquinos moved to St. Louis for LTC Aquino's assignment to ARPERCEN. The sworn statement also denied that Kinsey [Almond - Adams-Thompson's stepdaughter] was ever at her home or had ever been sexually assaulted by Mrs. Aquino. Mrs. Aquino's statement denied that Mrs. Aquino was separated from LTC Aquino at the post exchange on 12 August 1987 when viewed by Kinsey Adams-Thompson and Kinsey's parents. Mrs. Aquino also denied that she had ever been known as "Shamby". Is Mrs. Aquino's statement true?*

10a. Lilith Aquino's statement is true in all respects.

10b. *Can the Aquinos think of any other possible motive for the Adams-Thompsons to lie other than religious differences?*

10b. There are at least two possible reasons for the Adams-Thompsons to have lied at the time of their initial allegations:

(1) Religious prejudice: It must be remembered that Lawrence Adams-Thompson is not just a Christian layman but an ordained minister who takes his religion much more literally, passionately, and emotionally than the average person who considers himself a Christian. To such an individual as Adams-Thompson, "Satan" represents everything he hates and fears the most, and exists as a literal enemy rather than a merely symbolic one. As the chief official of the world's largest Satanic church, I would accordingly be an automatic object of his antagonism.

As the type of woman who would marry a Christian minister, Michele Adams-Thompson presumably shares this literal, fundamentalist approach to Christianity and religious prejudice against Satan and Satanism. The role of Michele in this affair merits specific investigation:

(a) Apparently Michele accompanied Kinsey to the Debbie Hickey "therapy" sessions in which sex abuse was alleged by Hickey. According to Hickey's notes, it was Michele (not the child or Hickey) who "raised the issue of a Satanic cult" into the "therapy" during the 2 June 1987 session.

(b) Hickey's notes of the 30 June 1987 "therapy" session state that "Kinsey had told her mother that Mikey wears an Army suit just like Daddy, with a stripe on the pants". This appears to be Michele making a statement to Hickey, not a spontaneous, initial comment by the child. This suggests to me that by this date it had already occurred to Michele to try to invent a story to involve the Presidio's well-known Satanist officer and his wife in the Presidio witch-hunt. [Note that "Satanic ritual child abuse" has been a staple accusation - and an inevitably unfounded one - of almost all of the child-care center witch-hunts since McMartin.] Even if the Adams-Thompsons had not seen my wife and myself in the PX in August, it is now apparent that they were planning to make allegations against us anyway, sooner or later, as the witch-hunt continued.

(c)   It is significant that, in the same 30 June 1987 "therapy" session, Hickey (not Michele) asked the child to pick out some officer rank, and the child selected a Chief Warrant Officer 2 insignia. Hickey then asked the child if she could remember a nametag, and the child said there was one with the letters "AK". Not anticipating that Hickey would ask these specific questions, Michele did not coach the child to select a Lieutenant Colonel insignia or to know how to spell my name.

(d)   From Hickey's notes of the "therapy" sessions, the "package" allegation-story does not appear as a single story in any session. Rather, over a 7-month period, a large grab-bag of fantastic, inconsistent, and incoherent stories was amassed. The story that the Adams-Thompsons told to the FBI on 13 August 1987 (FBI Form 302), after seeing my wife and myself in the Presidio PX, appears to have been a composite invented by them at that time to incorporate features from the therapy sessions that were least bizarre, to deliberately omit or change parts of these features which would lessen their credibility, and to invent other "accounts by the child" on their own initiative to reinforce the "package story". [This 13 August 1987 FBI Form 302 is apparently the first time this "package story", which was then given to SFPD Inspector Pamfiloff for his SFPD incident report, appears anywhere.]

For example [assuming that Kinsey Almond made statements as Hickey's notes claim]:

- Kinsey told of being taken on several trips: one to "Gary and Sassy's blue house" (7 April session), one to a "place with a blue swing set" (28 April), one to "Kathy's house" (12 May), one to a "house with real animals" (19 May), one to "Mr. Gary's house" (2 June), and one to a "Dr. Steve's house" (23 June). From this the Adams-Thompsons represented to the FBI and the SFPD only that Kinsey had given a single, believable account of one trip to a specific house.

- Kinsey mentioned several people besides Gary Hambright: "Shamby/Sassy" who has alternately brown (28 April) and "poopoo"-colored (7 April) hair, "Toto" who has green hair (28 April & 12 May), "Kathy" who has blonde hair and works at the day-care center, "Mikey" who wears officer uniform with Chief Warrant Officer 2 rank insignia and has a nametag with "AK" on it (30 June), an unnamed man "with hair on his face" (12 May), "Dr. Steve" (23 June), and another unnamed man wearing a dress (19 May). From this the Adams-Thompsons represented to the FBI and the SFPD only that Kinsey had identified a single couple, "Mikey and Shamby", and that "Mikey" wore a dress. They did not mention any feature of either "Mikey" or "Shamby" which they knew to be inconsistent with the actual appearance of my wife or myself (hair color, rank insignia, nametag letters, etc.). They did not mention that Kinsey had just as "credibly" mentioned someone with green hair.

- Kinsey mentioned several features of the house/houses to which she was supposedly taken: the color is blue (7 April), the house is Kathy's (12 May), the house is Dr. Steve's (23 June), the house has a blue swing set (28 April). Inside are real animals (19 May), dinosaurs that bit people (7 April), a golf book and golf balls (7 April), a Bible with "poopoo on it" and a "bad" cross "that went peepee" (19 May), a bathtub with lion's feet (2 June), a pot hanging from the ceiling with arms and legs hanging out of it (2 June), and that Mr. Gary cut a baby open and that there were 4 brown and black babies (10 August). From this the Adams-Thompsons represented to the FBI and SFPD only that Kinsey had been taken to a house "with a cross on the ceiling and a bathtub with lion's feet". They omitted mention of all the other features. In their story to the FBI and SFPD they evidently invented the following additional features, which to my knowledge do not appear anywhere in the "therapy" notes: hardwood floors, a living room with black walls, and filming Kinsey with a movie camera. [As I have previously noted in my earlier sworn statements, it is ridiculous to suppose that a 2-year-old infant would recognize or recall things like hardwood floors or a movie camera.]

As discussed in the *San Francisco Examiner* series of stories on "child abuse" witchhunts, which appeared just prior to the outbreak of the Presidio witch-hunt, allegations that "Satanic rituals" are involved began with the book *Michelle Remembers* and were sensationally introduced into the McMartin witch-hunt. Thereafter they became a staple of every copycat witch-hunt. Obviously Adams-Thompson saw an opportunity to victimize the Presidio's well-known Satanist officer and his wife in the Presidio witch-hunt when he saw us at the PX, and did so.

(2)   As a means for the Adams-Thompsons to divert attention and suspicion from themselves if either of them had been sexually maltreating the child in any way. David Finkelhor, Associate Director of the Family Violence Research Program at the University of New Hampshire, has written in *Child Sexual Abuse: New Theory & Research* that:

> The background factors most strongly associated with sexual victimization involved characteristics of the child's parents. For example, having a stepfather, one of the strongest risk factors, more than doubled a girl's vulnerability. Virtually half the girls with stepfathers were victimized by someone. Moreover this risk factor remained the strongest correlate of victimization, even when all other variables were statistically controlled.
>
> Victimized girls were much more likely to have mothers who were punitive about sexual matters. These girls warned, scolded, and punished their daughters for asking sex questions, for masturbating, and for looking at sexual pictures much more often than usual. A girl with a sexually punitive mother was 75% more vulnerable to sexual victimization than the "typical" girl in the sample. It was the second most powerful predictor of victimization, after having a stepfather, and was still highly significant when all other variables were controlled.
>
> At certain times in the past, moralists did express concern that children were being sexually abused as a result, in their view, of the liberalization of sexual values. Since they used the issue of child-molesting as a way of campaigning against other kinds of progressive reforms that most social-welfare professionals supported, the professionals tended to discount these alarms. Moreover, in many respects the moralists were mistaken about the problem, since they portrayed the greatest danger to children as coming from strangers and depraved individuals outside the family, not from within the family where, as recently documented, the more serious threat is.

Lawrence Adams-Thompson is the stepfather of Kinsey Almond. His wife Michele's assertive role in the marriage is suggested by her retention of her name "Adams" and the placement of it before Thompson's name, as well as her being the one to regularly give statements to the media rather than her husband. These statistical factors strongly suggest that, if Kinsey Almond has ever actually been sexually abused, the possibility that it was perpetrated within the family should be the initial focus of any investigation.

It is Michele Adams-Thompson who apparently took Kinsey to the Hickey "therapy" sessions, and who brought up the subject of a "Satanic cult" into those sessions (2 June). It is Michele who walked Kinsey past our San Francisco home for the "identification". The account that "Mikey wears an Army suit just like Daddy, with a stripe on the pants" is identified in Hickey's notes not as coming directly from Kinsey to Hickey, but rather as being told to Hickey by Michele. In one session Kinsey said to Hickey, "Don't tell my dad." [Why not?]

After making the allegations, the Adams-Thompsons have several strong reasons to continue to he in support of them:

(3) Reason #1 and possibly reason #2 as discussed above.

(4) Their false accusations have caused intense, extended damage to an innocent officer and his wife. If they now retract these accusations, they would be publicly exposed as having taken advantage of the lynch-mob atmosphere of the Presidio child-care scandal to try to defame and destroy that officer and his wife simply out of religious bigotry and personal maliciousness. Following the original SFPD raid on our home, the Adams-Thompsons had many opportunities to retract and apologize for the false allegations they made if they had any interest in doing so. Despite the abundant facts which immediately came to light showing the allegations to be conspicuously unsubstantiated (such as the completely incorrect description of the interior of our home), the Adams-Thompsons have consistently refused to retract or qualify their allegations in the least. Quite the contrary, Michelle Adams-Thompson has publicly blamed the Army, the FBI, and the SFPD for the fact that there is no evidence we are guilty of anything. In the 2 August 1988 *San Jose Mercury News* she said: "The district attorney's decision not to file charges is certainly not surprising in lieu (sic) of how the authorities have bungled everything else. No one agency has distinguished themselves (sic). It all seemed to be a really sad failure of all agencies to do their jobs properly."

(5) As I believe a thorough investigation will show, it is out of the question that Adams-Thompson made his allegations against my wife and myself "innocently".

(a) Based upon all official and public reports to which I have had access to date, there is a clear record that at no time prior to his 12 August 1987 attack on my wife and myself did Adams-Thompson take any actions which would show that he believed any September-October 1986 double rape/sodomy of his stepdaughter by anyone to have actually happened. [Examples would be taking the child to Letterman Hospital for a related emergency medical examination at that point in time, or SFPDIFBI/CID complaints by him dating to that period.]

(b) As shown in #10.b.(1)(d) above, the story the Adams-Thompsons gave to the FBI and SFPD on 12 August was deliberately and knowingly constructed by them to falsely accuse my wife and myself, and to omit any information which might not support this attack. Even after the raid on our home and the subsequent media publicity given to their fabricated story, the Adams-Thompsons remained silent about the elements of that story they had omitted, invented, and arbitrarily constructed - evidently in order to see my wife and myself further mauled in the press, with the resultant vandalism, death-threats, and legal difficulties with the SFPD which this entailed - to say nothing of the present CID investigation and the continuing disruption it has caused to our lives. [Mrs. Aquino and I have now been living in a continuous state of "criminal investigation" - and the consequent and relentless media intrusion into our personal lives - for over 1-1/2 years.]

The conclusion necessarily to be drawn from this is that Adams-Thompson definitely knew his allegations were false when he made them on 12 August 1987. This specific knowledge on his part is the essence of the court-martial charges I have preferred against him. Obviously he now has every possible reason to lie in support of the allegations he made, to keep from being court-martialed for his deliberately and intentionally malicious act.

(6) Religious prejudice in the Army is a violation of law. A confirmed religious discriminatory act by a commissioned officer would subject him to disciplinary action and possibly the loss of his commission. An act of sufficient harm to an innocent party might additionally subject him to prosecution. [This is again the basis for the UCMJ charges which I have preferred against Adams-Thompson.]

(7) I understand that Adams-Thompson was one of the original instigators of the entire Presidio child-care scandal. That witch-hunt has now caused serious harm to the individuals falsely accused during it, confusion and fear to many Presidio parents, psychological damage to many infant children who have been subjected to exhaustive questioning on revolting subjects and to "therapy" conditioning in lurid sexual fantasies, extensive disruption to the entire Presidio community, and the enormous expenditure of time, manpower, and funds by the FBI, the San Francisco Police Department, and the CID. If after all of this a human sacrifice cannot be found to justify the witch-hunt, the inevitable conclusion will be that it was all a fraud from the very beginning - simply the latest outbreak in the national epidemic of "day-care sex-abuse" witch-hunts which has swept the country during the last several years. That would change the public images of all of the witch-hunt leaders from crusaders and martyrs to callous, vindictive opportunists. The blame might well be concentrated on whoever started the hysteria in the first place. If Adams-Thompson is indeed the chaplain who originally advised the Tobins to make their original allegation, that blame might fail ultimately on him.

(8) I understand that 22 Presidio families - including the Adams-Thompsons -have filed $66 million in damage claims against the U.S. Army for alleged harm to their children at the day-care center. If any of these claims are granted, the parents may also be able to file additional monetary claims under California law. Obviously if the entire scandal is exposed as a fraud, with no evidence other than coached "therapy" by professional "molestation-finders" that anything ever happened to the children, the claims will be unsupported and no one, including the Adams-Thompsons, will get a cent.

On 15 March 1988 a $1.5 million claim against the government was filed, apparently by Adams-Thompson, as follows:

> [Name deleted in FOIA document] was sexually molested by Gary Hambright, Michael Aquino, Lilith Aquino, and others who have yet to be identified, while in the care and custody of the Presidio Child Development Center. The molestation took place at 123 Acme Avenue, San Francisco and probably at the Child Development Center and possibly elsewhere.

In addition to deliberately and knowingly telling a false "package story" to the FBI and SFPD, therefore, Adams-Thompson has filed a fraudulent claim against the government knowing that his allegations were merely fabricated by himself and his wife. This is therefore a deliberate attempt on his part to defraud the government.

l0c. *Do the Aquinos know of anyone who has ever heard Adams-Thompson denounce or criticize the Temple of Set?*

l0c. We neither traveled in his social circles nor made any inquiries about him while I was assigned to the Presidio. If he made any defamatory statements against ourselves or our religion, he would have had to be very circumspect about doing so. It is against Army Regulations for a chaplain to denounce a legitimate church. DA Training Circular 16-24, 9 June 1978, states:

> The commander is responsible for the religious life of the command, which includes meeting the religious needs of military personnel, their dependents, authorized civilians, and retired

personnel and their dependents. The staff officer responsible to the commander for seeing that this is accomplished is the chaplain.

Less familiar religions are included within this responsibility. The facilities provided by the commander should be made available to all religious groups for use as needed. Normal participation gives priority in scheduling to General Protestant and Catholic services. Other religious groups are accommodated in a cooperative manner so as to best meet the needs of all.

The chaplain can neither be required to perform any task which conflicts with the requirements of his/her own religious denomination, nor to participate in or conduct a service in conflict with his/her beliefs. However, the recognition of religious needs of others and the effort to meet these needs in terms of facilities, personnel, and planning is a responsibility of the chaplain. The Temple of Set is one such Satanic church specifically identified [as the "Congregation of Set"] in DA Pamphlet 165-13, *Religious Requirements and Practices of Certain Selected Groups: A Handbook for Chaplains*, April 1978. This has put Christian chaplains in a very awkward position. Satan and Satanism stand for everything they consider most intolerable, yet they are required by the Army to tolerate and even assist legitimate Satanic soldiers in practicing their faith.

In theory this means that Satanist soldiers could request the use of a post chapel for a Satanic Mass and expect help from the Christian chaplains in scheduling and decorating the facilities properly and in advertising the ceremony to the post community. In practice, appreciating the commotion this would create, the Temple of Set and Church of Satan have never made such requests, but as a diplomatic courtesy have advised their military members to conduct their meetings and services in private facilities.

The point here is that Adams-Thompson's entire religious profession, which he necessarily considers as taking precedence over his military one, is dedicated to denouncing and criticizing Satan and Satanism - and to destroying them if possible. It is virtually impossible for him to teach a Bible class, preach a sermon, or teach Sunday school without denouncing and criticizing the Devil in one way or another.

This is a social situation in which Christian priests and ministers, trained and accustomed to use the Devil as an acceptable object of hatred, have recently been forced by Army Regulations and United States law to tolerate Satanism as a religion of equal legitimacy and social respectability. Most chaplains have endeavored to adjust to this requirement gracefully and professionally. Adams-Thompson is obviously one of those who hasn't.

11. Does LTC or Mrs. Aquino know of any person who would say that CPT or Mrs. Adams-Thompson had a bad reputation for truthfulness or give an opinion that the Adams-Thompsons were untruthful?

11. There are many people who are sufficiently well-acquainted with my wife and myself to know that the Adams-Thompsons have lied flagrantly and persistently in their accusation against us. I have no knowledge of his or his wife's having a reputation for lying prior to this. I have, however, not had any previous social contact with them, traveled in social circles where they were discussed, nor had their previous history investigated.

The day after we learned from the SFPD report that Adams-Thompson had made the accusation that resulted in the raid on our San Francisco home, my wife and I called upon the Deputy Presidio Commander Colonel D. Peter Gleichenhaus (currently Inspector General, Headquarters, Sixth U.S. Army) to express our shock and anger. I recall that during that meeting Colonel Gleichenhaus mentioned that the Adams-Thompsons had a turbulent personal history at the Presidio, but I cannot remember specifics. You may wish to ask Colonel Gleichenhaus about their background.

12. In a letter dated 27 August 1987 to CPT Adams-Thompson, copy furnished to investigators and to the Commander, Presidio of San Francisco, LTC Aquino stated that the home at 123 Acme was closed up. Is this true? Was someone else using the home who could have brought children into the home without the knowledge of the Aquinos? Could you discuss whether it is possible that someone could have used 123 Acme to sexually/ritualistically abuse children in the absence of the Aquinos?

12.   As noted previously, 123 Acme is my wife's and my legal home of record. We keep it fully furnished, with all the utilities on, and leave the bulk of our belongings there. As assigned elsewhere by the Army, we rent a local apartment, but plan to travel back to our San Francisco home occasionally during the year for vacationing and business.

123 Acme is a building with one top flat (ours) and three smaller downstairs apartments which are rented out. When we moved to Washington in July 1986, we locked up the top flat. Prior to departing for such an extended period, we had extra security features added, such as a solid-core, deadbolted back door (similar to the front one) and a security alarm system installed by National Guardian Alarm and centrally monitored by them on a 24-hour basis from their San Francisco office. Any unauthorized entry into the flat would have triggered the monitoring service, resulting in a call to the police and our immediate notification. There have been no unauthorized entries since the system was installed.

Mr. William Butch (Lt. Commander U.S. Navy Reserve), Lilith's brother, and a lieutenant in a commercial security service in San Francisco) lived in one of the 123 apartments following our departure for Washington. After we departed for Washington, D.C. he supervised the building for us. He was given the key to the upstairs flat and the combination to the security system in case of an emergency.

From June 1986 until early January 1987, contractor Graham Marshall painted the entire exterior of the 121-123 building complex. It took a long time because he worked singlehandedly for the most part. Because he spent much time on ladders, scaffolding, and "bosun's chairs" on the roof and over the sides of the building, Mr. Butch habitually switched the upstairs flat alarm system off every morning [and on every night] to prevent Marshall's noise and impacts from setting off false alarms. [The system includes sound and vibration sensors.] The flat remained deadbolted. Marshall did not have access to the interior after July 1986.

There is no reason to suppose that any of the three lower apartments was used for sexual molestation or any other criminal purpose. Mr. Butch monitored the building and its other tenants as necessary. They were respectable individuals who caused no problems or disturbances during their lease periods. None of the apartments has any of the features alleged by Adams-Thompson (such as lion's-footed bathtubs, etc.). None of the other tenants had access to our flat.

[This question returns again to 123 Acme as though there is probable cause to think that these premises were involved in a crime. I accordingly wish to point out **again** that the alleged "description" which Adams-Thompson invented was completely inaccurate, and that there is no supporting evidence whatever that any crime involving anyone took place there. The inaccuracy of the alleged "description" shows clearly that it was merely fabricated by Adams-Thompson.]

13a.   *On 4 January 1988 LTC Aquino made a five-page sworn statement to MAJ Berry as support for the charges that were sworn by LTC Aquino. LTC Aquino denied that Kinsey Almond -Adams Thompson's stepdaughter] was ever at his home or had ever been sexually assaulted by him. LTC Aquino also denied that he had ever been known as "Mikey". Are these statements true? Is the following statement true (from 4 January 1988 sworn statement):*

> *7. I have never had anything to do with either Kinsey M. Almond (Chaplain Adams-Thompson's stepdaughter) or any other child involved with the Presidio daycare center. I have never molested any child in my life. I have never used or been known by the nickname "Mikey".*

13a.   All of these statements are completely, absolutely, and wholly true. I hereby swear to them again: I have **never** met Kinsey Almond/Adams-Thompson at **any** location at **any** time. I have **never** molested any child at the Presidio or off the Presidio, nor taken any Presidio day-care child **anywhere**, nor arranged for any such child to be taken **anywhere** for any purpose whatever, molestation or otherwise. My entire life history attests to my integrity and decency, and there is **no** principle in my religion which tolerates or advocates any harm to children or any abuse of them sexually.

Throughout my childhood I was nicknamed "Archy" by my parents (to distinguish me from my father, whose first name is also "Michael"). "Archy Ford-Aquino" is the name on my 1960 grammar-school graduation records at the Town School for Boys, 2750 Jackson Street, San Francisco. Since 1961 I have gone by my legal name of "Michael", and personal friends call me that. In the Army, where nicknames are virtually mandatory, I am called "Mike". No one has ever called me "Mikey". [I understand that the phrase "Mikey likes it" received considerable television and popular exposure in the last year or so, and that may be where this name was picked out.]

I further state that my wife Lilith Aquino has never used nor been called by the name "Shamby" [or "Sassy"], and I have known her since 1972. Her original name was Patricia, and she is usually called "Pat" by her parents. She chose the name of "Lilith" for herself in 1970, and made it her legal name in approximately 1974.

13b. [Is the following statement true]:

> *11. Adams-Thompson's statement that my wife did not appear until later in the PX parking lot is false, since at no time was she separated from me during our shopping trip.*

13b.

(1)   This statement is absolutely true. On that day we parked our car under the elevated approach to the Golden Gate Bridge, as we were always accustomed to parking there when going to the PX. There is less congestion there, and more spaces closer to the PX entrance are usually available. This was of all the more interest to us on 12 August 1987, as we were going to the PX specifically to purchase a microwave oven as a present for Lilith's daughter. Microwave ovens are heavy, and I didn't want to carry one any farther than necessary. At that time the microwave ovens in the PX were displayed in the front of the store a short distance back from the ID card-checking station. We went directly to the display and picked out an oven. A PX clerk brought that model from the stock in the back, and we took it to the check-out counter for purchasing. Then I carried the oven out to our car while Lilith walked immediately in front of me to clear the way and open the car-trunk when we got there. There were three glass doors that she had to open for me: one out of the PX itself, one into the PX "mall" area, and one out of the "mall" towards the bridge-approach parking lot. It would have been extremely difficult for me to get through those three sets of doors without her opening them for me.

Nor is there any reason why Lilith should have waited in the car while I went in alone to buy the oven. She is the cook in the family and knew what she was looking for in microwave features. And it was a present for her daughter, so she wanted to pick it out personally. And, since we had parked close by under the bridge approach, there is no way that she could have moved the car any closer to the mall doors for me.

(2)   Evidently Chaplain Adams-Thompson gave two different versions of this story, one to the FBI (contained in the FBI Form 302, 13 August 1987) and one to the SFPD (SFPD Incident Report) on the same day.

(a)   In his FBI version he said that I "made eye contact with Kinsey" in the PX. [I did not, and would not have recognized her if I had.] In his SFPD version he said only that the child saw me.

(b) In his FBI version he said that he and Kinsey saw my wife and myself together in the PX. In the SFPD version he said that he and Kinsey saw only me in the PX, and that my wife did not appear until later in the parking lot.

(c) In his FBI version he said that he "went to the car to wait for us, and saw them, and took the license number". In his SFPD version he said that he and Michele drove around to our car, where Kinsey supposedly identified my wife as "Shamby". And -

- As Adams-Thompson already knew who I was, it wouldn't have been necessary for him to take my car license number. There is no mention of the car or the license number in the SFPD report.

- The PX has two parking lots, one in front and one on the other side of the mall, under the bridge approach. How would Adams-Thompson have known in which lot to "wait for us"? If he and Michele drove around to the bridge-approach lot from the main lot after seeing us go through the mall, they wouldn't have had time to get there [for the supposed Kinsey "identification" of Lilith] before we drove away. It is a long drive around from the main PX lot to the bridge-approach parking area.

- If Adams-Thompson went to the vicinity of our car to wait for us, how would he have known which one it was? [It was not the car I had driven while assigned to the Presidio, but a rental car.]

(3) Adams-Thompson's account of the PX encounter is thus full of lies and inconsistencies. He even told two different versions of the story to the FBI and SFPD on the same day. Again this supports my contention that the "identification" details of the PX encounter were deliberately and maliciously invented by Adams-Thompson to support the attack which he and Michele had **already** decided [as is evident from the Hickey notes] to make on my wife and myself. While it is evident that Adams-Thompson himself saw us at the PX, no other item in either the version he told to the FBI or the version he told to the SFPD can be verified - including the presence of Kinsey Almond. The discrepancies between the two versions suggest that he saw us at the PX, then invented the "reaction" and "statements" by his stepdaughter.

14. *Although LTC Aquino has previously responded to this question in general terms, please again state whether LTC Aquino is aware of any parents or children related to the Presidio Child Development Center that have ever been in 123 Acme. I certainly recognize that if a parent (of a child that was in the CDC) viewed the inside of 123 Acme under innocent circumstances (for example at a party), then communicated specific information to their child, this information could potentially cause erroneous conclusions to be drawn by investigators.*

14.

a. No parents or children related to the child-care center have ever been in 123 Acme. My wife and I are private persons and did not socialize with other Presidio families except at garrison social functions such as military balls and "Hail and Farewells" at the officers club, post commander's home, etc. We never held any parties or receptions for Presidio personnel at our home at any time during my Presidio assignment from 1981 to 1986.

b. On 14 August 1987 San Francisco Police officer Glenn Pamfiloff, accompanied by other SFPD officers, FBI agents, and two CID agents, executed a search warrant on 123 Acme from 9PM to 1AM. A photographer accompanied the search and photographed every room and many individual articles in the entire residence. Photos of myself and my wife were also taken, and several photo albums of personal family and church photographs were confiscated. [All but a few photos have since been returned.] Almost certainly the photos taken by the photographer, together with some of those confiscated, were subsequently used in FBI/SFPD/CII) interrogation of Kinsey Almond [at which time Lawrence & Michele Adams-Thompson would also have seen them], the other Presidio children, parents, and/or "therapists" who were indoctrinating the children.

c. In the *San Francisco Chronicle*, 2 August 1988, Edward Lempinen wrote:

> There were apparent inconsistencies in [Kinsey Almond's] description, and nothing in the evidence or in interviews with at least 26 other young Presidio children "fully corroborated" the girl's account, Deputy District Attorney Michael Williams said.
> And although some children saw Aquino on TV and told their parents he was a "bad man", Williams said, none could pick him out of a police photo lineup.

This story verifies that the police photographs and other family and church photographs taken from our home were shown to Kinsey Almond, at least 26 other Presidio children, and presumably parents and "therapists" involved following 14 August 1987. I am quite certain you will find no accurate, detailed descriptions of our home whatever from children, parents, or "therapists" that predate 14 August 1987. [This news story also verifies that some of the children had been taught to call me a "bad man" during the months following the attack by Adams-Thompson. If this specific term was indeed used by more than one child, it is obvious that it was suggested to them by an interrogator or "therapist" - or simply picked up from one of the several television news reports that quoted this specific term from the Adams-Thompson allegations quoted in the original San Francisco Police incident report.]

d. On 10 April 1988 KTVU Channel #2 television broadcast a highly pre-publicized news special in prime-time entitled *Nightmare at the Presidio*. As it was a detailed documentary of the entire Presidio scandal, I am certain that it was viewed by virtually everyone in the Presidio community and probably most of the bay area as well. Included in that documentary were extensive camera interviews with my wife and myself at 123 Acme, and a TV camera tour of the flat. Any child, parent, or "therapist" description of the premises after 10 April would be the result of this film, if not the result of the previous raid photographs.

e. I myself have been described in, interviewed in, and photographed in the public media throughout my entire life, and more sensationally since I joined the Church of Satan in 1969 and then founded the Temple of Set in 1975. Within the Army, despite my efforts to avoid sensationalism, the controversial "officer/ Devil-worshipper" was inevitably an item of curiosity and gossip. After the press learned of Adams-Thompson's accusations, of course, media attention focused on the Temple of Set, my wife, and myself has been aggressive and continuous. Several books have been published this past year, among them Arthur Lyons' *Satan Wants You* with a photograph of my wife and myself at 123 Acme. In 1985 a documentary book by Nevill Drury, *The Occult Experience*, featured a chapter on the Temple of Set, an interview with Lilith and myself, and a photograph of ourselves at 123 Acme. A documentary film by the same title was released to educational television in October 1985, and featured an extensive interview with Lilith and myself at 123 Acme. This film was subsequently released as a commercial videotape and may presumably be rented from San Francisco video shops.

f. Beginning 29 October 1987, immediately after the Adams-Thompson story broke in the media, San Francisco TV channels #2 and #5 broadcast several evening news segments containing interviews with Lilith and myself, photos of 123 Acme, identification of its address, and discussions of the raid (including our black-walled bedroom) and the details of the Adams-Thompson allegations (including the "Mikey and Shamby" names).

g. On 24 November 1987 San Francisco Channel #2 broadcast an extensive news segment reading the Adams-Thompson allegations in detail from the SFPD report, again showing the exterior of 123 Acme, discussing our black-walled bedroom, and including interviews with Lilith and myself.

h. Since the Adams-Thompson attack Lilith and I have also been interviewed on the *Oprah Winfrey Show* (first broadcast 17 February 1988 and later re-broadcast), the highly-publicized Geraldo Rivera "Satanism" special on 25 October 1988, and many local television news and talk-show episodes.

i. In addition to the above television exposure of ourselves, our home, and the Adams-Thompson allegations in detail, there has been continuing and extensive coverage (including photographs of Lilith and myself) in the printed media, to include all bay area newspapers and national printed media such as *Newsweek*.

j. In summary it would have been easy for any interested person to describe the interior of our home and our own appearance, and to show broadcast TV-videotapes and photographs of this to children, following the initial SFPD raid on our home on 14 August 1987. Prior to that date it would have been possible to describe the general appearance of our home and ourselves by viewing the 1985 educational TV *Occult Experience* commercial videotape, or reading the accompanying book, or by talking with any one of our personal friends who had visited our rather exotic home.

15. *Does LTC or Mrs. Aquino have any connection with Gary Hambright, or any other 1986-1987 employee of the Presidio CDC?*

15. Neither my wife nor I have ever met Gary Hambright or any other employee of the Presidio day-care center, nor contacted them in any other way. We have never paid any money to anyone with any connection to the day-care center for any reason whatever. We have never set foot in the day-care center. We have never called it on the telephone, while I was assigned to the Presidio or before or subsequent to that assignment. We were not involved in any community programs at the Presidio which would have brought either of us into any contact with children.

16. *Did anyone use [the Aquino flat at] 123 Acme for conducting any kind of ritual between the hours of 0800 and 1700 in 1986 or 1987, while LTC Aquino was absent?*

16.

a. No. Nor does the interior of that flat contain a ceremonial chamber.

b. Religious ceremonies of the Temple of Set and the Church of Satan are customarily held in the evening. In my 20 years as a Satanist I do not ever recall having attended or even heard of any ceremony that was conducted during 8-5 "business hours".

c. When and where the Temple of Set may conduct rituals is ultimately irrelevant and immaterial. As has been previously, repeatedly, and exhaustively established, **none** of its rituals involve the abuse of children in any way, sexual or otherwise. I refuse to allow religious ceremonies conducted by the Temple of Set as part of its worship activities to be interpreted in any way as symptomatic of criminal activity. They have always been completely legitimate, and a right of our church under the Constitution, and we fully intend to continue them free from intimidation.

II. Concerning paragraph 4, page 1 of Captain Mark W. Harvey's 14 December 1988 letter to Mr. Shawn Hanson [containing the above questions]:

Before any questions are answered, allow me to inform you that LTC Aquino is suspected of a number of offenses relating to removal of children from the Presidio Child Development Center (CDC) in 1986 or early 1987 without the lawful authorization of their parents (kidnapping); then subsequently sexually assaulting these children with Mr. Gary Hambright and/or other unknown persons(s) (sodomy, rape, indecent assault on a child, conspiracy); then subsequently lying in sworn statements about these actions (false sworn statement); and preparing a false charge sheet against CPT Adams-Thompson (deliberate violation of a procedural rule); all in violation of various articles of the Uniform Code of Military Justice (UCMJ).

1. I have never removed or arranged to be removed from the Presidio day-care center any child for any purpose whatever, with or without parental knowledge or consent.

2. I have never sexually assaulted any child at any time anywhere. I have never assaulted, sodomized, or raped anyone of any age or sex nor participated in any agreement, arrangement, or conspiracy for anyone else to commit any of these crimes.

3. I have never met nor had any contact with Mr. Gary Hambright whatever.

4. I stand by all statements made in my sworn statements of 4 January 1988 and 23 August 1988 and reaffirm them to be the truth in every detail to the best of my knowledge.

5. Because of evidence which I obtained pursuant to my 23 June 1988 Freedom of Information Act request to the Staff Judge Advocate of the 25th Infantry Division, I concluded that, despite the facts described in paragraphs #15-17 in my 4 January 1988 statement, Adams-Thompson's responsibility for the obscene card mailed to me could not be established beyond reasonable doubt. Accordingly, in my letter to Major General Charles P. Otstott, Commanding General of the 25th Division on 23 August 1988, accompanying my 23 August sworn statement, I requested that Specification #2 of the charges against Adams-Thompson be dropped.

6. I am aware of no information or facts which cause me to alter my opinion that Specification #1 of the charges was properly and deservedly made, for the reasons given in my two sworn statements, particularly the updated 23 August 1988 one. I believe that statement to represent the truth, not just concerning Adams-Thompson's deliberately malicious and knowingly false attack upon my wife and myself, but concerning the nature of the entire Presidio childcare scandal. The contents of the Hickey notes, as related to me by Captain Hayes on 23 and 24 January 1989, further substantiate Lawrence and Michelle Adams-Thompson's deliberate and knowing fabrication of their "package story" to the FBI and SFPD. Thus I feel that it is not only probable but indeed conclusively demonstrated that Lawrence Adams-Thompson is guilty of Specification #1 of a violation of UCMJ Article #133 as I have charged.

7. While I have had no access to any records of the general Presidio investigation that have not been reported in the media, I have examined all media coverage of the scandal exhaustively since my wife and I were suddenly dragged into it. I have made extensive studies of the "child-abuse industry" epidemic of manufactured "day-care molestation" scandals across the nation. I am aware of and have several files on various religious hate-groups who are actively and aggressively trying to portray legitimate Satanists as child murderers or molesters in order to terrorize them and their families & children, and to persecute their religion out of existence. I consider the entire Presidio scandal to be just one more manufactured witch-hunt in this deplorable national epidemic, motivated by religious bigotry, financial greed, and petty ambitions for media attention by tile instigators,(and capitalizing upon the ignorance, confusion, and hysteria of parents who are unaware of this disgusting "industry".

8. The notes of Debbie Hickey, as related to me, are an appalling and atrocious abuse of the concept of "child therapy" - simply the same perverted, sex-obsessed indoctrination of day-care infants which has characterized all the other witch-hunts in this disgraceful national epidemic. If you will review the chart of "Similar Tales" contained in the *Memphis Commercial Appeal* series on the national "child-abuse industry" epidemic (Attachment #A to my sworn statement of 23 August 1988), you will see that virtually every "discovery" made by Hickey is merely a standard "therapist" indoctrination-theme for these witch-hunts - including all the features of her "play therapy" sessions with Kinsey Almond. This is not reputable psychiatry; it is unprofessional and deliberate fraud. I recommend that the CID submit all of Hickey's notes and records from the Presidio scare to Dr. Lee Coleman of the Center for the Study of Psychiatric

Testimony, Berkeley, California for a professional evaluation of their ethical and professional substance. That nothing more than Hickey's "play therapy" notes should be the "evidence" for the Presidio investigations is a flagrant malpractice of medicine, as with the similarly-twisted "therapy" which has fueled all of the other witch-hunts. Certainly there has been sufficient exposure of this malpractice for the Army to recognize it and refuse to tolerate its further infliction and exploitation. A person like Hickey should not be practicing psychiatry in the Army - nor for that matter in civilian society. To the extent that Hickey was aware of the "package story" which Adams-Thompson told the FBI and SFPD, and which he falsely attributed as a single, coherent story to her "play therapy" sessions with Almond, Hickey - by failing to come forward with the truth - has acted to obstruct justice and conspire against two innocent people.

9.   I don't think that the U.S. Army should pay one cent on the $66 million damage claims advanced by parents for crimes that never occurred.

10. Mrs. Aquino and I believe that the United States Army should not allow Chaplain Lawrence Adams-Thompson to escape responsibility for the extensive and excruciating damage he has willfully and maliciously caused to an innocent officer and his wife. We consider him unfit to be an Army officer or a member of the Corps of Chaplains. I formally request that the CID, on the basis of the facts now known to its investigators and discussed herein, recommend that Chaplain Adams-Thompson be court-martialed on Specification #1 of the court-martial charges I preferred against him on 4 January 1988, and additionally on a charge of a deliberate attempt to defraud the government of $1.5 million with a false claim for damages.

Affidavit

I, Lieutenant Colonel Michael A. Aquino, have read or have had read to me this statement which begins on page 1 and ends on page 18. I fully understand the contents of the entire statement made by me. The statement is true. I have initialed all corrections and have initialed the bottom of each page containing the statement. I have made this statement freely without hope of benefit or reward, without threat of punishment, and without coercion, unlawful influence, or unlawful inducement.

/s/ Michael A. Aquino

Subscribed and sworn to before me, a person authorized by law to administer oaths, this 27th day of January 1989.

Witnesses:
Major Gary M. Profit
Terry S. Swift
Michael O. Ogdon
HHC ARPERCEN
9700 Page Boulevard, St. Louis, MO 63132

Authority to Administer Oaths: AR 600-11

Appendix 46: Letter, Captain Thomas Hayes to Major General Eugene Cromartie 2/17/89

Department of the Army
US Army Trial Defense Service
Presidio Field Office
Presidio of San Francisco, California 94129

AFKC-ZM-JA-TDS (27-10)   17 February 1989

MEMORANDUM THRU

Command Judge Advocate, Headquarters 6th Region, Criminal Investigation Division Command, Presidio of San Francisco, California 94129

Commander, Headquarters, 6th Region, Criminal Investigation Division Command, Presidio of San Francisco, California 94129

FOR: Commander, Criminal Investigation Division Command, Washington, D.C.

SUBJECT: Status of CIDC Investigation Against LTC Michael A. Aquino

1. I write in my capacity as defense counsel to inquire concerning the status of the CIDC investigation of my client, LTC Michael Aquino. During my last conversation with the case agent I was told that the investigation may continue for another six months. I must express a sense of frustration with the pace at which the investigation is continuing and what appears to be a refusal to recognize some obvious facts that establish LTC Aquino's innocence.

2. The San Francisco Police Department search of my client's home took place in the Fall of 1987. Since that time, both the SFPD and the FBI have delved into LTC and Mrs. Aquino's background and have decided to close their investigations. I understand that CIDC representatives accompanied the SFPD on the search and assisted them to some extent in conducting their investigation. Then, after a period of 18 months has elapsed, the CIDC has opened an independent file and told the news media that LTC Aquino has been "titled." The public affairs officer went on to further define that term as being close to an "indictment." All these actions took place after LTC Aquino appeared on the "Geraldo" special concerning "satanic crime."

3. All of LTC Aquino's requests for access to the information upon which these allegations are based have been denied. He has been torn apart in the press, has borne tremendous expense for legal defense in attempting to regain possession of his personal belongings, has suffered damage to his career, and has received phone threats arising from these investigations. He has cooperated with all reasonable requests for information in an attempt to speed up the investigation process so that his name can be cleared.

4. Given the damage that both LTC Aquino and the families of the children that were apparently injured by Gary Hambright have suffered and continue to suffer, the speed with which the investigation is proceeding is too slow. To suggest that this matter will continue for another six months in the investigation stage is too much for all to bear. I can assure you that the Aquinos realize the need for thoroughness in gathering information, and they are willing to assist in every reasonable way. However I have begun to question the efforts of the CIDC to gain the cooperation of the agencies that have already examined this case to their satisfaction, namely the SFPD and the FBI. I would like to know if the CIDC has reviewed those case files and, if so, why is this investigation taking so long?

5. My second area of concern is the apparent refusal of the CIDC to evaluate key records and address their impact on the case. My review of some of the records made during the counseling sessions between LTC Hickey and the Adams-Thompson child causes me to question the basis for the entire investigation. After the child

recounted many bizarre stories during the period of February through June of 1987 of people with green hair and pots containing arms and legs, it was her mother that suggested that there may be some connection with "satanic worship". It was also her mother that first made mention of the child having told of a man in uniform with a name tag containing the letter "A". Where is the   medical evidence of trauma? Surely a child who had experienced the sodomous horrors described would suffer some injury. Unless of course these stories were planted in the child's psyche through parental suggestion.

6. This information from the counseling notes differs from the SFPD report filed by Investigator Pamfiloff wherein he recounted the child's father stating that the child had given this information directly to LTC Hickey during March or April. These may appear to be minor differences, yet they must be investigated by the CIDC because they provide evidence of a possible "set-up" orchestrated by the Adams-Thompsons. This would not be an extraordinary event given that the common, uninformed perception of LTC Aquino's religion is that he is a "devil worshiper" and CPT Adams-Thompson's duties as a Christian chaplain would set him against such activity.

7. I have enclosed a copy of a tape recording made by LTC Aquino last week during an interview with a news reporter from station WSVN in Miami, Florida. In the tape of the television interview, LTC   Aquino explained some of the precepts of his religion that provide a more informed view of his beliefs than are commonly perceived. You should find the tape helpful in dispelling some of the myths of him as a "devil worshiper". He utterly rejects any and all acts of violence or abuse towards any person. His attempts to clarify his religious beliefs and defend his name on television throughout this investigation attest to his bravery and innocence. We must all ask ourselves if we would have the courage to stand up for our right to the free exercise of our religion in the face of such adversity. As LTC Aquino so aptly points out, we tend to criticize the Jews in Nazi Germany for failing to speak out when they too were accused of participating in "blood sacrifice" and the torture of children. While there may be criminals in our society who abuse children and others, calling it part of their religious practices, LTC and Mrs. Aquino are not among them. I would hope that the CIDC has tried to determine whether Mr. Gary Hambright was.

8. LTC Aquino preferred charges against Chaplain Adams-Thompson for   making false statements against him. These charges were said to have been investigated by the San Francisco CIDC Field Office. When LTC Aquino asked to see that portion of the file pertaining to the charges he had preferred, his FOIA request was denied. I appeal that decision to you as the CIDC Commander and again request that LTC Aquino be provided that portion of the file so that he can be assured that his allegations were taken and investigated seriously.

9. As my client has stated repeatedly, he is willing and ready to assist the CIDC in any reasonable way. He merely requests that he be given some specific dates or reasonable time frame during which he is supposed to have abused the Adams-Thompson or any other child. He will examine his records to account for his location on that date. It is hard to believe that the families making these allegations could not provide some detail as to when their children were in the care of the Child Care Center, or that the facility would not have maintained some attendance records.

10. I request that my client be provided with some accounting of the delay in moving this investigation forward. Second, I request that you grant his appeal to the CIDC's rejection of his FOIA request for that portion of the file relating to his charges against CPT Adams-Thompson. Finally, the case agents must take notice of some of the obvious facts establishing LTC Aquino's innocence and provide him the chance to rebut specific allegations rather than the broad innuendo that has surfaced to date. Thank you for considering my client's position. We trust that the CIDC will keep the interests of justice to all at the forefront of this matter.

/s/ Thomas M. Hayes III
Captain, Judge Advocate
Senior Defense Counsel

Appendix 47: Letter, Michael Aquino to Major General Eugene Cromartie 3/6/89

Major General Eugene L. Cromartie
Commanding General, U.S. Army Criminal Investigation Command

March 6, 1989

Dear General Cromartie:

I have received a copy of Captain Thomas Hayes' 17 February 1989 letter to you, and would like to add some comments of my own.

I was first notified of this new CID investigation in late November 1988, when Special Agent Stephen Penaluna telephoned me about it from the San Francisco Field Office. I could not believe that anyone could still take Chaplain Adams-Thompson's lies seriously -much less consider them "probable cause" for opening yet a third formal criminal investigation based on them. I asked to speak with the person responsible for making the decision to open this investigation.

Penaluna passed me to Special Agent Robert Birck, who stated to me that he and he alone was responsible for making the decision. He went on to say that the CID had always intended to make this special investigation of the Adams-Thompson allegation as part of its more general investigation of the entire Presidio scandal, and that the CID had only now gotten around to it [over a year after the allegation was made!]. In answer to my specific question, he denied absolutely that this new investigation of me was the result of my appearance on Geraldo Rivera's October 25, 1988 "Satanism" television show. I took Birck at his word that the CID simply needed to "clear its books" of the matter.

I was subsequently informed by Captain Thomas Hayes, the U.S. Army Trial Defense Service attorney assigned to advise me, that the CID's data-base on the Adams-Thompson allegations was in a state of utter disarray. On January 1, 1989, accordingly, I took the initiative to provide the CID with a complete set of all of the relevant information I possessed concerning the affair, to include the San Francisco Police Department's investigation based on the Adams-Thompson allegation.

Major Mark W. Harvey, CID 6th Region Judge Advocate, further invited me to suggest any leads which the CID could follow in order to verify my wife's and my innocence. Accordingly on January 5, 1989 I provided him with a 9-page list of 34 leads, discussed in depth, any of whose resolution would all the more expose and validate the truth of the situation.[205]

I further offered to provide written answers to any pertinent questions which the CID might have for me. On December 14, 1988 the CID sent me a list of 16 questions, to which I responded on January 27, 1989 in considerable detail in the form of a sworn statement with accompanying supporting data.[206] Although I made it clear that I would respond to any additional pertinent questions which the CID might have, none have been forthcoming.

The investigation concerning me remained open. Two weeks ago Captain Hayes inquired of Special Agent Birck the reason for the delay, and how much longer the investigation was expected to continue. Birck responded that, while the CID recognized the absurdity of the "therapy" notes which Adams-Thompson invoked as the source of his allegation, "other leads" were now being followed, and that this could take as long as six additional months beyond the three already spent by the CID - to say nothing of the year-long investigations preceding it.

---

[205] Appendix #44.

[206] Appendix #45.

While the CID has not informed me of any specific allegation other than that by Adams-Thompson, I am in the position to know one thing conclusively: that neither my wife nor I has ever had anything to do with any of the Presidio day-care children, nor has either of us ever molested any child. Therefore there **cannot** be any "leads" which are anything beyond unsubstantiated accusations by the therapist who is trying to cover up the damage her incompetence has caused to two innocent people, and/or by parents who have coached children into "recognitions" following the massive national media exposure given me as a consequence of Adams-Thompson's original attack, in order to try to collect on $66 million of claims against the government for "molestation" of their children at the Presidio.

When Captain Hayes advised me of Birck's statement, I telephoned Birck myself to ask him exactly what the problem was. He said that he could not discuss the case with me over the telephone. I then offered to meet with him and his investigators in San Francisco, which he accepted.

Subsequently I was advised by Major Harvey that plans for such an interview were being indefinitely postponed, and that an interview might not be necessary at all. I was further advised that responsibility for the investigation was being removed from the San Francisco Field Office to the 6th Region Headquarters, and that a new special agent was being brought in to supervise it.

While all of this CID administrative reorganization may indeed be taking place, I am nonetheless coming reluctantly to several conclusions about the entire affair. I think it is appropriate to bring them first to your attention as CID Commander.

(1) As shown in my August 23, 1988 and January 27, 1989 sworn statements, Adams-Thompson's allegation was **not** substantiated by any objective, factual evidence whatever. Furthermore it has come to light that the source which he claimed for his story - a cohesive, rational account given by his stepdaughter to "therapist" Debbie Hickey - **never existed at all**, but was rather invented by him and Mrs. Adams-Thompson. The original accusation - the justification for naming Mrs. Aquino and myself "suspects" - has thus been exposed as a deliberate fabrication. Nevertheless the CID investigation of me continues.

(2) As it was Adams-Thompson's August 1987 attack which first associated my name with the Presidio witch-hunt in the media, I am certain that there are no other allegations or "identifications" which predate that time. Once Mrs. Aquino and I were publicly showcased in the press, of course, any number of copy-cat allegations could be generated, based simply on the many descriptions, television films, and photographs of ourselves and our San Francisco home which flooded the bay area and the nation. I cannot think that any such copycat allegations - all as unsupported as Adams-Thompson's - would justify the CID continuing to suspend an innocent officer in the limbo of an indefinite investigation status. What is to prevent any other crackpot, religious bigot, or claim-greedy parent from inventing still more accusations when these are discredited? Am I supposed to spend the rest of my military career as an automatic "investigatee" any time some vindictive crank feels an urge to disrupt my life?

(3) There is, quite simply, **no** factual or objective reason for continuing this investigation of me one moment further. Even if the CID initiated it in good faith, the facts clearing my name and that of my wife were quickly brought to light for any objective individual to see. No "great leap of faith" is required for this; the facts are both obvious and conspicuous. As a Military Intelligence professional myself, I know full well when facts are conclusive and when they are not. The facts established as a matter of record in this case verify conclusively the innocence of my wife and myself.

(4) Not only should this investigation be terminated without further delay, it should be accompanied by an official statement that clearly and unequivocally exonerates my wife and myself from Adams-Thompson's malicious allegation. The manufactured nature of those allegations has now been revealed through the details of the "therapist" notes. No termination of this investigation which allows **any** doubt concerning my wife's and my integrity and innocence to persist - such as an "insufficient evidence" statement when in fact there is **no evidence whatever** - is acceptable.

(5) In January 1988, after four months of attempts to achieve an administrative resolution of Adams-Thompson's deliberate, malicious attack on my wife and myself, I preferred court-martial charges against him. Special Agent Birck was given the responsibility to investigate those charges. After a five-month "investigation" he recommended against referring them for court-martial despite the clear evidence for doing so. My FOIA request to see Birck's report concerning the charges was denied. Nevertheless, during the present investigation concerning me, considerable additional information confirming Adams-Thompson's criminal actions has come to light - for example, the Hickey notes and the discovery that Adams-Thompson told different versions of his story to the FBI and to the San Francisco Police. As this information came from CID sources, it was certainly available to Birck when he was supposedly investigating the charges I preferred. Nevertheless he recommended against Adams-Thompson's court-martial on the grounds that "there was no evidence to substantiate the charges".

(6) Today, therefore, I remain under the professional and social stigma of "criminal investigation" despite the clear evidence that I am innocent, while Adams-Thompson remains free and immune from investigation or charges despite the clear evidence that he committed a deliberate, criminal act against another officer and his wife. Both of these situations are an abuse of the justice which the CID supposedly exists to safeguard for all soldiers and their families.

(7) It is easy to say that a CID investigation is not itself punitive but is simply a fact-finding procedure which shouldn't trouble me even if it continues for a year or more. Quite obviously this is **not** the case. My personnel file is, flagged and my security clearance is suspended. Within the Army I am stigmatized by being in a "criminal investigation" status - all the more so because of the supposed rationale for that investigation: the kidnapping, rape, and sodomizing of an infant child. Just the fact that this new investigation has been initiated has been used by the press to imply that I am "guilty after all" despite the termination of the previous investigations. Just six days ago, on a March 1, 1989 show dealing with child pornography, drugs, and prostitution, Geraldo Rivera showed film clips of me and introduced an ex-FBI agent who said that I was now under "grand jury investigation" for the Adams-Thompson allegation.

(8) My wife and I have now been subjected to more than a year and a half of death threats, vandalism, and severe emotional stress because of this endless, senseless "state of investigation". My professional reputation in the Army, previously immaculate and exemplary throughout my nineteen years' service, has been stigmatized horribly. Our parents and our own children have been seriously traumatized. My business interests in the San Francisco Bay Area have been affected, as one's social reputation is all-important in commercial dealings. I have sustained over $50,000 in attorney's fees and vandalism repairs. In short, Mrs. Aquino and I have suffered and are continuing to suffer atrociously because of Adams-Thompson's attack. You have the authority and the responsibility to end this persecution before it continues any further, and to recommend punitive action against the person criminally responsible for it.

(9) An additional factor in this is the effect upon my religion and its formally-constituted institution, the Temple of Set. From the time of its founding in 1975 to the present, its activities have been ethical in all regards and its community reputation a completely unblemished one. Adams-Thompson's attack against two of its most senior officials necessarily reflects upon the entire Temple - at a time when hysteria about "Satanic cults" is a nationwide fad among cranks and religious hate-groups. The safety and security of all Setians, their families, and their children are jeopardized the more you allow the erroneous impression to persist that we in any way tolerate, prescribe, or practice abuse of children. As our official literature verifies, we do **not** abuse children, nor even admit minors to membership. We are a legitimate, law-abiding, and sincere religion, and our members have the right to worship in their own fashion, free from fear of harassment or persecution.

(10) The same former FBI agent stated on the March 1 Geraldo show that the CID investigation concerning me was opened specifically because of Congressional pressure brought to bear on the Army following the October 1988 Geraldo special. If this is true, it flatly contradicts Birck's statement that he opened it on his own initiative as a routine step in the general Presidio investigation. Furthermore, the CID is supposed to open investigations based upon legitimate probable cause that a crime occurred, not on the basis of political or religiously-motivated arm-twisting. Congress has its own power to hold hearings and make investigations as it deems necessary; it should not

be using the Army's criminal investigative machinery for this purpose, nor as a means of persecuting or intimidating a soldier and his family because of their religious beliefs.

In summary, this investigation of me has now passed clearly beyond the point where I can see any legitimate reason whatever for keeping it open. Any good-faith doubts which the CID had to resolve have, by any rational standard, been alleviated. I therefore request that you terminate the investigation without further delay, and that you do so with a clear and unqualified exoneration of my wife and myself.

If you do not do this, I will have no choice but to conclude that the investigation is being kept open, and Adams-Thompson's criminal act concealed and protected, for no other reason than to persecute and intimidate my wife and myself because of our religion. I would then have no choice but to initiate formal complaints through the Inspector General system, concerning administrative misuse of the CID's investigative powers, and through the Army Equal Opportunity system, concerning religious discrimination and persecution.

I sincerely hope that such measures will not be necessary. My wife and I have suffered enough - and more than we ever should have at all. We want nothing more than to be left alone, to put our lives back together after the abuse we have endured for so long. I do not think that this is the least bit unreasonable.

As for Chaplain Lawrence Adams-Thompson: If as Commanding General of the CIDC you enforce its mandate to expose and recommend punishment for criminal acts by anyone regardless of branch or office, then you will title this individual for the vicious and malicious act he deliberately committed against a fellow soldier and his wife, and for the three false monetary claims based upon it, totaling over $2 million, through which he has deliberately tried to defraud the government.

Respectfully,
/s/ Michael A. Aquino
Lt. Colonel, Military Intelligence

cc-   Major General William F. Ward, Chief, U.S. Army Reserve
      Brigadier General Paul L. Babiak, Commanding General, ARPERCEN
      Lt. Colonel Wayne H. Price, U.S. Army Trial Defense Service
      Lt. Colonel Greg Rixon, Department of the Army Public Affairs Office
      Major Mark W. Harvey, Headquarters, Sixth Region, CIDC
      Captain Thomas M. Hayes III, Senior Defense Counsel, Trial Defense Service
      Ms. Irene Rapoza, Senior Analyst, San Francisco Police Commission
      Office of the Inspector General, ARPERCEN
      Command Equal Opportunity Office, ARPERCEN

Appendix 48: Letter, Captain Thomas Hayes to Special Agent Dan Cates 3/21/89

Department of the Army
US Army Trial Defense Service
Presidio Field Office
Presidio of San Francisco, California 94129

AFKC-ZM-JA-TDS (27-10)

21 March 1989

MEMORANDUM THRU Command Judge Advocate, Headquarters 6th Region, Criminal Investigation Division Command, Presidio of San Francisco, California 94129

FOR Special Agent Dan Cates, Criminal Investigation Division Command, San Francisco Field Office, Presidio of San Francisco, California 94129

SUBJECT: Status of CIDC Investigation Against LTC Michael A. Aquino; Proposed Flagging of Chaplain Adams-Thompson

1. I write to follow up on our meeting of 15 March 1989, at which you assured me of your neutrality and the need to thoroughly document this case before you make a decision concerning the titling of my client. As I stated in my February memo to MG Cromartie, LTC Aquino will cooperate in any reasonable way that he can to see this case wrapped up. He and Mrs. Aquino continue to suffer injury to their reputation and career as a result of the rumor and innuendo upon which this case is based.

2. As I pointed out at our meeting, several facts stand out in establishing that Chaplain Adams-Thompson and his wife have orchestrated the attack on the Aquinos. The notes made by LTC Hickey during the interviews with Kinsey Almond directly impeach the San Francisco Police Department report made by Investigator Pamfiloff based upon Chaplain Adams-Thompson's complaint. Kinsey had not mentioned a "Mikey" or "Shamby", according to LTC Hickey's notes, at the time that Chaplain Adams-Thompson had told the SFPD that Kinsey had made such comments. LTC Hickey's notes further mention that it was Mrs. Adams-Thompson who had initiated the theory of "satanic crime".

3. I think it only fair to request that Chaplain Adams-Thompson be flagged and investigated further. He must be confronted with these glaring inconsistencies. I must express some frustration at never having been provided that portion of the CID file pertaining to the investigation of Chaplain Adams-Thompson. After all, how could revealing that part of the file jeopardize the investigation into the alleged child abuse? The FOIA denial causes one to pause and consider whether a real investigation into LTC Aquino's charges against the Chaplain was ever conducted.

4. I will await your reply.

/s/ Thomas M. Hayes III
Captain, Judge Advocate
Senior Defense Counsel

Appendix 49: Letter, Major Mark Harvey to Captain Thomas Hayes 4/7/89

Department of the Army
Headquarters, Sixth Region
US Army Criminal Investigation Command
Presidio of San Francisco, California 94129-6600

7 April 1989

CIRF-JA

MEMORANDUM FOR Captain Thomas M. Hayes III, Senior Defense Counsel, Presidio Field Office, Presidio of San Francisco, CA 94129

SUBJECT: Status of USACIDC Investigation of Lieutenant Colonel Michael A. Aquino

1. This letter is in response to your request for information, dated 17 February 1989, regarding the United States Army Criminal Investigation Command's (USACIDC), investigation of Lieutenant Colonel (LTC) Michael A. Aquino.

2. On 25 October 1988, LTC Aquino appeared on the nationwide television Geraldo Rivera special on Satanism. The USACIDC inquiry regarding the allegations against LTC Aquino was initiated prior to October 1988. The investigation was not initiated in response to pressure by Congress or the media. USACIDC has not been improperly influenced by anyone either to start or continue the investigation.

3. The USACIDC investigation of LTC Aquino is not based upon his religious beliefs. The sole basis for the investigation of LTC Aquino is whether or not LTC Aquino violated the Uniform Code 0f Military Justice. As you are well aware, USACIDC is also interested in establishing whether or not anyone else violated the Uniform Code of Military Justice regarding the allegations of child sexual abuse.

4. I have previously informed you that USACIDC has reviewed the case files of the Federal Bureau of Investigation and the San Francisco Police Department. USACIDC will avoid redoing the work of other investigative agencies whenever possible. USACIDC has limited resources and cannot afford to waste time replowing the same ground that has been plowed by other agencies.

5. As you are aware, USACIDC recently transferred control of the LTC Aquino investigation to Sixth Region from the San Francisco Field Office and brought in a new investigator, who is now in charge of this investigation. These changes were made to expedite completion of the investigation. USACIDC is making significant progress toward the timely and thorough completion of the investigation.

6. On 13 December 1989 LTC Aquino was flagged. LTC Aquino has been under USACIDC formal investigation for about four months. This investigation is very complex, with many important witnesses scattered throughout the United States. LTC Aquino is not under any restriction by the Army. I regret that I am not able to predict when the USACIDC investigation will be completed; however I can say that it will require between 60 and 90 days to be finalized.

7. LTC Aquino has provided leads in his most recent sworn statement, and I have been assured that many of these leads have all ready been pursued.

8. LTC Aquino has declined to consent to release of his banking records. This decision by LTC Aquino may delay completion of the investigation because it is necessary to establish LTC Aquino's location in 1986 and 1987 using less reliable and efficient means than the Aquino's banking and credit card records.

9. LTC Aquino has decided that he is willing to be interviewed by USACIDC as soon as USACIDC is ready to conduct the interview. This decision reflects well on LTC Aquino, and should tend to expedite completion of the investigation.

10. I have provided your letter of 17 February 1989 to Headquarters, USACIDC.

11. On 6 April 1989 you told me that I did not have to go through you to communicate with LTC Aquino, and that I could discuss the merits of his case with him. After I have talked to LTC Aquino, I will inform you of the contents of any conversation that I have had with your client.

12. On 7 April 1989 LTC Aquino telephonically informed me that he had written a letter to LTC Hickey's superiors at Fort Lewis with a copy furnished to me, as well as the Office of the Surgeon General, requesting disciplinary action against LTC Hickey for lack of medical ethics and malpractice.

13. I informed LTC Aquino that I had seen the tape of the television program in Miami, and read his letter requesting retraction of misleading portions of the Miami program. I told LTC Aquino that I was certain that the lady on the television program that was in shadow was not LTC Hickey, and I did not know the identity of the lady.

14. I told LTC Aquino that I would complete this letter today and provide it to you. Nothing else of significance was discussed in our telephone conversation of 7 April 1989.

/s/ Mark W. Harvey
Major, Judge Advocate
Region Judge Advocate

Appendix 50: Letter, Michael Aquino to Major Mark Harvey 4/24/89

April 24, 1989

Dear Major Harvey:

Captain Thomas Hayes has just provided me with a copy of your 7 April letter to him, and I have some comments concerning it for consideration by Special Agent Cates and yourself:

(1) Per the enclosed letter to Geraldo Rivera, I am attempting to verify the statement on his show that Congressional or other pressure was brought upon the Army to open this third investigation of me. I will keep you advised of anything I learn in this regard.[207]

(2) Your statement that "the USACIDC inquiry regarding the allegations against LTC Aquino was initiated prior to October 1988" reflects only the *pro forma* technicality that the general investigation concerning the Presidio day-care center witch-hunt has remained open since 1986.

The CID investigation of me obviously began the month following the Geraldo "Satanism" show [as indeed you acknowledge in paragraph #6 of your letter]. I was first notified of this investigation by Special Agent Penaluna by telephone in late November 1988, at which time he required me to be photographed and fingerprinted by the CID office in Granite City, Illinois. He stated that the basis for his requirement was that the CID was opening a formal investigation of me. His account is verified by the fact that my records were not flagged until 13 December 1988. Furthermore, as recounted in my 6 March 1989 letter to General Cromartie, Special Agent Birck stated to me that he had personally made the decision to open this new investigation of me in November.

The allegations by Adams-Thompson were extremely serious: the kidnapping, rape, and sodomy of a 2-year-old infant. I do not think it likely that the CID, if it considered such allegations at all credible, would put them on a "back burner" for well over a year, with no attempt whatever to even ask me about them.

Two CID agents were present during the 14 August 1987 raid on our San Francisco home by the San Francisco Police Department, so I know that the CID knew sufficiently about the Adams-Thompson allegations to decide at that time whether it felt like taking them seriously. If it did, my records should have been flagged right then in August 1987.

Obviously the decision to open this investigation of me was made consequent to the Geraldo special. The statements by Penaluna and Birck, and the formal paperwork initiated by the CID, clearly establish this. The only question remaining is on whose orders, and because of what political influence brought to bear. As the answer to this question may establish whether the initiation of the investigation was improper and in violation of the 1st and 14th Amendments to the Constitution, and whether attempts have also been made to politically pre-influence its outcome in any way, I will continue to pursue it actively as long as I understand my wife, myself, and my religion to be objects of official intimidation and persecution.

(3) **Of course** the CID investigation of me is based on my religious beliefs. No non-Satanist Lieutenant Colonel would have been flagged and made the subject of a criminal investigation simply because of allegations by a chaplain which have long since been exposed as unsubstantiated and deliberately fabricated.

The CID knows and has medically confirmed that Kinsey Almond was never raped or sodomized as Adams-Thompson alleged to the FBI and SFPD. Therefore it is already proven that the supposed crime **never occurred at all**. Incidentally, if the CID has known this since Adams-Thompson made his initial allegations to the SFPD and

---

[207] Rivera did not respond to my inquiry.

FBI, why did the CID not communicate this critical information to an Army officer under severe police, media, and public attack for such a rape/sodomy?

The CID knows that **no** features of our San Francisco home match the "description" which Adams-Thompson represented as coming from his stepdaughter, but which was obviously his own fabrication. [As for the "black-walled living room", which the press tried to sensationalize as "verified", our living room is an entirely different pastel color. Our black/silver/red bedroom is not a living room. Moreover any mention of a "black room" is absent from the Hickey notes, and was obviously appended to the "package story" by Adams-Thompson on the hunch that, like Anton LaVey's famous black-roomed house in San Francisco, our home would also have one or more similarly-painted rooms.]

Obviously the sole basis for the "package story" manufactured by the chaplain is hate-propaganda concerning Satanism and its supposed interest in child-molestation, and his obvious motive, as a professional of a religion with a centuries-old doctrinal hatred of ours, of trying to harm my wife and myself and discredit the church to which we belong. Abundant examples of such hate-propaganda - from Sandi Gallant's videotaped lecture, to the revolting "Satanic child abuse" checklists of Gould and other "witch-hunting" therapists, to the vast media sensationalizing of such allegations from *Michelle Remembers* and the McMartin case forward - have been provided to you. Among the written questions which the CID posed to me, and to which I responded in my 27 January 1989 sworn statement, were questions concerning religious rituals and Adams-Thompson's religion-based motives.

(4) I appreciate your statement that "USACIDC is also interested in establishing whether or not anyone else violated the UCMJ regarding the allegations of child sexual abuse". In this regard, however, I am concerned about the following:

I have been officially informed that it is CID policy, made at the Washington, D.C. level, that no other flagging actions will even be considered while this investigation is in progress. As the act of requesting a flag signals the CID's official opinion that "credible allegations" exist, this *a priori* policy that no other flags will be considered places the statements and actions of Adams-Thompson in a protected status. Further, the insistence of the exclusive flag on my file carries with it the implication that Adams-Thompson's allegations, despite their abundant inaccuracies and inconsistencies, are nevertheless enshrined as "credible".

The effect of this policy, as it appears to me to date, is to preserve me in a "criminal investigation" status long after the false nature of the allegations should have become evident to any objective investigator, and to simply ignore all the evidence - as carefully and exhaustively provided to you in my sworn statements of 4 January 1988, 23 August 1988, and 27 January 1989 - which proves that Adams-Thompson deliberately and maliciously fabricated his "package story" and his allegations to the SFPD and FBI based upon it.

Any effort now by Adams-Thompson to say that he is or was "just repeating to the authorities what his stepdaughter told him" - a common dodge in child-abuse witch-hunts - is easily exposed as a lie to try to hide his criminal actions in August 1987. It has now been established exactly what Kinsey Almond originally said and did not say to Debbie Hickey, and none of Hickey's notes include anything resembling the "package story" which, embellished with technical details and sexual vulgarities beyond a 2-year-old's comprehension and carefully doctored to eliminate inconvenient therapy statements, Adams-Thompson told the FBI and SFPD had "come from his stepdaughter". If the Hickey notes are placed side-by-side with the the 13 August 1987 SFPD incident report and the FBI Form 302, it is clear that **the Hickey notes do not substantiate anything Adams-Thompson told the FBI and SFPD that they did**. Further, Adams-Thompson certainly knew that his stepdaughter was **a virgin without any signs of injury** at the time he gave the SFPD and FBI the story that she had been raped and sodomized by two adult males.

To date the CID has not even responded to Captain Thomas Hayes' 21 March 1989 letter to Special Agent Cates, through your office, requesting that Adams-Thompson be flagged on the basis of the clear evidence that he fabricated the "package story" and gave a deliberately and knowingly fraudulent account of Kinsey Almond's statements, actions, and therapy sessions to the SFPD and FBI.

To date the CID continues to refuse Captain Hayes and myself access to the CID investigation of Adams-Thompson which Special Agent Birck supposedly conducted in response to the UCMJ charges which I preferred against AdamsThompson. Neither Captain Hayes nor I have been advised of any legitimate reason why this investigation report should be denied to us. Obviously the quality, sincerity, and thoroughness with which this investigation was conducted bears directly upon the question of bias against me, and bias in favor of Adams-Thompson, in the present investigation. I once more reiterate my FOIA request, first made almost a year ago on 23 June 1988, for a full and complete copy of that CID investigative report in response to the UCMJ charges.

(5) I noted your comment that the CID has "reviewed the case files of the San Francisco Police Department". I would appreciate your confirming to Captain Hayes or myself that, in doing so, you have consulted directly and in specifics with Ms. Irene Rapoza, Senior Analyst, Office of Citizen Complaints, San Francisco Police Commission, concerning these case files and the conduct of the officers directly involved (Glenn Pamfiloff and Sandi Gallant) with them. As the CID is aware, I have filed an extensive and detailed series of administrative and legal complaints and court actions concerning the actions of Pamfiloff and Gallant, most currently the OCC complaints being investigated by Ms. Rapoza. Any CID review of SFPD "case files" in ignorance or disregard of Ms. Rapoza's analysis of those files will necessarily be biased and distorted.

I have requested Ms. Rapoza to make her findings available to the CID as much as possible. I am certain, in support of her own investigation, she would also welcome any information which the CID has which bears upon the conduct of Pamfiloff and Gallant.

(6) Concerning CID "review of the files of the FBI": On 8 February 1988 I made a FOIA request to the FBI for copies of all documents pertaining to myself and the Temple of Set, to include any and all paperwork generated by the San Francisco Field Office of the FBI. While receipt of my FOIA request was acknowledged, and while I received a 28 March 1988 form letter stating that "pertinent documents had been located", I have yet to receive a single such document. In answer to my several written and telephonic requests, I was told only that the FBI is backlogged and will eventually get around to my request "in six months to a year from the request date". It has now been well over a year since I made the request. Obviously the contents of the FBI files in question are potentially important to me, and presumably to you, in this present investigation. I request your assistance in expediting my FOIA request. It is request #FOIPA-29439 1, and the POC in the FBI Records Management Division is Mr. Willis Newton, telephone (202) 324-5767.

(7) I further noted your statement that "CIDC has limited resources and cannot afford to waste time replowing the same ground that has been plowed by other agencies". What exactly is Special Agent Cates' time-consuming, nationwide series of interviews with Presidio parents and children if not just such "replowing"?

All of the Presidio parents and children were interviewed by the FBI, and again by Pamfiloff in his quest to find some corroboration of the Adams-Thompson allegations. As reported in the 2 August 1988 San Francisco Chronicle, all these interviews produced **no identifications and no corroboration**.

Even that series of interviews, conducted by an SFPD officer with an obvious interest in justifying his aggressive actions against Mrs. Aquino and myself, was conducted months after all of San Francisco, including the Presidio parents and children, had been inundated by the flood of publicity given Mrs. Aquino and myself, our home, the Temple of Set, and the Adams-Thompson allegations. So why should Special Agent Cates be replowing this same ground yet again a year later? The only statements made by any children or by their parents with any credibility would be those before the media publicity avalanche.

Even prior to that avalanche, since the Hickey therapy notes establish that Mrs. Adams-Thompson had begun to introduce allegations about "a Satanic cult" and "an Army officer" into Kinsey Almond's therapy sessions as far back as 2 June 1987, the Adams-Thompsons had ample opportunity to spread such suggestions among other parents militantly active in the ongoing Presidio witch-hunt, either directly or through Almond's contact with other Presidio children after her mother and stepfather had begun to indoctrinate her with this idea.

(8) I take exception to your statement that "many important witnesses are scattered throughout the United States".

Since no crime ever occurred, there are no "witnesses" to anything. The original Adams-Thompson allegation, as detailed in the SFPD incident report, mentioned no "witnesses" at the fictional rape/sodomy/lion-foot-bathtub session, nor at the alleged PX "identification" incident. No "witnesses" were produced by Pamfiloff in his interviews in search of one. No Presidio parents other than the Adams-Thompsons have filed any claims on the basis of any alleged contact between my wife and myself and their children. The whole notion of "witnesses" suddenly being produced now, as still one more amendment to Adams -Thompson's continuously-changing "package story", is preposterous.

May I again observe that $66 million is no small temptation for someone to lie about almost anything, to say nothing of coaching a young child into similarly lying. This is all the more tempting since, as is the case in all previous "molestation" witch-hunts, parents and therapists have endeavored to hide behind statements supposedly "originating" from the child, thereby avoiding personal risk of being caught in the lies themselves and thus being subject to prosecution for perjury.

(9) The fact that I am not under any restriction by the Army is of course not nearly the whole story of our continuing ordeal.

Mrs. Aquino and I have been objects of intense and continuous vilification by hostile journalists since they first became aware of the Adams-Thompson allegations in October 1987. Under separate cover I am sending you copies of all the San Francisco newspaper stories written concerning the allegations from October 1987 to the present; you will find it a very thick stack indeed - with endless showcasing of the allegations and little if any attention to the inaccuracies and inconsistencies therein. Only lurid stories sell newspapers.

San Francisco has been the home of my family for many generations, ever since my grandfather was personal physician to the Crocker family. It is the city where I was born and lived most of my life, the city in which I earned my Eagle Scout badge, the city in which Mrs. Aquino earned her Honors Degree in college, and the city in which I earned an Adjunct Professorship at Golden Gate University after many years of teaching there.

Our family home, acquired by my grandfather, has now been the object of so much vandalism, telephonic threats, and hostile public attention that my wife is afraid to live there anymore. Its interior has been pawed through by a team of raiders who arrived late at night and tore the place apart until the early morning hours, photographing and confiscating our most personal and private church and family papers and articles - even including Mrs. Aquino's underwear.

In addition to over $50,000 of legal and vandalism-repair costs, we have now had 1-1/2 years of our lives completely convulsed by this vicious persecution. We are unable to live any kind of normal life. It is only with considerable effort that I am able to function in my present military assignment, and at both home and work I am constantly contacted by journalists wanting statements or interviews concerning the allegations and the past and present investigations.

As I pointed out to General Cromartie, existing under formal, public investigation for child rape and sodomy is not the same thing as existing under investigation for fudging on income taxes or stealing a typewriter. The social stigma associated with the crimes alleged by Adams-Thompson is easily the most extreme in society. Even when we are eventually exonerated, it will take years for this "image" to be corrected - and the harm caused us by it will never be wholly undone.

So please do not represent our experience as being a mild one in comparison with ordinary CID investigations - wherein, I might add, there **is** generally evidence that the crime in fact occurred in the first place, regardless of whether the investigatee is the culprit. I am now under investigation for the rape and sodomy of a child who has been medically established to be a virgin - and further "investigation" of this physiological miracle is supposed to take another two to three months beyond the 1-3/4 years since the CU) participation in the raid on our home?

(10) I provided leads not only in my most recent sworn statement, but also in my 5 January 1989 letter to you, which contained 22 leads pertinent to the Adams-Thompson allegations specifically and 12 leads pertinent to the Presidio witch-hunt generally. To date all the information which Captain Hayes has learned stemming from these leads has served to verify my innocence and document the deliberately manufactured and malicious nature of Adams-Thompson's allegations. This being the case, why am I still flagged - and why is Adams-Thompson **not** flagged?

(11) As I have indicated to the CID several times - in my sworn statement, through Captain Hayes, and directly to you - I have no qualms whatever about producing my banking records for any specific date on which a particular crime in a particular location has been alleged with some reason to believe it beyond unsubstantiated invention.

I do not see why, just because an Army chaplain who has already been caught in several lies and inconsistencies decides to revise his story to fit a time when I was still assigned to the Presidio before PCS assignment to Washington D.C., this should in and of itself be "reason" for the CID to request my records.

It is "necessary to establish LTC Aquino's location in 1986 and 1987" **only** if there is credible reason to think that I have committed some specific crime at some specific time and place. Then, as I have said all along, I will be pleased to provide any and all verifications of my location and actions which I can produce from my records, banking and otherwise. As an individual with a lifelong reputation of the highest integrity, I reject utterly the notion that my mere presence in my native city, where I have maintained my legal residence for 42 years, should somehow imply that I am involved in some crime which is alleged to take place in that city.

If, as I assume, you are familiar with the *modus operandi* of the continuing child-abuse witch-hunt epidemic around the United States, you know that a common tactic is to invent "crimes" tailored to whatever circumstances of the victim of the witch-hunt can be discovered or guessed at. The more a broad-brush "map" of my location and activities is provided to individuals such as Adams-Thompson and those with a similar vested interest in fabricating a case against me, the easier it is for allegations to be invented to fit that map. Indeed this appears **already** to be happening, with Adams-Thompson apparently trying to re-date his original allegations to May-July 1986 and hoping that no one will notice.

(12) Both Mrs. Aquino and I have always been willing to be interviewed by the CID. We will answer all questions for which we are satisfied the CID has a reasonable basis to ask. If no such basis is apparent to us, then we will ask the CID investigator to explain the basis and will discuss the facts surrounding that basis with the investigator, yourself, and Captain Hayes until the basis is either validated or invalidated.

In my 6 March 1989 letter to General Cromartie[208] , which to date has gone unanswered, I said that I would consider initiating an Inspector General complaint and an EEO complaint concerning the conduct of this investigation if, despite the facts which have long since established my innocence and the criminal culpability of Adams-Thompson, I continue to be investigated and Adams-Thompson continues to be sheltered against accountability for his criminal actions.

I have discussed this matter in detail with the Trial Defense Service, and I am advised that I have strong grounds for both complaints. In fact I have been advised to proceed immediately with both complaints. I have decided to postpone a decision on this matter pending developments in the next few weeks. If I have reason to believe that the CID is merely moving slowly and cautiously because of the political and public volatility of this case, and that an honest effort is indeed being made to resolve it factually and justly, then I would not want to complicate the situation even further with two investigations of the CID's actions to date in the court-martial investigation of

---

[208] Appendix #47.

Adams-Thompson and in the current investigation. On Captain Hayes' advice, however, I am keeping the Office of the Inspector General and the EEO ARPERCEN informed of the current situation.

Sincerely,
/s/ Michael A. Aquino
Lt. Colonel, Military Intelligence

cc- Major General William F. Ward, Chief, U.S. Army Reserve
Major General Eugene L. Cromartie, Commanding General, USACIDC
Brigadier General Paul L. Babiak, Commanding General, ARPERCEN
Lt. Colonel Wayne H. Price, U.S. Army Trial Defense Service
Lt. Colonel Greg Rixon, Department of the Army Public Affairs Office
Captain Thomas M. Hayes III, Senior Defense Counsel, Trial Defense Service
Ms. Irene Rapoza, Senior Analyst, San Francisco Police Commission
Mr. Bernard Zimmerman, Pillsbury, Madison & Sutro
Office of the Inspector General, ARPERCEN
Command Equal Opportunity Office, ARPERCEN

Appendix 51: Major Mark Harvey Memorandum for Record 5/18/89

CIRF-JA

Special Agent Daniel Cates Sixth Region, U. S. Army Criminal Investigation Command Presidio of San Francisco, CA 94129-6600

SUBJECT: Memorandum for Record, LTC Michael A. Aquino, CPT Thomas Hayes, Ms. Betty Narvaez, May 18, 1989

MEMORANDUM FOR RECORD: MAY 18, 1989

On Thursday, 18 May 1989, at about 0900 hours, LTC Michael A. Aquino called me at my office. LTC Aquino said that he had just had a phone conversation with his lawyer, CPT Hayes. Based on the telephone conversation with CPT Hayes, LTC Aquino decided that he should call me to discuss the questions that I had raised with Captain Hayes on May 17, 1989. Although I discussed the case with CPT Hayes on May 17, 1989, I did not solicit the phone call by LTC Aquino. Since LTC Aquino indicated that the call was based on an earlier consultation with his lawyer, I asked LTC Aquino some of the questions that I had not asked during the earlier interview.

BACKGROUND: On March 16, 1988, Detective Glenn Pamfiloff, San Francisco Police Department, interviewed Angelique Jefferson. This interview was tape recorded. At pages 16-17, Angelique states that she remembered four items from the time she observed ritualistic abuse of children, conducted by LTC and Mrs. Aquino: (1) shiny black lion-like statue; (2) white furry carpet; (3) bamboo furniture; and (4) an old fashioned tub, that one could see underneath. While Special Agents Penaluna and Cates, Captain Hayes and I were in LTC Aquino's apartment in Saint Louis, LTC Aquino showed us how his crystal ball worked and gave a tour of his ritual chamber. We observed a prominently displayed shiny black panther statue in LTC Aquino's ritual chamber beneath the altar. The statue was about eighteen inches tall. The lion-like statue was the only statue in the ritual chamber. None of the four characteristics allegedly observed by Angelique Jefferson appeared in any of the FBI photographs, or on the television program, "Nightmare at the Presidio".

I asked LTC Aquino about the statue of the black panther that is in his ritual chamber in his apartment in Saint Louis. LTC Aquino said that he purchased the statue about 2 months ago in connection with the Reserve Officers Wives' Club sale held in Saint Louis, and he did not have a black lion-like statue in his apartment or his mother's apartment in 1986. LTC Aquino said that he would attempt to obtain corroboration of this fact, then LTC Aquino would call me back. LTC Aquino further related that the reason he purchased the statue was because Lilith liked black cats. LTC Aquino also said that he paid $70 for the statue, and thought that he paid cash, rather than by check or credit card. LTC Aquino indicated that there was white carpet that was "fuzzy" in 1986 in his mother's apartment at 123 Acme Avenue. This was the same apartment that LTC Aquino moved into in January-February 1986. LTC Aquino was not sure whether there was bamboo furniture in his mother's apartment. LTC Aquino was sure that he did not have an old fashioned tub that a person could see underneath. LTC Aquino said that this white carpet was very worn and therefore he had it replaced it in 1986.

I asked LTC Aquino whether the front of his apartment building on Acme Avenue changed in 1986 or 1987, and LTC Aquino indicated that the exterior of the apartment was repainted; however, the painter used the same colored paint. (In other words there was no significant change in the exterior of 123 Acme Avenue between early 1986 and Kinsey's viewing of the apartment exterior in August 1987, when she was with the FBI.)

LTC Aquino indicated that the two most significant furnishings in his home or his mother's home in San Francisco were the white "Greek" statue of a male figure and the Egyptian throne type chair that has the carved lion figure heads on the arms. Both items appear in the FBI photographs taken in 1987. The statue of the male figure was made by LTC Aquino's mother in the 1930s, and has been in her apartment at 123 Acme Avenue for years.

According to LTC Aquino, the Egyptian throne has also been LTC Aquino's property for more than three years, and LTC Aquino felt that a child would recognize these furnishings if they had previously seen his apartment. However, LTC Aquino also felt that if a child claimed to recognize the Egyptian throne, it would not be significant because the Egyptian throne had been prominently displayed on television.

I asked LTC Aquino about the black masses that he conducted or attended. LTC Aquino said the black mass described by Wayne West as reprinted in Appendix 7 of LTC Aquino's book, *The Devil's Own* was conducted in 1970. The West black mass, which included a female in a nun's habit urinating into a chamber pot in front of the other ritual participants so that the urine could be sprinkled on those attending the black mass utilizing a phallic shaped object did occur generally in accordance with West's description in *The Devil's Own*. LTC Aquino related that the lady that was supposed to urinate into the chamber pot thought that she should drink alot of fluids prior to the ceremony to insure that she could urinate at the proper time in the ceremony. When the time came for her to urinate, she just kept urinating, delaying the ceremony. Anton Levey cast a spell which apparently helped to cause the flow of urine to stop. The spell caused those attending the black mass to laugh considerably. The West black mass was conducted under the direction of LTC Aquino, in 1970, at Anton Levey's house in San Francisco.

LTC Aquino conducted "one or two" other black masses as late a 1972 in Kentucky. These masses lacked some of the sexuality of the mass described by West in *The Devil's Own* and may not have included the use of a nude woman with spread legs, to receive the host, utilized as the "living altar."

LTC Aquino indicated that the wands seized in the search of his apartment were not placed into any bodily orifices at ceremonies.

MEMORANDUM FOR RECORD: MAY 18, 1989

On Thursday, 18 May 1989, at about 0940 hours, CPT Thomas Hayes, U. S. Army Trial Defense Service, called me at my office. CPT Hayes told me that he had a phone conversation with his client, LTC Aquino, about an hour ago and wanted to discuss any questions that I might have regarding the investigation of the allegations against LTC Aquino. I related that I had just talked to LTC Aquino, and CPT Hayes said that it was all right for me to question his client without going through CPT Hayes. I told CPT Hayes what LTC Aquino said in the phone conversation that I had just completed. CPT Hayes said that he did not object to future conversations by me with his client, LTC Aquino.

MEMORANDUM FOR RECORD: MAY 18, 1989

On Thursday, 18 May 1989, at about 1030 hours, LTC Michael A. Aquino called me at my office. LTC Aquino said that I should call Betty Narvaez, apparent owner of "Betty's Folly", whose name appeared on a sticker on the bottom of the black statue of the panther. LTC Aquino said that Betty Narvaez could be reached at (314) 831-0215. LTC Aquino measured the panther statue and said that it was 21.5 inches tall. LTC Aquino also said that the ritual with the chamber pot and the urinating woman in a nun's habit was not used in the ritual(s) in Kentucky. LTC Aquino was unsure whether a nude woman was used as a living altar in Kentucky, but thought that probably they were not because the altar by the Church of Satan at that time, in Kentucky, was probably not strong enough to support the weight of an adult female.

MEMORANDUM FOR RECORD: MAY 18, 1989

On Thursday, 18 May 1989, at about 1045 hours, I called Ms. Betty Narvaez, of "Betty's Folly", at (314) 831-0215. I described LTC Aquino and his alleged purchase of the black panther. Ms. Betty Narvaez recalled the purchase by LTC Aquino, stating that she recognized LTC Aquino from news programs. Her calendar showed that the purchase occurred on March 10, 1989, at an Reserve Officers Wives' Club Sale in Saint Louis. Betty said that she had personally created the mold for the statue years ago, and that similar statues using her mold of a panther had been sold throughout the United States. Betty said that LTC Aquino could have easily obtained a similar statue, and had it in his home in California in 1986. Nevertheless, LTC Aquino had not given her any indication that he had such a statue prior to March 10, 1989.

Appendix 52: Letter #1, Michael Aquino to Major Mark Harvey 5/31/89

May 31, 1989

Dear Major Harvey:

Captain Hayes has just FAXd me a copy of your Memorandum for Record of May 18, 1989. I have some corrections, clarifications, and comments concerning it:

(1) I do not think that it is appropriate for you to call my black panther statue "lion-like" when, immediately above, you quoted the Jefferson child as using that exact phrase. [Did the Jefferson child in fact use that exact phrase, or did she just say "lion", or did Pamfiloff use the term "lion" and just get some kind of acknowledgment from the child?] In any case, a black panther is not "lion-like" any more than it is "tiger-like". Panthers are black and have no mane, while lions are golden tan and have a mane. [This may seem "picky" of me, but my experience to date in this two-year investigative ordeal is that even the vaguest hint of anything which could be possibly interpreted as a "link" is quick to be blown up out of all proportion to common sense.]

(2) Only two front rooms of my mother's flat had the remains of white wall-to-wall carpet in them when Mrs. Aquino and I moved upstairs in January 1986. I say "remains" because, as I told you previously, my mother was very adamant about not changing anything in her flat during her later years. The carpets were in good condition at the time of their installation prior to my birth in 1946. By January 1986 they were as flat as runner-rugs and completely threadbare. During the last months of my mother's stay at home during her fight with cancer, she was increasingly unable to control her body, and the carpets were discolored accordingly despite daily cleaning. When Mrs. Aquino and I moved upstairs, therefore, these two carpets were thrown out immediately. On 1/18/86 I purchased the bright red and green rugs for those two rooms that appear in the photographs (Standard Brands sales invoice #795736, copy available) and put them in the two rooms until we could paint them.

(3) Since your question about bamboo furniture caught me by surprise, and since my mother had a great deal of furniture of all kinds in her flat, my initial response to you was that I was "not sure". I have since had time to recall her furnishings in detail and can state categorically that she had no bamboo furniture in the past few years. There was none in the flat when we moved into it, nor upstairs in the two roof rooms. As for Mrs. Aquino and myself, we dislike bamboo or rattan-type furniture and do not own any of it [and did not during our 1980-86 residence in San Francisco].

(4) Both tubs at 123 Acme, upstairs and downstairs, are modern in design and flush to the walls and floor. Both were installed by my mother many years prior to Mrs. Aquino's and my moving to San Francisco. The downstairs tub is at the point where the porcelain is wearing off through many years of use. The condition of the upstairs tub is better, but the type and condition of the tub itself, the fixtures attached to it should clearly establish that it predates 1980.

(5) I am not certain what the significance is supposed to be of your statement: "There was no significant change in the exterior of 123 Acme Avenue between early 1986 and Kinsey's viewing of the apartment exterior in August 1987, when she was with the FBI." In several sworn statements and letters I have pointed out the fallacies of that "viewing trip", among them:

- Almond was not taken to the house where she allegedly told investigators she was driven to, i.e. "Mr. Gary's house". Why was she not driven there for an "identification"?

- Almond was not shown several streets or buildings at random during the "identification trip". She was driven directly to 123 Acme and then "walked past it by her mother".

• During the same trip, Almond "identified" the red Isuzu rental car which we had had for only a couple of days as the car used for her alleged abduction to "Mr. Gary's house".

Given the absurdity, inconsistency, and factual inaccuracy of Almond's statements to date, and given the obvious interest of Michele Adams-Thompson in eliciting a response from Almond in front of 123, I think that this rehashing of the "identification trip" is pointless.

(6) "LTC Aquino indicated that the two most significant furnishings in his home or his mother's home in San Francisco were the white 'Greek' statue of a male figure and the Egyptian throne-type chair that has the carved lion figure heads on the arms."

I recall saying to you that these were two extremely eye-catching items, and that the throne (an exact replica of Pharaoh Tutankhamen's famous golden throne) has been remarked on by many visitors since I acquired it in the late 1970s. However neither you nor I can say that all people, or children, would regard these two articles, and especially the statue, as "the most significant" furnishings. Our home is full of antiques, curios, artwork, and rare magical artifacts. The same room that contains the Tut throne contains four Imperial Chinese dragon-chairs, a dragon-desk, and a dragon-table from the Pan-Pacific World's Fair. Many people have been more interested in them than in the Tut throne. Many people have been in our home and made no comment concerning any of the chairs - or the statue, for that matter.

As I have remarked before, I am increasingly exasperated with attempts to stretch Almond's statement about "a bathtub with lion's feet" into anything and everything connected with lions [or panthers]. A bathtub is **not** a chair. A lion's head carving on a chair is **not** a lion's foot on a bathtub. A tiny portion of a painting showing Anton LaVey's head on the front-view of a sphinx is still **not** a bathtub with lion's feet. We **do not and have never** had a bathtub with lion's feet, nor a "plastic lion bathtub". That should be the end of this line of inquiry.

The male statue is not white. It is painted with a pastel paint called "seashell" which could not be mistaken for white. Nor is the statue "Greek". It was created in Germany by my mother as a young woman, at which time she was studying under the great German sculptor Kolbe. It is rough and Expressionistic as opposed to the smooth, idealized sculpture of Greek and neo-Greek art.

I have responded to your comments concerning the *Missa Solemnis* (Black Mass) of the Church of Satan and Temple of Set in another letter to you of this date.

(7) "LTC Aquino indicated that the wands seized in the search of his apartment were not placed into any bodily orifices at ceremonies."

The two ceremonial wands belonging to Mrs. Aquino and myself, and purchased from "The Enchanted Crystal" decorative glass shop on Union Street in San Francisco, were not "seized in the search". They were looked at and photographed, but were not taken.

I am utterly revolted at the kind of mind that, when looking at these two beautiful works of art, could only propose that they must have been used for "placing into bodily orifices". This is one more example of the disgusting misrepresentation of our religion by people whose minds are apparently fixed firmly on whatever perversions they can visualize. Would you ask a question like this to a Catholic priest about the phallus-like aspergillum he uses in his religious ceremonies?

(8) Since I have never seen one of Betty Narvaez' statues prior to the one at the ARPERCEN sale, I don't see how she could say that "I could have easily obtained a similar statue and had it in my home in California in 1986". I have no idea where her wares may be sold apart from that one store in the St. Louis shopping center, or even if they are available anywhere in San Francisco. I did not have any similar statue in my San Francisco home. This was clearly evident in the raid, when our home was thoroughly ransacked and photographed. Why would I have bought another statue from her now if I already had one? If I wanted two, why would they not have been displayed together

as a set? I find this attempt to lead Ms. Narvaez into a random speculation about my ability to find her statues around the country as absurd as trying to transform lion-footed bathtubs into chairs: once again an attempt to manipulate the answer to an easily-dispensed-with question into something that insinuates exactly the opposite.

I have freely, truthfully, and candidly provided information to the CID on any and all questions that occurred to you - even those which clearly ranged beyond specific allegations to all areas of my personal, professional, and religious life. I have done so on the assumption that your investigation was and is a dispassionate and non-weighted search for the truth. It concerns me when I see indications that there is some sort of "lust for the hunt" here: that in the absence of any evidence whatever supporting Adams-Thompson's attack on my wife and myself, even the most outlandish and preposterous speculations are advanced as "something, anything to cling to". I hope that this is not the tone of this investigation, and that in raising these issues you were merely clearing the air of questions which, however ridiculous, others had raised to you.

Sincerely,
/s/ Michael A. Aquino
Lt. Colonel, Military Intelligence

cc-Captain Thomas Hayes

Appendix 53: Letter #2, Michael Aquino to Major Mark Harvey 5/31/89

Dear Major Harvey: May 31, 1989

Your memorandum of May 18, 1989 evidences your continuing interest in the *Missa Solemnis* (Black Mass) ritual of the Church of Satan as contained in Appendix #7 of my *Church of Satan* documentary history. While I have discussed the nature and purpose of that religious ceremony in the chapter of *COS* to which that appendix pertains, I should like to make some additional points concerning it.

(1) The Black Mass was and is an official, formal religious ceremony of the Church of Satan and the Temple of Set. As you know, it is not the ritual-murder ceremony described in Huysmans' *La-Bas* novel (the "stereotype Black Mass" of popular myth), but rather a psychodrama composed by Priest Wayne West for the Church of Satan. It of course involves no criminal or immoral activity whatever.

Our Black Mass possesses the same religious significance, and enjoys the same Constitutional protection, as any other religious ceremony in any other legally-recognized and credentialled church. While it was employed more by the Church of Satan than it has been by the Temple of Set, it forms a part of our religious heritage and, as such, is considered as sacred a practice as any other religious ceremony formally observed by the Temple of Set.

(2) At the time I presided at the 1970 Black Mass, I was an ordained Priest of the Church of Satan and as such was expected to perform official ceremonies of the Church for its membership. I was specifically asked to preside over the 1970 Black Mass at the Central Grotto of the Church by Anton LaVey, High Priest of the Church. This is no different from the responsibilities of priests, ministers, pastors, and rabbis from other religions, who are expected and required to conduct religious services for their respective congregations.

(3) The Black Mass - including the one in 1970 at which I presided as recounted in *The Church of Satan* - was not performed as a pageant for non-members of the Church of Satan. It was not performed for money, nor for mere entertainment, nor for any ulterior purpose. It was performed for the explicit reasons discussed in Anton LaVey's *Satanic Rituals*, as well as for those discussed in my *Church of Satan* history. Only adults who were members of the Church of Satan were in attendance, and these by prior request and invitation only.

In the *Satanic Rituals*, in the section concerning the Black Mass, LaVey writes: "While [the Black Mass] maintains the degree of blasphemy necessary to make it effective psychodrama, it does not dwell on inversion purely for the sake of blasphemy, but elevates the concepts of Satanism to a noble and rational degree. This ritual is a psychodrama in the truest sense. Its prime purpose is to **reduce or negate the stigma acquired through past indoctrination**. It is also a vehicle for **retaliation against unjust acts perpetrated in the name of Christianity**." [Emphasis mine.]

Allow me to discuss these two points in some detail:

(a) **Reduce past indoctrination**: The Satanic/Setian religion has always placed great importance on freeing the individual from crippling, self-destructive superstition and indoctrination. By satirizing and lampooning a vehicle of psychological control and intimidation used by a Satanist's former religion to keep him docile and fearful, we demonstrate the impotence of that vehicle and effectively free the individual from its domination. [I have gone into this principle in considerable detail in the relevant chapter in *COS*.]

It is for this reason that, as I believe I mentioned to you during your St. Louis visit, a Black Mass is tailored to its participants and audience by the officiating Priest. A Black Mass employing Christian symbolism would not be appropriate for persons with crippling inhibitions or superstitions stemming from Buddhist or Moslem indoctrination. The Christian-symbolism Black Mass, however, was naturally most appropriate within a Church of Satan membership which had generally come from a Christianity-conditioned background.

According to Captain Hayes, you are bothered by the element of humor in the Black Mass over which I presided, the implication presumably being that such humor somehow casts doubt on its being a sincere religious ritual. Nothing could be further from the truth. As discussed above, one of the prime purposes of the ritual is to eliminate fear [of the deity whose wrath was previously used to threaten an individual with pre-or posthumous punishment for "blasphemy"]. The ability to laugh at a sacred cow is thus important, indeed crucial. All religious ceremonies of the Church of Satan and Temple of Set enjoyed an atmosphere of pleasant and fearless spontaneity, wherein it was never felt necessary to "march to robotlike choreography". If something amusing occurred - like Anton LaVey's making "magical signs" to dissuade the "nun" from exceeding her role - it was no "sin" to chuckle at it. Nor did it prevent the same ceremony from returning to complete seriousness the next minute. And this brings me to the second point:

(b) **Retaliation against unjust acts perpetrated in the name of Christianity**: If you yourself are a Christian, it may seem insulting to you that the Church of Satan would practice a religious ceremony that criticizes everything which you hold most sacred. Permit me to point out, however, that the gander is more at fault than the goose in this instance: Christianity has been hurling the most vehement and unjustified abuse at Satan in its rituals, literature, statements, and actions for the past two thousand years. The Black Mass is a reaction and response to this; it is not an unprovoked initiative.

Although Christian intolerance and persecution of "heretics" date from antiquity, attacks on nonChristians grew steadily. More times than can be counted the populations of conquered "heathen" cultures were given the choice to convert or be put to the sword. Wars such as the Crusades were regularly funded and fought simply to spread this Christianity's sphere of control.

The Middle Ages and the Renaissance witnessed the uninterrupted slaughter of accused witches and Satanists throughout Europe. Not content with just killing "infidels" and "heretics", Christians invented history's most ghastly torture devices for prolonging their death agonies: iron masks that were heated red-hot then spiked to victims' faces, iron maidens, racks, boots, screws, and backbreaking wheels that are still preserved in scores of European museums. If unfortunates survived such torture, death by burning at the stake was their reward. The number of accused Satanists tortured and killed in the European witch-craze has been estimated by historians as at least 13 million.

I could go on about the Thirty Years' War, the extermination of whole pre-Columbian civilizations, and the Christian pogroms against Jews which set the stage for the Nazi holocaust of this century. But I trust the point is taken: Christianity's history is awash in blood - including in major part **our** blood as Satanists. We have good reason to reject it as a terrible plague of intolerance, misery, and cruelty - in historical impact a stark antithesis to the messages of peace, brotherhood, and love it insists that it represents.

Are things better now? Is "modern Christianity" benevolent, harmless, and tolerant? **This very investigation**, and the concurrent national campaign of hate and lies directed against our religion, are graphic evidence that, unless held in check by secular laws (such as the First Amendment), the more extreme elements of Christianity remain as intolerant of and dangerous to other religions as ever. It is the fanatic element within Christianity which accuses the Satanic religion of the most foul, perverted, and sexually-obsessed crimes it can invent. It has shown itself to be utterly contemptuous of "truth" and "justice" except as it defines them for its own advantage.

May I point out **again** that it is a **Christian** minister who falsely and maliciously attacked my wife and myself, without the slightest qualms or concern for the harm he has caused to two innocent strangers - and with arrogant confidence that, **because** he is a Christian minister and a chaplain, the CID would not dare to find fault with him for attacking a Satanist. Obviously he regards you as politically obedient tools - less dramatic than the rack or the iron maiden, to be sure, but just as effective in destroying a non-Christian religion within an Army which he regards as an essentially Christian preserve. It commissions and pays, after all, a Corps of Chaplains which is overwhelmingly

Christian. With government money (which is not supposed to support any religion) it builds Christian churches on military bases and funds activities in support of chaplains' efforts to further Christian indoctrination.

As you know from the media reports and other documentation I have provided you, Mrs. Aquino and I have not just been fighting for our good name against the malice of Adams-Thompson; Satanists across the country and in other countries have suddenly been forced to defend their persons, families, and religion against this surprising and unbelievably vicious assault - a wave of hate-propaganda and witch-hunts on a scale unmatched since the Nazis' campaign against the Jewish religion in the 1930s.

As I commented to you in St. Louis, the Temple of Set had thought to put the Black Mass out to pasture in 1975, as a theological statement which had happily become obsolete in the tolerant, New-Age atmosphere of the 1970s. All religions, we now supposed, could co-exist freely, cooperatively, and constructively. It seems we were naïvely over-optimistic. If you are taken aback by the vehemence of the Black Mass, kindly remember the very tangible horrors directed against us which have caused such a bitter statement to be necessary.

Sincerely,
/s/ Michael A. Aquino
Lt. Colonel, Military Intelligence

Enclosure: *A Manual of Exorcism*[209]

---

[209] Appendix #54. This was sent to Harvey to illustrate his own religion's (Catholicism) attitude towards Satanism.

Appendix 54: Catholic Church Rite of Exorcism[210]

A Manual of Exorcism
Very Useful for Priests and Ministers of the Church

The victim may be possessed by the Devil in two ways, namely: *per obsesionem*, and *per possesionem. Per obsesionem* is when the Devil is outside or around the person and then torments him with horrible faces, frightening shapes, and in other ways, as the exorcist will find out by experience. *Per possesione*m is when the Devil is inside the victim and possesses him. Then he torments him with blows, pains of the body, etc. This being understood, the symptoms according to Holy Scripture are:

First, the lack of obedience of the possessed person, his obstinacy and disobedience in relation to keeping the law of God and to the things regarding His holy service. Take the example of Saul, when David was playing the harp for him. Instead of thanking him, Saul threw a lance at him, attempting to take his life.

The second is a sudden illness, which excites him to a rage, biting his hands, throwing himself on the ground, in the fire, in the water, putting him in danger of depression and of taking his life, as they say about the lunatic of the Gospel and of others possessed by the Devil, referred to in Matthew, 8 and 17, Mark, 9, Luke, 11 and Acts 19.

The third is if the afflicted person really shakes and is upset in the presence of sacred objects such as the Cross, relics of saints, and also of the exorcist himself. This is more true when he is not aware or does not know that there are relics or sacred objects present.

Fourth: the hatred that the possessed person has toward spiritual things, such as not wanting to enter the Church, and if he does enter, leaving immediately, refusing to use holy water or to look at or kiss the statues of the saints and especially the Cross. They cannot say or hear holy words. If they are taken to hear Mass, they feel very disturbed and despondent. But when they are entirely in their senses, they confess that they love all these things, although with some confusion which hinders and restrains them.

Fifth: blaspheming God, His saints and relics; cursing the statues; abusing and insulting without reason those who accompany them; speaking and understanding Latin without having studied it; discussing the fine points of the deep mysteries of the faith and holy scripture, although uneducated; discovering and revealing secret things and hidden sins that only could be known by the person who committed them. In especially ignorant peasants, however, the Devil rarely speaks Latin in order to better disguise his presence and stratagems, or because the language does not help him very well, as Father Rafael de la Torre says: *quia lingua ad unum idioma habituata, est illi obedentior, et ad mutus illi placentes*, explained in Question 90, article 2.[211]

The symptoms which the authorities list for recognizing possession by the Devil are of three types. Some only arouse suspicion, others great conjecture, and others are conclusive. Those which only arouse suspicion are: sudden change of personality, such as having been a very pleasant, loving, quiet and peaceful person and now very belligerent and wild, given to disputes and quarrels, etc. They may have unusual, recurrent nightmares in which they have made a pact with the Devil or have called on him for service and help. Many times these symptoms are not conclusive, but in conjunction with others they give rise to great caution.

Those manifestations which cause great suspicion are: unaccustomed howling and hearing voices, horrible and ferocious visions; absence of feeling in the limbs, a loss of almost all the vital processes, and an extraordinary restlessness so that the sick person cannot be quiet and seeks out dark and solitary places. He may have an endurance and strength which exceed human power. He may also throw himself on the ground or in the water attempting to end his life, etc.

Those signs which are conclusive are: suddenly speaking foreign tongues or reading, writing and singing in ingenious ways without any special grace or miracle of God, and revealing secrets or noteworthy things which happened in foreign countries. In order for these symptoms to be conclusive, there must be no agreement with the Devil, as happens with wizards, who discover and reveal secrets without being possessed by the Devil. If, when they come to their senses, they cannot remember what they have said, or if they are told to be quiet and do not obey,

---

[210] Enclosed with Appendix #53.

[211] "quia..." because a tongue accustomed to a single language is more obedient to him [sc. a demon].

it is a sign that it is the Devil who is speaking. Likewise, if the person blasphemes in the presence, of sacred objects, or cannot say a prayer or tolerate having holy water put on him or having the sign of the cross made on his forehead, or hearing the exorcisms, the gospel or this verse of the canticle of Moses: *Deum, qui te genuit, dereliquisti, oblitus es Domini creatoris tui*[212] , or the other: *da laudem, et gloriam Deo*[213] .

ELEVENTH DOCUMENT:
OF EXORCISMS AND CONJURATIONS

Antiphon: O Lord, think not of my offenses, nor those of my parents; neither take revenge of our sins. Tob. 3.3
Our Father. V) And lead us not into temptation. R) But deliver us from evil. *Psalm 53* Save me, O God, by thy name, and judge me in your strength, etc. Glory be to the Father, etc. V) Save your servant, O Lord. R) Who puts his trust in you, O my God. V) Be for him, O Lord, a tower of strength. R) Against the face of the enemy. V) May the enemy accomplish nothing in him. R) And the son of iniquity not draw nigh to harm him. V) Send help to him, O Lord, from the holy place. R) And protect him from out of Sion. V) O Lord hear my prayer. R) And let my cry come unto thee. V) The Lord be with you. R) And with thy spirit.

Let us pray.

O God, who always hast mercy and forgiveness, receive our prayer that the compassion of your pity mercifully unbind this your servant, or handmaid, whom the bond of sin constrains.

Holy Lord, almighty Father, eternal God, Father of our Lord Jesus Christ, who hast sent the tyrant and apostate in exile to the fires of Gehenna, and hast sent your only begotten Son into this world to shred him raging into little pieces: quickly give ear to us, make haste to rescue man, made in your image and likeness, from ruin and the demon of midday. Lay terror, O Lord, on the beast that lays waste your vineyard. Give confidence to your servants to fight vigorously against the wicked dragon, lest he despise those who hope in you, lest he say as once he did through Pharaoh: "I know not the Lord, neither will I let Israel go" (Ex. 5.2). Let your powerful right arm force him to depart from your servant (or handmaid) N. +. Let him presume no longer to hold captive him whom you deigned to create in your image. Make room for the Holy Spirit by this sign + of our Lord Jesus Christ who with the Father and the same Holy Spirit hast deigned to create him, and in your Son to redeem him. Who lives and reigns for ever and ever. R) Amen.

If the demon has not shown himself when you finish saying this, proceed, saying:

God commands you and I adjure you, wicked and hateful spirits who still occupy this creature and vex him. by your obstinate rebellion; by God the Father + and the Son + and the Holy Spirit + , and by the holy Virgin Mary, Mother of God, and by all that can force and bind you in the name of Jesus Christ: to come out immediately and rise up directly by the right side between flesh and skin to the tongue, in such a way that he [the victim] suffer no injury or pain. Stand before me and obey me in all things as God's minister. Acknowledge your sentence and give honor to the living God.

While all are standing, say:

Again and again as minister of God I command you not to hurt this creature, or me, or another; and not to say anything except to the praise and glory of God. Again and again, by the power granted to me by Christ the Lord, I command you: let none of you come down to harm or dare to twist the face, tongue, cheeks, and ears of this creature of God.

Otherwise, in the power of the great and wonderful Adonai and the authority of our Lord Jesus Christ, through all that was said above: let there rise up against you in all his rage and fury either Lucifer, the wicked spirit himself, or another of the seven worse than himself, with all the tormenting spirits and penalties of hell; and as a brutal minister of God torture you violently with all the pains of hell until the day of judgment, by all that was said above. Amen.

Then proceed, saying the Gospel of Saint John, or another, over the possessed person and when finished say:
V) O Lord, hear my prayer. R) And let my cry come unto thee. V) The Lord be with you. R) And with thy spirit.

Let us pray.

---

[212] "Thou hast forsaken the God that begot thee, and hast forgotten the God that created thee."

[213] "Give praise and glory to God. Deut. 32.18.

Almighty Lord, Word of God the Father, Jesus Christ, God and Lord of all Creation, who gayest to your holy apostles the power to tread on serpents and dragons; who among the other commands of your wonderful works didst deign to say: "Be gone, demons;" (Lk. 10.18) and by whose power Satan fell like lightning from heaven: I call on your holy name with fear and trembling to give to me, your unworthy servant, once all my sins have been forgiven, a steady faith and power to approach this cruel demon with safety and the protection of your holy arm; through you, Jesus Christ, Lord our God,. who will come to judge the living and the dead and the world by fire. R) Amen.

When this prayer is over, the exorcist and the possessed person both cross themselves. The exorcist will put a part of his stole on the victim's neck, and putting his right hand on the victim's head, and showing him the cross with the other hand, he should say with great faith and confidence:

V) Behold the cross of the Lord; enemies, take flight. R)

The lion of the tribe of Juda, the root of David hath prevailed. V) O Lord, hear etc. R) And let etc. V) The Lord be with you. R) And with thy spirit.

Let us pray.

O God and Father of our Lord Jesus Christ, I call on your holy name and devoutly pray your mercy to grant me aid against this and every filthy spirit that troubles this your creature. Through the same Jesus Christ, your Son, our Lord, who lives and reigns with you in the unity of the Holy Spirit, God, for ever and ever. Amen.

EXORCISM

I exorcize you, filthy spirit, every invasion of the enemy, every phantasm, every legion, in the name of our Lord Jesus Christ +. He who ordered you sunk below the earth commands you to decamp and be gone from this creature of God + . He who rules the sea, the winds and the storms commands you. Hear therefore and tremble, Satan, enemy of the faith and of the human race, procurer of death, ravisher of life, corruptor of justice, root of evil, source of error, seducer of mankind, betrayer of nations, inciter of envy, wellspring of avarice, cause of strife, arouser of sorrows. Why do you stay, why resist, since you know that Christ the Lord has ruined your forces? Cower at him who was offered up in Isaac, sold with Joseph, slaughtered in the lamb, crucified in man: and from this emerged the victor. *The following crosses are made on the possessed person's forehead.* Therefore depart in the name of the Father + and the Son + and the Holy Spirit +; make room for the Holy Spirit through this sign of the cross of our Lord Jesus Christ: who with the Father and the same Holy Spirit lives and reigns, God, forever and ever. R) Amen.

V) O Lord, hear my prayer. R) And let etc. V) The Lord be with you. R) And with thy spirit.

Let us pray.

O God, the founder and defender of the human race, who hast created man in your image: look on this servant (or handmaid) sought out by the tricks of a filthy spirit, set about by the racing horror of the inveterate foe and ancient enemy of earth, struck by stupefaction of the senses of the human mind, upset by terror, and spurred on by dread of trembling fear. Oppose, O Lord, the power of the devil and remove his tricky snares. Let the impious tempter fly. May your servant by this sign of your name on the forehead be defended and safeguarded in soul and body.

The next three crosses will be made on the sick person's chest.

Guard + the contents of this breast. Rule + the bowels. Strengthen + the heart. Let the assaults of the opposing power evaporate from the soul. O Lord, grant at this invocation of your most holy name the grace that he who until now has inspired terror may recede in fright and vanish in defeat; and also that this your servant return his bounden service to you with a strengthened heart and a sincere mind. Through our Lord Jesus Christ, your Son, who lives etc. R) Amen.

EXORCISM

I adjure you, serpent of old, cursed dog, by the judge of the living and the dead, by the maker of the world, by him who has the power to send you into Gehenna: depart immediately with the army of your rage from this servant of God, N., who returns to the bosom of the church. Again I adjure you + *on the forehead*, not by my frailty but by the power of the Holy Spirit: go out from this servant of God, N., whom almighty God has made in his image. Give way, therefore, give way not to me but to the minister of Christ. His power forces you who yoked you with his cross. His arm fear, who trampling on the groans of hell brought out the souls into the light. The body of man be your terror + *on the chest*. The image of God be your dread + *on the forehead*. Do not resist, do not linger in this man: for Christ was pleased to dwell in man. Though you know me well to be a sihner, sneer not at me. God + commands you. The majesty of Christ + commands you. The Holy + Spirit commands you. The sign of the cross + commands you. The faith of the holy apostles Peter + and Paul and the other saints commands you. The blood + of the martyrs commands you. The continence + of the holy confessors commands you. The intercession + of all the holy men and women of God commands you. The power of the rites + of the Christian faith commands you. Depart, then, trespasser; depart, seducer skilled in every deceit and lie, you enemy of virtue, hound of the innocent. Give way, most cruel, give way, most impious, give way to Christ. In him you have not found a single one of your own works; he looted you, he overturned your kingdom, he bound you captive, he snatched away your vessels, he cast you into outer darkness where ruin was prepared for you and your henchmen. Why hang on in truculence? Why boldly refuse? You are guilty before almighty God whose statutes you have transgressed, guilty before his Son, our Lord Jesus Christ, whom you dared to tempt and rashly crucified; guilty before the human race to whom with blandishments you gave the poisoned cup of death.

Therefore I adjure you, wicked dragon, in the name of the lamb + without blemish who has walked on the asp and the basilisk, who has trampled underfoot the lion and the dragon: (Ps 91.13), depart from this man + *on the forehead*, depart from the church of God (*make a sign of the cross over the bystanders*) +; tremble and take flight at the invocation of the name of the Lord whom the lower reaches fear, to whom are subject the virtues and powers and dominions of heaven, whom the cherubim and seraphim praise with unwearied voices, saying: "Holy, holy, holy, Lord God of hosts." (Is. 6.3) The word made flesh + commands you. The child of the Virgin + commands you. Jesus of Nazareth + commands you who ordered you to depart, cast down and flattened, from the man after you had despised his disciples; for once he had separated you from that man you didn't dare, while he was present, to invade the flock of swine. Adjured in his name + now therefore depart from man whom he created. Adonai + commands you. Soter + commands you. Eloim + Eloa commands you: Jehovah + commands you. Agla + Sadai commands you. You are obstinate in wishing to resist +. You are obstinate in kicking against the pricks +. For the longer you take to leave, the greater your punishment grows; for you are spurning not men but him who rules the living and the dead, who is to come to judge the living and the dead and the world by fire, to whose command all give obedience. In his name it is right and just that every knee should bow, of those in heaven, on earth, and under the earth. R) Amen. Phil. 2.10

V) O Lord, hear etc. R) And let my cry etc. V) The Lord be with you. R) And with etc.

Let us pray.

O God of Heaven, God of earth, God of angels, God of archangels, God of prophets, God of apostles, God of martyrs, God of virgins, God who hast power to give life after death and rest after work; for there is no God but you, nor could there be any true God but you, creator of heaven and earth, who art true king and whose reign will have no end: I humbly beseech your majesty to free this your servant from unclean spirits, through Christ our Lord. Amen.

EXORCISM

I adjure you, every filthy spirit, every phantasm, every invasion of Satan, in the name of Jesus Christ + of Nazareth, who after baptism in the Jordan was led into the desert and vanquished you in your own house: I adjure you cease your attack on him + [the victim] whom he created from the slime of the earth to the honor of his glory, and in this miserable man tremble not at his human frailty but at the image of almighty God. Give in, then, to God who through his servant Moses drowned you and your malice in Pharaoh and his army in the deep. Give in to God + who through his faithful servant David put you to flight from King Saul with spiritual songs. Give in to God + who damned you in the traitor Judas Iscariot. Now is he touching you with divine lashes, in whose presence, trembling with your legions and crying out, you said: "What have we to do with thee, Jesus, the Son of the most high God? Art thou come here to torment us before our time?" (Mk. 1.24; 5.7). He is spurring you with unceasing flames, who at the end of time will say to the wicked: "Depart from me, ye cursed, into everlasting fire which was prepared for the devil and his angels." (Mt. 25.41) For you and your angels there will be undying worms. For you and your angels an unextinguishable fire is being prepared: because you are the inventor of damnable murder, the author of incest, the origin of sacrilege, the teacher of depraved deeds, the instructor of heretics, the inventor of all obscenity. Therefore, depart, wicked and depraved , depart with all your tricks, for God has willed man to be his temple.

Here the exorcist can strike the possessed person on the shoulders with the stole.

But why do you stay here longer? Give honor to God the Father almighty + to whom every knee bows. Make room for the Lord Jesus Christ who poured out his sacred blood for man. Make room for the Holy Spirit + who through his blessed apostle Peter openly humbled you in Simon the magician; who condemned your tricks in Ananias and Saphiras; who smote you giving honor to God in King Herod; who through his apostle Paul ruined you with the mist of blindness in Elymas the magician and bade you in a word to depart from the Snake Woman and perish. Now therefore depart +, depart, seducer. The underworld will be your home; your dwelling-place a serpent, to creep and grovel. Now is no time for delay. For behold, the triumphant Lord approaches quickly, and before him will burn a fire which shall precede him and consume his enemies round about. For though you might have fooled man, you cannot mock God. He casts you out, from whose eyes nothing is hidden. He expels you, to whose power all things are subdued. He shuts you out, who has prepared an everlasting Gehenna for you and your angels. From his mouth shall come forth a sharp sword, and he will come to judge the living and the dead and the world by fire. Amen. (Apoc. 1:16;19.15)

Next he will say the Magnificat, *and when it is finished he will say the following exorcism.*

May the undefiled Mother of God crush you and your pride, O apostate angels, she to whom the angel Gabriel was sent from God into a city of Galilee called Nazareth to announce, after a salutation, the conception of the Lord by saying: "Behold, thou shalt conceive and shalt bring forth a son, and thou shalt call his name Jesus; he shall be great, and shall be called the Son of the most High. This shall happen by the Holy Spirit coming over thee and the power of the most High overshadowing thee." And Mary answered: "Behold Mary, the handmaid of the Lord; let it be done to me according to thy word." (Lk. 1.26)

May she crush you and your pride who, when she found herself growing great with child arose and went into the hill country with haste into a city of Juda, and she entered into the house of Zacharias and saluted Elizabeth. And it came to pass that when Elizabeth heard the salutation of Mary, the infant leaped in her womb, and Elizabeth was filled with the Holy Spirit and she cried out saying: "Blessed art thou among women, and blessed is the fruit of thy womb."

May she conquer you and all your pride, who nine months after conception, while all things were in quiet silence and the night was in the midst of her course (Wis. 18.14/15), brought forth her firstborn son and wrapped him up in swaddling clothes and laid him in a manger because there was no room for him in the inn.

May she confound your boldness who remained a virgin before, during, and after childbirth.

May she blunt your impudence, in whom was ended the famous word of Eve's unhappiness: "In sorrow shalt thou bring forth children," (Gen. 3.16) for she brought forth the Lord in gladness. Eve sorrowed, but she rejoiced. Eve carried tears in her belly, but she bore inner joy: for the one gave birth to a sinner, the other an innocent and liberator of sinners. May she move against you by her achievements, whose lying-in was the beginning of salvation and signaled joy throughout the world: for she is the flower of the field from whom arose the precious lily of the valley, by whose birth the earlier order of creation was changed and guilt was extinguished; for from her is arisen the sun of justice, Christ our God, who by loosing the curse brought down the blessing, by confounding death endowed us with eternal life.

May she put you to flight, who in Cana of Galilee as the wine gave out said to her son: "They have no wine," (Jn. 2.3) and then to the servants: "Whatsoever he shall say to you, do ye." May she cast you out to the places suitable to you, O corrupters of a wounded mind; she who stood with Mary of Cleophas and Mary Magdalene by the cross of Jesus Christ her son, who as he saw her said: "Woman, behold thy son." (Jn. 19.6) then he said to his disciple John: "Behold thy mother." And from that hour the disciple received her into his own.

May she cast you down to suitable places, who, when she had paid off the debt of the flesh and was overcome by death, was taken up to the heavenly bridal chamber in which the king of kings sits on a starry throne.

Finally, may she drive you out, who just as Christ's magnificance is lifted above the heavens so is she raised above the choirs of angels to the realms of heaven. Trusting in her merits and prayers and by the authority of her son I command you to depart in haste and leave this creature of God loose and free of every wicked trick.

How long will you stay? Why do you linger? What are you bold enough to think? Take flight, you rebels against everlasting majesty; give way, you damned, to God and depart from this image of the holy Trinity for the places which God has prepared for you.

Here the exorcist will ask the demon why he does not want to leave, and he can proceed.

Say the litany of the saints, and when it is finished:

Christ hear us. Christ graciously hear us. Lord, have mercy. Christ have mercy. Lord have mercy. Our Father, etc. V) And lead us not, etc. R) But deliver us, etc. V) Lord hear, etc. R) And let my cry, etc. V) The Lord, etc. R) And with, etc.

Let us pray.

Grant us your servants, O Lord God, to rejoice in everlasting health of mind and body, and by the glorious intercession of the blessed Mary ever Virgin to be freed from current sorrow and enjoy eternal happiness. Through Christ our Lord. Amen.

O Virgin Mary who didst crush the serpent's head; who puttest demons to flight and scatterest evildoers, come to our aid lest this creature made in the image and likeness of your son be further tormented; and hear the prayers which we bring to the ears of your pity and mercy, so that by your intercession he may obtain the health he hopes for through the favor of Jesus Christ your son who was crucified and reigns for ever and ever. Amen.

Let us pray.

O glorious Virgin, mistress of heaven and earth, most holy mother of our Lord Jesus Christ, come to our aid lest this creature made in the image and likeness of your son be further tormented; and hear the prayers which we bring to the ears of your pity and mercy, so that under your protection, blessed lady, and by your only begotten son and your ineffable merits, he [sc. the victim] may not fear the torments of the devil, but gain the freedom he hopes for, preservation, and help against all evil spirits. Through our Lord Jesus Christ your Son who was crucified and now reigns for ever and ever. Amen.

Therefore, cursed devil, immediately acknowledge your sentence: give honor to the true and living God, give honor to our Lord Jesus Christ, give honor to the blessed Virgin Mary, and with your doings depart from this creature which our Lord Jesus Christ redeemed with his precious blood.

Declaration and Verdict

Otherwise, if you do not obey my orders, I condemn you eternally to the farthest depth of hell, and may your penalties increase a hundred thousand and a thousand times a thousand thousand times more than the pains of those who suffer in the deepest chasm. Again I command you to obey my orders under penalty of going for all time to the pool of fire and sulphur from the mouth of which comes out a sharp two-edged sword, and may it devour you through all time according to God's ordinance in that loathsome place.

I conjure you further by the aforementioned pains and by hundreds of thousands more, steadily increasing, to obey my earlier instructions; and this I command not by my own power and authority but in the name of him who cast you out of heaven for your pride and envy, and with the support of the faith and sanctity of the church for which I act as agent. Furthermore, I admonish all the princes and masters and every enemy who might have power over you: that (lest you overlook these imminent penalties and others in hundreds and hundreds of thousands, and thousands of hundreds of thousands, constantly increasing) should they not force you immediately, without delay, and instantly to obey my commands and then actually to depart from the body of this creature, N., and should you not obey: I will bring against you the sentence of your damnation, excommunication, and condemnation in the pool of fire and sulphur throughout eternity.

I curse and excommunicate, I cast out and smite you damned devils in the power of the most holy Trinity, the Father +, the Son +, and the Holy + Spirit.

May God the Father curse you, may God the Son curse you, and God the Holy Spirit; and may all your enemies among the devils and your leader Satan cast you out and smite you; be you cursed in this body and outside it, in the air, water, fire, earth, or wherever else you will be; and may you suffer intolerable pains and exceeding anguish unless you withdraw at once, with all your wicked tricks, from the body of this creature, N., never to return again.[214]

---

[214] I daresay this Rite of Exorcism was effective, because I can't think of any dæmons known to me who would sit still for more than a few minutes of this excruciating drivel.

Appendix 55: Letter, Captain Thomas Hayes to Commander 6RCID 5/31/89

Department of the Army
US Army Trial Defense Service
Presidio Field Office
Presidio of San Francisco, California 94129

AFKC-ZM-JA-TDS (27-10)   31 May 1989

MEMORANDUM THRU

Command Judge Advocate, Headquarters 6th Region, Criminal Investigation Division Command, Presidio of San Francisco, California 94129

FOR Commander, Headquarters, 6th Region, Criminal Investigation Division Command, Presidio of San Francisco, California 94129

SUBJECT: Request to Review CID File Prior to Titling Decision

1. I write in my capacity as defense counsel to make an unusual request. I have been in contact with your Command Judge Advocate, MAJ Mark Harvey, for many weeks monitoring the progress of the ongoing investigation of LTC Michael Aquino. I attended two exhaustive days of recorded interview with CID Agents Dan Cates, Steve Petaluna and MAJ Harvey at LTC Aquino's home in St. Louis. Because this is such an unusual case and the potential harm to LTC Aquino is so great, I request that he be provided a copy of the investigation before you, as the Region Commander, make a decision on whether my client should be placed in the title block of the report.

2. The case involves many bits and pieces of facts. The very nature of the allegations made by Chaplain Adams-Thompson through his daughter Kinsey, are so repugnant that it is easy to allow one's focus to shift from reality. Kinsey's lengthy ramblings to her psychologist, LTC Hickey, and the suspicious notes made by her   m o t h e r have been the grains from which many of the CID's concerns arose.

3. Recently MAJ Harvey was concerned at having seen a statue of a panther at LTC Aquino's home in St. Louis. It appears that one of the children reported having seen a statue of a lion in the place where abuse was alleged to have occurred. LTC Aquino immediately responded to MAJ Harvey's concern with a record of where he purchased the statue and the price paid long after he moved from San Francisco. Small details such as these that cause concern must be put to rest if there is to be a fair and just titling decision.

4. I request that the CID provide LTC Aquino a copy of the draft report prior to your final decision on titling. Even after a lengthy interview, there still may be bothersome questions. LTC Aquino only asks that he be given an opportunity to meet these concerns with answers and documentary evidence. If CID regulations would prohibit your office from producing a copy of the report for me before it is "final", LTC Aquino can arrange to review it at the Granite City, Illinois office. The CID could only be commended by those truly interested in the truth for arranging such a review. Please ask MAJ Harvey to call me when you have decided whether or not to honor this request.

/s/ Thomas M. Hayes III
Captain, Judge Advocate
Senior Defense Counsel

Appendix 56: Letter, Michael Aquino to Colonel Webster Ray 6/20/89

June 20, 1989

Colonel Webster D. Ray, Commander
6th Region USACIDC
Presidio of San Francisco
San Francisco, CA 94129

Dear Colonel Ray:

Captain Hayes of the Trial Defense Service has advised me of the following three recent developments:

(1) That your headquarters has denied my request to be permitted to review the investigative report concerning me for objectivity and accuracy prior to your making a decision whether or not to title me based upon it.

(2) That Major Harvey, your Region Judge Advocate, has told Hayes that there is nothing in the report on which court-martial charges against me could conceivably be supported.

(3) That Harvey has told Hayes that he nevertheless fully expects that I will be titled for the accusations by Chaplain Adams-Thompson anyway.

This surprising third statement by Harvey has prompted me to write this letter. Please permit me to speak candidly:

I am under no illusion whatever that either you or anyone else in the CID investigative or command structure thinks for a moment that I had anything to do with either the Adams-Thompson child or any other child. The evidence of my innocence, and of Adams-Thompson's deliberate malice in attacking Mrs. Aquino and myself, is both obvious and explicit.

Therefore, if Harvey's statement to Hayes is correct, the facts of the case are and always were irrelevant to any decision to title. Rather it appears that it was intended from the beginning that I be titled, and that Adams-Thompson's many violations of UCMJ #133 simply be ignored, no matter what the investigation itself might bring to light. From FOIA papers I have recently received from the government, it is evident that this CID investigation was ordered in November 1988 as a consequence of public and Congressional pressure to "deal with me" [in the words of one DA document] following my appearance on Geraldo Rivera's October 25, 1988 "Satanism" special to defend the legitimacy and ethics of my religion.

Evidently it was ordered that I be titled regardless of the outcome of the investigation in order to give the Army a lever to force me out of active service, either by threatening me with court-martial charges if I would not leave voluntarily or by using the titling as an excuse for administrative expulsion. The Adams-Thompson allegations, revived after being ignored by the CID for over a year, merely served as an available excuse. Whether or not this chaplain maliciously attacked an innocent officer and his wife is not deemed a problem which would trouble the Army. A finding by the. CID that a Christian chaplain committed a criminal act against a Satanist, however, would create a major public relations problem in which Christian activists around the country could be expected to criticize the Army vehemently and vociferously for such an "outrage".

I therefore perceive a situation in which a decision has been made to force me out of uniform so that the Army will no longer have to endure the the politically-awkward situation of having an active senior officer who is also a Satanist, the fact that he is as ethical as any other officer notwithstanding. On one hand, the DA Public Affairs Office will continue to issue statements, as it has, that my religious rights under the First Amendment are being scrupulously respected by the Army. On the other hand, a titling action will be used to force me out behind the scenes, ostensibly on grounds that have nothing to do with the First Amendment.

Obviously I do not expect you to confirm this scenario. I simply place it on the table as what I now understand the true situation to be. It is the purpose of this letter to communicate my own views on it, for consideration by you and the Department of the Army before you undertake any titling decision.

First, I appreciate the dilemma in which the Army finds itself - trapped on one hand by the legal requirements of the First Amendment and on the other by outside pressure to remove me from the Army. I further appreciate that, while the Army makes a reasonable attempt to respect civil and religious rights, it also cannot allow personal rights to jeopardize the functioning of the Army generally. If individual rights clash with the efficiency of the Army, it is ultimately those individual rights which must be abridged. That may not be how the law reads, but it appears to be how it is applied in practice.

I further appreciate that, while knowing of my religion for the last twenty years, the Army did not discriminate against me because of it, since the matter had not become a public issue. The attack by Adams-Thompson, coupled with the Presidio witch-hunt and the recent general national climate of anti-Satanic hysteria, changed all that, catapulting my presence into just such an issue. It may not have occurred by any action of mine, nor by the Army's, but it is there just the same.

I am prepared to cooperate with the Army on the constructive resolution of this situation, to include leaving active service at the end of my AGR tour if necessary.

However - and this is why I am writing this letter to you at this point in time - **under no circumstances** will I leave AGR service quietly if I am framed for a fictitious crime. If I am so titled, I will immediately and with all means at my disposal bring the details of this entire situation, to include the mishandling of the charges I preferred against Adams-Thompson, to all Army, civilian governmental, and public review agencies, officials, and private individuals concerned. This will include the widest possible media exposure, both domestic and foreign. I will also initiate any legal action against the Army which is available to me.

Any attempt to falsely title me in order to either intimidate me or force me out of uniform by administrative manipulation, therefore, will precipitate precisely what the Army presumably wishes to avoid: the explosion of this situation into a national scandal of the highest visibility - and ultimately of the greatest embarrassment to the Army. I have, after all, the truth and the documented facts to support me - and the means to ensure that they are made known. And I will not stop until my name is cleared, no matter how long it takes.

To date, while I have responded to media questions as necessary, I have intentionally avoided discussing the Army's handling of either the Adams-Thompson UCMJ charges or the current CID investigation with the press. This was on the assumption that, as Major Harvey originally indicated to me, the current investigation was a sincere effort by the CID to find the facts - which would inevitably result in the clearing of my name, the exposure of Adams-Thompson's malicious actions, and presumably the reactivation of the suppressed court-martial charges which I preferred against him.

In other words, I had no reason to discuss the situation with the press or public as long as I believed the Army to be acting in good faith to correct the existing injustice. If I now learn that my trust in the CID was misplaced - and that the investigation was simply an effort to manufacture anything at all, no matter how absurd, which could be used to support a titling of me - then I obviously have every justification to expose such misuse of the Army's criminal investigative machinery to the light of outside scrutiny and correction.

To preclude such a situation, it is not necessary for the CID to compromise its objectivity in any way, but simply to base its report and recommendation on precisely what it **should** be basing them on: **the truth**. I will therefore **not** be titled, and the concluding section of the report will state that there is **no** evidence that I am guilty of

any crime as alleged. Any language short of this - such as "insufficient evidence" - is not acceptable. [Language like that is merchandised by hate-groups as a *de facto* finding of "guilty but we can't prove it".]

I will not make any complaint, nor file any appeal, IG, or other action if Adams-Thompson is not titled in the report. Obviously he is guilty of a serious crime against Mrs. Aquino and myself. But apparently it is politically taboo for the Army to punish him because of it. He is a Christian chaplain, and the public image he has in consequence of the Presidio witch-hunt, no matter how ludicrous it may be, is of an aggrieved parent trying to protect his little girl from kidnapping, rape, and sodomy by Devil-worshipping pedophiles. Furthermore, to hold him officially accountable for his crime would reopen the question of whether the entire Presidio scandal was in fact as phony as the other copycat "child-care sex-abuse" scandals which have ravaged the country [to include many military installations] for the past several years. The Army has made it clear that it does not dare to ask this question, evidently for fear of public criticism by the militant parents who instigated these witch-hunts.

Again if I am fraudulently titled, however, this most assuredly will be an additional issue which I will insist upon bringing to widest possible official and public attention, to include the actions of "therapist" Lt. Col. Deborah Hickey in instigating and aggravating the hysteria in the case of the Presidio witch-hunt.

If I am not titled, and if the report concludes with a **clear** "no evidence" statement of exoneration, I will serve the remaining fourteen months of my AGR tour at ARPERCEN. My assignment as a resource manager is a low-visibility one, and there have been no public relations problems either internal to ARPERCEN or within the St. Louis community which would make it difficult for me to complete my tour. [Indeed both ARPERCEN and St. Louis generally have been very sympathetic to the ordeal which Mrs. Aquino and I have endured as a consequence of the Adams-Thompson attack.]

As General Ward, Chief of the Army Reserve, can confirm, I have been nonselected by the January 1989 AGR continuation board for retention in the AGR program past 30 August 1990. Since I substantially exceed all legitimate criteria for retention, I interpret this simply as one more move to force me out of uniform if the titling effort fails. I have retained an attorney to challenge the board action, and am confident in the outcome should a lawsuit be necessary. If I am not titled and am clearly exonerated, however, I would agree not to pursue this challenge, and instead to leave the AGR program on 30 August 1990. This date is sufficiently removed from the completion of the CID report that there will be no implication that I "left under threat".

Spectacles such as the Geraldo show are now most probably a thing of the past. With the exception of a small number of lunatic-fringe groups and individuals, the general populace now knows that the "Satanic child abuse" craze was a fraud no different from UFO abductions and Uri Geller's spoon-bending. Therefore my remaining time on active duty should pass quietly enough.

Obviously it is frustrating to me to see my AGR career destroyed by the action of one malicious individual, after I have devoted so many years and so much effort to qualifying and conducting myself as a conscientious and professional officer. Adams-Thompson, however, has evidently neutralized my ability to put my skills to effective use in the AGR program. Therefore it would appear appropriate for me to return to civilian life - as long as it is **quite** clear that I am doing so with no dishonor attached to my name, that of my family, or that of my church.

It is, I believe, in the interests of the Army to allow the situation to be resolved in this way. If it does not bring Adams-Thompson to justice, at least it does not compound his crime. As for my departure from the AGR program at the end of this tour, I am prepared to treat that as an unfortunate necessity driven by outside political forces over which neither the Army nor I have control.

Sincerely,
/s/ Michael A. Aquino
Lt. Colonel, Military Intelligence

Enclosure: Updated list of Adams-Thompson violations of Article 133, UCMJ.

cc- Honorable John 0. Marsh, Jr., Secretary of the Army
General Carl E. Vuono, Chief of Staff, U.S. Army
Major General William F. Ward, Chief, U.S. Army Reserve
Major General Eugene R. Cromartie, Commanding General, USACIDC
Mr. Gary R. Myers, Attorney
Captain Thomas M. Hayes III, Trial Defense Service

Appendix 57: Letter, Michael Aquino to Major Mark Harvey 7/4/89

July 4, 1989

Dear Major Harvey:

On June 30 Colonel Webster Ray, Commander of the 6th Region CID, informed Captain Hayes that he had decided to title me for the allegations made by Chaplain Adams-Thompson. Although you had stated to Hayes that Ray would not receive and review the CID investigative report until the week of June 26th (following Ray's return from TDY), Ray further told Hayes that he had made this decision **prior to departing on the TDY**. As the report had not been final-typed in its entirety even by the time Ray spoke to Hayes, it further confirms my impression that the report is merely incidental to a titling which had been pre-decided no matter what the investigation might bring to light concerning the truth of the situation. Contrary to what you said in your December 14, 1988 letter to Pillsbury, Madison, and Sutro, it now appears clear that the sole purpose of this investigation was to build - and if necessary fabricate - an argument to support that predetermined titling.

To date my requests to review the report, both in draft and in final form, have been denied. Until I am able to review it, I cannot comment upon its contents. I **can** comment, however, upon the contents of its cover-sheet as provided by you to Hayes. The following comments apply to Mrs. Aquino as well as myself:

"LOCATION OF OCCURRENCE: CHILD DEVELOPMENT CENTER (CDC), PRESIDIO OF SAN FRANCISCO; 123 ACME AVENUE; 208 DELORES STREET."

(1)   I have never been to the CDC nor had any contact with it, and the CID knows that there is **no** evidence to the contrary.

(2)   There is **no** evidence whatever that **any** crime as alleged ever occurred at our 123 Acme Avenue home. The pre-publicity "interior descriptions" of 123 assembled into a "package story" and attributed to Kinsey Almond by Adams-Thompson were all wrong, and a fraudulently backdated, post-publicity diary alteration by Mrs. Adams-Thompson to try to support that package story cannot change that fact. The surprise police raid yielded not a single item of pedophilia or anything indicating that I have the slightest interest in or involvement with this subject. As for the external "identification" of 123 by Almond in the company of her mother, her simultaneous "identification" of the rental car which the Adams-Thompsons had seen and mistakenly believed to be ours reveals both the spuriousness of the "identification" and the obvious coaching of the infant to "identify on cue.[215]

(3)   As I have never been to 208 Delores Street in my life, nor ever met nor had any other contact with Gary Hambright in my life, there can be no evidence to the contrary.

(4)   In his initial allegations against Gary Hambright in April 1987, Adams-Thompson specified the CDC as the location. He made **no** mention of any other location whatever.

(5)   In her "therapy" sessions with Debbie Hickey, Almond made **no** single coherent statement about being taken to any building remotely identifiable as 123 Acme Avenue. On the other hand, she rambled on about being taken to a variety of other houses owned by other people and with interior and exterior features totally unlike anything at 123.

CONCLUSION: All statements in "Location of occurrence" are deliberately false and unsubstantiated.

---

[215] As of this date I had still not seen, indeed did not know of the existence of the CID report of that "identification trip" which established that no such "identification" actually took place at all. The 6RCID, of course, was well aware of that document.

"DATE/TIME OF OCCURRENCE: ON OR ABOUT MAY-JULY 1986 BETWEEN 0730 AND 1600 HOURS."

(1)   The period of May-July 1986 passed without Kinsey Almond ever being taken for the kind of emergency medical care that a 2-year-old who had been raped and sodomized by 2 men (Chaplain A-T's package story) would have required. [While my FOIA request for access to the A-T medical records has been denied, it is reasonable to assume that, had any such incident occurred in May-July, the A-Ts would have noticed it immediately, emergency medical care would have been required, and the Presidio witch-hunt would have been instigated then instead of six months later.]

(2)   Similarly the period September-October 1986 passed without Almond being taken for such emergency medical care, and without the A-Ts noticing anything the least indicative of rape, sodomy, or any other molestation.

(3)   When ca. April 1987 the A-Ts first decided to participate in the Presidio witch-hunt by accusing someone (Hambright), they selected September-October 1986. When in August 1987 they decided to switch targets to Mrs. Aquino and myself, they retained the September-October 1986 accusation-dates. They retained these dates throughout the entire SFPD investigation and media coverage which followed.

(4)   As it quickly became clear that Mrs. Aquino and I had PCSd from the Presidio to Washington in July 1986, and had not been present in San Francisco on any date since then when Almond was at the day-care center, that fact in itself should suffice to absolve us from A-T's accusation. **The CID, however, just arbitrarily revised the dates of accusation to fit a time when we were still in San Francisco prior to PCS.** In this agenda-driven investigation, evidently, factual circumstances which disprove the allegations are *a priori* unacceptable and must therefore be ignored or quietly altered in the hope that no one would notice. I did notice.

(5)   No accuser has provided **any evidence whatever** that anything criminal took place at 123 during the May-July 1986 time period. On the other hand, an Army Lieutenant Colonel and his wife have stated under oath that nothing criminal occurred there, and there are no grounds in their lifelong records of unblemished truthfulness for the CID to impeach their credibility. Furthermore I provided the CID with the names of U.S. Navy Lt. Commander William Butch and Mr. Christopher Wise (Mrs. Aquino's brother and son) who lived constantly at 123 during all of 1986, and the CID never bothered to interview either of them. I further provided the CID with the name of my father, Mr. Michael Aquino Sr., who resided with us at 123 in July 1986 prior to our PCS to Washington. The CID never interviewed him either. Five adults with impeccable backgrounds were present on the 123 premises in the May-July 1986 time period, and all can verify that nothing criminal took place there. Nevertheless the CID chose to ignore three of these adults and without the slightest cause to treat the other two as liars, simply to perpetuate the myth of a May-July 1986 "crime period" **that was never the subject of anyone's original accusation**.

(6)   Two other individuals - a painting contractor and a general contractor - were also on the 123 premises daily throughout the May-July 1986 time period and were able to verify to the CID that they never saw any children brought there for any reason, much less sexual abuse ones. Assuming that the CID has interviewed both of these individuals as well, **there are now seven adults to verify that no crime occurred at 123 Acme Avenue during May-July 1986**. Yet the CID ignores this.

CONCLUSION: The "Date/time of occurrence" which appears on this cover sheet is not that of the actual A-T allegation, but was arbitrarily created by the CID in the absence of any such allegation. It is not substantiated by any evidence whatever, and is disproved by abundant evidence. **It therefore constitutes a deliberate and fraudulent fabrication by the CID.**

"DATE/TIME REPORTED: 12 AUGUST 1987, 1735 HOURS."

(1)   This is the date when Adams-Thompson told his personally-invented "package story" to the FBI, telling a different version of it to the SFPD on 14 August 1987 and a still-different version of it to the CID in 1989. Both FBI and SFPD versions of the original "package story" specified the September-October 1986 time period only, and provided no details whatever concerning 123 Acme Avenue that were accurate.

CONCLUSION: The "Date/time reported" is **not** the time when the "date/time of occurrence" was specified, nor when anything to validate 123 Acme as the location of any crime was specified. The **only** thing significant about the "date/time reported" is that on that date Lawrence Adams-Thompson made a vicious attack on two innocent people who didn't even know him or anyone in his family, and that all of the "evidence" that he offered was ultimately established to be wholly invented by him (the "package story"), unverified by examination (the interior of 123 and the physical condition of Almond as an unsodomized virgin), and/or falsely attributed to others (attribution of the "package story" to Debbie Hickey).

"INVESTIGATED BY: SPECIAL AGENTS STEPHEN PENALUNA AND DANIEL CATES."

(1)   Although the crimes specified in this accusation are among the most serious ones in society, the CID made no move to investigate them for over a year following A-T's attack. It is quite obvious that **no one** at the CID took the allegations seriously after the abortive SFPD raid and investigation. At no time from August 1987 to November 1988 did any representative of the CID even contact me to inquire about them.

(2)   In November 1988, immediately after my appearance on the Geraldo Rivera "Satanism" broadcast to defend my religion and the subsequent proliferation of confidential DA-level memos exploring options to "deal with" me, I was suddenly informed by Penaluna that this investigation was being opened. Though Special Agent Birck, Penaluna's superior, maintained that the investigation "had always been open", it is obvious that this is **not** the case and nothing had in fact been investigated in it. [An examination of verifiable time/date-stamped CID documents during August 1987-October 1988 should establish the facts here.] What this indicates is that this investigation was **not** opened on the basis of probable cause in August 1987, but **was** opened on the basis of a political agenda in November 1988.

(3)   The name of Major Mark Harvey must also be added to this line, as he participated directly in the investigation, to include correspondence with me and frequent discussions with me both by telephone and in person. Identification of all investigators involved is significant because, if it is established that the report deliberately conceals, falsifies, distorts, and/or omits any information crucial to the truth of the matter, the investigators either individually or collectively as appropriate will bear responsibility for such a violation of their responsibility under the law.

"TITLE: CONSPIRACY, KIDNAPPING, SODOMY, INDECENT ACTS OR LIBERTIES WITH A CHILD, INDECENT ACTS, FALSE SWEARING, INTENTIONAL NONCOMPLIANCE WITH ARTICLE 30 UCMJ (MALTREATMENT OF A SUBORDINATE), AND CONDUCT UNBECOMING AN OFFICER."

(1)   **There is no evidence to substantiate any one of these statements. All of them are false, and the CID knows full well that all of them are false.** If Colonel Ray signs this titling action, knowing that it is a complete falsehood and fabrication, he will be guilty of several false official statements in violation of Article 133 UCMJ and of other provisions of the UCMJ against defaming another soldier and participating in acts of religious discrimination in violation of the First and Fourteenth Amendments to the Constitution.

(2)   CONSPIRACY: There is **no evidence whatever** that I have conspired with anyone regarding the abduction of or harm to any child.

(3)   KIDNAPPING: There is **no evidence whatever** that I have either kidnapped any child or in any way orchestrated such a kidnapping.

(4)   SODOMY: I have **never** committed sodomy in my life, and there is **no evidence whatever to the contrary**. Major Harvey has confirmed to me that Kinsey Almond has been medically examined and found to be free from any sign of rape or sodomy (as her stepfather A-T alleged).

(5)   INDECENT ACTS OR LIBERTIES WITH A CHILD: There is **no** evidence that I have had any such contact with any child. There is nothing in my life history to suggest a pedophiliac disposition. Quite the contrary, at such times as I have been involved with young people - as for example an Assistant Scoutmaster and National Commander of the Eagle Scout Honor Society in the Boy Scouts of America, my contacts with them have always been ethical to an exemplary degree, frequently resulting in service awards and honors.

(6)   INDECENT ACTS: If this is intended to cover sexual frolics between consenting adults in private, then the CID will need to title every normally-sexed member of the United States Army. In my particular case, I am not and have never been a homosexual, and where women are concerned I have had sex with only my former and then my present wife - period.

(7)   FALSE SWEARING: I have sworn to charges against Adams-Thompson for the false and malicious attack he deliberately made against Mrs. Aquino and myself, and I swore to two detailed statements in support of those charges. I further swore to a detailed statement responding to CID written questions, and to oral statements made at the time of a personal interview with Cates, Penaluna, Harvey, and Hayes. **Every single one of these statements was and remains the truth**, and the evidence and documentation substantiating them as such was provided and explained in careful detail to the best of all information available to me. **Not a single statement therein was impeached to me or to Hayes by the CID at any time.**

On the other hand, as I have meticulously detailed to the CID, Chaplain Adams-Thompson **is** guilty of many knowingly false official statements, which is proven by the comparison of his statements of record to the SFPD, FBI, and CID; and by comparison of his allegations to such things as the physical condition of his stepdaughter and the actual contents of Debbie Hickey's "therapy" notes. He is an established liar not once, and not by honest accident, but many times over and deliberately so. In concealing this and failing to title him accordingly, the CID is acting to suppress a serious crime which he has committed against a fellow officer and his wife - and another crime against the U.S. government, for Adams-Thompson has also filed a fraudulent monetary claim against the government based upon his knowingly-false allegations.

(8)   INTENTIONAL NON-COMPLIANCE WITH ARTICLE 30 UCMJ -MALTREATMENT OF A SUBORDINATE: As this has never been mentioned to either me or Captain Hayes throughout the entire investigation, I assume it refers to the fact that, using the lawful means available to me as an Army officer, I sought to have Adams-Thompson brought to justice for his vicious crime against Mrs. Aquino and myself. As documentation clearly establishes, I first requested A-T himself to correct his actions. Then I requested his chain of command to take administrative corrective action where he was concerned. Then, only after exhausting all lesser alternatives and after consultation with the Command Judge Advocate of my headquarters, I preferred UCMJ charges against him. These charges were based strictly upon the truth as I understood it to be, and were amended on my own initiative in the single instance where one specification was later shown to be improbable.

The honest and factually-substantiated invocation of the Uniform Code of Military Justice is the right of every American soldier. **The CID has no business whatever titling a soldier for daring to seek justice under law.**

The CID, furthermore, was tasked by the 25th Infantry Division to investigate the charges I preferred against Adams-Thompson. Beyond the fact that the CID stated to the 25th Division that there was "no evidence to substantiate the charges", there is no indication that the CID conducted **any** *bona-fide* investigation in support of those charges whatever. My repeated FOIA requests for a copy of the "investigation report" have been consistently denied, despite the fact that I am both the injured party and the officer who signed the charge sheet as preferring official. Furthermore, as has come to light in the course of this present investigation, the CID was not only in the position to validate the evidence I provided in support of the charges, but in its own files possessed substantial **additional** information in support of the charges of which it took no initiative either to inform me or to inform the 25th Division. **Therefore the CID acted to suppress evidence of a crime and to prevent that crime from being referred for court-martial.**[216]

In a 5-month period - January to May 1988 - the CID claimed to know enough about the facts of the Adams-Thompson situation to recommend dismissal of the charges against him. At the same time they claimed not to know enough about that same situation to keep a "preliminary" investigation open on me and then in November 1988, following the Geraldo show, to open a 7-month intensive investigation of me. This makes it quite clear that the CID has been operating under a predetermined bias and agenda in which Adams-Thompson was prohibited from being found guilty and I was prohibited from being found innocent.

The titling of "false swearing ... maltreatment of a subordinate", therefore, is not only false in itself, but serves to cover up a serious breach of ethics by the CID in its mishandling and suppression of the UCMJ charges against Adams-Thompson.

(9)   CONDUCT UNBECOMING AN OFFICER: This phrase has surfaced only once in the investigation - by Major Harvey, a Catholic, in connection with a religious ceremony of the Church of Satan with which he personally disagrees. It is axiomatic that individuals of different religions disagree as to rituals and ceremonies, but the First Amendment to the Constitution provides that, as long as no criminal acts are committed, **adherents of any religion have the absolute right to worship whatever god they choose, however they choose.** AR 600-20, Paragraph 6-3 further states that:

> The policy of the U.S. Army is to provide equal opportunity and treatment for soldiers and their families without regard to religion [and similar factors] ... This policy applies both on and off post, extends to soldiers' working, living, and recreational environments (including both on- and off-post housing) ...

If Major Harvey or anyone else in the CID seeks to use the UCMJ as a means for religious persecution, discrimination, or intimidation, therefore, such misuse of the CID's titling powers constitutes a clear violation of AR 600-20 [and the Constitution] and **is itself an illegal act** for which the perpetrator is required to be held responsible.

CONCLUSION: All statements in the titling line are not only false, but are clearly contrary to the truth as the CID knows it to be. Specific elements of this titling line are deliberately present to conceal misuse of its investigative powers by the CID in the case of the Adams-Thompson UCMJ charges, and to intimidate me [and other Setian/Satanist members of the U.S. Armed Forces] against the free exercise of religion as guaranteed by the U.S. Constitution and AR 600-20.

This is a "crime" with **no** victim, as there is **no** sign of any damage whatever to the child who was alleged by Adams-Thompson to have been raped and sodomized by two men. There is **no** evidence that the child was ever kidnapped or sexually maltreated in any way, as would have produced instantaneous injury and emotional distress in the child at the time of such a traumatic experience.

---

[216] At this date I still had not succeeded in obtaining the CID "Report of Investigation" (Appendix #32), which verified my contentions here even more conclusively.

This is a "crime" in which the accuser, after no allegations at the supposed time of the sexual attacks, proposed one perpetrator, then on a malicious whim switched to two others several months later.

This is a "crime" in which the accuser, after letting the dates in question pass by without the slightest comment, clearly specified one set of dates (September-October 1986) both in his initial attempt to target Hambright and then in his subsequent attempt to target Mrs. Aquino and myself. **When the CID couldn't make these dates fit our location, they simply changed them.**

This is a "crime" in which the accuser **arbitrarily switched the location** from one place to another depending simply on whom he was accusing at the moment. From this cover sheet it further appears that the CID has now **arbitrarily added a third location on no evidence whatever**.

This is a "crime" with **no** motive. Neither Mrs. Aquino nor I have any history of the slightest interest in or involvement with child molestation or mistreatment. On the contrary, we have a lifelong record of sterling reputations where contact with young people is concerned. As is now quite clear to the entire United States - with the evident exception of the CID - the Temple of Set is a religious institution which neither involves children in any of its activities nor practices any harmful or illegal activity whatever.

Who, what, when, where, and why: **Not one** of these established - but rather **all exploded** by obvious lies, inescapable physical facts, and attempted latter-day alterations. For a titling such as this to be based upon an investigation such as this is utterly absurd -and a flagrantly grotesque abuse of the CID's investigative powers and responsibilities.

Finally - and most disgracefully - this is a "crime" in which the **real** criminal, Chaplain Lawrence Adams-Thompson, is being protected against accountability for his extremely destructive crime, and his associated effort to defraud the government, evidently because the Army simply does not have the courage to call a Christian chaplain to account for an extremely serious crime he committed against a soldier and his wife who happen to be legitimate Satanists. If this nation considers itself better than Nazi Germany, wherein there was one standard of justice for Christians and another for Jews, then it is incumbent upon us to prove it - not when it is politically convenient to do so, but when the Constitution **demands** that we do so.

The foregoing facts are provided to place the cover sheet to the CID report, and its titling of me, in the context of the truth which both the CID and all parties involved know it to be. These are the facts which will inevitably come out if this false and fraudulent titling action is not immediately and thoroughly removed. Ideally the CID should take the initiative to do this. Otherwise senior officials of the Army will be forced into a position where they have to defend the CID's conduct of this entire affair, which they will ultimately be unable to do - to the national embarrassment and discredit of the Army.

As stated in my June 20, 1989 letter to Colonel Ray, I am aware of the actual political forces behind this misuse of the CID. While I will not for a moment tolerate bogus criminal titling, I reiterate my willingness to work with the Army towards a constructive resolution to this situation which is in the Army's best interest and which does not compromise my own honor, that of my wife, or that of our religion.

Sincerely,
Michael A. Aquino
Lt. Colonel, Military Intelligence

cc-   Major General Eugene Cromartie
       Captain Thomas M. Hayes
       Mr. Gary R. Myers

Appendix 58: Letter, Michael Aquino to Major General Eugene Cromartie 8/3/89

August 3, 1989

Dear General Cromartie:

On 7/31/89, having heard nothing further concerning the titling decision, I telephoned Colonel Ray, CID 6th Region Commander. In answer to my questions, he stated the following:

(1) That he has signed the titling action.

(2) That before doing so he did read my 6/20/89 letter to him and my 7/4/89 fax message to his Region Judge Advocate Major Harvey addressing and refuting all items on the titling cover sheet. [Copies of these were provided directly to you.]

(3) That when signing the titling action he neither changed nor removed any of the entries on that cover sheet.

(4) That he made the decision to refuse my attorneys and/or myself the opportunity to review the CID investigation report despite our having informed him that it necessarily contains serious errors and/or deliberate fabrications if it purports to justify any item on the titling cover sheet. This request to review the CID report, under any conditions of security specified by the CID, was made by Captain Thomas Hayes via memorandum to HQ 6th Region dated 5/31/89.

(5) That he and he alone takes responsibility for the titling decision, and that he was not acting on instructions or expectations from you concerning that decision.

(6) That you will now review the report and the titling decision before its forwarding to the Crime Records Center, and that you have authority to remove the titling decision as part of that review.

(7) That he still refuses to grant either myself or my attorneys the opportunity to review the report prior to your review of it, so that, once more, we may detail for you the inaccuracies within it.

I hereby request that you immediately rescind Colonel Ray's titling action on the grounds that I am clearly innocent of all crimes as alleged and that there is no evidence to the contrary.

I further advise you that Colonel Ray, in signing this titling action, has knowingly and deliberately made a false official statement in violation of Article 133 of the Uniform Code of Military Justice. If each item on the titling cover sheet, as identified and refuted in my 7/4/89 fax message, is to be considered a separate statement, then Colonel Ray has signed his name to twelve separate false statements embracing "time, location, and nature of offense".

Although Colonel Ray has denied me and my attorneys the opportunity to review the report upon which he supposedly based his decision, there is no reason for me to await release of that report before drawing this conclusion. Exposure and critique of the report will merely serve to support the bogus nature of this titling action that much more conclusively.

As soon as I obtain this report which the CID seems so anxious to prevent my examining, I will immediately request that anything unsubstantiated, discriminatory, or prejudicial in it be removed - through the administrative appeals process, but through the federal courts if necessary. Such an action would necessarily require the authors and signatory of the report to justify each and every item so identified. If the report selectively omits information known to the CID which establishes my innocence, I will request that it be added and the conclusions of the report amended in accordance with it.

If, when examined in its entirety, the entire report appears to be merely a transparent attempt to frame me in order to give the Army an excuse to harass me and my wife in violation of our Constitutional rights, to cover up the extreme and inexcusable damage perpetrated by a Christian chaplain - not just to another officer and his wife but to other innocent people and to the Presidio community generally - and/or to cover up the CID's misuse of its investigative procedures in the case of the Presidio witch-hunt, the charges preferred against Adams-Thompson, and the post-Geraldo investigation of me, then I will request that the entire report be thrown out. Such a finding, by the Defense Department or the federal courts, would presumably set in motion an appropriate internal investigation of the CID for having allowed such an abuse of the investigative process to occur in the first place.

Even if the report contains complete fabrications and deliberately manufactured "evidence" concealed from my attorneys and myself, it will be no excuse for Colonel Ray to claim that he was ignorant of the facts or misled by the report's contents. Captain Hayes' 5/31/89 memorandum, my letter to Ray of 6/20/89, and my 7/4/89 fax message all alerted Ray to the serious inaccuracies in any report which purported to substantiate a titling of me. He was offered the opportunity to receive my analysis of the report prior to his making a decision, which he refused.

It is a matter of documented record that I have cooperated completely, voluntarily, and thoroughly with the CID throughout this entire investigation, providing CID representatives Major Harvey and Special Agents Cates and Penaluna not only full and complete answers to all of their questions before, during, and after their two-day face-to-face interview, but also abundant correspondence and other documentation to substantiate the facts as presented. In an investigation of me lasting nine months [or two years, if one believes the CID's statement that it was opened the moment the chaplain made his allegations], not a single allegation or shred of "evidence" has been produced which could not be easily refuted and disproved.

In addition to my many personal contacts with Major Harvey by telephone and correspondence, my attorney Captain Hayes was in continuous contact with Harvey, Cates, and Penaluna concerning the investigation. Prior to the final face-to-face interview here in St. Louis, Hayes requested and was granted access to the investigative file. Had there been any item of "evidence" in it which could possibly have misled the CID, he would have identified it and I would have addressed it accordingly.

During two days of face-to-face interviews involving myself and Mrs. Aquino in St. Louis, we repeatedly encouraged Harvey, Cates, and Penaluna to ask whatever questions they wished, even of no demonstrated relevance to the allegations. The interviews ceased when the CID investigators indicated that they had no further questions to ask. During the interview session, as in the other contacts with the CID, not a single statement of mine or Mrs. Aquino's was impeached despite exhaustive cross-examination by Harvey and Cates. Our substantiation of our innocence, as we have represented it consistently since the chaplain first attacked us, has remained conclusive.

During the time between the face-to-face interview and the writing of the report, both Captain Hayes and I spoke several times with Harvey and/or Cates. A few additional questions were asked, which were immediately and thoroughly answered in further verification of my innocence.

In short, Colonel Ray has **no excuse whatever** for the titling decision he made, unless he should state that he made it under duress from higher authority according to a predetermined agenda in intentional disregard of the truth.

My previous correspondence to the 6th Region CID and yourself has detailed the facts in support of my innocence and Chaplain Adams-Thompson's flagrant violations of Article 133 both exhaustively and conclusively. These facts speak quite adequately for themselves, and there is no reason to repeat them here. I do append to this letter a list of Adams-Thompson's specific lies, expanded/updated from the list which I originally compiled for CID investigators in May 1989 and updated with my 6/20/89 letter to Colonel Ray (copy to you).[217]

The CID knew of many of these actions by Adams-Thompson, as indeed Special Agent Cates stated openly to Hayes and myself during our joint review of the original draft of this list as presented to him during the 5/89 interview. Furthermore all items on the list are verified not by my personal supposition, but rather by an examination and comparison of official San Francisco Police, FBI, and CID documents and statements. The CID therefore has **no** excuse for not acknowledging AdamsThompson's crime and titling him accordingly.

In January of 1988, after first exhausting all administrative recourse through his commander, I preferred court-martial charges against Adams-Thompson for his malicious attack on Mrs. Aquino and myself. These charges were dismissed by the CO 25th Division on the basis of an official CID statement that "no grounds exist to substantiate the charges".

As is now quite clear, the CID was at that time in possession not only of considerable information to substantiate the points I made in my sworn statement, but also of considerable **additional** information unknown to me (such as the medically-established completely-unharmed condition of the child alleged by Adams-Thompson to have been raped and sodomized) to even more conclusively establish my innocence and the chaplain's guilt as charged in Specification #1. The CID's failure to provide this information to the 25th Division, or to advise me of it as the officer preferring the charges, constitutes an act of misprision of serious offense *(Manual for Courts Martial 1984,* Part IV, paragraph 95) and an act of deliberate obstruction of justice *(MCM IV* para 96), both in violation of Article 134 UCMJ.

In connection with that same action, the CID has to date, in violation of Title 5 U.S. Code, denied me a copy of the investigative report it states that it prepared concerning the charges preferred against Adams-Thompson. In addition to being a violation of Title 5, this denial is also a violation of Article 134 concerning misprision of serious offense and obstruction of justice, both in the case of the charges against Adams-Thompson and in the case of the subsequent CID investigation conducted against me. As the charges against Adams-Thompson were dismissed in May 1988, the CID's representation that its report is deniable because it is part of the general Presidio investigation is indefensible. If the investigation were considered "closed" enough to dismiss the charges against Adams-Thompson, then it is "closed" enough for the Freedom of Information Act to require immediate and thorough disclosure of the CID "investigation" of those charges.

In the face of the CID's concealment of that report, if it exists, I necessarily conclude that it is being denied me simply because my review of it would expose its thorough inadequacy, commencing with the CID's failure to even contact the two individuals -myself and Mrs. Aquino - who had provided sworn statements in support of it. If this is the case, then the conduct of that "investigation" constitutes a further violation of Article 134 UCMJ concerning misprision of serious offense and obstruction of justice.

I once more restate and renew my request of 6/23/88 that a complete copy of that report of investigation in support of the court-martial charges I preferred against Adams-Thompson be provided to be without further excuse or delay.

With reference to that same preferral of charges against Adams-Thompson, the CID later added to the titling against me the charge that I had sworn to false statements. Since the CID knew then and knows now that my sworn statements were true and verifiable in all respects, this addition to the titling sheet cannot be construed as other than an attempt to cover up the previous illegal acts of the CID suppressing the charges against Adams-Thompson. This deliberate misrepresentation of my sworn statements as false constitutes an additional violation of Article 134 concerning obstruction of justice, and also concerning communicating a threat *(MCM IV* para 110), to the extent that this additional titling was intended to intimidate me because I had dared to seek justice by invoking the UCMJ against a chaplain who had committed a serious crime against Mrs. Aquino and myself.

---

[217] Appendix #34.

As Colonel Ray's commander, and as Commanding General of the CIDC, you are responsible to identify violations of the UCMJ and take corrective action accordingly. You are also responsible to identify violations of professional ethics by CID personnel. I request that you do so with regard to the violations identified above, commencing with the immediate rescinding of the titling against me and the identification and removal of any and all false and fraudulent statements in the investigation report which purport to substantiate it. The present situation is a flagrant and extraordinary outrage of justice, which is all the more shocking because of the complicity of the CID in perpetrating it.

In connection with your disposition of the CID report concerning me, I once more request that you provide me with a copy of it prior to your decision, so that I may critique and annotate its statements and return it to you.

If you take no action to correct these violations of the UCMJ by CID personnel, then I will initiate a request to the Department of Defense Inspector General to review this entire affair, with additional attention to such memoranda, decisions, and actions at Headquarters, Department of the Army level as may have acted to orchestrate and prejudice the CID actions taken against me in violation of the First and Fourteenth Amendments to the Constitution and other applicable federal laws. I think that Senator Helms' 1/9/89 letter to Secretary Marsh (copy enclosed) is a most illuminating case in point.

As you know, I have to date avoided all comment to the public, press, or government outside of the Department of the Army concerning the CID's handling of this investigation. As unjustified as I felt the investigation to be, I accepted Major Harvey's word that it was an unbiased procedure designed to clear the air of an unresolved issue, which would result not only in my exoneration but in titling of Chaplain Adams-Thompson as the facts warranted. Obviously I was deceived.

In order to avoid public embarrassment of the Army, and to give you maximum flexibility in correcting the injustice done to me, I will not initiate comment outside of official channels. If the press should learn of Colonel Ray's titling decision and/or the contents of the report through any other source, however, and if they question me about it, I will not hesitate to respond with the truth, to include all relevant documentation and correspondence between myself and the CID.

Under no circumstances will I tolerate for a moment the further defamation of my wife, myself, or our church simply because the Army is trying to cover up the disgraceful misconduct of a Christian chaplain. It is outrageous that we have been subjected to two years of this ordeal already, with an attendant stream of vandalism, slander, death threats and malicious abuse from, the more ignorant and fanatic elements of the public. The safety and security of other members of our church and their families, both military and civilian, have been endangered as well.

The Army could have ended this ordeal at any time with a clear and unequivocal statement of the truth. Not only has it not had the courage to do so; it has, to its shame, acted to aggravate this injustice to an honorable and innocent Army family. This injustice will be corrected as the truth inevitably comes to light. The only question is how far the United States Army is willing to sanction misprision and obstruction of justice simply in order to cover up the criminal misconduct of Chaplain AdamsThompson.

Respectfully,
/s/ Michael A. Aquino
Lt. Colonel, Military Intelligence

Enclosures:
- Letter, Senator Jesse Helms to Secretary of the Army Marsh, 1/9/89.
- Chaplain Lawrence Adams-Thompson's Actions in Violation of Article #133.
- Fax message, Lt.Col. Aquino to Headquarters, Sixth Region CID, 7/4/89.

Copies to:

Honorable John 0. Marsh, Jr., Secretary of the Army
General Carl E. Vuono, Chief of Staff, United States Army
General Robert W. RisCassi, Vice Chief of Staff, United States Army
Lieutenant General Henry Doctor, Inspector General of the Army
Lieutenant General Charles W. Bagnal, Commanding General, WESTCOM
Major General William F. Ward, Chief, Army Reserve
Major General William K. Suter, Judge Advocate General of the Army
Major General Norris L. Einertson, Chief of Chaplains, Department of the Army
Mr. Joseph G. Hanley, Chief of Public Affairs, Department of the Army
Major General Charles P. Otstott, Commanding General, 25th Infantry Division
Colonel Bobby R. Sanders, Commander, ARPERCEN
Colonel Joseph V. Rafferty, Commander, Presidio of San Francisco
Colonel Webster D. Ray, Commander, 6th Region CID
Colonel John T. Lane, Inspector General, ARPERCEN
Lt. Colonel Nolan H. Goudeaux, Headquarters, Trial Defense Service
Captain Thomas M. Hayes III, Trial Defense Service, Presidio of San Francisco
Mr. Bob Mahoney, Public Affairs Office, 6th Army & Presidio of San Francisco
Mr. Gary R. Myers, Attorney
San Francisco Police Commission
Pillsbury, Madison & Sutro, Attorneys

Appendix 59: 6RCID Report of Investigation Cover Letter

Department of the Army
Headquarters, Sixth Region
US Army Criminal Investigation Command
Presidio of San Francisco, California 94129-6600

CIRFS-OP   11 August 1989

SUBJECT: CID Report of Investigation - Final "C" - 0610-88-C1D026-69259-5K3/6F3/6E2/6Al /5M2/5Y2/DIMIS

SEE DISTRIBUTION:

LOCATION OF OCCURRENCE: Child Development Center (CDC), Presidio of San Francisco (PSF), CA 94129; 123 Acme Avenue, San Francisco, CA; 208 Dolores Street, San Francisco, CA.

DATE/TIME OF OCCURRENCE: On or about May - Jul 1986, between 0730-1600.

DATE/TIME REPORTED: 12 Aug 87, 1735.

INVESTIGATED BY: SA Stephen H. PENALUNA, 3104 and SA Daniel S. CATES, 1843.

TITLE:

1. AQUINO, Michael A. (10); LTC; ###-##-####; 16 Oct 46; San Francisco (SF), CA; M; White; HHC, US Army Reserve Personnel Center, 9700 Page Blvd, St Louis, MO 63132; Conspiracy; Kidnapping; Sodomy; Indecent Acts or Liberties with a Child; Indecent Acts, False Swearing; Intentional Noncompliance with Art 30, UCMJ (Violation of Article), Maltreatment of a Subordinate and Conduct Unbecoming an Officer.

2. HAMBRIGHT, Gary Willard; Civ; 538-54-6534; 7Jul 53; Ellensburg, WA; M;   White; (NFl); Conspiracy (18 USC, Section 373), Kidnapping (18 USC 1201), Sexual Abuse (18 USC 2242 (B)).

3. AQUINO, Lilith; Civ; ###-##-####; 21 Apr 42; F; White; P0 Box 4507, St Louis, NO 63108; AKA: Patricia WISE, Patricia SINCLAIR, Lilith SINCLAIR; (DW of LTC Michael A (10) AQUINO, N, ###-##-####, HHC, US Army Reserve Personnel Center, 9700 Page Blvd, St Louis, MO 63132); Conspiracy (18 USC 373); Kidnapping (18 USC 1201); Sexual Abuse(18 USC 2242 (B)); False Statement (18 USC 1001).

VICTIM:

1. ADAMS-THOMPSON, Kinsey Marie Almond; "JUVENILE - THIS RECORD MAY BE RELEASED ONLY AS AUTHORIZED BY AR 195-2, PARA 4-3F"; Civ; 531-94-0177; 1 Sep 83; Renton, WA; F; White; (DSD of CPT Larry Parker ADAMS-THOMPSON, M, 562-76-3492, HHC, 4/27th Inf, 25th ID (L), Schofield Barracks, HI 96857); Kidnapping, Sodomy, Indecent Liberties, Sexual Abuse.

2. ADAMS-THOMPSON, Larry Parker; CPT; 562-76-3492; San Diego, CA; N; White; HHC, 4/27th Inf, 25th ID (L), Schofield Barracks, HI 96857; Intentional Noncompliance with Art 30, UCMJ (violation of Article 98, UCMJ); Maltreatment of Subordinate, and Conduct Unbecoming an Officer.

3. US Government; Conspiracy, False Sworn Statement, False Statement, Indecent Acts, and Conduct Unbecoming an Officer.

4. Previously deleted.

5. Previously deleted.

6. DORSEY, Emily Elizabeth; "JUVENILE - THIS RECORD MAY BE RELEASED ONLY AS AUTHORIZED BY AR 195-2, PARA 4-3F"; Civ; Privacy Act; 15 Jul 82; San Diego, CA;. F; White; 2123 Mendocino Blvd, San Diego, CA; (DD of CPT Thomas R. DORSEY, N, 566-90-8995, USA MEDDAC, Ft Eustis, VA 23604); Kidnapping, Sexual Abuse.

SYNOPSIS:

Investigation disclosed that L. AQUINO and HAMBRIGHT, acting in concert, transported K. ADAMS-THOMPSON, without parental permission, from the CDC, PSF, CA, to 123 Acme Ave, SF, CA, the residence of LTC and L. AQUINO, where LTC AQUINO was waiting. There, with the assistance of LTC and L. AQUINO, HAMBRIGHT forced K. ADAMS-THOMPSON to orally copulate him and indecently assaulted her.

On an undetermined date HAMBRIGHT transported E. DORSEY, without parental permission, to 208 Delores St, SF, CA. At that location he removed her clothing and fondled her vaginal area with his hand.

On 4 Jan 88, at Headquarters, ARPERCEN, 9700 Page Blvd, St Louis, MO 63132, LTC AQUINO filed charges against CPT ADAMS-THOMPSON for a violation of Art 133, UCMJ wherein LTC AQUINO alleged that CPT ADAMS-THOMPSON falsely accused him of sexually assaulting K. ADAMS-THOMPSON, charges he knew to be false since LTC AQUINO had in his possession a police report clearly indicating the accusations were made by K. ADAMS-THOMPSON, not her father.

On 4 Jan 88, 23 Aug 88, and 27 Jan 89, at Headquarters, ARPERCEN, 9700 Page Blvd, St Louis, MO 63132, LTC AQUINO rendered false written sworn statements by knowingly mis-stating the age of K. ADAMS-THOMPSON (while having a document in his possession which correctly stated her date of birth), and by denying having ever been to the CDC, PSF, CA. On 4 Jan 88 and 10-11 May 89, L. AQUINO, in sworn statements, falsely denied her participation in the cited offenses.

During a sworn interview conducted 10-11 May 1989, LTC AQUINO admitted to officiating at the West Black Mass, in 1970, while on active duty as a commissioned officer. By organizing and orchestrating a Black Mass ceremony involving public nudity; female public urination in the presence of males; placing a cracker into the vagina of a naked female serving as a "living alter"; LTC [sic] committed the offense of Conduct Unbecoming an officer and Indecent Acts.

During the course of this investigation Wesley K. WITHROW, Civ, 570-63-6261, and Brandon C. WITHROW, 557-71-3241, both residing at 642 Henderson Lane, Ukiah, CA, alleged LTC AQUINO, along with other adults, including their maternal grandparents, fondled their privates, placed their (the adult's) fingers in their, W. and B. WITHROW's, respective anuses and forced them to lie nude, on top of nude women and simulate intercourse. Additionally, both indicated they had observed LTC AQUINO, and others, engage in the ritualistic murder of numerous adults and children in San Francisco, CA, Sonoma County, CA, and Mendocino County, CA. Investigation did not substantiate the incidents occurred as alleged; therefore, based on coordination with the supported Staff Judge Advocate, W. WITHROW and B. WITHROW were previously deleted as victims in this report.

STATUTES:

18 USC, Section 1201 - Kidnapping.
Art 134, UCMJ - Kidnapping.
18 USC, Section 373 - Conspiracy.

Art 81, UCMJ - Conspiracy.
Art 77, UCMJ - Principal.
18 USC, Section 2242 (B) - Sexual Abuse.
Art 125, UCMJ - Sodomy
Art 98, UCMJ -Noncompliance with Procedural Rules.
Art 134 (87) UCMJ - Indecent Liberties with a Child
Art 134 (90) UCMJ - Indecent Acts with Another
Art 134 (79) UCMJ - False Swearing
Art 133 UCMJ - Conduct Unbecoming an Officer

BASIS FOR INVESTIGATION:

In November 1986, the San Francisco Field Office, USACIDC, initiated Report of Investigation (ROI) 0667-86-C1D026-69776, regarding the sexual assault/abuse of children attending the CDC, PSF, CA, by Mr Gary Hambright, a UA-05 care provider, employed at the CDC. During the investigation by the Federal Bureau of Investigation (FBI), USACIDC, and the San Francisco Police Department (SFPD), information surfaced that some of the victims had been taken to off-post dwellings, where they had been ritualistically abused. The victims provided fragmented information concerning the location and perpetrators of the sexual abuse. The name "Mike" or "Mikey" was mentioned during therapy sessions at Child Psychiatry, Letterman Army Medical Center (L.AMC). On 12 Aug 1987, Kinsey Adams-Thompson (hereinafter Kinsey), while in the Presidio Post Exchange with her parents, observed LTC AQUINO, and displaying fright, informed her mother, "That's the bad man, that's Mikey." The SFPD was the lead on this investigation, which USACIDC monitored and assisted (Sequence #0499-87-C1D026). In Sep 1988, SFPD terminated active investigation, as investigation to date had not generated sufficient evidence to convince civil authorities that prosecution had a high probability of conviction. On 21 Nov 1988, based on a briefing by the SFPD, consideration of medical evidence, FBI records; and coordination between USACIDC personnel and supported Staff Judge Advocate's Office, a determination was made that sufficient evidence existed to initiate this ROI.

On September 30, 1987, a 12 count indictment was returned by a grand jury located in San Francisco that alleged that Mr. Gary HAMBRIGHT sexually assaulted David TOBIN, Lee BALLWAY, Ryan BALLWAY, Kara BAILEY, Leticia COLE, Trinity HANRICK, Catherine HUYCKE, Larry STOUDEMIRE, Christopher FIELDS, and Cohn FOX at the Presidio CDC. Federal Rule of Criminal Procedure (FRCP) 6e prohibits the release of information obtained by the grand jury through the use of grand jury subpoenas, or presented to the grand jury through witness testimony. Certain information may or may not be presented in this ROI due to the application of the secrecy requirements of FRCP 6e.

Appendix 60: Analysis of 6RCID Report of Investigation Cover Letter

Final ROI Cover Letter Analysis
Lt. Colonel Michael A. Aquino

[A copy of this analysis was provided to the Commanding General, CIC
on November 30, 1989. Neither acknowledgment nor response was received.]

* * *

1. *Date*.

    a. This cover letter (Attachment #A) is dated 11 August 1989.

    b. On 5/31/89, concerned because of remarks he had heard from Major Harvey (SJA 6RCID) about the report, my Army attorney Captain Hayes requested that we be allowed to review and provide comments concerning it to Colonel Webster Ray, 6RCID commander, prior to his making any decision concerning it. [Attachment #B].

    c. On 6/12/89 the 6RCID denied this request. [Attachment #C].

    d. On 6/20/89 Harvey told Hayes that he fully expected Colonel Ray to title me for the Adams-Thompson allegations. Accordingly, realizing that I was simply the target of a pre-determined frame-up, I sent Colonel Ray the letter at Attachment #D.

    e. On 7/4/89 Hayes obtained from Harvey a copy of the draft of this cover letter. Accordingly I faxed the 6RCID, with a copy to Major General Cromartie, the detailed refutation of the draft at Attachment #E.

    f. On 7/6/89 Ray sent me a non-committal answer (Attachment #F), then informed Hayes on 7/31/89 that he would be titling me anyway.

    g. On 8/3/89 I sent Major General Cromartie the letter at Attachment #G, notifying him of the violation of Articles #133 & #134 UCMJ by Colonel Ray in his signing of the fraudulent titling. I also restated my request for an immediate copy of the report by which this titling was supposedly substantiated.

    h. On 8/11/89-8/28/89 the CID made distribution of this report, including its fraudulent titling action, to [at minimum] the Crime Records Center, Commanding General of Fort Leonard Wood, Commander of ARPERCEN, Commander of the Presidio of San Francisco, and Sergeant/Inspector Pamfiloff of the San Francisco Police Department (Attachment #H).

        (1) Neither I nor my attorneys were informed of this action, nor were we provided with a copy of the report.

        (2) The distribution of this report to Pamfiloff is especially improper because, **as the CID well knows**, this officer was **formally investigated by the San Francisco Police Commission** for his bias and flagrant misconduct of the original SFPD action in this case, allegations which the Commission finally **sustained** [Attachment #I]. While it is inappropriate for a fraudulent report such as this to be sent to the San Francisco Police in the first place, any such material should, under these circumstances, have been sent directly to the Investigating Officer of the Police Commission, Ms. Irene Rapoza.

i. On 11/20/89 I first learned that the fraudulent report had been distributed. My civilian attorney, Mr. Gary Myers, immediately telephoned Cromartie's headquarters and demanded a copy of the report without further delay. He was promised that a copy would be sent to me immediately.

j. I finally received a heavily censored and blanked-out copy of the report on 11/27/89 - **six months** after my initial request for it, and **three and one-half months** after it had been distributed by the CID.

k. Quite obviously it was the intention of the CID first to avoid receiving information that would specifically invalidate the statements of the report before the fraudulent titling action could be taken; then to distribute the defamatory report throughout my chain of command - and to Pamfiloff - to cause as much harm to myself, Mrs. Aquino, and our religion as possible; and finally to delay providing a copy of the report to me as long as possible, knowing that it would immediately be exposed for the transparent fraud that it is.

l. On 11/21/89, through the FOIA, I requested from the CID commanding general, Major General Cromartie, a copy of all regulations and directives which govern the distribution of CID investigative reports, both to the subject of the report and to other addressees [Attachment #J]. As of this date I have not yet received a response. Major General Cromartie is thereby in violation of the Freedom of Information Act.

2. *Location of occurrence.*

The report contains **no** substantiation that either Mrs. Aquino or I **ever** visited the Presidio day-care center, 208 Dolores Street (apparently the residence of Gary Hambright) or were involved in **any** way with alleged criminal activities connected with these or any other locations. The report contains **no** substantiation that **any** crime **ever** took place at 123 Acme Avenue (our home). The authors and approvers were and are fully aware of this. This entry thus constitutes deliberate obstruction of justice by the authors in violation of Article 134 UCMJ and the making of a false official statement in violation of Article 133 UCMJ.

3. *Date/time of occurrence.*

a. When Chaplain Adams-Thompson made his initial allegations against us in August 1987, he **specifically** indicated the time period "September-October 1986" (San Francisco Police Department incident report 8/14/87). When the CID verified that neither Mrs. Aquino nor I had been in San Francisco at any time during this period when Kinsey Almond had been at the day-care center, this **proved our innocence** and provided further evidence of Adams-Thompson's deliberate malice in making his accusations.

b. Instead, in an effort to cover up the Chaplain's crime and to fabricate a "case" against us, the authors **arbitrarily back-dated the date/time** to a period when Mrs. Aquino and I were still assigned to the Presidio. This constitutes an act of deliberate misprision of serious offense, falsification of evidence, and obstruction of justice by the authors in violation of Article 134 UCMJ and the making of a false official statement in violation of Article 133 UCMJ.

c. Furthermore, on FBI Form #FD-302 (1/14/87) (attachment #K), it is clearly established that **Almond was not assigned to Gary Hambright's class at the day-care center until September 1986. He had no control over Almond during the May-July 86 time-frame, hence could not possibly have abducted her at that time**. The authors possessed this document but concealed its existence from me and omitted mention of its significance in this report. They further concealed the existence and contents of this document from the 25th Infantry Division Investigating Officer inquiring into the original court-martial charges against Adams-Thompson. These acts constitute the deliberate concealment of evidence by the authors, hence misprision of serious offense and obstruction of justice in violation of Article 134 UCMJ.

d. In a 12/15/86 letter to Presidio parents (attachment #L), Lt. Colonel Myer, Director of Personnel & Community Affairs of the Presidio of San Francisco, further stated that Gary Hambright had **no** supervision over **any** children under the age of 3, **which Almond did not attain until September 1, 1986. Again this**

makes impossible the commission of any such crime as the CID report alleges in the May-July 86 time-period. Again the authors knew about this document but concealed its existence from me and omitted mention of its significance in this report. This constitutes the deliberate concealment of evidence by the authors in an act of misprision of serious offense and obstruction of justice in violation of Article 134 UCMJ.

4. *Date/time reported.*

    a. According to the SFPD incident report, FBI Agent Clyde Foreman informed SFPD Sergeant/Inspector Pamfiloff that Lawrence and Michele Adams-Thompson made their "package story" allegations to him on 8/13/87. All that they alleged to Foreman by telephone on 8/12/87 (FBI FD-302 L. Adams-Thompson, 8/13/87) was the 8/12/87 PX encounter.]

    b. The official FBI record of the Adams-Thompsons' allegations of kidnapping and child-abuse (FBI Form FD-302, 8/13/87) further verifies that this "package story" was **not** presented for the first time until 8/13/87.

        (1) This is **one day after** the Adams-Thompsons saw us in the Presidio PX. Why did it take the Adams-Thompsons a day to report what they represented as a serious crime?

        (2) **Why was there no mention whatever of this "package story" to anyone prior to this date, whether or not the Adams-Thompsons felt it timely to "identify" a target "Mikey/Shamby"?** The evidence quite obviously indicates that the Adams-Thompsons made their decision to manufacture a story to use Kinsey Almond for their personal profit in the Presidio child-care scam **subsequent to the 1/14/87 FBI interview.** In collaboration with Debbie Hickey, who supplied the "Satanic" propaganda and a rag-bag of fantasies for Adams-Thompson to pick and choose from in trying to create a plausible "package story", it is evident from the Hickey notes that **by June 87** the Adams-Thompsons had already decided to try to attack me. Their unexpected sight of Mrs. Aquino and myself in the PX on 8/12/87 simply gave them an opportunity to falsify that encounter as well and then present the hastily-thrown-together "package story" the next day. That it was a last-minute rush-job is also evidenced by the fact that Michele offered it in **one** version to the FBI on 8/13/87 and Lawrence offered it in a **different and inconsistent** version to the SFPD a day later on 8/14/87.

    c. Lawrence and Michele's allegations on 8/13/87 and 8/14/87 made no mention of the locations of the CDC or 208 Delores Street, and specified the time period of September-October 1986. Therefore not only is the "date/time reported" entry in this cover letter wrong, but its connection to the "location of occurrence" and "date/time of occurrence" is false.

    d. The authors of the report are aware of the significance of a day's delay in the making of the allegations by the Adams-Thompsons, and they possess the documents verifying this. They are aware of all the evidence verifying the bogus manufacture of the "package story" by the Adams-Thompsons. They know that on the dates when the Adams-Thompsons first made their allegations to the FBI and SFPD, those allegations specifically contradict other entries on this cover letter. This cover-letter entry thus constitutes falsification of evidence by the authors in violation of Article 134 UCMJ and a false official statement in violation of Article 133 UCMJ.

5. *Investigated by.*

    a. The names of only Sergeant Stephen Penaluna and Chief Warrant Officer Daniel Cates are cited here.

        (1) In actuality the principal role as investigator was played by Captain/Major Mark Harvey, the Staff Judge Advocate of 6RCID, who to my knowledge is neither trained nor qualified as a CID investigator. He is an attorney whose proper purpose is to advise the 6RCID commander on legal matters and to review the findings of authorized CID investigators for compliance with the law. During the entire

course of this investigation, my attorneys and I had far more investigative question/answer contact with Harvey than with either Cates or Penaluna.

(2) Penaluna, in fact, was originally the **sole** investigator assigned to the investigation in November 1988 (according to his own statement to me at that time). I was later told that Cates was brought down from Alaska, four months after the investigation was started, to take over the investigation because Penaluna was not considered sufficiently competent to conduct it on his own. This was told bluntly to my attorney Captain Hayes in informal conversation and was couched in more diplomatic language in Harvey's official letter. [See attachment #M, paragraph 5.]

(3) I was informed by Hayes that Cates returned to Alaska approximately **two months** before Colonel Ray reviewed the report. During this period it was **Harvey** who, judging by his repeated statements to Hayes, was in charge of its extensive re-writing and editing. **Therefore the actual author of the final report is evidently Harvey**, with Cates merely signing it *pro forma*. I think that, if the matter is researched, it will be found that Penaluna wrote little if any of it, and that he did not have the final say as to any of its contents or conclusions regardless of the placement of his name first among the authors.

b. The evident actual author of this report is thus a junior Army attorney without either CID investigative training or credentials, nor any background in fake "child-abuse" scams such as that at the Presidio. He was assisted by one CID agent who was considered incompetent to handle the investigation by himself, and a second CID agent who was brought into the investigation when it was apparently determined that Penaluna was not taking it towards the predetermined conclusion, and who left approximately two months before the report bearing his name was revised, edited, final-typed, and reviewed by the 6RCID commander. Nor is there any information known to me that either Cates or Penaluna have any special training in the handling of "mass Satanic day-care child-abuse" scams such as have become a major fad in the country since the Los Angeles McMartin fiasco.

c. As the narrative report is extremely [and illegally] prejudicial and defamatory to the Satanic religion of its targets (Mrs. Aquino and myself), the religious convictions of the authors are directly relevant and material. All were formally raised and trained as Christians in three of the most extreme and anti-Satanic churches of that religion.

(1) Penaluna is a Lutheran. The Lutheran Church, since its founding, has been the most intolerant of Protestant churches and was responsible for mass slaughters of accused Satanists in medieval Europe. In 1988 the Lutheran Church in the United States published a vicious propaganda document *How to Respond to Satanism* attacking the Satanic religion, accusing it of sponsoring ritual child-abuse, cannibalism, murder, and similar atrocities. Satanism is described as the mortal enemy of Christianity, to be attacked and eradicated in society at all costs.

(2) Cates is a Baptist. The Baptist churches, as the mainstream of modern "religious-right" fundamentalism, have been consistently in the forefront of the current nationwide campaign to slander and persecute the Satanic religion.

(3) Harvey, principal author of the CID report, is a Catholic. The Catholic Church is responsible for the torture and slaughter of millions of accused Satanists throughout history. In contemporary America it has a massive record of **convictions** of sex-crimes against children and official efforts to cover up such crimes [see Attachment #N]. Its official spokesmen during the current nationwide campaign to persecute the Satanic religion have published gutter propaganda of the crudest sort. The Catholic Church also employs a disgusting and offensive ritual, entitled the *Rite of Exorcism*, to further slander our religion and our deity. It was in response to the *Rite of Exorcism* that the Satanic *Missa Solemnis* was historically created. This explains Harvey's obsession with that religious ceremony - despite the fact that it has nothing whatever to do with the Adams-Thompson allegations - and his transparent effort to misuse the titling power of the CID to suppress it, threaten us, and consequently intimidate

other Satanists in the armed forces from daring to celebrate any religious ceremony unacceptable to his Catholic value system.

(4) All three authors have insisted that their religions did not affect the objectivity of this investigation. This is contradicted by the structure and content of the report itself.

(a) The **major portion** of the investigation report is quite obviously an attempt to distort, attack, and defame the Satanic religion, and to attack and defame Mrs. Aquino and myself for being adherents of it. Extensive narrative passages by Harvey [as boasted by him to Hayes during conversations between them at the Presidio Officers Club and elsewhere during his final writing of the report] are devoted to clumsy arguments why our religion should be denied the protection of the Constitution concerning its beliefs, practices, and ceremonies. The "logic" of these arguments recalls the similar "logic" used by the Nazis to justify their suppression, persecution, and extermination of the Jewish religion.

(b) In contrast, comparatively little space is devoted to the Adams-Thompson allegations *per se*, because of course there is **no** evidence to substantiate them and the authors declined to discuss the massive evidence exonerating us and proving the crimes of Lawrence and Michele Adams-Thompson. Such "evidence" as is presented boils down to the same thing again and again: **completely unsupported** statements by interested adults and/or "therapized" children **long after** the details of the Adams-Thompson attack had become common knowledge to anyone remotely interested in the Presidio scam, similar day-care scams around the country, or the anti-Satanism campaign still in vogue among the religious extremists of the country.

(c) A genuine religion dictates the moral principles of its adherents. If Cates, Penaluna, and Harvey insist that they have set the intense anti-Satanic bias of their religions aside in conducting this investigation, they are saying that their religions, and consequently the morals prescribed by them, may be selectively ignored when inconvenient. Hence none of these authors may be relied upon to state the truth when it is inconvenient - as of course it was in this fraudulent CID report.

(d) On the other hand, if Cates, Harvey, and Penaluna say that they did **not** compromise the dictates of their faiths in conducting this investigation, then the official position of all three of those faiths dictates that the Satanic religion and its representatives should be condemned *a priori*. "Thou shalt not suffer a witch to live." And of course **Christian** Chaplain Adams-Thompson and his **Christian** wife are at all costs to be protected from accountability for their crimes, which, since they were "against Satan and Satanism" are not only excusable but indeed commendable!

d. It is not necessary that a CID investigation such as this be conducted by "religious friends" rather than "religious enemies" of Satanism. The important thing is that the **religious neutrality** of **all** investigators be beyond question. In this case **none** of the three investigators was either a Satanist, an atheist, an agnostic, or a member of any religion other than Christianity - the religion with a 2,000-year old record of the most extreme hatred and persecution of Satanism.

e. The truthfulness of Major Harvey, as the principal author of this report, bears additional scrutiny.

(1) Harvey has in fact lied to me and my attorneys on several occasions. For instance, Harvey's 4/7/87 letter to Hayes (Attachment #O) contains numerous half-truths, deceptive statements, and outright lies. These are detailed in my 4/24/89 response to him (Attachment #P). [It was not until much later that I learned, via FOIA papers from the Department of the Army, just how flagrant Harvey's lies in his 4/7/87 letter were. [See Attachment #Q.]

(2) More recently, Harvey reiterated the lie to my Army attorney Captain Tinti on 9/29/89 that this investigation was not started consequent to post-Geraldo political pressure, and said that he "thought" I

was fingerprinted by the CID prior to the 10/25/88 airing of that show. Harvey **knew quite well** that the CID investigation of me was not opened until almost a month after that show, and that of course I was not ordered to be fingerprinted by the CID until that time.

(3) Harvey has repeatedly tried to find some way of reinterpreting inconvenient revelations of the investigation into something completely the opposite. In blunt terms, such efforts constitute an attempt to manufacture evidence in violation of Article 134 UCMJ.

(a) When he found that I had purchased a black panther statue in St. Louis long after the time when he could have tried to use it as "evidence" against me, he asked the artist who made the statue whether it was possible for me to have purchased an identical statue in San Francisco years previously.

(b) Adams-Thompson's "package story" to the SFPD included mention of a lion-footed bathtub, over which Pamfiloff was so confused that in the same report [on the same page] he wrote it up as both "a plastic lion bathtub" and "a bathtub with lion's feet". [In a supposed FBI FD-302 interview with Foreman 8/13/87 (still concealed from me), Almond purportedly said "bathtub with lion's feet", in which case either Adams-Thompson or Pamfiloff creatively and arbitrarily added "plastic lion bathtub" as an option the next morning.]

When Pamfiloff's midnight raid on our home failed to reveal either type of bathtub, and when CID interviews with workmen who had spent considerable time in all areas of our building still yielded no plastic lion bathtubs or lion's-footed bathtubs, Harvey went on a personal crusade for **anything** remotely lion-like.

Thwarted by the St. Louis-purchased panther statue, he proceeded to propose that a tiny figure in one corner of a painting hanging in our living room could qualify. That figure is a 2-3" frontal picture of a sphinx with Anton LaVey's head. Outside of the fact that there are two paws on the front, it bears no features of a lion whatever. Nor can the painting be used as a bathtub. Nor can Pharaoh Tutankhamen's golden throne be used as a bathtub. [If Harvey wishes to argue that Kinsey Almond cannot distinguish between an oil painting on the wall, a chair, and a bathtub, any other statements by her scarcely commend themselves for credibility.]

(c) Confronted with the inconvenient fact that Mrs. Aquino and I have consistently told the CID verified **truths** and that the Adams-Thompsons have just as consistently told the CID (and the SFPD and the FBI) a long string of verified **lies**, Harvey has tried doggedly to come up with some excuse for calling me a liar. After an intensive search he came up with the dazzling revelation (a) that I had been confused over Kinsey Almond's age, and (b) that I hadn't read a definition of my wife's name that he had managed to find. These "discoveries" are trumpeted at length in the CID report as if they prove something relevant, which of course they don't. These idiotic assertions by Harvey are addressed in my 10/18/89 letter to General Cromartie (Attachment #R).

(d) Harvey's defamatory distortion of the Satanic religion in the CID report, and his utter misrepresentation and quoting out-of-context of my words and actions therein, are examples of religious bigotry and propaganda at its most extreme. Harvey has **no** excuse for this display of prejudice, as in each case he knows from discussions with me and documentation provided by me that the truth is **not at all** as he has tried to misrepresent it in the report. In addition to Harvey's hate-propaganda against our religion constituting a violation of Article 133 UCMJ, it is quite clear that this officer stands in conspicuous and intentional violation of AR 600-20's requirement that all soldiers and their families be free to practice their religions as guaranteed by the Constitution.

6. *Title*.

    a.   Concerning myself, **none** of these crimes are proven or even substantiated in the least by this report. The report further omits massive amounts of information which **refute absolutely** the allegations. This titling is thus a **deliberately false official statement** by the authors, and Colonel Ray as signatory, in violation of Article 133 UCMJ. If each "title" is considered as a separate false statement, then the authors and Colonel Ray are guilty of eight violations of Article 133 in this titling statement alone.

    b.   The second paragraph identifies Gary Hambright. This report establishes **no connection whatever** between Hambright [or anyone else at the child-care center] and either Mrs. Aquino or myself. Hence the introduction of Hambright's name, and of **separate** allegations against him during the Presidio child-care hysteria, is a transparent effort by the authors and Colonel Ray to imply a connection between Hambright/ those allegations and Adams-Thompson's **separate** attack upon Mrs. Aquino and myself. Such an effort to color this ROI with "guilt by implication" constitutes a violation of Article 133 UCMJ (false official statement) and Article 134 (obstruction of justice).

    It is further significant that Hambright is **not** a proven or convicted criminal in the Presidio child-care scam. Although he was investigated for allegations made against him in that witch-hunt, **all of the allegations were either thrown out by the court or withdrawn by the prosecution**. Therefore Hambright is **entitled by law to the presumption of innocence**, and the authors' obvious attempts to find some way of connecting his life with ours on the assumption that this would "prove" something about us are properly exposed as mere propaganda trying to exploit the publicity accorded the Hambright accusations in the media. Such sleazy methods are not proper to an investigatory report such as this.

    c.   Mrs. Lilith Aquino.

       (1)   The titling of Mrs. Aquino, a civilian not subject to the UCMJ, by the CID is a violation of U.S. law.

       (2)   Concerning Mrs. Aquino, **none** of these crimes are proven or even substantiated in the least by this report. The report further omits massive amounts of information which **refute absolutely** the allegations. This titling is thus a **deliberately false official statement** by the authors, and Colonel Ray as signatory, in violation of Article 133 UCMJ. If each "title" is considered as a separate false statement, then the authors and Colonel Ray are guilty of eight violations of Article 133 in this titling statement alone.

       (3)   Mrs. Aquino and I take strong exception to the phrase "AKA Patricia Wise, Patricia Sinclair, Lilith Sinclair", which implies that these are "phony" aliases she uses. "Patricia Wise" was her maiden name, which [as the CID knows] she legally changed to "Lilith Sinclair" as an adult. She has **never** used the name "Patricia Sinclair". Upon her marriage to me in January 1986, she took my last name as is customary under the circumstances. "Lilith Aquino" is the **only** name she has used since then.

       (4) If it is CID practice to refer to all persons in a report by any names they have ever used, may I suggest:

- Lawrence Adams-Thompson, AKA Larry Thompson, Larry Adams-Thompson, Larry Parker Adams-Thompson.
- Michele Adams-Thompson, AKA Michele Adams, Michele Elise.
- Kinsey Almond, AKA Kinsey Adams, AKA Kinsey Adams-Thompson.

7. *Victim*.

    a.   "Kinsey Almond". The report not only does **not** substantiate that either Mrs. Aquino or I committed **any** crimes concerning this child [or any other child] in any way; it also does **not** substantiate that **anyone** committed **any** such crimes concerning that child. On 5/14/89 the CID obtained a copy of a medical examination of Almond performed on 3/12/87, stating that there was "**no physical evidence of abuse**". This contradicts **absolutely** the statement of psychiatrist Debbie Hickey that Almond was abused - which, upon examination, is clearly based **not** upon explicit testimony from Almond to Hickey, but rather upon nothing more than Hickey's personal whim as to what Almond's childish fantasies "mean". Identifying of Almond as a "victim" is thus a **deliberately false official statement** by the authors, and Colonel Ray as signatory, in violation of Article 133 UCMJ.

b. "Chaplain Lawrence Adams-Thompson". The report not only does **not** substantiate that either Mrs. Aquino or I committed any crimes concerning this individual in any way; it deliberately distorts my efforts to see him brought to justice under the UCMJ for the crime **he** committed against Mrs. Aquino and myself, and for his efforts to defraud the U.S. Government of several millions of dollars in fraudulent claims. This is thus a **deliberately false official statement** by the authors, and Colonel Ray as signatory, in violation of Article 133 UCMJ. It is further an act of misprision of serious offense and obstruction of justice by the 6RCID in violation of Article 134 UCMJ in that the 6RCID has **deliberately** concealed evidence of Adams-Thompson's crimes from the 25th Infantry Division (his UCMJ authority).

c. "U.S. Government": The authors and Colonel Ray as signatory are all aware that **nothing** in this report substantiates "conspiracy, false sworn statement, false statement, indecent acts, and conduct unbecoming an officer". This is thus a **deliberately false official statement** by the authors, and Colonel Ray as signatory, in violation of Article 133 UCMJ. It is further an act of misprision of serious offense and obstruction of justice by the 6RCID in violation of Article 134 UCMJ in that the authors have **deliberately** concealed the evidence of Adams-Thompson's crime which validates **all** of my statements, sworn and unsworn, concerning it.

d. Emily Dorsey. As with the insertion of Hambright's name into the titling block of this ROI, the insertion of Dorsey's name here is merely to associate allegations of kidnapping and sexual abuse (actually against **only** Hambright) with Mrs. Aquino and myself as the targets of this fraudulent ROI. Such an effort to color this ROI with "guilt by implication" constitutes a violation of Article 133 UCMJ (false official statement) and Article 134 (obstruction of justice).

8. *Synopsis.*

a. Paragraph #1.

(1) This investigation did **not** "disclose" that Lilith Aquino and/or Gary Hambright transported Kinsey Almond (name deleted but presumed from report), or any other child, **anywhere**. It did **not** "disclose" that I was involved in any contact with Almond [or any other allegedly-molested children] whatever. It did **not** "disclose" that Almond [or any other allegedly-molested child] has ever been present inside our San Francisco home. It did **not** "disclose" that Hambright has ever "forced Almond to orally copulate him and that he indecently assaulted her", with or without involvement by Mrs. Aquino and/or myself.

(2) Throughout this investigation the CID has been provided with massive amounts of information which expose **every single one** of these allegations by Lawrence and Michele Adams-Thompson as **a deliberate series of continuously- and clumsily-altered lies**. See Attachment #S, the original draft of which was presented to the authors during our personal interview with them in early May, well before the writing of this report. [Updated editions of this list have regularly been provided to the CID as well, as I have been able to obtain more information - including much which the CID attempted to conceal from me.]

b. Paragraph #2: Mrs. Aquino and I have never had any contact whatever with Gary Hambright [save to receive a 7/14/89 statement from him through the San Francisco Public Defender's Office in which he certifies that he has never had any contact with us - Attachment #T]. However, this paragraph is **not** substantiated by any evidence known to me, nor was Hambright ever prosecuted based upon these allegations.

As with the insertion of Hambright's name into the titling block of this ROI, and Dorsey's name into the "victim" heading, the inclusion of this paragraph in this ROI is merely to associate allegations of kidnapping and sexual abuse (actually against **only** Hambright) with Mrs. Aquino and myself as the targets of this fraudulent ROI. Such an effort to color this ROI with "guilt by implication" constitutes a violation of Article 133 UCMJ (false official statement) and Article 134 (obstruction of justice).

c. Paragraph #3.

(1) The 1/4/88 charges that I filed against Chaplain Adams-Thompson were based upon the information contained in my sworn statement of that date, which was and remains true as sworn. **Not a single item** in that sworn statement, or in my updated 8/23/88 one, has been impeached or disproved by the CID or anyone else. The authors know of the evidence supporting Specification #1 of the charges that I preferred against Adams-Thompson, and, in violation of Article 134 UCMJ, **deliberately concealed additional evidence supporting it, unknown to me at the time, from the Commanding Generals of the 25th Division and WESTCOM.** This is therefore a **deliberately false official statement** by the authors, and Colonel Ray as signatory, in violation of Article 133 UCMJ.

(2) The San Francisco Police Report of August 14, 1987 clearly identifies "Larry P. Adams-Thompson" as the "primary reportee" of the allegations. His statements are identified as "(R/P1)" throughout the narrative of the report.[218] Michele Adams-Thompson is identified as "(P2)" in the narrative. Kinsey Almond is identified as "(V)". Pages #2-3 of the report contain the narrative.

(a) On page #2 **all** of the statements to the SFPD were made either by Lawrence or Michele Adams-Thompson. "(V)" appears **only** where either Lawrence or Michele, in their statements to Foreman or Pamfiloff, were referring to her or **purporting** to repeat statements from her or describe actions by her.

(b) On page #3 there are **still** no direct statements by Almond to Pamfiloff. Rather Pamfiloff is writing down what he was **told** were Almond's statements to FBI Agent Foreman on the previous day. As this was all related to Pamfiloff second-hand, and as Lawrence Adams-Thompson is identified on page #1 of the SFPD report as the "primary reportee", it is clear that **he** made these statements to Pamfiloff.

(c) Other than the fact that Almond was present when Pamfiloff's discussion with Lawrence Adams-Thompson took place - as stated on page #2, lines #4-5 of the SFPD report, there is no indication that Almond said **anything whatever** to Pamfiloff.

(d) The authors' statement concerning this point is thus a **deliberately false official statement** by them, and Colonel Ray as signatory, in violation of Article 133 UCMJ.

d. Paragraph #4.

(1) As stated in my 10/18/89 letter to Major General Cromartie (Attachment #U), my inattention to Kinsey Almond's age is a quite understandable and honest mistake, which is not in the least material to the investigation. Considering that I now have a massive accumulation of letters, personal documents, and statements which I have provided to the SFPD and the CID since they decided to mount this shameful campaign against us, Harvey's focus on this as the only incorrect statement he has found is absurd.

---

[218] As personally confirmed to me by Glenn Pamfiloff in 1991, Kinsey Almond was **not even present** during his 8/14/87 interview with Larry A-T. See Chapter #4.

(2) I have in fact **never** been to the Presidio child-care center, **nor** has Mrs. Aquino. Since the report contains no evidence to substantiate that we have, this allegation is as false as all the rest.

(3) The claim of the paragraph that either Mrs. Aquino or myself has ever told a deliberate lie to the CID, or in any way concealed the truth with regard to this affair, is thus a false statement by the authors in violation of Article 133 UCMJ. By trying to misrepresent our sworn statements as false, furthermore, the authors and Colonel Ray as signatory further commit an act of misprision of serious offense and obstruction of justice in violation of Article 134 UCMJ.

e. Paragraph #5.

(1) As has been common knowledge within the Church of Satan and Temple of Set for 19 years, I indeed officiated at a Black Mass (*Missa Solemnis*) at the Central Grotto of the Church of Satan in 1970. I take exception to the word "admitted" in this paragraph, implying as it does that the CID "caught me at something". The *Missa Solemnis* was and is an official religious ceremony of the Church of Satan and Temple of Set, and the 1970 Mass was described in detail in my history *The Church of Satan*, published in 1983. The *Missa Solemnis* contains **no illegal elements whatever**. As such **it is protected by the First Amendment to the Constitution**, and has **no** business even being mentioned in this CID report, much less represented as "conduct unbecoming an officer" or "indecent acts".

(2) The authors allege that I officiated at the "West" Black Mass. The text of that ceremony (authored by Priest Wayne West), which I provided to the authors in St. Louis in May 1989 (as an appendix to *The Church of Satan*), was indeed the basis for the *Missa Solemnis* which I performed at the Church of Satan in 1970. As I informed Harvey, Cates, and Penaluna, however, I modified the ceremony as actually performed in several ways to **delete** elements which I personally considered unnecessary and/or inappropriate. Thus the ceremony as performed contained **no** disrobing, **no** masturbation, **no** consumption of bodily fluids of any sort, and **no** nudity (save for the Living Altar).

(3) The *Missa Solemnis* does **not** involve "public nudity". It is a **private** religious ceremony which was conducted **exclusively** for registered members of the Church of Satan. The 1970 ceremony was conducted within the home of Anton LaVey and was by invitation only to selected members of the Central Grotto of the Church of Satan.

(4) No "female public urination in the presence of males" took place during the *Missa Solemnis*. It was a closed, private ceremony. Furthermore the act of urination by the female involved had a specific religious significance and was not in the least for obscene or prurient purposes.

(5) Similarly the placing of a cracker into the vagina of the Living Altar had a specific and precisely-defined religious significance and was not in the least for obscene or prurient purposes. The cracker, as symbolic of Jesus Christ, was intended to symbolize the experience of physical love with a woman. If a Satanic religious ceremony involving the female vagina is affirmed to be "criminal" by the CID, then Judæo/Christian rituals of penis mutilation (circumcision) must **also** be held to be "criminal" - **and** acts of child abuse.

(6) On 5/10-11/89 during our interview with the authors, it became increasingly clear that Major Harvey was particularly obsessed with the subject of the *Missa Solemnis*, coming back to it again and again. Accordingly I took considerable time to discuss its history and purpose with him. Weeks later, upon hearing from my military attorney Captain Hayes that Harvey was **still** obsessed with the *Missa Solemnis*, I once more took the time to carefully review its religious significance to him (Attachment #V). Harvey and the other authors thus have **no excuse whatever** for misunderstanding the authentic religious purpose of the ceremony.

(7) For the authors to try to represent the private, legal, religious ceremonies of **any** legitimate church as crimes under the UCMJ is a flagrant and inexcusable violation of the First Amendment to the Constitution and of Army Regulation 600-20 in support of it. To the extent that such a representation by the authors is intended to constitute a threat that Satanists in the Armed Forces may not practice their religion freely and without intimidation or persecution, the authors have acted to communicate a threat in violation of Article 134 UCMJ (*MCM* IV, paragraph 110).

(8) Incidentally, although ceremonial nudity is not used by the Temple of Set and was only occasionally used by the Church of Satan, there are a great many non-Christian religions, with hundreds if not thousands of members in the armed forces, which worship **entirely** in the nude (cf. DA Pamphlet #165-13, *Religious Requirements and Practices of Certain Selected Groups*). If the CID proposes to prosecute everyone who takes his/her clothes off for a religious ceremony, Fort Leavenworth will shortly be filled to capacity with a great many unadorned bodies. [In an effort to minimize his Baptist affiliation, Cates recently insisted to Tinti that he is inclined towards the Native American Church. Native American religion includes many instances of nude/semi-nude ceremonies, and the NAC reportedly uses the hallucinogenic drug peyote as a religious sacrament. Perhaps that explains some of the "logic" in this CID report ...]

f.   Paragraph #6.

(1) Since this paragraph concludes that the copy-cat allegations by the Witherow children were "**unsubstantiated**", why are the allegations detailed so graphically and disgustingly here, save - again - to imply defamation of me?

(2) What the ROI **omits** to mention is that the apparent root of the Witherow situation is a long-running, bitter custody fight over the two children, in which allegations of "ritualistic sex abuse" were allegedly made by the husband against the children's mother and grandfather. From what I understand, the mother's mentally-impaired brother was ultimately charged and convicted. This affair occurred before the sensationalistic publicity of the Adams-Thompson attack evidently gave the Witherow father/ stepmother the idea to try to coach the children into fresh allegations based on whatever they could assemble from news media accounts.

(3) The new Mrs. Witherow - the father's new wife - is the founder and promoter of "Victims of Systems", apparently one more group of zealots dedicated to creating and promoting "child abuse" witch-hunts. Most notorious is the "Believe the Children" organization, originally founded to inflame the McMartin situation in Los Angeles. There were efforts to form additional lynch-mob groups of this sort in San Francisco at the time of the Presidio scam as well. This "Victims" group is evidently a similar effort by Witherow to glamorize the publicity she originally attained through use of the children, and to attempt - as with these fake allegations against me - to further capitalize on it. Why is **none of this** mentioned in the ROI?

(4) In short, paragraph #6 is worded in such a way as to insinuate its allegations to the reader without providing any of the truth to expose and discredit not only the allegations per se but the motives and ethics of their sources as well.

9.   *Statutes.*

This report substantiates the violation of **none** of the cited statutes by either myself or Mrs. Aquino. It substantiates the violation of **none** of the statutes by Gary Hambright in any connection with Mrs. Aquino or myself whatever.

10. *Basis for investigation.*

a. As the CID well knows, the allegation that children in day-care "molestation" scams are taken to off-site locations for abuse has a common, well-known, **and utterly-unsubstantiated** cliché of such scams for years. It is introduced simply to enable instigators and promoters of such scams to come up with some way of trying to get around the impossibility of child sex-abuse in the open and generally-supervised atmosphere of the average day-care facility. It is incorrect to represent this long-since-exposed fallacy as "information", and the authors are well aware of this.

b. **No** children have been established as the victims of **any sexual abuse whatever** in connection with the Presidio of San Francisco scam, and the authors are well aware of this.

c. "Fragmented information" is more properly described as random fantasies as is typical of preschool children. To the extent that the statements of the Presidio children - like other groups of children coached by parents, grilled by "therapists", and questioned endlessly by law-enforcement investigators in such scams - are similar to those of Kinsey Almond as represented by Debbie Hickey in six months of "therapy" intended to substantiate Hickey's initial diagnosis of "abuse", nothing but a confused jumble of nonsense resulted. The notion that this "substantiates" anything is preposterous. The medical and law-enforcement literature exposing this sham practice has now grown to enormous size, and it is significant of the investigators' incompetence that they are ignorant of it. [Indeed I provided copies of much of this information to the 6RCID, **all of which, of course, is omitted from the CID report entirely.**]

d. "Mikey".

   (1) As the CID is aware, I have **never** been known by the name "Mikey". That name was **never** initially mentioned by Almond, and was first introduced to Debbie Hickey by **Michele Adams-Thompson** on 6/30/87 after she had previously introduced the subject of "Satanism" to Hickey on 6/2/87.

   (2) According to the CID account of Adams-Thompson's 8/12/87 telephone call to the FBI, he referred to me as "LTC **Mike** Aquino". Only close personal friends and officers senior to me at the Presidio called me by such a nickname; my signature block was "Michael A. Aquino" and, as I habitually dislike nicknames, I avoided entering my name in any other way. Presumably Adams-Thompson, by his use of this name to the FBI, was trying to imply that there was already a connection to the alleged "Mikey".

   (3) Nor is there any information that any other child besides Almond ever mentioned either name **prior** to the massive publicity given the Adams-Thompson allegations (including the term "Mikey") in the San Francisco/national/international media. Nor does it make any sense that I would use my own name [**or** home, **or** wear an Army uniform (at a time when, according to the CID's desperate backdating, I was on leave status)] if I were going to commit crimes such as these.

   (4) Elsewhere in the CID report Harvey makes an issue the fact that the LaVeys, who were at that time as close as immediate family to me, called me "Mike" in conversational letters they wrote. Under the circumstances it would have been rather stilted for them **not** to have used this term. Similarly they signed such letters "Anton" or "Diane", rather than "Anton Szandor LaVey" or "Diane LaVey". I **never** said to the CID that no close friend of mine ever called me "Mike" throughout my entire life - just that I do not like or encourage the use of the nickname myself.

   (5) The CID report of the ludicrous "house identification" expedition of 8/13/87 reveals that Almond **did not** identify our home as her stepfather alleged to Pamfiloff the next day, and this report has her talking about "Mickie". We are now getting rather far afield from "Michael" or even "Mike".

e. There is **no** substantiation that Almond ever made **any** of the statements in the PX later alleged by Adams-Thompson to Pamfiloff as part of his "package story", **or was even present at the PX at all**. The entire account of the PX encounter by the adult Adams-Thompsons is full of lies, inconsistencies, and physical impossibilities as detailed at Attachment #W.[219] The authors, of course, are well aware of this.

f. In particular, in **none** of the original "package story" versions did either Lawrence or Michele Adams-Thompson allege that Almond had said the phrase "That's the bad man, that's Mikey."

g. The statement that "USACIDC monitored and assisted the SFPD investigation":

   (1) This is, from my knowledge, true only to the extent that two CID personnel wandered around curiously inside our home during Pamfiloff's 8/14/87 midnight raid.

   (2) Thereafter there was **no indication whatever** of any CID interest or involvement: no flagging of my file, no suspension of clearance, not so much as a single contact or question from the CID. If possible violations of all of these statutes were involved, it is absurd to think that the CID would allow such an officer to go about his Army duties for one year and three months without taking any action whatever.

   (3) According to my military attorney Captain Hayes, the **truth** is that in November 1988, when political pressure was suddenly put on the CID to frame me following the 10/25/88 Geraldo show, the files of the San Francisco Field Office of the CID concerning the Adams-Thompson allegations were a "complete mess". It was necessary for me to provide Harvey with a complete set of documents concerning the allegations, which I volunteered on the assumption that the CID's investigation was intended to be a *bona-fide* attempt to clear the air. I have not seen **any** evidence that the CID maintained **any** systematic file, much less a "monitoring/assisting" effort, prior to the Geraldo-inspired framing campaign.

h. The statement that "in September 1988 SFPD terminated active investigation" is **false**. The San Francisco District Attorney formally closed the SFPD investigation on **August 1, 1988**. This "September" lie was apparently written into this cover letter to attempt to conceal the fact that, for **three and one-half months** after the closing of the SFPD investigation, the CID did **nothing at all** about it - and in fact only initiated an investigation in November because of post-Geraldo political pressure.

i. The statement that "the [SFPD] investigation had not generated sufficient evidence to convince civil authorities that prosecution had a high probability of conviction" is **false**. The SFPD investigation, after a year, had produced **no evidence whatever** that any such crimes were ever committed at all, much less that they were committed by Mrs. Aquino or myself.[220] In fact the SFPD's initiation and handling of that investigation resulted in (1) an Internal Affairs investigation of the officers concerned within the Police Department, and subsequently (2) an investigation of those same officers by the San Francisco Police Commission. Attachment #X is the letter of findings against those officers by the Police Commission, **sustaining** the many violations by Pamfiloff in the SFPD investigation and the many violations by Gallant in her pre-Adams-Thompson campaign of defamation against ourselves, our church, and our religion.

j. As the SFPD uncovered **no** evidence of **any** crime, whatever briefing Pamfiloff/ Gallant gave the 6RCID on 11/21/88 **cannot** have provided any justification for the CID's opening a new investigation. [If this briefing is so significant, why is a transcript or summary of it not included in the ROI?]

k. There is **no** "medical evidence" to consider. Contrary to what Lawrence Adams-Thompson alleged in his "package story" to Pamfiloff, Kinsey Almond is a **virgin** showing **no** signs of rape by two adult males - **nor any medical sign whatever of any molestation**. Nor is there **any** evidence of the Adams-Thompson's taking Almond for **any** molestation-type medical treatment during either the September-October 1986 period or the CID-later-invented May-July 1986 period.

---

[219] Appendix #34.

[220] See also Glenn Pamfiloff's confirmation of this in 1991 & 2000 (Chapter #4).

l. It is interesting to see the CID admitting that it "considered the FBI records", because, throughout this investigation, the CID investigators were complaining to Hayes that the FBI records were **closed** to them, hence that they had to start "from the beginning". This admission by the CID that it **did in fact** have access to the FBI records makes this present titling effort that much more conspicuously fraudulent, as the CID **knew about the exonerating contents of the FBI Form FD-302, 1/14/87 at the time when it opened this investigation**.

m. Exactly what "coordination" took place on 11/21/89 between the 6RCID and the Presidio SJA remains somewhat murky. An undated memorandum from TJAG states only that "on 23 November 1988, LTC Craig Schwender, the SJA at the Presidio of San Francisco, reported that the CID titled LTC Aquino". Schwender also seriously misled TJAG concerning "the evidence", as is detailed in Attachment #Y, page #5. Consequently his objectivity in determining "probable cause" is impeached.

n. "Sufficient evidence" did **not** exist to initiate this ROI.

   (1) Quite the contrary, massive evidence existed, **and was known to the CID**, proving Mrs. Aquino and myself **utterly innocent** of Adams-Thompson's allegations **and proving Chaplain Adams-Thompson conclusively guilty of Specification #1 of the charges I preferred against him in January 1988**. The CID has deliberately acted to cover up Adams-Thompson's crime in violation of Article 134 UCMJ, and - by continuing to refuse to produce the report it prepared in response to those charges - is further acting to cover up this violation of Article 134.

   (2) Throughout this investigation the 6RCID suppressed and concealed from my attorneys and myself evidence that proved the innocence of Mrs. Aquino and myself, such as the FBI FD-302 1/14/87. Had the Federal Public Defender's Office in San Francisco not informed me of the existence of this document and provided me with a copy of it, I have no doubt it would continue to have been suppressed by the CID. Unsurprisingly it does **not** appear as an exhibit in the CID report.

11. Indictment of Hambright.

   a. What is the relevance of stating that Hambright was indicted for alleged crimes against children not the subjects of this ROI? He was never indicted for any alleged crime against Kinsey Almond - nor against Emily Dorsey, for that matter. Nor does any of this have anything to do with the Adams-Thompson attack against Mrs. Aquino and myself.

   b. Why does the CID ROI not go on to mention that all of these indictments against Hambright were ultimately **dismissed** by the court and never prosecuted?

   c. Once again the inclusion of this irrelevant, slanted paragraph is simply to add fraudulent, defamatory impact against Mrs. Aquino and myself.

Appendix 61: Analysis of 6RCID Report of Investigation Narrative

Lt.Col. Michael A. Aquino

December 22, 1989

Major General Eugene L. Cromartie
Commanding General, USACIDC
5611 Columbia Pike
Falls Church, VA 22041-5015

Dear General Cromartie:

Enclosed are my comments and corrections to the "Narrative" portion of the fraudulent Sixth Region CID report concerning Mrs. Aquino and myself.

As was the case with the cover letter to that report, the narrative does **not** substantiate the titling of either Mrs. Aquino or myself for any alleged crime whatever. To the contrary, it provides clear evidence of the crimes of Chaplain Lawrence Adams-Thompson as concealed to date by the Sixth Region, and of massive violations of Articles 133 and 134 of the UCMJ, and of CID regulations, by the report authors and Colonel Ray as signatory and Sixth Region commander.

I can continue in this manner through the entire report, if you insist, to the continued discredit and embarrassment of the U.S. Army CID in front of all commanders and Army executives with an interest in this affair. As you know, I will not for a moment tolerate crimes against my wife or myself, whether by Adams-Thompson or by a CID regional headquarters which has made its contempt for the United States Constitution, and its assumption of CID invulnerability from U.S. law and the UCMJ, quite clear.

This exercise is, however, a waste of my professional time, hence the taxpayers' time. I once more ask, that without further delay, you rescind the fraudulent report and remove the titling of Mrs. Aquino and myself.

As you know, I have re-preferred charges against Adams-Thompson for his crimes, and I expect that the 25th Division, after once having been embarrassed before the WESTCOM Commanding General because of the 6th Region CID's deliberate misinformation, will take greater care concerning the RCM 303 inquiry this time.

As for the criminal actions of Major Harvey, Chief Warrant Officer Cates, and Staff Sergeant Penaluna in preparing this report, and of Colonel Ray in signing it, it is your responsibility to investigate your Sixth Region headquarters and San Francisco Field Office and take corrective action as appropriate.

The U.S. Army Criminal Investigation Command has a crucial responsibility for the prevention and detection of crime in the Army. Because of the serious harm that could be caused to soldiers wrongly accused of crimes, it is incumbent upon all CID personnel to maintain the most rigorous ethics in their investigations. It may be easy for a senior officer such as myself to expose CID misconduct of an investigation, but the majority of CID investigations focus on junior soldiers who may not have such analytical skills. Such soldiers trust in the CID to conduct fair, impartial, and objective investigations, and indeed to set a standard for the entire Army by obedience to the law.

The conduct of the Sixth Region CID headquarters in this affair is absolutely disgraceful. That the same persons responsible for this appalling abuse of investigatory ethics should escape accountability for their actions, much less continue in positions of responsibility to investigate other U.S. Army personnel in the Sixth Region area, is an offense to the U.S. Army, and to the laws of this nation, which you as Commanding General should not tolerate.

Respectfully,

/s/ Michael A. Aquino
Lt. Colonel, Military Intelligence

Enclosure:
> • Comments concerning CID report "Narrative" with attachments.

Copies to:
> Honorable Michael P.W. Stone, Secretary of the Army
> General Carl E. Vuono, Chief of Staff, United States Army
> General Robert W. RisCassi, Vice Chief of Staff, United States Army
> Lieutenant General Johnny H. Corns, Inspector General of the Army
> Lieutenant General Charles W. Bagnal, Commanding General, WESTCOM
> Major General William F. Ward, Chief, Army Reserve
> Major General William K. Suter, Judge Advocate General of the Army
> Major General Norris L. Einertson, Chief of Chaplains, Department of the Army
> Major General Charles P. Otstott, Commanding General, 25th Infantry Division
> Major General Daniel R. Schroeder, Commanding General, Fort Leonard Wood
> Colonel Bobby R. Sanders, Commander, ARPERCEN
> Colonel William D. Swift, Commander, Presidio of San Francisco
> Colonel Carl L. Lockett, Commander, 6th Region CID
> Colonel John T. Lane, Inspector General, ARPERCEN
> Commander, U.S. Army Central Personnel Security Clearance Facility
> Lt.Colonel Nolan H. Goudeaux, Headquarters, Trial Defense Service
> Major Harold Brown, Tort Claims Division, U.S. Army Claims Service
> Captain Thomas Tinti, Trial Defense Service, Presidio of San Francisco
> Mr. Joseph G. Hanley, Chief of Public Affairs, OCAR, Department of the Army
> Mr. Bob Mahoney, Public Affairs Office, 6th Army & Presidio of San Francisco
> Mr. Gary R. Myers, Attorney
> San Francisco Police Commission
> Chief of Police Frank M. Jordan, San Francisco Police Department
> Captain Michael Hebel, Juvenile Division, San Francisco Police Department
> Pillsbury, Madison & Sutro, Attorneys

Corrections to 6RCID Narrative
Lt. Colonel Michael A. Aquino

[This analysis was provided to the Commanding General, CIC on December 22, 1989. Neither acknowledgment nor response was received.]

Statements by the Sixth Region CID (6RCID) are in *Italics*. My own responses to the 6RCID statements are in regular type

1. *Summary of Significant Information*

    1.1.

        a.   K. *ADAMS-THOMPSON [Kinsey Almond], as well as four other children, during the course of a previous investigation (0667-86-C1D026-69776), alleged that they were taken off-post and sexually assaulted by various people, including "Mr. Mike or Mikey".*

            (1)   In the original Hickey notes through 8/10/87, and in any other account prior to Adams-Thompson's invention of the "package story" on 8/12/87, Kinsey Almond **never** alleged that she was "taken off-post and sexually assaulted by various people including 'Mr. Mike or Mikey'". Rather Almond responded in many different and inconsistent ways to suggestive questions by Hickey. For the CID to represent one out of scores of combinations of such various responses as a single, coherent "allegation" is a clear falsehood. This information is omitted from the 6RCID report.

            (2)   There is no record of "four other children alleging that they were taken offpost and sexually assaulted by any 'Mr. Mike or Mikey'" anywhere in this CID report, nor in the media, nor in any other documents of which I am aware. This information is omitted from the 6RCID report.

            (3)   There is no record of Almond ever using the phrase "off-post" or otherwise specifying this. This information is omitted from the 6RCID report.

            (4)   In the pre-8/12/87 Hickey "therapy" sessions, Hickey prompted Almond through several different versions of "the trip": no trip at all [twice] (4/7), to "Sassy and Todo's house" (4/7), to a house with a garage, a tree house, a swing set, and a fence [none at 123 Acme] (4/7), to "Kathy's house" (5/12), to a "house with real animals" [none at 123 Acme] (5/19), to "Mr. Gary's house" (6/2), and to a "Dr. Steve's house" (6/23).

            (5)   None of the other children's accounts of any "trips" substantiate or corroborate the Almond responses as to location.

                (a)   The 6RCID deliberately omits this contradictory/discrediting information from this summary, instead insinuating that Almond and "four other children" **had** given a single, believable account of one trip to a specific house.

                (b)   There is no record of the 6RCID or anyone else ever trying to identify "Sassy", "Kathy", or "Dr. Steve" or search for such residences on- or off-post.

                (c)   In particular Almond specifically and repeatedly (6/2, 6/9) identified "Dr. Steve" as being with Hambright at "the house". Michele Adams-Thompson acknowledged that she knew "Dr. Steve" and that he was a neighbor of the Adams-Thompsons. No effort was made by the CID to investigate "Dr. Steve" or search his house.

(d)   On 5/12 Almond identified the house as "Cathy's". Jaime Parker said on 7/8 and 7/31 that the house was "Katie Fry's" (same first name), and on on 7/31 Parker's mother told Hickey that "Katie had approached her and said she used to take kids to her house to go to the bathroom when they would go to Sanchez Park". No effort was made by the CID to investigate "Katie/Cathie Fry" or search her house.

(e)   Therefore **two** specific (and one by two children) identifications of **actual** individuals occurred during Hickey's "therapy" sessions -**neither of which was investigated at all by the FBI or CID**. Why therefore was a **nonexistent** "identification" of Mrs. Aquino and myself pursued so frantically by the CID)?

(5)   There is **no** record in the Hickey notes of Almond **ever** using the name "Mr. Mike". On 7/8 Jaime Parker referred to a man at Katie Fry's house as "Frank", then on 7/17 called the same person "Mr. Mike". **No** effort was made by the CID to investigate a "Frank or Mike in connection with Katie Fry". [In the CID report #8.1 the CID states that it interviewed Jaime Parker and showed her photographic lineups and that she "was not able to provide any information of value to this investigation".]

(6)   There is **no** record in the pre-"package story" Hickey notes of Almond **ever** saying that "Mikey" was present at any of the locations to which Hickey reports Almond said she was taken. The allegation that "Mikey" was present first appears in the FBI FD-302 report on 8/13/87, upon Adams-Thompson's invention of the "package story". This information is **omitted** from the 6RCID report

(7)   This statement by the 6RCID report authors and signatory is thus a false official statement in violation of Article #133 UCMJ and an act to obstruct justice in violation of Article #134 UCMJ.

b.   *[Almond] reported that she had been taken to Mr. Gary's house by Mr. Gary in a green car.*

(1)   Almond has changed the color of the supposed car every time questioners have suggested a car-ride to her. It was "blue" (4/7), "red & white" (4/21), then "green" (8/13), then "red" (later that same 8/13 morning). Accordingly Almond's account of a car-ride, and the color of the supposed car, are **unreliable and unbelievable**. This information is **omitted** from the 6RCID report.

(2)   In the Hickey sessions prior to her stepfather's 8/13/87 "package story", Almond mentioned several features of the house/houses to which she was supposedly taken [**after first denying twice to Hickey that she was taken anywhere** (4/7)]: the color is blue (4/7), the house is Kathy's (5/12), the house is Dr. Steve's (6/23), the house has a garage, a tree house, a swing set, and a fence (4/28). Inside are dinosaurs that bit people (4/7), a golf book and golf balls (4/7), a *Bible* with "poopoo on it" and a "bad cross that went peepee" (5/19), a bathtub with lion's feet (6/2), a pot hanging from the ceiling with arms and legs and a penis hanging out of it (6/2), and that Mr. Gary cut a baby open and that there were a varying number of babies in alternating black and white colors (5/19, 5/26/, 8/10). **None** of these features match our house. The 6RCID **deliberately omits this contradictory/discrediting information**, instead insinuating that Almond had given a single, believable account of one trip to a specific house.

(3)   Our house on Acme Avenue is not, of course, "Mr. Gary's house". Gary Hambright has never resided or visited there. The 6RC1D **deliberately omits this contradictory/ discrediting information**.

(4) In point of fact Almond does **not** use the expression "Mr. Gary's house" herself **anywhere** in the Hickey notes. The phrase is always introduced (first 4/7) and used by **Hickey** to seek a response from Almond. [The 4/7 Hickey notes add that **Michele Adams-Thompson** had also proposed the "trip to Mr. Gary's house" theme to Almond prior to that session - and that Almond had **denied any such trip** to her mother as well.] Obviously neither Michele nor Hickey were about to let such an inconvenient denial stand. After her initial three denials of such a trip were ignored, Almond presumably realized that she was expected to say "yes".

(5) Gary Hambright cannot drive anyone anywhere, being an epileptic with neither a car nor a driver's license. The 6RCID **deliberately omits this contradictory/discrediting information**. Furthermore the 6RCID **concealed this information from my attorneys and myself**; I was advised of it only by the Federal Public Defender's Office.

(6) 1-1/2 years later, in another attempt to manufacture evidence in violation of #134 UCMJ and explain away the impossibility of Hambright driving, the Adams-Thompsons invented the idea of Mrs. Aquino driving the car and coached it into Almond, who in a 4/7-8/89 6RCID interview, obediently **contradicted her earlier 8/13/87 recitation** accordingly. [In that same interview she then **re-contradicted** herself by saying that it was "Mr. Gary" who took her.] This information is **omitted** from the 6RCID report.

(7) This statement by the 6RCID report authors and signatory is thus a false official statement in violation of Article #133 UCMJ and an act to obstruct justice in violation of Article #134 UCMJ.

c. *While there, Mr. Gary placed his penis into her bottom, her vagina, and her mouth.*

(1) There is **no** record in the pre-"package story" Hickey notes of Almond **ever** using the phrase "Mr. Gary placed his penis into her bottom, her vagina, and her mouth". This phrase first appears in the FBI FD-302 report on 8/13/87, **after** Adams-Thompson's invention of the "package story". This information is **omitted** from the 6RCID report. [On 4/7 Hickey said that Almond said that "she put Mr. Gary's penis in her mouth and Mr. Gary put his penis in her bottom".]

(2) As the 6RCID is well aware, from an FBI interview on 1/26/87: "**When Mrs. Adams-Thompson asked if Mr. Gary had been mean to her or tried to touch her, Kinsey replied negatively.**" As the FBI interview **closest** to the time-period specified in the Adams-Thompson allegations [**and** in the revised time-period invented by the 6RCID to manufacture evidence], this is the most reliable interview and is of course of vital importance. Yet **its existence was concealed from me by the 6RCID**, and it is **omitted altogether** from this 6RCID report.

(3) There is, of course, **no** corroborative evidence of any sort that Almond was **ever** taken to **any** house at **any** time per the Hickey notes, Adams-Thompson's "package story", or Almond's later attempted recitations thereof. The 6RCID is well aware of this, yet does **not** mention it in the report.

(4) As 6RCID is well aware, Almond has been medically examined and found to be **a virgin, with "no physical evidence of sexual abuse"**. [See item #5, *Adams-Thompson's Violations of #133 UCMJ*, 11/29/89.]

(5) This statement by the 6RCID report authors and signatory is thus a false official statement in violation of Article #133 UCMJ and an act to obstruct justice in violation of Article #134 UCMJ.

d. *According to [Almond], also present at the house were "Mikey" and "Shamby".*

(1) This allegation first appears in the FBI FD-302 report on 8/13/87, **after** Adams-Thompson's invention of the "package story". **Prior** to his fabrication of the "package story", there is **no** account of Almond herself **ever** linking "Mikey" and "Shamby" together, placing them in the same location, or even discussing them at the same time. This information is **omitted** from the 6RCID report.

   (a) "Shambee" first appears in the 1/27/87 Hickey Session, introduced by Almond as "her friend at school who was spanked by Mr. Rogers on TV".

   (b) "Mikey" was **never** mentioned initially by Almond, and there is no mention of this name whatever until 6/30/87 - **after** Michele introduced the idea of a "Satanic cult" to Hickey on 6/2/87. On 6/30/87 it is **Michele** - not Almond - who introduces "Mikey" to Hickey, alleging that "Mikey is Shambee's husband". **None** of this was mentioned by Almond **herself** during that session, nor did Hickey ask her questions about any of it.

(2) In the Hickey sessions Almond states **no** feature of "Shambee" or "Mikey" to suggest any identification with either Mrs. Aquino or myself. In fact **Almond never gives any physical description of "Shambee" or "Mikey" at all**. The oft-quoted statement that "Mikey wore an Army suit with a stripe on the pants" was made by **Michele** to Hickey on 6/30/87 and **never** repeated by Almond herself to Hickey.

(3) The 6RCID's unqualified attribution of this part of the Adams-Thompson "package story" to Almond is thus an attempt to manufacture evidence and obstruction of justice in violation of Article 134 UCMJ.

e. *She stated "Mikey" had put his penis into her mouth, bottom and vagina (Paragraph 4.1, this report).*

(1) This is a statement **by FBI Agent Clyde Foreman** writing a report of his interview with Almond on 8/13/87. The exact words are **not** necessarily Almond's. Almond said (6/30/87) that Mikey "put his penis in her mouth and peed on her, and put poo-poo in her mouth". During all of the preceding sessions she had made the **same** statements concerning (a) Hambright, (b) "little boys", (c) all of the children at "the house", (d) Sassy, (e) Todo, (f) the cross, (g) the bible, (h) the female doll, (i) the penis in the pot hanging from the ceiling with arms and legs in it, and (j) Dr. Steve.

(2) As 6RCID is well aware, Almond has been medically examined and found to be a virgin, with no physical evidence of sexual abuse. [See item #5, *Adams-Thompson's Violations of #133 UCMJ*, 11/29/89.]

(3) Although Adams-Thompson alleged in his 8/13/87 "package story" that the multiple rape/sodomy happened between 1 September and 31 October 1986, **there is no evidence that he ever noticed anything wrong with Almond, nor took her for an emergency medical examination of this nature at any point during that period [nor during the 6RCID-later-invented MayJuly 86 period]**.

(4) Although two rapes and two sodomies, which Adams-Thompson alleged were committed by two adult males, would also have severely traumatized a 3-year-old, **there is no published evidence that either Lawrence or Michele ever noticed anything wrong with Almond nor took her for psychiatric help during September/October 1986 [nor during the 6RCID-later-invented May-July 86 period]**.

(5)   The 6RCID's unqualified attribution of this part of the Adams-Thompson "package story" to Almond is thus an attempt to manufacture evidence and obstruction of justice in violation of Article 134 UCMJ.

f.   *[Almond] and Dana Smith, during therapy, mentioned the name "TODO" as one of their assailants (paragraphs 14.1 and 143, this report).*

(1)   There is **no** evidence in the CID report that Dana Smith ever mentioned the name "Todo". There are no "therapy" or interview notes concerning Smith provided as an exhibit to the report. In the CID report #8.1 the CID states that it interviewed Dana Smith and showed her photographic lineups and that she "**was not able to provide any information of value to this investigation**".

(2)   Nowhere in the Hickey/Almond notes is "Todo" described as having "assailed" either Almond or any other child in any way. Almond's only description of "Todo" is that he had first "blond" (4/27/87) and then "green" (4/28/87) hair. The 6RCID **deliberately omits** this contradictory/ discrediting information.

(3)   The 6RCID's statement here is thus deliberately false in violation of Article 133 UCMJ and, as used, is an obvious attempt to manufacture evidence and obstruct justice in violation of Article 134 UCMJ.

g.   *On 13 Aug 87, [Almond] identified a red 1987 Isuzu Mark I automobile, CA license 2ENS452, as "Shamby's" car, in which [Almond] had ridden with "Shamby" (paragraph 4.1, this report).*

(1)   **This fact exposes the "package story" as Adams-Thompson's invention of the previous day, and also exposes the coaching of Almond to make a bogus "identification".** The 8/13/87 6RCID report by SA Potter editorially states that Almond picked out the red Isuzu as "Mrs. Shamby's" car and said that she had ridden in it with her. This was of course after Michele and Lawrence Adams-Thompson had connected that car with us at the PX on 8/12/87, but before they discovered it to be only a rental car which we had had for only a couple of days previously.

(2)   Neither Mrs. Aquino nor I owned or drove a red car during the single weekend trip we made to San Francisco during the September-October 1986 time period (alleged to be the time of the incident in Adams-Thompson's "package story"). We drove a rental car, which was not red or any color close to red [as verified by its rental company receipt].

(3)   Neither Mrs. Aquino nor I owned or drove a red car during the 6RCIDreinvented May-July 86 period. We drove our own car, which was not red or any color close to red.

h.   *On 7-8 Apr 89, [Almond] stated Mr. Gary's house contained a bath tub with lion's feet and a shower with a glass door (paragraph 4.1, this report).*

(1)   This is thus **exculpatory** evidence. Our home in San Francisco contains neither a bathtub with lion's feet nor a shower with a glass door, as the 6RCID knows. Our bathtub is a modem, built-in tub with no feet at all, and it has a shower curtain.

i.   *On 7-8 Apr 89, [Almond] stated she went to Mr. Gary's house on several occasions and that Evan and Cohn Fox, Kara Bailey, and Kelly Quigley were present on most of those occasions (paragraph 4.1, this report).*

(1) Not later than April 1987 Adams-Thompson made his first, pre-"package story" allegation against Gary Hambright for sexually abusing Almond. "Such act or acts took place sometime in September or October 1986 at the Child Development Center, Presidio of San Francisco." [Letter, Presidio CDS Director to Hambright, 4/17/87]. Adams-Thompson was **specific about the time and location**, and **no** allegation was made of the child being transported elsewhere or of anyone else being involved.

(2) As the 6RCID well knows, the allegation that children in day-care "molestation" scams are taken to off-site locations for abuse has been a common, well-known, and utterly-unsubstantiated cliché of such scams for years. It is introduced simply to enable instigators and promoters of such scams to come up with some way of trying to get around the impossibility of child sex-abuse in the open and constantly-supervised atmosphere of the average day-care facility.

(3) In the original Hickey notes there was no clear mention of any more than a single "trip", alternately to "Mr. Gary's", "Kathie's", and "Dr. Steve's" house; and the "house" changes its appearance, decor, and inhabitants every time another interrogator leads Almond through the drill. Clearly **the whole notion of an actual trip or trips credibly recounted by Almond is utterly discredite**d.

(4) Per Captain Hayes (telephone discussion 5/5/89), the Fox and Quigley children were videotape-interviewed by SA Cates and **both denied** this account. This further impeaches Almond's truthfulness and reliability. This information is **omitted** from the 6RCID report as provided to me.

(5) The 6RCID's unqualified attribution of this part of the revised AdamsThompson "package story" to Almond is thus an attempt to manufacture evidence and obstruction of justice in violation of Article 134 UCMJ.

j. *On 7-8 Apr 89, [Almond] stated Mr. Gary had threatened her with a gun, saying he would shoot her with it if she ever told her parents what had happened (paragraph 4.1, this report).*

(1) Such a significant and presumably-frightening "event" as this was never mentioned by Almond in the Hickey notes, nor by Adams-Thompson in his initial "package story". Obviously it is a tacked-on addition, years later, to add additional drama to the allegations. Like "offsite transport", "being threatened with weapons" is an invariable, routine feature of "day-care child molestation" scams generally.

(2) Hickey **herself** introduced the general subject and specific term "gun" into the Almond "therapy" sessions, asking Almond on 4/7/87 "if there was a gun there". Almond's response was, "Yes, Mr. Gary told Sassy he would kill her." ... which makes no sense if the CID is trying to equate "Sassy" with "Shambee" and propose her as a conspirator with Hambright.

* * * * *

What this "Summary of Significant Information" **actually** reveals is that:

- **No** information exists to substantiate the report or the titling action.

- **Abundant** information exists to **disprove** the allegations and expose AdamsThompson as a deliberate, malicious liar.

- The 6RCID authors and signatory were all in possession of the exculpatory information cited above, yet omitted mention of it.

- Manufacture of evidence by both Adams-Thompson and the 6RCID, as evidenced above, is a violation of Article 134 UCMJ.

- Omission and suppression of the evidence cited by me above, in that such acts by the 6RCID shelter Adams-Thompson from accountability for his crime against Mrs. Aquino and myself, constitute multiple acts of Misprision of Serious Offense and Obstruction of Justice by the 6RCID in violation of Article 134 UCMJ.

- Attempts by the 6RCID to shelter Adams-Thompson from accountability for his crime are further attempts by the 6RCID to cover up its own violations of Articles 133 and 134 UCMJ in its "investigation" of the 1/4/88 court-martial charges against him. Hence this 6RCID report, furthering this 6RCID cover-up attempt, is also in this respect a violation of the Misprision of Serious Offense and Obstruction of Justice provisions of Article 134 UCMJ.

This "Summary of Significant Information" is thus **a deliberate, willful series of false official statements in violation of Article #133 UCMJ, and a series of acts in violation of Article #134 UCMJ**.

* * * * *

Evidence

k. *On 12 Aug 87, [Almond] identified Lt. Colonel Aquino and Mrs. Aquino as "Mikey" and "Shamby" respectively (paragraph 4.1, this report).*

 (1) Paragraph 4.1 contains **no evidence whatever** that Almond "identified" anyone on 12 Aug 87 (the date of the alleged incident in the Presidio PX) or was even present herself at the PX on that date. All that is established is that **Lawrence and/or Michele** Adams-Thompson were present in the PX that day and saw us there, preparatory to their invention of the "package story" later that same day. As part of that "package story", the Adams-Thompsons alleged Almond's involvement at the PX, changing their accounts of this involvement, and changing the numbers of persons there, several times from 8/13/87 until the present. [See Section #C "The August 12, 1987 Presidio Post Exchange Incident", *Chaplain Lawrence AdamsThompson's Actions in Violation of Article 133, UCMJ*, updated 11/29/89.]

 (2) The 6RCID is aware of this information, yet **omits** mention of it here. Hence this unqualified 6RCID statement is a false official statement in violation of Article 133 UCMJ and an act of obstruction of justice in violation of Article 134 UCMJ.

l. *On 12 August 1987, Captain Adams-Thompson reported [Almond] had identified Lt. Colonel and Mrs. Aquino as "Mikey" and "Shamby" at the PX, PSF, CA. He also noted Lt. Colonel and Mrs. Aquino got into a red 1987 Isuzu Mark I automobile, CA license 2ENS452, which [Almond] identified as "Shamby's" car (paragraph 3.1, this report).*

 (1) All this establishes is that Adams-Thompson made a **personal** allegation to the 6RCID after seeing Mrs. Aquino and myself at the PX and noticing the car in which we drove off.

 (2) As noted above, there is **no** evidence that Almond made any such "identification" at the PX, or was even present.

(3) Adams-Thompson's assumption that the red Isuzu was ours, and his consequent coaching of Almond to "identify" it to support his allegations, led to her doing just that the next morning. As Adams-Thompson did not know at the time, of course, the Isuzu was a rental car which we had had for only a couple of days, and had not even been registered to the rental company until 7/87. This is **conclusive evidence** both of the Adams-Thompsons' coaching of Almond to support their "package story" and of the deliberate falsification of that "package story".

(4) The 6RCJD is aware of this information, yet **omits** mention of it here. Hence this unqualified 6RCID statement is a false official statement in violation of Article 133 UCMJ and an act of obstruction of justice in violation of Article 134 UCMJ.

m. *On 13 August 1987, [Almond] identified Hambright as Mr. Gary from a photographic lineup (paragraph 4.1, this report).*

(1) This statement is not evidence of any crime committed by Mrs. Aquino or myself.

n. *On 13 August 1987, [Almond] identified 123 Acme Avenue, San Francisco, California, as the location to which she was taken by Mr. Gary (paragraph 4.1, this report).*

(1) Although this "identification" was hyped repeatedly in the media immediately after Adams-Thompson made his attack, no evidence to substantiate it was ever produced from the time of his attack until November 1989, when I finally managed to obtain a [heavily censored] copy of this 6RCID report concerning myself.

(2) The 6RCID report of that "identification trip", as finally exposed upon my obtaining of this 6RCID report concerning myself, establishes that Almond **did not make any such identification of 123 Acme Avenue.** The **only** "identification" she made was of the red Isuzu, which, as noted above, was an impossible and obviously pre-coached "identification". [See Section #D "The 123 Acme 'Identification' Trip", *Chaplain Lawrence Adams-Thompson's Actions in Violation of Article 133, UCMJ,* updated 11/29/89.]

(3) The 6RCID is aware of this information, yet **omits** mention of it here. Hence this unqualified 6RCID statement is a false official statement in violation of Article 133 UCMJ and an act of obstruction of justice in violation of Article 134 UCMJ.

o. *On 7-8 April 1989, [Almond] identified a female who is not a suspect in this investigation as "Shamby" from both photographic and video line-ups (paragraph 9.19, this report).*

(1) This is **exculpatory** evidence, substantiating Mrs. Aquino's innocence and discrediting **any** "identification" of "Shamby" by Almond.

(2) If such great emphasis is being placed in children's "identifications" to substantiate the Presidio scam and justify the titling of two innocent persons despite the overwhelming evidence proving our innocence, then why was the person so "identified" by this child automatically ruled "not a suspect in this investigation"? This was a repeated identification - both photographic and video. Was **this** "identified" person's photo subsequently shown to other CDC children? Was a search warrant sought for **her** home? Was an "identification" trip made to **her** home? Was a strenuous effort made to find any conceivable way of "titling" or indicting **her**? It is no argument that she might be a CID or other law-enforcement official, as such persons are no more privileged or exempt from suspicion than anyone else.

(3) On 1/27/87 Almond said to Hickey that "Shambee" was "her friend at school whom she played with", "who had its neck broken", and who was spanked by Mr. Rogers on TV.

p.   *On 7-8 April 1989, [Almond] identified Lt. Colonel Aquino as "Mike" from both photographic and video line-ups as the individual whom she had previously identified in the PX, PSF, CA (paragraph 9.19, this report).*

(1)   The use of a photographic line-up by the 6RCID **after** 1-1/2 years of Almond being exposed to my face in the media, and of course by coaching and reinforcement from Adams-Thompson and Michele, is absurd. The technique used is further in explicit violation of CID Regulation CIDR 195-1 (1 November 1986), which states:

(a)   "A line-up is appropriate **when the witness does not know the identity of the perpetrator**." [5-1 1.a.(2)]. By April 1989, of course, it would be absurd for Almond not to recognize my name and face as a consequence of their continuous media exposure and the obvious interest of her stepfather and mother in reinforcing her support of their "package story" in preparation for the 6RCID performance.

(b)   "The persons portrayed in the photographs should be reasonably similar in appearance." [5-11 d. (1) (b)]. All other individuals on the photo line-up as used by the 6RCJD, as seen by Captain Hayes, **look nothing like me whatever**. Not one of them has either of my two most distinctive features (a pronounced widow's peak and sharplyupturned eyebrows). To call such persons "similar in appearance to me" would be like calling Mr. Spock "similar in appearance" to the other crewmen in *Star Trek*. When suggesting a video lineup in his 10/17/88 letter, Major [then Captain] Harvey said specifically that the alternate persons "will not need to all have pointed eyebrows and the widow's peak". In fact none of them had either of these crucial features.

(2)   In viewing the videotape of this 6RCID interview (a videotape which I have not personally seen), JAG Captain Thomas Hayes has stated that, when shown my picture, Almond said, "That's him!" in a happy, excited voice "as though she were expecting to be rewarded for her performance". She showed no sign of displeasure or distress whatever.

(3)   There is, of course, **no** record of Almond "identifying" my face to anyone from a line-up **before** April 1989.

(4)   Following the August 1987 Adams-Thompson attack, Inspector Pamfiloff showed a photographic lineup to 26 other Presidio children. **Not one of these children "identified" my photograph.** This is also significant since, at the time of her April 1989 interview, Almond was reciting a revised version of the "package story" **to include several other children**.

(5)   Obviously a "photo identification" by Almond in April 1989 is **no evidence whatever** in substantiation of Adams-Thompson's allegations, or the 6RC1D titling action taken against me.

(6)   This statement in the "evidence" section is thus **no "evidence" at all** -except of 6RCID's violation of CIDR 195-1 and consequent attempt to manufacture evidence in violation of Article 134 UCMJ.

q.   *On 7-8 April 1989 [Almond] was unable to identify 123 Acme Avenue, San Francisco, California from a photographic line-up as the location to which she had been taken (paragraph 9.19, this report).*

(1)   This is **exculpatory** evidence.

(2)   In fact, as noted above, Almond **never "identified" 123 Acme in the first place**, as alleged by the 6RCID and SFPD.

(3)   From the morning of August 13, 1987, of course, both Lawrence and Michele Adams-Thompson knew exactly what the exterior of 123 Acme looked like, as did Almond, who had been taken there and shown it by her mother on 8/13/87 [and possibly on 8/12/87 as well].

r.   *On 7-8 April 1989, [Almond] stated she had been taken by "Shamby" and Mr. Gary to Mr. Gary's house, in a red car, which was "Shamby's" (paragraph 4.1, this report).*

(1)   This statement does not substantiate any "titling" of Mrs. Aquino or myself.

(2)   "Shambee" was never associated with Mrs. Aquino by Almond in six months of Hickey "therapy" sessions. It was **Michele Adams-Thompso**n who first proposed to Hickey that "Shambee" be changed from "a friend at school" to "the wife of an Army officer" on 6/30/87.

(3)   This 4/7-8/89 statement once more impeaches the reliability of **any** statements by Almond, as "Shamby" is now added to the car which formerly contained just "Mr. Gary", the house remains "Mr. Gary's", and the color of the car changes from several other colors cited in the Hickey notes.

(4)   Obviously the Adams-Thompsons added "Shamby" as a driver of the car upon discovering that Gary Hambright is an epileptic who cannot drive and doesn't own a car (information **concealed** from me by 6RCID).

(5)   As already established, neither Mrs. Aquino nor I either owned or rented a red car during the time of either Adams-Thompson's original "package story" allegation (September-October 1986) or the 6RCID-later-invented allegation (May-July 1986).

s.   *On 7-8 April 1989, [Almond] denied that "Mikey" and/or "Shamby" had ever done anything bad to either her or to other children in her presence (paragraph 4.1, this report).*

(1)   This is **exculpatory** evidence, of course, even **if** the mysterious "Mikey" and "Shamby" are assumed to be myself and Mrs. Aquino (which is merely the Adams-Thompson "package story" allegation, is **not** otherwise substantiated, and is **contradicted** by statements from other Presidio day-care children). Hence it does **not** support the allegations of this 6RCID report or the 6RC1D titling of Mrs. Aquino or myself.

t.   *On 14 August 1987 123 Acme Avenue, San Francisco, California was verified to be the residence of Lt. Colonel and Mrs. Aquino (paragraph 5.A.1., this report).*

(1)   This is not "evidence" which supports any alleged "crime" whatever. 123 Acme has been our family home for three generations!

u.   *On 14 August 1987, during the conduct of a search, photographs were exposed depicting the interior of the 123 Acme Avenue, San Francisco, California which do not support the bath tub or shower with a glass door as reported by [Almond] (paragraph 5.A.3., this report).*

(1)   This is **exculpatory** evidence, which substantiates our innocence and the deliberate falsification of the "package story" by Adams-Thompson.

(2)   The supposed interior of "Mr. Gary's house" was proposed to the SFPD on 8/14/87 by **Lawrence Adams-Thompson, not** by Almond.

(3)   No "shower with a glass door" was included in the original 8/12-14/87 "package story" invented by Adams-Thompson. This additional revision to the many revisions of the "package story" first appears 1-1/2 years later, after the Adams-Thompsons knew that 123 Acme has a modern, not an old-fashioned tub. [Nevertheless our bathtub still does not have a glass door, but just a shower-curtain.]

v.   *On 4 January 1988, 23 August 1988, 22 November 1988, 27 January 1989, and 10-11 May 1989, Lt. Colonel Aquino rendered sworn written statements and sworn testimony in which he denied any criminal misconduct and denied ever being known as "Mike" or "Mikey" (paragraph 6.1, this report).*

(1)   This is a **false statement by the 6RCID** in violation of Article 133 UCMJ. It is correct that I denied ever being called "Mikey", and that is the truth. It is **not** correct that I denied ever being called "Mike". As explained in my sworn statement of 1/27/89 (in answer to 6RCID questions), my childhood nickname was "Archy", and, as I dislike nicknames, I habitually use "Michael" rather than "Mike" personally and among junior acquaintances. Persons older and senior to me, (particularly in the Army, where anything beyond a one-syllable nickname would be regarded as an affectation), occasionally take the liberty to call me "Mike". I see nothing the least bit peculiar or sinister in that.

(2)   Paragraph 6.1 of the 6RCJD report reports my statement to the 6RCID that "while his military contemporaries frequently call him 'Mike', he does not like this name and is not called that by any person(s) outside his military acquaintances".

    (a)   Elsewhere in the 6RCID report Major Harvey makes a considerable fuss about Anton and Diane LaVey having addressed me as "Mike" in their personal correspondence with me [but not to any other officials or members of the Church of Satan] during the 1969-1975 time of our close friendship. As the LaVeys and I were all then as close as family, this is not the least surprising. After my estrangement from the LaVeys in 1975, my statement to the 6RCID, which is in the present tense, remains exactly true as stated.

    (b)   Indeed Anton LaVey singled out this well-known preference of mine for highlighting in his book *The Compleat Witch* (Dodd, Mead 1970/71, page #61), in which he said: "'Mike' is an all-around guy, whereas 'Michael' is serious and romantic."

(3)   The Hickey notes establish that as far back as June 1987 it had occurred to the Adams-Thompsons to fabricate allegations against me, based simply upon the well-known fact that I was a prominent Satanist and that it had become an accepted and widespread tactic of "day-care child molestation" scams to allege "Satanic ritual" responsibility and involvement.

(4)   I stand absolutely by all of my sworn statements as identified above as containing the truth as it was known to me at the time of the statement in question. Not a single statement in any of these sworn statements has been impeached by the 6RCID or anyone else.

w.   *Lt. Colonel Aquino reported his residence at 123 Acme Avenue, San Francisco, California and the property at 121 Acme Avenue, San Francisco, California underwent major structural changes and painting commencing about December 1985 and being completed about Jan 87 (paragraph 6.1, this report).*

(1)   This is not "evidence" which supports any alleged "crime" at all.

x.   *During interview, while under oath, Lt. Colonel Aquino stated he taught classes for the Golden Gate University from 1979 until the fall semester 1985 (paragraph 6.1, this report).*

    (1)   I made **no** such statement under oath to the 6RCID, and their allegation that I did so is thus a false official statement in violation of Article 133 UCMJ.

    (2)   What I told 6RCID is that I began teaching at Golden Gate University in the Fall Semester 1980. [It would have been impossible for me to have begun teaching there in 1979, as we did not even move to San Francisco until 1980 and I did not receive my Ph.D. (enabling me to qualify to teach at GGU) until 1980.]

y.   *On 4 January 1988 and 11 May 1989, Mrs. Aquino rendered a sworn written statement and sworn testimony in which she denied any criminal misconduct (paragraph 6.2, this report).*

    (1)   This is not "evidence" which supports any alleged "crime" whatever. Mrs. Aquino's statements were and are **completely true**, and are substantiated by all of the evidence, including abundant evidence which 6RCID has omitted from its report in violation of Article 134 UCMJ.

z.   *It was ascertained 123 Acme Avenue, San Francisco, California is two miles in distance from the Child Development Center, Presidio of San Francisco, California, requiring 7 minutes 14 seconds driving time (paragraph 5.A.1., this report).*

    (1)   This is not "evidence" which supports any alleged "crime" whatever. There is nothing special about "7 minutes, 14 seconds" in terms of the "package story" or any other variation on it, and there are thousands of residences in San Francisco which are within an equal or shorter driving time from the Presidio day-care center - including, of course, on-post housing itself.

aa.   *On 8 April 1989, Michele Adams-Thompson stated [Almond] had identified Lt. Colonel and Mrs. Aquino as "Mikey" and "Shamby" on 12 August 1987 in the PX, Presidio of San Francisco, California (paragraph 7.8, this report).*

    (1)   This is merely Michele's reciting of the "PX story", 1-1/2 years later. That story has been shown to be so compromised by the Adams-Thompsons' efforts to revise it since first alleging it, that it is of no evidence of anything **except their efforts to prop up and adjust their original lies**. [See Section #C "The August 12, 1987 Presidio Post Exchange Incident", *Chaplain Lawrence Adams-Thompson's Actions in Violation of Article 133, UCMJ*, updated 11/29/89.]

ab(1).   *On 12 April 1989 Joshua Thompson [a son of Adams-Thompson by previous marriage] identified a female who is not a suspect as the female identified as "Shamby" by [Almond] at the PX, Presidio of San Francisco, California, on 12 August 87. Further, he identified Lt. Colonel Aquino as the male identified by [Almond] as "Mikey" (paragraph 7.10, this report).*

ab(2).   *On 12 April 1989 Timothy Thompson [another son of Adams-Thompson by previous marriage] identified a female who is not a suspect as the female identified as "Shamby" by [Almond] at the PX, Presidio of San Francisco, California, on 12 August 87. Further, he identified Lt. Colonel Aquino as the male identified by [Almond] as "Mikey" (paragraph 7.11, this report).*

    (1)   Although they made several statements to the FBI, the 6RCID, and the SFPD in August 1987 at the time they saw us in the Presidio PX, the Adams-Thompsons made **no mention whatever of the presence or involvement of the two boys until 1-1/2 years later**. Clearly the two boys, and still another Adams-Thompson child, were added to the story later on to try to prop it up, and the boys instructed by their father and/or Michele to parrot the story. The two boys were

approximately 9 and 13 at the time of the PX incident, hence would have been important witnesses at **that** time.

(2) Obviously **by April of 1989 the entire Adams-Thompson family** ought to know quite well what both Mrs. Aquino and I look like. Even so, both boys "identified" **another woman other than Mrs. Aquino** as having been present in the PX, which impeaches their credibility concerning the "identification" of myself.

(3) Again, if such sacred emphasis is being placed in children's "identifications" to substantiate the Presidio scam and justify the titling of two innocent persons despite the overwhelming evidence proving our innocence, then why was the person so "identified" by these boys automatically ruled "not a suspect in this investigation"? Was **this** "identified" person's photo subsequently shown to other CDC children? Was a search warrant sought for **her** home? Was an "identification" trip made to **her** home? Was a strenuous effort made to find any conceivable way of "titling" or indicting **her**? It is no argument that she might be a CID or other law-enforcement official, as such persons are no more privileged or exempt from suspicion than anyone else.

ac. *On 12 April 1989 Mrs. Jennifer L. Thompson [A-T's previous wife] related she is aware of no information which would indicate that Captain Adams-Thompson, for religious or other reason(s), would attempt to alter or influence the testimony of [Almond] regarding this matter (paragraph 7.12, this report).*

(1) This is an absurd statement for Jennifer to make. As she is well aware, if Adams-Thompson cannot convince Almond to recite his "package story", he faces exposure and possible criminal prosecution for it, both from the Army and the San Francisco Police Department. That would not be in her sons' interests, of course, nor in hers if she receives any alimony or child-support from him.

(2) Furthermore, as I expect Jennifer is also well aware, the Adams-Thompsons have made **several million dollars in fraudulent claims** against the government based on his "package story". If that story is exposed, Lawrence and Michele Adams-Thompson once again face possible criminal prosecution for it - and **no** Adams-Thompson (including, of course, Jennifer and the two boys) would become instant multi-millionaires.

(3) Lawrence Adams-Thompson is a Christian clergyman with an central and compelling bias against the Satanic religion.

ad. *During the course of this investigation no child who attended the Presidio of San Francisco Child Development Center and was interviewed, with the exception of [Almond], identified either Lt. Colonel or Mrs. Aquino as one of their assailants (paragraphs 4, 7, and 8, this report).*

(1) This is **exculpatory** evidence which further discredits Almond's statement to the contrary, substantiates our innocence, and contributes to the exposure of the Adams-Thompson "package story" as a fabrication.

ae. *During the course of this investigation no child who was interviewed identified 123 Acme Avenue, San Francisco, California from a photographic line-up, as a location to which they had been taken (paragraphs 8 and 9, this report).*

(1) This is **exculpatory** evidence which further discredits Almond's statement to the contrary, substantiates our innocence, and contributes to the exposure of the Adams-Thompson "package story" as a fabrication.

af(1). *On 19 April 1989, Evan Fox denied ever leaving the Presidio of San Francisco Child Development Center with anyone other than his parents and denied ever being sexually assaulted (paragraph 8.1, this report).*

af(2). *On 19 April 1989, Cohn Fox denied ever being sexually assaulted off-post.*

af(3). *On 23 April 1989, Kara Bailey denied recognizing either Lt. Colonel or Mrs. Aquino, or having ever been sexually assaulted at the Presidio of San Francisco Child Development Center (paragraph 8.1, this report).*

(1)   This is all **exculpatory** evidence which substantiates our innocence.

(2)   This is also a misleading understatement of paragraph 8.1 of the 6RCID report. Its initial two sentences are: "During the course of this investigation the following children who were reported victims of ritualistic sexual abuse, at various locations in CA, were interviewed and provided the opportunity to view photographic line-ups. **None were able to provide any information of value to this investigation.**"

ag.   *Kelly Quigley was not interviewed based on the desires of her parents (paragraph 18.1, this report).*

(1)   This statement is not evidence of any alleged crime whatever.

ah.   *On 5 January 1989 and 20 January 1989, Ms. Blood denied ever having seen any human sacrifice and/or children in Temple of Set rituals (paragraph 8.3, this report).*

(1)   This statement is **exculpatory**, not evidence of any alleged crime. Regarding the rest of Linda Blood's statements to the 6RCID, however:

(2)   Ms. Blood is also an individual whose extreme and aggressive personal hostility towards Mrs. Aquino and myself is well known and documented to the 6RCID. She has repeatedly demonstrated both her irrational hatred of us and her willingness to lie about ourselves, herself, and the Temple of Set as long as her statements about her own past involvement do not jeopardize her own present media posture as an "anti-cult crusader". Ms. Blood was expelled from the Temple of Set for unacceptable sexual behavior, after only a few months as a member.

(3)   The 6RCID's use of Blood's testimony in this investigation, despite the fact that she knows no more about the Adams-Thompson attack than any other member of the newswatching public, and despite their knowledge that she is a hostile, irrational, and unreliable individual, further evidences the 6RCID's **deliberate and prejudicial conduct of this investigation**. The evidence provided by me to the 6RCID showing Blood to be an unreliable source of information is **not** presented in the report: recordings of years of obscene, sado-masochistic, and threatening messages left on on our telephone answering machine [and my aged mother's], her counseling by the Lexington, Massachusetts Police Department because of this, etc.

(4)   Nor did the 6RCID make **any** effort to include in the report interviews with any of the thousands of reputable persons over the last 43 years who can attest to my integrity and that of Mrs. Aquino. Except where unavoidable, the report contains **only** propaganda designed to defame us, by persons with an obvious interest in doing so.

ai.   *On 31 January 1989 Ms. Cynthia Angell reported she has been informed the Sayer children, Bridgette and Charles, reported having been sexually abused at the Presidio of San Francisco Child Development Center in the presence of or under the direction of a person they characterize as "Michael Keno" (paragraph 8.4, this report).*

(1) Angell is an attorney for the father in yet another child-custody case in which "Satanic child abuse" tactics are being employed against the other parent in an attempt to win custody. The details of Angell's statement are evidence of **no crime whatever** by Mrs. Aquino or myself, and were, like the other Sonoma/Mendocino copy-cat allegations, simply an attempt to try to exploit the massive publicity given the Adams-Thompson attack on us during the previous year and a half. It is noteworthy that in **none** of the Sonoma/Mendocino attacks were there **any** Aquino-oriented statements or allegations until **long after** the Adams-Thompson attack had become a massive media event throughout the entire country and northern California in particular.

(2) On 13 November 1990 Angell appeared on the Geraldo Rivera show and twice falsely stated that she had "issued a subpœna for Michael Aquino". When on 19 November 1990 my attorney Mr. Matthew Wertheim asked her for a copy of such "subpœna", she never responded. [Nor was any such subpœna ever served on me.]

(3) #8.4 of the CID report relates Angell's account of her "Satanic kidnapping" seriously. Further on the Geraldo show Angell said: "They, they, put me, they, one man got into my car, pushed a gun up against my side, told me to take a drive. As I drove, he told me that I'd been investigating things that I shouldn't be investigating, that I was involved in something I shouldn't be involved in, and that unless I dropped this case immediately that they would kill me. They took me outside of the town, at which point I was blindfolded, put into another car - there were two men at that point - they drove me around for two, perhaps three hours and simply threatened me and told me that these things were real and that I shouldn't pursue the case any further."

  (a) At first Angell says that **two** men kidnapped her. Now she says that only **one** man kidnapped her, and that the second man appeared only at a switch to a second car. Yet before "that point" she said "**they**" took me". So did the second man just "appear" in her car while she was driving it?

  (b) After Angell had already had a good look at the two men during the "quite lengthy" drive, why should they **then** bother to blindfold her? Why should it take 2-3 hours to make 30-seconds-worth of threats? Why should criminals try to convince a witch-hunt attorney that "these things were real" if their interests lay in promoting the view that "Satanic child abuse" is **not** real?

  (c) Obviously Angell did not drop the case, and by the time she went on Geraldo (11/13/90) she cited no further threats against her. Nor, obviously, was she murdered. In fact she felt confident enough to go on *Geraldo Rivera* and tell a detailed story about the supposed "abduction".

(4) I think it is reasonable to say that the truthfulness and ethics of Angell are impeached.

aj. *On 14 February 1989 Louis D. Seago, a former member of the Temple of Set, stated he has no knowledge of the use and/or abuse of children during his tenure with the Temple. Further, he indicated he is aware of neither Lt. Colonel nor Mrs. Aquino having any sexual preferences which include children. He did, however, state it would be typical of Lt. Colonel Aquino to connect with someone of opposing ideology and elicit them to engage in an activity which would conflict with their beliefs. He further advised Lt. Colonel Aquino had spoken of a ritual chamber in the apartment of 121 Acme Avenue, San Francisco, California (paragraph 8.5, this report).*

(1) Seago's correct name is "Lewis D. Seago" aka "L. Dale Seago".

(2)   As with Blood, Seago is a hostile individual who was expelled from the Temple of Set for unethical behavior by a vote of the majority of the Priesthood.

(3)   As a Captain in the USAR, **Seago was later forced to undergo psychiatric examination for misconduct at Fort Huachuca, with findings sufficiently adverse to discredit his reliability as a witness.** The 6RCID is well aware of this, yet **omits** mention of it in this report.

(4)   As the 6RCID knows, but as it **also omits to mention** in this report, Seago deliberately contributed to the scare-propaganda of the 10/25/88 Geraldo Rivera "Satanism" show by stating on camera to Rivera that "a Satanic organization was active on the Presidio and that the authorities were aware of it". Seago used the pseudonym of "Joseph" on that show, but identified himself on camera as an officer in the U.S. Army, and Rivera acknowledged that his identity would be concealed by keeping his face off-camera.

    (a)   There was, of course, **no** Satanic organization active at the Presidio. The Temple of Set held no activities there at all, and, following Seago's expulsion, I was the sole member of the Temple at that installation.

    (b)   Seago's false and deliberately alarmist allegation was extremely embarrassing to Presidio Commander Colonel Joseph Rafferty, who was shown on camera denying any knowledge of Satanic activity there immediately after Seago's statement. Rafferty had no knowledge of what Seago had said, or who he was, until the broadcast aired on television - at which moment I placed an immediate telephone call to Rafferty to verify Rafferty's statement and identify Captain Seago to him.

(5)   Seago has no grounds whatever to suggest that I would "connect with someone of opposing ideology and elicit them to engage in an activity which would conflict with their beliefs". It is well-known that I discuss and debate theological, philosophical, military, and political science issues with colleagues; indeed my skill and success at doing so have been singled out for OER/AER entries and academic evaluations. As for "eliciting someone to engage in an activity in conflict with his beliefs", that is preposterous and quite unsubstantiated. Nor does such a vague statement, even if it were true, constitute evidence of any "crime" whatever.

(6)   There is not and has never been any ritual chamber at 121 Acme Avenue, and so of course I could not have discussed this with Seago.

ak.   *On 14 February 1989, Mr Jack Cooper, an Estate Probate Appraiser, indicated he had appraised the properties at 121 and 123 Acme Avenue, San Francisco, California. He advised he has no recollection of any bath tub with lion's feet or a shower with a glass door. Nor did he recall any ritual chamber (paragraph 8.6, this report).*

    (1)   This evidence is **exculpatory**.

al.   *On 21 February 1989, Mr Donald Corwell, who installed the security system in LTC AQUINO's residences, indicated he had no recollection of any bath tub with lion's feet or a shower with a glass door. Further, he did not recall any ritual chamber (paragraph 8.7, this report).*

    (1)   This evidence is **exculpatory**.

am.   *On 6 December 1988, CID Special Agent Penaluna obtained airline tickets pertaining to Lt. Colonel and Mrs. Aquino for the period 14-18 June 1986 (paragraph 11.1, this report).*

    (1)   This statement is not evidence of any alleged crime whatever.

an. *Between 1 March 1989 and 8 April 1989 attempts were made to obtain the original of a diary containing disclosures made by [Almond] to Michele Adams-Thompson. It was determined that the original diary was made of notes on various scraps of paper which were later combined and copied. The present whereabouts of the original documents is unknown (paragraph 11.2, this report).*

(1)　The existence of this "diary" is merely alleged by Michele Adams-Thompson, and "disclosures made to her by Almond" are also nothing but long-after-the-attack inventions made by her in an attempt to support her and her husband's equally-invented "package story".

(2)　In paragraph 11.2 of the 6RCID report it is stated that Adams-Thompson refused to give 6RCID the original diary on the advice of his civilian attorney. Why refuse, if it provided important evidence substantiating serious crimes committed against his stepdaughter? If, on the other hand, analysis of the diary and its entries would have **exposed his and Michele's "package story" as a fabrication**, then his refusal to provide it to the 6RCID is quite understandable.

(3)　Five days after Adams-Thompson's refusal to give the original diary to the 6RCID, Michele Adams-Thompson now told the 6RCID that the original diary had been "lost" (paragraph 11.2 of the 6RCID report). It is very curious that a diary which Adams-Thompson acknowledged having a week earlier, and in which he had been advised of the 6RCID's special interest, would suddenly "become lost".

(4)　What **actually** happened and why is quite clear:

(a)　Michele provided the 6RCID a photocopy of a page from the purported "original diary" in which (**out in the margin, not** in the body of the entry of that date) she wrote that Almond had said something about "a room with soft walls".

(b)　Michele **never** mentioned nor provided any such diary entry to the SFPD during its original investigation 1-1/2 years previously.

(c)　**After** all of the media publicity surrounding the raid on our home, of course, and after being shown the FBI/SFPD photographs of all rooms in our home on 10/291987, the Adams-Thompsons knew that we have a little room with padded walls (originally decorated thus by my father when the room included a wetbar).

(d)　If Michele could provide some kind of "accurate interior description" which **appeared** to predate the raid, it would be useful to the sale of the "package story". Hence she wrote the entry in the margin after-the-fact, and provided only a photocopy of the page to the 6RCID so that laboratory analysis could not be used to compare the ages of the ink, the type of writing instrument, etc.

(5)　The doctored photocopy of a page of Michele Adams-Thompson's "lost" diary is evidence only of the continuing effort of the Adams-Thompsons to try to substantiate their disintegrating "package story" by belated revisions to it, hence this manufacture of evidence by them in violation of Article 134 UCMJ.

ao. *During the course of this investigation a credit check was conducted on Lt. Colonel Aquino and the Temple of Set. No contact could be established between either Aquino or the Temple and Hambright, or other employees of the Presidio of San Francisco Child Development Center (paragraph 13.1, this report).*

(1)   This is **exculpatory** evidence in that it substantiates what we have said about there being no contact whatever between ourselves and either Gary Hambright or the Presidio daycare center.

(2)   It must again be said that neither Hambright nor anyone else connected with the day-care center has been convicted of any crime in connection with the Presidio "molestation" scam, nor even brought to trial on same. Hambright is therefore entitled by law to the presumption of innocence, and his name should not be used, as the 6RCID is obviously trying to do in this report, as "evidence" of a "crime" all by itself.

ap.   *On 3 January 1989 information was received indicating a review of Lt. Colonel Aquino's medical records had disclosed no treatment for any sexual transmitted diseases (paragraph 14.2, this report).*

(1)   I do not see the relevance of this entry to the report, nor is it evidence of anything relative to the Adams-Thompson allegations. Kinsey Almond has been medically established as showing no physical signs of sexual abuse whatever (paragraph 14.4, 6RCID report).

aq.   *On 4 March 1989 coordination was effected with Sergeant/Inspector Pamfiloff, San Francisco Police Department, who advised he had interviewed Staff Sergeant Clifton Jones, who reported Lt. Colonel Aquino was absent from his duty position from 1100-1400 on Tuesday and Thursday, due to his teaching commitments. Further, he established children in the Presidio of San Francisco Child Development Center were not under direct supervision from 1200 through the remainder of the day. Additionally, he provided a handwriting enhanced page from the notebook of Mrs. Aquino which read "wants to call Dave (Dale) and ask if he is the source of that porn stuff... (unreadable)" (paragraph 175, this report).*

(1)   GGU teaching.

(a)   SSG Jones' memory is understandably unreliable, as he was not expected to monitor my noontime teaching schedule. From semester to semester I sometimes taught on Monday/ Wednesday, othertimes Tuesday/Thursday.

(b)   Under the arrangements I had with the Presidio commander and my own director, I was on a very tight schedule to change to civilian clothes, drive downtown to the Sutter/ Stockton garage, park, walk 6 blocks to the GGU campus, teach class from 12 noon to 1:15, and then reverse the process to get back to my desk at the Presidio headquarters building by 2PM. [GGU also kept a meticulous record of the attendance of every professor, with missed sessions to be made up.] It is absurd for Pamfiloff to imply that in the middle of such a tight, supervised scheduled I would have had the time to commit a crime such as that alleged by Adams-Thompson.

(c)   Moreover, as GGU records substantiate, I had **stopped teaching there long before** either the Adams-Thompson-alleged time period or the 6RCID-invented time period. [The death of my mother in December 1985 left me with too many estate responsibilities to continue teaching in addition to my Army responsibilities.]

(2)   PSF CDC children not being under direct supervision after noon:

(a)   What does "direct supervision" mean? Certainly the center must have kept track of children left there sufficiently well for them not to wander off the premises and get lost or be hit by a car! If what Pamfiloff means is that the children were in a "general play" environment rather than in specific classes, that does not mean that they would have been any the less supervised by adults, or that it would have been any the easier for them to be kidnapped, repeatedly raped & sodomized, and returned back to the CDC without anyone noticing anything unusual!

(b)   During the original "package story" September-October 1986 time period, it has been proven that Mrs. Aquino and I were in Washington, D.C. on all dates on which Almond was left at the CDC.

(c)   Gary Hambright, as verified by a 12/15/86 letter from Lt. Colonel Walter W. Myer, Director of Personnel and Community Activities, HQ Presidio, **at no time during his entire employment at the CDC supervised children under the age of 3**. As Kinsey Almond did not turn 3 until 9/1/86, **Hambright could not have had her under his care or control during the 6RCIDinvented May-July 1986 time period**. Also during that time period, as verified by the San Francisco Public Defender's Office, Almond was only a "drop in" child, being left at the center for irregular and unscheduled periods of time by her parents. A would-be kidnapper would have no way of knowing when they would return to pick up the child.

(3)   *A handwriting enhanced page from the notebook of Mrs. Aquino which read "wants to call Dave (Dale) and ask if he is the source of that porn stuff... (unreadable)" (paragraph 17.5, this report).*

(a)   This "enhanced" page was shown to both Mrs. Aquino and myself by the 6RCID. It is a blank portion of notebook paper showing impressions apparently from the sheet above it which is no longer in existence. Both Mrs. Aquino and I found the "enhanced" portion unreadable and could not recognize it conclusively.

(b)   Shortly after his expulsion from the Temple of Set, Dale Seago made contact with Linda Blood, which resulted in a renewed barrage of pornographic messages from her on our telephone answering machine. The note was most probably an unacted-upon memo to consider calling Seago and ask him about the Blood calls.

(c)   Nevertheless this page has no relevance at all to the Adams-Thompson allegations or to this 6RCID investigation generally.

ar.   *On 9 March 1989, during a review of the notebook of Mrs. Aquino (which was seized by the San Francisco Police Department during the search of the Aquino residence) the name "Mike Todo" was located (paragraph 19.10, this report).*

(1)   This notebook page, as explained to the 6RCID by Mrs. Aquino, showed a list of names and phone numbers of persons who had telephoned to inquire about an apartment at 121 Acme which we had been advertising in the *San Francisco Chronicle*. It would have been easy for the 6RCID to check this information by calling the phone numbers on that notebook page. [We were told that they did try the "Mike Todo" number and found it disconnected. This is not surprising if he had been shopping for an apartment at the time he gave that number!]

as.   *On 23 March 1989 it was ascertained Lt. Colonel Aquino was in a continuous leave status from 2 June 1986 until 18 July 1986 (paragraph 19.11, this report).*

(1)   All officers (including myself) selected for resident attendance at the Industrial College of the Armed Forces August 1986-1987 were informed that there would be almost no opportunity to take leave during the school year. As I had accumulated quite a bit of leave-time, therefore, I took the excess prior to my departure from the Presidio. I don't see anything the least bit

sinister in that, particularly since there was a lot of painting and construction work going on at Acme which required daily attention from me.

at. *On 23 March 1989 the employment history of Lt. Colonel Aquino with Golden Gate University was obtained, which reflects he was employed in a teaching capacity from Spring 1979 until Fall 1982 (paragraph 19.12, this report).*

    (1)   Paragraph 19.12 of the 6RCID report contains substantial misinformation, apparently because the GGU person from whom it was obtained consulted incomplete or incorrect records. I commenced teaching at GGU in the Fall Semester 1980, after receiving my Ph.D. that summer from the University of California, and I taught until 1985, when the serious illness and then death of my mother made it impossible for me to continue. Almost all of my weekday courses were taught in the noon-1:15 time period, and I also taught occasional evening courses at two GGU offcampus sites in the Bay Area. I have of course copies of all of my GGU contracts on file to verify this.

au. *On 13 April 1989 it was determined that the 1987 Isuzu identified by [Almond] was first registered on 22 July 1987 to Budget Rent-a-Car Systems (paragraph 20.7, this report).*

    (1)   This is **exculpatory** evidence.

av. *On 29 March 1989 it was determined neither Lt. Colonel Aquino or Mrs. Aquino have ever had a red sports type car registered in CA (paragraph 20.6, this report).*

    (1)   This is **exculpatory** evidence.

aw. *On 5 May 1989 Mr. Anton LaVey was interviewed and throughout the course of the interview he referred to Lt. Colonel Aquino as either "Mike" or "Mikey" (paragraph 7.16, this report).*

    (1)   Anton LaVey has made no secret of his intense hatred for me and the Temple of Set since I exposed his intentions to financially exploit the Church of Satan for his personal profit in 1975. That scandal resulted in the mass resignations of almost every official of the Church, and brought about its end as a functioning organization. [The same persons who resigned from the Church because of LaVey's attempted corruption of it formed the Temple of Set as a corrective religious institution immediately thereafter.]

    (2)   It is regrettable, but not particularly surprising, that Anton LaVey would say everything he could to try to harm to Mrs. Aquino and myself via his interview with the 6RCID. He has made it abundantly clear over the years that he has not the slightest hesitation about lying when it suits his purposes.

    (3)   Paragraph 7.16 of the 6RCID report contains a number of other deliberately defamatory lies by LaVey, all easily refuted, which will be addressed in a critique to that paragraph.

    (4)   For the **third** time in this ROI (Blood, Seago, LaVey) the CID includes statements from persons **whose common thread is that they are well-known personal enemies of myself, Mrs. Aquino, and the Temple of Set**. Two of them were expelled from the Temple in disgrace for ethical misconduct (and have personal records of sexual abnormality themselves), and the third has an intense and widely-advertised hatred of Mrs. Aquino, the Temple of Set, and myself. Clearly, by highlighting **only these three** individuals as "character/Temple of Set" references, and by concealing their personal histories, abnormalities, and biases, the CID is attempting to assassinate our character and to defame the Temple of Set rather than to paint an

accurate and objective picture. This is clearly an obstruction of justice in violation of Article 134 UCMJ.

ax. *A comparison of the telephone toll charges to the telephone of Lt. Colonel Aquino with that of Hambright disclosed no charges for calls to any number identified with Hambright. Further, no charges to any worker of the Presidio of San Francisco Child Development Center were located in Lt. Colonel Aquino's telephone records (paragraph 19.19, this report).*

    (1)   This is **exculpatory** evidence.

ay. *A comparison of available telephone toll charges to the telephone of Hambright disclosed no charges for call to the number of either Lt. Colonel Aquino or the Temple of Set (paragraph 19.19, this report).*

    (1)   This is **exculpatory** evidence.

az. *Angelique Jefferson identified two of her assailants as "Shamby" and "Mikey" to her mother (paragraphs 19.18.A and 19.18.C, this report).*

    (1)   The detailed accounts in 19.18 are so utterly preposterous, and so clearly fictitious, that for the CID to single out "Shamby" and "Mikey" for mention in this summary is nothing more than an attempt to insinuate, hence manufacture evidence where in fact there is **none**. This is an act of obstruction of justice in violation of Article 134, UCMJ.

    (2)   These statements are from Jefferson's mother in a "journal" dated 13/14 December 1988 - **well over a year after** the Adams-Thompson attack was widely sensationalized in the media and it had been announced that the CID was opening yet another investigation of them.

    (3)   Like the other Sonoma/Mendocino copy-cat allegations, this one is simply an attempt to try to exploit the massive publicity given the Adams-Thompson attack on us during the previous year and a half. It is noteworthy that **in none of the Sonoma/Mendocino attacks were there any Aquino-oriented statements or allegations until long after the Adams-Thompson attack had become a massive media event throughout the entire country and northern California in particular**.

ba. *The names "Shamby" and "Mikey" were identified in local news media, prior to the report by Ms. Hartnett, Angelique Jefferson's mother (paragraphs 6.1 and 17.13, this report).*

    (1)   This is **exculpatory** evidence and impeaches Hartnett's allegations "on behalf of Jefferson" above.

bb. *On 21 May 1989, during the course of an interview, Master [Steven Jr.?] Quigley identified Lt. Colonel Aquino from a photographic line-up as an individual he had seen in the Child Development Center, Presidio of San Francisco, California (paragraph 7.17, this report).*

    (1)   On 21 April 1988 the parents of this child, Steven and Lisa Quigley, filed claims totaling $4,500,000 against the government for alleged "abuse" of Kelley and Steven Jr. in the Presidio scam. Clearly they have a strong motive for encouraging their children to promote anything (such as the Adams-Thompson attack against us) to support the scam.

    (2)   If this is one of the same Presidio day-care children to whom Pamfiloff showed a photographic line-up without any "identifications" of me over a year earlier, the reliability of this child's "later memory", or his truthfulness, is impeached.

(3)   As established in #1.1 p. (1) above, the 6RCID's use of a photo line-up technique in this investigation is **invalid and in specific violation of CIDR 195-1**.

(4)   By May 191989 my face had become well-known to everyone with an interest in the Presidio scam, so it is easy for anyone to make off-the-cuff allegations (all completely unsupported, of course).

(5)   As I have stated repeatedly, I have never been to the Presidio day-care center, hence this child's statement is untrue.

(6)   Why in the **entire** 6RCID report are there **no interviews with any adult who worked at the day-care center**? Is it because **no such adult ever saw Mrs. Aquino or myself there**? As is common knowledge, I have a unique appearance and was well-known around the Presidio during the five years I was assigned there. [Gary Hambright has already gone on written record that he has never seen us or met us either there or anywhere else, and Mrs. Aquino and I have sworn repeatedly to this same truth.]

1.2

a.   *On or about 4 January 1988 Lt. Colonel Aquino falsely swore a charge with two specifications on a DD Form 458 against Captain Adams-Thompson, alleging a violation of Article 133, UCMJ on the part of Captain Adams-Thompson. Lt. Colonel Aquino alleged Captain AdamsThompson had made false accusations against Lt. Colonel Aquino and had sent a derogatory postcard to Lt. Colonel Aquino. Subsequently, in a later sworn statement, Lt. Colonel Aquino withdrew the second specification regarding the postcard, based on information he obtained indicating Captain Adams-Thompson was not at the Presidio of San Francisco, California on the post date of the card (paragraph 6.1, this report).*

(1)   This is **a clear and deliberate lie by the 6RCID** in violation of Article 133 UCMJ. The charges that I preferred against Adams-Thompson in January 1988, and my sworn statement in support of them, were based **absolutely on the truth** as known to me at that time.

(2)   As has since been uncovered by me via the Freedom of Information Act, **the 6RCID deliberately suppressed the investigation of the charges against Adams-Thompson and misled the Commanding Generals of the 25th Infantry Division and WESTCOM concerning them**. This act by the 6RCID constitutes a clear act of Misprision of Serious Offense and Obstruction of Justice in violation of Article 134 UCMJ.

(3)   **This attempt to obstruct justice was continued at the CIDC headquarters in Washington, D.C.**, wherein the Staff Judge Advocate represented to me that no such CID report of investigation had ever existed. When I responded with documentary evidence that it did exist, the CIDC headquarters had no alternative but to send it to me - after illegal refusals for well over a year.

(4)   Accordingly the 6RCID effort to title me for "false charges" against Adams-Thompson in this report is merely one more effort to cover up serious corruption in the 6RCID and its San Francisco Field Office. If the 6RCID were to admit that the charges and sworn statements were true, then its whole attempt to whitewash Adams-Thompson and frame Mrs. Aquino and myself would be exposed for what it is.

Evidence

b.   *Sworn statements of Lt. Colonel Aquino, in which he alleges Captain AdamsThompson falsely accused him (exhibit 5, 6, and 8).*

        (1)   **All true** on the basis of all information known to me at the time of the statements in question. I since acquired considerable **additional** evidence documenting and substantiating Adams-Thompson's crimes, and re-preferred charges against him accordingly. **None of this evidence has ever been refuted by the CID.**

c.   *Review of both FBI and San Francisco Police Department files which indicate the allegations made against Lt. Colonel Aquino were made by [Almond] (paragraphs 4.1, this report).*

        (1)   A **direct lie** by the 6RCID in violation of Article 133 UCMJ. The original San Francisco Police Department incident report, and Pamfiloff's independent verification, states that it was **Lawrence Adams-Thompson** who told him the "package story" on 8/14/87.[221]

        (2)   My attorney was not provided with copies of the 8/13/87 FBI Form FD-302s in which Agent Foreman interviewed all three Adams-Thompsons (Lawrence, Michele, and Kinsey Almond) until 4/17/9 1, and I personally did not see them until September 1991.

        (3)   There are several discrepancies and inconsistencies between the 8/13/87 Adams-Thompson FBI interviews and the 8/14/87 Adams-Thompson SFPD interview, exposing the "package story" as a hastily-invented fabrication which Lawrence and Michele continued to reinvent and refine - with the CID's help - as time passed. See *Chaplain Lawrence Adams-Thompson's Actions in Violation of Article 133, UCMJ.*

        (4)   By the time these 8/13/87 FBI interviews took place, Lawrence and Michele Adams-Thompson had had over 24 hours to coach Almond into making the statements they desired.

        (5)   As these interviews took place after the "123 Acme identification trip", Almond had had all the more coaching on what she was expected to say, and Michele - having been taken to 123 Acme that morning -could insert a description of its exterior [only!] into her interview.

        (6)   Several allegations of the "package story" appear **only in the statements of Lawrence and Michele** to Foreman. The falsehood of these elements is detailed in my analysis of these FBI FD-302s and in *Chaplain Lawrence Adams-Thompson's Actions in Violation of Article 133, UCMJ.* The "package story" invented by the adult Adams-Thompsons **bears no resemblance whatever** to the pre-Presidio-PX Hickey notes, which further substantiates the invention of the "package story" on 8/12/87 and its modification before Lawrence AdamsThompson's re-telling of it to Pamfiloff on 8/14/87.

        (7)   The FBI FD-302 interview of Kinsey Almond herself contains **no identification of either Mrs. Aquino or myself, or allegations specifying us, either in the PX or in any other context**.

d.   *Statement of Lt. Colonel Aquino indicating, at the time of the preferral of the charges, he had in his possession a copy of the San Francisco Police Department incident report (exhibit 5 and paragraph 6.1, this report).*

---

[221] As documented in Chapter #4, Kinsey Almond/A-T was not even present during the Pamfiloff interview of Larry A-T.

(1) As stated above, the San Francisco Police Department incident report **verifies that it was Lawrence Adams-Thompson making the "package story" allegations to Pamfiloff, not Almond**.

e. *Statement of Captain Adams-Thompson in which he relates he felt as though Lt. Colonel Aquino's charges against him were an attempt to have him coerce his daughter, [Almond] into refuting her original statement (paragraph 42, this report).*

(1) As Adams-Thompson well knows, by the time UCMJ charges are preferred, it is too late for the charged person to "retract" his crime -and no longer the prerogative of the charging officer to accept such retraction. Such misuse of the UCMJ as a "threat" would itself be a violation of the UCMJ.

(2) It is noteworthy that Adams-Thompson was **not** asked any questions, nor did he offer any answers, to the substantive issues in Specification #1 of those 1/88 charges. All that he said was that he "felt threatened" by them. [No doubt any soldier facing court-martial charges "feels threatened" accordingly.]

1.3

a. *Wesley and Brandon Witherow reported Lt. Colonel Aquino, along with other adults, including their grandparents, fondled their privates, placed their (the adults')fingers in their (Wesley and Brandon Witherow's respective anuses, and forced them to lie nude on top of nude women and simulate intercourse. Additionally Brandon Witherow stated he was forced to perform fellatio on Lt. Colonel Aquino and others. Wesley and Brandon Witherow identified a location on top of a hill near Ukiah, California where they had reportedly observed their grandfather bury the remains of his victims. Wesley and Brandon Witherow also identified a location (possibly a stock pond) where the remains of persons who had been ritualistically murdered reportedly had been placed. Wesley and Brandon Withe row identified the Hopland Baptist Church, near the intersection of Highway 101 and Highway 175, as the location where they reportedly observed the ritualistic murder of a boy named "Timmy", whose remains were buried in front of the church. Wesley and Brandon Witherow both identified Angelique Jefferson as having been an individual they had seen at several of these occasions. Wesley and Brandon Witherow stated that they and their mother, Lori Derryberry, stayed at the home of Lt. Colonel Aquino in San Francisco, California for about a month. Wesley Witherow stated that he observed Lt. Colonel Aquino, assisted by his grandfather Jack Derryberry, while in the Derryberry home, kill an unidentified female. Wesley Witherow stated he observed Lt. Colonel Aquino ingest controlled substances (he believed) through injection and inhalation through the nose, at various locations on unspecified dates. Brandon Witherow stated that Lt. Colonel Aquino, J. Derryberry, and the other adults placed the bodies of their victims in the pond in Hopland, California. Brandon Witherow stated that J. Derryberry used underwater swimming gear to place the bodies under the water, and then he would place wood on top of them. Brandon Witherow stated that Lt. Colonel Aquino purchased a white Chevrolet Camaro for his mother, Lori Derryberry. Both B. and Wesley Witherow reported Hambright was present at the Jubilation Day Care Center in Fort Bragg, California (where they were taken by J. Derryberry), the Presidio of San Francisco Child Development Center, and Lt. Colonel Aquino's home (at all of which locations they reported they were sexually abused) (paragraphs 43 and 4.4, this report).*

(1) The evidence cited below "in support of" this "significant information" substantiates **none of it whatever**. Indeed the evidence exposes all of it as a fabrication. Hence inclusion of this paragraph as "significant information" is clearly inappropriate and obviously with defamatory intent, hence an obstruction of justice in violation of Article #134 UCMJ.

(2)   The Witherow "Satanic child-abuse" allegations were merely part of a custody battle, as is a common tactic in such battles. The two boys were living with their mother (Lori Derryberry) and her father until May 1986, when as a result of abuse-accusations by their father and his new wife (Debi Witherow) they were placed with their father. This battle began prior to the Adams-Thompson attack, with of course no Aquino-targeting allegations until more than a year after the Adams-Thompson sensationalizing in the media. Debi Witherow is a member of the McMartin activist group "Believe the Children" and herself subsequently founded a similar "child-abuse" scam-promotion group in northern California named "Victims of Systems".

(3)   According to the *San Jose Mercury-News* 5/17/89, two persons (Daryl Ball and Charlotte Thrailkill) are in prison in Sonoma Country, convicted [on a plea-bargain] in 1988 of molesting Angelique Jefferson and five other children. There is no indication that anything resembling Dee Hartnett's (Jefferson's mother) 1989 Aquino-targeting allegations appeared in the Ball/Thrailkill investigation/prosecution/trial, in connection with either Jefferson or any of the other children. Again no Aquino-targeting allegations were made by Dee Hartnett until more than a year after the Adams-Thompson sensationalizing in the media.

(4)   Dee Hartnett (Angelique Jefferson's mother) and Debi Witherow (the children's stepmother) knew one another and appeared in both television and newspaper interviews together.

Evidence

b.   *On 10 January 1989 Brandon Witherow and Wesley Witherow identified Lt. Colonel Aquino from a lineup as "Mike" or "Michael", having observed him on many occasions involved in the ritualistic abuse of children and adults (paragraphs 9.4 and 9.5, this report).*

(1)   By 1/10/89 **anyone** with an interest in "child-abuse" scams could easily "identify" me from 1-1/2 years' abundant photo and video publicity of me following the Adams-Thompson attack on Mrs. Aquino and myself. This "evidence" is evidence only of the lack of ethics in the adults currently controlling the two Witherow children.

c.   *On 15 March 1989 Wesley Witherow identified Lilith Aquino as being the girlfriend of Lt. Colonel Aquino from a still photo lineup (paragraph 9.15, this report).*

(1)   In March 1989 a similarly-worthless "identification". This statement is not evidence of any alleged crime by Mrs. Aquino or myself whatever.

d.   *On 15 March Wesley Witherow identified Lt. Colonel Aquino as Michael Aquino from lineups (paragraph 9.15, this report).*

(1)   In March 1989 a similarly-worthless "identification". This statement is not evidence of any alleged crime by Mrs. Aquino or myself whatever.

e.   *On 15 March Wesley Witherow identified the photograph of the Hopland Baptist Church as such (paragraph 9.15, this report).*

(1)   This statement is not evidence of any alleged crime by Mrs. Aquino or myself whatever.

f.   *On 15 March Wesley Witherow identified 1579B Pershing Drive, Presidio of San Francisco, California as being similar to the residence of Lt. Colonel Aquino. (However, he did not identify Lt. Colonel Aquino's house.) (paragraph 9.15, this report).*

(1)   This statement is not evidence of any alleged crime by Mrs. Aquino or myself whatever, but it serves to further impeach the reliability and truthfulness of Witherow.

g.   *On 15 March 1989, when observing the video lineup, Wesley Witherow identified female #2 (who is not a suspect) as the same person he identified in the female still photographs (paragraph 9.15, this report).*

(1)   This statement is not evidence of any alleged crime by Mrs. Aquino or myself whatever.

h.   *On 15 March 1989 Wesley Witherow was shown interior photographs of the Aquino home, and failed to identify it as such (paragraph 9.15, this report).*

(1)   This statement is not evidence of any alleged crime by Mrs. Aquino or myself whatever, but it serves to further impeach the reliability and truthfulness of Witherow.

i.   *On 17 May 1989 Wesley Witherow identified Hambright from a photographic lineup (paragraph 9.29, this report).*

(1)   This statement is not evidence of any alleged crime by Mrs. Aquino or myself whatever.

j.   *On 17 May 1989 Wesley Witherow provided descriptions of the Presidio of San Francisco Child Development Center and the Jubilation Day Care Center which are not accurate descriptions of either location. (paragraph 4.4, this report).*

(1)   This statement is not evidence of any alleged crime by Mrs. Aquino or myself whatever, but it serves to further impeach the reliability and truthfulness of Witherow.

k.   *On 15 March 1989 Wesley Witherow stated he observed J. Derryberry kill "Timmy" at the Hopland Baptist Church. However Brandon Witherow stated that Lt. Colonel Aquino killed "Timmy" at that location by cutting off his head (paragraphs 4.3 and 4.4, this report).*

(1)   A completely unsubstantiated, false, and freshly-invented allegation, along with the other sensationalist ones in #4.3-4.4, acknowledged as "unsubstantiated" by the CID.

l.   *Details provided by Angelique Jefferson which are contained in the journal kept by her mother Dee Hartnett, regarding the murder of "Timmy" also differ substantially from those of Brandon and Wesley Witherow (paragraph 19.18A, this report).*

(1)   This statement is not evidence of any alleged crime by Mrs. Aquino or myself whatever, but it serves to further impeach the reliability and truthfulness of the Witherow and Jefferson children.

m.   *On 16 March 1989 Brandon Witherow identified a female who is not a suspect and Lilith Aquino from lineups as people with whom his mother, Lori Derryberry, was acquainted (paragraph 9.16, this report).*

(1)   This statement is not evidence of any alleged crime by Mrs. Aquino or myself whatever. Neither I nor Mrs. Aquino have ever met any of the Witherows, Jeffersons, and/or other "child-abuse" scam promoters/ profiteers in northern California.

n.   *On 16 March 1989 Brandon Witherow identified Lt. Colonel Aquino as Mike Aquino from lineups (paragraph 9.16, this report).*

(1)   In March 1989 a similarly-worthless "identification". This statement is not evidence of any alleged crime by Mrs. Aquino or myself whatever.

o.   *On 16 March 1989 Brandon Witherow identified Apartment #7, 120 Portola Street, San Francisco, California as possibly being the location of Lt. Colonel Aquino's residence (paragraph 9.16, this report).*

(1)   This statement is not evidence of any alleged crime by Mrs. Aquino or myself whatever, but it serves to further impeach the reliability and truthfulness of Witherow.

p.   *On 17 May 1989 Brandon Witherow identified Hambright from a photographic lineup (paragraph 928, this report).*

(1)   This statement is not evidence of any alleged crime by Mrs. Aquino or myself whatever.

q.   *On 17 May 1989 Brandon Witherow provided descriptions of the Presidio of San Francisco Child Development Center and the Jubilation Day Care Center which are not accurate descriptions of either location (paragraph 43, this report).*

(1)   This statement is not evidence of any alleged crime by Mrs. Aquino or myself whatever, but it serves to further impeach the reliability and truthfulness of Witherow.

r.   *On 14 August 1987 photographs were exposed depicting the interior of 123 Acme Avenue, San Francisco, California which do not correspond with the description of the interior of the apartment identified by Wesley and Brandon Witherow as being that of Lt. Colonel Aquino (paragraph 5.A.3, this report).*

(1)   This statement is not evidence of any alleged crime by Mrs. Aquino or myself whatever, but it serves to further impeach the reliability and truthfulness of the Witherows.

s.   *The pond located at parcel number 48-180-03, which was identified by B. and Wesley Witherow as being the location where bodies were disposed under water, was determined to never have contained any water (paragraph 5.B.2, this report).*

(1)   This statement is not evidence of any alleged crime by Mrs. Aquino or myself whatever, but it serves to further impeach the reliability and truthfulness of the Witherows.

t.   *Examination of the area surrounding the church at Hopland, California disclosed no evidence of bodied being buried at that location (paragraph 17.15, this report).*

(1)   This statement is not evidence of any alleged crime by Mrs. Aquino or myself whatever, but it serves to further impeach the reliability and truthfulness of the Witherows.

u.   *Records pertaining to the Hopland Baptist Church revealed construction of same was not completed until late 1987 (paragraph S.C. this report).*

(1)   This statement is not evidence of any alleged crime by Mrs. Aquino or myself whatever, but it serves to further impeach the reliability and truthfulness of the Witherows.

v.   *On 4 January 1988, 23 August 1988, 27 January 1989, and 10-11 May 1989 Lt. Colonel Aquino rendered sworn written statements and sworn testimony denying any involvement in criminal misconduct (paragraph 6.1, this report).*

(1)   This statement is not evidence of any alleged crime by Mrs. Aquino or myself whatever.

w.   *On 4 January 1988 and 11 May 1988 Mrs. Aquino rendered a sworn written statement denying any involvement in criminal misconduct (paragraph 6.2, this report).*

(1)   This statement is not evidence of any alleged crime by Mrs. Aquino or myself whatever.

x.   *On 19 December 1988 Angelique Jefferson identified a location in the immediate vicinity of that identified by Brandon and Wesley Witherow as being near the pond in which the remains of people were disposed (paragraph 5.B, this report).*

(1)   This statement is not evidence of any alleged crime by Mrs. Aquino or myself whatever, but it serves to further impeach the reliability and truthfulness of Jefferson and expose the collaboration between the adults manipulating the Jefferson and Witherow children.

y.   *On 17 May 1989 Angelique Jefferson identified Mrs. Aquino from lineups as Lilith (paragraph 9.17, this report), whom she said had been involved in ritualistic murders which she had witnessed.*

(1)   In May 1989 a similarly-worthless "identification". A completely unsubstantiated, false, and freshly-invented allegation, acknowledged as "unsubstantiated" by the CID.

z.   *On 17 May 1989 Angelique Jefferson reported she had seen both Brandon and Wesley Witherow at various locations where she had observed children sexually abused and people murdered (paragraph 7.1, this report).*

(1)   This statement is not evidence of any alleged crime by Mrs. Aquino or myself whatever, but it serves to further impeach the reliability and truthfulness of Jefferson and expose the collaboration between the adults manipulating the Jefferson and Witherow children.

aa.   *On 17 May 1989 Angelique Jefferson identified one of her assailants as Charlotte Thrailkill (paragraph 7.1, this report).*

(1)   This statement is not evidence of any alleged crime by Mrs. Aquino or myself whatever.

ab.   *On 17 May 1989 Angelique Jefferson identified Lt. Colonel Aquino as the leader of many of the rituals to which she had been taken by Thrailkill and Daryl Ball (another of her assailants) (paragraph 9.17, this report).*

(1)   In May 1989 a similarly-worthless "identification". A completely unsubstantiated, false, and freshly-invented allegation, acknowledged as "unsubstantiated" by the CID.

ac.   *On 17 May 1989 Angelique Jefferson reported that she had been taken to Lt. Colonel Aquino's residence in San Francisco, California by Thrailkill and Ball; however she was unable to recognize same from a photographic lineup (paragraphs 7.1 and 9.17, this report).*

(1)   A completely unsubstantiated, false, and freshly-invented allegation, acknowledged as "unsubstantiated" by the CID, but the failed "Aquino residence identification" serves to further impeach the reliability and truthfulness of Jefferson.

ad.   *On 17 May 1989 Angelique Jefferson described the interior of Lt. Colonel Aquino's residence in San Francisco, California; however her description did not agree with either that of the Witherow children or with photographs exposed during a search of the residence (paragraphs 4.3, 4.4, 7.1, and 5A.3, this report).*

(1) This merely further impeaches the reliability and truthfulness of the Jefferson and Witherow children and exposes the collaboration between the adults manipulating them.

ae. *On 16 March 1989 Debi Witherow (the stepmother of Brandon and Wesley Witherow) indicated Wesley Witherow had admitted he had lied during a portion of his statement to USA CIDC on 15 March 1989 (paragraph 7.5, this report).*

(1) This statement is not evidence of any alleged crime by Mrs. Aquino or myself whatever. However it does provide additional evidence of Debi Witherow's intense feud with the Witherow children's mother's family, as in #7.5 she blames their tendency to lie upon them.

af. *On 22 April 1989, during the course of an interview, it was noted the color scheme in the Derryberry residence does not match that provided by Brandon and Wesley Witherow (paragraph 7.14, this report).*

(1) This statement is not evidence of any alleged crime by Mrs. Aquino or myself whatever. However it does further impeach the reliability and truthfulness of the Witherow children.

ag. *On 5 January 1989 Ms. Blood advised she never observed any children or human sacrifice in Temple of Set rituals (paragraph 8.3, this report).*

(1) This statement is not evidence of any alleged crime by Mrs. Aquino or myself whatever.

ah. *On 14 February 1989 Mr. Lewis D. Seago reported he had no knowledge of the use and/or abuse of children during his tenure with the Temple of Set (paragraph 85, this report).*

(1) This statement is not evidence of any alleged crime by Mrs. Aquino or myself whatever.

ai. *On 14 February 1989 Mr. Jack Cooper, estate probate appraiser, provided a description of the interior of Lt. Colonel Aquino's residence which is not consistent with that of Brandon and Wesley Witherow (paragraph 8.6, this report).*

(1) This statement is not evidence of any alleged crime by Mrs. Aquino or myself whatever. However it does further impeach the reliability and truthfulness of the Witherow children.

aj. *On 21 February 1989 Mr. Donald Corwell, who installed the security system in Lt. Colonel Aquino's home, provided a description of the interior of Lt. Colonel Aquino's residence which is not consistent with that of Brandon and Wesley Witherow (paragraph 8.7, this report).*

(1) This statement is not evidence of any alleged crime by Mrs. Aquino or myself whatever. However it does further impeach the reliability and truthfulness of the Witherow children.

ak. *On 17 March 1989, while listening to the audio portion of a video lineup, Angelique Jefferson recognized the voice of Lt. Colonel Aquino (paragraph 9.17, this report).*

(1) In March 1989 a worthless "identification", as my voice had been broadcast on many television and radio interviews by then. This statement is not evidence of any alleged crime by Mrs. Aquino or myself whatever.

al. *A comparison of the telephone toll charges of Lt. Colonel Aquino from 5 April 1983 through 1988 disclosed no toll charges to any suspects in Mendocino or Sonoma County, California (paragraph 19.19, this report).*

  (1) This statement is not evidence of any alleged crime by Mrs. Aquino or myself whatever.

am. *Ms. Donna Ryan, Assistant District Attorney, County of Sonoma, California reported she had received no information during the course of her investigation which would tend to support the allegations by Angelique Jefferson that she was taken to Mendocino County, California (paragraph 153, this report).*

  (1) This statement is not evidence of any alleged crime by Mrs. Aquino or myself whatever.

an. *During the course of the Santa Rosa Police Department and the Sonoma Country District Attorney's investigations, Angelique Jefferson identified the "barn" as being in Sonoma County, California, not in Mendocino Country as alleged to USA CIDC (paragraphs 15.3 and 20.4, this report).*

  (1) This statement is not evidence of any alleged crime by Mrs. Aquino or myself whatever. However it does further impeach the reliability and truthfulness of Jefferson.

ao. *During the course of the Santa Rosa Police Department and the Sonoma Country District Attorney's investigations, the house with the black bedroom and the red car (both of which she associated with Lt. Colonel Aquino to USACIDC) were identified by Angelique Jefferson as belonging to Gino (NFI), AKA "Pappy". Additionally "Pappy" was purported to be the leader of the rituals to the Santa Rosa Police Department by Angelique Jefferson, while she reported "Mike" to be the leader to USA CIDC (paragraphs 15.3 and 20.4, this report).*

  (1) This statement is not evidence of any alleged crime by Mrs. Aquino or myself whatever. However it does further impeach the reliability and truthfulness of Jefferson.

ap. The *descriptions provided by Wesley Witherow of one of the women who brought Angelique Jefferson to Ukiah, California is an accurate description of Charlotte Thrailkill, one of Angelique Jefferson's known assailants (paragraph 17.11, this report).*

  (1) This statement is not evidence of any alleged crime by Mrs. Aquino or myself whatever. However it does further expose the collaboration between the adults controlling the Witherow and Jefferson children.

aq. *Lt. Colonel Aquino was on leave from 2 June 1986 until 18 July 1986, a period during which Angelique Jefferson was sexually assaulted by Thrailkill and Ball (paragraph 19.11, this report).*

  (1) This statement is not evidence of any alleged crime by Mrs. Aquino or myself whatever.

ar. *A review of the transcripts of the testimony of Wesley and Brandon Witherow disclosed no mention of Lt. Colonel Aquino, "Mike" (or any person having a similar name), or murder(s) (paragraph 19.14, this report).*

  (1) This statement is not evidence of any alleged crime by Mrs. Aquino or myself whatever.

as. *The Ukiah Police Department file regarding the abuse of the Witherow children disclosed they were in the company of their alleged assailants only on 25 January 1986 and 18 May 1986 (during 1986) (paragraph 205, this report).*

(1)   This statement is not evidence of any alleged crime by Mrs. Aquino or myself whatever.

at.   *On 18 May 1986 Lt. Colonel Aquino inducted a Priest into the Temple of Set at his residence in San Francisco, California (paragraph 6.1, this report).*

(1)   This statement is not evidence of any alleged crime by Mrs. Aquino or myself whatever.

au.   *The Santa Rosa investigative file regarding Angelique Jefferson indicated she was assaulted by Thrailkill and Ball after February 1986 (paragraph 20.4, this report).*

(1)   This statement is not evidence of any alleged crime by Mrs. Aquino or myself whatever.

av.   *Thrailkill reported she met Ball between Christmas 1985 and New Year 1985-1986 (paragraph 63, this report).*

(1)   This statement is not evidence of any alleged crime by Mrs. Aquino or myself whatever.

1.4

a.   *On 10 April 1989 E. Dorsey related Hambright had taken her to 208 Dolores Street, San Francisco, California, where he removed her clothing and fondled her vaginal area with his hand. She further related he had done this in the Child Development Center, Presidio of San Francisco, California (paragraph 45, this report).*

(1)   This statement is not evidence of any alleged crime by Mrs. Aquino or myself whatever.

Evidence

b.   *On 10 April 1989 Emily Dorsey identified 208 Delores Street, San Francisco, California from a photographic line-up of buildings and houses (paragraph 9.20, this report).*

(1)   This statement is not evidence of any alleged crime by Mrs. Aquino or myself whatever.

c.   *The San Francisco Police Department incident report reflects Hambright resided at 208 Delores Street, San Francisco, California (exhibit 5).*

(1)   This statement is not evidence of any alleged crime by Mrs. Aquino or myself whatever.

d.   *Ms. Dorsey, the mother of Emily Dorsey, related Emily Dorsey attended the Child Development Center, Presidio of San Francisco, California (paragraph 7.9, this report).*

(1)   This statement is not evidence of any alleged crime by Mrs. Aquino or myself whatever.

e.   *Ms. Devon Runyan reported she had observed Hambright fondle Emily Dorsey at the Child Development Center, Presidio of San Francisco, California (paragraph 7.13, this report).*

(1)   This statement is not evidence of any alleged crime by Mrs. Aquino or myself whatever.

(2)   On 16 March 1988 Dennis and Gretchen Runyan filed claims totaling $4,500,000 against the government for alleged "abuse" of their children Devon and Dena in the Presidio scam. Clearly they have a strong motive for encouraging their children to promote anything (such as the Adams-Thompson attack against us) to support the scam.

1.5

a. *On 10 January 1989 Kristopher Byrd indicated "Mike" had led church services which he attended while in the care of Barbara and Sharon Orr (paragraph 9.6, this report).*

(1) After local, regional, national, and international news media had been sensationalizing the Adams-Thompson allegations for well over a year, it is scarcely surprising that instigators of other "day-care sex abuse" scams such as that at the Presidio would try for a piece of the action.

Barbara and Sharon Orr, according to a major national study conducted by the *Memphis Commercial Appeal,* were two sisters who operated a day-care center in Fort Bragg, California. In January 1985, at the height of the scam-epidemic, they were suddenly attacked by the usual collection of parents and "therapists".

Under the usual, Debbie Hickey-kind of "therapy", children dutifully recited "rituals in which animals and babies were sacrificed and children placed on meat-hooks and held underwater. Barbara On was alleged to have cut the children with a long, jeweled knife and sucked their blood. Parents took their children into graveyards to search for clues. One mother upbraided authorities for declining to send scuba divers offshore in the Pacific Ocean to look for a submarine entrance to an underground amusement park."

Obviously there were no missing babies, nor meat hooks, nor knife-cuts, nor underground amusement parks to be found. Nevertheless the instigators of the scam informed the *Commercial Appeal* three years later that they had a "long term plan to keep the children in therapy and determine if they would ever qualify as credible witnesses".

No charges were ever filed against the Orrs, but they were of course terrorized and professionally ruined. According to the 1/21/88 *Commercial Appeal:*

> Barbara On, 35, said she deteriorated physically during the ordeal, suffering from stress and severe depression. She said she contemplated suicide, but was inspired by others who said they were falsely accused of abuse. "I guess that's what really motivated me - getting mad, saying 'No, I'm not going to do this to myself'," she said.
>
> Ms. Orr said she has lost forever the ability to enjoy the company of children. She's afraid to be left alone with, or show any affection toward a child. "It's something I don't think I'll ever be able to get over," she said.

(2) The 6RCID knows that the attack on the On sisters is one of the **filthiest and ugliest** examples of the "day-care sex abuse" scams, and that there is **not the slightest evidence that the Orrs are guilty of anything**. Accordingly, efforts by one of the instigators of that scam to piggyback on Adams-Thompson's efforts in the Presidio scam are evidence of nothing but the greed and viciousness of that instigator.

(3) The 6RCID has **no** business representing such a transparent, copycat attack as "evidence", **nor** of presenting a distorted picture of the attack on the Orrs in disregard of the actual evidence in that affair.

Evidence

b. *On 10 January 1989 Kristopher Byrd identified Lt. Colonel Aquino as "Mike" from photographic lineups (paragraph 9.6, this report).*

(1) In January 1989 a worthless "identification". This statement is not evidence of any alleged crime by Mrs. Aquino or myself whatever.

Appendix 62: Gary Myers' Appeal of the 6RCID Report of Investigation

Memorandum for: Major General Eugene L. Cromartie
                          Commanding General, USA Criminal Investigation Command
From: Lt. Colonel Michael A. Aquino
Through: Gary Myers, Esq.
Date: 31 January 1990
Subject: Appeal of Titling Action - CID Report of Investigation

SUMMARY

1. This is an appeal from a CID Titling Action regarding Michael and Lilith Aquino (hereafter "Respondent").

2. The Relief sought is:

    a. The total expungment of the CID Report of Investigation from the U.S. Army Crime Records Center, and

    b. A communication in writing to all parties on the distribution list of such report that such report has been expunged with further instructions to so inform any party in any subsequent chain of distribution.

3. Due to impropriety or the appearance of impropriety on the part of certain elements of the CID and the JAGC, Respondent requests that this appeal be reviewed by elements outside the JAGC and the CID infrastructure. A specific request is hereby made that the General Counsel of the Army be such reviewing authority.

4. The bases for the appeal are as follows:

    a. That the complete defense of alibi exists with regard to the allegations of Conspiracy, Kidnapping, Sodomy, Indecent Acts or Liberties with a Child, and Sexual Abuse.

    b. That there is no evidence of False Swearing or False Statement; Intentional Noncompliance with Act 30, UCMJ, Maltreatment of a Subordinate or Conduct Unbecoming an Officer, and Indecent Acts.

    c. That Lilith Aquino is a civilian, not subject to the UCMJ, and is therefore not a proper party for titling by the United States Army which has no jurisdiction over Lilith Aquino.

    d. That this titling action resulted from political influence brought upon the United States Army by Senator Jesse Helms of North Carolina.

    e. That elements of the Army Judge Advocate General's Corps, the Office of the Surgeon General, and the CID acted improperly with regard to this investigation.

    f. That Respondent was investigated in a timely fashion by the San Francisco Police Department and the FBI and no attempt to prosecute was made and that the CID investigation was so stale as to be tainted.

    g. That Respondent was titled even though the CID knew no charges were contemplated by command and was so informed prior to the date of titling, and that the Army knowingly allowed the Statute of Limitations to run prior to titling.

DISCUSSION

This section will address the specific bases for appeal set forth in the summary above. Sub-topic e., the improper conduct of elements of the Judge Advocate General's Corps, the Office of the Surgeon General and the CID will be addressed as it arises in each of the other sub-topics.

a. *That the complete defense of Alibi exists with regard to the allegations of Conspiracy, Kidnapping, Sodomy, Indecent Acts or Liberties with a child, and Sexual Abuse.*

If ever there were a case of investigators attempting to fit a preconceived conclusion into later-discovered facts, **this** is that case.

All relevant allegations pointed to the **fall of 1986** in San Francisco for the alleged abuse of Kinsey Almond, the then-three-year-old stepchild of Captain Adams-Thompson, Army chaplain.

But when the CID and Major Mark Harvey, JAGC, discovered that they could not fit the Satanist Respondent into that fall because Respondent was not in San Francisco, the CID and Harvey, with Adams-Thompson's silent concurrence, created a new scenario and a new time frame.

Since Respondent was on leave and in San Francisco from 3 June 1986 to 18 July 1986, the CID and Harvey did this:

> "Further investigation shifted the time of Almond's kidnapping from CDC from the fall of 1986 to June-July 1986. This change was based on the CDC records and the canceled checks maintained by Mrs. Adams-Thompson." Report p. 56.

Neither the CDC records nor the checks could form a basis for shifting the focus of the investigation. The records and checks just show that the child was at the day care center in June, July, September, and October of 1986. They are passive records. There is no dynamic associated with them that allows one to conclude June-July was preferable to September-October.

The "shift" is **unsupported**. The lack of support is of no moment, however, because the investigation missed critical exculpatory evidence which was readily discoverable by the investigators but which they chose not to pursue.

The investigators were told that in the June-July period Respondent had substantial work done on the interior and exterior of his home at 123 Acme, San Francisco, "the crime scene", and the place where Kinsey Almond was allegedly abused. Report at 26. Respondent delivered to the the investigators the names, addresses and telephone numbers of the artisans who worked at the home and the property contiguous to it, also owned by Respondent.

Both the CID and Harvey, who acted in a conflicting role as both investigator and JA to the CID, followed certain of these leads and ignored others. Those that were followed were followed **only** for the limited purpose of seeking inculpatory evidence. Report P. 70, 71 and 95. **No** attempt was made to seek exculpatory evidence, but such exculpatory evidence was there among the ignored.

Respondent has the absolute defense of alibi for the June-July time period.

E. Graham Marshall was a painter in San Francisco who was hired by Respondent in the Spring of 1986 to paint first the interior and then the exterior of 121 Acme and the alleged crime scene, 123 Acme, San Francisco, California. E. Graham Marshall's affidavit is attached at Exhibit A.

Kinsey Almond was at the CDC on the following dates in June and July of 1986: June -10; July - 2, 9, 11, 17. This information comes from the checks Mrs. Adams-Thompson, Almond's mother, wrote to the CDC. Major Harvey informed counsel that the June 10th date was the most critical because Kinsey Almond said that certain of her friends were with her at Respondent's home, and June 10th was the only date all those named friends were at the CDC with Kinsey Almond.

None of the other children named by Almond - the Bailey, Fox and Quigley children - confirmed Almond's story. In fact Kinsey Almond's story **remains uncorroborated** with respect to Respondent.

On June 10, 1986 E. Graham Marshall, the painter from San Francisco, as was his practice, went to Respondent's home, the alleged crime scene, to work on the interior. This is what happened, from Marshall's affidavit:

22. I specifically and distinctly recall being at 123 Acme on June 10, 1986.
    a. On June 10, 1986 I specifically recall staining cabinets in the observation room. These cabinets were stained a dark color.
    b. I arrived between 7:45 and 9:00 AM as usual.
    c. Since June 10, 1986 was a completion day, I did not go to lunch.
    d. After completion of final touch-up, including cabinet and window sill work, Michael Aquino and I discussed proposals for work to be performed on the exteriors of 121 and 123 Acme.
    e. I did not leave the premises until after 4:00 PM.
23. At no time whatsoever did I see any children enter or leave 123 Acme on June 10, 1986.

Marshall remembers June 10, 1986 because of the exterior contract he typed that evening, then signed, dated, and delivered to Respondent on June 11, 1986 following his completion day, June 10, 1986. (Exhibits II and III of the Affidavit)

Marshall's affidavit clearly states that Marshall was at Respondent's home, the alleged crime scene, every day that Kinsey Almond was at the CDC in July. On this point his Affidavit is clear - there were **no** children. There was **no** crime committed by Respondent.

Counsel has requested the checks Mrs. Adams-Thompson wrote to the day care center to determine, by their amount on each date, how long Kinsey Almond was at the day care center. The cost per hour is known, so by merely dividing the cost per hour into the total amount of any given check, the number of hours on each date could be ascertained.

This evidence is critical for the purpose of determining whether anything could have happened to Kinsey Almond within the time she was at the day care center. A brief time would serve as exculpatory evidence.

The CID and Major Harvey saw the checks and failed to preserve the evidence either by making copies or by keeping the originals. Exhibit Al.

There is no evidence that the CID examined the potentially exculpatory nature of the checks.

Now the Adams-Thompsons have refused to deliver copies of the checks to the CID. They too perhaps have discovered the exculpatory nature of the checks.

This set of circumstances strongly suggests:

1. A failure of basic investigatory standards by the CID and Major Harvey,
2. A knowing failure to examine evidence for exculpatory implications, and
3. A confirmation that the Adams-Thompson rendition of events is suspect and that their motives are other than what they have espoused to date.

But this is not the end of the story. An analysis of the September-October 1986 time-frame is required to better understand the motives of Captain Adams-Thompson and Mrs. Thompson, the CID, Major Harvey, JA, and LTC Hickey, M.C., psychiatrist at the Presidio.

The Respondent was in Washington, D.C. in September and October 1986 when the acts complained of actually were alleged to have occurred. Report at p. 26.

Gary Hambright, an alleged co-conspirator, was employed by the Presidio day care center in September of 1985. From September of 1985 through November of 1986 Hambright supervised children in the three-years-and-older age group. At **no** time did Hambright supervise or have control over two-year-olds. See Exhibit B, which is an official government document confirming the above statements.

Kinsey Almond, the alleged victim was born September 1, 1983. She became three on September 1, 1986. **From September 1, 1986 to November 1986 she was under Hambright's supervision and at no other time.** Further, during this period Kinsey Almond was at the day care center on only four days. (See Exhibit C)

The initial interviews with the Adams-Thompson family by law enforcement agencies and by LTC Deborah Hickey, a psychiatrist with the Medical Corps (see excerpt of FBI Hickey notes at Exhibit F) reveal conclusively that the Adams-Thompsons stated that they noticed changes in their daughter's behavior **beginning in September** of 1986. See Exhibits D, E and F and Report at 18.

Exhibit D is the San Francisco Police Department Incident Report dated 08/14/87. Attention is drawn to the upper right-hand corner of the cover sheet, where Adams-Thompson advised that **the dates of occurrence were between 09/01/86 and 10/31/86**.

Exhibit E is an FBI Report confirming the fall dates. The FBI Reports of the Adams-Thompson and Hickey interviews are critical as they were provided to the FBI in January of 1987, before Respondent was implicated by Adams-Thompson in this matter, and are therefore the most credible evidence of alleged dates.

The CID report not only fails to mention these pivotal facts, but also intentionally seeks to cover up these facts.

Respondent was in Washington, D.C. during the September through November period of 1986, returning to San Francisco only for one weekend during this period when there was no chance of seeing Kinsey Almond.

There is no evidence of any kind in the report that Respondent knew or had any association with Hambright.

Almond was under Hambright's control only in September and October of 1986. Respondent was not in San Francisco during this period. This clearly-exculpatory information is knowingly excluded from the report.

Major Harvey, JAGC, who wrote the report, and the CID commander who signed the report said at page 26 of the report:

> The number of times that Almond received care at the CDC in the Fall of 1986 is irrelevant because LTC Aquino was out of the State of California the majority of the Fall of 1986.

If this statement is true, then why does **all** the evidence point to the fall time frame, and why is there **no** evidence that anything happened or could have happened before September 1, 1986?

The inescapable truth of the matter is that **once the investigators discovered that an alibi defense existed for the fall of 1986, they attempted to contort the truth, with the Adams-Thompsons' support, to gain a result not supported by fact**. Major Harvey writes at page 56 of the report:

> Further investigation shifted the time of Almond's kidnapping form the CDC from the Fall of 1986 to June-July 1986. This change was based upon the CDC records and the canceled checks maintained by Mrs. Adams-Thompson.

The CDC records show that Hambright was not in control of Almond in the June-July 1986 period. The checks prove nothing other than that Almond was at the day care center.

The reason for the shift is that this was the only way to implicate Respondent. The evidence does not support the "shift".

The above conclusion is supported in the following particulars:

1. The Adams-Thompsons stated that Kinsey Almond had identified Lilith Aquino's car on 13 August 1987 while at 123 Acme. This was of course not possible, since the car was rented for only a few days and could not have been used to transport the child in 1986. This fact is disregarded by the report. See pages 6 and 58 of the Report.

2. At page 6 of the Report there is a definitive statement made that Almond identified the Respondent's house as the one she was taken to by Hambright. The facts are that Hambright did not and could not drive due to epilepsy, and that the "identification" of the house was as follows:

    > "Approximately 10-15 feet before coming to the front of 123 Acme Avenue, Almond began to appear frightened and wanted to be held by her mother. Almond was picked up by her mother but continued to stare at the front of 123 Acme Avenue." (See page 140 of the Report)

    A three-year-old child is with her by-now-furious mother, "appears" to be frightened, is held by her mother in front of the Respondent's residence, and stares right along with her mother. This is not an identification of anything. The mother knew the address and she knew her child. The presence and intervention of the mother made the procedure worthless.

3. During the Spring and Summer of 1986, extensive renovation was done on the Aquinos' house by artisans, whose names were given to the CID. The CID did no in-depth investigation of these artisans, who were at the Aquino house virtually every working day in June and July of 1986. The CID knew when Almond was at the day care center, yet they did nothing to confirm that workmen were crawling all over the Aquino home during the June and July period.

4. The report relies heavily upon a manifestly stale investigation. After the FBI and the SFPD dropped their investigations of Respondent in 1988, the Army, under political pressure from Senator Helms, commanded a belated investigation in November of 1988.

    The CID and Major Harvey rely upon interviews of Almond in April of 1989 to substantiate the titling action. This child was three years old in 1986, and **after more than two years** the CID is willing to accept what she says about events that occurred in 1986 as though those events happened yesterday. Not only is her memory utterly suspect under such a circumstance, as her conflicting statements demonstrate, but also she has had an opportunity to see pictures of Respondent and to be influenced by parents and therapists.

What **is** telling, is found on page 8 of the report:

"During the course of this investigation, **no** child who attended the PSF CDC and was interviewed, with the exception of Almond, identified either LTC or Mrs. Aquino as one of their assailants." (paragraph 4, 7, and 8 this report).

"During the course of this investigation, **no** child who was interviewed identified 123 Acme Ave. SF, CA, from a photographic line-up, as a location to which they had been taken (paragraph 8 and 9, this report)." (emphasis added)

5. What the report does **not** say, and what **was** supported by medical examination, is that Kinsey Almond **was found to be a virgin**. Her supposed early statements to the therapist, LTC Hickey, to the contrary are therefore simply untrue. Report page 26.

   LTC Deborah Hickey, M.C. did nothing to abate the hysteria surrounding this incident. She apparently was the therapist for multiple numbers of the day care center children. Upon information and belief she diagnosed her own child as being sexually abused. Following that revelation she continued to treat these children. The continuation of treatment under that circumstance is violative of her professional ethical standards and makes any diagnosis or conclusion on her part inherently suspect. This scenario is not mentioned in the report.

6. The Adams-Thompson story of the PX encounter between Almond and Respondent was investigated by no law enforcement agency. **No** attempt was made to interview clerks or cashiers or other employees of the PX, or to determine if others had seen the events described by Adams-Thompson occur. Report p. 25 and 26.

   There was a presumption made by law enforcement that Adams-Thompson was truthful without any background check to determine if he or his wife might have a motive for singling out Respondent on religious or other grounds. This failure is inexcusable given the seriousness of the charges. There is no doubt that Adams-Thompson knew Respondent and of Respondent's religious beliefs prior to the alleged encounter in August of 1987. See page 215 of the Report, page 2 of Adams-Thompson's sworn statement at Exhibit 12 of the Report.

   What is of note in this regard is that Almond was in therapy with LTC Hickey starting in January of 1987. In June of 1987, whether through LTC Hickey or Mrs. Adams-Thompson, the notion of Satanism was introduced into the mix. See the alleged "diary" remarks at page 27 of the Report. Six short weeks later Adams-Thompson was telling police that the Satanist Aquino was the man who his daughter identified as being a child molester.

7. There is good reason to believe that the Adams-Thompson account is suspect.

   (a) There is **no third party corroboration** of anything alleged by the Adams-Thompsons or Almond.

   (b) Adams-Thompson has changed his story regarding who in his family was at the PX, to include in April of 1989 his two sons, who were used then to shore-up the PX events. Report at 25.

   (c) The Adams-Thompsons conveniently dropped the notion that the September-October time frame was the critical time frame.

   (d) Mrs. Adams-Thompson's "diary", which was "lost", is a suspect document, as there is nothing to sustain the notion that anything written in the "copies" was done contemporaneously with alleged events. Nor do references to padded rooms show anything more than comments written **after** it was discovered that an upholstered room existed in Respondent's home. Report at 27.

(e) The Adams-Thompsons did not have their child in daily day care. Almond was dropped off and picked up at **random**. There was no way for Respondent to know when Almond would be at the day care center, or when she would be picked up. It is difficult to envision a circumstance less conducive to the removal of this particular child from the day care center with any certainty that her parents would not return or that her absence would go unnoticed. In fact **all the day care workers denied that Hambright absented himself with children**. See page 56 of the Report. **Nor is there any credible evidence that Respondent ever appeared at the day care center.**

b. *That there is no evidence of False Swearing or False Statement; Intentional Noncompliance with Art. 30, UCMJ, Maltreatment of a Subordinate, or Conduct Unbecoming an Officer, and Indecent Acts.*

These sections of the report are little more than attempts at character assassination of Respondent, and are further intended to inflame the reader and mask the vacuous findings of the principal charges.

1. The indecent acts complained of are at 42 and 43 of the Report and relate to a religious procedure carried out by Respondent in 1970. At Page 42 Major Harvey writes:

> Upon learning that Major Harvey considered the black mass "an indecent act" and "conduct unbecoming an officer" and therefore violative of the UCMJ, LTC Aquino wrote a letter attempting to place his activities under the protection of the First Amendment.

Major Harvey wrote this report. This is a clear statement of bias on the part of Harvey. Yet he did not remove himself from the investigation or from being counsel to the investigation.

None of the cases cited to support Harvey's viewpoint has anything to do with First Amendment Rights, and therefore all are irrelevant.

If Harvey and the CID understand First Amendment freedoms, they have an extraordinary way of showing that understanding. Page after page of quotations from Satanic literature is irrelevant. Pulling out-of-context quotations to meet their viewpoint is unacceptable conduct by an officer of the court and members of law enforcement.

2. Much time is spent by Harvey and the CID attacking Respondent's credibility. Harvey becomes philosopher, psychiatrist, and moralist as he plows through this and that justification for denying that Respondent had any credibility at all.

The Report admits at page 45 that there is **no corroboration of evidence**. Instead Harvey and the CID tell us that "Aquino's familiarity with the widespread use by the Nazis of distortion, lies, and manipulation are factors that should not be ignored."

The truth is that LTC Michael Aquino has an **exemplary** record as an Army officer, all of which is well-documented, to include high evaluations for integrity and ethical conduct.

3. Harvey and the CID could find no negative comments from any member of the Armed Forces about Respondent. What they did find were three persons with whom Respondent had been in conflict on ethical grounds, then treat their statements as truth without an examination of underlying factors.

Seago, Blood and LaVey, all Satanists, were good enough to disprove Respondent's credibility for Harvey and the CID. Report pp. 84, 85, 88, 89, 90 and 91.

The problem is that in each case Respondent provided Harvey and the CID with exculpatory information which was totally ignored and which showed bias on the part of each of the witnesses.

Harvey and the CID were willing to treat as fact, without investigation, any negative representation made by these three:

- LaVey, as head of the Church of Satan, began commercializing the Church by selling priesthoods. Respondent on ethical grounds disagreed causing a schism in the church and a demise of LaVey's influence.

- Blood is a woman of suspect mental stability who has been restrained by law enforcement from harassing Respondent by phone.

- Seago was removed from Respondent's church for cause.

All of this was known by Harvey and the CID and ignored or minimized.

4. The report is so rambling that it is difficult to ascertain exactly what false swearing was supposed to have occurred.

    Apparently Respondent alleged Almond was two years old when she was actually three. This was not material. See Report page 31.

    Page 30 of the Report is truly insightful. There it is suggested that a false statement was made when Respondent, a non-lawyer, was not clear on the form of dismissal of Hambright's charges.

    Further on page 30 of the Report it is suggested that Respondent made a false statement regarding who filed the complaint - Adams-Thompson or his stepdaughter Almond. Again this is not material. More importantly, a review of the SFPD Incident Report shows **Adams-Thompson** as the reporting entity.

    In summary, **there is not one material statement made by Respondent which remotely raises itself to the level of false swearing** - the knowing misrepresentation of a material fact.

5. The interplay between Adams-Thompson and Respondent was grounded in fact and not a violation of the UCMJ.

    Upon information and belief Adams-Thompson has filed a claim for a substantial sum with the Army as a result of all this on behalf of Almond, his wife and himself. Money is a recognized motive in many offenses.

    Respondent sought vindication from Adams-Thompson because Adams-Thompson was wrong. Respondent did not threaten Adams-Thompson; he charged him as is his right to do.

    The greeting card referred to at page 29 of the report was sent on September 2, 1987 from San Francisco, the very date Adams-Thompson arrived in Hawaii. A simple phone call from Adams-Thompson to a cohort in San Francisco solves the problem with the postmark on the card.

    The reality is further that Adams-Thompson and his wife were the prime movers in this matter. Adams-Thompson was a person reporting an alleged crime. The SFPD Incident Report shows "Larry R. Adams-Thompson" as the reporting entity.

The truth is that Adams-Thompson's motives have never been examined. Certainly with these investigators in charge of the investigation, this Protestant minister who has charged a Satanist will never be investigated.

c. *That Lilith Aquino is a civilian, not subject to the UCMJ, and is therefore not a proper party for titling by the United States Army which has no jurisdiction over Lilith Aquino.*

This sub-topic is self-explanatory.

d. *That this titling action resulted from political influence brought upon the United States Army by Senator Jesse Helms of North Carolina.*

This Report was drafted without apparent regard for the consequences of close scrutiny. This results from individuals who possess either no judgment or from individuals who by dint of some sense of invincibility conclude that whatever they do has official sanction, thereby precluding the prospect of negative repercussions.

Somewhere, and most probably at the highest levels of the Army, Respondent was declared a "Free Fire Zone".

The involvement of Senator Helms and the flurry of activity by the Army subsequent to that involvement make both the Senator and the Army suspect.

On August 1, 1988 the San Francisco District Attorney announced that no charges would be filed against Respondent. Prior to this time there was no active CID investigation of the Respondent.

On October 26, 1988 Wayne Bowles from Senator Helms' office complained to Secretary Marsh about Respondent.

The letter is reproduced here in its entirety. So offensive is this letter to the facts of this case and to the Constitution that it should not occupy space as a mere exhibit. (Original at Exhibit G)

Jesse Helms
North Carolina

United States Senate
Washington, D.C. 20510

October 26, 1988

The Honorable John O. Marsh, Jr.
Secretary of the Army

Dear Secretary Marsh:
I am writing first as a citizen of the great nation of ours and secondly as an employee of our federal government, concerning a cancer in the military, specifically a cancer within the Army.
Last evening I viewed a program hosted by Geraldo Rivera on Satanism and Witchcraft. I was appalled to learn that a Colonel Aquino of the United States Army was a founder of the Temple of Set, a satanic cult. I believe he is stationed in St. Louis.
To my view, this is disheartening. Here is a military man who has taken an oath to defend God and country who practices a religion that is completely contrary to the oath he swore to uphold. If you or any member of your staff saw this telecast I am confident your reaction was identical to mine.
This individual should not be allowed to remain in the Army, his military service record notwithstanding. I am respectful of any individual's right to his first amendment prerogatives to worship. However, I cannot believe the Constitution is intended to protect those individuals who have a belief system that espouses the killing and sacrifice of infants and the ritual torturing of children.

I would appreciate your looking into the existence of satanic worship in the Army and it's [sic] adherents. Perhaps it may be necessary to hold Congressional hearings to consider appropriate legislation in this matter.

> Kindest regards,
> Sincerely,
> /s/ Wayne Ronald Boyles, III
> Legislative Assistant to Senator Jesse Helms

The Army recognized that Bowles was simply a surrogate for the Senator by responding directly to Senator Helms and bypassing Bowles in a letter of December 8, 1988. This letter represents a rational Constitutional standard. Exhibit H.

Helms decided to keep the heat on the Army, and on January 9, 1989 wrote a letter to the Secretary of the Army.

This letter is also included in its entirety, as paraphrasing does not do the letter justice, particularly given its source. (Original at Exhibit I)

Jesse Helms
North Carolina

United States Senate
Washington, D.C. 20510

January 9, 1989

Dear Jack:

Except for two or three trips back to Washington, I've been working out of our Raleigh office since the Senate adjourned in late October. Yesterday in going through a stack of material sent to me in Raleigh, I ran across a December 27 clipping from *The Washington Times* about a Lt. Col. Michael Aquino who identifies himself as a "Satanist" and who claims that this is his "religion".

Either the man needs psychiatric help, or the Army doesn't need <u>him</u>. The fact that he has twice appeared on national television seems to me to demonstrate that he doesn't have all four wheels on the ground.

This is not a matter of freedom of religion. Satanism is not a religion.

I tried yesterday to reach you at your home through the White House switchboard, but learned that you are in Germany. When you get back, would you give me a ring? Maybe there's something I missed in translation, but I do not understand how the Army decided to "stand by" Colonel Aquino - if indeed the newspaper account is accurate.

The most charitable thing that can be said of the colonel is that he is a nut. If that is the case, I might have some sympathy for him but I still do not believe that he should be "handling budgets" for the Army Reserve Personnel Center - or anywhere else. Perhaps I am dismayed at his arrogance as much as anything else.

In any event, please let me have the Army's side of it - and I sure would appreciate a call from you.

> Sincerely,
> /s/ Jesse

The Judge Advocate General of the Army physically met with Senator Helms to discuss the Aquino matter in late January or early February of 1989 after discussion with the Secretary of the Army. Exhibit J.

In response to Respondent's request for letters sent to the Army by Helms, Helms sought refuge behind the Senate's Legal Counsel. Exhibit K.

By November 9, 1988 the Army was already taking action on the Helms surrogate letter. Exhibit L.

On November 23, 1988 the CID began its investigation. There is no evidence that the CID had any interest in investigating the Respondent from August 1, 1988, the date San Francisco publicly stated no charges would be brought, until November 23, 1988.

The investigation did not get into full swing until March of 1989. By this time the investigation was clearly stale. Respondent nonetheless cooperated fully with the investigation, including allowing an interview in his home in St. Louis where he and Lilith Aquino answered all questions propounded by the CID and Major Harvey, who was present for the interrogation.

The Army apparently did not expect Respondent's cooperation, as is evidenced by the memorandum at Exhibit M.

It is significant that at no time did Respondent fail to be responsive to reasonable inquiries made by the CID.

On November 29, 1988 a high-level meeting at the Pentagon was held to discuss the Aquino matter, including the following persons: TJAG, ODCSPER, DACH, PA, OCLL, M&RA, CC. Exhibit N.

There can be little doubt that the Army adopted a policy of appeasement in its dealings with Senator Helms. Respondent was expendable. The solution was twofold, namely to deny Respondent continuation as an AGR officer and to title Respondent without ever charging him. The way to accomplish that was to allow the Statute of Limitations to run prior to the titling, and to use the Statute of Limitations as an excuse for avoiding a public trial that surely would end in an acquittal.

The test for continuation as an AGR officer was merely "fully qualified", which Respondent was without doubt, but when the Continuation Board improperly asked if Respondent was flagged and was improperly told "yes", due to the investigation, there was a basis for denial and Respondent was denied. Exhibit M.

f. *That Respondent was investigated in a timely fashion by the San Francisco Police Department and the FBI, and no attempt to prosecute was made, and that the CID investigation was so stale as to be tainted.*

A timely investigation is critical in any criminal matter both for purposes of preserving physical evidence as well as testimony. Both the FBI and the SFPD conducted timely investigations of Respondent. A decision was made not to prosecute.

Respondent complained of the conduct of the SFPD regarding the manner in which the investigation was conducted and the premature declarations of Respondent's guilt by elements of the SFPD. The Office of Citizen Complaints of the San Francisco Police Commission sustained those complaints. See Exhibit 0.

This demonstrates the obvious; namely, that law enforcement unchecked in an atmosphere tantamount to hysteria can go too far in attempting to ascribe guilt. That happened with the SFPD and it has happened here.

g. *That Respondent was titled even though the CID knew no charges were contemplated by command and was so informed prior to the date of titling, and that the Army knowingly allowed the Statute of Limitations to run prior to titling.*

This is more than passing strange. The CID had ample opportunity to finish its investigation and get Respondent titled long before the Statute of Limitations ran.

In a phone conversation with Major Harvey, Counsel for Respondent learned that **the Army had decided not to charge Respondent before the titling action was completed**. Assuming the accuracy of Major Harvey's representation, why then proceed with a titling action?

There is only one available answer and that lies in the interplay between the Army and Senator Helms. The titling action for such heinous crimes effectively destroys Respondent's career and labels him for life. Helms is satisfied.

By knowingly allowing the Statute to run, there is an excuse for no prosecution, and no chance for Respondent's vindication in a public forum.

Knowing that the matter would not be prosecuted gave Harvey and the CID license to say or conclude whatever they wished.

Further license was provided by the very nature of the case - "a Satanist accused of child abuse". Who would not be repelled by the mere thought of such a circumstance? The answer is simple - those who understand and believe both in the presumption of innocence and in the Constitution of the United States.

Appendix 63: Complaint for Declaratory Judgment and Damages

United States District Court for the Eastern District of Virginia
Alexandria Division

Michael A. Aquino, Plaintiff
v.
The Honorable Michael P.W. Stone, Secretary of the Army
Department of the Army, Washington, D.C.,
Defendant

Also Serve:
The Attorney General Of   the United States
Department of Justice, Washington, D.C.
and
The United States Attorney
South Washington Street
Alexandria, Virginia

Complaint for Declaratory Judgment and Damages

This is an action for declaratory judgment to amend the titling action and to remove Plaintiff's name from the title block of United States Army Criminal Investigation Command (USACIDC or CID) Report of Investigation (ROI) Final "C"-0610-88-CID- 026-69259 5K3/6F3/6EZ/6A1/5M2/5Y2/DIMIS. This is also an action for damages, reasonable attorney's fees and costs.

For a discussion of the substance and import of a titling action, see Exhibit I.

All plaintiff's administrative remedies have been exhausted.

Jurisdiction and Venue

Jurisdiction is conferred on this Court by 28 U.S.C. §1331(a) and by The Administrative Procedure Act, as amended, 5 U.S.C. §552a(g)(1)(A) & (C).

Venue is proper in this District as the claim arose in this District, and both the agency records and control over the agency records are situated in this District.

Parties

1. Plaintiff, Michael A. Aquino, is a Lieutenant Colonel in the United States Army Reserve.
2. Defendant, the Honorable Michael P. W. Stone, in his official capacity is the Secretary of the Army.

Facts

1. Plaintiff, then an active duty Lieutenant Colonel in the United States Army, was titled by the U.S. Army CID on August 11, 1989 for Conspiracy, Kidnapping, Sodomy, Indecent Acts or Liberties With a Child, Indecent Acts, False Swearing, Intentional Noncompliance With Article 30, Uniform Code of Military Justice, Maltreatment of a Subordinate and Conduct Unbecoming an Officer.

2. Plaintiff sought to amend the titling action and requested that Plaintiff's name be removed from the title block.

3. The CID granted relief in part and denied relief in part. Plaintiff remains titled for Conspiracy, Kidnapping, Sodomy, Indecent Acts and False Swearing.

4. Plaintiff now seeks *de novo* judicial review of both the titling action and Defendant's failure to accurately amend the titling action.

5. Defendant's knowing failure to accurately amend the titling action was a willful and intentional action designed to cover up Defendant's improper and baseless investigation of Plaintiff and to continue to hold up Plaintiff to ridicule.

6. The result of such inaccurately maintained records and the willful and intentional misconduct of the Defendant was that Plaintiff was denied by an Army board action the opportunity to continue Plaintiff's career on active duty, to be promoted in the normal course and to retire at the end of Plaintiff's active duty career, all of which has damaged Plaintiff. See 5 U.S.C. §552a(g) (4) (A).

Cause of Action

7. The titling of Plaintiff as well as the failure to accurately amend the titling action was an abuse of discretion by the Defendant, was arbitrary and capricious, and there was no substantial evidence on the record to provide probable cause to believe any offense had been committed by Plaintiff.

The willful and intentional failure to accurately maintain this titling action has caused Plaintiff to lose Plaintiff's active duty Army career and attendant benefits to include retirement benefits.

Prayer for Relief

That this Honorable Court declare the CID titling of Plaintiff to have been without merit and the Defendant be ordered to amend the titling action and to remove the Plaintiff's name from the title block of the aforesaid CID/ROI and to publish said removal pursuant to applicable regulations.

That this Honorable Court award the Plaintiff actual damages for the willful and intentional misconduct of the Defendant.

That reasonable attorney's fees and costs be awarded the Plaintiff.

> Respectfully submitted,
> /s/ Gary R. Myers, Esq.

November 15, 1990

Appendix 64: District Court Interrogatories

Introduction - M. Aquino

Prior to the filing of briefs, plaintiff was permitted to submit 26 written questions to defendant. While the judge was able to see and consider these questions and answers when deciding the case, he was not able to see any critique or rebuttal of the CID's written answers.

I originally wrote the critique below for my attorney, on the possibility that he might have some opportunity to introduce it to the court. He did not.

*This entire set of CID responses is filled with "it's possible that", "it's conceivable that", "may have been", etc. Having no facts or even probabilities at all to work with, the CID tries to justify "probable cause" on the basis of **possibilities alone** - and most of these are so remote and/or so inconsistent with established fact as to be incredible.*

The responses also cite only those statements by Kinsey and Michele which are accusatory in the latest version of the CID's "scenario". All of the many inconsistent and unsupportive statements by both of these two individuals are ignored as though they didn't exist.

The critique is here formatted as "footnotes" to the CID's answers.

QUESTION ONE

Myers Question

Please describe how CDC records and canceled checks maintained by Mrs. Adams-Thompson shifted the time of Almond's kidnapping from the CDC from the fall of 1986 to June-July 1986. As part of your response, describe all evidence which caused the fall of 1986 to be the initial focus of the investigation, why such evidence was ultimately disregarded, and how plaintiff was linked to CDC records and Mrs. Adams-Thompson's canceled checks by the CDC.

CID Response

The joint investigation of Lieutenant Colonel and Mrs. Aquino by the San Francisco Police Department (hereinafter "SFPD") and the Federal Bureau of Investigation (hereinafter "FBI") was monitored and assisted by the San Francisco Field Office, United States Army Criminal Investigation Command (hereinafter "CID").[222]

---

[222] False statement. The CID began its investigation on 11/23/88, at which time it followed the required official procedures of notifying me, notifying my commander to suspend actions on ("flag") my personnel file, and notifying the Army Intelligence & Security Command to suspend my security clearance.

After 11/23/88 CID investigators Penaluna and Harvey complained to my Army attorney Captain Hayes that "they had nothing", that "the FBI files were closed to them", and that "they had to start from scratch". Hence the 100%-ignorant nature of Harvey's list of questions initially submitted to me in January 1988. Later on, when Cates was added to the CID team, he said to Hayes that "previous investigations were not important; he would conduct this one from scratch".

No official from either the FBI or the SFPD has ever made any reference whatever to any such "monitoring and assistance".

This response by the CID is clearly intended to support the fiction that the CID investigation was not a Helms-driven political scheme commencing November 1988.]

This activity is documented under CID sequence number 0499-87-CID026 (See Basis for Investigation, page 4, Report of Investigation Number 0610-88-CID026-69259). [Hereinafter CID Report of Investigation 0610-88-CID026-69259 titling LTC Aquino will be referred to as "CID Aquino ROI".][223]

The SFPD prepared Report Number 870910025 (hereinafter "SFPD Aquino ROI"), which documented the FBI and SFPD conclusion that Kinsey Adams-Thompson was sexually molested by LTC Michael A. Aquino, Mrs. Lilith Aquino, and Mr. Gary W. Hambright during 7:30 AM to 4:00 PM, Monday-Friday, between September 1, 1986 and October 31, 1986 (SFPD Aquino ROI at top of pages 1 and 2). [A copy of the SFPD Aquino ROI is Attachment A to Exhibit 5 (sworn statement of LTC Aquino dated 4 Jan 1988) of the CID Aquino ROI.][224]

The SFPD Aquino ROI was based upon FBI interviews, which are discussed in detail in the SFPD Aquino ROI and pages 18-19, 24-27, 58-59, paragraphs 2.2.1, 2.2.3, 4.1 CID Aquino ROI.[225]

The initial date of incident was based on Mrs. Adams-Thompson's comment that Kinsey had wet herself at the Child Development Center (CDC) and began to have nightmares in the fall of 1986.[226]

Kinsey also made derogatory comments about Gary Hambright in the fall of 1986 (page 18, CID Aquino ROI).[227]

---

[223] Only **one** document bearing CID sequence number "0499-87-CID026" appears in the CID ROI. This is Agent Potter's 1/2-page report of the "123 Acme identification" trip on 8/13/87 (ROI Exhibit #E-1). This report states that it was made "in conjunction with" an 8/13/87 FBI interview of Kinsey Almond, and makes no reference to any CID actions. [The FBI 8/13/87 interview also makes no reference to any CID actions.]

CID attorney Captain Harvey's 10/17/88 letter (ROI Exhibit #G-3) makes no reference to any CID sequence number, nor to any pre-11/23/88 investigation, monitoring, or assistance of any sort by the CID.

[224] The SFPD document referred to is an **incident report** (i.e. a report of a complaint), **not** a "report of investigation" [by the SFPD officer recording the complaint]. This SFPD incident report stated **no** "FBI and SFPD conclusion" concerning the truth of Chaplain Adams-Thompson's (the interviewee) allegations.

[225] The SFPD incident report does not identify, quote from, nor include as attachments any FBI interviews. The story that Chaplain Adams-Thompson alleges to the SFPD is inconsistent with all FBI interviews concerning Kinsey Almond.

The CID ROI "discussion" of the FBI interviews distorts, excuses, and embellishes their actual contents to conform to the agenda of the ROI author. Consequently these "discussions" are relevant only to the CID bias and agenda, and are not reliable as summaries of the actual FBI reports.

[226] The initial date-window of Chaplain Adams-Thompson's fabricated allegations was restricted to 9/1-10/31/86, because that was the **only** period when Kinsey was under Hambright's supervision at the CDC.

Omitted from the CID ROI, and kept secret from my attorneys and myself until we discovered them independently, were FBI interviews of Lawrence, Michele, and Kinsey Adams-Thompson on 1/14-15/87.

In her 1/14/87 FBI interview - two months past the accusation date-window - Michele made the **retroactive** "wetting" and "nightmares" comments. Significantly the A-Ts did **not** register or report any concern about any aspect of Kinsey's behavior **during** or **prior to** the 9/1-10/31/86 window. By the time of this 1/14/87 interview the "abuse" witch-hunt against Hambright, encouraged by the A-Ts [as one of the five activist parents circularizing others at the Presidio to promote the witchhunt] was fully underway. Michele's "sudden recall" of "bedwetting/nightmares" is thus non-credible.

On 2/19/87 the FBI interviewed the therapist Debbie Hickey, who was also specific about the 9/1-10/31/86 window.

On 4/23/87 Hickey provided a sworn affidavit in which she states that the two adult A-Ts were specific about the 9/1-10/31/86 window to her when she interviewed them on 1/13/87.

[227] False statement. What appears on page #18 of the CID ROI is the ROI author's comment that Kinsey told her **mother** that she "did not like Mr. Gary", which is only an allegation from **Michele** in her 1/14/87 FBI interview. When Kinsey herself was interviewed by the FBI on 1/15/87, she made no derogatory comments about Hambright at all.

Mrs. Adams-Thompson made her statements to the FBI in August 1987, and her recollection of the timing of Kinsey's nightmares or wetting her panties may have been incorrect.[228]

Another explanation is that a psychological reaction to the sexual assaults is not uncommon.[229]

The August 13 and 14, 1987 FBI interviews of the Adams-Thompsons were considered highly reliable in regard to Kinsey's identification of LTC Aquino at the post exchange and the subsequent identification of the Aquino residence (pages 26-27, CID Aquino ROI).[230]

The identification of Mrs. Aquino as "Shamby" was less reliable because this identification was "suggestive" because of her proximity to LTC Aquino when the identification was made.[231]

Once a determination had been made that the identification was reliable, it was important to determine when LTC Aquino and Gary Hambright were in San Francisco.[232]

If it could be established that LTC Aquino, Kinsey Adams-Thompson, and Gary Hambright were not together, then the allegation would be unfounded.[233]

---

[228] Michele A-T's statement about Almond's "nightmares and wetting" was made in her 1/14/87 FBI interview - just **two months** after the accusation window. By falsifying the origin of the statement to 8/87, the CID attempts to manufacture "evidence" of a "blurred accusation window" in violation of the law.

[229] There is no record whatever of any "psychological reaction to a sexual assault" by Almond either prior to or during the 9-10/86 accusation window. There is no evidence of any sexual assault on Almond, period. There is only the say-so of "therapist" Hickey in her 2/18/87 FBI interview, which Hickey justified by comments about her 2/3/87 session with Almond which are not accurately taken from her actual notes of that session.

[230] Throughout the CID investigation I provided the CID with increasing documentation as to just how **unreliable** the 8/13-14/87 interviews of the A-Ts actually were. See "A-T's Violations of #133 UCMJ" (originally provided to the CID on 5/10/89) for numerous inconsistencies, prop-up-revisions, and obvious falsifications - including **no** evidence that Almond was even at the PX or behaved there as the A-Ts alleged, and including the fact that Almond made **no** "identification" of our residence at all.

[231] Again there is **only** the allegation by the A-Ts that Almond made any such "identification", and abundant evidence that this was simply one more A-T lie. Nor after the A-T allegations did Almond ever pick out Lilith from any photo/video-lineup. The A-Ts are 100% inconsistent as to when anyone saw Lilith anywhere [see "A-T's Violations of #133 UCMJ"].

"Proximity to me": Michele specified in her 4/10/89 CID statement that Lilith was standing next to our rented car **"alone"** when they first saw her and Almond made her alleged "identification" of her.

Moreover, as Lilith and I had been constantly together in the PX, why wouldn't Almond have "IDd" her at the same time as she "did" me?

[232] As noted, the CID knew that the "identification" was anything **but** reliable.

The CID now says that its next step was to try to find a date when both Hambright and myself were in San Francisco. This is a **reversal** of appropriate investigative procedure, which would be to see whether I could be placed in the same **precise location** - not just "city"! - as Almond **during the accusation window** (the only period when Hambright had any control over Almond).

In short, the CID not only created a nonexistent "crime" but [repeatedly] moved its date [and location] around to try to escape the valid alibis which kept proving our innocence.

[233] It was **indeed** "established that LTC Aquino, Kinsey Adams-Thompson, and Gary Hambright were not together" during both the accusation window and the CID-attempted re-dating and re-locating. Therefor the A-Ts' allegations **were** unfounded, and, as evident from their deliberate lies to investigators, intentionally and maliciously fabricated. [See "A-T's Violations of #133 UCMJ".]

Accordingly it was important to establish the dates when Kinsey received care at the Presidio CDC.[234]

Ultimately LTC Aquino admitted in a sworn statement that he was in San Francisco throughout June-July 1986 (pages 56-57, CID Aquino ROI).[235]

Employment records at the Presidio CDC established that Gary Hambright was at the CDC throughout June-July 1986.[236]

Mrs. Adams-Thompson paid for daycare for Kinsey by check, establishing that Kinsey received daycare during April-July 1986.[237]

This shift in dates for the occurrence of the offense is discussed at paragraph 2.8.2, pages 56-57, CID Aquino ROI.[238]

QUESTION TWO

Myers Question

Please describe what steps were taken by defendant to verify or discredit the alibi provided by E. Graham Marshall, the painter, who provided an affidavit.

CID Response

On March 27, 1990 Major Mark W. Harvey, Region Judge Advocate, Sixth Region, CID, Presidio of San Francisco, CA 94139 telephonically interviewed E. Graham Marshall. With the consent of Mr. Marshall, the interview was tape-recorded.

Mr. Marshall indicated that LTC Aquino could have brought a child into the large front room of Mr. Butch's apartment, on the lower level of 123 Acme, without Mr. Marshall being aware of it (pages 6-7, Marshall interview).

In 1986 Mr. William T. Butch, a member of the Temple of Set and LTC Aquino's brother-in-law, moved into the street-level apartment at 123 Acme. LTC Aquino owned Mr. Butch's apartment. LTC Aquino and Mrs. Aquino had lived in the street-level apartment at 123 Acme before LTC Aquino's mother passed away (para. 8.17, CID Aquino ROI). After LTC Aquino's mother's death, LTC and Mrs. Aquino moved upstairs into his mother's residence, and Mr. Butch moved into the street-level apartment at 123 Acme. The police never searched Mr. Butch's apartment, and no pictures of Mr. Butch's apartment were shown to any children. According to LTC Aquino, the Butch

---

[234] The dates when Almond was under any supervision by Hambright whatever were established from the A-Ts' checks. An immediate comparison of those check dates to Lilith's and my verified location in Washington, D.C. on the same dates would have **proved our innocence immediately and absolutely**. Instead the CID did not even bother with obtaining the checks until late in its investigation, and long after it had set in motion harmful acts against me (such as fixing of the AGR continuation board). In short, proof of our innocence was **never of the least interest** to the CID.

[235] I did not "admit"; I **stated** - as was of course routine information from my assignment, leave, and financial records. Here again the CID is working on its falsified "back-dating" to a period many months prior to the 9-10/86 accusation window.

[236] However the CID also knew that Hambright had no supervision of Almond until September 1986, so his merely being at the CDC before then is irrelevant.

[237] As Hambright had no supervision of Almond until September 1986, Michele A-T's checks to the CDC before then are irrelevant.

[238] Paragraph 2.8.2 of the ROI simply repeats the above: that, upon finding that Lilith and I were on the other side of the U.S.A. on all possible dates during the 9-10/86 accusation window, the CID then manufactured a new date months earlier, based on **nothing** more than determining when I **had** been in San Francisco. Such "manufacture of evidence" is a violation of law.

apartment was used for one Temple of Set ritual, the ordination of a Temple of Set priest (middle of page 71, CID Aquino ROI).[239]

During Kinsey Adams-Thompson's Monday, May 15, 1989 interview, Kinsey repeated her earlier assertion that she was taken to a room with soft walls. However Kinsey contended that the room with padded walls on the top of 123 Acme was the correct room.[240]

Kinsey described the walls as being like blankets on a bed (of a rougher fabric type).[241]

The draping of walls is recommended by LTC Aquino in his writings, and an old photograph seized by the FBI during the search of the Aquino residence shows a ceremony, ritual, or play in which a draped room is used by the Aquinos.[242]

---

[239] That ordination tool place in June of 1986, at just the time the CID's 1991-invented scenario proposes the Butch apartment might have been "the place". At the beginning of the CID investigation, I gave Butch's name and occupancy of that apartment to Harvey (in response to his written questions), and when the question of the ritual came up I also gave them the name of the Priest who was ordained - Mitchell Wade of Berkeley, CA (now dead of illness). Wade told me that Penaluna telephoned him and asked him what kind of bathtub the apartment had, and nothing else. No one interviewed Wade in person or asked him anything else about the apartment.

And of course neither the CID not anyone else ever interviewed Bill Butch on the decor of his apartment or anything else. He had been living in that lower apartment since January of 1986, together with Lilith's son Christopher Wise (whom nobody interviewed either).

[240] No 5/15/89 interview of Almond ever took place. (ROI 4.1).

A CID interview of Almond did take place on 5/11/89. In violation of Discovery, neither a transcript nor a taped copy of this interview was provided to Plaintiff by the CID. Nor is a verbatim transcript of this interview included in the CID ROI. At Exhibit 45 is only Harvey's **memorandum alleging** what Almond said.

In this Harvey memorandum Almond **rejects** what was apparently a photograph of the vinyl-walled wetbar on the 123 roof that Harvey showed to her (from the 8/14/87 FBI photos taken during the search warrant). Therefore the CID's response here that Almond "contended that the room with the padded walls on the top of 123 Acme was the correct room" is a lie.

Almond **never** made any "earlier assertion" that she was taken to a room with soft walls. There is no mention of this, or anything like it, in (a) her 1/26/87 FBI interview, (b) her 8/13/87 FBI interview, (c) any of the 1/27-8/10/87 Hickey "therapy" sessions, or (d) the 10/15/87 FBI interview.

Nor did either of the A-Ts allege a "room with soft walls" **at any time prior** to their learning of the actual appearance of our home **following** the search warrant and its photographs.

After seeing the photographs on 10/15/87, Michele A-T sent a photocopy of her diary to Major Harvey of the CID.(ROI Ex.13). In the **margin** of the 6/30/87 entry, and clearly **not** part of the original entry, is "At bed: Gary had 'soft walls' mommy ... she's confused". (ROI Ex. 42). Here is evidence of Michele's deliberate attempt to manufacture "evidence".

In her 4/10/89 CID interview Michele A-T said that after photocopying her diary for Harvey, she "either misfiled or threw away the original". This is not sensible, because the original would obviously be important as evidence. It makes sense **only** if Michele had added the marginalia or other comments **after** the dates indicated, and feared that laboratory analysis would reveal this. No such analysis is possible with a photocopy.

[241] Again, the CID illegally concealed any verbatim transcript of what Almond said in her 5/11/89 interview. Harvey's interpretation (ROI Ex.45) says only "a cloth-like substance" and makes no mention of "like blankets on a bed (of a rougher fabric type)".

[242] The specific photograph is neither included in the CID ROI as any kind of "evidence", nor otherwise identified. However the plaster and fiberboard walls in our residence could not hold heavy hangings, such as blankets, without damage. Accordingly we have never used such hangings for any temporary purpose here, as examination of the walls would easily verify. The CID made no attempt or request to examine any walls in 123 for signs of such hangings as they allege here. Had they done so, they would have found no high-up holes in the original 1930-vintage plaster at all.

This interview is discussed at paragraph 2.2.3, page 27, and Exhibit 45, CID Aquino ROI.[243]

The large living room of Mr. Butch's apartment on the street level of 123 Acme is the most logical location for Gary Hambright and LTC Aquino to have committed the sexual assault of Kinsey Adams-Thompson.[244]

This room could have been draped with blankets, and Kinsey would not have recognized any of the building's interior contents.[245]

Based on the interviews of Mr. West (paragraph 8.17, CID Aquino ROI), Mr. Marshall, LTC Aquino (paragraph 6.1, CID Aquino ROI), and Kinsey Adams-Thompson, the CID determined that the apartment on the upper level of 123 Acme was probably **not** the apartment where the sexual offenses occurred. If the sexual offenses did occur in the upper apartment of 123 Acme, the FBI photographs taken in August 1987 were of little use because such significant redecoration had occurred between the alleged time of the offenses (summer 1986) and the time of the photographs (August 1987).[246]

---

[243] As detailed above, this Almond interview is differently described in this Response, in the ROI narrative at 2.2.3, and in Harvey's memorandum at ROI Ex.45. A verbatim transcript or tape was concealed or destroyed.

[244] If this room is so "logical", why was no investigative attention paid to it **at all** by the SFPD, the FBI, or the CID **prior to** Graham Marshall's affidavit exonerating our own flat as any possible "crime scene"? Prior to Marshall's statement, the CID maintained adamantly and exclusively that the alleged "crime" had been committed **there**, even to the extent of trying to manufacture evidence such as statuary being there when it had not been (ROI P. 72-73) and transform Almond's original 8/13/87 FBI interview statement about "a bathtub with lion's feet" into "any pictures of lions" (CID question #5, M. Aquino sworn statement 1/27/89).

Nor did the SFPD, FBI, or CID ever attempt to interview William Butch. However on 4/4/91 Butch provided a sworn affidavit that he would have been home in the daytime on 6/10/86 because of his work schedule, that his apartment did not have padded or draped walls, and that he never saw any children in the apartment. (Appeals Exhibits P. 258-9).

And, as shall be repeated every time the CID or anyone else insinuates to the contrary, **there is no evidence whatever that Hambright, Lilith, or I ever sexually assaulted Almond anywhere, anytime**. Note also Almond's medical examination of 3/12/87 - a brief time after the 9-10/86 accusation window - verifying her to be a virgin with no signs of any sexual abuse whatever (ROI Ex.18).

[245] An examination of the front room of Butch's apartment, had the CID considered its suggestion serious enough to even request it [which it obviously did not], would have revealed the original, unbroken plaster around the tops of all walls in the room - indeed throughout the entire apartment. Also in his 4/4/91 sworn affidavit, Butch stated that his apartment did not have padded or draped walls. (Appeals Exhibits P. 258-9).

During the search warrant execution not a single "black blanket" or "black wall hanging" appeared, either on or off any wall, as is evident from the photographs - since the contents of all of our closets and drawers were strewn out into the open for the photographing.

The Temple of Set's ceremonies can be, and are, conducted in surroundings of **any** color - not just black. If asked, we could produce hundreds of members who have attended ceremonies in either the downstairs or the upstairs flat with their perfectly normal tan walls. I have plenty of photos of other Church of Satan & Temple of Set ceremonial rooms showing non-black walls, including my own previous residences.

[246] As shall be repeated every time the CID or anyone else insinuates to the contrary, **there is no evidence whatever that Hambright, Lilith, or I ever sexually assaulted Almond anywhere, anytime**.

"If the sexual offenses occurred in the upper apartment, the FBI photos taken in August 1987 were of little use ..." Then why did the CID try so strenuously for so long to allege that Almond "identified" **anything** from them - which of course she did **not** in the 10/29/87 FBI interview of her?

"The alleged time of the offenses" was **not** "summer 1986", but **September 1-October 31, 1986** - determined by the **only** timespan when Hambright had Almond under his supervision at the CDC. The "summer 1986" re-date was simply an arbitrary maneuver by the CID to manufacture "evidence" and obstruct justice in violation of the law. [See notes to Response #1.]

QUESTION THREE

Myers Question

Please state the dates and times on those respective days that Kinsey Almond was at the CDC during the June-July 1986 time-period. Does the defendant possess copies of or original checks written by the Adams-Thompsons to the Presidio CDC for the above time period for the care of Kinsey Almond? Did the defendant ever see or possess such checks? Why does the defendant not now possess such checks or copies of such checks?

CID Response

In April 1987 [sic. - should be 1989] the checks were shown to Special Agent Dan Cates, who noted the respective days that Kinsey was at the CDC during April-August 1986, but did not retain copies of the checks.[247]

Defendant does not now possess copies or the original checks written by the Adams-Thompsons to the Presidio CDC for the above time-period for the care of Kinsey. The Adams-Thompsons have declined to provide copies of such checks. If copies of the checks are obtained from the Adams-Thompsons, they will be provided to plaintiff.[248]

QUESTION FOUR

Myers Question

Please describe all evidence linking Plaintiff to Mr. Gary Hambright.

CID Response

Kinsey Adams-Thompson said that she was sexually molested by both Gary Hambright and LTC Aquino.[249]

Kinsey Adams-Thompson identified Gary Hambright from a photographic lineup (paragraph 9.19, CID Aquino ROI).[250]

---

[247] This indicates that as of April 1989 the CID knew that the **only possible** accusation window of 9-10/86 was **absolute proof** of our innocence, hence they discarded it entirely in their agenda to frame us. [Cates didn't show any interest in checks pertinent to the accusation window.]

[248] Copies of the checks were obtained 4/8/91 (ROI Exhibit G1). They verify that Lilith and I were in Washington, D.C. on all dates during 9-10/86 when Almond was at the CDC under Hambright's control or supervision, hence are additional absolute proof of our innocence. Presumably this is why the A-Ts refused so long to provide them.

As Almond was not under Hambright's control or supervision during any time other than 9-10/86, the check dates/amounts outside that accusation window are irrelevant - except to show how the CID went about picking a three-months-prior date for their 1989 "revision" agenda.

[249] While after being repeatedly coerced by Hickey Almond recited Hickey's indoctrination that Hambright molested her, Almond **never** recited that she was sexually molested by me in any interview transcript included in the ROI and provided under Discovery. Harvey's "interpretations" of her 1989 interview are noncredible in view of Harvey's bias, agenda, and frequent lying throughout the investigation.

[250] Almond's identification of Hambright is not surprising, since she was in his class during the 9-10/86 period, and since her parents, Hickey, and investigators kept focusing her on him constantly thereafter.

On April 7-8, 1989 Kinsey Adams-Thompson identified LTC Aquino as the "Mike" or "Mikey" that had sexually assaulted her with Gary Hambright (paragraph 9.19, CID Aquino ROI).[251]

On May 21, 1989 Steven L. Quigley told USACIDC that he observed LTC Aquino in the Child Development Center (CDC) on two occasions (paragraph 7.17, CID Aquino ROI).[252]

Gary Hambright worked at the CDC. LTC Aquino had no known reason for being at the CDC. LTC Aquino repeatedly denied under oath that he had ever been in the CDC.[253]

QUESTION FIVE

Myers Question

Please describe all evidence which points to plaintiff acting in concert with any person, and name those persons.

---

[251] As this 4/89 interview occurred after two years of her parents and a series of SFPD, FBI, and CID investigators pushing videos and photos of Lilith and myself on this child, her picking out my face in 4/89 is hardly surprising. Nor, for the same reason, does it prove anything at all.

What **is** relevant is that **prior** to her mother Michele's introduction of descriptions of me (whom she and her husband knew from my Presidio assignment) into Hickey's 6/30/87 session, Almond never mentioned any "Mikey" whatever, and never recited the name "Mike".

When Almond had started to recite "Mikey" after 6/30/87, there is no evidence whatever that she herself associated the name with me. There were only her **parents'** allegations in their planned scheme, and then two years of their obviously pushing Almond to echo this allegation. If she actually did so two years later in 1989, the CID was sufficiently disappointed in her performance not to include any direct quotation from her in the ROI to this effect, and to conceal either a transcript or a tape from me in this lawsuit.

[252] By May 1989 the A-T allegations had long been an international media circus, and anyone with an interest in promoting the Presidio "abuse" scam could allege anything. What is relevant is that there is no record of Quigley making any reference to me, or anyone resembling me, **before** the media publicity.

Neither a transcript nor a tape of any statement whatever by Quigley was provided in the CID ROI under Discovery, in violation of law. If Quigley said he had seen me at the CDC, he simply told a lie, as I have never been there at any time.

What **is** known about Quigley is that according to a 6/23/88 list of claims against the CDC for alleged abuse, the Quigley family had filed for a total of **$4.5 million** in claims. So it obviously had a substantial vested interest in promoting anything supporting the Presidio "abuse" scenario. The CID **omits this motive and bias** of the Quigleys from the ROI or this Response, of course.

In the referenced para 7.17 of the ROI, Quigley is described as saying that "Mikey" was not in uniform at the CDC. Almond, on the other hand, recited her mother's story that "Mikey" wore an Army officer's uniform. Obviously either Quigley or Almond is noncredible as a "witness" accordingly.

Nor did Almond herself, in any of her coached recitals of allegations, **ever** allege that I had been to the CDC. [The A-T story was that Lilith and I had been at our home, and that Hambright had driven Almond there.] Another contradiction between the A-T and Quigley versions.

And - conspicuous by its absence: There were obviously a great many children and several teachers at the CDC - **none** of whom **ever** referred to anyone identifiable as Lilith or myself **before** the A-T publicity. Thereafter the CID could get only one of the children - Quigley - to cooperate with them in a 3-year-stale "remembered identification"!

[253] I have indeed never been to the CDC, and until the attack on Lilith and myself, did not even know where it was located on the Presidio.

As indeed I have repeatedly sworn under oath, I never knew nor had any association or contact with Hambright at all.

On July 14, 1989 Gary Hambright provided the following handwritten statement via his attorneys: "To whom it may concern, I, Gary Willard Hambright, have never seen or met Michael A. Aquino at the Presidio Day Care Center or anywhere else. He, Aquino, has never taken any child, to my knowledge, from the Presidio Day Care Center nor did I take children to his home."

CID Response

From January to August 1987, Kinsey Adams-Thompson told LTC Deborah Hickey that she was sexually molested by "Mr. Gary" or "Gary" (Gary Hambright),[254] "Mikey" or "Mike" (LTC Aquino),[255] and "Shamby" or "Todo" or "Sassy" (Mrs. Aquino).[256]

Sometimes Kinsey related that other persons were at the house where she was molested (pages 20-24, CID Aquino ROI).[257]

The only person known by name that there is probable cause to believe acted in concert with LTC Aquino is Mr. Gary Hambright.[258]

On August 13, 1987 Captain and Mrs. Adams-Thompson told Special Agent Foreman that they observed Kinsey Adams-Thompson's identification of LTC Aquino as the "Mikey" that had sexually molested her, and identified Mrs. Aquino as "Shamby", another person that had sexually molested her.[259]

Other evidence is described in pages 24-27, 58-61, 100-101, CID Aquino ROI; Stmt of Mrs. Adams-Thompson, CID Aquino ROI; pages 2-3, SFPD ROI.[260]

Other children stated that they departed the CDC with Mr. Hambright to go to another location where bizarre sexual and nonsexual activities occurred.[261]

Other children stated that other adults, apparently not employed at the Presidio CDC, took them to the Aquino residence or the residence of other adults and sexually molested these children.[262]

---

[254] False. See transcript and analysis of Hickey notes.

[255] False. See transcript and analysis of Hickey notes. Note here the CID's own unsubstantiated association of "Mikey" or "Mike" with my name.

[256] False. See transcript and analysis of Hickey notes. Note here the CID's own unsubstantiated association of "Shamby", "Sassy", or "Todo" with Lilith's name. "Todo" appears on a completely unconnected list of persons who telephoned concerning an apartment we had available.

[257] This is not evidence of anything whatever concerning Lilith and myself.

[258] There is in fact **no** probable cause to associate Hambright with Lilith and myself in any way - save as coincidental victims of the Presidio "abuse" witch hunt.

[259] A deliberately false allegation by the A-Ts. See "A-T's Violations of Article #133", Section #C.

[260] The PX encounter on pages 24-27 is exposed in "A-T's Violations of Article #133", Section #C. The PX encounter is exposed as indicated, and the two-years-later Almond CID interview is meaningless because of conditioning and contamination of Almond. Pages 100-101 cite a two-years-later photo lineup shown to Almond, in which her by-then-unsurprising notice of me is even more contradicted by her **non**-"recognition" of a photo of our home and her "identification of a female (who is not a suspect) as 'Shamby'".

All statements by Michele A-T - who has been caught in innumerable lies, and who has a clearly vested interest in not being convicted of felonies for false statements to law-enforcement officers and making false monetary claims against the government - are evidence of nothing except her own motives and actions in furtherance of them.

Concerning the SFPD Incident Report (again misrepresented by the CID here as a "ROI"), see annotations #3 & #4 to Response One. The SFPD report is simply a record of what Lawrence A-T alleged to the interviewing officer.

[261] While this statement has no relevance to Lilith or myself, based on all published information to date concerning the Hambright allegations, there is no evidence that he ever sexually abused any child at the CDC or elsewhere.

[262] The CID ROI includes no such allegations which predate the A-T allegations publicity. The CID ROI indicates that all such post-A-T allegations were originally alleged-to-be-hearsay by parents with an emotional, financial, and/ or publicity stake in either the Presidio or other "child abuse" witchhunts.

Some of these statements are partially consistent with going to the residence of LTC and Mrs. Aquino.[263]

Some of the children related that the adults in the residence wore masks and costumes.[264]

Some of the children related that when they saw LTC Aquino on television, they remembered that LTC Aquino was at the residence where they saw the adults in costumes.[265]

For a variety of reasons the CID determined that these children's descriptions were not sufficiently credible to formally list these children as the victims of crimes committed by LTC and Mrs. Aquino.[266]

In order to protect the privacy of these other adults and children, neither their names nor the incidents discussed in the CID Aquino ROI are further discussed.[267]

The CID did not determine that there was probable cause to believe that these other adults acted in concert with LTC Aquino and Mr. Gary Hambright.[268]

For example, one of the children, we will call her Angela, testified that her baby-sitter and a friend sexually molested her. After Angela's baby-sitter was convicted of child sexual abuse and sentenced to twenty years confinement, Angela alleged that LTC and Mrs. Aquino acted in concert with the convicted child molesters.[269]

CID developed sufficient evidence to show that Angela's allegations against LTC and Mrs. Aquino lacked probable cause.[270]

Several children in Northern California made similar allegations against the Aquinos. These allegations were also unsubstantiated.[271]

---

[263] No such "consistencies" predate previous media, parental networking, or investigator exposure of the information, and none whatever predates the A-T allegations publicity.

[264] The theme of "adults wearing masks and costumes" was a standard feature of 1980s' "Satanic Ritual Abuse" scams from McMartin onward, and was routinely advertised by both "therapists" and "cult cops" who promoted such scams.

[265] Rather the **parents** of children previously used in either the Presidio or other "abuse" scams alleged such statements by their children. Again, not a single such allegation predates the A-T publicity.

[266] As the ROI indicates, such aspects of the children's supposed allegations as could be checked resulted in nothing but lies, nonexistent locations, and other invalidations of the children's [and their manipulating parents'] credibility.

Accordingly for the CID to invoke the names and/or stories of such children/parents in the ROI as "evidence" of anything is unjustified, and as such a deliberate attempt by the CID to manufacture "evidence" in violation of law.

[267] The names of all the children and their parents were provided in the uncensored ROI provided during Discovery. What this revealed was that all of the parents/children named were principally involved in either the Presidio or previous "abuse" scams, with massive financial claims, publicity-mongering, etc. The CID's original concealment of their names was actually to conceal this discrediting of them as objective, uninvolved information sources.

[268] In fact what an examination of the "other adults" revealed was that they had not the slightest connection with Hambright or myself. Nor, as the CID knows, is there any evidence that Hambright and I even knew each other, much less "acted in concert".

[269] From the uncensored ROI this is the pre-Presidio case of Angelique Jefferson. What the CID omits to mention here is that Jefferson's babysitter and friend maintained their innocence of Jefferson's mother's allegations, but plea-bargained out of fear of prosecutorial threats. When the CID interviewed them in prison, they both continued to deny ever having molested anyone. The same mother's invention of allegations against Lilith and myself came **after** the A-T publicity, was **not** substantiated by anything in the previous Jefferson case, and was **disproved** by abundant impossibilities in the mother's attempted fabrications.

[270] Accordingly for the CID to invoke the names and/or stories of such children/parents in the ROI as "evidence" of anything is unjustified, and as such a deliberate attempt by the CID to manufacture "evidence" in violation of law.

[271] Accordingly for the CID to invoke the names and/or stories of such children/parents in the ROI as "evidence" of anything is unjustified, and as such a deliberate attempt by the CID to manufacture "evidence" in violation of law.

QUESTION SIX

Myers Question

Please provide the names, addresses, phone numbers, and ages of all persons deemed by Defendant through the CID to be victims of Plaintiff. The age requested is the age at the date of contact with Plaintiff.

CID Response

The "victim block" of the CID Aquino ROI lists the only victim established by the probable cause evidentiary standard, which is used as the reporting standard by the CID. The listed victim is Kinsey Marie Almond Adams-Thompson, dependent stepdaughter of Captain Larry Parker Adams-Thompson. Kinsey's date of birth is September 1, 1983. When the offenses occurred between September 1, 1985 and September 1, 1986, Kinsey was between 2 and 3 years old.[272]

There were children who alleged in interviews with the SFPD, FBI, CID, and medical personnel working at the Letterman Army Medical Center that they were sexually abused while away from the Presidio Child Development Center (CDC).[273]

The focus of the CID Aquino ROI was on allegations relating to offenses outside the CDC that were committed by either LTC Aquino or Mr. Gary Hambright or both. However none of the other children's information was considered by the CID to be sufficiently reliable to meet the probable cause standard. Accordingly the other children interviewed were not listed in the "victim block" of the CID Aquino ROI.[274]

The Adams-Thompsons are represented by Mr. Jack London of the law firm of Morrison and Forster, San Francisco, CA. Mr. London's telephone number is (415) 677-7415. The Adams-Thompsons may be contacted through their attorney.

QUESTION SEVEN

Myers Question

Please describe the dates and times when the aforesaid persons in Question #6 were in direct contact with Plaintiff, and what offenses Plaintiff committed during each such contact.

---

[272] As the CID ROI reveals, there is in fact not a single item of evidence establishing probable cause to believe that Lilith or I committed any crime whatever.

Note here also the CID's repeating of its 1989 revision of the original 9-10/86 A-T allegations to fit their agenda prohibiting any finding of our innocence and the A-Ts' crime.

[273] No published information to date verifies that any child connected with the Presidio "abuse" scam was actually sexually abused, and the "timeline" factor indicates that the entire scam was based on nothing more than the same opportunism which had instigated previous "abuse" scams.

[274] This "unreliability", however, did not prevent the CID from bringing up the falsified stories of these copycat parents and their coached children, and highlighting them as much as possible in the ROI for propaganda in furtherance of the CID agenda.

CID Response

LTC Aquino and Kinsey Adams-Thompson had no scheduled direct contact. Gary Hambright was Kinsey's child care provider,[275] and Kinsey reported that she was sexually abused by Mr. Hambright and LTC Aquino.[276]

Steven Quigley stated that he saw LTC Aquino at the Child Development Center on two occasions (paragraph 7.17, CID Aquino ROI).[277]

The evidence in the Aquino ROI shows that these offenses probably occurred during the period between April and August 1986.[278]

QUESTION EIGHT

Myers Question

Please describe all evidence for each person named in the Question #6 above which demonstrates that such person was kidnapped or sexually abused.

CID Response

See response to Question #1.[279]

In addition, Kinsey was interviewed or discussed the allegations of sexual abuse with her mother,[280] therapists at Letterman Army Medical Center,[281] the FBI,[282] and the CID.[283] These multiple interviews are discussed in detail throughout the CID Aquino ROI. Restating or summarizing this evidence is burdensome and the Defendant wants to avoid the possibility of summarizing facts which Plaintiff may deem significant. However, attention is invited to the following pages, paragraphs, or exhibits of the CID Aquino ROI:

---

[275] Hambright was Almond's child care provider at the CDC **only** during the period 9-10/86, during which time Lilith and I were verified to be in Washington, D.C. on all dates Almond attended the CDC.

[276] Almond **never** reported that she was sexually abused by Hambright and myself. This story was invented by her parents and simply alleged to their child when Chaplain A-T told it to the SFPD on 8/14/87.

[277] See annotation #4 to Question #4.

[278] There is **no evidence whatever** supporting the CID's 1989 invention of a pre-9/86 date for the originally-9-10/86 A-T allegations, except that our innocence of the allegations was proven beyond doubt, and this was unacceptable per the CID's agenda.

[279] See annotations to response to Question #1.

[280] There is only Michele A-T's word for this, and the adult A-Ts were caught in numerous lies concerning their fabricated allegations against Lilith and myself, all of which the CID ignored in its agenda. Additionally the A-Ts filed $3 million in fraudulent claims against the government, which gave them both a strong incentive to lie and a proportionate incentive to prevent their lies from being exposed. See A-T Violations.

[281] Only **one** therapist at Letterman - Debbie Hickey - whose notes established that she coached Almond into "allegations" when the child herself denied them. Thereafter Hickey further "interpreted" what Almond recited in Hickey's own desired scenario. See analysis of Hickey notes.

[282] Almond never identified or accused Lilith or myself of anything in any FBI interview. See Exhibit G-3, FBI Interviews.

[283] Almond was never interviewed by the CID until April 1989, by which time the A-Ts had had two years to prepare her responses, and both incentive ($3 million claims) and defensive (their commission of criminal actions: false statements, fraudulent claims) motives to do so.

a. Pages 18-27.[284]

b. Paragraph 3, Interview of Complainant.[285]

c. Paragraph 4.1, Interviews of Kinsey Adams-Thompson.[286]

d. Paragraph 6.1, 6.2, 6.5; Interviews of LTC Aquino, Mrs. Aquino, and Mr. Gary Hambright.[287]

e. Paragraphs 7.7, 7.8; Interviews of CPT and Mrs. Adams-Thompson.[288]

f. Paragraph 7.17, Interview of Mr. Steven Quigley.[289]

g. Paragraphs 9.19, 9.21, 9.22, 9.30; views of lineups by Kinsey Adams-Thompson, Joshua Thompson, T. Thompson, S. Quigley.[290]

h. Exhibit 1, AIR of SA Potter.[291]

i. Exhibit 2, Stmt of CPT Adams-Thompson.[292]

j. Exhibit 5, Stmt of LTC Aquino, dated 4 Jan 1988.[293]

k. Exhibit 6, Stmt of LTC Aquino, dated 23 Aug 1988.[294]

l. Exhibit 8, Stmt of LTC Aquino, dated 27 Jan 1989.[295]

m. Exhibit 9, Stmt of LTC Aquino, dated 10 May 1989.[296]

---

[284] Pages #18-27 contain only Hickey's, the adult A-Ts', and Harvey's opinion that Almond was kidnapped or assaulted. There is **no** evidence.

[285] Paragraph #3, page #38 contains only Larry A-T's fabricated allegation of the "PX encounter", as well as his admission that he himself knew and recognized both Lilith and myself when he saw us at the PX. There is **no** evidence of Almond's kidnapping or assault.

[286] Paragraph 4.1 contains Harvey's distorted and selective accounts of (a) the 8/13/87 FBI interview of Almond, (b) the 8/14/87 trip to 123 Acme in which Almond made no identification of it, (c) the 4/7-8/89 CID interview of Almond, worthless because of her two years' conditioning and coaching by her parents and others, and also because of Harvey's concealment of the original tape and inaccurate "paraphrasing" of it (ROI Exhibit #45). There is **no** evidence of Almond's kidnapping or assault.

[287] There is **no** evidence of Almond's kidnapping or assault in any of these interviews.

[288] There is **no** evidence of Almond's kidnapping or assault in any of these interviews.

[289] There is **no** evidence of Almond's kidnapping or assault in this interview.

[290] As these photographic lineups were conducted in violation of several CID regulations concerning their suitability, as well as two years after all of the children [of financially motivated and legally jeopardized parents] knew of the A-T attack on Lilith and myself via its massive publicity, they are worthless. They constitute **no** evidence of Almond's kidnapping or assault.

[291] The 123 Acme trip report by SA Potter establishes (a) that Almond did **not** "identify" 123, and (b) that her mother and the investigators who took her there rigged the trip to coach her to do so, then lied about the failed results. See "A-T Violations". This constitutes **no** evidence of Almond's kidnapping or assault.

[292] This contains **no** evidence of Almond's kidnapping or assault.

[293] This contains **no** evidence of Almond's kidnapping or assault, and it contains significant evidence that no such events ever occurred and were deliberately and maliciously fabricated by the A-Ts.

[294] *Ibid.*

[295] *Ibid.*

[296] *Ibid.*

n. Exhibit 10, Stmt by L. Aquino, dated 4 Jan 1988.[297]
o. Exhibit 12, Stmt of CPT Adams-Thompson, dated 10 Apr 1989.[298]
p. Exhibit 13, Stmt of Michele Adams-Thompson, dated 10 Apr 1989.[299]
q. Exhibit 18, Medical Examination of Kinsey Adams-Thompson, dated 12 Mar 1987.[300]
r. Exhibit 23, Chart depicting PCD, TDY, and Leaves of LTC Aquino.[301]
s. Exhibit 38, Medical Records of Psychiatric Treatment of Kinsey Adams-Thompson.[302]
t. Exhibit 42, Diary of Michele Adams-Thompson.[303]
u. Exhibit 45, MFR interview of Kinsey Adams-Thompson by CPTs Harvey and Boomer.[304]

QUESTION NINE

Myers Question

Please describe the involvement of LTC Deborah Hickey, MC, in diagnosing the persons named in Question #6 above. Describe the persons diagnosed and the diagnosis in each case along with any physical or psychological evidence to support the diagnosis.

CID Response

LTC Deborah Hickey, MC diagnosed Kinsey Adams-Thompson as a victim of sexual abuse. Significant therapy sessions are documented in CID Aquino ROI on pages 20-24. The therapy sessions were conducted from January to at least August 1987. The known dates are provided with Question #11.[305]

---

[297] *Ibid.*

[298] This contains only Larry A-T's 2-year-later allegations, adapted to the 1988-89 CID agenda. It contains **no** evidence of Almond's kidnapping or assault.

[299] This contains only Michele A-T's 2-year-later allegations, adapted to the 1988-89 CID agenda. It contains **no** evidence of Almond's kidnapping or assault.

[300] Kinsey Almond's 3/12/87 medical examination indicates that there was "**no** physical evidence of abuse" and verifies that the A-Ts **knew this, and concealed it**, at the time they devised their faked story to alleged to the SFPD and FBI in 8/87.

[301] This verifies that I was not in San Francisco at any time during the possible allegation window of 9-10/86 when Almond was at the CDC.

[302] Exhibit 38 are selected and **incomplete** pages from the Hickey "therapy" notes. They contain **no** evidence of Almond's kidnapping or assault, but abundant evidence of Hickey's attempt to manufacture such "evidence" by indoctrinating it into the child.

[303] This contains photocopies which Michele A-T alleged to be her diary, provided to the CID two years later, with obviously-faked marginal additions. This is **not** evidence of Almond's kidnapping or assault.

[304] This contains only Harvey's allegations of what Almond said in her CID interview two years later. It is worthless both because of the child's conditioning by her parents and Harvey's personal bias and official agenda.

[305] Hickey diagnosed Almond as a victim of sexual abuse despite Almond's initial, repeated denials, a medical examination showing her to be a virgin with no signs of any sexual abuse, and the lack of any medical emergency during the 9-10/86 accusation window [or the 1989-invented CID backdate] that would have resulted from a sexual assault on Almond.

The Hickey "therapy" session notes included with the Discovery CID ROI are extremely censored. Nevertheless even the ones provided show that Hickey simply harassed Almond into reciting what she desired, then further "interpreted" the recitations in her own "diagnosis". See analysis of Hickey notes, and Hickey's Affidavit.

LTC Hickey had a significant role in the diagnosis of Kinsey Adams-Thompson.[306]

LTC Hickey had numerous therapy sessions in which Kinsey mentioned ritualistic abuse by Mr. Gary, Mikey, Shamby, and persons by other names.[307]

There was no physical evidence, such as vaginal or rectal tears, semen samples, or sexually transmitted diseases to support the diagnosis of sexual abuse (CID Aquino ROI, Exhibit 18).[308]

The psychological evidence is contained within the medical records of Kinsey Adams-Thompson. Matters that a child should not know about are discussed by Kinsey during therapy.[309]

The medical records are lengthy. A shorter summary is contained at pages 20-24 of the CID Aquino ROI.[310]

QUESTION TEN

Myers Question

Please confirm or deny that LTC Hickey diagnosed her own children as being abused.

CID Response

On June 8, 1987 during dinner, Jennifer Simmons, born on October 4, 1984, was asked by her mother, LTC Hickey, about school (daycare at the CDC). Jennifer told LTC Hickey about an incident in which a teacher whom she identified as Miss Nancy had taken pictures of her and a fellow student named Michael. These photographs were taken at "Miss Nancy's house". Jennifer stated that Michael had kissed her or bit her on the vagina while at Miss Nancy's house. On June 22, 1987 Jennifer Simmons did not provide any information of investigative value to SA Foreman of the FBI. This information is documented at paragraph 6.9.1 and Exhibit 166, CID Hambright ROI 0667-86-CID026-69776. The CID has never listed Jennifer Simmons or any of LTC Hickey's children as "victims" in any CID ROIs.[311]

The Defendant is not aware of any "diagnosis" as "abused" or "not abused" concerning LTC Hickey's children.[312]

---

[306] Hickey was in fact the **only** Letterman "therapist" conducting the 8-month indoctrination of Almond.

[307] All such statements were either made by Hickey or Almond's mother, or tutored into Almond for her to recite. See Hickey Notes analysis.

[308] This is proof that Almond was **never** sexually assaulted as the A-Ts, Hickey, and the CID deliberately falsified.

[309] There is no "psychological evidence" other than the Hickey notes, and these show simply that Almond was harassed into reciting Hickey's and Michele A-T's "abuse" scenario. These two persons provided all of the sexually-perverse information to Almond "that a child should not know about".

[310] Harvey's page #20-24 summary is agenda-edited, and the actual Hickey notes provided as an ROI exhibit are severely censored, in suppression of evidence and violation of Discovery.

[311] The question asked about Hickey's **children** (plural), and the CID responds concerning only one daughter. News media - Channel 2 television - reported both that Hickey had so "diagnosed" her own **children** and had refused to be interviewed.

If Hickey, a physician, immediately examined Jennifer's vagina, obviously there were no bite wounds.

If this dinner conversation about the day's school happened on 6/8/87, how is it that Hickey did not contact the school or the police about "Miss Nancy"? How is it that "Michael" or his parents were not contacted [or, if contacted, denied the story]? Obviously the story proved false, otherwise "Miss Nancy" would have been arrested.

In its answer the CID uses the plural - "any of LTC Hickey's children" - but answers the question only concerning Jennifer.

[312] Again the plural is used, indicating more than one Hickey child. Also the CID is **indeed** aware of Hickey's "abuse diagnosis" concerning at least Jennifer, as it admits in the next paragraph.

If LTC Hickey were questioned, she would say that she believed that her daughter was sexually abused in connection with the Child Development Center at the Presidio, but not apparently in connection with LTC Aquino's case.[313]

QUESTION ELEVEN

Myers Question

Please describe why LTC Hickey was permitted to continue in her role as psychiatrist to the persons named in Question #9 above when her own children were part of the event. Describe the time-period that LTC Hickey was involved with any person named in Question #9 above.

CID Response

LTC Deborah Hickey, Medical Corps (MC) diagnosed Kinsey Adams-Thompson as a victim of sexual abuse.[314]

Significant therapy sessions are documented in CID Aquino ROI on pages 20-24. The therapy sessions are documented within CID Aquino ROI in Exhibit 38 as being conducted on the following dates:

a. January 20 and 27, 1987
b. February 3 and 24, 1987
c. March 24 and 30, 1987
d. April 7, 21, and 28, 1987
e. May 12, 19, and 26, 1987
f. June 2, 9, 23, and 30, 1987
g. July 2 and 7, 1987
h. August 10, 1987

The CID was required by Child Psychiatry, Letterman Army Medical Center (LAMC), to select pages from the Kinsey Adams-Thompson patient record based on relevance to the investigation. The pages in the LAMC patient record were numbered from 1 to at least 64. Thirty pages of the medical record had relevancy to the investigation and were photocopied and marked Exhibit 38. (This is the reason that there are skips in the page numbers at the bottoms of Exhibit 38.) CID Aquino ROI further summarizes Exhibit 38 by quoting some of the most significant therapy sessions on pages 20-24 of CID Aquino ROI.[315]

---

[313] In short, the CID's evasive answer to Question #10 is "yes".

From its response, it is also clear that in the case of Jennifer, this "diagnosis" was made on nothing more than a dinner remark which evidently proved to be physically and factually unsubstantiated.

[314] Hickey's diagnosis was made solely on the basis of Hickey's predetermined agenda, in which she accepted no responses from Almond that denied sexual abuse. Hickey's psychological diagnosis was also completely contradicted by Almond's 3/12/87 physical examination, which found no signs of any sexual abuse. Hickey would certainly have been aware of this finding.

[315] In other words, only 32 pages (half or less, going by the CID statement of "at least 64") of the entire Hickey notes concerning Almond were included in the ROI, leaving one to wonder what was contained in all the **other** pages. Clearly, "significant" in the jargon of the CID means "only those pages that could be interpreted to frame the Aquinos". The concealing of the other pages implies that what was on those pages would, if known, demolish the CID's, Hickey's, and the A-Ts' efforts even more transparently than the revealed pages.

Harvey makes another effort to focus attention on his selective and deliberately misleading interpretation of the Hickey notes on pages #20-24 of the ROI, rather than on the more difficult-to-read notes themselves.

The distortion and bias of Harvey's passages, and the true significance of just the **revealed** Hickey notes, are discussed in my "Hickey Notes Analysis".

LTC Hickey had numerous therapy sessions in which Kinsey mentioned ritualistic abuse by Mr. Gary, Mikey, Shamby, and persons by other names.[316]

In June 1987 medical personnel at Letterman Army Medical Center were advised by LTC Hickey that she was concerned about her own possible lack of objectivity caused by the revelations of Jennifer. LTC Hickey's supervisors at Letterman Army Medical Center decided that due to LTC Hickey's strong rapport with her patients, she should be allowed to continue to provide therapy to Kinsey Adams-Thompson and other children, in the best interests of the children.[317]

QUESTION TWELVE

Myers Question

Please describe with precision what false swearing Plaintiff allegedly engaged in.

CID Response

The incidents regarding the false swearing and a discussion of misleading statements are provided at pages 2 and 28-38 of CID Aquino ROI. The false swearing relates to false portions of oral and written statements provided by LTC Aquino.[318]

The written false statements are dated January 4, 1988, August 23, 1988, and January 27, 1989, and were made at the Army Personnel Center, St. Louis, MO (Exhibits 5, 6, and 8, CID Aquino ROI). In these three written statements LTC Aquino falsely stated: (a) that he had never gone to the Presidio Child Development Center, (b) that he did not sexually assault Kinsey Adams-Thompson, (c) that he had never knowingly met Kinsey Adams-Thompson, and (d) that he did not bring or arrange for Gary Hambright to bring Kinsey Adams-Thompson to his building, 123 Acme.[319]

On January 4, 1988 and August 23, 1988, LTC Aquino made sworn statements deliberately understating Kinsey's age in an effort to undermine her credibility with LTC Aquino's and CPT Adams-Thompson's military chain of command. On May 10 and 11, 1989, by the legal materials LTC Aquino provided to the CID and the oral

---

[316] Hickey had numerous sessions in which she and Michele A-T repeatedly coached Almond to recite their scenarios concerning Hambright, Mikey, Shamby, other persons, and ritualistic abuse. See my "Hickey Notes Analysis".

[317] No copy of such a request by Hickey is provided by the CID. No copy of her superiors' answer is provided. The supervisors are not named.

The conspicuous reason is that it is a clear breach of medical ethics for such a conflict of interest to be allowed to persist once identified, reflecting both on Hickey and on the unnamed superiors.

Further, if Hickey believed Jennifer's dinnertime remarks despite the obvious proofs that nothing had happened to her [see annotations to Question #10], this further establishes Hickey's incompetence to make "abuse" diagnoses and her own agenda to conclude "abuse" in utter disregard of complete physical and circumstantial evidence to the contrary.

This CID Response also indicates why Hickey's later chain of command refused to open an investigation into the medical competence and ethics of her conduct during the Presidio scam. If her actions were continuously sanctioned by these unnamed superiors, they would have been implicated along with her in any finding of malpractice. See my letters to Hickey's CoC.

[318] **Not a single inaccurate statement by m**e is identified by the CID except for my accidental mistake concerning the age of Almond, as discussed below. As I simply denied the A-Ts' false allegations concerning Lilith and myself, and as the CID had a predetermined agenda to sell those allegations, it just followed that the CID automatically called any statement that I made in refutation of those falsehoods and that agenda "false swearing".

[319] All these sworn statements by me are **true**, and included abundant evidence to prove that truth. At the time additional proofs, as I would later discover, were still concealed from me by the CID.

and written statements which he made, LTC Aquino showed that he was acutely aware that the younger he made Kinsey appear, the more likely she was not to be believed. In LTC Aquino's January 4, 1988 sworn statement LTC Aquino stated, "Adams-Thompson alleges that he made the accusation based solely on comments elicited from his 3-year-old stepdaughter (who was age 2 in October 1986)". (See page 30 and Exhibit 5, CID Aquino ROI.) In LTC Aquino's August 23, 1988 sworn statement at paragraph 19, LTC Aquino states "Adams-Thompson alleges that he made the accusation based solely on comments elicited from his 3-year-old stepdaughter (who was age 2 in September 1986)". (See page 30 and Exhibit 6, CID Aquino ROI.) Kinsey celebrated her third birthday on September 1, 1986. LTC Aquino had in his possession the SFPD Aquino ROI that correctly indicated Kinsey was born on September 1, 1983. During the May 10 and 11, 1989 interviews, LTC Aquino explained that his incorrect statements about Kinsey's age were due to confusion about newspaper accounts related to David Tobin's age (pages 31, 72, CID Aquino ROI).[320]

The January 4, 1988 sworn statement falsely states that CPT Larry Adams-Thompson made the allegation that LTC Aquino molested his daughter. LTC Aquino had the SFPD Aquino ROI in his possession when he made this statement. Accordingly LTC Aquino knew that Kinsey, rather than her stepfather, made this allegation against LTC Aquino.[321]

The charges sworn by LTC Aquino on January 4, 1988 against CPT Larry Adams-Thompson were false (a copy of the charges is at Exhibit 5, CID Aquino ROI). The CID's basis for believing these charges to be false are described at pages 29-30, CID Aquino ROI.[322]

In paragraph 13a of LTC Aquino's sworn statement of January 27, 1989 (Exhibit 8, CID Aquino ROI), LTC Aquino states that he goes by his legal first name of "Michael". In the Army, LTC Aquino states that he is called "Mike", and never "Mikey". In *The Church of Satan*, at page 272, Diane LaVey, at that time LTC Aquino's personal friend, called LTC Aquino "Mike".[323] During a CID interview Mr. Anton LaVey referred to LTC Aquino as "Mike"

---

[320] That the CID would try to make such a big issue out of my ignorance concerning Almond's precise age illustrates how desperate the CID was to find **any** mistake by me in the several sworn statements and scores of signed letters and oral statements by me on the A-T scam.

Since Almond was said to be 3 at the time her parents concocted their accusations against Lilith and myself (August 1987), and since the alleged date-window of those accusations was almost a full year earlier (September-October 1986), I assumed that Almond would have been 2 during that date-window. I didn't bother to do precise math from her birthdate as indicated on the SFPD Incident Report (**not** "ROI"). [However, as I included that Incident Report as an exhibit to my sworn statements, I can hardly be said to have concealed Almond's true age.]

The fact that Almond was 3-and-1/6th rather than 2 during the 9-10/86 accusation window is immaterial. Her credibility is not significantly different because of this.

Ironically, if Almond's credibility is to be invalidated during age 2, then the CID's 1989-revision of the accusation date to June 1986 would also roll back Almond to the middle of age 2, hence invalidate her credibility about anything she "recalled" about that period. Indeed in the ROI the CID **itself** admits: "Kinsey's confusion over who may have gone with her to the Aquino residence, and other details, is not surprising when one recalls that she was less than 3 when she was abducted from the CDC." (ROI 2.6, page #48).

With regard to Tobin, what I told the CID was that the Tobin child had been reported in the media as age 2, and that before Lilith and I learned of the A-Ts' being behind the attack on us, we assumed that the Tobin parents were responsible, as they had been aggressively in the media promoting the Presidio witch-hunts immediately prior to the surprise raid on our home.

[321] **Larry A-T** indeed invented and made the accusations against Lilith and myself to the SFPD recorded in the 8/14/87 Incident Report. Almond was not even present.

[322] The charges sworn by me on 1/4/88 were **true**, and the CID's basis for denying that truth is that it contradicted the CID's predetermined agenda.

[323] What I said concerning my name is completely accurate.

or "Mikey". Mr. LaVey's interview is at paragraph 7.16, CID Aquino ROI. The CID discussion of this offense is at pages 36-37, CID Aquino ROI.[324]

On May 10 and 11, 1989, at his residence in St. Louis, LTC Aquino made a false oral sworn statement to Special Agent Dan Cates of the CID. Paragraph 6.1, CID Aquino ROI, summarizes the most significant aspects of LTC Aquino's sworn oral statement. In the May 10 and 11, 1989 statement LTC Aquino again falsely denied: (a) going to the Presidio Child Development Center, (b) sexually assaulting Kinsey Adams-Thompson, (c) knowing Kinsey Adams-Thompson, and (d) knowing Gary Hambright.[325]

On May 10 and 11, 1989, at his residence in St. Louis, MO, LTC Aquino falsely stated that only LTC Aquino, Mrs. Butch, and Mrs. Aquino had the security access code of the upper-level apartment of 123 Acme. See lines 7-9, page 71, CID Aquino ROI.[326]

QUESTION THIRTEEN

Myers Question

Please describe all psychological medical evidence to support that any person described in Question #6 above was sexually abused.

CID Response

LTC Deborah Hickey, Medical Corps (MC) diagnosed Kinsey Adams-Thompson as a victim of sexual abuse.[327]

Significant therapy sessions are documented in CID Aquino ROI on pages 20-24. The therapy sessions are documented within CID Aquino ROI in Exhibit 38 as being conducted on the following dates:
a. January 20 and 27, 1987
b. February 3 and 24, 1987
c. March 24 and 30, 1987
d. April 7, 21, and 28, 1987
e. May 12, 19, and 26, 1987
f. June 2, 9, 23, and 30, 1987
g. July 2 and 7, 1987
h. August 10, 1987

The CID was required by Child Psychiatry, Letterman Army Medical Center (LAMC), to select pages from the Kinsey Adams-Thompson patient record based on relevance to the investigation. The pages in the LAMC patient record were numbered from 1 to at least 64. Thirty-two pages of the medical record had relevancy to the investigation and were photocopied and marked Exhibit 38.

LTC Hickey had numerous therapy sessions in which Kinsey mentioned ritualistic abuse by Mr. Gary, Mikey, Shamby, and persons by other names.

---

[324] Letters from Anton LaVey during the entire time of our 6-year friendship, contained in *The Church of Satan* provided to the CID, also verify that he called me only "Michael" or "Mike" during that time. **Only** during his 1989 interview with the CID - at which time he hated me obsessively for exposing his 1975 corruption of the Church, as the CID also knew - did he maliciously and repeatedly use the term "Mikey" to refer to me. The CID was also provided with several documents by me proving all other character-attacks by LaVey during that interview false, which certainly impeaches his use of "Mikey" during that interview as well.

[325] All of these sworn statements made to SA Cates were **true**.

[326] The CID's reason for calling this a "lie" is that the security alarm company, which monitored entry of the access code and was responsible for calling the police if it were incorrectly entered, **also** knew the code. **Of course** it did for the entire alarm system to work!

[327] See annotations #1-3 to Question #11, as the CID merely repeats those Responses here.

LTC Hickey used "play therapy", a process of using play to gain information from the child. The information is then used to resolve stress, which is often deeply suppressed by the child. The therapist uses nonleading questions to resolve or clarify issues for the child. This methodology is discussed at pages 19-20, CID Aquino ROI.[328]

The psychological evidence is contained within the medical records of Kinsey Adams-Thompson. Children under the age of five should not be aware of matters related by Kinsey Adams-Thompson to LTC Hickey, absent sexual abuse.[329]

QUESTION FOURTEEN

Myers Question

Please describe in detail the substance of the conversation held between Senator Helms and Major General Overholt, TJAG, in late January or early February of 1989, which is noted at Exhibit J of Plaintiff's Request for Amendment of the Titling Action.

CID Response

Defendant presently has not located any records which contain the substance of a conversation between Senator Helms and Major General Overholt, TJAG, in late January or early February of 1989. A review for these records is ongoing, and any records discovered will immediately be provided to Plaintiff's counsel.[330]

QUESTION FIFTEEN

Myers Question

Please describe in detail why the CID investigation did not commence until November of 1988. Include Senator Helms' role as well as the role of the Secretary of the Army, Mr. Marsh, and the Army Staff including TJAG, ODCSPER, DACH, PA, OCU, MSRA, SC.

CID Response

In October or November 1988 the CID learned that the investigations previously conducted by the SFPD and FBI suffered from two significant weaknesses:[331]

---

[328] Even in 1989 the nationwide use of "play therapy" to instigate and pursue "daycare abuse" and "Satanic ritual abuse" witchhunts was notorious for its use of coaching, harassing, and leading of children to recite whatever was demanded of them. Abundant literature exposing this quack technique was provided to the CID. Since then, the technique has been exposed even more widely, leading to its complete discrediting in the medical profession in the way that it was used in the 1980s witchhunts.

[329] Children under the age of 5 are quite capable of reciting whatever disgusting sexual items are taught to them, as the Hickey notes verify that Hickey did to Almond.

[330] No document was ever provided indicating that the CID had made such a request to either TJAG or Senator Helms, nor were any documents [or a statement that no such documents exist] provided to Plaintiff. In short, the CID simply kept this crucial evidence of the Helms-driven agenda buried.

[331] In its Responses to Questions #1 and #15, the CID maintains that it "monitored and assisted the SFPD and FBI investigations". [No documentary evidence that it did either for either agency was included in the ROI.] If the CID continues to insist that it "monitored and assisted" the SFPD & FBI, how is it that these "two significant weaknesses" were not seen in the **1-1/4 years** before the CID opened its own investigation? There is no documentary evidence in the ROI that the CID **ever** complained to the SFPD or FBI about such "significant weaknesses", or indeed about anything at all in their investigations.

(a) failure to present the abused children with an adequate lineup,[332] and

(b) failure to establish the locations of LTC Aquino, Mr. Gary Hambright, and the abused children during the April-October 1986 period.[333]

Based on the SFPD request for CID investigative action to resolve these two weaknesses,[334] the CID determined that a video lineup and photographic lineup should be shown to each CDC child that told any investigative agency or medical authority that they left the CDC with a CDC employee or other stranger.[335] Since this would be a very significant effort, the Sixth Region CID decided to open a formal CID investigation.[336] There was no communication from anyone in Washington, D.C. that recommended to the Six Region CID that an investigation by the CID should be opened.[337] The Commander, Sixth Region, based upon recommendations from the Office of the Staff Judge Advocate, U.S. Army Garrison, Presidio of San Francisco and the Staff Judge Advocate, Headquarters, Sixth Region CID, decided to open the CID Aquino ROI.[338]

---

[332] CID lie. The 8/2/88 *San Francisco Chronicle* states: "But there were apparent inconsistencies in [Almond's] description, and nothing in the evidence or in interviews **with at least 26 other young Presidio children** 'fully corroborated' the girl's account, [Deputy District Attorney Michael] Williams said. And although some children saw Aquino on TV and told their parents he was a 'bad man', Williams said, **none could pick him out of a Police photo lineup**."

[333] First, there was and is **no** evidence that **any** children were abused in connection with the Presidio day-care witch-hunt. Secondly, the only accusation of "abuse" against Lilith and myself was made by the A-Ts, naming just a **single** child (Almond). Thirdly, Almond was under Hambright's supervision **only** during 9-10/86, so dates prior to 9/1/86 were irrelevant. Fourthly, there is **no** documentary evidence in the ROI that the SFPD "failed to establish my location" during the 9-10/86 accusation window. My duty station, and finance & leave records, would certainly have been available to the SFPD from the Army - or from me directly if the SFPD had communicated specific accusation dates to my attorney [it did not].

[334] There is no documentary evidence in the ROI of any SFPD request for the CID to take any action whatever, including to "resolve any weaknesses" of its investigation.

[335] Showing a lineup to any Presidio CDC children after 1-1/4 years of massive international publicity of Lilith and myself, to include our photo and video pictures, was in violation of CID regulations. The CID conduct of such lineups violated several other CID regulations as well. See "CID Lineup Regulations".

[336] The CID states here that its **only** rationale for opening its investigation was to conduct illegal lineups in violation of its own regulations and to falsify a new accusation date because of our proven innocence during the 9-10/86 accusation window.

[337] As instructions to open a fraudulent CID investigation to intimidate and frame an innocent officer and his wife are a felony, the issuance of such instructions would indeed not be routinely recorded, but would have been clandestine. That the CID investigation was opened immediately after Senator Helms' demand to the Secretary of the Army that my career be destroyed - **with no prior CID interest whatever** - the circumstantial evidence of such clandestine instructions is inescapable. Also inescapable is that in this Response the CID avoided all mention of the Helms-Marsh letters, as well as of ODCSPER, DACH, PA, OCU, MSRA, SC (as specified in the Plaintiff question). That these offices were indeed involved is evidenced by the Department of the Army briefing they all participated in on 11/23/88 (the day the CID investigation was opened). (See Burton paper & attendance record).

[338] No such recommendations are included or referenced in the ROI, nor provided to Plaintiff in Discovery in this lawsuit. If such recommendations were, as the CID alleges, based on the "two significant weaknesses" discussed above, then the Commander, 6RCID, the SJA Presidio, and the SJA 6RCID are guilty of conspiracy to violate CID evidentiary regulations (lineup procedures) and manufacture false "evidence" (the 1989 "backdating").

From February to May 1988 the SFPD conducted an investigation of the off-Presidio allegations of child sexual abuse.[339] The CID role was to monitor this investigation and assist as needed.[340] The main investigative activity was by Detective Pamfiloff of the SFPD, who conducted numerous taped interviews of children from the Presidio Child Development Center.

From June to August 1988 the SFPD file was at the office of the District Attorney, San Francisco for review and a prosecutive decision regarding LTC Michael Aquino, Mrs. Lilith Aquino, and Mr. Gary Hambright.

In mid-August 1988 the SFPD file was returned to Detective Pamfiloff. Prosecution was declined absent additional evidence, which would require substantial additional investigative effort.[341]

From September to October 1988, Headquarters, Sixth Region and personnel from the San Francisco Field Office discussed the allegations against the Aquinos with Detective Pamfiloff, the San Francisco District Attorney's Office, the United States Attorney's Office, and the Federal Bureau of Investigation.[342]

From October 31, 1988 LTC Aquino was fingerprinted and photographed by CID.[343]

On November 1 through 3, 1988, copyright coordination was conducted by CID to use a tape of LTC and Mrs. Aquino from the Oprah Winfrey Show for a video lineup.[344]

On November 15 and 17, 1988 Detective Pamfiloff provided briefings to Headquarters, Sixth Region and Office of the Staff Judge Advocate, United States Army Garrison on the SFPD investigation.[345]

On November 23, 1988 Colonel W.D. Ray, Commander, Sixth Region, directed the opening of a formal investigation of LTC Michael A. Aquino, Mrs. Lilith Aquino, and Mr. Gary Hambright for kidnapping and sexually assaulting children from the Presidio Child Development Center.[346]

---

[339] The SFPD investigation was opened 8/14/87 with Larry A-T's false accusations to Pamfiloff. It was closed 8/1/88 with the San Francisco District Attorney's announcement that no charges would be filed. The shorter, falsified date-span stated here by the CID is presumably to suggest that the SFPD investigation was too brief.

[340] For the third time the CID falsely insists that it "monitored and assisted" the SFPD & FBI investigations.

[341] The SFPD investigation was formally closed not in "mid-August" but on 8/1/88, when the San Francisco District Attorney announced that no charges would be filed (*SF Chronicle* 8/2/88). This is another attempt by the CID to fabricate a shorter timespan between the SFPD closing and the CID opening on 11/23/88.

[342] No documentation of any such discussions is included or referenced in the ROI, nor provided to Plaintiff in Discovery in this lawsuit.

[343] Since the CID investigation was not opened until 11/23/88, the CID's fingerprinting me on 10/31/88 without alerting me to any such investigation or advising me of my Constitutional rights was a violation of its own regulations and federal law. Additionally, that as there was no further reference to my fingerprints in the ROI, they were very obviously not found anywhere at the CDC (which was presumably thoroughly checked for prints at the beginning of the witch-hunt in November 1986). Additionally, this 10/31/88 fingerprinting was conducted soon after Secretary of the Army March received Senator Helms' 10/26/88 letter demanding that my career be destroyed.

[344] As above, why was the CID conducting investigative actions concerning me without first formally opening an investigation and advising me of my rights? Additionally CID plans to conduct a video lineup in 1989 are in violation of CID regulations concerning lineups. [See CID Regulations.]

[345] No documentation of any such briefings by Pamfiloff is included or referenced in the ROI, nor provided to Plaintiff in Discovery in this lawsuit.

[346] As the CID's stated reasons for opening its investigation were to conduct illegal lineups and falsify accusation dates [see above], then Ray's direction was in violation of federal law. At this time the CID possessed conclusive evidence that neither Lilith nor I had assaulted Almond (not "children") as the A-Ts alleged.

On November 25 and 26, 1988, a Sixth Region, CID investigative plan and Department of Defense Inspector General subpoenas were drafted at Headquarters, Sixth Region, CID.[347]

On November 30 and December 1, 1988, Headquarters CID conducted meetings to discuss the investigation of LTC Aquino. The November 30 meeting was attended by Sixth Region and Headquarters CID personnel; the meeting on December 1 included representatives from the Criminal Law Division, OTJAG, and the Army General Counsel's Office.[348]

Attendees at both meetings agreed that the initial titling decision and the investigative plan were appropriate. No one said anything at the meetings about any interest by Senator Helms, the Army Staff, or the Secretary of the Army in the outcome of the investigation.[349] The goal of the investigation was to correct the weaknesses of the previous investigations.[350] These investigative efforts could clear LTC Aquino or they could generate sufficient evidence for a court-martial.[351] The interests of justice would best be served by making the best possible investigative effort to corroborate or refute the allegations of Kinsey Adams-Thompson and the other children.[352]

QUESTION SIXTEEN

Myers Question

Please describe why Plaintiff was denied continuation as an AGR officer. Include a description of whether or not the Continuation Board knew of Plaintiff's flagging or the CID investigation. If the Continuation Board was informed of Plaintiff's flagging or the CID investigation, state whether such knowledge were properly before the board. If such knowledge were before the board, state why such knowledge was given to the board.

---

[347] No documentation of any such investigative plan is included or referenced in the ROI, nor provided to Plaintiff in Discovery in this lawsuit. Indeed the CID attempts to present a 10/17/88 letter from Harvey (Defendant Ex. #G-3) as its "investigative plan", although that letter consists simply of Harvey's suggestions for various violations of law by the CID in the conduct of any investigation. [Ref. Harvey Investigative Letter]. The use of Inspector General subpoenæ is reserved to IG investigations, and their deliberate misuse by the CID to circumvent law-enforcement subpoena requirements is illegal.

[348] No documentation of any such meetings is included or referenced in the ROI, nor provided to Plaintiff in Discovery in this lawsuit. If such meetings occurred, and if representatives from TJAG and the Army General Counsel's Office agreed with the CID's conspiracy to manufacture and falsify evidence, then these representatives and offices thereby proved their participation in the conspiracy - and probable direction of it, as they are superior to the CID in the Army chain of command.

[349] Concerning the initial titling decision, see Note #8 above. As above, there was no "investigative plan". As the letters from Helms to Marsh were confidential and in violation of federal law, they would certainly not be identified or discussed except at the highest levels of the Army, as the Judge Advocate General of the Army's personal briefing of Helms evidences. [Ref trip to brief Helms].

[350] There were no such "identified weaknesses" See note above.

[351] As evidenced from the ROI and all other CID actions connected with this case, the CID never made any attempt whatever to clear Lilith and myself, and instead suppressed or ignored all exculpatory evidence and manufactured false "evidence" in its agenda to frame us for a nonexistent crime. For instance, the CID's corruption of the AGR continuation board took place **at the very beginning** of its investigation. [Ref AGR board].

[352] The CID, however, ignored the interests of justice in the conduct of this investigation, in favor of its predetermined agenda. Again, the allegations were not made by Almond, or any other CDC child, but by the A-Ts.

CID Response

Plaintiff was not found fully qualified in accordance with AR 135-18, paragraph 4-11.[353] There is no record reflecting whether the Continuation Board knew of Plaintiff's flagging or a CID investigation.[354]

QUESTION SEVENTEEN

Myers Question

Please state why Plaintiff was denied promotion to full colonel. State whether or not Plaintiff's titling was before the promotion board.

CID Response

Plaintiff was not found fully qualified in accordance with AR 135-55, paragraph 3-9.[355] There is no record reflecting whether Plaintiff's titling was before the promotion board.[356]

QUESTION EIGHTEEN

Myers Question

Please describe in detail what steps Defendant, through the CID, has taken to corroborate the Adams-Thompsons' rendition of events. State what corroborating evidence exists to support the Adams-Thompsons' rendition of events.

CID Response

See response to Questions #1 and #8.[357]

In addition, Kinsey's statements were corroborated by interviews of CPT and Mrs. Adams-Thompson, who established Kinsey's shocked reaction to sighting LTC Aquino in the Presidio Post Exchange (paragraph 7.7 and 7.8, CID Aquino ROI).[358] The receipt from the Post Exchange as well as LTC and Mrs. Aquino's statements establish that the Aquinos were present in the Presidio Post Exchange on August 12, 1987 (paragraph 6.1 and 6.2, CID Aquino ROI).[359] Kinsey's recognition of 123 Acme as the place where she was taken by LTC Aquino

---

[353] I was fully qualified in accordance with AR 135-18.

[354] I was informed by the SJA, ARPERCEN that he had been asked by the board whether I were flagged and had answered "yes" in violation of AR 135-18. When writing this response, the CID was also aware - but concealed from Plaintiff - that it had deliberately corrupted the Continuation Board. [See Harvey/Tate statement.]

[355] Promotions to full colonel are on a "best qualified", not a "fully qualified" (as are AGR continuation decisions) basis.

[356] This response evades a direct answer. As the CID knows, all promotion board records are destroyed at the conclusion of each board. As with its corruption of the AGR board, the CID would know if it had similarly corrupted the promotion board, but again takes refuge behind a "no record" answer.

[357] See annotations to Questions #1 and #8.

[358] As the adult A-Ts were the only ones who on 8/14/87 alleged that the "PX sighting reaction" by Almond ever occurred [neither Almond nor anyone else made any statement about it for two years, after which time the A-Ts had had ample opportunity to train her into reciting the story], the A-Ts cannot "corroborate" their own story.

[359] The fact that Lilith and I were present in the PX on 8/13/87 corroborates no crime whatever.

corroborated her allegations.[360] LTC Aquino's leave throughout the summer of 1986, and LTC Aquino's statement that he remained in San Francisco during this leave eliminated a possible alibi defense (paragraph 6.1, CID Aquino ROI).[361] Mr. Gary Hambright's presence at the Presidio CDC on a daily basis made it possible for Mr. Hambright to remove children from the Presidio CDC.[362] The Presidio CDC's failure to maintain proper care of the children (parents indicated that the Presidio CDC often did not know the locations of their children; when it was time to pick up the children, the parents had to look all over the CDC to find them).[363] Steven Quigley also placed LTC Aquino at the Presidio CDC (paragraph 7.17, CID Aquino ROI).[364] Other children interviewed by the CID and medical personnel described ritualistic sexual abuse similar to that suffered by Kinsey Adams-Thompson (pages 48-55, CID Aquino ROI).[365] The interior contents of the Aquino residence provide limited corroboration of the statements of Kinsey Adams-Thompson.[366] Some of the items that Kinsey Adams-Thompson told LTC Hickey were contained in the house where she was sexually assaulted were found and photographed by the FBI during the search conducted

---

[360] No corroboration. Almond did not recognize 123 Acme, despite the FBI's and her mother's attempts to coach her into such an "identification". See 123 Identification trip.

[361] First, an alibi defense for any time-period prior to 9-10/86 is unnecessary, because Almond was never under Hambright's care or control at the CDC prior to that time. Second, Graham Marshall indeed provided an absolute alibi defense for the 1989-invented CID "backdate" to 6/10/86. Third, all of the other children who were at the CDC with Almond on 6/10/86, whom in 1989 she said "were taken with her" contradicted the A-Ts' falsified story (para 2.6-7, CID ROI).

[362] Children at the CDC were assigned to specific teachers in specific classes, and only children 3 years and older were assigned to Hambright (Presidio HQ letter to parents). Almond did not turn 3 until 9/1/86. Secondly, the A-Ts both stated to the FBI in their original interviews closest to the 9-10/86 accusation window that they noticed nothing wrong with Almond until that 9-10/86 period (A-Ts' original 1/87 FBI interviews). Third, Hambright denies the A-Ts' allegations (Statement of Hambright). Fourth, all other CDC teachers and staff denied that Hambright abused children or that they watched his classes while he took any children away anywhere (para. 2.8.1, CID ROI).

[363] While some parents may have had to look "all over" the CDC to find their children, descriptions of the CDC indicate that it was a single, small building with a fenced playground. That is hardly significant of "failure to maintain proper care", particularly if children were allowed to play with one another freely. Additionally the A-Ts never complained at any time that they couldn't locate Almond. Additionally Almond was always an unscheduled "drop-in" attendee, so any "abductor" would not have known when her parents would return.

[364] No corroboration. See Annotations to Question #4.

[365] Almond never mentioned "ritualistic sexual abuse" prior to being taught it by Hickey and Michele A-T, as the Hickey notes verify. No other Presidio children alleged that Lilith or I had committed any crime whatever. Finally, "therapist"- and parent-network-taught "descriptions of ritualistic sexual abuse" were a standard feature of all "abuse" witchhunts of the 1980s, and particularly after McMartin.

[366] No corroboration. The actual contents of our home were not described in any way by Almond before her parents and investigators knew exactly what it looked like from FBI photos taken during the 8/14/87 search warrant execution.

in August 1987 (page 22, and paragraph 19.10, Aquino CID ROI).[367] However this corroboration was limited due to the redecoration by the Aquinos and the passage of time between the sexual assault and the search by the FBI (pages 47-48, CID Aquino ROI).[368]

Additionally, Kinsey made references to Satanism by hand gestures to her mother and LTC Hickey (page 23, Exhibit 42, CID Aquino ROI).[369] LTC Aquino's writings and statements provide ample corroboration that he is involved in the Temple of Set, whose source is the Church of Satan.[370] Kinsey said that she was taken by Mr. Gary Hambright to a room with blankets on the walls (Exhibit 42, Diary of Mrs. Adams-Thompson, Exhibit 45 MFR by Major Harvey, CID Aquino ROI).[371] Aspects of Temple of Set worship include religious activities in a draped room (pages 27 and 29, CID Aquino ROI).[372] Religious ceremonies for the Temple of Set were conducted in 123 Acme in the apartment on the street level (paragraph 8.16, CID Aquino ROI).[373]

QUESTION NINETEEN

Myers Question

---

[367] First, Almond never told Hickey that she was sexually assaulted, except to recite Hickey's promptings that she was. Secondly, no corroboration. Many if not all homes contain "toys/stuffed animals, computer, guns". Of the other items that Harvey lists, they were either not ever mentioned by Almond to Hickey [see Hickey analysis] or did not exist in our home as Harvey describes them. What page #22 evidences is simply another effort by Harvey to manufacture "evidence" in obstruction of justice.

ROI paragraph #19.10 states that a notebook page containing the name "Mike Todo" in a list of names and phone numbers. As the CID was informed, this list was of persons who called concerning an apartment-vacancy advertisement. The CID did not bother to contact any of the persons on the list, including Todo, to verify this. That the CID did not consider this as anything other than a device to continue the frame of us is verified by the fact that they didn't make any attempt to contact Todo.

[368] First, there was no sexual assault at our home. Secondly, Harvey has no grounds whatever to state that our repairs and repainting "limited" the [nonexistent] "corroboration".

[369] No, **Michele A-T**, who wrote this in her diary after Hickey reports that Michele provided her with papers about "Satanic ritual abuse" [even if one assumes the photocopies of the "lost" diary provided in 1989 to be genuine], knew about this sign. There is no account anywhere of Almond using it spontaneously prior to her mother's interest in this theme.

[370] The fact that I have been a senior religious official in the Church of Satan and Temple of Set has been well-known and publicized since 1970 and 1975 respectively, including throughout the Army, and thus "corroborates" nothing.

[371] This is not a statement by Almond, but an allegation by **Michele A-T** in an obviously-manufactured marginal note in the photocopy of her "lost diary" provided in 1989 [**after** the A-Ts had been informed by the FBI that our home included a room with upholstered walls]. No "corroboration".

[372] No activities of the Temple of Set, as abundantly documented throughout its records since 1975, include "Satanic ritual abuse". As the CID knows, no children are permitted to join the Temple, or to participate or even be present at any of its activities, ritual or nonritual. Secondly, no draped room was found in the search warrant execution. Thirdly, the original plaster walls in our apartment [and that of Butch, to which the CID tried in 1991 to "relocate" the "crime"] would have shown nail or other high-up damage from hanging drapes or blankets. The CID never bothered to look, nor to request to look. Nor, had it looked, would it have found any such damage. Nor were any black blankets or drapes found in our home during the search warrant execution. Also many Temple of Set members who had attended religious ceremonies at our home could easily have testified that we never covered any part of our walls for them, nor did Butch. The CID never requested or attempted any such interviews.

[373] The simple fact that religious ceremonies for the Temple of Set were conducted at the homes of Priests of that religion "corroborates" nothing.

Please state why Plaintiff remains titled when Plaintiff's wife, a supposed co-conspirator, was dropped from titling for lack of probable cause. State whether Defendant believes Plaintiff acted alone.

If Defendant does not believe Plaintiff acted alone, then state with whom Plaintiff acted.

If Defendant does not state that Plaintiff acted with Plaintiff's wife, state what evidence points to Plaintiff acting without Plaintiff's wife, and state how Defendant concluded the titling conduct was done without participation of Plaintiff's wife.

CID Response

Kinsey Adams-Thompson's medical records indicate that Kinsey Adams-Thompson said that Mr. Gary Hambright, "Mikey", "Shamby", "Todo", "Kathy", "Dr. Steve", and/or "Sassy" were at the bad house where she was sexually molested.[374] Once Kinsey said that "Mikey" and "Shamby" were married (page #24, CID Aquino ROI).[375] On another occasion, Kinsey said that Sassy was Todo's girlfriend (page 21, CID Aquino ROI).[376]

The Defendant believes that Mr. Gary Hambright, LTC Michael Aquino, "Shamby", and possibly others conspired to remove Kinsey Adams-Thompson from the CDC for purposes of ritualistic sexual abuse.[377]

The decision to delete Mrs. Aquino from the subject block was based upon Kinsey's inability to pick Mrs. Aquino out of the video lineup (paragraph 9.19, CID Aquino ROI).[378] On August 12, 1987 Kinsey identified Mrs. Aquino as "Shamby".[379] However, Mrs. Aquino's proximity to LTC Aquino when viewed by Kinsey Adams-Thompson in the Presidio Post Exchange parking lot made this identification too suggestive to be reliable by itself.[380]

---

[374] Harvey refers to Hickey's "play-therapy" notes, not to physical medical examination records. As the CID provided only those pages of the Hickey notes that it felt it could use in the frame attempt, the annotations here may be supplemented by even more exculpatory facts in the illegally-concealed pages. Concerning these names, see in the analysis of the Hickey notes why none of them refer in the least sensibly to Lilith or myself.

[375] Per the Hickey notes it is **Michele A-T**, not Almond, who introduces the name "Mikey" on 6/30/87, then alleges "Mikey" as "Shambee's husband", then proceeds with hints that "Mikey" is an Army officer. Obviously the A-Ts had decided to accuse Lilith and myself in the witch-hunt by this time, and here Michele began to lay the groundwork.

[376] Almond never - even in the A-Ts' falsified "PX encounter" - referred to me as "Todo" or Lilith as "Sassy". Moreover Almond's comments concerning "Todo" and "Sassy" in the Hickey notes are so irrational as to be meaningless. See Hickey notes analysis.

[377] If the CID believes this in disregard of the massive and conclusive evidence that no such crime ever occurred, then the CID is incompetent. More obviously, of course, the CID is simply reciting a predetermined agenda in which all factual evidence is irrelevant.

[378] The decision to delete Lilith from the subject block was based upon my attorney Gary Myers reminding the CID that its titling of a civilian is illegal under *Posse Comitatus* law. When the CID learned that a lawsuit would follow any less-than-complete retraction of its fraudulent ROI, it removed what it thought were the most conspicuous and indefensible titlings, such as Lilith as a civilian and all titlings of me based on my religion *per se*. Almond's 1989 ability to recognize either Lilith or myself after two years of parental and investigator prompting is as irrelevant here as elsewhere.

[379] On 8/6/87 the A-Ts recognized Lilith and myself in the Presidio PX and falsely alleged "reaction/ recognition" by Almond, in keeping with their plan which first appeared on 6/2/87 with Michele laying the groundwork for Aquino accusations with Hickey. See PX expose and Hickey notes expose.

[380] As Lilith and I were together the entire time at the PX, including within the store, then by the same logic Almond's "identification" of me beside Lilith would have been "too suggestive to be reliable by itself". See PX expose.

The Defendant believes that Mrs. Aquino is the most likely suspect to be "Shamby". However, this belief falls slightly short of "probable cause".[381] During the video lineup, Kinsey's statement that woman #2 was "Shamby" indicates that Kinsey believed a woman of very similar appearance to Mrs. Aquino was "Shamby".[382] Defendant has given Mrs. Aquino the benefit of the doubt.[383] It is possible that a female of similar description to Mrs. Aquino was involved in the ritualistic sexual abuse of Kinsey Adams-Thompson at 123 Acme without the participation of Mrs. Aquino.[384] In recognition of this possibility, the Commanding General of CID decided to remove Mrs. Aquino from the title block.[385] Defendant does not believe Plaintiff acted alone. Defendant believes Plaintiff acted with Mr. Gary Hambright and with other unnamed and unidentified persons, who may include Mrs. Aquino.[386]

QUESTION TWENTY

Myers Question

Please state why June 10, 1986 is viewed as the critical date in this matter.

---

[381] If "Shambee" as Almond initially described her in the Hickey notes is either "a friend of hers at school who was spanked by Mr. Rogers on TV" and "had its (sic) neck broken" [probably a doll], then there are no grounds for the CID to consider Lilith "Shambee". On 7/7/87 Hickey asked Almond if Shambee worked at the school. Almond's answer - and the next three pages of the Hickey notes - were concealed by the CID and not provided to Plaintiff in Discovery.

[382] No, Almond's statement that woman #2 was "Shamby" indicates that Almond thought woman #2 was "Shamby". So why did the CID not title woman #2 if a single 1989 lineup response from Almond constituted "probable cause" to title, overwhelming all other considerations and evidence?

[383] The CID never gave Lilith any "benefit of the doubt" from the beginning, and in disregard of all serious evidence titled her for kidnapping and child molestation simply because she was married to me and to fulfill its agenda to intimidate me and destroy my career, the CID threatened and humiliated my wife as well.

[384] There is no evidence that Almond was ever sexually abused and/or kidnapped to 123 Acme by Lilith or myself. If the CID now changes its tune to portray Lilith as (a) evidence that Almond's alleged "PX identification" was unreliable and (b) uninvolved with the A-Ts' "kidnap/rape" scenario, then it would have to explain why Lilith, who lived in our home and provided a sworn statement that no such "kidnap/rape" ever occurred, was not believed. Secondly, as Almond's failure to "recognize" Lilith is called significant, the CID has no grounds to insinuate that a resemblance to her is significant.

[385] In light of the rampant violations of law throughout the ROI, the CID Commanding General's sudden attack of gallantry is ludicrous. Lilith's name was removed from the titling block for the reasons annotated above.

[386] In fact, Defendant knows that no such "crime" took place at all, and "believes" only the Helms mission it was given to do.

CID Response

June 10, 1986 is viewed as a significant date in the investigation, but not necessarily a critical date.[387]

Kinsey Adams-Thompson was one of the three children receiving care at the CDC on June 10, 1986.[388] Each of the three children said that at least one of the other two were (sic) with them at the "scary house".[389] Page 48, CID Aquino ROI explains why this date was considered the most likely date of the offense.[390] See also pages 19-24[5], 48-49[6], and 52-53[7], CID Aquino ROI to cross-reference the statements of the children.

---

[387] When the CID discovered that Lilith and I were in Washington, D.C. on all dates during the A-T 9-10/86 accusation window when Almond was at the Presidio daycare center, providing an absolute alibi proving our innocence and the A-Ts' conspiracy to make false allegations and defraud the government, the CID [in 1989] examined my Army records to find out when I **had** previously been in the city of San Francisco - three months before the 9-10/86 window - and simply created a new accusation date, as finding us innocent was not permitted in its agenda. When the CID says that 6/10 is "significant but not critical", it means that it was now treating the accusations as applicable to any date whatever. Had 6/10 proved inconvenient, the CID would clearly have either produced another date out of thin air or simply ignored the entire date-question, treating the A-T accusations as valid for all of 1986 [at least]. This CID mindset appears in Harvey's initial 12/14/88 letter to me, which asks not only for "all dates when LTC and Mrs. Aquino lived in San Francisco" but also "the dates when LTC and Mrs. Aquino were in San Francisco between January 1986 and July 1987".

[388] There is no evidence in the ROI or elsewhere as to how many children attended the CDC on 6/10/86, but presumably it was more than three.

[389] The CID focuses on these three because of their alleged statements that "at least one of the other two were (sic) with them at the 'scary house'". Apparently the entire CDC teaching staff denied that any such abduction took place, and all of the [presumably many] other children at the CDC denied seeing any such abduction either. This **preponderance of the evidence** is concealed by the CID.

The CID identifies the "other two" as Evan Fox and Kara Bailey. The CID states that the 6/10/86 revised date was invented in 1989 because that was "one date that Pamfiloff indicated Almond, Fox, and Bailey were present together in the CDC". No indication as to how Pamfiloff concluded this is given in the ROI or elsewhere. However in the same ROI paragraph (2.6, page #48) the CID states that "there are gaps in the records obtained from the Presidio CDC which make it difficult to reliably show when Kinsey Adams-Thompson, Kara Bailey, and Evan Fox were together in the CDC". So the CID can't even **reliably** state that 6/10/86 is such a date.

Fox' pre-CID interviews contain such scrambled and inconsistent statements as to be meaningless. (CID ROI 2.6.1, pages #48-51). On the other hand on 4/19/89 Fox **denied** to the CID "that he was removed from the CDC without his parents' permission by Mr. Hambright or the Aquinos" (CID ROI 2.6.1.(e), page #51). The Fox parents had a compelling motive to push the image of the Presidio scam as actual molestation, as they had filed $6 million in claims based upon this.

Bailey, like Fox, made no alleged references to anything remotely suggesting Lilith and myself until **after** the A-T accusation publicity, when Bailey's mother (a close friend of the A-Ts, ROI 2.6.3) made allegations on Kara's behalf in support of the A-Ts' allegations. Thereafter Bailey was interviewed by Pamfiloff and "either would not or could not identify LTC or Mrs. Aquino" and "repeatedly said she did not recognize the pictures from the Aquino/ Acme residence" (ROI 2.6.3). On 4/23/89 Bailey **denied** to the CID "that she was removed from the CDC without her parents' permission by Mr. Hambright or the Aquinos" (ROI 2.6.3, page #53).

So not only did Lilith and I, Hambright, the entire rest of the teaching staff of the CDC, and all other children at the CDC deny any 6/10/86 "kidnapping & sexual abuse", but **so did both Evan Fox and Kara Bailey, whom Almond supposedly said were with her**. Against this there is **only** Almond's two-years-later, parental/"therapist"-coached, and internally-contradictory answers to CID questioning, which "confusion" the CID states "is not surprising when one recalls that she was less than 3 when she was abducted from the CDC" (ROI 2.6, page #48.

[390] The CID's rationale for picking 6/10/86 for its 1989 invented date was **only** that Almond, Bailey, and Fox supposedly attended the CDC that day. However both Bailey and Fox denied that any such "kidnapping & sexual abuse" ever occurred, on that or any other day [see previous note].

QUESTION TWENTY-ONE

Myers Question

Please state who wrote the CID Report of Investigation. Give addresses and phone numbers of such persons.

CID Response

Major Mark W. Harvey
Headquarters, Sixth Region
U.S. Army Criminal Investigation Command
Presidio of San Francisco, CA 94129-6600
(415) 561-3812
Major Harvey wrote pages 15-57 of the ROI.[391]

Special Agent Steven Penaluna and Daniel S. Cates
Alaska Field Office, Sixth Region
Fort Richardson, Alaska 99505-7840
(907) 863-3148
Special Agent Cates wrote the remainder of the ROI.
Special Agent Steven Penaluna assisted in the preparation of the ROI.[392]

Master Warrant Officer Manfred Meine
Headquarters, Sixth Region
U.S. Army Criminal Investigation Command
Presidio of San Francisco, CA 94129-6600
(415) 561-3207
Master Warrant Officer Meine reviewed the ROI and made minor corrections [393] prior to approval by Colonel W.D. Ray, Sixth Region Commander.[394]

QUESTION TWENTY-TWO

Myers Question

Please state the exact role that Major Mark Harvey played in this investigation.

---

[391] In fact Harvey most probably wrote the **entire** ROI, as evidenced by his repeated bragging to my Army attorney Captain Hayes that he was doing so, as well as a comparison of the bias and writing styles of pages #15-57 with the rest of the ROI.

[392] Presumably the fiction that Cates and Penaluna had anything to do with the ROI besides shuffling papers and refilling Harvey's coffeecup is put forward here because only Cates' - not Harvey's [or Penaluna's or Meine's] - appeared as "Preparer" of the ROI (ROI page #134). Presumably it is illegal for a CID ROI to be signed by someone who did not in fact write it, just as it is illegal for the actual author to conceal his identity [and accordingly motives and biases].

[393] There is no "Master Warrant Officer" rank in the U.S. Armed Forces, and no indication that Meine had any role in this ROI or investigation whatever.

[394] Ray violated the law by signing a deliberately and obviously fraudulent ROI. See pretitling correspondence with Ray.

CID Response

Major Harvey is the region judge advocate for the Sixth Region, US Army Criminal Investigation Command, Presidio of San Francisco, California. His duties include providing legal advice to investigators and reviewing investigations for legal sufficiency, including titling determinations such as this one. In the course of these duties Major Harvey discussed the investigation with representatives of the San Francisco Police Department, the FBI, other military attorneys, his military superiors, and with LTC Aquino, his military defense counsel Captain Thomas Hayes, and his civilian counsel Mr. Gary Myers. Major Harvey interviewed most of the significant witnesses in the investigation and wrote pages #15-57 of the ROI.[395]

QUESTION TWENTY-THREE

Myers Question

Please state whether or not a claim on behalf of Kinsey Almond has been filed with the Army Claims Service, and if so in what amount.

CID Response

A claim on behalf of Kinsey Adams-Thompson has been filed with the Army Claims Service for the amount of $1,500,000.[396]

QUESTION TWENTY-FOUR

Myers Question

Describe in detail for each offense listed below what evidence Defendant relied upon to conclude that probable cause existed to believe Plaintiff committed such offenses: (a) Conspiracy, (b) Kidnapping, (c) Sodomy, (d) Indecent Acts, (e) False Swearing.

CID Response

See response to Questions #1 and #8.[397]

Kinsey told the FBI, LTC Hickey, and her mother:[398]

---

[395] In other words, Harvey conducted the "investigation" and wrote the ROI, which he represented to my Army attorney Captain Hayes as "approved" before Colonel Ray had even seen it, much less affixed his signature to it. See Ray correspondence.

[396] In fact the A-Ts filed claims for a total of **$3 million** - twice the amount the CID admits here. The CID's falsification of the amount is obviously to minimize the A-Ts' obvious financial motive for fabricating their accusations.

[397] See Annotations to Questions #1 and #8.

[398] Kinsey told the FBI and Hickey **none** of the following, as evidenced by the FBI reports and the Hickey notes included in the ROI. As for Michele A-T, there are only her allegations that Almond made any accusatory statements to her whatever, and these Michele allegations are impeached by Almond's own recorded statements to the contrary to the FBI and Hickey - as well as Michele's own forged/"lost" diary, $3 million motive, and own contradictory statements when trying with her husband to fabricate the accusations. See A-T Violations.

(a) that "Mr. Gary" (Hambright), "Mikey" (LTC Aquino) and "Shamby" (dark haired white female) removed her from the Presidio Child Development Center to a house identified as 123 Acme (conspiracy and kidnapping);[399]

(b) that while at a house identified by the FBI as 123 Acme, "Mr. Gary" and "Mikey" forced Kinsey to commit sodomy on them (conspiracy and sodomy);[400]

(c) that while at a house identified by the FBI as 123 Acme, "Mr. Gary" and "Mikey" committed indecent acts upon Kinsey when they forced her to touch their penis (sic) (conspiracy and indecent acts).[401]

The evidence that supports false swearing is provided in the response to Question #12.[402]

The CID Aquino ROI contains relevant evidence that tends to corroborate these essential facts.[403]

QUESTION TWENTY-FIVE

Myers Question

State when and when the offenses of conspiracy, kidnapping, sodomy, and indecent acts occurred, and describe what evidence supports each conclusion.

CID Response

The most probable location of the offense is the street level apartment, rented by Mr. Butch and owned by LTC Aquino at 123 Acme. See response to Question #2.[404]

The time of the offenses was May, June, July, or August 1986. This is based on the belief that Mr. Gary Hambright and LTC Michael Aquino were both in San Francisco during these months, and that Kinsey Adams-

---

[399] Almond never described me as "Mikey" to either Hickey or any investigator at the time of her parents' 1987 accusations. Almond made no mention of "Shambee"'s hair-color or race in the Hickey notes. [On 4/7/87 Almond said that Shambee and Sassy were the same person, then described Sassy as having blonde hair (4/7), then "black hair like Hickey" (who has brown hair) (4/28), then blonde hair again (5/12). Almond also said that Sassy had "yellow eyes like Hickey" (who has green eyes) (4/28). Lilith has neither blonde nor brown hair, nor yellow or green eyes.

Almond never "identified" 123 Acme as anything at all, despite the repeated prompting of the FBI and Michele A-T to get her to do so. See 123 Acme portion of A-T Violations and ROI Exhibit #1.

[400] As noted above, 123 Acme was never identified as any "crime scene" whatever. There is no evidence that Hambright and/or I ever "forced Kinsey to commit sodomy". There are only her parents' fabricated accusations.

[401] *Ibid*.

[402] There was no false swearing. See Annotations to Question #12.

[403] The ROI contains no evidence whatever corroborating either the original A-T accusations or the CID's 1989 attempts to revise them to fit its agenda. See in particular Annotations to Question #18.

[404] The first speculation of the Butch apartment was in 1991, **after** Graham Marshall testified that no children were present in our apartment. There is no evidence supporting the CID speculation at all. See Annotations to Question #2.

Thompson received care from the Presidio CDC at diverse times during these months.[405] There is evidence that Kinsey departed the Presidio CDC on at least one occasion with Mr. Hambright.[406] The specific date is unknown.[407]

See response to Question #24.[408]

QUESTION TWENTY-SIX

Myers Question

State specifically what evidence supports the identification of Plaintiff as a participant. State what person made the identification, to whom, when, and under what circumstances.

---

[405] Hambright had no supervision or control over Almond until September 1986. See January 1987 FBI interviews with the A-Ts (CID Lawsuit Exhibit #G2 - omitted from the original ROI), as well as Presidio DPCA letter 12/15/86. The fact that Hambright and/or I were in the same large city, and during a time when Hambright had no supervision or control over Almond whatever, is not evidence of anything except CID efforts to manufacture "evidence". Finally, if Almond indeed received care at the CDC during May-August 1986, why did the CID not investigate or interview the CDC teachers who **did** supervise her during that period? **All** such teachers - none of whom were ever indicted or convicted of any crime whatever - **denied** witnessing any such "kidnapping or abuse" of Almond at any time (ROI 2.8.1).

[406] There is no evidence other than Almond's coached recitations during the Hickey notes. On 4/7/87 Almond denied **twice** to Hickey being taken anywhere. Only after Hickey then continued to badger her did she agree with Hickey. Secondly, whether Almond was ever taken anywhere by Hambright or anyone else at any time is **not** "evidence" of any crime whatever by Lilith or myself.

[407] If "the specific date is unknown", then the CID's stated refusal to remove my name from the titling block "because the evidence of my alibi on 6/10/86 is not persuasive" is unjustified, as here the CID says that 6/10/86 is no more "known" than any other date.

[408] See Annotations to Question #24.

CID Response

The evidence that supports the identification of Plaintiff as a participant is contained in the FBI interviews, which are discussed in detail in the SFPD Aquino ROI[409] and pages 18-19[410] , 24-27[411] , 58-59, and paragraphs 2.2.1, 2.2.3, 4.1 of the CID Aquino ROI.[412]

See also page 13 of the sworn statement by LTC Aquino, dated January 27, 1989 (Exhibit 8, CID Aquino ROI).[413]

See responses to Questions #1 and #8.[414]

---

[409] None of the FBI interviews of Almond mentioned or discussed in the ROI even mention my name, much less describe or "identify" me. The 1/26/87 FBI interviews of the A-Ts mention neither me nor anyone resembling me. The 8/13/87 interviews of the A-Ts postdate their decision to fabricate accusations against Lilith and myself [evidenced in Michele A-T's 6/2/87 "Satanic cult" & 6/30/87 "Mikey the Army officer/Shamby's husband" suggestions to Hickey]. Hickey notes.

[410] ROI pages 18-19 discuss the 1/14/87 Almond FBI interview. This interview neither mentions my name nor describes or includes anyone resembling me. It is noteworthy rather as the investigative interview closest to the 9-10/86 accusation window, in which Almond denies any abuse whatever.

[411] ROI pages 24-27 discuss the 8/13/87 FBI interviews. These interviews all post-date the decision by the A-Ts to invent fictitious accusations against us as proved by Michele A-T's 6/2/87 and 6/30/87 suggestions to Hickey. Additionally in these interviews:

(a) Almond mentions nothing whatever about any "PX identification by her" (supposedly only the previous day), and does not "identify" me either by photo-lineup or otherwise. This interview also contains comments by Almond reciting her mother's previous 6/2/87 and 6/30/87 suggestions to Hickey, which do not appear at all in any investigative interview or "therapy" notes about Almond prior to then.

(b) The A-Ts give their own falsified accounts of the "PX encounter". See A-T Violations exposing this.

(c) Contrary to Harvey's narrative on page #26, there is no "FBI report" at ROI Exhibit #1. Rather there is only the narrative of CID Agent Potter, which establishes that Almond did **not** "identify" 123 Acme. See A-T Violations, 123 section.

Page 27 also refers to a 8/14/87 FBI interview of Almond. No such interview appears as an exhibit to the ROI nor was provided to Plaintiff in Discovery with all relevant FBI interviews.

Page 27 also refers to the 2-years-later CID interviews of Almond, which are (a) neither "FBI" interviews nor reliable because of the elapsed time and the vested interest by the A-Ts in continuing to coach and reinforce Almond during that interval.

[412] Pages 58-59 merely repeat interpretations of the 8/13/87 FBI and 4/89 CID interviews. Paragraph 2.2.1 merely comprises pages 18-19. Paragraph 2.2.3 merely comprises pages 24-27. Paragraph 4.1 merely comprises pages 58-59. See the annotation above.

[413] This page of my 1/27/89 sworn statement merely acknowledges that Lilith and I were in the Presidio PX on 8/12/87 and that one or both of the adult A-Ts obviously saw us there.

[414] See Annotations to Questions #1 and #8.

Appendix 65: Myers District Court Brief

United States District Court for the Eastern District of Virginia
Alexandria Division

Michael A. Aquino, Plaintiff
v.
The Honorable Michael P.W. Stone, Secretary of the Army
Department of the Army, Washington, D.C.,
Defendant

Civil Action No. 90-1547-A

Brief in Support of Plaintiff's Claim

Status of the Case

On November 15, 1990, Plaintiff filed a complaint seeking damages and a declaratory judgment to amend the titling action and to remove Plaintiff's name from the title block of United States Army Criminal Investigation Command (USACIDC or CID) Report of Investigation (ROI) final "C" -0610-88-CID026-69259 5K3/6F3/6E7/6A1/5M2/5Y2/ DIMIS under 5 U.S.C. #552 a(g)(1)(A) & (C) of the Administrative Procedure Act.

The statute specifically provides for *de novo* judicial review. This Honorable Court, therefore, is not limited to mere review of the agency action, but has the statutory authority instead to examine the underlying factors which gave rise to the agency action and to make an independent determination of the propriety of the titling action.

The parties have agreed to limit the attention of this Honorable Court to the record, exhibits obtained through discovery, interrogatory answers, briefs and oral argument.

Statement of Facts

Plaintiff, then an active duty Lieutenant Colonel in the United States Army, was titled by the CID on August 11, 1989 for "Conspiracy, Kidnapping, Sodomy, Indecent Acts or Liberties with a Child, Indecent Acts, False Swearing, Intentional Noncompliance with Article 30 - Uniform Code of Military Justice, Maltreatment of a Subordinate and Conduct Unbecoming an Officer" (Defense Exhibit D).

Plaintiff sought to amend the titling action, and requested that Plaintiff's name be removed from the title block (Plaintiff's Exhibit 1). The CID granted relief in part and denied relief in part, keeping Plaintiff titled for "Conspiracy, Kidnapping, Sodomy, Indecent Acts, and False Swearing" (Plaintiff's Exhibit 4). The test for titling is that of "probable cause" (AR 195-2, para. 4-4b).

Argument

There is no probable cause to believe Plaintiff should be titled for any offense.

"Probable Cause: Reasonable cause; having more evidence for than against. A reasonable ground for belief in the existence of facts warranting the proceedings complained of." - *Black's Law Dictionary*, 5th Edition, 1979

This is a story about bias, fear, scapegoating, and political influence converging to destroy the life and career of a competent and dedicated Army officer who held beliefs incompatible with the American mainstream.

That Plaintiff was an outstanding officer is not debated (Plaintiff's Exhibit 13). That he adopted Satanism as his religion is equally clear.

In April of 1986 a little girl, age 2, named Kinsey Almond, was taken for the first time to the Presidio Child Development Center (CDC) by her mother, Mrs. Adams-Thompson (Defense Exhibit G-1). Her father, an active-duty captain in the Chaplain's Corps, was a Presbyterian minister.

Kinsey was a sporadic, infrequent visitor to the CDC during April, May, June, July, and August of 1986, attending a total of 13 times - only once in June (June 10th) - and staying for an undetermined number of hours, varying from three hours to seven hours and fifty minutes (Defense Exhibit G-1). Kinsey was not a regular, and there was no certainty as to when she would be there or how long she would stay.

By September of 1986 Kinsey was three, and she went to a new class at the CDC headed by a man named Gary Hambright. After several weeks Kinsey's parents noted behavioral changes in Kinsey. **All was well before September.**

In the Fall of 1986 and Winter of 1987 she started telling her parents that she did not want to see Mr. Gary (New Defense Exhibit 15, not previously provided by the Government, attached hereto).

By January of 1987 her parents took Kinsey to a psychiatrist out of concern for her behavior.

The psychiatrist concluded on April 23, 1987:

"From the sessions I have had with Kinsey to this date, I have concluded that she participated in and witnessed sexual and, at times, perverted activities involving **an** adult and herself and other children enrolled at the Center with her. **I also have concluded that she has a great fear of a person at the school she identifies as "Mr. Gary" and that "Mr. Gary" is the adult with whom Kinsey experienced these activities."** (emphasis added)

There is **not the slightest mention of any person, to include Plaintiff, other than "Mr. Gary"**. Not a hint of other adult involvement is made.

An interview of the parents conducted by the FBI on January 26, 1987 confirms that the **Fall of 1986** was when Kinsey's problems began (Defense Exhibit G-2).

Although Kinsey had told her psychiatrist that she was raped and sodomized, a medical examination of this 3-year-old child in March of 1987 revealed **no evidence of physical abuse to either her vagina or rectum, and her hymen was intact** (Defense Exhibit E-18, p. 5; Defense Exhibit E-38, therapist's notes).

The FBI, with the San Francisco Police Department (SFPD), in January of 1987 began a full-scale investigation of the Presidio CDC and Gary Hambright. Multiple children came forward to tell of abuse.

Kinsey's father knew Plaintiff and of Plaintiff's belief in Satanism (Defense Exhibit E-12, p. 2).

Kinsey's mother kept a diary, which she says she copied, then lost the original. Defense Exhibit 42 is therefore what Kinsey's mother says are copies of pages from a diary kept by her contemporaneously with events. There is no proof that this is true, and no ability to test the original for authenticity if such an original ever existed.

Kinsey's mother's explanation of how she lost the diary is fascinating:

"I originally kept my journal on scraps of notebook paper. In **January 1989** I photographed my journal at the request of CPT Mark Harvey [CID military counsel]. I was so pleased how my journal looked after the loose notes were photocopied, I may have either misfiled or thrown away the original loose notes.

Sometime in early August 1987 I recopied (by hand) some of the original notes onto loose papers because they were not legible." (emphasis added) (Defense Exhibit 13)

Plaintiff's involvement in this case, brought on by Kinsey's parents, began August 12, 1987. The notes have no credibility, and were probably done after Plaintiff was involved.

Nonetheless this "diary" starts on June 26, 1987, to suggest that Kinsey was involved with two other persons named "Mikey" and "Shamby"; and on June 26, 1987 the "diary" says Kinsey's conduct suggested the occult was part of Kinsey's problem (Defense Exhibit E-42).

Incredibly this circumstance is not developed, because Kinsey is sent off to her grandparents on July 7, 1987 until August 9, 1987. The "diary" appears to stop for that month also, because Exhibit 42 is blank for that period. So it appears the "diary" was tailored to report on Kinsey or at least the mother's perceptions of Kinsey.

Interestingly, in the therapist's notes at Defense Exhibit 38 for June 30, 1987, Kinsey's mother told the therapist of "Mikey" and "Shamby" but said nothing of the occult. In fact the mother asked the therapist whether Satanic cults were involved on June 2, 1987 - fully 24 days before her allusion to the occult in her diary. This occurred in response to the therapist's inquiry as to why Kinsey was talking about dead people, had said her neighbor Dr. Steve had spanked Mr. Gary, and had said Dr. Steve was with Mr. Gary at Mr. Gary's house.

If there were such great concern for the occult on June 26, 1987, why was it not raised with the therapist on June 30, 1987? It is incredible that such a startling discovery would not have been revealed at that time, given the question asked on June 2, 1987.

What is even more telling is this: On July 2, 1987 the therapist met with Kinsey's mother alone, and there is no indication of Satanism or the occult in the conversation. But the therapist notes: "Met c mo. Pt talking c mo frequently now about events. Ma keeping track." The "keeping track" reference suggests that the procedure was a new event.

Kinsey went to her grandmother's on July 7, 1987, returned on August 9, 1987, and saw the therapist only on August 10, 1987. There was no mention of the occult. That therapy session closed with these notes:

> "Pt then said that I had "broken the lamp" and we needed to "talk about it". Pt. began to lecture me in a quiet controlled tone of voice and finally said "Honey, I'm sorry but this requires a spanking" and called Larry to "come up here" to give me a spanking." (Defense Exhibit 38).

"Larry" is, of course, Kinsey's father. The point is: At **no** time prior to August 12, 1987 did Kinsey's mother reveal Kinsey's supposed allusions to the occult to the therapist.

On August 12, 1987 Kinsey's parents reported to the FBI that Kinsey identified Plaintiff and Plaintiff's wife as "Mikey" and "Shamby" respectively, while shopping at the Presidio PX.

No law enforcement agency ever attempted to investigate the identification scene for corroborating witnesses.

On the 13th of August 1987 Kinsey's parents gave a statement to the FBI (Defense Exhibit G-3) and to the SFPD August 14, 1987. **Noteworthy is the fact that Kinsey's father told the police the dates of the criminal conduct were September 1, 1986 to October 31, 1986 (Plaintiff's Exhibit 1-D). This conformed to the statement made by Kinsey's mother to the FBI on January 26, 1987 (Plaintiff's Exhibit 1-F).**

There is **no** evidence that Kinsey **ever** personally identified Plaintiff as "Mikey" to any law enforcement agency by photo, line-up, or otherwise during August, September, or October of 1987. Kinsey's parents' statement that Kinsey identified Plaintiff was **not corroborated in any fashion** to include Kinsey's own identification.

These alleged crimes were believed to have taken place outside the CDC, because the children interviewed said they were taken to a house.

The FBI sought an identification of the house lived in by Plaintiff. On August 13, 1987 Kinsey was taken to Plaintiff's home in San Francisco. Although in the Report of Investigation (ROI) the CID says a positive identification was made (Defense Exhibit D, p. 7), the fact is that **no** identification was made.

The FBI agent on the scene reported:

"Approximately 10-15 feet before coming to the front of 123 Acme Avenue, Almond began to appear frightened and wanted to be held by her mother. Almond was picked up by her mother but continued to stare at the front of 123 Acme Avenue." (Defense Exhibit E-1).

This is not an identification of anything. The mother knew the address, and she knew her child. The "identification" is worthless.

Additionally it should be noted that Kinsey identified the Plaintiff's rental car as "Shamby's" while doing the house identification, which, of course, was impossible - since the car was not rented by Plaintiff in 1986 and neither Plaintiff nor his wife ever owned a red car. (Defense Exhibit E-1).

The FBI and the SFPD thoroughly investigated the case, and on August 1, 1988 the San Francisco District Attorney announced no charges would be filed against Plaintiff.

Prior to this time there was no active CID investigation of the Plaintiff.

On October 26, 1988 Wayne Bowles from Senator Helms' office complained to then-Secretary of the Army Marsh about Plaintiff.

The letter is reproduced here in its entirety. (Original at Plaintiff's Exhibit 1-G):

Jesse Helms
North Carolina

United States Senate
Washington, D.C. 20510

October 26, 1988

The Honorable John O. Marsh, Jr.
Secretary of the Army

Dear Secretary Marsh:

I am writing first as a citizen of the great nation of ours and secondly as an employee of our federal government, concerning a cancer in the military, specifically a cancer within the Army.

Last evening I viewed a program hosted by Geraldo Rivera on Satanism and Witchcraft. I was appalled to learn that a Colonel Aquino of the United States Army was a founder of the Temple of Set, a satanic cult. I believe he is stationed in St. Louis.

To my view, this is disheartening. Here is a military man who has taken an oath to defend God and country who practices a religion that is completely contrary to the oath he swore to uphold. If you or any member of your staff saw this telecast I am confident your reaction was identical to mine.

This individual should not be allowed to remain in the Army, his military service record notwithstanding. I am respectful of any individual's right to his first amendment prerogatives to worship. However, I cannot believe the Constitution is intended to protect those individuals who have a belief system that espouses the killing and sacrifice of infants and the ritual torturing of children.

I would appreciate your looking into the existence of satanic worship in the Army and it's [sic] adherents. Perhaps it may be necessary to hold Congressional hearings to consider appropriate legislation in this matter.

Kindest regards,

Sincerely,
/s/ Wayne Ronald Boyles, III
Legislative Assistant to Senator Jesse Helms

The Army recognized that Bowles was simply a surrogate for the Senator by responding directly to Senator Helms and bypassing Bowles in a letter of December 8, 1988. This letter represents a rational constitutional standard (Plaintiff's Exhibit 1-H).

Helms decided to keep the heat on the Army, and on January 9, 1989 wrote a letter to the Secretary of the Army. This letter is also included in its entirety. (Original at Exhibit 1-I):

Jesse Helms
North Carolina

United States Senate
Washington, D.C. 20510

January 9, 1989

Dear Jack:

Except for two or three trips back to Washington, I've been working out of our Raleigh office since the Senate adjourned in late October. Yesterday in going through a stack of material sent to me in Raleigh, I ran across a December 27 clipping from *The Washington Times* about a Lt. Col. Michael Aquino who identifies himself as a "Satanist" and who claims that this is his "religion".

Either the man needs psychiatric help, or the Army doesn't need <u>him</u>. The fact that he has twice appeared on national television seems to me to demonstrate that he doesn't have all four wheels on the ground.

This is not a matter of freedom of religion. Satanism is not a religion.

I tried yesterday to reach you at your home through the White House switchboard, but learned that you are in Germany. When you get back, would you give me a ring? Maybe there's something I missed in translation, but I do not understand how the Army decided to "stand by" Colonel Aquino - if indeed the newspaper account is accurate.

The most charitable thing that can be said of the colonel is that he is a nut. If that is the case, I might have some sympathy for him but I still do not believe that he should be "handling budgets" for the Army Reserve Personnel Center - or anywhere else. Perhaps I am dismayed at his arrogance as much as anything else.

In any event, please let me have the Army's side of it - and I sure would appreciate a call from you.

Sincerely,
/s/ Jesse

The Judge Advocate General of the Army physically met with Senator Helms to discuss the Aquino matter in late January or early February of 1989 after discussion with the Secretary of the Army (Plaintiff's Exhibit 1-J).

In response to Plaintiff's request for letters sent to the Army by Helms, Helms sought refuge behind the Senate's Legal Counsel (Plaintiff's Exhibit 1-K).

By November 9, 1988 the Army was already taking action on the Helms surrogate letter (Plaintiff's Exhibit 1-L).

On November 23, 1988 the CID began its investigation. There is no evidence that the CID had any interest in investigating the Plaintiff from August 1, 1988 - the date San Francisco publicly stated no charges would be brought - until November 23, 1988. The investigation did not get into full swing until March of 1989.

At Plaintiff's Exhibit 2, p. 27 is Defendant's interrogatory answer as to why the CID initiated the investigation. The CID tells us that the FBI and SFPD investigation were deficient. Here is an extremely-high-profile case which is on television and on newspapers daily, and the CID wants this Honorable Court to believe the FBI and the SFPD did not do their job.

By March of 1989 the investigation was clearly stale. Plaintiff nonetheless cooperated fully with the investigation, including allowing an interview in his home in St. Louis, where he and Lilith Aquino answered all questions propounded by the CID. The Army apparently did not expect Plaintiff's cooperation, as is evidenced by the memorandum at Plaintiff's Exhibit 1-M.

It is significant that at no time did Plaintiff fail to be responsive to reasonable inquiries made by the CID.

On November 29, 1988 a high-level meeting at the Pentagon was held to discuss the Aquino matter, including the following persons: TJAG, ODCSPER, DACH, PA, OCLL, M&RA, GC (Plaintiff's Exhibit 1-N).

There can be little doubt that the Army adopted a policy of appeasement in its dealings with Senator Helms. Plaintiff was expendable. The solution was twofold: namely to deny Plaintiff continuation as an AGR officer, and to title Plaintiff without ever charging him. The way to accomplish that was to allow the Statute of Limitations to run prior to the titling, and to use the Statute of Limitations as an excuse for avoiding a public trial that surely would end in an acquittal.

The test for continuation as an AGR officer was merely "fully qualified", which Plaintiff was without doubt (Plaintiff's Exhibit 1-M, p. 7-9, memo from LTC John Burton). But when the Continuation Board improperly asked if Plaintiff were flagged, as such a question falls outside the Board's proper review, and was improperly told "yes, due to the investigation" (Plaintiff's Exhibit 1-M, p. 4), Plaintiff was denied (Plaintiff's Exhibit 10).

The CID had ample opportunity to finish its investigation and get Plaintiff titled long before the Statute of Limitations ran.

In a phone conversation with military counsel to the CID, Counsel for Plaintiff learned that the Army had decided not to charge Plaintiff **before the titling action was completed**. Assuming the accuracy of the representation, why then proceed with a titling action?

There is only one available answer, and that lies in the interplay between the Army and Senator Helms. The titling action for such heinous crimes effectively destroyed Plaintiff's career and labeled him for life. Helms was satisfied.

By knowingly allowing the Statute to run, there was an excuse for no prosecution, and no chance for Plaintiff's vindication in a public forum.

Knowing that the matter would not be prosecuted gave the CID license to say or conclude whatever they wished.

By the time the CID got involved, **all relevant allegations pointed to the Fall of 1986 in San Francisco for the alleged abuse of Kinsey**.

But when the CID discovered that they could **not** fit the Satanist Plaintiff into that Fall because Plaintiff was **not** in San Francisco, the CID - with Kinsey's parents' silent concurrence - created a new scenario and a new time frame.

Since Plaintiff was on leave and in San Francisco from June 3, 1986 to July 18, 1986, the CID and Harvey did this:

"Further investigation shifted the time of Almond's kidnapping from CDC from the Fall of 1986 to June-July 1986. This change was based on the CDC records and the canceled checks maintained by Mrs. Adams-Thompson." (Defense Exhibit D-1, p. 56).

Neither the CDC records nor the checks could form a basis for shifting the focus of the investigation. The records and checks just show that the child was at the day care center in June, July, August, September and October of 1986. They are passive records. There is no dynamic associated with them that allows one to conclude June-July was preferable to September-October.

The "shift" is **unsupported**. The lack of support is of no moment, however, because the investigation missed critical exculpatory evidence which was readily discoverable by the investigators but which they chose not to pursue.

The investigators were told that in the June-July period Plaintiff had substantial work done on the interior and exterior of his home at 123 Acme, San Francisco, "the crime scene" and the place where Kinsey was allegedly abused. (Defense Exhibit D-1, p. 26) Plaintiff delivered to the the investigators the names, addresses, and telephone numbers of the artisans who worked at the home and the property contiguous to it, also owned by Plaintiff.

The CID followed certain of these leads and ignored others. Those that were followed were followed only for the limited purpose of seeking inculpatory evidence (Report P. 70, 71, and 95). No attempt was made to seek exculpatory evidence, but such exculpatory evidence **was** there among the ignored.

Plaintiff has the **absolute defense of alibi** for the June-July time period.

E. Graham Marshall was a painter in San Francisco who was hired by Plaintiff in the Spring of 1986 to paint first the interior and then the exterior of the alleged crime scene, 123 Acme, San Francisco, California. (Graham Marshall's affidavit is attached as Plaintiff's Exhibit 1-A).

Kinsey was at the CDC on the following dates in June and July of 1986: June 10; July 2, 9, 11, 17. This information comes from the checks Kinsey's mother wrote to the CDC (Plaintiff's Exhibit 6).

What is critical to understand is that June 10, 1986 became the focus of the entire investigation. Kinsey had told investigators that other children had been with her in the "house". The only date Kinsey and the children named were together at the CDC during the time Plaintiff was in San Francisco was June 10, 1986.

In every CID status report provided by the government, the only date named for the offenses alleged is June 10, 1986 (Plaintiff's Exhibit 5). There is absolutely no consideration of another date by the CID.

On June 10, 1986 E. Graham Marshall, the painter from San Francisco, as was his practice, went to Plaintiff's home, the alleged crime scene, to work on the interior. This is what happened from Marshall's affidavit (Plaintiff's Exhibit 1-A):

"22. I specifically and distinctly recall being at 123 Acme on June 10, 1986.
    a. One June 10, 1986 I specifically recall staining cabinets in the observation room. These cabinets were stained a dark color.
    b. I arrived between 7:45 and 9:00 AM as usual.
    c. Since June 10, 1986 was a completion day, I did not go to lunch.
    d. After completion of final touch-up, including cabinet and window sill work, Michael Aquino and I discussed a proposal for work to be performed on the exteriors of 121 and 123 Acme.
    e. I did not leave the premises until after 4:00 PM.
23. At no time whatsoever did I see any children enter or leave 123 Acme on June 10, 1986."

Marshall remembers June 10, 1986 because of the exterior contract he typed that evening, then signed, dated, and delivered to Respondent on June 11, 1986 following his completion day June 10, 1986. (Exhibits II and III of the Affidavit)

Marshall's affidavit clearly states that Marshall was at Plaintiff's home, the alleged crime scene, every day that Kinsey was at the CDC in July. On this point his Affidavit is clear: There were **no** children. There was **no** crime committed by Plaintiff.

In addition the checks show rather clearly that Kinsey was an infrequent visitor to the CDC and that her stays varied in time. What the CID wants this Honorable Court to believe is that Plaintiff, in concert with Gary Hambright, took this child, who in June was not in his class, from the CDC, not knowing when she would be there and not knowing how long she would stay, molested her in Plaintiff's home, and successfully returned her to the CDC without anyone knowing that she, Gary Hambright, or other children were gone.

Now, of course, the CID had to deal with Graham Marshall's Affidavit. At Plaintiff's Exhibit 13 is the titling opinion from the Army's Office of the Judge Advocate which served as the basis to find that there was no probable cause to title Mrs. Aquino, the Plaintiff's wife, notwithstanding the fact that Kinsey had positively, at least according to her parents (Defense Exhibit E-42, August 12, 1987; Defense Exhibit E-12), identified Mrs. Aquino as "Shamby".

One line is devoted to the Affidavit: "The evidence of alibi offered by LTC Aquino is not persuasive."

No, and why not? The only investigation the CID did to confirm the Affidavit is a phone call from the CID's lawyer to Graham Marshall at Plaintiff's Exhibit 7.

This transcript created a new problem for the CID. The alibi held up. Marshall was there in Aquino's home on June 10, 1986 for the entire day, and he never did see any kids.

For the second time in this scarred and disgraceful investigation, the CID conformed new-found facts to the desired result.

Plaintiff's home had an apartment on the first floor. Plaintiff's brother-in-law, a Navy Commander, lived there. The apartment had never been searched by the FBI, SFPD or CID. There was never a hint that the apartment could be the crime scene. The pictures at Defense Exhibit E-3 taken by the government were of Plaintiff's home in the upper floors.

Now, after three years of investigation, with Plaintiff already titled, the CID lawyer suggests to Marshall at page 7 of the transcript that Plaintiff could have taken children into the Plaintiff's brother-in-law's apartment without Marshall's knowledge. Marshall said, "It's conceivable."

Based on that statement the Army concluded that the alibi was "not persuasive".

Now, of course, the crime scene is Bill Butch's apartment. For an exhaustive discussion of the 1991 version of the crime scene, see Defendant's Answers to Interrogatories at Plaintiff's Exhibit 2, p. 4-6. Everyone should have known it all along. But, as is usual in sloppy, incompetent, and preconceived result-directed investigations, the CID failed again to investigate.

If the CID had investigated by contacting Bill Butch, Plaintiff's brother-in-law, the CID would have discovered what Bill Butch always knew. Butch's apartment looked nothing like what the children described. Beyond that, Bill Butch worked all night on June 10, 1986, went home, went to bed, and got up in the afternoon. He never saw any children at the Plaintiff's home. Defense Exhibit 8, Affidavit of Bill Butch.

So lightly regarded was the apartment during the investigation that Bill Butch was never interviewed by the FBI, the SFPD, or the CID.

Beyond all of the above, there is no evidence of any kind in the ROI that Plaintiff knew or had any association with Hambright.

Kinsey was under Hambright's control **only in September and October of 1986**. During June and July she had another teacher (Defense Exhibit 1-B). Plaintiff was not in San Francisco during September-October 1986. **This clearly exculpatory information is knowingly excluded from the ROI.**

In June, how did Hambright get this child out of someone else's class? There is no explanation.

The CID said at Defense Exhibit D-1, p. 26 of the ROI: "The number of times that Almond received care at the CDC in the Fall of 1986 is irrelevant, because LTC Aquino was out of the State of California the majority of the Fall of 1986." If this statement is true, then **why does all the evidence point to the Fall time frame, and why is there no evidence that anything happened or could have happened before September 1, 1986**?

The inescapable truth of the matter is that **once the investigators discovered that an alibi defense existed for the Fall of 1986, they attempted to contort the truth, with Kinsey's parents' support, to gain a result not supported by fact**.

What is telling is found in Defense Exhibit D-1, p. 8 of the ROI.

"During the course of this investigation, no child who attended the PSF CDC and was interviewed, with the exception of Almond, identified either LTC or Mrs. Aquino as one of their assailants (paragraph 4, 7, and 8 this report).
"During the course of this investigation, no child who was interviewed identified 123 Acme Ave., SF, CA from a photographic line-up as a location to which they had been taken (paragraph 8 and 9, this report)." (Emphasis Added).

The CID and Major Harvey rely upon interviews of Almond in April of 1989 to substantiate the titling action. This child was three years old in 1986, and after more than two years the CID is willing to accept what she says about events that occurred in 1986 as though those events happened yesterday. Not only is her memory utterly suspect under such a circumstance, as her conflicting statements demonstrate, but also she has had an opportunity to see pictures of Plaintiff and to be influenced by her parents and others.

The ultimate reality is that **Kinsey's parents** were the moving force in this entire matter. They now have a claim filed with the government for $1.5 million on behalf of Kinsey and $1.5 million on behalf of themselves.

Conclusion

There is not the slightest hint of probable cause to title Plaintiff.

Respectfully submitted,
/s/ Gary R. Myers
Attorney for Plaintiff

May 16, 1991

- 428 -

Appendix 66: TJAG/CID District Court Brief Statements Analysis

False Official Statements by Major Patrick Lisowski in
Memorandum in Support of Defendant's Motion for Judgment on the Record
U.S. District Court, Eastern District of Virginia
Case #90-1547-A
- identified as of December 16, 1991 by Lt.Col. Michael A. Aquino -

Page 3:   *#4. On August 12, 1987 Kinsey was at the Presidio Post Exchange (PX) with her parents. At about 4:00 PM, as they walked through the store, Kinsey ran to her parents, frightened, and told them that she had seen "Mikey" from "Mr. Gary's house". Kinsey's mother picked her up, and Kinsey pointed at the plaintiff, LTC Michael Aquino, and identified him as "Mikey". Kinsey said she was afraid and wanted to leave the store. CPT Adams-Thompson recognized LTC Aquino from his prior assignment at the Presidio. He took Kinsey from Mrs. Adams-Thompson and carried her out of the store to the parking lot. When the Aquinos exited the store, Kinsey identified Mrs. Aquino as "Shamby", another person who she saw with "Mr. Gary". After returning home, Kinsey said that she was afraid that "Mikey" and "Shamby" would come to her home and hurt her.*

1.   The supposed "PX encounter" is here presented as established fact, when Lisowski knows that in August 1987 the "details" of Kinsey Almond's presence and supposed actions were merely unsubstantiated/uncorroborated [by Almond or anyone else] allegations by Lawrence and Michele Adams-Thompson (A-T). All that is established fact is that Mrs. Aquino and I were at the PX and that one or both of the adult A-Ts saw us there, that this took place **after** it had been decided to merchandise Almond as a "victim" in the ongoing Presidio scam, and **after Michele** had already introduced the subject of Satanism (6/2/87) and insinuations concerning me (6/30/87) into her discussions with Debbie Hickey.

2.   The adult A-Ts offered at least three conflicting and inconsistent versions of what Almond is supposed to have said in the PX [see enclosed list of A-T Violations of Article #133 UCMJ, Section C]. This in itself discredits this effort by them as obviously manufactured on the spur of the moment and revised thereafter to try to adjust to inconvenient facts as they emerged.

3.   The version that Almond "told her parents that she had seen 'Mikey' from 'Mr. Gary's house' was invented by **Michele** for **her** statement to FBI agent Foreman on 8/13/87. One day later Lawrence A-T gave two completely different versions to the CID and the SFPD [A-T Violations #44-46].

4.   In **none** of the preexisting versions of what Almond said or did at the PX was it said that "Kinsey's mother picked her up and she pointed at Lt.Col. Aquino". This is a new fabrication in this brief by Lisowski.

5.   The supposed statement by Almond that "she was afraid and wanted to leave the store" was not invented until Lawrence A-T's 4/10/89 interview with the CID - over 1-1/2 years after the PX encounter date.

6.   "When the Aquinos exited the store, Kinsey identified Mrs. Aquino as 'Shamby', another person who she saw with 'Mr. Gary'." This alleged identification is demolished in A-T Violations #50-59.

7.   "Shambee" (Hickey's spelling)

- appears in the Hickey notes first on 1/27/87, introduced by Almond as "her friend at school" who was spanked by Mr. Rogers on TV. Almond added that Shambee "also had its neck broken", indicating that "Shambee" is either an imaginary "friend" or perhaps a doll.

- There is no record of the FBI/SFPD/CID interviewing either teachers or other children at the Presidio day-care center to see if anyone used or was known by the name "Shambee".

- There is no mention of "Shambee" by any other child.

- On 4/7/87 Almond said that Shambee and Sassy were the same person, and that Sassy was Todo's girlfriend. After this neither Almond nor Hickey used the name "Shambee" anymore, discussing only "Sassy".

- "Shambee" is reintroduced as "Mikey's wife" by **Michele A-T** on 6/30/87.

- On 7/7/87 Almond told Hickey that "Nancy and Shambee were good mothers"

- On 7/7/87 Hickey asked Almond if Shambee worked at the school. Almond's answer - and anything else she may have said as a follow-up on the next three pages of Hickey's record - **has been concealed by the CID**.

8.   Almond's "statement after returning home" is again only an allegation by the adult A-Ts, not established fact as stated here by Lisowski.

Pages 3-4.   *#5. FBI Agent Foreman interviewed Kinsey at 9PM the next day, August 13th. She told him that "Mikey wears Army clothes like my daddies [sic]" and that "Mikey" put his penis into her mouth, bottom, and vagina just like "Mr. Gary".*

1.   This is not substantiated by any entry concerning "Mikey" in the Hickey notes until 6/30/87, following Michele A-T's introduction of the idea of a "Satanic cult" to Hickey on 6/2/87.

2.   On 6/30/87 it is **Michele, not Almond**, who introduces "Mikey" to Hickey, alleging that "Mikey is Shambee's husband". Michele then alleges to Hickey that Almond told her that "Mikey wore an 'Army suit' with a stripe on the pants". **None** of these allegations by Michele were checked by Hickey in her 6/30 direct questioning of Almond, and Almond herself made **no mention of any of them** during the session.

3.   To Hickey - inconsistent with the Foreman interview - Almond said that Mikey "put his penis in her mouth and peed on her, and put poo-poo in her mouth". During all of the preceding sessions she had made the same statements concerning (a) Hambright, (b) "little boys", (c) all of the children at "the house", (d) Sassy, (e) Todo, (f) the cross, (g) the bible, (h) the female doll, (i) the penis in the pot hanging from the ceiling with arms and legs in it, and (j) Dr. Steve.

Page 4.   *#5. Kinsey told her mother that "Mikey" was the "blood man" because he had put blood on her and licked it off.*

1.   This alludes to **Michele A-T**'s 8/13/87 statement to Foreman, **not** Almond's.

2.   The elaboration "because he had put blood on her and licked it off" is **not** in that Michele A-T 8/13/87 statement.

3. Calling "Mikey" the "blood man" is not in any of the Hickey notes, either by Almond or by Michele. Clearly it was a later invention by Michele.

Page 4.   *#5. Mrs. A-T also recalled that Kinsey had described "Mikey" as having "eyebrows that went up".*

1. Again this is from the **Michele** interview, **not** the Almond one. All it indicates is that **Michele** knew what I looked like after seeing me at the Presidio and in the PX.

2. Lisowski tries to create the impression that everything in paragraph #5 of his brief was from direct statements of Almond to Foreman. As shown here, this is **not** the case at all.

Page 4.   *#6. In addition to the identification at the PX ...*

1. Again, there are **only** the allegations of the two adult A-Ts that Almond ever "identified" me at the PX, or was even there at all. Lisowski suggests that this "Almond PX identification" is established fact.

Page 4.   *#6. Kinsey identified plaintiff out of a five-person photo lineup and video lineup.*

1. When? **Only 1-1/2 years later** during the CID 4/7-8/89 interview, after Almond had certainly been exposed to my picture and video image endlessly by her parents, therapist(s), investigator(s), and anyone else with an interest in furthering the scam.

2. During the St. Louis interview of us in May 1989, the CID showed us the photo-lineup used. It contains several other persons besides me, **none** of whom has either my distinctive widow's peak nor distinctive upturned eyebrows. Some had beards and mustaches. My photo was placed in the direct center of the lineup. Under such circumstances, such a "photo lineup" is so staged as to be worthless.

3. The lineup was in explicit violation of CID regulation 195-1, which states that:

    • "a lineup is appropriate when ... the witness does not know the identity of the perpetrator ..."

    • "the persons portrayed in the photographs should be reasonably similar in appearance."

    • "there should be three or more viewings with the positions of the photographs varied each time."

    • "The special agent conducting the photo lineup will identify in the ROI narrative which photographs were used, their positions in the lineup, and the results."

    • All of these CIDR 195-1 requirements were violated in this case. Where the "ROI narrative" is concerned, the only discussion - which does not meet the above requirements - is on pages #101-2 of the ROI.

4. Since in the same CID interview Almond failed to "identify" either Mrs. Aquino (about whom the adult A-Ts alleged she had been so certain at the PX) or 123 Acme (which was supposed to "terrify" her), what does this say about the value of any "lineup identification" of me?

Pages 4-5. *#7. After Kinsey's interview she was taken to the vicinity of plaintiff's house, which is about two miles, a seven-minute drive from the CDC. G.E. D-5 (Crime Scene Examination) at 65. Accompanied by her mother and two investigators, and starting about one and a half blocks from plaintiff's house, Kinsey walked down the street where plaintiff lives. Upon approaching plaintiff's house, Kinsey appeared to be frightened and asked to be held by her mother. After being picked up she continued to stare at the front of 123 Acme Avenue, where plaintiff lived. Kinsey said that the area was familiar and she had been there before. When asked if this was "Mr. Gary's" house, she answered yes, and stated that "Mr. Gary" had driven her there, where she met "Mikey" and "Shamby". G.E. E-1 (SA Potter's Report); G.E. D-4 (Interview of Victim) at 59.*

    1.   The supposed "123 Acme Avenue identification trip" is demolished in items #60-72 of A-T Violations.

Page 5.   *#8. Captain A-T reported the PX identification and Kinsey's statements to the San Francisco Police Department (SFPD), and, based on this evidence, a magistrate determined that probable cause existed to issue a search warrant for the top apartment at 123 Acme Avenue, plaintiff's residence. G.E. D-5 (Crime Scene Examination) at 65, G.E. E-5 (SFPD Incident Report dated August 14, 1987, following Aquino statement dated January 4, 1988). During the search the FBI photographed the interior of the apartment and some weapons, masks, and ceremonial items observed there. G.E. E-3. The three other apartments in the house and the house next door at 121 Acme Avenue were not searched, although later investigation disclosed that plaintiff owned both buildings G.E. D-19 at 119.*

    1.   The search warrant specified 123 Acme, not merely the "top apartment". The SFPD, the CID, and the FBI could have search the entire building that night. I specifically asked them if they wanted to, and they declined.

    2.   The other premises at 123 and 121 Acme were all leased to tenants at the time. The SFPD/FBI/CID made no effort to see these premises nor to interview any of the tenants throughout the investigation.

    3.   The fact that "weapons, masks, and ceremonial items" were observed in our home is irrelevant. Many if not most homes contain [like ours] one or more legal firearms - particularly homes of professional military families. Commercial Halloween-style masks are also neither unusual nor "evidence", nor is it unusual for a religious official to have "ceremonial items" in his home. What **is** relevant and pertinent is that in **none** of the Hickey sessions did Almond discuss or mention either "masks" or "ceremonial items".

    4.   "Weapons, masks, and/or ceremonial items" were not identified in the search warrant as relevant to the investigation.

    5.   No "weapons, masks, or ceremonial items" were confiscated in the search.

    6.   These three "sinister images" are clearly introduced into the brief by Lisowski only for dramatic effect.

Page 5.   *#9. Although Kinsey's reactions to the photographs are not conclusive, the photographs do show a number of items that corroborate Kinsey's and the other children's descriptions of the house where they were taken: (1) masks, (2) guns, (3) toy animals or dinosaurs, (4) a lion picture on the wall and lions on the Egyptian throne, (5) a computer, (6) cameras, (7) a black room with soft walls, and (8) a robot. G.E. E-38 (Excerpts of Kinsey's medical records) at 31, 32, 38; G.E. D-14 at 109; G.E. D-2 at 22.*

    1.   "Kinsey's reactions to the photographs are not conclusive ...":

- The FBI did not show Almond any photos of other buildings or interiors other than 123.

- Almond made **no identifications at all** from the photos. When she made a comment about a photo in one of the two sessions, it was either contradicted or invalidated by her comment or lack of one concerning the identical photo in the other session.

- Almond asked the FBI agent if the photos were of **his** house!

- Almond noticed items in the photos which didn't even **exist** until after October 1986.

- During the same session Almond identified "sisters" of hers who did not exist, despite Michele's hasty effort to coach her through a revised response.

2. "Masks": Discussed above. Also a generic staple of all "Satanic child molestation" scams nationwide by this time.

3. "Guns": Discussed above. Also a generic staple of the scams.

4. "Toy animals or dinosaurs": Almond **never** mentioned toy animals [except the ones she was playing with in Hickey's office]. Neither were "toy animals" mentioned in the Hickey, Michele, or Lawrence A-T allegations.

5. "A lion picture on the wall and lions on the Egyptian throne": On 8/13/87 Almond told FBI agent Foreman that the house had "a bathtub with lion's feet". She made no other mention of lions whatever, in any context.

   - As the search verified, our bathtub does not have lion's feet [or feet of any kind].

   - Attempts to stretch "a bathtub with lion's feet" into anything whatever with lions on it in our residence are fraudulent and a deliberate attempt to obstruct justice by concealing exculpatory evidence (the actual design of our bathtub) and manufacturing false "evidence".

   - This attempt to manufacture "evidence" is all the more significant because, of this entire list of "relevant items", **only "a bathtub with lion's feet"** was actually mentioned by Almond to Foreman on 8/13/87. She mentioned **none** of the other items to him.

6. "A computer": Not mentioned by Almond to Foreman on 8/13/87 nor alleged by Lawrence A-T to the SFPD on 8/14/87. As with legal weapons, personal computers are a common feature of many, if indeed not most homes today.

7. "Cameras": Again an item generic to almost every home.

8. "A black room with soft walls": As with the lion-theme above, an attempt by Lisowski to manufacture evidence by deliberately distorting facts.

   - In the 5/18/87 Hickey notes Almond said that she saw "a cross and it was a bad one that went peepee".

   - On 8/14/87 Lawrence A-T changed this into "a living room with black walls and a cross on the ceiling" to make it sound less ridiculous to the SFPD.

   - When the SFPD searched our home, they found the living room was beige and had no cross on the ceiling. Our bedroom was black/silver/red, but is only big enough for our bed, could not be mistaken for a "living room", and also contains no cross on the ceiling, white or otherwise, "peepeeing" or otherwise.

- After the A-Ts learned that the little room on our roof has upholstered walls (not in black!), Michele forged an entry in her diary to make it sound as though Almond had said something about "a room with soft walls" before the date of the raid. The marginal location of the diary notation, and the different writing instrument obviously used, reveal the forgery.

- Lisowski's manipulation of all of this into "a black room with soft walls" appears for the first time in this brief.

9. "A Robot": Not mentioned in the search warrant. Not mentioned by Almond. Nor, as far as I know, mentioned by any other child in the Presidio "abuse" scam.

Pages 5-6. *#10. One of the items seized by the SFPD during the search was a notebook. G.E. D-5 at 65. That notebook contained the name "Mike Todo". G.E. D-14 at 109. Kinsey and another child mentioned "Todo" as one of the persons at "Mr. Gary's" house. G.E. D-19 at 120. During an April 7, 1987 interview with MAJ Hickey, months before the PX identification, Kinsey stated that "Shamby" and "Sassy" were the same person, and that "Sassy" was "Todo's" girlfriend. G.E. D-2 at 21, G.E. E-38 (as numbered at page bottom).*

1. One page from Mrs. Aquino's telephone notebook contained a list of names and telephone numbers, one of which was for a "Mike Todo". As Mrs. Aquino explained to the CID in her May 1989 interview, that page of the notebook contained a list of persons and their telephone numbers who called in answer to an ad in the *San Francisco Chronicle* for rental of one of the 121 Acme flats. The flat was eventually rented to someone else.

2. We never met this "Todo", and apparently Mrs. Aquino spoke to him only once on the phone. In the CID interview she suggested that the CID trace him through the phone number he gave - and for that matter verify the nature of the list by calling the other persons on it.

3. The CID responded that Todo's phone number was disconnected, but apparently they made no effort whatever to trace him through telephone company records, or for that matter to verify the flat-rental-ad nature of the list with any of the other names on it.

4. Kinsey Almond's statements to Hickey concerning "Todo" and "Sassy" are so incoherent and inconsistent as to be worthless:

- Almond said Sassy had **blonde** hair (4/7/87), then that Sassy had "**black** hair like Hickey" (who has **brown** hair) (4/28/87), then that Sassy had **blonde** hair again (5/12/87).
- Almond said Sassy "had **yellow** eyes like Hickey" (who has **green** eyes) (4/28/87).
- Almond switched Sassy's name to "Cathy" (5/12/87), then back again to "Sassy" in the same session.
- Said Sassy and Todo were white and had **blonde** hair (4/7/87), then that Sassy had "**black** hair like Hickey" (who has **brown** hair) and Todo had **green** hair (4/28/87).
- Said Sassy and Todo lived [at the house] and then said that they **didn't** (4/7/87).
- Said Sassy and Todo had "**two**" toys, then said they had "**all kinds of**" toys (4/7/87).
- Said Sassy and Todo had "dinosaurs that bite and hurt" (4/7/87).
- Said Sassy "had **yellow** eyes like Hickey" (who has **green** eyes) (4/28/87).
- On 4/7/87 said that she went to **Sassy** & Todo's house. On 5/12/87 said that the lady's name was **Cathy** and that it was her house (no mention of Todo).

Pages 6-7. *#12: Based upon these sworn charges against CPT A-T and other statements made by plaintiff as the investigation continued, CID investigated plaintiff for false swearing. Specifically, plaintiff falsely stated that Kinsey was two years old in October 1986 when she was in fact three. G.E. E-5, G.E. D-1 at 10. Plaintiff admitted that he incorrectly stated Kinsey's age, but claimed it was a mistake. G.E. D-6 at 72.*

1. **None** of the exhaustive statements and evidence that I presented in the two sworn charge packets were ever refuted, for the simple reason that, as the CID records themselves reveal, **they were never investigated by the UCMJ authority at all** in violation of the *Manual for Courts-Martial*. It is clear that from the beginning the CID used the charge packets only to see if they could find some technicality somewhere - such as my mistake concerning Almond's age - to use to frame a case against me.

2. The **only** discrepancy found was my reference to Almond as "2" at a time when she was "3". As explained to the CID during the May 1989 interview, when they first brought this to my attention, A-T's attack on me came in August 1987 when the child was 3. Since the time period he specified (September-October 1986) was almost a year previously, I assumed that Almond had been age 2 at that time. It simply did not occur to me to check her exact birthdate and note that it was precisely at the September 1 turning-point. I can perhaps be forgiven for having no knowledge of or interest in Almond whatever until her parents suddenly attacked my wife and myself in August 1987. Nor does the distinction between 2-11/12 years and 3-1/12 years of age strike me as chronologically significant. Also as an enclosure to my charges and sworn statements I included a copy of the SFPD Incident Report, which of course contained Almond's birthdate.

Page 7. *#12. Plaintiff also stated that he had "never used or been known by the nickname 'Mikey'". G.E. D-5 at 2. In addition to the children's identification of him as "Mikey", however, Mr. Anton LaVey, a friend and associate, referred to plaintiff as "Mikey". G.E. D-2 at 37, G.E. D-7 at 85.*

1. I have never been known by or used the nickname "Mikey", Even as a young child, my nickname was "Archy" (to distinguish me from my father, Michael Sr.). The diploma of my graduation from Town School for Boys, San Francisco shows "Archy Ford-Aquino", as do all of my yearbooks, etc. at that elementary school.

2. According to SFPD investigator Glenn Pamfiloff, **not one child** of all the ones he interviewed during his investigation of the A-T allegations identified me.

3. Kinsey Almond herself **never** "identified" me until the April 1989 CID interview, by which time her recognition of a photo of me was academic because of coaching and prior exposure.

4. Anton LaVey is not by any stretch of imagination a "friend and associate". LaVey referred to me as "Mikey" to the CID only because, since I exposed his financial exploitation of the Church of Satan in 1975, he hates me intensely and has made it repeatedly and publicly clear that he does.

    - I retain on file all of my correspondence with him prior to 1975. The only first names he **ever** used therein was "Michael" and occasionally "Mike".

    - By the time LaVey was interviewed by the CID, the "Mikey" allegations of A-T had been all over the San Francisco news media. Because of his interest in and hatred for Mrs. Aquino and myself, LaVey simply tailored his responses to try to harm us. His attitude of hatred was so obvious to the CID agent (SA Cates) interviewing him that Cates remarked "He certainly doesn't like you very much!" to me later.

- LaVey is a habitual and deliberate liar, who routinely falsifies anything of convenience to him. See in particular the exposé of numerous LaVey falsehoods in *Rolling Stone* #612 (9/5/91) and also the court papers and judicial findings in *Hegarty v. LaVey* (San Francisco County Superior Court #SCV-891863).

Page 7.   *#12. Plaintiff made other statements controverted by evidence, including that only three people had access to the security code to his upper apartment and that he had never been to the CDC.*

    1.   I made **no** "other statements controverted by evidence". [And **only** my incidental mistake concerning Almond's age was incorrect - a single, immaterial error amidst thousands of pages of letters and statements to which I have signed my name concerning the A-T attack.]

    2.   Only three persons who lived at or checked on 123 Acme/Upper - Mrs. Aquino, her brother, and myself - had the security code to our flat. Obviously National Guardian Security Systems - the company which installed and monitored the system - did too. That is all.

    3.   I have not in fact ever been to the CDC. There is no physical evidence to the contrary, nor statement from any adult (parent, CDC worker, other person) to the contrary. During the Presidio scam prior to the A-T attack on us, no child ever mentioned me, my name, or even a description of anyone like me. "Identifications" and "remembered sightings" after the A-T attack became a media circus mean nothing.

Page 7.   *#13. On August 12, 1988 the San Francisco district attorney's office closed its investigation of child abuse at the CDC.*

    1.   In the ROI the CID said "In September 1988 SFPD terminated active investigation." I confronted CID Commanding General Cromartie with this lie in my 11/30/89 letter to him. So now Lisowski quietly moves it to 8/12?

    2.   8/12 is **still** a lie. It is cited to try to narrow the inconvenient gap between the closing of the SFPD investigation and the Geraldo Rivera/Senator Helms-driven opening of the CID investigation. In fact the actual date when the SFPD District Attorney's Office announced that no charges would be filed against me was 8/1/88.

Page 7.   *#13. In September 1988 CID investigators met with representatives from the SFPD, etc. to discuss the status of the investigation.*

    1.   **What** "investigation"? The SFPD one had been closed over a month earlier. The CID one would not be opened until late November.

Page 7.   *#14. On October 17, 1988, at the request of CID Special Agent Penaluna, the local Army investigator, MAJ Mark Harvey drafted an Investigation Plan for plaintiff's case. The memorandum discussed plans for continuing the investigation of plaintiff in light of the completion of the SFPD investigation and the perceived weaknesses of that investigation. G.E. G-3 (CID Investigative Plan).*

    1.   The letter authored by Major Harvey at G.E. G-3 is **not** a "CID Investigative Plan" itself, but is merely a recommendation for "additional investigative actions".

    2.   Harvey's letter makes **no** reference whatever to "completion of the SFPD investigation" **nor** to "perceived weaknesses of that investigation".

    3.   Harvey's letter includes the recommendation to "get the names of the children that articulated a colorable connection to the Aquinos". In fact no children interviewed by the SFPD identified

either Mrs. Aquino or myself. Harvey's use of the term "colorable" is significant, as Webster's defines that word as "having an appearance of truth; **feigned**, **factitious**, **counterfeit**". Harvey thus suggests that the CID hunt for anything that can be represented as evidence even if it is in fact **not**.

4. Harvey's statement that he "will prepare DODIG subpœnas" for use in a CID investigation is illegal. My Army attorney Captain Hayes informed me that Department of Defense Inspector General subpœnas are reserved for use in Inspector General investigations, which this was clearly **not**.

Pages 7-8: *#14. On October 26, 1988 Wayne Boyles III, Legislative Assistant to Senator Jesse Helms, wrote a letter to the Secretary of the Army complaining about plaintiff's appearance on a Geraldo Rivera television show about Satanism and witchcraft. P.E. 1, Exhibit G. The CID investigation of plaintiff was underway before any involvement by Senator Helms' office.*

1. False statement by Lisowski. The letter from Boyles was dated 10/26/88. The CID investigation was opened 11/23/88 - almost a month **after** the Boyles letter. (Department of the Army Judge Advocate General's Information Paper, 11/23/88).

Page 8: *#15. On April 7 and 8, 1989 the CID interviewed Kinsey. After viewing a photographic lineup, she identified plaintiff as "Mikey" but did not pick out Mrs. Aquino as "Shamby".*

1. The improper design and use of this photographic lineup has been discussed above.

Page 8. *#15. After viewing a video lineup Kinsey again identified plaintiff, and again did not identify Mrs. Aquino as "Shamby". G.E.D-9. (Identification lineups) at 100-101.*

1. After learning of this "video lineup" from the CID in May 1989, I requested through my Army attorney Captain Hayes to be able to see it, particularly since the photo lineup was so obviously "stacked". My request was denied.

2. Under court rules of disclosure I should have been provided with every exhibit of the CID ROI, to include the photo and video lineups. In violation of the law these two exhibits, which the CID has represented as so important and relevant, were **not** provided to me. Apart from my brief glimpse of the photo lineup in May 1989, they have been concealed to this day.

3. If my face was **the only one common to both** the photo and the video lineups, it is all the less surprising that Almond had no trouble picking it out, aside from abundant prior exposure and coaching.

Page 8: *#15. Kinsey stated that "Shamby" and "Mr. Gary" took her to "Mr. Gary's house" and that "Mikey" was there.*

1. Every element of this aged (almost three years from the "CID-invented re-dating" of May-June 1986) statement has changed along the way in an effort to make it "fit" revealed facts:

   • In her 1/14/87 FBI statement, Almond said nothing about being taken anywhere by anyone or having anything done to her anywhere. Since this denial was obviously unacceptable to her parents, she was immediately placed in "therapy" with Hickey, the abuse-finder for the Presidio scam.

- By the third (2/3/87) "play session", Almond now announced that she had performed fellatio on "Mr. Gary" at the CDC. There is no mention of going anywhere else, or of any other adult being involved.

- It took Hickey and the A-Ts two more months to get Almond to agree to an off-CDC location. Finally on 4/7/87 Hickey asked Almond **twice** if she ever went anywhere with Hambright. Both times Almond said **no**. When Hickey refused to accept these answers, Almond **only then** said yes - to "Sassy's house". In the same session Almond described the house as "blue" and the bathtub as "blue" (neither correct concerning 123 Acme).

- There is no mention of "Mikey" by Almond whatever, at "the house" or anywhere else, for over two more months of "therapy". On 6/2/87 Michele A-T proposes a "Satanic cult", and then on 6/30/87 Michele introduces "Mikey" as "Shambee's husband".

- On 6/2/87 and 6/9/87 Almond said that the man at the house with Hambright was "Dr. Steve". As it turns out, "Dr. Steve" is the only real person specifically and repeatedly identified by Almond as being at the house with Hambright. Michele admitted that "Dr. Steve" was a neighbor of theirs at the Presidio of San Francisco. Neither Hickey [per her notes] nor Michele reported this identification to the FBI/CID/SFPD. There is no record that "Dr. Steve" was ever questioned, served with a search warrant, or titled on the strength of this **authentic, unsolicited identification** by Almond.

- Clearly Lisowski's succinct statement, which includes no mention of this extensive coaching and revision whatever, is false and misleading.

Page 8: #15. *She described the house as blue-gray in color, the same color as plaintiff's house at 123 Acme Avenue.*

1. On 4/7/87, after Hickey twice refused Almond's denials that she had been taken anywhere, Almond agreed that she had been taken to a house and that it was **blue** (not "blue-gray") in color.

2. On the morning of 8/13/87 Michele A-T and Almond were taken to 123 Acme Avenue and saw that it was entirely **dark "battleship" gray** in color.

3. Almost two years later, on 4/7-8/89, Almond reportedly told the CID (exact transcript not provided) that the house was now "blue-gray". Clearly she had been coached to make the color try to fit 123 Acme as it was now known to be.

4. Again Lisowski's statement to the court omits this sequence and attempted manufacture of evidence.

5. Lisowski personally describes "blue-gray" as "the same color as 123 Acme", which in 1986 was solid dark "battleship" gray. Another deliberate false statement by Lisowski.

Page 8:   *#16. On May 11, 1989 Kinsey was reinterviewed by CPT Boomer and MAJ Harvey, judge advocates at the Presidio. She said that "Mikey" told her to touch "Mr. Gary's" penis and that "Mikey" forced her to stay in the room with soft walls, and blocked the door so she could not leave. She stated that she had found the house with FBI Agent Foreman and that the house was blue and gray. Id. at 60-61.*

    1.   In the Hickey "therapy" session in which Michele introduced "Mikey" (6/30/87), Almond did not say that "'Mikey' told her to touch 'Mr. Gary's' penis", nor did she say that "'Mikey' forced her to stay in the room with soft walls and blocked the door so she could not leave". Almond said nothing about "Mikey" to Hickey at any other "therapy" session, nor did she ever say anything about "a room with soft walls" - to Hickey or Foreman. As noted above, the "room with soft walls" was added to the ever-evolving scam-story by Michele after learning about our rooftop room after the search.

    2.   As I pointed out to Major Harvey in a 5/18/89 telephone conversation when he mentioned the Michele diary forgery to me, that little wetbar-room has picture windows that make its interior visible to scores of apartment windows across the street, and it does not have a lock to lock someone inside it.

    3.   As demonstrated in A-T Violations Section #D, Almond did not "find 123 Acme with Foreman". She was taken directly to it, driven by it unsuccessfully, and finally walked to it by Michele and halted and coached concerning it by Michele.

Pages 8-9:   *#17. On May 15, 1989 CID agents and legal advisors met with LTC Craig Schwender, Staff Judge Advocate for the Presidio, and reviewed the investigation and evidence with him. LTC Schwender opined that there was probable cause to title LTC Aquino for the offenses of indecent acts with a child, sodomy, conspiracy, kidnapping, and false swearing. G.E. D-16 at 113. LTC Schwender also opined that there was sufficient evidence to title Mrs. Aquino for sexual abuse, conspiracy, and kidnapping.*

    1.   There was, as abundantly demonstrated to date, not a shred of evidence to title either Mrs. Aquino or myself for any of these offenses.

    2.   The CID and the U.S. Army has no legal authority to title a civilian (Mrs. Aquino) in any case.

    3.   Prior to this meeting, Schwender has already evidenced his bias in the investigation:

- On 1/13/89 Schwender told TJAG that "the CID feels that Lt.Col. Aquino's cooperation will be short-lived." There was no basis for this remark whatever. I willingly and actively cooperated with the CID right up to June 1989 when I realized that the investigation was fraudulent.

- On 1/13/89 Schwender told TJAG about Michele A-T's forged diary entry as though its authenticity were established beyond question.

- On 1/26/89 Schwender falsely told TJAG that Major Harvey had found some documents by me that "speak about the doctrine of the Temple of Set of using urine and feces in connection with their rituals". There was and is no such doctrine, and the Temple of Set has never used urine or feces in any of its rituals.

Page 9:   *#18. The final Report of Investigation (ROI) was issued on August 11, 1989. G.E. D at 1-4. On January 4, 1990 Major Harvey spoke with the staff judge advocate at Fort Leonard Wood, MO to determine what action the commander of Fort Leonard Wood had decided to take in the case. The commander took no action against plaintiff as a result of the investigation. G.E. B at 3.*

1. My attorney Mr. Gary Myers was informed by Headquarters, Department of the Army that the decision not to court-martial me was made **prior to the titling decision** (i.e. prior to August 1989). In that case the account of the "decision by the Fort Leonard Wood commander on 1/4/90" is false, intended as a cover-up of the illegal conduct of the investigation process.

2. On 10/2/89 the flag was removed from my personnel file at ARPERCEN. Such a flag would have remained in place unless a decision **had already been made** that there would be no charges preferred against me.

3. Lisowski's account is thus false and obstructs justice by concealing this additional misuse of investigatory/court-martial procedures.

Page 16: *The facts in the administrative record … [through page 17] … present at "Mr. Gary's" house.*

1. As demonstrated herein and previously in abundant communications to the Army, **every single sentence in these three paragraphs is completely and deliberately false**. Altogether these paragraphs contain at least nine separate false statements (if one counts by sentence), more if each sentence is broken down into phrases of known falsehoods.

Appendix 67: Gary Myers' District Court Reply Brief

United States District Court for the Eastern District of Virginia
Alexandria Division

Michael A. Aquino, Plaintiff
v.
The Honorable Michael P.W. Stone, Secretary of the Army
Department of the Army, Washington, D.C.,
Defendant

Civil Action No. 90-1547-A

Plaintiff's Reply to Defendant's Memorandum in Support of
the Defendant's Motion for Judgment on the Record

Argument

Plaintiff is in substantial agreement with Defendant that an issue is raised here as to the applicability of the provisions of the Privacy Act as to this matter given the exemption provisions of 5 U.S.C. #552a(J)(2) and implementing regulations found at 32 C.F.R. #505.5, ID A 0508.11a USA CIDC. Plaintiff further agrees that if this Honorable Court finds that if the Privacy Act does not apply, then the standard of review to be applied is under the Administrative Procedure Act (APA), 5 U.S.C. #702, and specifically 5 U.S.C. #706(2)(A), which is the "arbitrary, capricious, abuse of discretion, or otherwise not in accordance with law" standard. Neither damages nor attorney's fees and costs are contemplated by the APA. *De novo* review under the circumstances of this case would be available only under the Privacy Act.

Plaintiff brought suit under the Privacy Act because firstly Plaintiff is of the belief that the exemption promulgated by the Secretary of the Army at 32 C.F.R. 505.5, ID A0508.11a USACIDC does not apply to this case, and secondly the conduct of the Defendant was so egregious as to take this case outside the exemption.

The exemption at 32 C.F.R. 505.5 provides in part:

(1) **Sysname**: Criminal Investigation and Crime Laboratory Files.
(2) **Exemption**: All portions of this system of records which fall within 5 U.S.C. 552a(j)(2) are exempt from the following provisions of Title 5 U.S.C. Section 552a:(c)(3), (c)(4), (d), (e)(1), (e)(2), (e)(3), (e)(4)(G), (e)(4)(H), (e)(5), (e)(g), (f), and (g).
(3) **Authority**: 5 U.S.C. 552(j)(2).
(4) **Reasons**: (a) ... (b) From subsections ... (g) [allowing suit under the Privacy Act] **because access might compromise ongoing investigations**, reveal classified information, investigatory techniques or the identity of confidential informants, or invade the privacy of persons who provide information in connection with a particular investigation. **The exemption from access necessarily includes exemption from amendment**, certain agency requirements relating to access and amendment of records, and **civil liability** predicated upon agency compliance with those specific provisions of the Privacy Act. The exemption from access necessarily includes exemption from other requirements. (Emphasis added)

This exemption has nothing to do with the circumstances of this case. Plaintiff knew he was being investigated and did not file an amendment request until **after** Plaintiff was titled and the ROI was sitting in the Crime Records Center in completed form. In fact the ROI was given to Plaintiff by Defendant in order for an amendment request to be filed.

In the original ROI given to Plaintiff, certain matters were deleted with the notation "Privacy Act". These matters were later given to Plaintiff as a result of Plaintiff's discovery request for documents by the Defendant without protest.

Succinctly stated, none of the reasons for exemption applies in this case:

1. There is and was no ongoing investigation to be protected.

2. There is and was no classified information.

3. There is and was no unrevealed investigatory techniques or confidential informants.

4. There is and was no invasion of any person's privacy.

What **is** for certain is that a bogus ROI sits in the Crime Records Center showing Plaintiff as having committed all manner of heinous acts, which ROI can be revealed to the public under the Freedom of Information Act and which labels Plaintiff for life.

The rationale for exemption may apply **during** an investigation, but there is no necessity for such an exemption when the ROI is revealed and the titling has been accomplished.

The Plaintiff has dealt with most of the Defendant's *Statement of Facts* in Plaintiff's initial brief. Nonetheless clarification is required in certain areas:

1. The only supposed identification of Plaintiff by Kinsey in 1987 was related to law enforcement by Kinsey's parents. Kinsey in 1987 - the time most proximate to the alleged event - never identified Plaintiff to anyone in law enforcement. In 1989 the CID says Kinsey identified Plaintiff, but by then Kinsey had multiple opportunities to see pictures of Plaintiff, and the identification is worthless.

2. Kinsey never identified Plaintiff's house. The FBI agent in charge of the investigation did not report a positive identification (Defense Exhibit D-1). A CID agent along for the ride said in the 1989 ROI that Kinsey positively identified the house as "Mr. Gary's" house where she met "Mikey" and "Shamby".[415] Where is this striking information in the FBI report? Where is the CID report of the events of that day? This never happened. Kinsey supposedly said Mr. Gary drove her there. Gary Hambright did not have a driver's license.[416]

---

[415] In fact there is no statement by the CID agent that Kinsey said anything about or otherwise "identified" our house in any way whatever. The CID agent's trip report instead states that Kinsey was driven directly to our block, then walked and driven by the house repeatedly with no statement or gesture from her whatever. The CID agent reported only that Kinsey's mother Michelle (who knew our address beforehand) picked Kinsey up and held her in front of our house to suggest to the law enforcement personnel that there was an identification. It is rather an additional indication of the adult A-Ts' active effort to push their faked allegations.

[416] According to his Federal Public Defenders, Gary Hambright was an epileptic who neither had a driver's license nor knew how to drive nor owned an automobile.

3. There is absolutely no proof of any kind that the CID investigation of Plaintiff began before Jesse Helms' office got involved. The "investigative plan" at Defense Exhibit G-3, dated 17 October 1988, is a concept that got reduced to practice with Senator Helms' intervention.[417]

4. The search warrant for Plaintiff's home was for the **entire** house - not, as the Defense now suggests, for the top apartment alone.[418] The Bill Butch apartment was simply never considered "crime scene" material until 1991, when Plaintiff's home as the "crime scene" could no longer withstand scrutiny.

Under the Uniform Code of Military Justice, the elements of the offenses for which Plaintiff has been titled are as follows (*Manual for Courts Martial* 1984):

[Here are reprinted Articles 81 (Conspiracy), 125 (Sodomy), 134 (False Swearing) (Indecent Acts or Liberties with a Child) (Kidnapping) (Indecent Acts with Another).]

Conclusion

For the reasons indicated it is respectfully requested that judgment for the Plaintiff be entered.

Respectfully submitted,
/s/ Gary R. Myers
Counsel for Plaintiff

---

[417] What during this lawsuit the CID tried to represent as a pre-Helms "investigative plan" was in fact a 1-1/2-page letter by CID attorney Captain Mark Harvey suggesting various ways to manufacture and falsify "evidence", illegally employ Inspector General subpoenæ, and rig photo/video lineups in violation of CID Regulation CIDR 195-1 (11/1/86) to influence any possible court action against Lilith and myself.

[418] During the execution of the search warrant, moreover, I specifically asked investigators if they wished to go anywhere or see anything else in the entire building, and they all refused. They were interested only in our apartment.

Appendix 68: District Court Oral Arguments

United States District Court for the Eastern District of Virginia
Alexandria Division

Michael A. Aquino, Plaintiff
v.
The Honorable Michael P.W. Stone, Secretary of the Army
Department of the Army, Washington, D.C.,
Defendant

Civil Action No. 90-1547-A

Hearing on Motions

May 31, 1991

Before: Claude M. Hilton, Judge

Appearances:
Gary R. Myers, Counsel for the Plaintiff
Patrick Lisowski and Richard Parker, Counsel for Defendant

The Clerk: Civil action 90-1547-A, Michael Aquino versus the Honorable Michael P.W. Stone.

Mr. Parker: Good morning, Your Honor. Richard Parker for the United States. With me is Major Patrick Lisowski from the Army Litigation Division. Major Lisowski is a member in good standing of the Bar of Pennsylvania. Accordingly, I move his admission *pro has vice*.

The Court: All right, the motion is granted. Who wants to go first? You have both got motions for summary judgment.

Mr. Myers: Your Honor, the plaintiff in conversation with the defendant has agreed to go first. To the extent necessary, I wonder if I might reserve two minutes for rebuttal?

The Court: All right.

Mr. Myers: Your Honor, this is a case that elicits immediate emotional response. It is a titling action by the United States Army against a former active duty officer who has been accused of heinous acts against small children, conspiracy, sodomy, indecent acts against small children. What makes it more different is the religion predicated upon the worship of Satan.

I want to say that, with respect to this individual and because there are multiple buzz-words associated with this particular case, it is imperative that the Court recognize in Exhibit 13 the status and character of this man. You will find there the efficiency reports of this man through his military career. Each and every one is outstanding. His last one refers to him as a man of the highest moral and ethical standards. I believe that a review of his military record will show that.

The church of which he is the head is the Temple of Set. It has been recognized by the Internal Revenue Service. There has been no secrecy associated with it.

The man is a Ph.D. in Political Science. He is an intellectual. The dogma that he predicates his religion upon comes from Egyptian and pre-Egyptian theology having to do with the anti-Christ view of things. But nonetheless not a dogma that suggests abuse of children, animals, or any other form of heinous conduct is appropriate.

And I want to predicate all that I do today on those two simple statements, because we are not dealing here with an individual who has gone outside the mainstream of American Society with regard to conduct. He has gone outside the mainstream of American Society in a protected Constitutional fashion with respect to religion.

Now the Government in their brief suggests that although we have brought this suit as the plaintiff on the Privacy Act, that it is an inappropriate vehicle, and that the APA should be used so that you are limited to an "arbitrary and capricious" standard. We believe that you need not get to the "arbitrary and capricious" issue. We believe that the Privacy Act applies.

If one examines the case of *Ryan versus the Department of Justice* decided by the Fourth Circuit in 1979, there you will find, Your Honor, that the exemption from the Privacy Act which the Government relies upon was scrupulously examined by the Fourth Circuit. That court concluded that the exemption is only viable if the reasons for the exemption apply to the particular case.

The reasons for the exemption of the Privacy Act in this case as stated in the C.F.R. applicable to this case are as follows:

- If there is an ongoing investigation.
- If there are classified matters to be revealed.
- If there are informants to be protected.
- If there are individual privacy rights to be protected.
- If there are investigatory techniques to be protected.

None of those reasons apply to this case:

- This is an investigation that was completed, completely and fully.
- Matters that were a part of the Privacy Act in the prior investigation were given to the plaintiff upon discovery requests for documents.
- There is no ongoing investigation. This case comes before you after the investigation is utterly and totally completed.
- There are no confidential informants, no privacy rights to be protected, no national secrets to be revealed.

So we believe as the plaintiff that the appropriate forum is the Privacy Act with its attendant damage provisions.

Moving now, if I may, Your Honor, to certain questions that give rise to why we are here:

You have read the briefs. I am not going to belabor you with the facts. But it is more than passing strange that the brief from the plaintiff, which laid out with particularity egregious misconduct of the military in this case, was not rebutted - not rebutted.

There is no "probable cause" in this case, Your Honor, which is the test, to conclude that this man has done anything. The plaintiff through counsel has been able to identify three separate and distinct alibis, all of which have held up.

The defendant in this case attempted to title the plaintiff's wife based upon the same eyewitness testimony of the little girl who is supposed to have been molested. And yet that woman, Mrs. Aquino, was taken off the title block by the Army, notwithstanding the eyewitness testimony of this little girl.

I point out to you, Your Honor, that this case was a *cause celebre* in the San Francisco Bay Area and most of the west coast. It received huge amounts of publicity. The FBI and the San Francisco Police Department were inextricably involved in it for month upon month. Nothing came of it.

What did happen after they closed their cases was that Senator Jesse Helms, because of the high-profile nature of my client, initiated an inquiry to then-Secretary Marsh regarding my client. And you have Senator Helms' letter in front of you.

And I say this to you, Judge, very simply what happened was this: A couple of parents who had a little girl decided that Michael Aquino was a reasonable target. And the CID, which is the Army investigative branch, in league with their superiors started a campaign to make certain that Senator Helms was satisfied and that this Satanism would be eliminated from the Army. And that is exactly what happened. And I stand on every line and sentence that you have in that brief before you.

Now as a result of all of this, the parents of this little girl have filed $3 million in claims from the United States Government.

There is not one other child at the Presidio Day Care Center, not one other child out of a multitude of nearly 20 who alleged abuse, who could "identify" Michael Aquino or his wife other than this little girl who was then three years old. And when did this little girl "identify" Michael Aquino? Not in 1987, when all this happened - when the FBI was there. Her parents said she identified him, supposedly, in 1989.

Now we are talking about the memory of a very small child. And I ask you to take judicial notice at least of what two- and three-year-olds can and cannot remember.

There is not the slightest prospect, Your Honor, that my client engaged in any form of misfeasance or malfeasance. As an Army officer he was utterly superior, but they threw him out. And the way they threw him out was this: He came up for continuation as an AGR officer, meaning a National Guard officer.[419] The test for that was whether or not he was "fully qualified". And you will find a memo in the file, part of the exhibits, showing that he clearly **was** "fully qualified". And there was a billet for him to fill.

But what the Army did was that they advised this continuation board that Michael Aquino had been flagged. **Improper**. The **only** matter that is supposed to be before that continuation board is his OMPF, which is basically his personnel file. **Improper**.

There is an interesting memorandum detailing the scenario of events that occurred in the Aquino matter which I have provided to the Court as an exhibit, which was obtained under the Freedom of Information Act.

Judge, this is simply a case where there are no conspirators. There never was any evidence that Michael Aquino was in any way, shape, or form associated with a Mr. Gary Hambright, who was at the Presidio Day Care Center. Mrs. Aquino was dropped from the titling block for lack of "probable cause". Whom did he conspire with?

This child was examined by medical doctors and found to be perfectly fit physically. Although she said she was raped, although she said she was sodomized, there is no evidence of that.

Michael Aquino could not have done this. This child was only in Mr. Hambright's class in September and October of 1987. And Michael Aquino was here in Washington during that period of time.

---

[419] AGR = Active Guard & Reserve, a fulltime active duty program for both the Army Reserve and the Army National Guard. I am an Army Reserve officer.

What the CID did was they tried to figure out when Aquino **was** in San Francisco and convert the facts to **that** date. The only date that they found to be meaningful was June 10, 1987. Plaintiff has provided an absolute alibi for that date.

Your Honor, my practice is limited to military law. And I know the men who are making these decisions, and they are not evil men. It is not the evil men we have to worry about. It is the well-intentioned ones who bend to pressure. And that is what has happened in this case.

No matter what standard you choose to employ - whether it be the "arbitrary and capricious" standard because you do not feel that the Privacy Act applies here [and we strenuously suggest that it does] - you must conclude, Your Honor, that it **is** "arbitrary and capricious" - I say this respectfully, of course - "arbitrary and capricious" not to title Mrs. Aquino and to title Dr. Aquino when the same little girl identified them both.

No, there was an agenda here, Judge. The Army carried out that agenda. They made certain that the man would never go to trial, because they titled him after the Statute of Limitations ran. They had the best of all worlds. They satisfied Senator Helms, they satisfied their own needs, and they left this man with no career.

And that is what happened in this case, Judge. And I believe that the factual representations we have made, all of which are supported by documentation, none of which are speculative, all of which are unrebutted by the Government, are dispositive.

Thank you.

The Court: All right.

Mr. Lisowski: Your Honor, at the outset I would like to say that the Government has not chosen to respond to every allegation that plaintiff makes because the Government feels very strongly that there is absolutely no credence to most of those allegations at all, and that to respond to those is not necessary. The facts of the case are fairly straightforward.

This case comes down to two issues, Your Honor: Does the Privacy Act exemption apply; and, if so, were the Government's actions "arbitrary and capricious"?

The Government agrees with plaintiff's counsel, and plaintiff has conceded, that if the Privacy Act exemption **does** apply - the (j)(2) exemption - then the "arbitrary and capricious" standard is the correct one to apply in this case. And if that is the correct standard under the APA, then plaintiff is entitled to no damages. Plaintiff seeks the broader *de novo* review, and he seeks the glimmer of hope that he can recover some damages under the Privacy Act.

The *Ryan* case states that there are two requirements for a proper exemption: First, that the Secretary promulgate regulations, which the Secretary of the Army has done in 32 C.F.R. 505.5. And secondly, that those regulations state the reasons why records are exempt. And the Army has also done that.

I think a case that is better on point here, Your Honor, is the *Wentz* case that is cited in the Government brief. *Ryan* involved a Privacy Act issue of access and wrongful disclosure. The *Wentz* case involves a plaintiff who was seeking to amend a law-enforcement record, which is more directly on point here. And in *Wentz* the Court noted that the (j)(2) exemption is a general exemption which is designed to apply to a whole system of records, which is the case here.

And the Court in *Wentz* also noted that in examining this issue, the Privacy Act exemption or the Privacy Act provision for amendment of records falls under 552a(d). And that subsection is entitled "Access to Records". And access, as is stated in the regulation, necessarily includes amendment.

So it is not inconsistent for the Government in their exemption regulations to also address access to records. And under the subsection in the Privacy Act statute, it is consistent then for that access to also include amendments to records, and the reasons are the same.

For that reason, Your Honor, the Government urges that the Privacy Act exemption does apply in this case.

Even if Your Honor were to find that the exemption does not apply, the Privacy Act still allows a plaintiff only to amend factual determinations. And in this case, Your Honor, clearly the facts are not in dispute. The little girl made the identification at the Post Exchange while she was shopping with her parents.[420] And the dispute that the plaintiff has is with the evaluation and determination of those facts.

And the Privacy Act is not meant to allow a plaintiff who disagrees with a determination to change, shape, or color that determination to his own likings. It is meant to allow the plaintiff to attack facts that are in error. And plaintiff is only allowed to attack the determination if he can discredit each and every one of the underlying facts. And plaintiff has not done so in this case.

Additionally, Your Honor, if you find - once again assuming that the Privacy Act did apply - plaintiff would would not be entitled to damages. He has the very formidable barrier that in order to prove damages, he has to show causation. And the only causation that is mentioned here in the record is purely speculative, on whether or not the Continuation Board may have known that the plaintiff was flagged or titled, whether or not that would be improper. And that certainly doesn't meet the high hurdle of causation. And it doesn't come close to meeting the even higher hurdle of showing that the Army acted willfully and intentionally in doing so.[421]

Finally, Your Honor, the only way one can rule for the plaintiff in this case is to adopt the plaintiff's view of the facts. And that means that you have to assume or you have to believe that a mother and a father instructed their daughter to fabricate this story of child molestation and to identify or pick out someone who they didn't like, and talk their daughter or embed in her somehow the fact that this was the man that molested you.

If you look at the facts, Your Honor, Colonel Aquino left the Presidio San Francisco in the end of the summer of 1986. He was assigned here in Washington, D.C. After Washington, D.C. his follow-on assignment was to go to St. Louis. He was only back in the Presidio in San Francisco during that summer. Plaintiffs would not even know that he was back there. He had left the Presidio. How would they know that their daughter would see that person in the Post Exchange in San Francisco in the summer of 1987 when he had left that area for a year and he was being reassigned to St. Louis?[422]

---

[420] There were **only** the allegations of her parents that Kinsey Almond made any "PX identification". No PX personnel corroborated any "PX encounter" whatever, and the parents gave several conflicting, inconsistent, and physically impossible versions of their statement to investigators. [Major Lisowski was aware of this at the time of this hearing.]

[421] As Lisowski knew at the time of this hearing - but which he and the CID had illegally concealed from Myers and myself - the CID had taken a far more deliberate and direct role in illegally fixing the AGR continuation board. In a book which I discovered only after this district court hearing, CID chief investigator Major Mark Harvey stated:
> "[Aquino's] name is now entered in our records as the perpetrator. We don't have to do anything about it - in fact we aren't going to force a court martial in this case. There are two reasons for that: the first is that it would not be good for the kids to have to go to court now and be cross-examined. **The second is simply that his secondment to the Regular Army is ending: we just won't renew his contract, so in effect we are getting rid of him that way.**" (Tim Tate, *Children for the Devil*, 1991)

[422] As noted in #2 above, there is no evidence that the child Kinsey Almond noticed Mrs. Aquino or myself during our August 1987 visit to the Presidio PX. One or both of the **adult** Adams-Thompsons obviously did notice us, and recognized us from official Presidio social events during the pre-June 1986 period when both Chaplain A-T and I were assigned to the garrison.

And yet this girl, in a completely public setting, identifies this man as "Mikey", a man who sodomized her and having her place her mouth on his penis. There wouldn't be any tears or anything in her vagina or anus for that kind of sodomy.[423]

Based on the facts, Your Honor, you would have to believe that there was a giant conspiracy between the parents, the daughter, the psychiatrist, the child psychiatrist that treated the girl, between the CID agents who investigated the case, between the military policemen and investigators who reviewed the case, and between the officials in the Army Criminal Law Division who also reviewed the case.[424]

And finally, Your Honor, plaintiff is not left without a remedy here. The Privacy Act requires and Army Regulation 195-2 provides that remedy: That if the plaintiff disagrees with a determination that is made, he should be allowed to state the reasons for his disagreements, and those reasons should be appended to that official record. As you can see by the volume of this administrative record that you have, Appendix F, which is part of the Criminal Investigation Division report of investigation, includes all of the submissions made by the plaintiff which state his side of the story and the reasons why he disagrees with this.

---

[423] See notes above. Almond made **no** verified "PX identification", and no "identification" whatever until **two years** later, when the CID alleged that she picked my picture out of an [CID regulation-illegal] photo-lineup. By that time, obviously, her parents had had plenty of time to teach her to choose any photo or video of me presented to her.

Lisowski ignores the facts that rape and rectal sodomy of a 2-year-old child, as her stepfather alleged, would **definitely** leave physical damage evidence, and that a medical examination of Kinsey shortly after the "allegation window" indicated "**no evidence of abuse**".

Lisowski also ignores the fact that rape, rectal, or oral sodomy would presumably be so traumatic to a child as to cause instantly-noticeable psychological damage. Almond was never taken to any doctor for any such complaint at the time of the allegation window.

[424] "**The parents**": had a $3 million get-rich-quick scheme in mind. Later, when the Helms-driven agenda began, they were obviously pleased to cooperate in this convenient revival of their scheme.

"**The daughter**": made **no** "identification" of me until two years after her parents initiated their scheme, and **never** any "identification" of Lilith. In her interview with the CID on 7-8 April 1989, "Almond denied that 'Mikey' and/or 'Shamby' [the names her parents tried to twist into labels for ourselves] had ever done anything bad to either her or to other children in her presence." (CID Report)

"**The psychiatrist**": As revealed by her own session notes, Hickey had her own agenda of "diagnosing" Presidio children brought to her by refusing to accept any denials from them, and continuing to harass them until they said what she wanted them to say. The Army Medical Corps refused without any explanation my request that Hickey's mass-diagnoses of "abuse" throughout the entire Presidio episode be examined for professional incompetence.

"**The CID agents who investigated the case**": had a predetermined agenda to frame Lilith and myself, stemming from Helms' demands on the Secretary of the Army, and immediately evidenced by CID fixing of the AGR continuation board **at the very beginning** of the supposedly-unbiased "investigation". The CID's massive criminal actions, such as manufacture and suppression of evidence, misprision of serious offense, and numerous false official statements [including to this court], also speak for themselves. Even before the opening of the CID investigation, CID attorney Mark Harvey sent a letter to the CID San Francisco Field Office suggesting ways in which CID regulations could be violated and "evidence" manufactured concerning Lilith and myself.

"**The Army Criminal Law Division**": On 11/23/88 (the same date on which the CID investigation of me was opened) Lt.Col. John Burton of the Department of the Army Judge Advocate General's Office (TJAG) sent a secret [from me] briefing paper to the Director of the Army Staff exploring several excuses for eliminating me from active service, such as "conduct unbecoming" and "moral or professional dereliction" and advising possible bases under which I could be expelled. Burton's paper was secretly briefed to TJAG, ODCSPER, DACH, OCAR, PA, OCLL, M&RA, and GC in a secret [from me] meeting held in the Pentagon on 11/29/88. The Judge Advocate General of the Army - a 3-star general - personally traveled to Helms' office on 2/1/89 "to discuss LTC Aquino's status".

But the proper way to dispose of this case, Your Honor, is to examine the (j)(2) exemption under the Privacy Act, and to conclude that this (j)(2) exemption applies under the *Ryan* case and the *Wentz* case under either or both cases to this case at hand, and that the Army did not act "arbitrarily and capriciously" in making its determination.

Your Honor, plaintiff has a lot better chance in this case of fitting a camel through the eye of a needle than showing that the Army acted "arbitrarily and capriciously" in their determination that Lt. Colonel Aquino sexually abused this child. This is not a case of a witch hunt or a warlock hunt, and it is not a case of religious discrimination. Plaintiff was not titled because he the chief priest or the High Priest of the Temple of Set. It is completely irrelevant, Your Honor.[425] He was titled in this report of investigation because the evidence shows that he committed indecent acts with a child, and that he conspired with others to take this child away from the day care center, take them to his apartment, and that's where he sexually abused her.[426]

Thank you, Your Honor.

The Court: All right.

Mr. Myers: If I may, Judge. There is **no** evidence that this child has told anyone **herself** that she identified Michael Aquino. The **parents** say this.

But let me point out to you, Your Honor: This little girl at the same time advised the psychiatrist that her next door neighbor, who was a doctor, Dr. Steve, was part of this effort as well.[427]

---

[425] To summarize just a few of the religious prejudicial actions and influences in this case:

On or about 12/8/88, in response to publicity concerning my religion in October 1988, the Office of Secretary of the Army Marsh sent letters to at least thirty senators and representatives stating that "the Army by no means encourages 'devil worship'". The Secretary of the Army thus stated an official position of prejudice against a legitimate religion in direct violation of the First and Fourteenth Amendments to the Constitution and in violation of AR 600-20 (prohibiting religious discrimination in the Army) - and did so specifically with reference to me and coincidentally with the just-opened CID "investigation".

On 12/2/88 - also just after the opening of the CID "investigation" - Vice Chief of Staff of the Army General Arthur Brown, the second-highest-ranking officer in the Army, sent a letter to the president of NBC denouncing the Temple of Set and equating the legitimate Satanic religion with "lawlessness" and "vandalism". Brown cited an official position paper from the Army's Office of the Chief of Public Affairs containing numerous religious defamations and distortions, as well as denial of Constitutional protections.

Major Mark Harvey, author of the CID ROI, devoted major portions of it to misrepresenting and attacking my religious beliefs and actions, and the Temple of Set generally. Prior to writing the ROI he bragged to my Army attorney Captain Thomas Hayes that he was certain he could "get around" my Constitutional First Amendment religious protections.

[426] There was in actuality **no evidence whatever** of any child sexual abuse, kidnapping, conspiracy, or involvement of our home in any way - as Lisowski well knew at the time of this hearing.

[427] In the Hickey notes of Almond's "therapy" sessions, Almond makes no reference to us or a house like ours, but **does** say that she was taken to the house of a "Dr. Steve", whom her parents later indicated was a neighbor of theirs on the Presidio. There is no indication that "Dr. Steve" was ever made a subject of investigation by anyone based on Almond's **actual** allegations.

This little girl identified the car that the Aquinos "owned" as the one that Mrs. Aquino drove her in. It was a **rented** car. It **could not** have been their car. It was rented for the weekend that they were out there. The little girl's testimony is utterly incredible.[428]

And it wasn't this little girl alone who is supposed to have gone to the Aquino home, Judge. It was multiple children. And the only day the Army has in their investigation was June 10. Yet **no** other child could identify Dr. Aquino or Mrs. Aquino or the home they lived in - **no** other child. And yet they were supposed to.[429]

The Army glibly talks about a conspiracy. With **whom**? Mrs. Aquino couldn't have been in it. The Army decided not to title her. There is no evidence that Gary Hambright even knew Michael Aquino. With whom? It is easy to say conspiracy, but with whom? And upon what factual predicate?

No, Judge. This isn't a neat and tidy little case where we can just sweep it away and say "we did a wonderful job here protecting the public interest". This was a concerted effort to bury this plaintiff. And the facts that I have put in that brief are **not** "speculation", Judge. They come from government documents. Each and every fact is supported by exhibit number. And each and every fact comes from the government. Not "speculation", Judge. This is a serious matter.

Thank you.

The Court: All right. I will look at this further, and I will get an answer to you all in some reasonable time.

Mr. Lisowski: Thank you, Your Honor.

Mr. Myers: Thank you, Judge.

The Court: If we have no further business, we will adjourn until Monday morning.

Hearing Concluded

---

[428] To clarify: When Lilith and I visited the Presidio PX in August 1987, we rented a car for our brief stay in the city. The A-Ts saw us with this car at the PX and - not realizing it was just a rental car - alleged that Almond "identified" it as the one she had been abducted in the previous year.

[429] In fact the two other children that Almond said were with her during her "abuse" denied in all interviews that any such kidnapping or abuse had happened **at all**.

Appendix 69: District Court Decision

United States District Court for the Eastern District of Virginia
Alexandria Division

Michael A. Aquino, Plaintiff
v.
The Honorable Michael P.W. Stone, Secretary of the Army
Department of the Army, Washington, D.C.,
Defendant

Civil Action No. 90-1547-A

Order

This matter came before the court on cross motions for summary judgment. For the reasons stated in the accompanying memorandum opinion, it is hereby ordered that plaintiff's motion for summary judgment is denied and that defendant's motion for summary judgment is granted and this case is dismissed.

/s/ Claude M. Hilton
United States District Judge
Alexandria, Virginia

July 1, 1991

Memorandum Opinion

This is a civil action brought by the plaintiff, Aquino, against the defendant, the Secretary of the Army, pursuant to the Privacy Act of 1974, 5 U.S.C.A. #552a(g). Plaintiff alleges that the United States Army Criminal Investigation Command (CID) has refused to amend a Report of Investigation (ROI) which states that the plaintiff was the subject of an investigation for sexual child abuse and related crimes. Plaintiff seeks to remove his name from the title block of the ROI, to recover damages for the alleged willful and intentional misconduct of the Army for refusing to accurately maintain this record, and to recover attorney fees and costs.

This matter came before the court on defendant's motion for summary judgment. The Secretary of the Army asserts that the plaintiff has failed to state a claim under the Privacy Act because the ROIs are exempt from the amendment and civil liability provisions of the Privacy Act. If the Privacy Act exemption applies, plaintiff's only remaining remedy for relief is pursuant to the Administrative Procedure Act (APA), 5 U.S.C.A. #702, where the standard of review of the defendant's refusal to amend the ROI is whether or not the defendant acted "arbitrarily and capriciously". Plaintiff argues that the Privacy Act does apply in this case because the rationale for the exemption is not present in this case. Therefore the standard of review of the Army's actions is *de novo*.

Plaintiff is a Lieutenant Colonel in the United States Army Reserve. His name appears in the title block of a CID ROI for indecent acts with a child and related offenses. Kinsey Marie Adams-Thompson appears in the victim block of that report. She and her parents were interviewed by an FBI agent about allegations of child abuse at the Child Development Center (CDC) in 1987 because Kinsey told a doctor at the base that a CDC employee, Gary Hambright, had sexually molested her. Later an investigation of LTC Aquino and his wife also commenced.

In January 1988 plaintiff made a written sworn statement denying the allegations against him and preferring sworn charges against Captain Adams-Thompson, the child's father. Plaintiff charged Captain Adams-Thompson with conduct unbecoming an officer because the Captain reported the allegations of child abuse to the San Francisco Police.[430] Based on these sworn statements, plaintiff was investigated for false swearing.[431]

Although the San Francisco Police Department (SFPD) closed its investigation and filed no charges against the plaintiff or anyone else, the CID investigators drafted an investigative plan for plaintiff's case.[432]

After the investigation the evidence was reviewed by LTC Schwender, Staff Judge Advocate for the Presidio. He determined that there was probable cause to title LTC Aquino with offenses of indecent acts with a child, sodomy, conspiracy, kidnapping, and false swearing.[433]

The final ROI was issued in August 1989. In January 1990 plaintiff appealed the titling determination. Plaintiff's amendment request was reviewed internally. Colonel Gilligan, who reviewed the amendment request, recommended deleting plaintiff from several charges which had been investigated.[434] The commanding general of the CID adopted those recommendations in September 1990.[7] However plaintiff remains titled for "indecent acts with a child, sodomy, conspiracy, kidnapping, indecent acts, and false swearing".

Under the Privacy Act an individual may gain access to, and may request amendment of his record or any information which is contained in a system of records maintained by an agency. 5 U.S.C.A. #552a(d)(1)&(2). Under 5 U.S.C.A. #552a(g) an individual is permitted to bring a civil action against the agency in the United States district courts whenever any agency determines not to amend an individual's record in accordance with his request. However an agency may exempt law enforcement records from the application of #552a(d)&(g) under subsection 552a(j)(2). To properly exempt a system of records from the Privacy Act requirements, "an agency must: (1) promulgate rules, pursuant to the rule-making requirements of #553(b)(1),(2),&(3),(c)&(e) ... and (2) state the reasons in the rule itself why the system of records is to be exempt from a provision of the Act". *Ryan v. Department of Justice*, 595 F.2d 954,957 (4th Cir. 1979). In this case the parties have not challenged the exemption of the entire system of records, specifically criminal investigation files, but the plaintiff does challenge the applicability of that exemption in this case.

---

[430] In fact I **twice** preferred formal charges against Chaplain A-T - first on 1/4/88 and again on 11/29/89. The two specifications were for (1) "knowingly and with malicious intent make false statements and representations defaming the characters of Lt. Colonel Michael A. Aquino and Mrs. Lilith Aquino", and (2) filing "one ore more false claims, based upon the false statements and representations identified in Specification 1, such claims totaling at least $750,000 and possibly as much as $3 million, and such claim or claims thus constituting a deliberate attempt by him to defraud the United States Government". Both preferrals of charges were summarily and illegally dismissed by his superiors without a full *Rule for Courts Martial* #303 investigation. Such dismissals thus constitute both "obstruction of justice" and "misprision of serious offense" violations of Article 134, UCMJ. Requests for correction of the dismissals, up to the 3-star general level, were brushed aside or ignored altogether.

Two additional factual corrections: (1) Lawrence Adams-Thompson was Kinsey Almond's stepfather, not her father. (2) There is no evidence that the fake story told by him to the S.F.P.D. existed in any form prior to his own utterance of it. Therefore he **invented**, rather than "reported" it.

[431] All of the statements in my two sworn charges against Chaplain Adams-Thompson were and remain true, and the CID never rebutted a single one of them, during this lawsuit or at any other time.

[432] No such "investigative plan" was ever produced by the CID during the discovery phase of this lawsuit. The CID claimed that a 1-1/2-page letter by Captain Mark Harvey, proposing ways to violate the law in order to frame a case against me, was an "investigative plan"; very obviously it was not.

[433] Schwender made these decisions **before** the investigation (TWX, FOUO, 6RCID to USACIDC, 11/22/88). **No** SFPD or FBI justification was included in the ROI.

[434] Gilligan may have in fact recommended deleting **all** titlings but was overruled by unidentified senior authorities. See my 10/18/90 letter to Brigadier General Thomas Kilmartin in Chapter #7.

Plaintiff argues that the reasons listed for the exemption in 32 C.F.R. #505.5 do not apply in this case.[a] Plaintiff asserts that there is and was no ongoing investigation to be protected, there is and was no classified information, there is and was no unrevealed investigatory techniques or confidential informants, and there is and was no invasion of any person's privacy. Accordingly plaintiff asserts that there is no necessity for the exemption when the ROI is revealed and the titling is accomplished.

The Army, though, has completely exempted this entire system of records from the civil remedies provisions of the Privacy Act. The Army promulgated rules at 32 C.F.R. #505.5 and complied with the requirement for stating the reasons for the exemption in the rule. Within that exemption the Army has exempted the failure to amend a criminal investigation from the civil remedies provision of the Privacy Act. "By requiring the agency to state the reasons in the rule itself for exempting a system of records from a provision of the Privacy Act, the extent of the exemption intended can be fully ascertained." *Ryan*, 595 F.2d at 958. Furthermore "the exemption authorized by 5 U.S.C. #552a(j)(2) is a general exemption which applies to a whole system of records of the agency, and therefore the Privacy Act 'does not require that a regulation's rationale for exempting a record from disclosure apply in each particular case'". *Wentz v. Department of Justice*, 772 F.2d 335,337 (7th Cir. 1985), *cert. denied*, 475 U.S. 1086 (1986) (quoting *Shapiro v. Drug Enforcement Agency*, 721 F.2d 215,218 (7th Cir. 1983)).

In *Wentz* the appellant argued that since a certain document had already been revealed to him, the exemption to amendment had no relevancy to him. 772 F.2d at 337. The court rejected this argument, since the rationale of the exemption need not apply in each particular case. Further, in the appellant's original copy of the document requested, certain portions of the document were deleted and only included in the Justice Department's copy. Thus the exemption would be applicable in certain situations. *Id*. at 338.

Similarly plaintiff's original ROI had certain matters deleted with the notation "Privacy Act". Although the plaintiff received the full copy in discovery,[435] there may be occasions when the Army copy would contain information that would not be contained in an individual's copy, and the exemption would be applicable. In addition, since the exemption need not apply in each particular case, the exemption applies to plaintiff's case as well.

Because the exemption from the Privacy Act specifically covers the entire system of records in which plaintiff's ROI is contained, plaintiff cannot bring an action for civil remedies pursuant to the Privacy Act. Therefore the applicable standard of review of the Army's decision not to amend the plaintiff's ROI is whether the Army acted "arbitrarily and capriciously".

The Army reviewed plaintiff's request to amend the ROI under Army Regulation 195-2 since the ROIs are exempt from the amendment provisions of the Privacy Act.[b] Thus plaintiff's only remaining remedy is under the APA. The APA does not waive sovereign immunity from claims for monetary relief. See, e.g., *Rhodes v. United States*, 760 F.2d 1180,1184 (11th Cir. 1985); *Ghandi v. Police Dept. of Detroit*, 747 F.2d 338,343 (6th Cir. 1984), *cert. denied*, 484 U.S. 1042 (1988); *Doe v. Civiletti*, 635 F.2d 88,94 (2nd Cir. 1980). Therefore plaintiff is only entitled to injunctive-type relief based on a review of the Army's refusal to delete his name from the ROI title block.

Under the APA plaintiff is not entitled to *de novo* review of his claim because such review is only afforded under the APA when seeking enforcement of nonadjudicatory agency action and when the factfinding procedures are inadequate. See 5 U.S.C.A. #706(2)(F). Thus the court should determine whether the Army's action was "arbitrary, capricious, an abuse of discretion, or otherwise not in accordance with law". 5 U.S.C.A. #706(2)(A). Under this standard of review the Army decision maker is afforded considerable deference. The inquiry is confined to whether the decision challenged was based on relevant factors and whether there was a clear error in judgment. *Heisig v. United States*, 719 F.2d 1153 (Fed. Cir. 1983); *Sidoran v. Commissioner*, 640 F.2d 231 (9th Cir. 1981).

---

[435] Actually I did **not** receive a full copy. Omitted, for example, were the illegal CID lineup pictures. Some important evidence, such as the **complete** Hickey notes, was also omitted from [possibly the original as well] ROI because they may have contained information contradicting the ROI's agenda.

The facts in the administrative record support the conclusion that the CID decision not to remove plaintiff's name from the title block was not arbitrary or capricious. There was sufficient evidence from which the Army decision maker could determine that probable cause existed to believe that the plaintiff committed the offenses. The fact that reasonable minds may differ over the conclusions reached does not mean that Army decision makers made a clear error in judgment. See *Motor Vehicle Mfrs. Ass'n v. State Farm Mutual Automobile Ins. Co.*, 463 U.S. 29, 43 (1983); *Benvenuti v. Department of Defense*, 613 F. Supp. 308, 311-12 (D. D.C. 1985), *aff'd*, 802 F.2d 469 (Fed. Cir. 1986).

An appropriate order shall issue.

/s/ Claude M. Hilton
United States District Judge
Alexandria, Virginia

July 1, 1991
Judge's Footnotes

a. 32 C.F.R. #505.5 provides in part:

(2) **Exemption**: All portions of this system of records (Criminal Investigations and Crime Laboratory Files) which fall within 5 U.S.C. #552a(j)(2) are exempt from [5 U.S.C. #552a(d)&(g)] ...

(4) **Reasons**: ... (b) From subsections ... (d) ... and (g) because access might compromise on- going investigations, reveal classified information, investigatory techniques or the identity of confidential informants, or invade the privacy of persons who provide information in connection with a particular investigation. The exemption from access necessarily includes exemption from amendment, certain agency requirements relating to access and amendment of records, and civil liability predicated upon agency compliance with those specific provisions of the Privacy Act. This exemption from access necessarily includes exemption from other requirements.

b. Army Regulation 195-2, Criminal Investigation Activities, para. 4-4b (Oct. 30, 1985) provides:

b. *Amendment of CID reports*. CID reports of investigation are exempt from the amendment provisions of the Privacy Act and AR 340-21. Requests for amendment will be considered only under the provisions of this regulation. Requests to amend CID reports of investigation will be granted only if the individual submits new, relevant, and material facts that are determined to warrant revision of the report. The burden of proof is on the individual. Requests to delete a person's name from the title block will be granted if it is determined that probable cause does not exist to believe that the individual committed the offense for which titled as a subject.

Appendix 70: Gary Myers' Court of Appeals Brief

[Note: This was a mammoth, telephone-book-size document, with extensive citations and appendices. Only the case-fact sections are reproduced here (without their also-extensive footnotes).]

In the United States Court of Appeals for the Fourth Circuit

No. 90-1547-A

Michael Aquino, Plaintiff-Appellant,
v.
The Honorable Michael Stone, Secretary of the Army, Defendant-Appellee

**On Appeal from the United States District Court
for the Eastern District of Virginia**

BRIEF FOR APPELLANT

Issues Presented for Review

I. Whether the district court erred in denying application of the Privacy Act to a request for expungement on the basis that an Army regulation exempts criminal investigatory records from civil actions compelling expungement of inaccurate information in such records.

II. Whether, assuming the district court correctly concluded that the exemption regulation bars this action under the Privacy Act, the court erred in concluding that the Army's findings were not arbitrary and capricious under the Administrative Procedure Act.

Standard of Review

The appropriate standard of review with respect to issues I and II is *de novo*. As this circuit previously has recognized, "summary judgments are reviewed *de novo* on appeal." *Miller v Federal Deposit Insurance Corporation*, 906 F.2d 972, 974 (4th Cir. 1990); *Higgins v Dupont De Nemours & Co.*, 863 F.2d 1162, 1166-67 (4th Cir. 1988); *Felty v Graves-Humphreys Co.*, 818 F.2d 1126, 1127-28 (4th Cir. 1987). Moreover statutory interpretation is reviewed *de novo* in other circuits. *U.S. v Horowitz* 756 F.2d 1400 (9th Cir. 1985) *cert. denied* 106 S.Ct. 74, *U.S. v Montova* 827 F.2d 143 (7th Cir. 1987), *U.S. v Robinson*, 887 F.2d 656 (6th Cir. 1989).

Jurisdiction

The district court had jurisdiction over this case under the Privacy Act, 5 U.S.C. 552a (g), and this court has appellate jurisdiction under 28 U.S.C. 1291 (appeal from a final decision of the district court).

Statement of the Case

A. Nature of the Case and Prior Proceedings

Plaintiff filed a complaint on November 15, 1990 seeking damages and a declaratory judgment to amend the titling action and to remove Plaintiff's name from the title block of United States Army Criminal Investigation Command (USACIDC or CID) Report of Investigation (ROI) final "C"-0610-88-CIDCO26-6925 5K3/6F3/6E7/6A1/5M2/5y2/DIMIS under 5 U.S.C. § 552a(g) (1) (A) & (C) of the Administrative Procedure Act

(APA). The plaintiff was titled for Conspiracy, Kidnapping, Sodomy, Indecent Acts and False Swearing. Plaintiff contended the Privacy Act provides for *de novo* judicial review of the amendment request, or if the ROI is found exempt under subsection (j) (2) of the Act, then the action is reviewable as an agency action under the APA.

The Army argued that its failure to amend or expunge the ROI was exempted under the provisions of the Privacy Act allowing agencies to exempt criminal investigatory records pursuant to 5 U.S.C. 552a(j) (2) and the Army's implementing regulation. 32 C.F.R. § 505.5, ID-A0508.1aUSACIDC. The Army also argued that it had not acted arbitrarily or capriciously in refusing to amend the ROI, and that there was no basis for an award of damages. Both sides moved for summary judgment.

By order entered July 1, 1991 the district court agreed with the Army, finding the ROI exempt from amendment under the Privacy Act. It also found that the Army had not acted arbitrarily or capriciously in refusing to amend the ROI under the APA, and that there was no basis for an award of damages. Plaintiff appealed.

B. The District Court Decision

The district court first rejected the plaintiff's argument that the (j) (2) exemption is not viable when the reasons listed in the Army's exemption regulation do not apply in the particular case. The court also rejected the plaintiff's argument that there is no necessity for the exemption when the ROI is fully revealed and the titling action is completed. The court, interpreting *Ryan v Dept of Justice*, 595 F.2d at 954, 958, (4th Cir. 1979), held that the Army regulation had completely exempted the entire CID record system by promulgating rules and complying with the requirement to state the reasons for the exemption in the rule. The court further found that the exemption under subsection (j) (2) is a general exemption which applies to a whole system of records, and that the Privacy Act does not require a regulation's rationale to apply in each particular case, citing only *Wentz v Dept. of Justice*, 772 F.2d 335, 337 (7th Cir. 1985), *cert. denied*, 475 U.S. 1086 (1986) and *Shapiro v Drug Enforcement Agency*, 721 F.2d 215, 218 (7th Cir. 1983).

Under the APA standard of review, the court found that the Army's refusal to amend the ROI was not arbitrary and capricious, relying on the "considerable deference" traditionally afforded Army decision-makers under *Heisig v U.S.*, 719 F.2d 1153 (Fed. Cir. 1983); *Sidoran v Commissioner*, 640 F.2d 231 (9th Cir. 1981). The court then stated that the facts supported the CID decision not to amend the ROI and there was sufficient evidence of probable cause to believe that the plaintiff committed the offenses. Finally the court held that sovereign immunity is not waived under the APA, so there was no basis for an award of damages. By order the court dismissed the case, denying the plaintiff's motion for summary judgment and granting the Army's motion for summary judgment. The plaintiff's appeal followed.

C. The Statutory Scheme and the Army Exemption Regulation

Under the Privacy Act an individual may gain access to, and may request amendment of his record or any information which is contained in a system of records maintained by an agency whenever he believes the records are not "accurate, relevant, timely or complete". 5 U.S.C. § 552a(d) (1) and (2). Under subsection (g) an individual is permitted to bring a civil action against the agency in the U.S. district courts whenever any agency refuses to amend the records. However an agency may exempt law enforcement records from the application of subsection (d) and (g) under subsection (j) (2) if the system of records is

... (2) maintained by an agency or component thereof which performs as its principal function any activity pertaining to the enforcement of criminal laws ... and which consists of ... (B) information compiled for the purposes of a criminal investigation ....

Under the more inclusive language of subsection (k) of the Act, an agency can exempt records from specific provisions (including (d)) if the system of records is

... (2) investigatory material compiled for law enforcement purposes, other than material within the scope of subsection (g) (2).

To properly exempt a system of records, both sections require that the agency "promulgate rules, pursuant to the rulemaking requirements of § 553(b) ... and state the reasons in the rule why the system of records is to be exempted from a provision of" the Act.

The Army has promulgated a regulation, 32 C.F.R. § 505.5, exempting ROIs as part of its CID record system, and has stated the specific reasons why the record system is exempt. The regulation provides in part:

(2) **Exemption** - All portions of this system of records (Criminal Investigations and Crime Laboratory Files) which fall within 5 U.S.C. § 552a(j)(2) are exempt from (5 U.S.C. § 552a(d) and (g) ....

(4) **Reasons** - ...(b) From subjections (d) ... and (g) because access might compromise ongoing investigations, reveal classified information, investigatory techniques or the identity of confidential informants, or invade the privacy of persons who provide information in connection with a particular investigation.

D. Relevant Facts

Plaintiff is a lieutenant colonel in the United States Army Reserve. His name appears in the title block of a CID ROI for Conspiracy, Kidnapping, Sodomy, Indecent Acts with a Child and False Swearing. II app. 227. The test for titling is that of probable cause. AR 195-2, para. 4-4b, add. A-11.

Kinsey Adams-Thompson appears in the victim block of that report. She and her parents were interviewed by an FBI agent about allegations of child abuse at the U.S. Army Presidio, California, Child Development Center (CDC) in 1987 because Kinsey told a doctor at the Fort that a CDC employee, Gary Hambright, had sexually molested her.[436] II app. 514. Multiple children came forward to tell of abuse at the CDC and were subsequently interviewed by the FBI. I app. 13. Later, an investigation of LTC Aquino and his wife also commenced.

Plaintiff adopted Satanism as his religion and started the Temple of Set. Kinsey Adams-Thompson's father is an active-duty captain in the Army Chaplain Corps and was a Baptist minister. I app. 12. Captain Adams-Thompson was familiar with and knew plaintiff and his Satanist beliefs when he was stationed at the same military post, Presidio, California. II app. 409.

In August 1987, Kinsey's parents reported to the FBI that Kinsey has identified plaintiff and plaintiff's wife while shopping at the Presidio PX. II app. 352. Plaintiff was on leave from his current duty station in St. Louis, MO. I app. 44.

In January 1988, plaintiff made a written sworn statement denying the allegations against him and preferring sworn charges against Captain Adams-Thompson, the child's father. II app. 301, 390. Plaintiff charged Captain Adams-Thompson with conduct unbecoming an officer because the Captain reported the allegations of child abuse to the San Francisco police.[437] Based on these sworn statements, plaintiff was investigated for false swearing.

In August 1988, the San Francisco district attorney's office and FBI closed their investigations without filing any charges against plaintiff or anyone else. I app. 17.

---

[436] As evidenced in the [incomplete] Hickey notes (Appendix #12), Kinsey initially denied [as she had previously to the FBI] that Hambright had molested her. Only after repeated insistence by Hickey did Kinsey say what Hickey wanted.

[437] Not "conduct unbecoming", but rather "making a false official statement" [to investigators from the FBI/SFPD].

In September 1988 CID officials met with representatives from the SFPD, the local district attorney's office, the U.S. Attorney's Office, and the FBI to discuss the status of the case. I app. 7.[438]

The investigation immediately received national and international attention in various newspapers and tabloids.[439] In September and early October, plaintiff appeared on several nationally broadcasted TV talk shows including the "Geraldo Rivera Show" and "Oprah Winfrey Show." II app. 117, 119.

In October 1988 a CID Investigative Plan for plaintiff's case was drafted in light of the perceived weaknesses of the previous investigation. II app. 528.[440]

Also in October 1988 a staff aide to Senator Jesse Helms sent a letter to the Secretary of the Army complaining about plaintiff's appearance on these TV shows about Satanism and witchcraft. The staff aide asked for personal attention into the matter and raised the possibility of future Congressional hearings to consider legislation. II app. 117-18. A subsequent letter was sent by Senator Helms to the Secretary in the same fashion in January 1989. II app. 119-20.

In November 1988 a high-level meeting took place in the Pentagon to discuss the Aquino matter. II app. 121. The Judge Advocate General of the Army met with Senator Helms to discuss the matter in early 1989. II app. 120. The Statute of Limitations ran on all alleged crimes June 1989. I app. 12-13, 44-45.

The Final ROI was issued in August 1989, determining that there was probable cause to title LTC Aquino and his wife with the above-noted offenses. I app. 44 at n. 3, II app. 286.

Mrs. Aquino was later dropped from the ROI on all charges on the basis of insufficient probable cause. II app. 287-288.

Plaintiff was denied continued active-duty status as an AGR officer after a Continuation Board was informed of "flagged status" due to the investigation. I app. 12.

Plaintiff appealed the ROI in January 1990. The Commanding General of the CID adopted final recommendations on the ROI in September 1990, dropping some titled offenses. Plaintiff remains titled for Conspiracy, Kidnapping, Sodomy, Indecent Acts and False Swearing.

Plaintiff filed his complaint in Federal District Court, Eastern District of Virginia in November 1990.

Introduction and Summary of Argument

By adopting the Army's argument allowing a blanket exemption of its investigatory records to reject plaintiff's request for amendment under the Privacy Act, the district court has done significant damage to the language and structure of the Act and the Army's own regulations. This holding must be overturned.

---

[438] So the CID would much later claim in order to imply that its investigation of me had pre-dated Helms' communiqués to Secretary of the Army Marsh. However not a single piece of documentation from either the CID or any of these other agencies was ever produced to substantiate this claim.

[439] This publicity refers to the FBI & SFPD investigations of A-T's allegations, which were opened the moment he made them in August 1987. The Army CID's investigation was not opened until November 1988, post-Helms.

[440] There was no "Investigation Plan" - only a memo from Captain Harvey suggesting possible illegal ways to try to incriminate me. No mention whatever was made in that letter of "perceived weaknesses" or of any other investigation at all. See Appendix #66.

The district court's decision has effectively granted the Army an exemption not found in the statute's and regulations' plain language. The result nullifies Congress' intent to subject all agency rulemaking to the notice and comment requirements.

Moreover the Army's unprecedented liberal interpretation of the statute is inconsistent with every circuit, and contrary to the history and purpose of the Privacy Act exemption provisions. This court must act firmly to correct this error because the district court's holding is sweeping and categorical, and sets this circuit on a path at odds with clear judicial trends.

Ryan and *Wentz* provide no support for the district court's conclusion that the reasons for a Privacy Act exemption need not apply in each case. To the contrary, *Ryan* has been clarified and extended by other circuits to mean that the reasons for exempting a system of records must affirmatively be demonstrated to be present in each particular record for which exemption is invoked. Secondly, *Wentz* has been harmonized with this judicial trend while limiting the case's holding to its unique facts.

The clear judicial trend is to utilize standards developed under the Freedom of Information Act to determine whether records are exempt from access and disclosure under the Privacy Act. This circuit has consistently recognized this direction of the law by adopting necessary precedents from other circuits. The facts of this case call for this circuit to take the next logical step in that judicial trend and apply these standards to the plaintiff's request for amendment of his records under the Privacy Act.

Accordingly, as we now show, the ROI plaintiff seeks to amend is not exempt under the Act and implementing Army regulation. Therefore the district court's decision must be reversed with instructions to apply the Privacy Act.

Alternatively we also show that, if exempt under the Privacy Act, the district court erred in finding the Army's refusal to amend the ROI not arbitrary and capricious under the Administrative Procedure Act. The district court's decision must be reversed with instructions to consider all the relevant factors in its review of the Army's titling action, or to state its reasons for its findings.

Argument

I. The amendment provisions of the Privacy Act apply to the records in this case.

To reverse the district court's holding rejecting Aquino's request for amendment of a Report of Investigation, this Court must first determine that the Privacy Act and the Army's regulation do not allow the Army to exempt itself from a civil action seeking amendment or expungement of its Criminal Investigation and Crime Laboratory records.

A. The plain language of the Privacy Act and the Army's own regulation prohibit the Army from exempting itself for a failure to amend or expunge the ROI.

1. The language of the Statute and Army regulation prohibit "Blanket Exemptions" of law enforcement record systems.

[Extensive, detailed, and source-cited legal text skipped here.]

... The language of subsection (j) (2) (B) of the Privacy Act states that agency record systems qualify for exemption only if courts and agencies have defined "law enforcement purpose."

2. A law enforcement purpose is satisfied by passing the *Pratt* Test and by falling within the reasons stated in the agency's implementing regulation.

The *Pratt* test for "law enforcement purpose" was initially devised in a FOIA exemption 7 context by the D.C. Circuit. *Pratt v Webster*, 673 F.2d 408, 420-421 (D.C. Cir. 1982). The case has broad applicability because it held "that federal agencies, including the FBI, must meet the threshold requirements of the exemption." *Id*. at 416.

Several circuits, including the 4th Circuit, have adopted the *Pratt* test in evaluating exemption 7 of the FOIA.

The *Pratt* test rejects an automatic blanket exception for the law enforcement exemption. The blanket exemption has also been referred to as the "*per se* rule". Instead, the agency must make "a two-fold threshold showing, and then must show that the document fits into one of the six subsections". *Freeman* at 1122. This threshold inquiry mandates analysis "in [each] case with respect to [each] investigative file".

We first address the threshold requirements of the *Pratt* test.

a. Part I

The threshold inquiry is the first half of the *Pratt* test, and consists of two criteria. First, "the agency must demonstrate a connection between its investigation of an individual and the existence of a possible ... violation of federal law". *John Doe* at 1353 citing *Pratt* 673 F.2d 420. Secondly, the "nexus between the investigation and one of the agency's law enforcement duties must be based on information sufficient to support ... a colorable claim of its rationality". *Pratt* at 421.

This second requirement is not met where the agency offers a "pretextual or wholly unbelievable" basis for a claim. A pretextual. basis exists when there is "evidence that would suggest that the [agency] was motivated by anything other than genuine investigatory concerns". *John Doe* at 1354.

In applying this threshold inquiry, the Privacy Act dictates a standard that all records concerning individuals be maintained "with such accuracy ... and completeness as is necessary to assure fairness". 5 U.S.C. § 552a(g) (1) (C). "The Act was designed to create a code of fair information practices ...." *Smiertke v U.S Dept. of Treasury*, 447 F. Supp. 221, 224 (D.D.C. 1978), *remanded on other grounds*, 604 F. 2d 698 (D.C. Cir. 1979). "An agency, we think it plain ... dishonors the Privacy Act standard of 'accuracy... necessary to assure fairness' if it collects and keeps without careful investigation derogatory information from unreliable sources or of a kind that could be run to earth with a reasonable degree of certainty." *Jane Doe v U.S.* 821 F.2d 694, 699 (D.C. Cir. 1987) (*en banc*) (court review of State Dept. refusal to amend ROI under Privacy Act). The *Jane Doe* court also noted,

> The reasonable record-keeper, guided by a standard stressing fairness, should be particularly vigilant in requiring independent, reliable verification of undocumented, damaging bits of information gathered from third parties. *Jane Doe* at n. 14 (emphasis added) *citing in support Doe v U.S Civil Service Comm'n* 483 F. Supp. 539, 579-80 (S.D.N.Y. 1980).

Also particularly relevant to the present case, the court in *Jane Doe* stressed that in certain cases involving "Communist associations, homosexual relations or child abuse [allegations are] generally susceptible of objective inquiry, so that an agency would be remiss ... if it sought no independent verification. We have underscored this very point." *Id*. at n. 20 (rebuttal to dissent of Wald, C.J.) (emphasis added).

In applying this threshold inquiry to agencies whose principle function is not law enforcement, the courts have employed a more stringent test, so the "court must scrutinize with some skepticism the particular purpose claimed for disputed documents under exemption." *Pratt* at 418. These are "mixed-function agencies" such as the U.S. Army or National Labor Relations Board, whereas the FBI or Drug Enforcement Agency function principally as criminal law enforcement agencies.

To fulfill the "nexus criteria" under this higher standard of scrutiny, the "law enforcement purpose must relate to some type of formal proceeding, and one that is pending". This "pending proceeding rule" has been construed to apply in the 4th Circuit in the FOIA exemption 7 context. The *Pratt* court concurred and found that for mixed-function agencies to satisfy the law enforcement test, "it is necessary for the investigation to lead to a criminal prosecution or other enforcement proceeding ...." *Id.* at 421, n. 33.

We now turn to the second half of the *Pratt* test.

b. Part II

The second half of the *Pratt* test requires the agency to fit the records at issue within one of six subsections. The subsections are the categories listed in FOIA Exemption 7, and identify six types of disclosure-related harms deemed to be the only valid reasons for the law enforcement exemption. *Id.* at 417.

Fitting the records at issue into one of the categories is a distinct element of the *Pratt* test.

3. Proper analysis under Section (j) (2) of the Privacy Act utilizes standards developed under the FOIA in determining whether records are exempt from amendment.

There is a clear judicial trend to apply legal standards developed under the law enforcement exemption 7 of the FOIA to construe agency regulations under exemption (j) (2) of the Privacy Act.

In *Doe* the court "borrowed" the *Pratt* test for law enforcement purposes, noting the "test adapts well to the Privacy Act context because the language of subsection (k)(2), the more inclusive of the Act's two exemption provisions, is virtually identical to that of FOIA exemption 7".

Moreover these courts applied the whole *Pratt* test in the Privacy Act context. *John Doe* at 1356 ("[I]n both contexts there is a threshold inquiry as to whether disputed material is properly characterized as compiled for law enforcement purposes.")

Application of the *Pratt* test analogized the application of the six categories under the FOIA exemption 7 to application of the reasons requirements under § 552a (j). *Exner* at 1209; *John Doe* at 1356-57; *Andrews* at 1413-14.

The only difference between the two exemptions is that under FOIA 7 the reasons are expressly restricted by statute, while under § 552a(j) (2) Congress granted agencies "broad discretion" to promulgate their reasons in exemption regulations.

For example, the harms are listed under FOIA 7, so treatment of records is "fairly straightforward". However "(i]n creating subsections (j) and (k) of the Privacy Act, Congress did not delineate the agency interests justifying exemption ...." *John Doe* at 1357.

Even though agencies possess discretion under the Privacy Act, the courts still found that "holding the [agencies] to the specific reasons stated in [their] exemption regulation(s) ... fully appropriate" and "reflects Congress' intent that agencies only employ Privacy Act exemptions where truly necessary".

a. The legal foundation for the judicial trend of applying FOIA standards in the Privacy Act context was laid by the 4th Circuit in *Ryan* and *Local 2047*.

The bedrock cases of *Ryan* and *Local 2047* are responsible in part for the articulation and extension of the *Pratt* doctrine and its application in construing exemptions under the Privacy Act.

The *Ryan* rationale was directly relied on, its rationale followed or extended, by all circuits confronting the issue. *Exner* at 1207, 1209, (citing *Ryan* apply FOIA standard to Privacy Act exemption; reason for exemption must be consistent with reasons in regulation); *Fendler* at 553 (agency must rely on reasons in regulations); *Andrews* at 1411, 1413-1414 (citing *Ryan* to extend rationale to routine use of exemption; cited *Local 2047* to apply FOIA standards to interpret Privacy Act exemption); *Nakash* at 1365 (citing *Ryan*); *Castenda* at 86 (applying reasons stated in regulations); *John Doe* at 1357 (apply FOIA standard to Privacy Act exemption; FBI rationale for exemption must be justified by reasons in regulations); *Simon* at 23 (agency must explain its reasons in detail for each document to justify exemption, citing *Exner*); *Tijerina* at 796 (reasons cited in regulation must be served to justify exemption from civil liability).

The 4th Circuit is following the trend it set in *Ryan* and *Local 2047* since it has already taken the necessary steps.

First, by adopting the *Pratt* test in a FOIA exemption 7 context, the Circuit established the precursor to extending the test in a section (j) (2) context. *Freeman* at 1123.

Secondly, this Circuit has rejected the "blanket exemption" approach in a "reverse" FOIA exemption 4 case (has the same effect as a Privacy Act exemption from access). *Hercules v Marsh Secy. of the Army* 839 F.2d 1027, 1029 (4th Cir. 1988) (reverse FOIA action to enjoin U.S. Army by government contractor who claimed exemption from access on statutory provision, 5 U.S.C. § 552(b)(4)). In *Hercules* the court found that merely invoking exemption categories was insufficient since they were "not a mandatory bar" to access. *Id.* at 1029. The court, after applying the Army's regulation to the records at issue, held the exemption did not apply because its underlying reasons had not been satisfied. *Id.* at 1029-30 (failed to establish "likelihood of harm" from disclosure). Thus this Circuit should apply the *Hercules* FOIA standard to reject "blanket exemptions" in the Privacy Act context, or at least be consistent with its underlying principle when construing agency exemption regulations under the Act.

Finally, several circuits have clarified and extended the *Ryan* and *Local 2047* rules to require the reasons for Privacy Act exemptions be affirmatively demonstrated to be present for each particular record. Although not binding upon this circuit, their rationale is persuasive and thoroughly supported by the legislative history and purpose underlying the Privacy Act.

This development of the law calls for the logical extension of the *Pratt* test to the (j) (2) law enforcement exemption of the Act. With this in mind we apply the *Pratt* test to the facts in this case.

4. **The ROI fails to qualify for exemption under the Pratt test and reasons stated in the Army regulation.**

a. **The plain language of the statute and regulation prohibit a blanket exemption.**

The district court adopted the Army's argument that its regulation "has completely exempted this entire system of records from the civil remedies provision of the Privacy Act". By accepting the Army's remarkable proposition, the district court has in effect allowed the Army to promulgate an exemption not found in the regulation's plain language: an automatic blanket exemption from amendment requests.

The Army has not provided in its regulation **any** justification for completely and wholly exempting its investigatory records from the individual amendment request provision of subsection (d) of the Act, and this court should not condone such a usurpation of the rulemaking process.

Instead of providing a blanket exemption, the Army's regulation exempts a record only if amendment would have one of five adverse effects.

No agency was granted a blanket exemption under the Privacy Act, not even the Central Intelligence Agency, which must still subject portions of its entire record system to the reasons stated in its regulation.

The district court, by adopting the Army's proposition, also accepted its erroneous interpretation of caselaw and flawed understanding of the Act and its own regulation.

The Army argued that the exemption justification need not apply to Aquino's specific amendment request, but may be invoked because it applies **generally** to all amendment requests, regardless of the particular facts in each case. The Army relies for this contention not on the language of its regulation, which exempts only specified records or files from amendment, or on cases that interpret similar regulations with the statute, but on cases discussing exemption provisions of the Act which **permit** the Army to claim a general exemption for a system of records. I app. 48, 84-85, 9192.

If this Court were to accept the Army's contention, it would sanction the wholesale exemption of entire record systems, no matter how **narrow** or **specific** an agency's stated justification for such exemption. Such an interpretation would eliminate the necessity for the statutorily-mandated justification and render the notice and comment requirements of the Act a nullity. Indeed this argument, which amounts to a justification for exemption stated only in this litigation, admits that the Army's regulation does not currently allow the maintenance of such a general exemption.

The caselaw relied upon by the district court and Army to permit a blanket exemption does not stand for the proposition which they contend, nor have they justified their inconsistent interpretation of these cases.

First, both completely ignored the *May* court's holding that both harmonized *Wentz* with other circuits and distinguished *Wentz* by limiting its application to its unique facts. Furthermore, not only has *Wentz* never been followed, but the district court's and Army's interpretation is directly contradicted by the unanimity of caselaw from other circuits that has clearly rejected blanket exemptions.

Secondly, *Wentz* cannot be relied upon in this case because it did not involve an interpretation of the language of the agency's regulation *vis-à-vis* the statute. For the same reason, neither can the district court rely on *Shapiro* 721 F.2d 215 (7th Cir. 1983), *vacated on other grounds sub nom*, *U.S Dept. of Justice v Provenzano*, 469 U.S. 14 (1984) (consolidating *Shapiro* and *Wentz* No. 83-5878) (court found that issue was moot whether exemption (j) (2) of the Privacy Act was a withholding statute under exemption 3 of the FOIA by enactment of P.L. 98-477, 98 Stat. 22O9.

The district court failed to recognize the broader implication of the legislation that mooted the question before the Supreme Court. The new law was enacted specifically to correct bad caselaw; to stop courts from reading Privacy Act exemption (j) (2) too broadly.

Shapiro can be distinguished on the same basis as *Wentz*: the holdings are limited by their unique facts. The *Kimberlin* court thus concluded in *Shapiro* "the reason given for denying an individual access to his [DEA] files ... was found sufficiently specific to satisfy the reason-giving requirement of § 552a(j) (2) ... because access to such records would alert a subject to the existence of an investigation ..."

The *Shapiro* holding can be further limited to those agencies whose "principal function is law enforcement", thus excluding mixed-function agencies such as the Army. *Shapiro* at 217-18.

However if the *Shapiro* case cannot be distinguished or its holding limited, then it is simply wrong. The court's broad interpretation is based merely on the label attached to section (j) (2) making it a "general" exemption as opposed to a "specific" exemption. This reasoning is untenable because it completely ignores other contextual elements of the statute and their interrelationship with the limiting language of the agency's regulation. *Id.* at n. i. Secondly, the terms only mean that agencies have an option to exempt records from "specific" provision of the Act or from all provisions "generally" permitted.

Finally, the district court and Army have distorted the *Ryan* holding by advancing an interpretation inconsistent with every other circuit relying on the case. These other circuits have clarified and extended *Ryan* to mean only that the rationale for exempting a system of records must affirmatively be demonstrated to be present in each particular record.

We next determine whether the Army's rationale for exempting the ROI is present in this particular case. The appropriate standard of review for making this determination, based on the *Pratt* test, is more rigorous than the deferential standard applied to criminal law agencies. In this case the Army is a mixed-function agency, so the court "must scrutinize with some skepticism the particular purpose claimed". *Pratt* at 418; *Freeman* at 1123. Finally, it is proper to challenge the "law enforcement purpose" of the Army under *Pratt* on appeal as the issue was fully preserved at the district level.

b. Part I - The ROI fails to qualify under the threshold inquiry.

The Army fails to satisfy the first prong of the threshold inquiry because its proffered evidence connecting Michael Aquino with the existence of a possible violation of federal law is tenuous at best, and entirely based on "undocumented, damaging bits of information gathered from third parties". *Jane Doe* at n. 14.

The Army has plainly "dishonored the Privacy Act standard of accuracy ... necessary to assure fairness" because it has collected and kept without careful investigation derogatory information from unreliable sources without "requiring independent, reliable verification." *Jane Doe* at 699, n. 14.

Moreover, in cases involving child abuse, allegations are generally susceptible of objective inquiry, "so any agency would be remiss if it sought no independent verification." *Jane Doe* at n. 20. Contrary to this standard, the Army's ROI finding of probable cause "connecting" Michael Aquino to crimes rests upon uncorroborated, third-party allegations, innuendo, and ignores critical exculpatory evidence. The finding flies in the face of the Army's own regulations requiring the "quality and quantity of all available evidence" be tested for both "relevancy and materiality".

The factual record is replete with unverified information:

(1) **no evidence of physical abuse of Kinsey Adams-Thompson.** I app. 13, 11 app. 416-422;

(2) **no evidence that Kinsey ever personally identified Michael Aquino** as "Mikey" to any law enforcement agency by photo, lineup or otherwise immediately after her parents had **alleged** an identification was made while shopping at the Presidio PX. **Thus Kinsey's parents' statement of the alleged identification was not corroborated** in any fashion, nor did any law enforcement agency ever attempt to investigate the identification scene for corroborating witnesses. I app. 13, 15-16, 38, 62; II app. 520, 523;

(3) **Kinsey never identified Michael Aquino's house.** I. app. 16-17, 63; II app. 298 (item 4), 352;

(4) **no proof of authenticity of alleged copies of the diary,** where the original was lost, allegedly kept by the mother contemporaneously with events. I app. 13-14;

(5) **The Army chose to ignore Michael Aquino's substantiated, absolute alibi defenses** on dates of alleged criminal conduct. Marshal Affidavit, I app. 24-27, II app. 102-04, 127-28 (painter performed work at crime scene on alleged day of crime); Butch Affidavit, I app. 27, II app. 258;

(6) **No evidence in the ROI of association, agreement, overt act or knowledge of other co-conspirator** Gary Hambright. Mrs. Aquino was dropped from the titling action for lack of probable cause. I app. 27, II app. 300 (item 4);

(7) **no corroboration from *any other children* interviewed on identity of Michael Aquino or his residence.** I app. 28, II app. 299 (item 4). **And see** "CID Investigative Plan: 17 Oct 1988 (requirement that **other** children identify Aquino from video lineup; requirement that "testimony of multiple children ... **will** factually **corroborate** the allegation."). 528-29 (items 1(e), 2).

Without establishing any shred of inculpatory evidence linking Michael Aquino to any crimes, the Army cannot reasonably conclude under the *Pratt* test that its investigation has "demonstrated a connection between Aquino and the existence of a possible violation of law." *Pratt* at 420.

The Army investigation fails to satisfy the "nexus to a colorable claim of its rationality" because there is undisputed evidence suggesting a pretextual basis for its titling action. The factual record indicates that Army investigators and high-level officials "were motivated by other than genuine investigatory concerns" and thus orchestrated a "campaign of appeasement" to remove Michael Aquino from the Army.

First, a highly-publicized and thorough investigation of the same case by the FBI and San Francisco Police Department in August 1988 was terminated after finding no probable cause. No charges were filed. I app. 17.

The following October Senator Jesse Helms viewed Mr. Aquino on several TV talk shows. Senator Jesse Helms then pressured the Army's highest officials to specifically get rid of Michael Aquino or risk embarrassing "Congressional hearings into this matter to consider appropriate legislation ...." I app. 17-20 (letters from staff aide and Senator).

In November the Army CID investigation was initiated on the simple premise that the FBI and SFPD investigation "was deficient". I app. 20.

On November 29, 1988 a high-level meeting took place at the Pentagon to discuss the Aquino matter and included seven senior Army and Defense Dept. officials and Congressional liaison officers. I app. 21. These officials adopted a policy of appeasement with Senator Helms. The solution was to deny Michael Aquino continuation as an AGR officer and to title him without ever charging him. The method was to allow the statute of limitations to run prior to titling, and use it as an excuse to avoid a public trial likely to end in acquittal. Discontinuation from AGR status was effected by improperly including reference to the investigation in the Continuation Board's review. I app. 21, II app. 264-66.

The second. pretextual grounds for the investigation point to Kinsey's parents as the only other moving force. This conclusion is inescapable because no other children interviewed by the FBI, SFPD, or Army CID **ever corroborated** identification of Michael Aquino and his residence. I app. 28-29. Also significant was that prior to any investigation, Kinsey's father, an Army chaplain, knew Michael Aquino and his belief in Satanism as both were stationed at the Presidio Army Post. I app. 13, II app. 409.

As a result of applying the rigorous standard of review to the evidence, it cannot be concluded that the Army investigation leading to a titling action constituted a legitimate law enforcement purpose under the *Pratt* threshold inquiry. The Army's law enforcement purpose is at best questionable, and certainly could not meet the probable cause standard stated in its own regulation.

c. Part III - The ROI fails to satisfy the reasons stated in the Army's regulation.

Assuming the ROI satisfies the *Pratt* threshold inquiry, it still fails to qualify under the "law enforcement purpose" test because it does not "fall within" one of the reasons stated in the Army's regulation. 32 C.F.R. § 505.5(2), (4)(a)-(g).

It is fully appropriate to hold the Army "to the specific reasons stated in its exemption regulation" and to allow exemption only if, and to the extent, amendment would result in one of the specified listed harms. *John Doe* at n. 17.

The Army is also limited to those exemption reasons which it has filed and explained, and cannot claim new ones in this lawsuit to serve a purpose not the subject of a prior rulemaking process.

The Army must make an affirmative showing that amendment of the ROI would result in one of the harms listed in its regulation; "bare conclusory allegations are not sufficient". *Irons* at 471. The Army, however, has ignored this requirement, offering only a bare-bones argument that the whole record system is exempt regardless of the nature of the documents therein.

Finally, since the Army is a mixed-function agency, the ROI must relate to some type of formal, pending proceeding.

The Army regulation provides five justifications for immunizing the ROI from the access and amendment provisions of subsection (d). The regulation mirrors exemption 7 of the FOIA, and recites the adverse effects that disclosure would have upon law enforcement. 32 C.F.R. § 505.5(2)(4)(b).

The first adverse effect is that disclosure and amendment would harm "ongoing investigations". As the FBI conceded in *Doe*, the Army must here concede that these access-related concerns do not apply where "the agency refuses to expunge information that has already been disclosed to the person seeking expungement". *John Doe* at 1357. Moreover,this justification has nothing to do with the circumstances of this case. Mr. Aquino knew he was being investigated and did not file an amendment request until after he was titled and the ROI was sitting in completed form at the Crime Records Center. I app. 61-62. The rationale for this exemption protects the ROI prior to its completion and during related ongoing investigations, but there is no necessity for such an exemption when the ROI is revealed, the titling action is completed and no allegations of ongoing investigations or pending, formal proceedings have been made. *NLRB* at 232; *Masonic Homes* at 18-19. Nor is the "mere hypothetical possibility of a future enforcement proceeding sufficient" to bring the disclosed ROI within a law enforcement purpose. *Lame v U.S. Dept. of Justice*, 645 F.2d 917, 920 (3rd Cir. 1981) (rule applied to mixed-function agencies). This principle flows from the remedial purpose of the Privacy Act which requires **all** records maintained by an agency, not just those "immediately needed", to be accurate, timely, relevant and complete." *R.R. v Dept. of the Army*, 482 F. Supp. 770, 774 (D.D.C. 1980).

None of the other justifications listed in the Army regulation apply to this case, nor has the Army alleged **any** reasons consistent with these justifications to exempt the ROI from amendment. In effect the Army is asking this court to accept an unprecedented liberal interpretation of the Act and its regulation: namely the Army maintains that any amendment of investigatory records in its CID system, **whatever the nature** of information collected and **no matter what length of time** records have been maintained, would in **all** cases be exempt. This contention overstates the Army's Privacy Act statutory duty to assure fairness by verifying differing accounts of events against the factual record. *Jane Doe* at 701, (D.C. Cir. 1987) (*en banc*).

This court should overturn the district court's decision accepting this unprecedented interpretation of the Army's exemption regulation and the Privacy Act. The court should also find that the Army has not met its burden to qualify its ROI within the "law enforcement purpose" exemption (j) (2), and remand with instructions to apply the amendment provisions of the Privacy Act.

II. Even if the ROI is exempt, the District Court improperly applied the Administrative Procedure Act's review standard of "arbitrary and capricious". 5 U.S.C. 706(2) (A)

A. The district court abused its discretion by failing to state the reasons for Its decision in finding the Army's action not arbitrary and capricious.

The district court failed to adequately explain the reasons why it found the CID decision not to remove Michael Aquino's name from the title block not arbitrary and capricious. This appellate court's institutional interest in reviewability demands articulation of the district court's reasons. *Farmington Dowel Products Co. v Forster Mgf. Co.* 436 F.2d 699, 701-02 (1st Cir. 1970).

Under this standard of review of arbitrary and capricious, the district court must make a searching and careful inquiry in determining whether the Army took a "hard look" at all relevant factors when it titled Michael Aquino. *Citizens to Protect Overton Park v Volpe, Sec'y of Transportation*, 401 U.S. 402, 417 (1971) (hereinafter *Overton Park*). *Hutto Stockyard In. v U.S. Dept. of Agriculture*, 903 F.2d 299, 305 (4th Cir. 1990).

This judicial inquiry must include "the whole record" to ensure the Army's decision was not a clear error of judgment. However the Supreme Court in *Overton Park* cautioned that "since the bare record may not disclose the factors that were considered or the [agency's] construction of the evidence, it may be necessary for the District Court to require some explanation in order to determine if the [agency] acted within the scope of [its] authority".

The district court, however, ignored this principle by providing only general, conclusory statements without pointing to any specific factors relied upon by the Army to title Michael Aquino. Without any visible, underlying basis for its conclusions, the court merely recites excerpts of the Army's Brief, "[t]he facts support ... the CID decision ... there was substantial evidence from which the Army decision-maker could determine probable cause ...."

Neither did the district court address whether its consideration of relevant factors included application of the Army's own regulations.

Since Michael Aquino's case was dismissed on summary judgment, the absence of any discussion of relevant factors is remarkable. The district court's lack of reasons is even more startling, considering that a finding of probable cause under the ROI in this case, is equivalent to a criminal indictment involving five felonies.

As a result of the district court's failure to state its reasons for finding that the Army's decision was not arbitrary and capricious, this court has insufficient basis on which to review its decision. The district court's order granting summary judgment for the Army must be vacated, and the case remanded with instructions that the district court adequately explain its reasons for affirming the Army's finding of probable cause in the ROI involving Michael Aquino.

B. Assuming reasons were sufficiently stated by the district court, the Army is not afforded considerable deference when it is acting outside its special function.

The district court adopted the Army's argument that under the arbitrary and capricious review standard, "the Army decision-maker is (traditionally) afforded considerable deference."

On examination, these cases do not really help the Army, rather they can be distinguished as all involving appeals from Boards of Military Records from within the various branches of the military. These cases involve agencies acting pursuant to their enabling statutes, and thus are "entitled to considerable deference when exercising [their] special functions of applying general provisions of the Act to the complexities of [internal activities]". *NLRB v Brown* 380 U.S. 278, 291-292 (1965), quoted *U.S. Dept. of Health and Human Services v FLRA* 844 F.2d 1.087, 1094 (4th Cir. 1988).

The present case, however, involves a direct appeal from the Army CID to a Federal District Court pursuant to law enforcement activities, thus there is no special function or expertise entitling the Army decision-makers "considerable deference". The Army in this case is operating outside of its primary function, acting as a mixed-function agency, whereas in the cases above, the agencies' activities clearly fell within the military services' enabling statutes. The present case is an action brought independent of any enabling statutes, under the Privacy Act, 5 U.S.C. § 552a(g).

1. The district court failed to consider pre-decisional bias in the titling action as a relevant factor.

Since the Army's decision refusing to amend the ROI is not entitled to special deference, the court must take a "hard look" at the "whole record" ensuring that all relevant factors were considered.

Relevant factors would necessarily include any procedural requirements and any "unique" or "extraordinary" circumstances having an adverse effect on the titling action. *Overton* at 412-413 ("truly unusual factors in a particular case ... reached extraordinary magnitudes" thus it was appropriate to justify giving weight to that factor" *quoted in Maryland Wildlife Federation v Dole* 747 F.2d 229, 244 (4th Cir. 1984) (Winter, J. dissenting) (noting the majority's consideration of unique and extraordinary circumstances as relevant factors under the APA arbitrary and capricious review standard).

Such an example would be pre-decisional bias, particularly when there is evidence suggesting that high-ranking deciders within the agency, or other outside, inappropriately effected the impartiality of the process. *See FTC v Cement Institute*, 333 U.S. 683 (1948); *Gilligan, Will & Co. v SEC* 267 F.2d 461 (2d Cir.) *cert. denied*, 361 U.S. 896 (1959) (circuit decision is the most frequently quoted test for bias: "whether a disinterested observer may conclude that the agency has in some measure adjudged the facts as well as the law of a particular case in advance of hearing it.")

Such is the present case, where there is undisputed, substantial evidence pointing to improper influence and political pressure exerted on the titling process by Congressional officials and staff and high-ranking Army officials not normally involved in criminal investigations. I app. 17-22. The bias resulted from a concerted effort of appeasement of the Army in response to Senator Jesse Helms. Senator Helms, who after seeing Michael Aquino on several TV talk shows, decided that the Army must get rid of the officer. There is undisputed evidence that the Secretary of the Army and other high-level officials were personally involved in management and oversight of the titling action. I app. 17-19. The appeasement was to avoid embarrassing Congressional hearings on "this matter" threatened by the Senator. I app. 18-19. The evidence of pre-decisional bias is even more convincing because prior to commencement of the CID investigation, the FBI and San Francisco police had completed their investigation of the same matter without filing any charges, indictments or making any arrests. I app. 17.

Despite the undisputed, substantial evidence of predecisional bias, the district court's opinion makes no reference to it. Nor does the opinion even hint that it considered bias as a relevant factor in its review of the Army's action refusing to amend the titling action. Nor does the Army dispute in its Brief the existence of Congressional influence and involvement by high-level Army officials.

It is quite probable that in response to the unexpected publicity and congressional intervention in this particular case, the Army decided to amend its Access and Amendment Refusal Authority regulation to delegate responsibility for handling such requests under the Privacy Act. This amendment was filed five weeks after Michael Aquino's trial hearing (or six months after filing his complaint).

The delegation to much lower level supervisors suggests that the Army now seeks to avoid further high-profile Privacy Act requests by adding another layer of review while "keeping a lid" on potentially embarrassing requests. Moreover this recent change removes higher-level officials from the opportunity to exert pre-decisional bias. The timing of this Army amendment with the filing of this complaint and past notoriety suggests that the Army did recognize some degree of inappropriate activity in Privacy Act requests in general.

In sum, the district court failed to consider the relevant factor of pre-decisional bias in its review of the Army's titling action. This court should vacate the district court's order for summary judgment and remand with instructions to consider all relevant factors, or to adequately state its reasons why it chose not to consider this factor.

Conclusion

For the foregoing reasons, the district court's grant of summary judgment rejecting plaintiff's Privacy Act amendment request should be reversed, and the case should be remanded with instructions to apply the Act's amendment provisions.

Alternatively, the district court erred in finding the Army's refusal to amend the ROI not arbitrary and capricious under the Administrative Procedure Act. The district court's decision should be reversed with instructions to consider all the relevant factors in its review of the Army's titling action, or to state its reasons for its findings.

Respectfully submitted,
/s/ Gary Myers, Esq.
/s/ John A. Wickham, Esq.
Gary Myers and Associates
Attorneys for Appellant Michael Aquino

Appendix 71: TJAG/CID Court of Appeals Brief Statements Analysis

False Official Statements by Major Patrick Lisowski to the
U.S. Court of Appeals for the Fourth Circuit
Case #91-1164
Cited in the Opinion of the Court on February 26, 1992
- identified as of March 23, 1992 by Lt.Col. Michael A. Aquino -

[The following statements by the court in its published opinion are identified in regular type to pages in that decision, and then in Italics to false statements by Lisowski in his brief relied upon by the court to reach that decision. Where no Italics are cited, comments relate to documents provided as "truthful" by Lisowski to the court. This analysis is not a complete listing of all false statements by Lisowski in the brief, but rather of only those which were singled out by the court for reference in its Opinion.]

1. Page 2: "Lieutenant Colonel Michael Aquino, formerly of the U.S. Army Reserves ..." *Page 11: "Appellant-Plaintiff Michael A. Aquino was a Lieutenant Colonel in the United States Army Reserve; he is now retired from the Army."*

   A. I remain a Lieutenant Colonel in the the Active/Selected U.S. Army Reserve. This false statement by Lisowski clearly conveys the impression that I was either forced out of the Reserve or voluntarily retired from it due to this scam.

   B. The obvious implication is that my suit is less important because I am no longer a serving officer, and that all parts of the Army accepted and agreed with the CID's fraudulent report.

   C. The truth is that I refused to allow my career to be terminated by the scam. My chain of command agreed with me, continuing throughout the investigation and subsequent to the titling to issue me officer efficiency reports **of the highest evaluation, and with special commendation of my moral standards**.

   D. After the fraudulent titling action my file was unflagged, I served the remainder of my scheduled AGR tour, and went on to my present assignment in the USAR as an Individual Mobilization Augmentee in the Selected Reserve.

2. Page 3: "Although the SFPD discontinued its investigation of the Aquinos in September 1988 for lack of sufficient evidence, the CID continued ..." *Page 15: "In September 1988 CID investigators met with representatives from the SFPD, the U.S. Attorney's Office, and the FBI to discuss the status of the investigation." Page 22: "The record shows that the CID's plans for the investigation ... were initiated in October 1988, well before the Army received a letter from Senator Helms' office."*

   A. In fact the CID did not "continue" an investigation of Mrs. Aquino and myself, but **initiated** it on **November 23, 1988** following the Helms pressure. The 8/12/88 date (revised from the earlier-attempted CID ROI falsehood of 9/88) is to try to narrow the inconvenient gap between the closing of the SFPD investigation and the Geraldo Rivera/Senator Helms-driven opening of the CID investigation. In fact the actual date when the SFPD District Attorney's Office announced that no charges would be filed against me was **8/1/88**. Therefore the CID investigation was opened almost **four months after** the SFPD investigation was closed. Moreover the FBI **never** announced **any** investigation of us whatever. This is clearly a fraudulent attempt by Lisowski to imply an "unbroken chain of investigation" in which the Army's actions were endorsed by the FBI. Such was **not** the case.

B.   The **sole** document produced by the CID to suggest that an investigation was underway prior to Helms' influence was a 10/17/88 letter by Major Harvey suggesting ways to manipulate a lineup and court-martial in order to obtain a conviction, and proposing illegal use of Inspector General subpœnas.

- As the CID investigation was **not authorized and opened until 11/23/88**, by **what** authority and under **whose** directions was Harvey proposing such manipulation and illegal subpœnas?

- If, as Lisowski states, CID plans for the investigation were initiated a month prior to that investigation's being officially authorized, it would be most interesting to see the **entire** paper trail ... to include the signatures of those persons who instigated it. Why didn't Lisowski produce **those** complete "CID plans"? Why are **none** of them contained or even mentioned in the ROI as exhibits? Why was there **no mention whatever** of Harvey's "supposedly-significant" 10/17/88 letter in the ROI?

3.   Page 3: "... and the applicable 3-year statute of limitations had expired in June 1989." *[Lisowski, district court brief, page 9:]* "*The final Report of Investigation (ROI) was issued on August 11, 1989. G.E. D at 1-4. On January 4, 1990 Major Harvey spoke with the staff judge advocate at Fort Leonard Wood, MO to determine what action the commander of Fort Leonard Wood had decided to take in the case. The commander took no action against plaintiff as a result of the investigation. G.E. B at 3.*"

A.   My attorney Mr. Gary Myers was informed by TJAG that the decision not to court-martial me was made **prior to the titling decision** (i.e. prior to August 1989). In that case the account of the "decision by the Fort Leonard Wood commander on 1/4/90" is false, intended as a cover-up of the illegal conduct of the investigation process.

B.   On 10/2/89 the flag was removed from my personnel file at ARPERCEN. Such a flag would have remained in place unless a decision **had already been made** that there would be no charges preferred against me.

C.   Lisowski's account is thus false and obstructs justice by concealing this additional misuse of investigatory/court-martial procedures.

4.   Page 3: "... on the grounds that the identifications of her by the children were inadequate ..." *[Lisowski, district court interrogatories, page 37:]* "*The decision to delete Mrs. Aquino from the subject block was based upon Kinsey's inability to pick Mrs. Aquino out of the video lineup. On 8/12/87 Kinsey identified Mrs. Aquino as 'Shamby'. However, Mrs. Aquino's proximity to LTC Aquino when viewed by Kinsey Adams-Thompson in the Presidio Post Exchange parking lot made this identification too suggestive to be reliable by itself. The defendant believes that Mrs. Aquino is the most likely suspect to be 'Shamby'. However this belief falls slightly short of 'probable cause'. During the video lineup, Kinsey's statement that woman #2 was 'Shamby' indicates that Kinsey believed a woman of very similar appearance to Mrs. Aquino was 'Shamby'. Defendant has given Mrs. Aquino the benefit of the doubt. It is possible that a female of similar description to Mrs. Aquino was involved in the ritual sexual abuse of Kinsey Adams-Thompson at 123 Acme without the participation of Mrs. Aquino. In recognition of this possibility, the Commanding General of CID decided to remove Mrs. Aquino from the title block. Defendant does not believe plaintiff acted alone. Defendant believes plaintiff acted with Mr. Gary Hambright and with other unnamed and identified persons, who may include Mrs. Aquino.*"

A.   "*Identifications*" = plural? "*Children*" = plural? There is not a **single** "identification" of Mrs. Aquino by **any** child in the ROI - only the "identification by Kinsey Almond" **alleged** by the adult Adams-Thompsons.

B.   If the decision to delete Mrs. Aquino's name from the titling had indeed been based on Almond's "*inability to pick Mrs. Aquino out of the video lineup*", then Mrs. Aquino would not have been titled in the **original** ROI. On 8/12/87 it is again **only** the allegation by the **adult** Adams-Thompsons that the "PX parking lot identification" ever occurred, and the numerous changes, inconsistencies, and fabrications in their accounts - known to the CID - eliminate that altogether as a reliable account. [See *Chaplain Adams-Thompson's Actions in Violation of Article 133 UCMJ*, 11/29/89, #C, #37-59.]

C. *"Mrs. Aquino's proximity to LTC Aquino when viewed by Kinsey Adams-Thompson in the Presidio Post Exchange parking lot made this identification too suggestive to be reliable by itself."*

As a matter of fact (*A-T UCMJ #133 Violations*, items #50-57), the A-Ts are 100% inconsistent as to when anyone saw Mrs. Aquino anywhere. As far as the "proximity to LTC Aquino" dodge is concerned, Michele A-T specified in her 4/10/89 CID statement that Lilith was standing next to our car **"alone"** when they first saw her and Almond made her alleged "ID" of her. [And, as Mrs. Aquino and I had been constantly together in the PX, why wouldn't Almond have "IDd" her at the same time as she "did" me?]

D. *"The defendant believes that Mrs. Aquino is the most likely suspect to be 'Shamby'."*

"Shambee" (Hickey's spelling):

-   appears in the Hickey notes first on 1/27/87, introduced by Almond as "her friend at school" who was spanked by Mr. Rogers on TV. Almond added that Shambee "also had its neck broken", indicating that "Shambee" is either an imaginary "friend" or perhaps a doll.

-   There is no record of the FBI/SFPD/CID interviewing either teachers or other children at the Presidio day-care center to see if anyone used or was known by the name "Shambee".

-   There is no mention of "Shambee" by any other child.

-   On 4/7/87 Almond said that Shambee and Sassy were the same person, and that Sassy was Todo's girlfriend. After this neither Almond nor Hickey used the name "Shambee" anymore, discussing only "Sassy".

-   "Shambee" is reintroduced as "Mikey's wife" by **Michele A-T** on 6/30/87.

-   On 7/7/87 Almond told Hickey that "Nancy and Shambee were good mothers"

-   On 7/7/87 Hickey asked Almond if Shambee worked at the school. Almond's answer - and anything else she may have said as a follow-up on the next three pages of Hickey's record - **has been concealed by the CID**.

On page #8 of his brief to the district court, Lisowski stated the following "significance" of "Shamby": *"Kinsey stated that 'Shamby' and 'Mr. Gary' took her to 'Mr. Gary's house' and that 'Mikey' was there."* Every element of this aged (almost three years from the "CID-invented re-dating" of May-June 1986) statement has changed along the way in an effort to make it "fit" revealed facts:

-   In her 1/14/87 FBI interview, Almond said nothing about being taken anywhere by anyone or having anything done to her at all. Since this denial was obviously unacceptable to her parents, she was immediately placed in "therapy" with Hickey, the official abuse-finder for the Presidio scam.

-   By the third (2/3/87) "play session", Almond now announced that she had performed fellatio on "Mr. Gary" at the CDC. There is no mention of going anywhere else, or of any other adult being involved.

- It took Hickey and the A-Ts two more months to get Almond to agree to an off-CDC location. Finally on 4/7/87 Hickey asked Almond **twice** if she ever went anywhere with Hambright. Both times Almond said **no**. When Hickey refused to accept these answers, Almond **only then** said yes - to "Sassy's house". In the same session Almond described the house as "blue" and the bathtub as "blue" (neither correct in the case of 123 Acme).

- There is no mention of "Mikey" by Almond whatever, at "the house" or anywhere else, for over two more months of "therapy". On 6/2/87 **Michele** A-T proposes a "Satanic cult", and then on 6/30/87 **Michele** introduces "Mikey" as "Shambee's husband" and a military officer.

- On 6/2/87 and 6/9/87 Almond said that the man at the house with Hambright was "Dr. Steve". As it turns out, "Dr. Steve" is the only real person specifically and repeatedly identified by Almond as being at the house with Hambright. Michele admitted that "Dr. Steve" was a neighbor of theirs at the Presidio of San Francisco. Neither Hickey [per her notes] nor Michele reported this identification to the FBI/CID/SFPD. There is no record that "Dr. Steve" was ever questioned, served with a search warrant, or titled on the strength of this **authentic, unsolicited identification** by Almond.

- Clearly Lisowski's succinct statement, which includes **no mention of this extensive coaching and revision whatever**, is false and misleading.

E. *"During the video lineup, Kinsey's statement that woman #2 was 'Shamby' indicates that Kinsey believed a woman of very similar appearance to Mrs. Aquino was 'Shamby'."*

- CID regulation 195-1 states that "the persons portrayed in the photographs should be reasonably similar in appearance." Lisowski states here that even if Mrs. Aquino was **not** selected in a lineup, the mere fact that someone else on the same lineup was selected **implies the selection of Mrs. Aquino**! In this case the lineup technique is totally invalid, as there is no way for any targeted person to survive it.

- Numerous other violations of CID regulation 195-1 were committed, and ignored by the CID & TJAG, in this case. [See *False Official Statements by Major Patrick Lisowski to the U.S. District Court*.]

F. *"It is possible that a female of similar description to Mrs. Aquino was involved in the ritual sexual abuse of Kinsey Adams-Thompson at 123 Acme without the participation of Mrs. Aquino. In recognition of this possibility, the Commanding General of CID decided to remove Mrs. Aquino from the title block."*

- *"Possibility"* clearly does **not** equate to "probable cause".

- Even so, evidence has shown that it was **impossible** for Almond to have been *"ritually sexually abused at 123 Acme"*, as she shows **no** signs of **any** "abuse" except as coached into her by Hickey and her parents, there are **no** valid "identifications" of either the interior or exterior of 123, the Aquinos were in **Washington, D.C.** at the originally-alleged date, and on the CID-invented-backdate there were **two separate, uncontested witness statements** that **no** children were present anywhere in 123.

- If Mrs. Aquino is removed as a suspect, then her sworn statement that she was also present with Lt.Col. Aquino on the CID-invented-backdate and that no children were present, or molested anywhere at any time, constitutes a **third** uncontested witness statement.

- The Commanding General of CID did not *"decide to remove Mrs. Aquino from the title block"*. According to my attorney, who was in regular contact with the CID at this time, **the CID's legal counsel informed my attorney that he had recommended total expungement of all titlings**. In defiance of this, the decision to make only a partial expungement was made by Colonel Francis A. Gilligan, Chief, Criminal Law Division TJAG, on 7/30/90 and was merely obediently accepted by the CID.

  - •• According to the TJAG chronology, this is the same Colonel Gilligan who on 12/5/88 was bypassing the UCMJ authority at Fort Leonard Wood to work directly with Lt.Col. Schwender at the Presidio, in apparent contradiction of the TJAG paper proposing "no top-down guidance" [see #13 below]. Since Gilligan had a vested interest in defending an investigation in which he personally had been involved from the beginning, his resistance to expunging it is understandable.

- In fact Mrs. Aquino was originally titled by the CID simply because it was thought useful to do so in order to reinforce the predetermined fraudulent titling of myself, destroy her inconvenient presence as a witness to my innocence, and further intimidate me by creating a dangerous threat to my wife.

- In fact the titling of Mrs. Aquino was removed **only** when TJAG realized that a federal lawsuit was imminent. The titling of civilians by the CID is **expressly prohibited** by Department of Defense Directive #5525.7, Appendix #3, and obviously TJAG was not enthusiastic about having the CID violation exposed in court.

G. *"Defendant believes plaintiff acted with Mr. Gary Hambright and with other unnamed and identified persons, who may include Mrs. Aquino."* There is **no evidence whatever** - apart from the adult Adams-Thompsons' unsupported allegations - connecting Mrs. Aquino or myself with Gary Hambright in any way.

5. Page 3: *"... the evidence of alibi offered by LTC Aquino was not persuasive."*

   A. This quotes a statement in Colonel Gilligan's 7/30/90 letter to the CID. This specifically refers to a deposition by a commercial painter, Graham Marshall, who was present in the our flat with Mrs. Aquino and myself on the CID-invented-backdate and verified that there were **no** children there at any time. In order to get around this inconvenient alibi, the CID's Major Harvey telephoned Marshall and said, "**Let me propose a scenario, and you tell me if there is anything that wouldn't fit. I mean this is a possible scenario. I am not asking you to say whether you think that this happened or not.**" Harvey then proposed to Marshall that a child could have been taken into the downstairs (Butch) apartment. Marshall said, "It's conceivable."

   B. Harvey's **speculative invention** of another location, not supported by any evidence whatever from Marshall or anyone else, is the **only** basis for the "not persuasive" claim by Gilligan.

   C. On 4/4/91 William Butch, a professional civilian security officer and a Commander USNR, resident of the Harvey-invented apartment, provided a sworn affidavit verifying that he had been home the entire day and there were **no** children present there either. Commander Butch's affidavit was **never challenged or refuted** by the CID; it was **simply ignored by Lisowski altogether** in his attempts to defend the CID/TJAG - a clear act of obstruction of justice in violation of #134 UCMJ.

6. Page 3-footnote: "In 1990 a continuation board of the Army Reserve recommended discontinuing Aquino's service in the Reserve, and he was processed out of the Army." *Page 11: "Appellant-Plaintiff Michael A. Aquino was a Lieutenant Colonel in the United States Army Reserve; he is now retired from the*

Army." [Lisowski, district court interrogatories, page 31:] "There is no record reflecting whether the AGR Continuation Board knew of plaintiff's flagging or a CID investigation."

A.   I remain a Lieutenant Colonel in the the Active/Selected U.S. Army Reserve. [See #1A-D above.]

B.   Indeed there **is** a record showing corruption of the AGR Board by TJAG, and **Lisowski knew of its existence**. It is Exhibit #M in my original administrative appeal of the fraudulent titling, and consists of an official TJAG chronology of the investigation. The entry for 1/24/89 states: "MAJ Phillips, ARPERCEN Command Judge Advocate, related that a continuation board was held and that the board did ask if LTC Aquino was flagged. The response was affirmative." Provision of such information to the board by MAJ Phillips was in violation of AR 135-18 and the OCAR LOI to the board, which specifically provides that the OMPF (which does **not** include flagging actions) be used as the basis for evaluation. The provision of flagging information to the board by TJAG was clearly an effort - and a successful one - to prejudice the board's decision in my case.

C.   In Tim Tate's *Children For the Devil* Major Harvey, CID Judge Advocate for the investigation, is quoted: "We aren't going to force a court martial in this case … [Aquino's] secondment to the Regular Army is ending; we just won't renew his contract, so in effect we are getting rid of him that way." An explicit acknowledgment of the manipulation and misuse of the AGR continuation board process and purpose in violation of AR 135-18.

7.   Page 6: "… based on a legitimate concern that federal laws have been or may be violated." *Page 18: "The evidence in the record clearly supports the determination that there is probable cause to believe that Michael Aquino sexually molested a child." Page 40: "Despite plaintiff's contentions, this investigation was not a 'witchhunt'. The sole reasons for the investigation and the CID decision to title plaintiff are the facts demonstrating that plaintiff sexually abused young children."*

A.   As is clear from the disclosure of the Hickey notes, all exposed and documented behavior of the Adams-Thompsons prior to the opening of the CID investigation, and the medical findings showing Almond to be a virgin with no medical signs whatever of molestation, there was **never** such a "legitimate concern" by the CID. They knew from the outset that we were innocent. **The entire conduct of the investigation consisted of an attempt to conceal or ignore all evidence substantiating our innocence, and to manufacture "evidence" to support the fraudulent titling.** There were and are **no** facts "demonstrating that plaintiff sexually abused young children". See (1) Adams-Thompson's Violations of #133 UCMJ, (2) ROI cover letter analysis, and (3) ROI Summary of Significant Information analysis.

B.   No better example of the predetermined bias and agenda of the investigation can be given than the 10/17/88 letter from Major Harvey - **prior to the opening of the supposedly "unbiased" investigation** - proposing ways to manipulate a video lineup and an eventual court-martial to secure a conviction. There is **no mention whatever** of **any** possibility that an investigation might prove our innocence.

   •   This same Major Harvey on 12/14/88 wrote to my attorney: "If LTC Aquino has **not** committed these offenses, USACIDC hopes to establish his innocence and assist in clearing his name … If LTC Aquino provides certain leads or evidence that shows the allegations to be without merit, I will insure that USACIDC personnel follow those leads, to the maximum possible extent, in order to properly document his innocence."

   •   **All such exculpatory evidence and leads provided were ignored or concealed in order to fabricate the titling and cover up the actual UCMJ violations by Adams-Thompson, Hickey, and CID/TJAG investigatory personnel.**

C.   Lisowski deliberately specifies the word *"children"* (plural) to imply that there were **multiple** "victims" - which is not even alleged by the fraudulent ROI.

8.   Page 8: "... the testimony of [Almond] that 'Mikey' had sexually molested her ..."

     A.   There was **no** mention by Almond of a "Mikey" whatever, anywhere, anytime until **Michele Adams-Thompson introduced the name and military association** in the 6/30/87 Hickey session. Everything that Almond herself then said to Hickey about "Mikey" she had previously said randomly about many other people and objects. Thereafter it is a simple case of Michele continuing to coach her daughter to use the name and allegations in an effort to support the desired framing of the Satanist officer and his wife she and her husband knew about and had decided to victimize.

9.   Page 8: "... on her identifications of Aquino as 'Mikey' ..." *Page 12: "In addition to the identification at the post exchange, Kinsey identified plaintiff out of a five-person photo-lineup and video lineup."*

     A.   The adult Adams-Thompsons' ever-mutating accounts of the "PX identification" make it obvious that it was merely their invention, not an "identification". [It is **impossible** for it to have been an identification, since we have **never** seen the child and to this day have no idea what she looks like.]

     B.   Almond made **no** "identifications" of me whatever until she was shown an illegally-designed photo-lineup by the CID **1-1/2 years later**, after her parents had had ample opportunity to condition her to support their scam and attempted financial defrauding of the government.

     C.   It is also preposterous to credit a child at age 4 with an accurate "identification" recalled from age **2-1/2** (her age at the CID-invented-backdate).

10.   Page 8: "... and of the Aquinos' apartment building as the location of the alleged crime ..." *Page 13: "Kinsey said that the area was familiar and that she had been there before. When asked if this was 'Mr. Gary's' house, she answered yes, and stated that Mr. Gary had driven her there, where she met 'Mikey' and 'Shamby'."*

     A.   Almond made **no** such "identification" and **not one of these alleged statements** - as is verified in the CID report of the staged "identification trip". This is therefore a **direct lie** by Lisowski. The supposed "123 identification trip" is exposed in detail in *Chaplain Adams-Thompson's Violations of #133 UCMJ*, Section #D, items #60-72.

11.   Page 8: "... and on other evidence from Aquino's apartment partially matching the child's descriptions of the locale of the crime." *Page 13: The photographs were shown to Kinsey. Although her reactions to the photographs are not conclusive, the photographs do show a number of items that corroborate K's and other children's descriptions of the house where they were taken.*

     A.   What "crime"? All the evidence reveals that there **never was any crime**.

     B.   In switching the location of the alleged crime from our flat to Commander Butch's flat, the Army acknowledges that Marshall's alibi is indeed "persuasive" as regards our flat. Therefore any objects in our flat are acknowledged as irrelevant. Or does the CID propose to shift furnishings and personal articles at will, just as it shifts locations and dates at will?

     C.   As detailed on page #5 of my summary of Lisowski's false statements to the district court, **nothing** in our flat matched **anything** Almond alleged, or which was specified in the SFPD search warrant as relevant. What is this "**partial** match/corroborate" business? Is this a new way of blessing Harvey's creative efforts to transform a "bathtub with lion's feet" into anything whatever with any part of a lion on it?

D. Concerning "the house" [to which Almond was alleged to have been taken]:

- On 4/7/87 Hickey asked Almond **twice** if she ever went anywhere with Hambright. Both times Almond said **no**. When Hickey still persisted, Almond then said **yes** - to Sassy and Todo's house.

- On 4/7/87 Almond said that Sassy & Todo's house "was **upstairs** and there were **no stairs around**".

- On 4/7/87 Hickey asked Almond if the house "had a garage, a tree house, and a swing set, and a fence", and Almond said, "Yes." [Our home in San Francisco has **none** of these.]

- In Hickey's notes concerning other Presidio children, accounts concerning "trips to a house", its description, and people connected with it vary markedly. For example, in the 5/31/87 Hickey entry concerning Jaime Parker: "[Jaime's mother said] Jaime visited Trinity, and Trinity lives in the general area of Katie and may be confusing stories. Then said Katie had approached her and **said she used to take kids to her house** to go to the bathroom when they would go to Sanchez Park."

- There is no record of any FBI/SFPD/CID investigation of "Katie" or search warrant ever served on her house to investigate its design, decor, bathtub, etc.

12. Page 8: "... the Army's factual bases were not so wholly unreliable as to render the titling & amendment-refusal decisions arbitrary or capricious." *Page 40: "Despite plaintiff's contentions, this investigation was not a 'witchhunt' ... The Army has been aware of plaintiff's religious beliefs throughout his Army career and has not interfered with his religious practices. The sole reasons for the investigation and the CID decision to title plaintiff are the facts demonstrating that plaintiff sexually abused young children."*

A. As is clear from the disclosure of the Hickey notes, all exposed and documented behavior of the Adams-Thompsons prior to the opening of the CID investigation, and the medical findings showing Almond to be a virgin with no medical signs whatever of molestation, there were no factual bases whatever for the titling, making it indeed arbitrary and capricious. **The entire conduct of the investigation consisted of an attempt to conceal or ignore all evidence substantiating our innocence, and to manufacture "evidence" to support the fraudulent titling.** There were and are **no** facts "demonstrating that plaintiff sexually abused young children". See (a) Adams-Thompson's Violations of #133 UCMJ, (b) ROI cover letter analysis, and (c) ROI Summary of Significant Information analysis.

B. As Lisowski is certainly aware, there were indeed previous attempts by Army officials to discriminate against me because of religious bias. This has extended from a general officer attempt to deny me an ROTC teaching post (an act of discrimination immediately corrected by his superior, the TRADOC CG) to innumerable "command performance" attendance requirements at military functions opened and closed by Christian religious invocations which I was expected to endorse by standing in an attitude of prayer. I challenged and eventually corrected the more serious incidents and endeavored to ignore the minor ones for the sake of professional courtesy. That does not mean that I did not find them intrusive and offensive to my religion.

C. The Adams-Thompson affair was national news. Obviously my "unacceptable" religion now indeed made me the target of a witch-hunt to appease Jesse Helms and allies of his possessing sufficient influence to orchestrate and manipulate TJAG/CID investigations. The alternative would have been not only the exonerating of a Satanist senior-grade officer, but the prosecution of a Christian chaplain for crimes committed against him and subsequently the exposure of the Presidio "Satanic child abuse" scam altogether, as just one more in the series of such predatory scams throughout the 1980s.

D. The entire "Satanic child abuse" myth started by the now-discredited book *Michelle Remembers* has long since been exploded nationwide by such definitive studies as Lanning's FBI Academy analysis and Robert Hicks' *In Pursuit of Satan: Police and the Occult*. This shameful witchhunt against Mrs. Aquino and myself, and the equally dishonorable efforts of TJAG to try to prop it up long after it has been exposed for the sham that it is, constitute the sole remaining memorial to this shabby episode of hate-crime.

13. Page 9: "The report recommended, 'Do not issue top-down guidance to Aquino's command or the continuation board ...'"

   A. This quotes from the information paper presented by Lt.Col. John Burton to a secret DA meeting on 11/23/88 timed to coincide precisely with the opening of the CID investigation directed against me. It is **not** a "report" of any decisions taken at that meeting.

   B. As shown above, illegal information was **in fact** fed to the AGR continuation board by TJAG's ARPERCEN representative, with the result that I was illegally denied AGR continuation in violation of AR 135-18.

   C. The recommendation of "no top down guidance" in the paper was made **only with respect to ARPERCEN**, the headquarters where I was assigned. ARPERCEN had **no** UCMJ authority over me. That authority was held by the Commanding General of Fort Leonard Wood, who as evidenced by the TJAG chronology played only a bystander role in the investigation. Even the flagging decision was made by LTC Schwender at the Presidio of San Francisco, location of Sixth Region CID headquarters, with a Major Cork from FLW flying out to the Presidio to "concur".

14. Page 9: "'... allow CID to continue its inquiry ...'"

   A. A further quote from the TJAG paper: It is interesting that it refers to a **continuation** of CID investigation on the same date that that investigation was supposedly **opened**. Why are **all** pre-"opening" CID documents excluded from the ROI?

15. Page 9: "'... allow the local command to determine whether charges should be preferred and an Article 32 investigation conducted.'"

   A. A further quote from the TJAG paper. My attorney Mr. Gary Myers was informed by Headquarters, Department of the Army that the decision not to court-martial me was made **prior to the titling decision** (i.e. prior to August 1989). In that case the account of the "decision by the Fort Leonard Wood commander on 1/4/90" is false, intended as a cover-up of the illegal conduct of the investigation process.

   B. On 10/2/89 the flag was removed from my personnel file at ARPERCEN. Such a flag would have remained in place unless a decision **had already been made** that there would be no charges preferred against me.

16. Page 9: "More significantly, the Region Judge Advocate at the Presidio developed the plan for continuing the investigation of the Aquinos prior to 10/17/88 (sic) when the letter from Helms' aide was written."

   A. This again refers to the 10/17/88 letter by Major Harvey suggesting ways to manipulate a lineup and court-martial in order to obtain a conviction, and proposing illegal use of Inspector General subpœnas. It is **not** a "CID investigation plan" as represented by Lisowski. **No** such pre-11/23/88 "investigation plan", or **any** other CID/TJAG/DA documents concerning this investigation whatever dated prior to 11/23/88 were included in the ROI or provided in discovery upon this lawsuit.

B.   The letter from Jesse Helms' office was dated 10/26/88. The CID investigation was opened 11/23/88 - almost a month later.

17.   Page 9: "Moreover the CID reached its decision 'to initiate this report of investigation' on November 21, 1988, before the meeting at which the high-level officers of the Army decided how to respond to the pressure from Senator Helms' aide."

    A.   The Secretary of the Army was in possession of the first letter from Helms' office almost a month before the 11/23/88 (not 11/21/88) meeting. There is no indication whatever that a decision concerning a response to that letter was made at that meeting, or that the letter was even discussed at the meeting.

    B.   In fact the two letters from Helms and his assistant were considered sufficiently important that on 1/17/89 Major General Overholt, the Department of the Army Judge Advocate General, was summoned to Secretary of the Army Marsh's office to discuss it personally. It was subsequently considered sufficiently important so that General Overholt met personally with Senator Helms to discuss it.

Appendix 72: Court of Appeals Decision

Published

**UNITED STATES COURT OF APPEALS
FOR THE FOURTH CIRCUIT**

Michael A. Aquino, Plaintiff-Appellant
v.
Michael P.W. Stone, Secretary of the Army, Defendant-Appellee

No. 91-1164

Appeal from the United States District Court
for the Eastern District of Virginia, at Alexandria.
Claude M. Hilton, District Judge.
(CA-90-1547-A)

Argued: December 2, 1991
Decided: February 26, 1992

Before SPROUSE and NIEMEYER, Circuit Judges, and BUTZNER, Senior Circuit Judge.

Affirmed by published opinion. Judge Niemeyer wrote the opinion, in which Judge Sprouse and Senior Judge Butzner joined.

Counsel

Argued: Gary Rowland Myers, Gary R. Myers & Associates, Washington, D.C., for Appellant. Major Patrick W. P. Lisowski, Army Litigation Division, United States Army, Arlington, Virginia, for Appellee. **On Brief**: John A. Wickham, Gary R. Myers & Associates, Washington, D.C., for Appellant. Dennis Edward Szybala, Assistant United States Attorney, Alexandria, Virginia, for Appellee.

Opinion

Niemeyer, Circuit Judge:

Lieutenant Colonel Michael Aquino, formerly of the U.S. Army Reserves,[441] filed suit under the Privacy Act of 1974, 5 U.S.C. § 552a (1988), against the Secretary of the Army seeking to amend an Army report of a criminal investigation about him and to recover damages caused by inaccuracies in the report. He also sued under the Administrative Procedure Act, 5 U.S.C. § 701, *et seq.* (1988), to review the Secretary's refusal to amend the report. The district court entered summary judgment for the Secretary, concluding that criminal investigatory files are

---

[441] This is the first of several factual errors in this Opinion, indicating the judges' carelessness in reviewing the actual facts of the case. Their decision appears to have been based on technicalities of the Army's CID investigation exemption claims, with only cursory - and as noted inaccurate - mention of the underlying facts in this instance. In this sentence: I was not "formerly of the U.S. Army Reserves (sic)"; I continued to be a USAR officer - just not on full-time active duty. Far from being an incidental error, this misstatement by the Court is of critical importance, as it indicates that in making their decision, the judges assumed that some sort of legitimate administrative censure or sanction **had** been taken against me as a consequence of the CID investigation. [They repeat this assumption later in their Opinion.]

exempt from the provisions of the Privacy Act that were invoked by Aquino, and that the Secretary's decision not to amend was not arbitrary or capricious. Finding no reversible error, we affirm.

I

In November 1986 the San Francisco Police Department (SFPD), the Federal Bureau of Investigation (FBI) and the U.S. Army Criminal Investigation Division Command (CID) began investigating charges that Gary Hambright had sexually molested several of the children entrusted to his care as an employee at the Child Development Center on the Army base known as the Presidio.

On August 12, 1987 Army Captain Larry Adams-Thompson reported to the authorities that his three-year-old daughter, who had attended the Child Development Center during the period of Hambright's alleged crimes, had become visibly frightened upon seeing LTC Aquino and his wife at the Army's post exchange that day and called them "Mikey" and "Shamby".[442] In a subsequent interview by an FBI agent, the girl implicated "Mikey," "Shamby" and "Mr. Gary" in the sexual molestation of her and other children at "Mr. Gary's house".[443] The investigation of Hambright was expanded to include Aquino and his wife.

Although the SFPD discontinued its investigation of the Aquinos in September 1988 for lack of sufficient evidence,[444] the CD continued[445] and in August 1989 issued a report of investigation designating both Aquinos in the "title block" of the report and describing the various child-abuse and related criminal offenses investigated.[446]

---

[442] As previously detailed, the **only** source of this allegation were the two adult A-Ts, who changed the details of their account several times over the years.

[443] In her 8/13/87 FBI interview, Kinsey mentioned the names "Mikey", "Shamby", and "Mr. Gary", but made no mention of the "supposedly-the-day-before & traumatic PX incident" whatever. She did not associate the names "Mikey" and "Shamby" with the Aquinos either by name or by description. Moreover in her original 1/26/87 FBI interview (2/3 year closer to the alleged 9/1-10/31/86 Hambright-supervision window), Kinsey stated that Hambright had not hurt her in any way, made no mention of being taken anywhere away from the day-care center, and made no mention of either "Mikey" or "Shamby" or anyone resembling them. These names were produced only later in the Hickey "therapy" sessions, and in different and non-associated contexts.

[444] The SFPD closed its investigation a month previously, on 8/1/88.

[445] The CID did not open its investigation until 11/23/88, as evidenced not only by FOIA documents but by the official flagging of my personnel file, security clearance suspension, etc. which were all required upon a formal CID criminal investigation. The CID took no interest whatever in the A-T allegations for the previous 1-1/3 years since A-T made them, as detailed in this documentation. Here the court is simply reciting the CID lie in order to evade the reality that there was no CID interest until **after** the Helms-Secretary of the Army contact.

[446] As detailed in my analysis of the CID ROI herein, it actually contained no evidence whatever that either Lilith or I had committed any such crimes at all, and ignored all of the facts evidencing the A-Ts' fabrication of their allegations.

The report concluded that the investigation was closed because all further leads involved adults who refused to cooperate,[447] and the applicable three-year statute of limitations had expired in June 1989.[448]

Thereafter, on January 31, 1990, the Aquinos requested that the CID remove their names from the title block of the report. While the CID deleted Mrs. Aquino's name entirely, on the ground that the identifications of her by the children interviewed were inadequate,[449] it did not delete LTC Aquino's name. The CID also removed from the report charges arising out of allegations that Aquino made against CPT Adams-Thompson.[450] All the child-abuse charges remained, because "[t]he evidence of alibi offered by LTC Aquino [was] not persuasive".[451]

Aquino filed suit in the district court under the Privacy Act, 5 U.S.C. § 552a(g), to compel the Army to amend the investigatory report about him and for damages resulting from his discharge from the service,[452] which he attributes to the inaccurate records about him.[453] [In 1990 a continuation board of the Army Reserve recommended

---

[447] No such "non-cooperative adults" were ever identified by the CID. The ROI mentioned no such adults at all. The CID was also aware that pertinent adults, such as all of the other teachers at the day-care center, had directly and absolutely denied that Hambright had either abused children or taken any of them off the premises at any time.

[448] This statute of limitations applied **only** to the CID-creatively-revised 6/10/86 "crime date", back-dated **only** because the A-Ts' original 9/1-10/31/86 accusation-window could not be made to fit our 3,000-miles-away location. Had the CID truly believed that we had committed such serious crimes, of course, it could easily have finalized its ROI **before** the statute deadline. Moreover my "making of false statements" [in sworn testimony of our innocence and the ATs' guilt] was still **very much within** statute deadlines, so I could have been prosecuted for that - except that everyone involved knew I was telling the **truth**. This "statue of limitations expiration" was simply a dodge used by the CID to have an excuse for not initiating any prosecution based on the ROI.

[449] "Identifications" (plural)? "Children" (plural)? There is not a **single** "identification" of Lilith by **any** child in the ROI . There is only the "PX identification" alleged **only by the adult** A-Ts.

[450] Incorrect. The several sworn statements and detailed evidence that I had made concerning A-T's deliberate falsification of his allegations and attempted defrauding of the U.S. government with false claims based on them were never investigated nor refuted by the CID, but instead treated as "false swearing" by me. This "false swearing" was left in the ROI titling after the administrative appeal, because to remove it would imply that my sworn statements were indeed **true** (which they were).

[451] Graham Marshall's alibi of our 123 Acme residence was **absolute and unequivocal**, and the CID could not refute it. Their only way around it, on the spur of that moment, was to "relocate" the already-"backdated" "crime" to another apartment in the same building, whose resident, US Navy Commander William Butch, denied any such "crime" as well, and whose apartment of course fitted nothing of the strenuously-attempted "interior description" that the CID had tried for months to fabricate concerning our own flat. Accordingly this phrase "not persuasive" was used only because there were **no possibly factual grounds whatever** for rejecting Marshall's alibi.

[452] As noted above, not "discharge from the service" but discontinuation from the full-time AGR program.

[453] Not to "inaccurate records" *per se*, but to the fraudulent "CID investigation" commenced against us, and to Major Harvey's **explicit admission** [in Time Tate's book] that the CID had intentionally used the AGR continuation board to "get rid" of me - a manipulation which took place at the **beginning** of the CID's supposedly-not-predetermined "investigation".

discontinuing Aquino's service in the Reserve,[454] and he was processed out of the Army.][455] He also sued under the Administrative Procedure Act to review the action of the Secretary of the Army in developing the investigatory report about him and in refusing to amend it.

On cross motions for summary judgment, the district court granted the Army's motion and denied Aquino's, holding that the files sought to be amended by Aquino were exempt from the Privacy Act provisions under which Aquino sued. On its review of the Army's action under the Administrative Procedure Act, the court concluded that "[t]here was sufficient evidence from which the Army decision maker could determine that probable cause existed to believe that [Aquino] committed the offenses" and that therefore the Army's decisions to create the report and not amend it were not arbitrary or capricious.[456]

This appeal followed, but Aquino has now abandoned his claim for damages.[457]

II

The Privacy Act of 1974 was enacted to "protect the privacy of individuals identified in information systems maintained by Federal agencies" by giving the individuals information about and access to records about them and permitting them "to have a copy made of all or any portion thereof, and to correct or amend such records". Pub. L. No. 93-579, § 2(a)(5), (b)(3), 88 Stat. 1896, 1896 (1974). The Act authorizes civil actions in federal court to compel compliance with the Act and, in the case of "intentional or willful" violations, to award damages. See 5 U.S.C. § 552a(g)(1), (4).

Aquino contends that evidence collected by the Army CID did not justify its creating an investigation report titled under his name, and that those involved with the investigation were motivated to remove him from the Army because he is the founder of the Temple of Set, a satanist religion.[458] Because, he argues, the Army did not have probable cause to link him with the crimes described in the report, the report should be amended and his name deleted from its caption because the information is not "accurate, relevant, timely, or complete" as required by 5 U.S.C. § 552a(d)(2).

The Secretary contends that Aquino cannot proceed under the Privacy Act because the records that Aquino seeks to amend are criminal investigation records which are exempt from the Act under 5 U.S.C. § 552a(j)(2).

The Privacy Act authorizes agencies to exempt from many of its provisions, including those applicable here, criminal investigative record systems maintained by the agency or a "component" thereof. The record systems must be "maintained by an agency or component thereof which performs as its principal function any activity pertaining to the enforcement of criminal laws" and must consist of "information compiled for the purpose of a criminal

---

[454] The AGR board recommended only that I not be offered another AGR contract after my current one expired in August 1990 - 1-1/4 years hence from the board date. There was no disciplinary finding that my current AGR tour should be curtailed, and after its conclusion I was simply transferred back to the part-time Army Reserve as a Lt. Colonel in full standing.

[455] Again the Court makes this critically-false statement. I remained an officer in full standing in the U.S. Army Reserve until I requested transfer to the Retired Reserve in 1994; and in 2006 I was permanently retired from the Army as a Lt. Colonel, Army of the United States (Ret).

[456] As my attorney Gary Myers noted in his brief to this Appeals Court, the district judge cited **not one single example** of such "sufficient evidence" or "probable cause to believe".

[457] I had **not** abandoned that claim at the time of this appeal. Indeed the appeal was in part to **enforce** it.

[458] Strictly speaking, the Temple of Set is not a "Satanist" religion, having no interest in Judæo-Christian superstition or mythology. But the instigators of the "Satanic Ritual Abuse" mania, the A-Ts, Jesse Helms, and the CID did not bother to draw such actual and factual distinctions.

investigation". See 5 U.S.C. § 552a(j)(2). To implement its election to exempt criminal investigative record systems, the agency must promulgate rules to do so and give reasons why the systems are to be exempted. See 5 U.S.C. § 552a(j).

The Army has promulgated a rule, 32 C.F.R § 505.5(e)(r), to exempt the CID's system of records known as the Criminal Investigation and Crime Laboratory Files, which includes reports of investigations. The rule applies to "[a]ll portions of this system of records which fall within 5 U.S.C. § 552a(j)(2)". The rule also sets forth the reasons for the exemption:

> [A]ccess might compromise on-going investigations, reveal classified information, investigatory techniques or the identity of confidential informants, or invade the privacy of persons who provide information in connection with a particular investigation.[459]

See 32 C.F.R § 505.5(e)(r)(4)(b).

Aquino argues that the exemption may be given effect only if the Army promulgates rules which would require it to give, on a case by case approach, reasons for exempting each document or set of documents which it chooses to include within the exemption. In short, he argues that documents must be processed individually in a manner specified by rule such that each time an exemption is invoked, an authorized reason for the exemption must be given.

In support of his argument he cites *Doe v. FBI*, 936 F.2d 1346, 1353 (D.C. Cir. 1991). In that case the court was presented with the problem, not present here, of providing a method by which the FBI could protect exempt records which were contained in non-exempt files. The FBI had an employment application file with respect to Doe, which contained criminal investigation records of Doe. The court stated, "The critical question, then, is whether the FBI's investigatory information on Doe lost its exempt status when it was subsequently used, in altered form, for a non-law enforcement purpose", i.e. to process an employment application. 936 F.2d at 1356. The court remanded the case to the district court to determine whether the cumulative burden to the FBI from processing amendment requests, one of the FBI's reasons for exemption, applied to non-law enforcement records containing law enforcement information as a class. *Id.* at 1358. We are not presented with any of those issues in this case.

While we can understand that Aquino would want a more individualized evaluation of his file to justify the CID's claim of exemption, particularly when he believes that an investigatory report is inaccurate, we do not think that the Privacy Act was intended to provide an amendatory procedure for records about investigations into violations of the criminal laws. The Army effectively promulgated rules to exempt criminal investigatory files, and Aquino makes no contention that his records are not contained within the "system of records" exempted. Section 552a(j) provides that any agency may promulgate rules "to exempt any system of records within the agency" from specified Privacy Act provisions if the agency

> ... include[s] in the statement required under §553c of this title [requiring notice to interested persons giving them an opportunity to participate in the rule making], the reasons why the system of records is to be exempted from a provision of this section.

(emphasis added). This the agency has done.

Aquino does not suggest that the rule-making process was defective. Nor does he contend that the reasons stated by the rule are not adequate. Aquino's principal complaint centers on his contention that the investigation itself was improperly motivated and that information reported was in some respects false, but he does not controvert the authenticity of the records or the fact that a criminal investigation was conducted.

---

[459] As detailed in Gary Myers' briefs, the CID ROI in this instance fulfills **none** of these tests.

In these circumstances, we cannot conclude that a statute aimed at protecting the privacy of records can be made the vehicle to challenge whether an underlying criminal investigation was properly motivated. It is sufficient for the Privacy Act exemption that the records are authentic and were generated in connection with the CID's investigation into a possible violation of the criminal law based on information sufficient to support at least "a colorable claim" that the subject committed the violation. Cf. *Pratt v. Webster*, 673 F.2d 408, 421 (D.C. Cir. 1982) (interpreting 5 U.S.C. § 552(b)(7) (1976) to require that an agency "establish that its investigating activities are realistically based on a legitimate concern that federal laws have been or may be violated").[460]

Because we conclude that the files in this case were generated for the purpose of a law enforcement investigation by a component of the Army, the CID, whose primary purpose it was to investigate violations and that such files were exempted by regulation promulgated under § 552a(j) of the Privacy Act, the refusal by the CID to amend those files cannot give rise to a civil action under § 552a(g)(1)(a).

III

Aquino also sued under the Administrative Procedure Act to review the Secretary's decisions to title an investigatory report with his name and refuse to amend it.

We are in some doubt about whether an action to compel the amendment of documents under the Administrative Procedure Act is available when Congress provides specifically for that type of suit under the Privacy Act. Cf. *Block v. Community Nutrition Inst.*, 467 U.S. 340, 345-48 (1984) (rejecting Administrative Procedure Act (APA) review of milk marketing orders in suits by consumers because extensive non-APA statutory scheme of review implicitly precludes them). We need not decide this issue, however, because we agree with the district court that the decisions meet the applicable standard under the Administrative Procedure Act.

Although the decisions to investigate and subsequently to title a report of the investigation in Aquino's name fall within the prosecutorial discretion of the CID, the decision not to amend the title block constitutes informal adjudication. We therefore agree with the parties and the district court that the appropriate standard of review under the Administrative Procedure Act is whether the decision was "arbitrary, capricious, an abuse of discretion, or otherwise not in accordance with law". See 5 U.S.C. § 706(2)(A) (1988); *Duke Power Co. v. United States Nuclear Regulatory Comm'n*, 770 F.2d 386, 389 (4th Cir. 1985) (*per curiam*). Under this standard "the court must consider whether the decision was based on a consideration of the relevant factors and whether there has been a clear error of judgment". See *Hutto Stockyard, Inc. v. United States Dep't of Agric.*, 903 F.2d 299, 307 (4th Cir. 1990) (quoting *Citizens to Preserve Overton Park, Inc. v. Volpe*, 401 U.S. 402, 416 (1971)).

Under the applicable Army regulations, the CID names an individual as a suspect in the title block of a report of investigation of a crime if there is "probable cause to title", which exists when "considering the quality and quantity of all available evidence, without regard to its admissibility in a court of law, the evidence points toward the commission of a crime by a particular person ... and would cause a reasonably prudent person to believe that the person ... committed the crime". CID Reg. 195-1, Criminal Investigation: CID Operations, Glossary-4 (November 1, 1986) (as amended April 1, 1989).

Generally, to amend a report an individual must adduce "new, relevant, and material facts that are determined to warrant revision". Army Reg. 195-2, Criminal Investigation Activities, & 4-4b (Oct. 30, 1985). More particularly, to remove the individual's name from the title block, the individual carries the "burden of proof" that "probable cause [as defined by regulation] does not exist to believe that the individual committed the offense for which titled as a subject". *Id*.

In its initial decision to include Aquino in the title block of the report of investigation, the CID relied principally upon the testimony of CPT Adams-Thompson's daughter that "Mikey" had sexually molested her, on her

---

[460] And this *Pratt* test, as Gary Myers' extensive and detailed briefs and arguments to the district and appeals courts verify, was certainly not met by the CID or its ROI in this instance.

identifications of Aquino as "Mikey", and of the Aquinos' apartment building as the location of the alleged crime, and on other evidence from Aquino's apartment partially matching the child's descriptions of the locale of the crime.[461] The Army denied Aquino's request to amend the report on the basis that Aquino's "evidence of alibi", the testimony of the men working in the Aquinos' apartment at the time of the alleged offenses, was not persuasive.[462] The Army's considerations in both decisions clearly were relevant and their factual bases not so wholly unreliable as to render either decision arbitrary or capricious.[463]

Aquino contends that both decisions to title a report in his name and not to amend were tainted by consideration of the irrelevant factor of his satanist religious beliefs.[464] He points to a letter dated October 26, 1988, from an aide to U.S. Senator Jesse Helms to the Secretary of the Army expressing distress that satanists, and Aquino in particular, were members of the Army Reserves. In a follow-up letter, dated January 9, 1989, Senator Helms himself argued strongly for removing Aquino from the Army. Aquino also notes that on November 29, 1988 certain high-level officers within the Army met to discuss his case in response to letters from the Senator's aide and others. And finally the record contains an unattributed document suggesting that the continuation board deciding whether Aquino could continue serving in the Army Reserves learned that his records had been "flagged". [On appeal Aquino seeks to "supplement the record" with further evidence that, he argues, demonstrates anti-satanist bias on the part of an Army officer involved in the investigation of his case. Because we review appeals from summary judgment only upon the record available to the district court, see Fed. R. App. P. 10(a), we deny his request to supplement the record and refuse to consider the offered additional materials.][465]

This evidence supports the finding, which we must accept on review of summary judgment, that some pressure was put on the top of the Army to remove Aquino. It does not, however, require the inference that this pressure was communicated down the ranks to the CID, which conducted the investigation and created the report of investigation, or was otherwise a factor in the investigation. Indeed the record contains strong evidence to the contrary. The report presented at the high-level meeting on November 29, to which Aquino alluded, recommended, "Do not issue 'top

---

[461] **All** of these "reliances" were proven to be false, falsified, coerced from Kinsey by the "therapist" and interrogators, and/or contracted by known & numerous undisputed facts - as detailed earlier and in detail throughout this documentation. All of this was explained in explicit detail to the district and appeals courts by Gary Myers in his briefs and oral arguments.

[462] "Not persuasive" - discussed above: the CID's fallback phrase for a conclusion based upon no facts whatever, and indeed refuted by the facts.

[463] A statement by this appeals court only possible after it has so repeatedly, extensively, and unquestioningly rubber-stamped the CID's falsification of the facts and manufacture of "evidence" in its ROI and now to these two federal courts.

[464] As previously noted, I was not a Satanist, but a Setian at the time of the A-T incident. The two religions are completely distinct from one another. Again the appeals court does not bother to show any awareness of this distinction.

[465] This refers to the statement by Major Mark Harvey in Tim Tate's book (available only after the district court action) in which Harvey admitted the CID's illegal tampering with the AGR continuation board. While technically within its rights to ignore this development, the appeals court hardly bolsters its recited-denial of CID board tampering by suppressing this clear evidence to the contrary.

down' guidance to [Aquino's command or the continuation board] .... Allow CID to continue its inquiry; allow the local command to determine whether charges should be preferred and an Article 32 investigation conducted." [466]

More significantly, the Region Judge Advocate at the Presidio developed the plan for continuing the investigation of the Aquinos prior to October 17, 1988, when the letter from Senator Helms' aide was written.[467] Moreover, the CID reached its decision "to initiate this [report of investigation]" on November 21, 1988, before the meeting at which the high-level officers of the Army decided how to respond to the pressure from Senator Helms' aide.[468] The evidence of political pressure advanced by Aquino does not support his conclusion that it precipitated the investigation about him.[469]

We cannot conclude from the record before us that the Army's decision to title an investigative report with Aquino's name or its subsequent decision not to remove his name from the title block of the report were the result of other than relevant considerations. Since it is not the role of the courts to second-guess an agency's decision, absent a clear error of judgment, not present in this case, we conclude that the district court acted properly.[470]

The decision of the district court granting the Secretary's motion for summary judgment and denying Aquino's is accordingly

AFFIRMED.

---

[466] This statement naïvely ignores the fact that the CID's "investigation" was initiated **prior** to this meeting (on 11/23/88), and clearly **not** on the initiative of the CID's San Francisco Field Office (which had shown no previous interest in the A-T allegations whatever). Moreover the CID's principal "task officer" for this fraudulent investigation, Major Mark Harvey, not only acknowledged to Tim Tate that he **had** taken [unlawful] action to "get rid of me" by using the AGR continuation board **at the beginning of the CID "investigation"**; he also informed my Army attorney Captain Hayes that I would be "titled" **in advance of** the nominal titling officer's receipt, much less review of the ROI; and he informed my civilian attorney Gary Myers that I would not be court-martialed **half a year in advance of** the nominal court-martial authority's (the Major General commanding Fort Leonard Wood) announced decision. Under the circumstances only a complete fool, or someone participating in this same predetermined agenda, would venture a statement such as the court's here.
Note also that while this quote was taken from one of several information papers which were presented at this secret Pentagon meeting, the **official results and recommendations** of that meeting were **never** disclosed to me in my FOIA requests.

[467] As previously documented herein and explained by Gary Myers to the district and appeals courts, this so-called "CID investigation plan" was nothing more than a memorandum from then-Captain Mark Harvey suggesting ways in which the laws concerning court testimony and lineups could be evaded by the CID in any action which might be taken against me. There was no reference to any pre-existing, current, or imminent CID official investigation whatever.

[468] Helms' first letter was sent 10/26/88 (not "10/17/88" as the court says here), which was well in advance of the opening of the CID "investigation" on 11/23/88.

[469] The timing and force of the Helms-Marsh communiqués, not to mention Marsh's sending of the Judge Advocate General of the U.S. Army to Capitol Hill to brief Helms personally in response to his demands, strike me as pretty *prima facie* evidence in this regard. Since neither Secretary Marsh, Senator Helms, or General Overholt provided me with records of their conversations and decisions at this time in response to my FOIA requests, one must assume they didn't want me to see any such records. If they had all simply discussed the day's weather in Washington, I daresay my FOIA requests would have been fulfilled as required by the law.

[470] After the glaring omissions, misstatements, and factual falsehoods through this Opinion, this "conclusion" borders on sheer slapstick.

Appendix 73: Gary Myers' Petition for Rehearing *en Banc*

[Note: This document, like Myers' Appeal brief, contained extensive case citations in footnotes. Only the basic text sections are reproduced here.]

In the United States Court of Appeals for the Fourth Circuit

No. 91-1164 (Judgment entered on appeal: February 26, 1992)

Michael Aquino, Plaintiff-Petitioner,
v.
The Honorable Michael Stone, Secretary of the Army, Defendant-Petitionee

On Petition for Rehearing from the United States Court of Appeals for the Fourth Circuit

Petition for Rehearing and Suggestion for Rehearing *en Banc*

March 11, 1992

PETITION FOR REHEARING

Introduction

In counsel's judgment, this Court's decision affirming the district court's rejection of plaintiff's request for amendment of his records and damages under the Privacy Act and granting the Army's motion for summary judgment, is an opinion in direct conflict with another decision of this Court and of other Courts of Appeals, and the conflict is not addressed in the opinion.

The Court's opinion conflicts with its prior decision in *Ryan v Department of Justice* and those other Circuits that have relied upon it as a landmark case to clarify or extend its rationale in construing exemptions under the Privacy Act.

Even more striking in the present case, is that this Court cites no authority, legislative or otherwise, to support its decision. Instead the Court simply makes a bare, conclusory remark that "we do not think that the Privacy Act was intended to provide an amendatory procedure for records about investigations into violations of the criminal laws".

The legal consequences of this decision are twofold:

- First, the law on this issue now internally conflicts within this Circuit, and with those that have interpreted *Ryan*.

- Secondly, a whole new body of law has been created without legal or policy justification that grants criminal law enforcement agencies virtual immunity under the Privacy Act. What the Court proclaims instead is that in such circumstances, the only appropriate "vehicle to challenge whether an underlying criminal investigation was properly motivated" is the minimal "arbitrary and capricious" standard under the Administrative Procedure Act.

Finally, the Court has overlooked a key provision and entitlement in the Privacy Act by concluding, without any affirmative evidence to the contrary, that Michael Aquino no longer contemplates damages in his claim. I at 4.

For the foregoing reasons counsel additionally submits a Suggestion for Rehearing *en Banc*.

Argument

I. *Ryan* stands for the proposition that specific law enforcement records are exempt from the Privacy Act amendment provisions **only** if the agency's reason for withholding the specific records is "consistent with one of the reasons listed in the [agency's exemption] regulation".

The holding of *Ryan* and its significance were fully set forth in Petitioner's brief and reply brief on appeal. In *Ryan* the court's examination of the document's contents apparently proved that granting access "would compromise ongoing investigations and reveal investigatory techniques". Since this reason was actually listed as one of the adverse effects listed in the Department of Justice's exemption regulation, the court upheld the exemption.

The landmark status of the *Ryan* decision has been affirmed by its application, interpretation, and extension in several other circuit court decisions involving Privacy Act exemptions. Using the same language, the *Exner* court upheld the law enforcement exemption, agreeing with the lower court "because [it] found that the material here had been withheld for reasons consistent with those set out in the implementing regulation". *Id.* at 1202, 1206-07.

In a concurring opinion that included a detailed analysis of case law, legislative history, and executive branch implementation, Judge Pregerson clarified and supported the *Exner* holding by interpreting the Fourth Circuit's recent *Ryan* case. *Id.* at 1207-1209. Judge Pregerson interpreted *Ryan* to mean that "the reason for withholding the document was consistent with at least one of the adverse effects listed in the statement of reasons". *Id.* at 1209. Although there was no express authorization for courts to view such documents *in camera* for purposes of the *de novo* review, Pregerson added that such a power of inspection was implied. Otherwise "for a court to uphold an asserted investigatory record exemption without inquiring into whether the information in the document justifies the exemption would make judicial review meaningless".

In *Andrews* the court extended the *Ryan* rationale to apply in the context of the routine use exemption, citing the decision in support: "Any release of documents in reliance on routine use, as defined in the regulations enacted under the Privacy Act, ... **must be for reasons consistent with the reasons stated in the rule**". *Id.* at 1413-14 [emphasis added].

In *Nakash* the court extended the *Ryan* rationale again, applying it to narrowly read the exemption from civil liability, limiting it to only where the reasons apply under the situation. Applying *Ryan* in conjunction with another decision, the court here denied the exemption because "none of the purposes the [agency] cited [as reasons] are remotely served by allowing the agency to escape civil liability for violations of the disclosure and accuracy requirements of the Act". *Id.* at 1365 (citing with *Ryan*, *Tijerina v Veterans Administration*, 821 F.2d 789, 796 (D.C. Cir. 1987).

The *Ryan* rationale of applying the reason in the exemption regulation has been continued in several other Circuits:

- *Castenda* at 986 (7th Cir.) ("Bureau of Prisons exempted itself from 552a because [access ... would jeopardize legitimate correctional interests [quoting entire regulation] ... these reason apply with equal force.");

- *Nemetz* at 104-05 ("general allegations are insufficient to support exemption from access ..." Records are exempt only to the extent the statute and regulation apply to this case, so "evidence must be presented [*in camera*] ... in affidavits stating facts in support of their claim exemption ... [as] to this information".);

- *Hernandez* at 409 (found the Army's law enforcement records were exempt primarily on grounds that the reasons in the regulation applied: the investigation was ongoing, and a related civil action was pending).

Finally, one authority has interpreted *Ryan* to mean that an

"... agency is limited to those exceptions which it has filed and explained, and cannot claim new ones during a lawsuit to serve [another] purpose, though reasonable, was not the subject of a proper exemption process earlier." - 2 *Federal Information Disclosure* (O'Reilly's) §21.07 at 21-27 (1990).

In other words, only those reasons authorized in the exemption regulation can be invoked to deny access of particular records.

A. The *Aquino* decision conflicts with *Ryan* because it advances an argument completely at odds with its plain language: that an agency may exempt law enforcement records if the reasons for withholding the particular record are inconsistent with every one of the reasons listed in the agency's regulation.

In *Aquino* this Court concludes that when exempting law enforcement records from an access request, it is not necessary for an agency to give an "authorized reason" to justify the exemption. *Aquino* at 5. "Authorized" here naturally means those reasons listed in the agency's exemption regulation. Thus it can be inferred that reasons that are inconsistent with this "authorized" list can indeed apply to justify denial, so that even if none of the adverse effects listed in the regulation apply, the agency can still deny access.

The court implies that it is not even necessary to review individual requests for access to law enforcement records to determine whether any of the authorized reasons for exemption still exists or still applies. Rather it is only sufficient that reasons for exempting the entire system were stated in the regulation when it was originally promulgated. As a result, an agency may decide to withhold law enforcement records at its discretion, regardless whether the reason for such action is consistent or inconsistent with the reason in the regulation.

This *Aquino* rationale, then, flies in the face of the *Ryan* "consistency rule" and all the other similar interpretations given by the circuits above.

The impact of the *Aquino* decision is alarming, considering that the Court cites no authority - legislative, policy, or otherwise - to support its argument. The Court only makes the conclusory remark that the Privacy Act was not intended to be an "amendatory procedure" to gain access to criminal investigative records. *Id*. at 6. The Court directs instead that the APA is the appropriate vehicle, with its highly deferential "arbitrary and capricious" review, to challenge whether an investigation was properly motivated. *Id*.

The result is a totally new body of law that renders meaningless the statutory right to *de novo* review under the Privacy Act for requests for access or amendment to law enforcement agencies. Relegated to such a minimal standard of judicial review under the APA, it highly unlikely that unlawful or improper investigations or refusals to amend would be exposed.

The consequence is a virtual grant of immunity to law enforcement agencies, since they will be free to operate without the threat of the more rigorous *de novo* review.

The question arises, then: Upon what authority does the *Aquino* Court rely? *Ryan* certainly does not stand for the rule that reasons "inconsistent" with the regulation may be relied upon to justify exemptions.

The legal difficulty lies in that the *Aquino* decision is not clear whether it has overruled *Ryan* by silence or chosen to ignore it. The Circuit, however, cannot simply ignore the uniformity of application and interpretation of *Ryan* by other courts, and the judicial trend that has extended its rationale to include other exemptions under the Privacy Act.

The significance for this Circuit is that there is an internal conflict on the question whether the law enforcement exemption under the Privacy Act applies to certain records when the reason for refusing access or amendment to those records is inconsistent with all the reasons stated in the regulation.

The last legal issue the Court in *Aquino* overlooked is the claim for damages, as sought in the original complaint at the district court. The Court here states that "Aquino has now abandoned his claim for damages". *Aquino* at 4. The Court points to no legal rationale or affirmative evidence from Michael Aquino on appeal why the original claim for damages should not be considered. On the contrary, the claim for damages comes from the statute itself, under the Privacy Act. Appellant never relinquished or in any way indicated abandonment of his statutory claim. Petitioner was no less damaged by the Army's failure to amend its inaccurate records when he appealed to this Court than when he filed his complaint in the district court.

For the foregoing reasons petitioner requests a Rehearing, and additionally submits a Suggestion for Rehearing *en Banc*.

Respectfully submitted,
/s/ Gary Myers, Esq.
/s/ John A. Wickham, Esq.
Gary Myers and Associates
Attorneys for Petitioner Michael Aquino

Appendix 74: Letter, M. Aquino to General Gordon Sullivan 7/1/92

Lt. Colonel Michael A. Aquino, USAR

July 1, 1992

General Gordon R. Sullivan (Certified)
Chief of Staff, United States Army
Headquarters, Department of the Army
Pentagon Building
Washington, D.C. 20310-0200

Dear Sir:

I am writing to ask your personal intervention to correct a serious injustice and violation of Army Regulations and federal law committed against me by the Judge Advocate General and Criminal Investigation Command of the Army. I have exhausted all lower avenues of the chain of command prior to making this request of you.

The facts are summarized as follows. Detailed documentation of any of these points can be provided on request. I affirm that they are accurate under penalty of perjury.

In August 1987 an Army Christian chaplain, Captain Lawrence Adams-Thompson, made a knowingly-false and malicious accusation of child-molestation against my wife and myself. I am High Priest of the Temple of Set, an ethical and law-abiding Satanic church incorporated in California. An additional motive in Adams-Thompson's effort was his attempt to defraud the U.S. government of $3 million in false damage claims as subsequently filed by himself and his wife.

The chaplain's accusation was promptly investigated, amidst considerable national publicity, by the San Francisco Police Department. That investigation was closed on 8/1/88 with no charges filed. Because of the bias and violations of SFPD procedure in the investigation, I subsequently filed a complaint with the San Francisco Police Commission, and that complaint was sustained.

Following the close of the SFPD investigation, pressure was then put on the Army by Senator Jesse Helms to destroy my reputation and career as a soldier. On 11/23/88 - almost four months after the SFPD investigation was closed, and over a year after the chaplain's allegations - the CID opened a new investigation.

Although it possessed from the outset conclusive evidence of our innocence and of the chaplain's deliberate false accusation, the CID nevertheless issued a Report of Investigation (ROI) titling Mrs. Aquino and myself for the accusation in August 1989. The same ROI viciously misrepresented our church and religion and titled me for conduct unbecoming an officer accordingly. No court-martial charges were preferred against me as a consequence of this ROI, however.

While the CID investigation was in process, TJAG, in explicit violation of Army Regulations, influenced an AGR continuation board at the U.S. Army Reserve Personnel Center to discontinue me as a serving AGR officer. Also while the investigation was in process, the JAG officer controlling the investigation for the 6th Region CID secretly released confidential information from the investigation to a tabloid reporter in an effort to further harm Mrs. Aquino and myself.

Upon learning of the fraudulent titling actions contained in the ROI, I filed an administrative request with the Commanding General CIC for their removal. On 9/28/90 the CIC, as directed by TJAG, removed the chaplain-accusation titling from my wife and the religion-titlings from both of us. I remained titled for the chaplain-accusation.

I immediately filed suit in federal court to have this remaining fraudulent titling removed. The briefs and oral arguments filed by the TJAG attorneys in the district court contained extensive and deliberate lies in an effort to conceal the misconduct of the CIC investigation and to preserve the fraud of the titling. Based on this deception, the federal district judge declined to order removal of the titling.

I appealed immediately to the Court of Appeals. Again the TJAG attorneys deliberately lied to the court, and the court cited those lies as justification for its refusal to reverse the district court decision.

I declined to appeal to the U.S. Supreme Court, since there seemed little point in doing so as long as TJAG continued to lie to the courts and the judicial system appeared incapable of or uninterested in exposing these lies.

In February 1992 I filed a complaint with the Inspector General of the Army concerning these repeated violations of law and Army regulations by TJAG/CIC. After refusals by subordinate officers to act on the complaint, Acting DAIG Major General Bean personally declined to do so via his 5/7/92 letter to me (enclosed). It is his position that TJAG is responsible for investigating itself.

My attorneys and I requested TJAG to investigate and take corrective action concerning the remaining fraudulent titling, the lies in two federal courts by TJAG attorneys, and the illegal release of information by the TJAG attorney to the tabloid journalist. In responding letters (enclosed), TJAG said that such internal investigations would be conducted.

On 5/18/92 I wrote to Major General Fugh, TJAG, to request confirmation that these investigations were in fact being conducted. Well over a month has now passed with no response whatever to my letter (enclosed).

These are the facts. It appears to me that, in a continuing effort to cover up its many violations of law and Army Regulations throughout this entire affair, TJAG has simply decided to bury the truth and take no further actions whatever. It is for this reason that I am now writing to you.

An Army chaplain has committed serious crimes against a fellow officer and against the United States Army and, as far as I know, remains a serving officer on active duty. TJAG and CIC, in response to political pressure, fraudulently titled my wife and myself for a fictitious crime and then lied in court to cover up this fraud. The Inspector General of the Army adamantly refuses to investigate. TJAG, having deceived the courts and having nothing to fear from a DAIG investigation, feels that it can now safely ignore the truth - and the law.

No such crime as alleged by the chaplain was ever committed. I am an innocent officer who has been grievously harmed by TJAG/CIC for political - and illegal - reasons. I earnestly request that you, as the senior officer of the Army and ultimate guardian of its ethics, order the remaining fraudulent titling removed and those officers who have brought discredit and dishonor upon the Army by their actions in this case held accountable.

Respectfully,
/s/ Michael A. Aquino
Lt. Colonel, Military Intelligence, USAR

Appendix 75: Letter, M. Aquino to General Gordon Sullivan 8/20/92

Lt. Colonel Michael A. Aquino, USAR

August 20, 1992

General Gordon R. Sullivan
Chief of Staff, United States Army
Headquarters, Department of the Army
Pentagon Building
Washington, D.C. 20310-0200

Dear Sir:

In supplement to my 7/1/92 letter to you (copy enclosed) : I have just received the enclosed 8/14/92 letter from Colonel Lane of TJAG's Standards of Conduct Office. This is the same Colonel Lane who authored the 3/12/92 letter provided as an enclosure to my 7/1/92 letter to you.

As previously noted, Major Mark Harvey of TJAG authored a deliberately false and fraudulent ROI, whose many falsehoods and unjustified titlings were subsequently exposed. During the course of the CID investigation this same Major Harvey provided confidential CID information, and defamatory falsehoods, to a London tabloid journalist who subsequently published them. If such actions by Major Harvey indeed constitute "no violation of the Army Rules of Professional Conduct for Lawyers", then those Rules are an impotent farce.

Nevertheless what is actually happening here is quite clear: If TJAG acknowledges Major Harvey's unethical and illegal actions, then all of TJAG's efforts to protect the fraudulent ROI, including the cover-up of the actual violations of Army law and regulations by Chaplain Adams-Thompson, and the extensive lying by TJAG attorney Major Lisowski to two federal courts, would be exposed. TJAG evidently thinks this would be far more inconvenient and unpleasant than merely continuing the cover-up to perpetuate a flagrant and vicious injustice to two innocent, decent, and honorable people: my wife and myself.

Accordingly it is not surprising to me that I was never advised of the name of the "Preliminary Screening Official" tasked to "determine the facts", nor did any such "official" ever contact me to obtain further documentation and substantiation of Harvey's actions. Under the circumstances Colonel Lane's 8/14/92 letter to me is ludicrous.

The questions, as posed in my 7/1/92 letter to you, therefore remain: Are you, as Chief of Staff and senior officer of the United States Army, content to allow such disgraceful, unethical, and unprofessional conduct by your Judge Advocate General's office? Are you satisfied to have such individuals as Major Mark Harvey, Major Patrick Lisowski, and Chaplain Lawrence Adams-Thompson wearing the uniforms of commissioned officers in the Army? Is the good name of an officer who has served the United States and its Army faithfully and honorably for 23 years of the least concern to you?

If you do not insist upon truthfulness, integrity, and justice in the Army, who will?

Respectfully,
/s/ Michael A. Aquino
Lt. Colonel, Military Intelligence, USAR

Appendix 76: Court Opinion Concerning Kinsey's Trust Assets, 2007

MEMORANDUM OPINION
No. 04-06-00497-CV"
Peter J. PARENTI, Appellant
v.
Kinsey MOBERG, Appellee
From the Probate Court No. 1, Bexar County, Texas
Trial Court No. 2001-PC-3017B
Honorable Polly Jackson Spencer, Judge Presiding
Opinion by: Alma L. López, Chief Justice
Sitting: Alma L. López, Chief Justice
Sandee Bryan Marion, Justice
Rebecca Simmons, Justice
Delivered and Filed: May 30, 2007

AFFIRMED A jury found Peter J. Parenti liable for breaching his fiduciary duty to Kinsey Moberg and for knowingly aiding and abetting Moberg's mother and stepfather in breaching their fiduciary duty to Moberg. Parenti raises four issues on appeal, contending that: (1) Parenti had no fiduciary duty to Moberg; (2) Moberg was not entitled to mental anguish damages; (3) the award of attorney's fees from an underlying probate action as actual damages was improper; and (4) the exemplary damages award is grossly excessive. We affirm the trial court's judgment.

Background

Kinsey Moberg was sexually assaulted when she was a young child. Her mother and stepfather, Michele Adams-Thompson and Larry Adams-Thompson (collectively "the Thompsons"), filed suit in California against the federal government on behalf of themselves and Moberg regarding Moberg's assault. The parties reached a settlement, which was approved by the California court. Consistent with the settlement, the court ordered the federal government to pay $334,720 to the Thompsons "on their own behalf and on behalf of their minor child, [Moberg]." The Thompsons kept fifty percent of the money and created a trust for Moberg with the remaining fifty percent. Peter Parenti was hired to draft the trust, which was titled "The Kinsey Almond Adams-Thompson Living Trust" ("the Trust"). The Thompsons were named as trustees. The Trust provided that Moberg would become a co-trustee when she turned eighteen but that she would not have exclusive control of the Trust until she was fifty years old. The Trust also provided that if Moberg did not accept and sign the Trust within one month of turning eighteen, the Trust assets would go to the Thompsons unless Moberg was disabled or the Thompsons waived the requirement or extended the deadline for her to sign.

When Moberg was thirteen years old, she moved in with her biological father. Later, as Moberg approached her eighteenth birthday, her father's attorney sent a letter to Parenti requesting that Parenti send a copy of the Trust to Moberg or her father. Moberg had not seen a copy of the Trust since it was executed when she was twelve years old. Parenti responded in a letter that the trust documents prohibited the trustees from disclosing the trust documents except pursuant to a court order. He also stated in the letter that he advised Moberg's mother as trustee that if she disclosed the documents to Moberg, she could be sued for damages. In addition, the letter stated that Parenti would provide a copy of the Trust to Moberg when she turned eighteen and became a co-trustee.

Moberg turned eighteen on September 1, 2001. Seventeen days later, Parenti sent her a letter stating that she should soon receive a copy of the Trust and explaining her responsibilities as a co-trustee and beneficiary of the Trust. Ten days after that, Moberg was served with a lawsuit filed against her by her stepfather, who was represented by Parenti. The lawsuit was a declaratory-judgment action seeking a judicial declaration that the Trust was valid and that the terms of the Trust should be followed, including a specific request for enforcement of the provision stating that Moberg must accept and sign the Trust by a certain date or all assets of the Trust would be distributed to the

Thompsons. The deadline for her to sign the Trust was extended to November 1, 2001. Moberg filed a counterclaim against the Thompsons for breach of their fiduciary duties and to declare the trust unenforceable.

The probate court ultimately terminated the Trust and ordered all trust assets distributed to Moberg. Moberg then brought this suit against Parenti for breach of fiduciary duty and for aiding and abetting the Thompsons in breaching their fiduciary duty. After a jury trial, the jury found that an attorney-client relationship existed between Parenti and Moberg in the creation of the trust and that Parenti was liable on both of Moberg's claims. The jury awarded Moberg $55,000 in damages for the attorney's fees she incurred in the declaratory-judgment suit. The jury also awarded Moberg mental anguish damages in the amount of $5,000 and exemplary damages in the amount of $300,000. Because Moberg had previously been awarded $13,500 of the attorney's fees she incurred in the declaratory-judgment action, the trial court applied a credit of $13,500 to the damages awarded by the jury. The trial court also reduced the exemplary damage award to $200,000. This appeal followed.

Independent Ground to Support Judgment

On appeal, Parenti challenges only one of two theories of liability submitted to the jury. The jury found Parenti liable under both theories. When a separate and independent ground that supports the judgment is not challenged on appeal, the appellate court must affirm. See Nobility Homes of Tex., Inc. v. Shivers, 557 S.W.2d 77, 83 (Tex. 1977); San Antonio Press, Inc. v. Custom Bilt Mach., 852 S.W.2d 64, 65 (Tex. App.-San Antonio 1993, no writ).

Parenti does not raise a separate issue challenging the jury's finding that Moberg was Parenti's client. Parenti's challenge to that finding is subsumed in his issue challenging the jury's finding that he failed to comply with his fiduciary duty to Moberg, which was only one of the theories of liability submitted to the jury. The second theory of liability - knowingly aiding and abetting Moberg's parents in violating their fiduciary duty to Moberg - does not rest on the existence of an attorney-client relationship between Parenti and Moberg but only upon the existence of a fiduciary relationship between Moberg and her parents. Therefore, based on the manner in which Parenti presented his issues and based on his failure to challenge the second theory of liability, this court is unable to reach the issue of whether an attorney-client relationship legally existed between Parenti and Moberg. Accordingly, this opinion should not in any way be read as addressing that issue.

Because Parenti fails to challenge the second theory of liability, which is a separate and independent ground that supports the judgment, we affirm the trial court's judgment as to liability. Nobility Homes of Tex., Inc., 557 S.W.2d at 83; San Antonio Press, Inc., 852 S.W.2d at 65. We now turn to Parenti's remaining issues regarding damages.

Mental Anguish Damages

In his second issue, Parenti contends that the trial court erred in awarding Moberg mental anguish damages because: (1) Moberg's actual damages were economic; (2) the evidence in support of an award of mental anguish damages is legally insufficient; (3) there is no causal link between Parenti's conduct and Moberg's mental anguish.

A. Recovery of Mental Anguish Damages When Actual Damages are Economic

Parenti argues that Moberg cannot recover mental anguish damages because her actual damages are economic in nature. In support of his argument, Parenti cites two cases in which the Texas Supreme Court held that mental anguish damages are not recoverable in cases involving certain negligence claims. See Douglas v. Delp, 987 S.W.2d 879, 885 (Tex. 1999) (holding that plaintiff cannot recover damages for mental anguish when mental anguish is consequence of economic losses caused by attorney's negligence); City of Tyler v. Likes, 962 S.W.2d 489, 497 (Tex. 1997) (mental anguish based solely on negligent property damage not compensable as matter of law). However, Moberg did not allege negligence in this case. Further, courts have held that mental anguish damages are recoverable in some cases where the defendant's conduct is intentional or malicious. See Likes, 962 S.W.2d at 495 (stating that mental anguish damages are recoverable for some common law torts involving intentional or malicious conduct); Farmers & Merch. State Bank of Krum v. Ferguson, 617 S.W.2d 918, 921 (Tex. 1981) (upholding award of mental anguish damages under section 4.402 of the UCC for wrongful dishonor where jury found bank acted with malice); Beaumont v. Basham, 205 S.W.3d 608, 620 (Tex. App.-Waco 2006, pet. denied) (holding that plaintiff could recover mental anguish damages under the Theft Liability Act where jury found defendants acted with malice when they committed theft). Here, the jury found that Parenti acted with malice, and Parenti does not challenge that finding. Therefore, because the jury found that Parenti acted with malice, we hold that the trial court did not err in awarding mental anguish damages to Moberg. See Likes, 962 S.W.2d at 495; Ferguson, 617 S.W.2d at 921; Basham, 205 S.W.3d at 620.

B. Legal Sufficiency of Evidence to Support Mental Anguish Damages

Parenti asserts that the evidence is legally insufficient to support a finding that Moberg suffered mental anguish. To survive a legal sufficiency challenge, Moberg was required to show by direct evidence "the nature, duration, and severity of [her] anguish, thus establishing a substantial disruption in [her] daily routine," or show by other evidence "a high degree of mental pain and distress that is more than mere worry, anxiety, vexation, embarrassment, or anger." Parkway Co. v. Woodruff, 901 S.W.2d 434, 444 (Tex. 1995). Moberg testified that she became physically sick when she received the declaratory-judgment action brought by her stepfather and signed by Parenti. She testified that she thought Parenti was her lawyer and that she was shocked to see that he was representing her stepfather against her. She testified that she had trouble sleeping and that she had to miss work at times because she was crying and vomiting to such an extent that she could not work. She stated:
"I told my husband to call in because I couldn't speak because I was crying too hard and I had been up all night and I just couldn't stop throwing up. And it was several days just like that. I didn't go back right away. And it continued for a while, because this stuff tends to follow you and kind of snowball as it gets going. So I can't remember when it actually stopped, because I just, instead of - I guess I gained control of myself physically at one point, and then it was just not being able to sleep and not, you know, wanting to eat a lot. And so I just - I - was able to put in my normal work day and still try and get stuff done. I guess you could say I was coping. I was able to learn to cope with it."
We conclude that Moberg's testimony that she cried, lost sleep, vomited, and missed work for "several days" is sufficient to support the jury's finding. See Ortiz v. Furr's Supermarkets, 26 S.W.3d 646, 653 (Tex. App.-El Paso 2000, no pet.) (stating that mental anguish damages are warranted where mental anguish causes plaintiff to have difficulty eating, sleeping, working, socially interacting, or carrying on any other activity that, until time of alleged injury, she could accomplish on daily basis without difficulty). Because evidence exists in the record to support the jury's finding, we decline to sit as a thirteenth juror and overturn the decision of the jury. See Gainsco County Mut. Ins. Co. v. Martinez, 27 S.W.3d 97, 108 (Tex. App.-San Antonio 2000, pet. dism'd by agr.). We therefore overrule Parenti's legal sufficiency challenge.

C. Causation

Parenti contends that Moberg did not provide evidence establishing that her mental anguish was caused by Parenti. Moberg testified that her mental anguish was the result of being served with the declaratory-judgment action. Parenti argues that Moberg did not differentiate between the mental anguish caused by the Thompsons' lawsuit and that caused by Parenti's involvement in the lawsuit, and that it is more likely that her anguish was the result of being sued by her own parents. Parenti cites two Texas Supreme Court cases in support of his argument. See Gunn Infiniti, Inc. v. O'Byrne, 996 S.W.2d 854, 861 (Tex. 1999) (mental anguish damages not recoverable where plaintiff's testimony indicated his anguish was result of issues unrelated to defendant's DTPA violations); Arthur Andersen & Co. v. Perry Equip. Corp., 945 S.W.2d 812, 817 (Tex. 1997) (stating that consequential damages must be related to misrepresentation). Both cases stand for the same proposition: that a plaintiff's mental anguish must relate to the defendant's conduct. Here, Parenti's argument fails because Moberg's testimony does relate to Parenti's conduct. The jury found Parenti liable for knowingly aiding and abetting the Thompsons in the violation of their fiduciary duty to Moberg, and Parenti does not challenge that finding on appeal. Moberg's testimony that her mental anguish was caused by a lawsuit that was filed by her stepfather and drafted and signed by Parenti directly relates to the jury finding that Parenti knowingly assisted the Thompsons in violating their fiduciary duty to Moberg.

D. Conclusion Regarding Mental Anguish Damages

We emphasize once more that Parenti does not challenge the jury's finding of malice. Applying the governing law, without the benefit of reviewing the unchallenged finding, we hold that the trial court did not err in awarding Moberg mental anguish damages. See Likes, 962 S.W.2d at 495.

Attorney's Fees From Previous Case As Actual Damages

In his third issue, Parenti contends that the trial court erred in awarding Moberg attorney's fees from a previous case as actual damages because: (1) the previous judgment awarding attorney's fees was res judicata; (2) Moberg is entitled to only one satisfaction of her attorney's fees award; and (3) it is improper to award attorney's fees that were incurred in a prior suit. Parenti also contends that the trial court erred in excluding evidence of Moberg's previous attorney's fees award.

A. *Res Judicata*

Res judicata precludes relitigation of claims that have been finally adjudicated, or that arise out of the same subject matter and that could have been litigated in the prior action. Amstadt v. U.S. Brass Corp., 919 S.W.2d 644, 652 (Tex. 1996). *Res judicata* requires proof of the following elements: (1) a prior final judgment on the merits by a court of competent jurisdiction; (2) identity of parties or those in privity with them; and (3) a second action based on the same claims as were raised or could have been raised in the first action. Id. Here, *res judicata* does not apply because Parenti does not establish that he was a party or in privity with a party in the declaratory-judgment suit. Parenti was not a party in the declaratory-judgment suit because he was serving as an attorney representing a party in that suit. With respect to privity, people can be in privity in at least three ways: (1) they can control an action even if they are not a party to it; (2) their interest can be represented by a party; or (3) they can be successors in interest, deriving their claim through a party. Id. at 653. Parenti has not cited, and we have not located, any authority for the proposition that Parenti fits into any of the three categories. Because Parenti cannot show that he was a party or in privity with a party in the declaratory-judgment suit, *res judicata* does not apply.

B. One-Satisfaction Rule

Parenti argues that the one-satisfaction rule bars Moberg's recovery of attorney's fees from the declaratory-judgment suit as actual damages in this case because the trial court already awarded Moberg some of the same attorney's fees she requested in the declaratory-judgment suit. The purpose of the one-satisfaction rule is to prevent a plaintiff from obtaining more than one recovery for the same injury. See Stewart Title Guar. Co. v. Sterling, 822 S.W.2d 1, 7 (Tex. 1991). Here, Moberg's injury was that she was required to incur attorney's fees in defending against a declaratory-judgment action brought by her stepfather.

The record shows that in the declaratory-judgment suit, the trial court awarded some of the attorney's fees requested in that case. Parenti contends that the trial court's award in the declaratory-judgment suit constitutes full satisfaction for Moberg's injury. However, the record does not provide us with sufficient information to determine that the trial court's initial award of attorney's fees in the declaratory-judgment suit constitutes a full satisfaction of Moberg's damages. The record is unclear as to the trial court's reasoning for awarding only some of the attorney's fees requested by Moberg in the declaratory-judgment action. In fact, at a pre-trial hearing in this case, the trial court indicated that it could not remember why it awarded only some of the attorney's fees presented to it in the declaratory-judgment suit. The court stated that it was unsure if it had awarded only some of the fees because it felt that amount was reasonable or whether it was because there was one party not before the court at the time. The record also does not include the trial court's final judgment in the declaratory-judgment suit. It is at least clear that Moberg's total recovery of attorney's fees was no more than the amount she actually incurred in the declaratory-judgment suit because the trial court's judgment in this case shows that the court credited the amount awarded in the declaratory-judgment suit to the award in this case. Without further information in the record about the trial court's award of attorney's fees in the declaratory-judgment suit, we cannot conclude that the award of damages in this case violates the one-satisfaction rule.

C. Awarding Attorney's Fees From First Suit as Damages in Second Suit

Generally, expenses incurred in prosecuting or defending a suit are not recoverable as costs or damages unless recovery is expressly provided for by contract or statutory provisions. Turner v. Turner, 385 S.W.2d 230, 233 (Tex. 1964). However, equitable principles may allow the recovery of attorney's fees where a party was required to prosecute or defend the previous suit as a consequence of a wrongful act of the defendant. See Massey v. Columbus

State Bank, 35 S.W.3d 697, 701 (Tex. App.-Houston [1st Dist.] 2000, pet. denied); Nationwide Mut. Ins. Co. v. Holmes, 842 S.W.2d 335, 341 (Tex. App.-San Antonio 1992, writ denied); Baja Energy, Inc. v. Ball, 669 S.W.2d 836, 838 (Tex. App.-Eastland 1984, no writ). Here, Moberg's stepfather filed a declaratory-judgment action against her seeking a judicial declaration that the Trust was valid and enforcement of the trust provisions. Parenti drafted the Trust and served as the stepfather's attorney in the declaratory-judgment action. Moberg was required to defend herself in the declaratory-judgment suit, in which the court ultimately concluded that the Trust was unenforceable and should be terminated. In the case before us, Moberg alleged that Parenti aided and abetted her mother and stepfather in breaching their fiduciary duties to Moberg by knowingly creating an invalid trust and then filing a declaratory-judgment action against Moberg seeking a declaration that the Trust was valid. The jury found Parenti liable on this claim, and Parenti does not appeal that finding. Because of Parenti's actions, Moberg was required to pay attorney's fees in defending the declaratory-judgment action. Therefore, we conclude that based on equitable principles, the trial court did not err in awarding Moberg her attorney's fees from the declaratory-judgment suit as actual damages in this case. See Massey, 35 S.W.3d at 701; Baja Energy, 669 S.W.2d at 838.

D. Exclusion of Evidence Showing Previous Attorney's Fees Award

Parenti contends that the trial court erred in excluding evidence of the attorney's fees awarded to Moberg in the declaratory-judgment suit. We review the trial court's decision to exclude evidence for an abuse of discretion. Tex. Dep't of Transp. v. Able, 35 S.W.3d 608, 617 (Tex. 2000); City of Brownsville v. Alvarado, 897 S.W.2d 750, 753 (Tex. 1995). An abuse of discretion occurs when the trial court acts without regard to any guiding rules or principles. Alvarado, 897 S.W.2d at 754. If error is found in the exclusion of evidence, we examine the entire record to assess the harm caused by the error. See Cortez v. HCCI-San Antonio, Inc., 131 S.W.3d 113, 119 (Tex. App.-San Antonio 2004), aff'd, 159 S.W.3d 87 (Tex. 2005). We reverse based on the erroneous exclusion of evidence only if the proponent of the evidence shows error that was calculated to cause and probably did cause the rendition of an improper judgment. Tex. R. App. P. 44.1(a)(1); Alvarado, 897 S.W.2d at 753; Vela v. Wagner & Brown, Ltd., 203 S.W.3d 37, 52 (Tex. App.-San Antonio 2006, no pet.). Accordingly, the proponent of the evidence must demonstrate that the excluded evidence was both controlling on a material issue and not cumulative of other evidence. Able, 35 S.W.3d at 617; Williams Distrib. Co. v. Franklin, 898 S.W.2d 816, 817 (Tex. 1995). Erroneous evidentiary rulings are usually not harmful unless the case as a whole turns on the particular evidence in question. Alvarado, 897 S.W. 2d at 753-54; Sommers v. Concepcion, 20 S.W.3d 27, 41 (Tex. App.-Houston [14th Dist.] 2000, pet. denied).

We need not decide whether the exclusion of the evidence was improper because even assuming the trial court erred, we conclude the error was harmless. In the judgment in this case, the trial court credited the amount already awarded to Moberg in the declaratory-judgment suit to the amount awarded to her by the jury in this case. Because the amount previously awarded to Moberg was never made a part of the judgment against Parenti in this case, Parenti cannot demonstrate that the case turned on the excluded evidence or that the exclusion of the evidence probably caused the rendition of an improper judgment. Accordingly, we hold that any error in the exclusion of the evidence was harmless.

Parenti also argues that the court should have admitted affidavits of Moberg's attorneys detailing attorney's fees in the declaratory-judgment suit because the affidavits were admissible based on inconsistent statements. However, Parenti does not provide citations to the record in support of his argument. Although Parenti cites to Moberg's testimony about the amount of attorney's fees she had to pay in the first action, he did not seek to admit the affidavits at that point in the record, and he does not cite to a place in the record where he did seek to admit the affidavits. As a result, he has waived this argument. See Tex. R. App. P. 38.1(h) (requiring brief to contain appropriate citations to record); Flume v. State Bar of Tex., 974 S.W.2d 55, 62 (Tex. App.-San Antonio 1998, no pet.) (failure to cite to relevant portions of record waives appellate review).

Exemplary Damages

In his final issue, Parenti challenges the $200,000 exemplary damage award on the ground that it deprives him of due process under the Fourteenth Amendment to the United States Constitution because it is grossly excessive. In determining whether an exemplary damages award violates due process, we consider three guideposts: (1) the degree of reprehensibility of the defendant's misconduct; (2) the disparity between actual or potential harm suffered by the plaintiff and the exemplary damages award; and (3) the difference between the exemplary damages awarded by the jury and the civil penalties authorized or imposed in comparable cases. State Farm Mut. Auto. Ins. Co. v. Campbell, 538 U.S. 408, 418 (2003); Tony Gullo Motors I, L.P. v. Chapa, 212 S.W.3d 299, 308 (Tex. 2006); Baribeau v. Gustafson, 107 S.W.3d 52, 63 (Tex. App.-San Antonio 2003, pet. denied).

A. Reprehensibility of Parenti's Misconduct

The reprehensibility of the defendant's misconduct is the most important of the guideposts. State Farm, 538 U.S. at 419; Tony Gullo Motors, 212 S.W.3d at 308. In determining the reprehensibility of Parenti's conduct, we consider whether: (1) the harm caused was physical as opposed to economic; (2) the tortious conduct evinced an indifference to or reckless disregard of the health or safety of others; (3) the target of the conduct had financial vulnerability; (4) the conduct involved repeated actions or was an isolated incident; and (5) the harm was the result of intentional malice, trickery, or deceit, or mere accident. State Farm, 538 U.S. at 419; Tony Gullo Motors, 212 S.W.3d at 308. Here, the third and fifth factors are met. First, Moberg was financially vulnerable at the time that Parenti filed the declaratory-judgment action against her on behalf of her stepfather. She had only recently graduated from high school, turned eighteen, and moved into her own apartment when she was served with the lawsuit. As a result of the action, she had to enter into a contingency-fee contract to hire an attorney. By the time the court ultimately terminated the Trust and ordered the trust assets distributed to Moberg, she had incurred approximately $54,000 in attorney's fees.

Second, the jury found that the harm to Moberg was the result of malice, and Parenti does not appeal that finding. The record shows that Parenti was untruthful in a letter to an attorney representing Moberg's father in a custody dispute. The attorney had requested that Parenti send a copy of the Trust to Moberg or her father. In response, Parenti stated that the Trust prohibited the trustee from disclosing the trust documents to anyone except pursuant to a court order. However, Parenti admitted on the stand that his statement was not true. The Trust actually provided that the trustee was not required to disclose the trust documents to anyone who was not a beneficiary, did not have the approval of a beneficiary, or was not requesting the documents pursuant to a court order. Parenti stated that he made the false statement because the attorney was representing Moberg's father in a child support and custody dispute against Moberg's mother. When asked if he made the false statement to frustrate the attorney's attempt to get information that he needed, Parenti answered, "[n]ot necessarily." Parenti's letter also includes the statement that he advised Moberg's mother as trustee that if she were to violate the prohibition in the Trust, she could be sued for damages. However, since there is no such prohibition in the Trust, he also was untruthful with his client. Further, Parenti contradicted his letter when he testified at trial that the reason he refused to disclose a copy of the Trust was because the Thompsons refused to give him permission for the disclosure.

The record also includes a letter from Parenti to the attorney representing Moberg's mother in the custody dispute. In the letter, Parenti states that Texas courts are notorious for upholding the terms of such a trust, that Moberg's challenge to the Trust would likely be unsuccessful, that the trustees could defend the Trust with trust assets, that Moberg "would be spending her education money on litigation which is a very expensive way to get an education," and that Moberg "would end up paying all court costs and all attorney's fees on both sides of any litigation." Moberg's expert, Chris Heinrichs, testified that it was incorrect for Parenti to state in the letter that Moberg's challenge would be unsuccessful. Heinrichs testified that a minor has the right upon turning eighteen to void an agreement that she entered into or that was entered into on her behalf when she was a minor. Further, even though Parenti demonstrated in the letter that he knew that a lawsuit involving the validity of the Trust would be expensive for Moberg, he himself drafted a petition for a declaratory judgment against her on behalf of her stepfather before she had even seen a copy of the Trust. The petition drafted by Parenti requested among other things that the court award attorney's fees and enforce the forfeiture provision in the Trust requiring Moberg to sign the Trust by a certain date or lose the trust assets to the Thompsons. Thus, if the declaratory-judgment action had been successful and Moberg had refused to sign a trust that she felt was objectionable, she would have lost the trust corpus and been required to pay her attorney's fees and Parenti's fees. If she had signed the Trust, she would still be required to pay her attorney's fees and Parenti's fees.

Heinrichs also testified that the Trust itself had improper provisions. He testified that he had seen the property of a minor withheld until she turned eighteen, twenty-one, or twenty-five, but that he had never seen it withheld until she turned fifty as it was here. In addition, Heinrichs testified that it was improper for Parenti to put estate-planning provisions in the Trust because the law does not allow a minor to write a will. Heinrichs also stated that the provision stating that Moberg's father could never be a beneficiary or heir under the Trust was not permitted by law.

After considering Parenti's conduct as a whole, we conclude that the evidence of Parenti's wrong-doings supports the exemplary damages award.

B. Disparity Between Actual or Potential Harm and Exemplary Damages

The U.S. Supreme Court has declined to adopt a bright-line ratio between actual or potential damages and exemplary damages, but it has stated that few awards exceeding a single-digit ratio will satisfy due process. State Farm, 538 U.S. at 425. The Court has also concluded that an exemplary damages award of more than four times the amount of compensatory damages might be close to the line of constitutional impropriety. Id. Here, the jury awarded Moberg $55,000 in actual damages and $5,000 in mental anguish damages, for a total of $60,000 in compensatory damages. Because the $200,000 exemplary damages award is less than four times the compensatory damages award, the disparity between the two awards is within the Supreme Court's accepted ratio. Further, the potential harm to Moberg is much more substantial. If the Thompsons would have enforced the forfeiture provision in the Trust, Moberg would have lost the entire trust corpus, which was approximately $162,000 at the time it was distributed. Thus, the ratio between the potential harm to Moberg and the exemplary damages award is well within the accepted ratio.

C. Difference Between Exemplary Damages and Civil Penalties in Similar Cases

Section 41.008(b) of the Texas Civil Practices and Remedies Code caps exemplary damages at the greater of: (1) noneconomic damages plus two times economic damages, not to exceed $750,000; or (2) $200,000. See Tex. Civ. Prac. & Rem. Code Ann. § 41.008(b) (Vernon Supp. 2007). Thus, the $200,000 exemplary damages award in this case does not violate the statute's limitations. Although Parenti points out that the Deceptive Trade Practices Act (DTPA) authorizes only three times the amount of actual damages as exemplary damages, he does not cite caselaw or provide examples of DTPA claims that are comparable to the claims in this case, nor does he provide any other cases similar to this case that would support his argument. We therefore conclude that the third guidepost supports the exemplary damages amount awarded in this case. See Springs Window Fashions Div., Inc., v. Blind Maker, Inc., 184 S.W.3d 840, 891 (Tex. App.-Austin 2006, pet. granted, remanded by agr.) (holding exemplary damage award reasonable because within amount authorized by section 41.008(b)); Citizens Nat'l Bank v. Allen Rae Inv., Inc., 142 S.W.3d 459, 486 (Tex. App.-Fort Worth 2004, no pet.) (fact that exemplary damage award was within amount authorized by section 41.008(b) supported award).

Because each of the three guideposts supports the exemplary damages award, we hold that the award does not violate Parenti's due process rights.

Conclusion

We affirm the trial court's judgment.

Alma L. López, Chief Justice

Made in the USA
San Bernardino, CA
15 October 2014